Learning Resources Center
Carroll
1601 W
Westminster, MD 21157

W9-BKT-675

WITHDRAWN

Traditional Japanese Theater

TRANSLATIONS FROM

THE ASIAN CLASSICS

COLUMBIA

UNIVERSITY

PRESS

NEW YORK

Traditional Japanese Theater
An Anthology of Plays

EDITED BY

Karen Brazell

TRANSLATORS

James T. Araki

Monica Bethe

James R. Brandon

Karen Brazell

Janet Goff

Carolyn Haynes

Stanleigh H. Jones, Jr.

Ayako Kano

Eileen Katō

Donald Keene

Don Kenny

Jane Marie Law

Samuel L. Leiter

Richard McKinnon

Carolyn Anne Morley

Mark Oshima

Royall Tyler

Columbia University Press
Publishers Since 1893
New York   Chichester, West Sussex
Copyright © 1998 Columbia
University Press
All rights reserved

Columbia University Press wishes to express
its appreciation for assistance given by the
Japan Foundation and the Pushkin Fund
toward the cost of publishing this volume.

Library of Congress Cataloging-in-
Publication Data

Traditional Japanese theater: an anthology of
plays / edited by Karen Brazell ; translators,
James T. Araki . . . [et al.].
    p.   cm.   — (Translations from the
Asian classics)
Includes bibliographical references
ISBN 0-231-10872-9 (alk. paper). —
ISBN 0-231-10873-7 (pbk. : alk. paper)
1. Japanese drama—Translations into
English. I. Brazell, Karen. II. Araki, James T.
III. Series.
PL782.E5T73   1997
895.6'2008—dc21   97-23964

♾

Casebound editions of Columbia University
Press books are printed on permanent and
durable acid-free paper.

Composition by William Meyers
Printed in the United States of America

c 10 9 8 7 6 5 4 3 2 1
p 10 9 8 7 6 5 4 3 2 1

To Donald Keene

Contents

Preface

Anthologizing is a highly developed art in Japan. Since ancient times, poetry anthologies have placed poems in new contexts, established genres, defined and redefined the canon, and enhanced (or diminished) poets' reputations. Prose collections, never as numerous or predominant as poetic anthologies, created brief tales around poems, introduced stories and legends from various parts of the Asian continent, and provided exemplary materials for such diverse groups as preachers and brides. Collections of noh chantbooks (*utaibon*), increasingly popular with the development of woodblock printing in the seventeenth century, usually included some musical notation to aid amateur performers and served to define the repertoires of each of the schools of actors. The most famous kabuki collection, *Eighteen Kabuki Plays* (Kabuki jūhachi ban, 1832), defined the *aragoto* (bravura) style of the Ichikawa family.

This book does what Japanese anthologies have never done, however, for it brings together in a single volume plays from noh, kyōgen, the puppet theater, and kabuki. In earlier eras, these theatrical forms were vaguely connected as performance arts (*geinō*), but only in modern times have scholars and theater people begun to consider them part of a single literary or artistic category, what we in the West call "drama" (*engeki* in modern Japanese). Even today, however, most people (including the fans) specialize in one form or another. The concept "traditional Japanese theater" is therefore anachronistic; however, it is useful, for looked at as a group, these plays reveal a great deal about the nature of each genre, and their common characteristics, techniques, and aesthetics present a type of theatricality different from that of Western Europe.

In the title of this book, I use the term *theater* instead of *drama*, for until this century these texts were not read as dramatic literature; they were performance scripts. Although a book cannot effectively present performance, this anthology suggests some of the characteristics of the theatricality of the plays by providing extensive descriptions of stage business and lavish illustrations. Because it is practically impossible to describe everything that occurs on the stage, different translations emphasize different aspects of the performance. Consequently, the more plays by different translators one reads, the better idea one will have of what occurs on stage. Films and videotapes have much to offer, but unfortunately very few tapes of entire performances are readily available.

Because there are are so many excellent plays in the repertoires, selecting the items for this anthology has been a challenging task. I have chosen to present plays that are well known and regularly performed in the hope that readers will encounter them in other contexts and even see them performed as international productions become more commonplace. The selection emphasizes the more literary plays; many others in all genres are equally or more effective on stage. Many of the plays I have chosen repeat similar themes, characters, or events, for recognition and rediscovery are particularly important aspects of aesthetics in Japan. To reencounter Heike warriors, *yamabushi* (mountain priests), thunder gods, or ghosts in new settings; to re-view scenes of exorcism, extortion, suicide, or jealous rage with different characters is to deepen understanding and enjoyment. The four plays in part 1 were grouped together to reveal some of the differences among the theatrical genres by showing their representations of the figure of a thunder god and the motif of transformation. The rest of the plays are grouped by genre, with traditional categories ordering the plays of a single genre in part 2 and rough chronology in part 3. Readers should not feel constrained by this arrangement; any play will serve as a good introduction or a fitting conclusion.

To translate is to interpret, especially when the source and target languages are temporally, spatially, and culturally so distant that even basic grammatical constructs convey very different sorts of meaning. Japanese does not make distinctions in tense, gender, or quantity in the same ways that English does. Its word order is very different, and its suffixes often indicate levels of honorifics or politeness not found in English. Complex word play and frequent use of onomatopoeia are characteristics of many scripts. In translating into English much has to be transformed and many choices have to be made; rarely is there a single "right" translation of any given sentence. Consequently, to give a fuller sense of the qualities of Japanese theater, I have chosen to use works by translators who do not necessarily have the same goals and who have chosen to employ different English styles in their translations. For example, Royall Tyler uses modern colloquial language to emphasize the humorous and quotidian aspects of kyōgen plays, whereas Don Kenny, who translates kyōgen for English production, emphasizes the formulaic and archaic aspects of the scripts. Both styles of translation convey important qualities of kyōgen. To gain a good understanding of a specific play, particularly noh plays whose language is poetically dense, it is helpful to read more than one translation. All the noh plays and many of the kyōgen plays presented here have been translated elsewhere; the bibliography lists other volumes of translations. Most puppet and kabuki productions are composed of individual acts or scenes taken from several plays. This anthology likewise presents parts of longer works. In several cases, however, I have chosen selections from plays that are translated in their entirety elsewhere. References to these complete translations are provided in the brief introductions to the individual plays and in the bibliography.

Not only are there several ways to interpret, and hence to translate, each of the plays in this book, but the plays themselves are written in a wide variety of styles. For one writer to effectively express such diversity is almost impossible. Consequently, I have included plays translated by seventeen different people. These people have also chosen to give different types of information along with their translations of the scripts. Monica Bethe and James R. Brandon give unusually detailed information about musical forms; Samuel L. Leiter and Carolyn Anne Morley pay particular attention to acting styles. As editor I have attempted to impose similar formats on the plays and to ensure that approximately equal amounts of stage business are described for most plays, but I have not tried to efface individual differences among the translators.

Even matters so apparently straightforward as transcribing Japanese into the roman alphabet are in practice rather complicated. I employ a modified Hepburn system of transcription: before bilabials (*b*, *p*, and *m*) I use *m* rather than *n*, because that is closer to the usual pronunciation—hence *Yamamba* and *Komparu* rather than *Yamanba* and *Konparu*. Many words are pronounced with either voiced or unvoiced consonants (*ōguchi* or *ōkuchi*, *kazura* or *katsura*). I have usually given both options and briefly explained any difference in connotation that might exist. Word divisions are not fixed in Japanese, so many compounds may be transcribed as single, multiple, or hyphenated words. This becomes a particular problem with technical terms. General principles are difficult to apply, but I have attempted to be consistent. Gender pronouns can also be confusing when male actors play all the roles. I use *he* to refer to the actor *qua* actor, but *he* or *she* as appropriate when the referent is the character. In the body of the text, Japanese words are only italicized on first occurrence.

As its name implies, the Glossary of Theatrical Terminology and Index to Illustrations serves two distinct functions. It defines theatrical terms that are used in this book, and if the term is often used in translation (for example, *bridgeway* or *wave pattern*), the English term is also listed as a cross reference. In addition, there are references to figures that illustrate the visually definable items. Readers who wish to study costumes, props, or gestures can find the appropriate illustrations by using this index.

In Japan, anthologies are often compiled by committee, and in a sense that is true of this work, for the translators have played an unusually active role in its creation. Some translated pieces specifically for this volume, others revised translations originally published elsewhere, and all permitted changes in formatting and descriptions of stage business to enhance the unity of presentation. I often turned to the translators for information about their plays or areas of expertise. Without their full cooperation this volume would not have been possible. In the end, however, I made the final decisions, and hence any mistakes or infelicitous choices are my responsibility.

Many other people were also generous in providing suggestions, information, and help. I would especially like to thank Barbara Curtis Adachi, Susan Matisoff, Kyoko Selden, Haruo Shirane, Joshua Young, students in several classes who read and commented on early versions of the text, and the readers for Columbia University Press. Inspiration to begin this undertaking was provided by Helen Tartar. Along the way, encouragement came from numerous colleagues who teach Japanese theater in English translation. Finally, Jennifer Crewe of Columbia University Press took matters into her capable hands to enable this project to become a reality. I have received editorial assistance from Michael Bourdaghs, John R. Ziemer, Steven Dean Shurtleff, and Susan Specter. Most of the final copy editing was carefully done by Margaret Yamashita, and design work was by Linda Secondari. Ron Harris, assistant managing editor at Columbia University Press, supervised the editing and production of this work. His patient dedication and good sense were essential to the transformation of an unwieldy and complex manuscript into a book. Many good suggestions, much editorial assistance, and constant moral support were also provided by George Gibian, for whose generous help and congenial companionship I am most grateful.

For permission to reprint translations I would like to thank the University of California Press for the *Hamamatsu-ya* and *Devils Island* scenes and the kōwaka version of *Atsumori*; Columbia University Press for *Amijima*, *Dōjōji*, and scenes from *Coxinga*, *Chūshigura*, and *Sugawara and the Secrets of Calligraphy*; the Cornell University East Asia Program for *Thunderbolt*, *Mushrooms*, and *Cicada*; the University of Hawaii Press for *Saint Narukami*, *Suma Bay*, and *The Snail* (the last was published in the *Asian Theater Journal*); and The Japan Times Ltd. for *Delicious Poison*. *Two Daimyō* was originally published by Uniprint of Tokyo.

Obtaining appropriate illustrations for this volume was a major undertaking. Again the translators were of great assistance: Monica Bethe, Janet Goff, Eileen Katō, Donald Keene, Don Kenny, and Jane Marie Law were of particular help in obtaining photographs, as were Kyoko Selden and Rebecca Jennison. Helpful suggestions for writing the captions were given by Monica Bethe, James R. Brandon, Samuel L. Leiter, and Mark Oshima. Barbara C. Adachi generously allowed me to select photos from her magnificent collection; Orita Kōji of the National Theater (Kokuritsu gekijo) in Tokyo made possible the use of numerous photos by Aoki Shinji; Masuda Shōzō and Richard Emmert selected photos for this project from the excellent collection of the Noh Research Archive of Musashino Women's College (Musashino joshi daigaku nō kenkyūjo); and Takahashi Junko assisted in obtaining photos from the National Bunraku Theater (Kokuritsu bunraku gekijo). Their assistance is greatly appreciated, as is that of the photographers acknowledged in the captions and the hundreds of performers whose skill in these and other productions served as the basis for the descriptions of stage business accompanying the translations.

This book is dedicated to Donald Keene, examples of whose translations appear in its pages. Donald Keene is the senior translator among us and one of the best in the business. He has translated all genres of Japanese literature, from the earliest to the most recent, with great skill and sensitivity and has written masterfully about the entire range of Japanese literature in both English and Japanese. I studied under Donald Keene as a graduate student and have benefited from his advice, his assistance, his friendship, and his inspiration in the many years since. Several others among the translators were also his direct students; most of us have known him personally, and all of us have admired and learned from his work. Thank you, Donald.

PART 1

An Introduction to
Traditional Japanese Theater

Japanese Theater: A Living Tradition

Traditional Japanese theater is living theater. Although its roots go back a millennium and its forms have changed considerably over time, the major genres—noh, *kyōgen*, kabuki, and the puppet theater—can claim continuous performance traditions. The theatrical arts were, and continue to be, passed down from parent to child, from master to disciple, with each new generation learning by imitation the skills of the previous one and each preserving both performance practices and theater artifacts from earlier periods. Only after they have totally mastered traditional performance practices do players experiment with innovations, the most successful of which may then become part of the continuing tradition.

In addition to producing classical plays according to time-honored conventions, performers sometimes research and reproduce old works that have been dropped from the repertoire, or they participate in the production of completely new works. Many of these new plays use traditional practices to dramatize nontraditional subject matter. For example, in 1956 the Japanese version of both *Hamlet* and Puccini's *Madame Butterfly* were produced in the puppet theater (Jones 1976, 1983), and in 1991 a new noh play about heart transplants, written by Dr. Tomio Tada and scored by noh actor Cumas Hashioka, premiered in Japan. Three years later, noh performers presented it in the United States.

Experimentation is not limited to traditional performers. The author Mishima Yukio remade thirteen noh plays into modern theater, and Suzuki Tadashi, one of the best-known modern directors, developed a training regime based on traditional theatrical practices. The work of both men has achieved international acclaim. In the West, playwrights, choreographers, directors, and performers—such as William Butler Yeats, Vsevolod Meyerhold, Sergei Eisenstein, Max Reinhardt, Berthold Brecht, Benjamin Britten, George Balanchine, and the Théâtre du Solei—have experimented with practices and materials from the Japanese theater. There also are groups that produce traditional plays in English. Two of the translators of plays in this anthology are leaders in this field: Don Kenny leads an international kyōgen troupe that performs in both Japanese and English, and James R. Brandon regularly produces English kabuki with students in Hawaii, often with the assistance of professional kabuki actors. Traditional Japanese forms and performers are now active players on the world stage.

The traditional Japanese theater troupes, which perform at the Vatican, in London theaters, and in New York's Central Park, as well as in Japan, are composed almost entirely of men. Throughout Japanese history, most performing arts groups have been limited to a single sex, and although female performers have played crucial roles in the development of all types of theater, the major professional stages have been largely the preserve of men. Women perform most often in the more informal settings of teahouses, banquets, and recitals. In addition to professional actors, many men and women practice the arts of traditional theater as hobbies and, long before the advent of karaoke, would entertain one another with a bit of noh chant or a short kabuki dance. These amateurs, including many non-Japanese, are an important part of the economic backbone of traditional theater; they provide support by taking lessons with actors and regularly attending professional performances.

Theater as a distinct performance genre with well-developed texts appeared in Japan only after poetry, narrative literature, and a sophisticated poetics had flourished for more than six hundred years. During the early, pretheater period (ca. 700–1350), both religious and secular performing arts prospered. In addition, many of the early literary arts had performance aspects: stories, for example, were often read aloud in conjunction with displays of illustrations, or they were proclaimed from Buddhist pulpits as part of elaborate ceremonies. Court poetry was frequently recited aloud and sometimes composed in the voices of figures in screen paintings. Music and dance were important parts of both sacred and secular culture, and troupes of entertainers—acrobats, monkey trainers, puppeteers, and comic mimes—traversed the countryside amusing people of all classes. When a full-fledged theater did develop in the fourteenth century, it was, as one might expect, quite unlike its counterparts elsewhere in the world.

The introduction to this book traces the development of theater in Japan, suggests some of its general characteristics, and describes the stages on which the major genres are performed. More detailed descriptions of the genres, particularly of their performance aspects, are given in the introductions to parts 2 and 3.

Historical Perspectives

The earliest recorded Japanese performance, a sacred event depicted in the *Kojiki* (712) and the *Nihonshoki* (720), occurred in the mythological age of the deities. To induce the Sun Goddess to come out of a cave where she had hidden herself in anger at her brother's misbehavior, a female deity named Uzume put on a costume, stamped on an overturned bucket, became possessed, and, according to one version of the story, revealed her genitals. The divine audience roared in appreciative laughter, and the Sun Goddess, her curiosity aroused by this merriment, emerged from

FIGURE 1.1. A shrine priestess (*miko*) performs kagura before the inner sanctuary of Ima Hiei Shrine in Kyoto on November 14, 1991. The dancer holds bells (*suzu*) and a sword. (Photo by David Boggett.)

FIGURE 1.2. Bugaku dances continue to be presented to the deity and the public at Imagumano Shrine in Kyoto, where Kannami and his son Zeami performed noh for the shogun Yoshimitsu in 1374. Folded strips of paper (*gohei*) and straw ropes mark off sacred space. (Photo by Karen Brazell.)

the cave, thereby restoring light to the universe. This heavenly performance has long been proclaimed the origin of theater. Uzume later descended to earth to prepare the way for Ninigi, the mythological ancestor of the imperial family, and became the progenitor of a line of female shamans. These shamans and their successors, especially those known as *miko* and associated with Shinto shrines, were central to the ritual performance events generally known as *kagura*. Many types of kagura, which include music, song, dance, and some mime, are still in ritual use at Shinto shrines today (figure 1.1).

Performing arts imported from the Asian continent by way of China and Korea were popular in the imperial court during the Nara (710–784) and Heian (794–1186) periods. *Gigaku*, known today only through surviving masks and a few documents, was first introduced as a performing art in the sixth century by an immigrant from the Korean peninsula who had studied in China. It flourished under the patronage of the Nara court. The performances, which were held at Buddhist temples, consisted of a procession of masked figures followed by dances and mimes accompanied by flutes, drums, and cymbals. The lion dance (*shishi mai*), which remains popular today, was a featured part of the performances. *Bugaku* largely replaced gigaku in the Heian period and became the ceremonial music of the court.[1] This form of music and masked dance included elements from China, Korea, and even India and Tibet. The dances were sometimes performed by Heian aristocrats, who placed a high value on acquiring artistic skills. The hero of *The Tale of Genji* (Genji

1. Bugaku refers to the dance that is accompanied by *gagaku* music. I use bugaku as a generic term.

monogatari), for example, is praised for his splendid performance of a bugaku dance as well as for his poetic and musical skills. Although its continental proto-types have disappeared, bugaku is preserved today by shrines, the imperial house-hold, and amateur groups in Japan (figure 1.2).

Another entertainment imported from China, known as *sarugaku* or *sangaku*, included acrobatics, magic, music, dance, comic pantomime, and trained animal acts, especially those using monkeys. The well-known scholar Fujiwara no Akihira (d. 1066) wrote *A Record of New Sarugaku* (Shinsarugakuki), which describes a rich variety show including solo sumo wrestling, rice-planting songs, puppets, lion dances, and what appear to have been comic sketches of various types of people, such as an aged local magistrate putting on airs, a respectable older woman blush-ingly covering her face with a fan, someone pounding his belly after having overeaten, a reverend monk coveting a gaily colored stole, and a respected nun seeking diapers for her soon-to-be-born infant. Sarugaku performers were usually itinerants, who often had connections with religious institutions. Many of them lived as social outcasts in segregated areas (*sanjo*), along with other entertainers (puppeteers, dancers, storytellers) and various other social pariahs (such as butch-ers, prostitutes, and undertakers).

The second half of the twelfth century was a time of social and political disrup-tion. Civil wars, which provided a rich source of material for later dramatists, ripped apart the basic fabric of Japanese life. In the ensuing medieval society (ca. 1185 to 1600), the warrior replaced the aristocrat at the center of power, and high-ranking women lost their economic independence and the prominent role they had occu-pied as both writers and readers of elite literature. Areas outside the capital grew in economic and political importance, with the result that travel increased markedly. Sharply increased communication with the continent accelerated the importation of ideas and artifacts. The literary language for prose narratives evolved from the women's style of the classical period, which used mostly Japanese diction and gram-matical forms, to a mixed style that included many Chinese loan words and gram-matical constructions. New sects of Pure Land and Zen Buddhism gained popu-larity, and large religious complexes that combined Buddhist and Shinto practices prospered as cultural centers. Services centering on the chanting of the *nembutsu* (the invocation *namu Amida Butsu*, "Hail Amida Buddha") became popular and increasingly included performance elements, some of which developed into long-lasting folk traditions. The Mibu Temple in Kyoto, for example, traces its perfor-mance tradition (called *Mibu dainembutsu kyōgen*) back to a nembutsu service held in the third month of 1300 (see figure 2.62).

In the medieval period, some of the performing arts that had been on the periphery of court culture moved toward center stage. Interaction increased be-tween folk and aristocratic entertainments, religious and secular arts, and male and female performers. One good example is the popular song known as *imayō*. In the Heian period these were sung by lower-class female performers who were some-times summoned to court to entertain the aristocrats. In the twelfth century the retired emperor GoShirakawa (1127–1192) became so intrigued by this art that he studied under a woman singer named Otomae (1085–1169), sponsored imayō events at court, and compiled an anthology of the songs and practical imayō criticism

(*Ryōjin hishō*). His efforts paid off: the songs remained so popular at the imperial court that a century later *The Confessions of Lady Nijō* (Towazugatari) depicts two emperors singing imayō. Unfortunately, GoShirakawa's anthology survives only in fragments, so our knowledge of the nature of these songs is limited.

Another type of song called *sōka* (or *sōga*) was created in Kamakura, headquarters of the military rulers between 1185 and 1333. Especially popular with the warrior class, the lyrics of these songs drew on past literature as well as contemporary activities. Some of them consist of lists of the virtues of almost anything—from blossoms to hawks and gambling; some feature interwoven strands of images and phrases from classical literary works; and others are poetic travel accounts enumerating the major sights along popular routes. The songs served as cultural mandalas for the Kamakura elite and remained popular for a century or more—even the noh actor and playwright Zeami (1363–1443) mentions them in his works. They probably influenced the development of the noh theater by providing precedents for its poetic language, and they may also have influenced its music and rhythms, although we cannot be sure of this because we know little about how sōka were performed.

Female dancers were crucial to the flowering of the performing arts in the medieval period. The *shirabyōshi* donned male court caps and white (*shira*) robes, danced to percussion accompaniment, and sang songs, including imayō. Although little is known about the nature of their performances, the dancers themselves figure prominently in the life and literature of the period. Shizuka Gozen, Giō, and Hotoke are immortalized in *The Tale of the Heike* and in the noh plays *Yoshino Shizuka, Futari Shizuka, Futari Giō,* and *Hotoke no Hara.* In his treatise entitled *Three Elements* (Sandō), Zeami places the artistic accomplishments of the shirabyōshi Giō, Gijo, and Shizuka alongside those of the famous Heian-period poets Lady Ise and Ono no Komachi. Other noh plays, such as *Dōjōji* (included in part 2), feature unnamed shirabyōshi, and the heroines in plays like *Izutsu* (part 2) and *Matsukaze* are modeled on the shirabyōshi figure, as the women dance wearing the caps and gowns of their lovers.

The successors of the shirabyōshi were the *kusemai* dancers whose art integrated song and dance more closely and had a lively rhythm. It so impressed the noh actor Kannami (or Kan'ami, 1333–1384) that he himself studied with the kusemai performer Otozuru (dates unknown) and incorporated into noh the rhythms and structures of her art. This innovation was an important step in the development of the classical noh theater, but it also hastened the demise of kusemai as an independent art. The kusemai texts preserved today were probably heavily influenced by the noh. The performers, however, were immortalized by the depictions of kusemai dancers in such noh plays as *Hyakuman* and *Yamamba* (in part 2). These and other plays also appear to have incorporated earlier kusemai into their structures.

In addition to these song (*utaimono*) and dance (*mai*) genres, recited narratives (*katarimono*) had an important place in medieval entertainments. These narratives were recited to the rhythmical accompaniment of a closed fan tapped against the palm of the hand, a hand drum (*tsuzumi*), the plucking and striking of the harsh lute-like *biwa*, or, later, to the sounds of *shamisen* (also pronounced *samisen*). The first popular performers of recited narratives were biwa priests (*biwa hōshi*), men who were generally blind and may have taken the Buddhist tonsure. These biwa priests

probably were originally ritual specialists who placated unsettled spirits, especially the malignant spirits of the dead.
By the eleventh century there were at
least two general types of biwa priests:
those who followed military troops and
sang battle songs and those who chanted Buddhist pieces at temples, especially those around Kyoto. These two
aspects of the biwa priests' art were
combined in battle tales couched in
Buddhist terms. The most successful
was *The Tale of Heike*, which wove the
stories of hundreds of men and women
who lived and died during the civil
wars of the late twelfth century—wars
that the Heike lost—around Buddhist
themes of impermanence, karmic retribution, and salvation. The first version
of this tale, now lost, was written between 1219 and 1222 and was followed
by various reciter's versions, the most
influential of which was dictated by the
talented biwa priest Kakuichi (d. 1371)
to his disciple Teiichi a few months before his death. Zeami thought highly of
this work and broadened its dissemina-
tion and its fame by treating it as a
"classical" source to be drawn on in
composing noh plays. *The Tale of the
Heike* (whose recitation came to be
called *heikyoku*) provided a rich mine

FIGURE 1.3. Rice-planting songs (*taueuta*), a component of early *den-gaku* (literally, "field music"), are still performed each spring. In June 1992, at Fushimi Inari Shrine in Kyoto, festively clad women transplant rice as priestesses dance behind them. (Photo by David Boggett.)

of materials for later theater and literature, including the plays about the plight of
Shunkan and the death of Atsumori translated here.

After 1333, when the shogunal headquarters moved from Kamakura to an area
of Kyoto called Muromachi, military patronage of the arts increased as these leaders attempted to prove that they, like the aristocrats who had ruled before them,
were a cultural elite and therefore had a legitimate right to power. Under the
patronage of the Muromachi military rulers (1333–1574), the first major theatrical
genres developed. In the mid-fourteenth century *dengaku*—a performance art that,
like sarugaku, combined song, dance, and mime—was enthusiastically supported
by the first Ashikaga shogun, Takauji (1305–1358) (figure 1.3). A performance attended by the shogun in the summer of 1349 on the broad riverbed in the center of the
capital has been vividly described. At one point, a child actor wearing a monkey
mask, a gold and red brocade robe, and fur slippers entered the arched bridgeway
to a lively beat and leaped gracefully up onto the handrail. At this, the audience rose

up with stamps and cries of appreciation, which caused the stands to collapse, killing and injuring scores of people and inciting others to loot and fight. A quarter century later, the reputation of the actor Kannami, the head of one of several saru-gaku troupes, attracted the attention of the third shogun, Ashikaga Yoshimitsu (1358–1408). Kannami and his son Zeami performed for the shogun at the Imagu-mano Shrine in Kyoto in 1374. Yoshimitsu's admiration for Kannami's artistic skill and his attraction to the young Zeami led the shogun to patronize their art. Thus sarugaku noh became part of the cultural life of the capital.

The literary aesthetics of the capital's elite culture was based on the classical poetic tradition of *waka* and included the newer linked verse (*renga*). Zeami, who must have received more education than the average poor actor, proved talented at poetry, and he soon attracted the attention of litterateurs and arbiters of court taste such as Nijō Yoshimoto (1320–1388). The plays that Zeami composed and per-formed furthered the poetic and cultural ideals of the time. The concept of pro-found and refined beauty known as *yūgen*, which first emerged as an important aes-thetic ideal in twelfth-century poetics, achieved three-dimensional representation on the noh stage, and the poetic techniques of imagistic association (*engo* and *yori-ai*) and allusive variation (*honka dori*) were expanded in noh texts.

Although Zeami incorporated into his noh many techniques and much materi-al from the poetic tradition, he did not limit himself to that legacy. The classical works that he used as sources were often filtered through medieval commentaries, handbooks, and legends. In addition to classical literature, Zeami and succeeding playwrights also drew heavily on more recent works, most notably *The Tale of the Heike*, but also tale literature (*setsuwa bungaku*) and sacred texts. Religious prac-tices and beliefs also influenced the structure of Zeami's plays. The two-act noh play in which a spirit or ghost appears in the form of an ordinary person in act 1 and in its "true" form as a deity or a dead person in act 2 owes much to shamanistic prac-tices, memorial services, and records of dreams and visions. Plays featuring the ghosts of dead people often include depictions of suffering in a Buddhist-style pur-gatory, and when demons take center stage, exorcism is almost sure to follow. Some of the main characters in noh plays are ordinary, living people, but even then the experiences enacted are usually extraordinary, with altered states of consciousness caused by obsessive grief, love, loyalty, or devotion, a favorite subject.

Kyōgen plays are normally interspersed between noh plays in a day's program. Quotidian experiences are the stuff of these plays, which feature husbands and wives, masters and servants, merchants, blind people, *yamabushi* (mountain priests), and even animals and plants. Popular songs of the period (*kouta*) were worked into kyō-gen plays, and conversely, songs sung in kyōgen became popular outside the theater. Noh and kyōgen have common origins, and it is easy to see the beginnings of kyō-gen in the comic mimes performed in the Heian period. Although the two theaters developed as companion arts, the early history of kyōgen is shadowy. Zeami's holo-graphs of several complete noh texts have survived, although the earliest extant kyō-gen scripts, the *Tenshō kyōgen bon* of 1578, are simply brief plot outlines. Full kyō-gen texts were written down only in the Edo period (1600–1868); consequently, some of what is claimed to be an expression of Muromachi society may in fact be more typical of a later period. It is clear, however, that in the century after Zeami, kyōgen enjoyed growing popularity in the numerous public performances typical of that period. In the late fifteenth and the sixteenth centuries, noh and kyōgen were performed by both male and female professional troupes as well as by amateur and semi-amateur (*te sarugaku*) actors. Teaching amateurs quickly became an economic factor in preserving the theater, as it continues to be today.

Late medieval records mention noh plays staged with puppets. Although both string marionettes and mechanical dolls were known in Japan, hand-operated puppets have been the focus of most of the artistic development. Puppets served as mediums in Shinto rituals to express the words and perform the actions of the gods, and puppet performances were presented as offerings to please and petition the deities; any humans who happened to be around could also enjoy the performances. Puppeteers (*ebisu kake*) connected with the Ebisu Shrine at Nishinomiya (between modern Osaka and Kobe) and specializing in plays about the deity Ebisu were particularly well known. This troupe staged noh plays in 1555 and was invited to play at the imperial palace. Other puppeteers (*hotoke mawashi*) were connected with temples and presented tales about Buddhist deities and related themes. Not, however, until puppeteers joined forces with *jōruri* chanters and shamisen players was the puppet theater truly established.

To trace that development, we need to return to the history of recited narratives. The recitation of *The Tale of the Heike* to the accompaniment of the biwa (heikyo-ku) gradually declined in popularity and was partially replaced by a genre called *kōwaka*. The performers of kōwaka might be viewed as male successors to the kuse-mai entertainers. They also danced to the rhythmic accompaniment of a drum or fan, but their recitations were mostly battle tales, among which episodes from the *Heike* played a major role. Nothing is known about the movements accompanying this recitation, for only remnants of the performing art have survived. Dance, however, seems to have been secondary to the telling of the tales. Kōwaka gained prominence in the fifteenth century, and by the sixteenth century its popularity sometimes rivaled noh among warrior audiences. But thereafter, its decline was swift, and its performance practices have largely been lost, although some fifty texts remain. As the kōwaka *Atsumori* (translated in part 2) exemplifies, the plots of these tales suggest an intermediary stage between noh and the kabuki and puppet theaters, with the focus having moved from the individual warrior, his memories, and his search for salvation to a larger web of social relationships and obligations.

Other recited narratives attained broad popular appeal. One such genre, *sekkyō bushi* (literally "sermon ballads"), consisted of stories recited by itinerant entertainers accompanied by a variety of musical instruments, initially a bamboo instrument called the *sasara* and gongs (*shō*). In one type of tale popular with these reciters (*honji mono*), the main character was revealed to be a manifestation (*suijaku*) of a deity, the honji or true form. These stories also included their share of human emotions, especially grief caused by separation from a loved one. As these entertainers attracted more urban audiences, they added new musical instruments and finally puppets to their presentations, but their art was eventually overshadowed by the popularity of the livelier music of jōruri performances.

The most popular recited narrative in the sixteenth century was a piece entitled *A Tale in Twelve Episodes* (Jūnidan sōshi), which relates the story of Lady Jōruri and

Minamoto Yoshitsune, the warrior who helped the Genji win the twelfth-century wars and who was then attacked by his brother Yoritomo, the first Minamoto shogun. This tale was probably first recited to biwa music, but by about 1570, the shamisen had been introduced from the Ryūkyū Islands, and the nature of recited narratives underwent a radical change. This new instrument, with its sharp, almost percussive sound, was deemed better suited to accompany narrative chanting than was the more melodious biwa. When shamisen accompaniment was added to the recitation of A *Tale in Twelve Episodes*, jōruri chanting was born, the name attesting to the popularity of the story's heroine. At some point, probably around the turn of the seventeenth century, this type of narrative recitation and the art of puppetry were combined, and the puppet theater, which also came to be called jōruri—or more formally, doll (*ningyō*) jōruri—was on its way to becoming a fully developed theatrical form.

Another element involved in the creation of new theatrical forms was the growth of group dances called *odori*. In contrast to the term *mai* (literally "turning" or "circling"), which was used for the dance forms described thus far, odori (literally "jumping" or "leaping") refers to a style of dancing in which the feet maintain less constant contact with the floor. Odori-type dancing as a religious practice was advocated by the priest Kūya (903–972) and was popularized by Ippen (1239–1289). This activity, called *nembutsu odori*, involved group dancing to the chanting of the nembutsu and the singing of Buddhist hymns with drum, gong, and rattle accompaniment. First performed by groups of priests and then by masses of parishioners as well, it was particularly popular during the summer festival of the dead (*obon*) as a ritual to pacify malignant souls. It continues to be a popular part of these summer festivals.

A parallel art called decorative dancing (*furyū odori*) consisted of mass processions of dancers in fancy costumes with masks and decorated props—typically, enormous umbrellas, elaborate floats, and the music of drums, flutes, and gongs. The popularity and ostentatiousness of these processions led to periodic government prohibitions, but they continued to be held well into the Tokugawa period and linger today in more sedate forms such as the Gion Festival held each July in Kyoto. These two performance types were sometimes combined into a syncretized form known as decorative nembutsu (*nembutsu furyū*). In this combination, popular songs joined religious ones, and costumes and masks added to the pleasure of the event and the effectiveness of the ritual propitiation of the deities and the souls of the dead. The nembutsu furyū tradition led directly to the development of the kabuki theater.

The second half of the sixteenth century, like the late twelfth century, was a period of major transitions and prolonged civil war. The three consecutive military leaders of this tumultuous period were patrons and devotees of the performing arts and used these arts to promote their own personal and political agendas. Oda Nobunaga (1534–1582), the first of the three, was particularly partial to kōwaka. Before an important battle in 1560, he reportedly danced a felicitous section of the kōwaka *Atsumori*, and in 1582 he sponsored a competition between kōwaka and noh, which was won by the former group. On another occasion he is said to have dressed up as a celestial maiden and danced with the masses in a furyū nembutsu during an obon festival. His successor, Toyotomi Hideyoshi (1536–1598), proved to be the most enthusiastic thespian. Not only did he sponsor and participate in ostentatious furyū events, but he was also passionately fond of noh. In 1593 he celebrated the birth of a son by acting in sixteen noh plays in front of the emperor GoYōzei. His eventual successor, Tokugawa Ieyasu (1542–1616), joined him in presenting a new kyōgen play. The next year Hideyoshi performed at the imperial palace again. This time in addition to doing traditional pieces, he starred in five plays about his own life, which he had commissioned. Besides celebrating his military exploits, the plays expressed his mother's claim that she owed her salvation to the prayers of her filial son! Such self-aggrandizement did little to further Hideyoshi's eternal fame, however, as the plays were never staged again after he died four years later without leaving a secure heir.

Tokugawa Ieyasu laid the groundwork for both the perpetuation of the Tokugawa shogunate and the role of noh as the ceremonial "music" (shikigaku) of the military rulers, a function similar to that of bugaku in the Heian period. Immediately after he became shogun in 1603, Ieyasu ordered three days of celebratory noh and kyōgen performances, a practice that his successors continued. Although Ieyasu himself performed in his earlier years (his earliest recorded performance was in 1571, when he was twenty-nine), later he preferred to remain a spectator and earned a reputation as a discerning and appreciative critic. He carried on Hideyoshi's policy of supporting the four schools (za) of noh—Kanze, Hōshō, Komparu, and Kongō—with relatively generous grants of rice stipends and estate rights, which were continued until the Tokugawa shogunate was overthrown in 1868 and which made government-sponsored actors the equivalent of members of the warrior class. Under Ieyasu's immediate successors, the most famous noh actor of the seventeenth century, Kita Shichitayū Osayoshi (1586–1653), was patronized and permitted to found the Kita troupe, the fifth and last of the official noh schools, all of which are still active. In addition to noh actors, these schools originally included musicians, kyōgen players, and semiamateur performers (te sarugaku); all were male.

In 1603, the year in which Ieyasu was named the first Tokugawa shogun, a woman known as Okuni starred in an epoch-making event: she performed what was referred to as "kabuki dance" (kabuki odori) on the dry riverbed of the Kamo River in Kyoto. Although this is the first time that phrase appears in extant records, the word kabuki, which literally means "to tilt" or "to slant," was commonly used to refer to unusual or outlandish behavior or dress.[2] This seems an apt description of Okuni's performance, as early pictures show her dancing in Portuguese-style trousers, wearing a "southern barbarian" (that is, foreign) style coolie hat, with a gong in her hand and a Christian cross around her neck. An early-seventeenth-century source (Kabuki zōshi) claims that Okuni's performances included scenes depicting the more kabuki-like aspects of a samurai dandy, alleged to be Okuni's recently deceased lover, and a nembutsu odori (perhaps dedicated to her lover's ghost).

2. The way of writing the name of the theater was soon changed to the more felicitous ideographs for "song, dance, and art" (ka-bu-ki).

Kabuki odori excited the popular imagination, and troupes of female performers proliferated. The settings of these performances included teahouses and public baths, and the shamisen was soon added to the flute and drum accompaniment. Ranking members of the samurai class vied to become patrons of the actresses. On at least one occasion there was a serious riot as rival warriors thronged the kabuki stage seeking favors from the actresses. Declaring such behavior improper for members of the ruling class, the shogunate took action against the actresses and, in 1629, prohibited women from appearing on the stage. This prohibition effectively ended the direct participation of women in the major theatrical genres, although female dancers continued to perform in the more private settings of the banquet hall and the teahouse.

The prohibition against female performers brought new visibility to troupes of young men (*wakashu*), who had been competing with the women. These youths made major innovations in the rapidly developing art of kabuki, including the introduction of acrobatic skills and juggling known as *hōka* and kyōgen-like scenarios developed with the help of independent noh and kyōgen actors. The third Tokugawa shogun, Iemitsu, was a particularly active patron of young men's kabuki. Like the women kabuki dancers, however, the youths were displaying themselves as available for prostitution, and once their protector Iemitsu died, they too were banned.

After 1652, only adult males could appear onstage. The passage between youth and adulthood was marked by shaving the front part of the head, an act usually undertaken in the late teens. Not surprisingly, however, some young kabuki actors became adults prematurely. To hide their bald spots, actors playing female roles covered the front part of their heads with purple cloths; remnants of this practice still appear in modern costuming (see figure 1.29). Males playing female roles had to register with the government to ensure that women did not appear onstage, a practice that helped speed role specialization, particularly that of female impersonators (*onnagata*). Eliminating women and young men from the stage reduced the direct sexual allure of the performances and led to significant innovations designed to attract wider audiences. The actors created more sophisticated, dialogue-oriented scenes to supplement the song and dance and depicted contemporary events onstage, the most popular of which were prostitute procurement, love suicides, scandalous murders, and fights among warriors.

The Tokugawa clan chose Edo (present-day Tokyo) as its headquarters, and early in the seventeenth century many entertainers decided to try their luck in this new city, among them several well-known jōruri chanters. The audiences they found in Edo—somewhat rougher than those in Osaka and Kyoto—were part of a growing class of urban dwellers, mostly merchants and artisans, who were eager to assert their own cultural identity. One early reflection of this was the creation of a bombastic martial hero named Kimpira, whose lively exploits in several popular puppet plays exemplify the frontier spirit of this new city. In 1673 a young kabuki actor, Ichikawa Danjūrō I (1660–1704), made his debut in Edo playing the role of Kimpira, and his bravura style (*aragoto*) of acting—performed with vivid red and black makeup (*kumadori*)—created a sensation. Danjūrō developed his acting style in some fifty plays he wrote under the name Mimasuya Hyōgo. Two of these, *Saint*

Narukami (1684) and *The God Fudō* (1697), became sources for the play *Saint Narukami and the God Fudō*, a section of which is translated in this volume. Danjūrō died in a manner befitting the creator of the bold aragoto style: he was stabbed to death onstage by a fellow actor.

Danjūrō lived during the Genroku era (roughly 1680 to 1720), one of the liveliest cultural periods in Japanese history and a time of prosperity for noh and kyōgen and of rapid progress in the development of the newer genres. The shogun from 1680 to 1709 was Tokugawa Tsunayoshi (1646–1709), an eccentric leader who was something of a noh "fanatic." By his time noh had been established as the official ceremonial music (shikigaku), with formal performances regularly scheduled to ensure prosperity for the country and long life for the rulers. Tsunayoshi's involvement with noh, however, went well beyond any official relationship. He was an impassioned performer; in 1697 alone he was the main actor (*shite*) seventy-one times in twenty-three different plays and performed independent noh dances 150 times! Furthermore, Tsunayoshi insisted that his retainers and the feudal lords (*daimyō*) also practice noh and sponsor players and performances. He granted dozens of actors the status of samurai and made some of them quite wealthy, but he would also banish performers or reduce their stipends if they displeased him, and his abrupt summons to actors to serve in his castle sometimes disrupted orderly lines of succession in the schools. His taste for unusual noh (which was shared by his immediate successor) resulted in the revival of many old plays, more than one hundred of which still remain in the repertory of at least one school. Some of these plays (like *Kinuta*, *Semimaru*, and *Ohara gokō*) are now highly valued pieces. The publication of five hundred noh plays and 150 summaries of kyōgen also encouraged the appreciation of the plays as literature. Noh's popularity spread far beyond Edo, the shogunate, and the five official schools. Many daimyō—even in places as distant as Sendai—were active noh supporters, and provincial members of the warrior class and their families (including wives and daughters) would take up noh chanting or drumming. In Nara, temple performers (*negi*) were increasingly active; subscription noh (*kanjinnō*) performances, open to the public for a fee, were particularly popular in Osaka, and the imperial palace in Kyoto sponsored competitive performances. A document published in 1687 (*Nō no kimmōzui*) lists 274 noh and kyōgen performers residing in Kyoto. Noh had become a nationwide success.

The popularity of noh, however, was mostly limited to members of the warrior class, which left the majority of the townspeople of Osaka, Kyoto, and Edo open to newer forms of theater. A disastrous fire in 1657 destroyed most of Edo and its theaters and encouraged some of the leading jōruri chanters to return to their roots in Osaka, which remains the home of the puppet theater even today. An outstanding kabuki actor in Kyoto, Sakata Tōjūrō (1644–1709), enhanced a category of plays about prostitutes (*keisei goto*) by creating a gentle, amorous, and humorously ineffective male lover. *Love Letter from the Licensed Quarter* (Kuruwa bunshō, 1712) is a good example of a prostitute play featuring Izaemon, the role that Tōjūrō created, and the courtesan Yūgiri. Tōjūrō's gentle, understated acting style is called *wagoto*, in contrast to Danjūrō's bold and exaggerated aragoto. In the kabuki version of the play *Love Suicides at Amijima* (1721; translated here), Jihei is played in wagoto style (see figure 3.15). Sakata Tōjūrō's ideas about his art and comments on

FIGURE 1.4. The role of Sukeroku, as defined by Danjūrō II, combines the gentle chic of the wagoto style in the costume and the pose on the left, with a hint of the aragoto style in the makeup and the glaring pose (*mie*) on the right. The purple crepe headband (*hachimaki*) rakishly tied is a symbol of the dashing man about town. (Photos by Aoki Shinji.)

the life of a female impersonator by the famous onnagata Yoshizawa Ayame (1673–1729) are recorded in *The Actor's Analects* (Yakusha rongo), the best Tokugawa work on acting.

The interplay between the Kyoto and Edo styles of kabuki is well illustrated by the history of the play *Sukeroku* (the full name is *Sukeroku yukari no Edo zakura*). The love suicide of the courtesan Agemaki and her lover Sukeroku was depicted in kabuki plays in Kyoto in the late seventeenth century. In 1713, an Edo play—with Ichikawa Danjūrō II (1688–1758) in the role of Sukeroku—ignored the suicide and concentrated instead on Sukeroku's rivalry with another samurai, named Ikyū. The gentle Kyoto lover takes on a decidedly Edo air swaggering about, bragging, and using Edo colloquialisms and bantering insults. Three years later, Danjūrō revised the play, adding a long entrance scene performed with a large umbrella, possibly to take advantage of the development of the rampway (*hanamichi*), which at about this time was extended to reach from the stage to the rear of the audience. Danjūrō, skilled in both the aragoto style his father had developed and the Kyoto wagoto, combined the two in this Sukeroku. Instead of the padded aragoto costume, Sukeroku wears a chic black kimono and ties a purple silk band around his head. His makeup includes narrow black and red lines over his eyes, alluding to the aragoto style (figure 1.4).

As the preceding comments may suggest, kabuki is very much an actor-oriented theater, which accounts for the actors' rather cavalier treatment of scripts, especially in the early days of the theater's history. Although playwrights were first listed in theater programs as early as 1680, their function was more limited than this recognition might imply. Some parts of the play were left to the actors to improvise, and other sections appear to have been freely reworked by them. Since no kabuki scripts from the Genroku period have survived, it is impossible to know what they contained. It is clear, however, that the role of the playwright was not to create a literary masterpiece; instead, his task was to provide a vehicle for the actors' art.

The puppet theater, in contrast, centered on the chanter and his text. In 1684 the celebrated jōruri chanter Takemoto Gidayū (1651–1714) opened a theater in Osaka. Gidayū's innovative style of chanting became the standard, called *gidayū bushi* in his honor. Gidayū's influence goes deeper than his prominence as a performer, however; his understanding of music and theater, including his knowledge of noh, helped him create a new musical structure for puppet plays, which he developed in collaboration with the playwright Chikamatsu Monzaemon (1653–1724).

Chikamatsu, the first known playwright who was not a performer, wrote both kabuki and puppet plays. Among his early puppet plays was *Kagekiyo Victorious* (Shusse Kagekiyo), produced in 1686 by Gidayū in his new theater. From about 1688, however, Chikamatsu served mainly as a staff playwright for the kabuki actor Sakata Tōjūrō, creating some of his prostitute plays. In 1703 he returned to writing for the puppets. The reasons for this change are not known, although commentators hypothesize that he objected to the many liberties the kabuki actors took with his texts. Perhaps he realized that Tōjūrō would soon leave the stage (he died in 1709), or perhaps he was attracted to the rising popularity of Gidayū. Whatever the initial reasons for his switch, it became permanent with the resounding success of his *Love Suicides at Sonezaki* (Sonezaki shinjū), presented at Gidayū's theater in 1703. The kabuki theater had been producing love-suicide plays for at least twenty years, but the subject had been avoided in the more conservative puppet theater. Nevertheless, when Chikamatsu, who happened to be in Osaka, heard of the suicide of the shopkeeper Tokubei and the courtesan Ohatsu, he quickly produced a puppet play for Gidayū. Although *Love Suicides at Sonezaki* opened only three weeks after the actual event, a kabuki play on the subject had already premiered. Such rapid responses led to the nickname "overnight pickles" (*ichiyazuke*) for plays about current events.

Chikamatsu's "pickle" was so successful that it ensured the fortunes of the young Takemoto Theater and inaugurated the writing of domestic plays (*sewa mono*) for the puppet theater. In contrast to earlier pieces, which tended to depict historical events and feature superhuman characters such as Kimpira, these plays portray the tragedies of ordinary life. After this success Chikamatsu moved to Osaka and dedicated all his efforts to the puppet theater. He continued to write domestic plays, including his masterpiece *Love Suicides at Amijima* (Ten no Amijima shinjū, 1721; translated in part 3), but he did not limit himself to them. After Gidayū's death, when a successful play was needed to launch the career of Gidayū's young successor, Chikamatsu composed the period piece (*jidai mono*) *The Battles of Coxinga* (Kokusen'ya kassen; partially translated in part 3). It exceeded all expectations by running for a record seventeen months.

FIGURE 1.5. Three-man puppets with movable features were not created until the second quarter of the eighteenth century. In *Sugawara and the Secrets of Calligraphy*, Matsuomarō has a Bunshichi head with movable eyeballs and eyebrows. (Photo by Barbara C. Adachi.)

In the early eighteenth century, great strides were made in the development of puppets. The hand-held puppets of Chikamatsu's time were small enough to be operated by one person and were of relatively simple construction; only in the 1690s were they given functional arms. String marionettes and mechanical dolls sometimes were mixed with the hand-operated puppets for special effect. From 1705 on, the puppeteers performed in full view of the audience, and the chanter and shamisen player moved from behind a curtain to a platform at stage left. It was not until after Chikamatsu's death in 1724 that the puppets' eyes, mouths, and fingers were made to move, and only in 1734 did puppets operated by three men appear (figure 1.5). The early eighteenth century was the heyday of the puppet theater and probably the only time in theater history when, in Osaka at least, inanimate dolls enjoyed greater fame than live actors.

In Chikamatsu Monzaemon's day, the chanter reigned supreme in the puppet theater. But by the mid-eighteenth century that too had changed, thanks partly to a puppeteer named Yoshida Bunzaburō (d. 1760), who introduced the three-man puppet and began using an extension rod to operate the puppet's left arm. Bunzaburō gained considerable influence in the Takemoto Theater, then managed by the playwright Takeda Izumo II (1691–1756), who was particularly interested in the visual aspects of performance. A crisis occurred one day in 1748, when Bunzaburō requested that the chanter prolong a passage so the dolls would have more time to act. Considering the request an insult, the chanter refused. Izumo, uncertain how to adjudicate this dispute, finally ruled in favor of the puppeteer, precipitating the departure of the chanter to a rival theater.

Izumo and his fellow playwrights clearly wrote for the puppets. Although they were less literary than Chikamatsu Monzaemon, they had an unerring sense of the theatrical. They normally worked in groups. Izumo, Namiki Senryū (1695–1751; also called Sōsuke), and Miyoshi Shōraku (1696–?) together produced what are considered the three greatest works for puppets: *Sugawara and the Secrets of Calligraphy* (Sugawara denjū tenarai kagami, 1746), *Yoshitsune and a Thousand*

Cherry Trees (Yoshitsune sembon zakura, 1747), and *Chūshingura* (Kanadehon chūshingura, 1748), scenes of which are anthologized in part 3. After the death of a somewhat younger colleague, Chikamatsu Hanji (1725–1783)—an admirer but not a relative of Chikamatsu Monzaemon—no other great playwrights wrote for the puppets, and their popularity declined. The two major puppet theaters in Osaka folded in 1765 and 1767, handing over their facilities to kabuki actors, and for a century the puppet tradition was kept alive only in small urban theaters and in the countryside.

Shogunal authorities, who kept a close watch over the activities of the urban classes, did not hesitate to regulate the theater. As we have seen, two important governmental decisions had already greatly affected the growth of theater: the prohibition of women onstage and the decision to make noh and kyōgen the official performing art of the warrior class. Suspicious of the possible adverse effects of theater on behavior—arguments that are familiar even today—the government also censored the content of plays. In 1722 the love-suicide theme, a staple of both the kabuki and the puppet theater, was proscribed, and performers were not allowed to portray members of leading families or important current events. In order to circumvent the censorship, playwrights disguised current events by setting them in the past. Accordingly, *Chūshingura*, which enacts a vendetta carried out in 1703, was set in the fourteenth century, and the names of the characters were altered just enough to avoid problems with the law but not enough to prevent recognition by the audience. Various historical periods and people were selected as conventional settings or worlds (*sekai*), and the employment of these worlds—even when it was not really necessary—became increasingly popular, particularly in Edo, the castle town of the shogun.

During the peak of the puppet theater's success, kabuki borrowed heavily from it, especially in Osaka and Kyoto. (The influence actually went both ways, as is described in the introduction to part 3.) Popular puppet plays were often reproduced on the kabuki stage within a month of their premieres, with puppeteers and jōruri musicians sometimes assisting in the preparation of the kabuki versions. Gidayū-style music was adapted wholesale, sometimes used even for plays written originally for kabuki, and this in turn affected the movements of the actors. One playwright influential in kabuki's adaptation of puppet techniques was Namiki Shōzō (1730–1773), who became a disciple of Namiki Senryū for a year or so before Senryū died in 1751. After his teacher's death Shōzō returned to writing for the kabuki theater, but the puppet influence is clear in his later plays, in which he incorporated gidayū-style narrators. He is best known, however, for his employment of elaborate stage machinery. Starting in 1753 he began to make extensive use of stage traps (*seri*), which had been around for almost half a century, and he is credited with the first effective use of the revolving stage (*mawari butai*) in 1758, almost a century and a half before it appeared in German theater. These mechanisms, along with the already existing rampway (hanamichi) through the audience, played a large part in developing kabuki's spectacular aspects.

Meanwhile in Edo, the local culture was making itself felt in the theater. One good example is the history of the piece *Sukeroku*. In the 1716 Edo production, already discussed briefly, the play was set in the world (sekai) of the Soga brothers;

that is, the hero Sukeroku was revealed to be a disguise (*yatsushi*) for the historical and legendary figure Soga no Gorō (aka Tokimune, 1174–1193). The anachronistic identification of a typical Tokugawa-period dandy with a twelfth-century warrior was readily accepted. In a later revision (1753) the playwright Fujimoto Tobun (1716–1763) went a step further and inserted *Sukeroku* in a long play about the Soga brothers, an example of the Edo practice of combining domestic pieces (sewa mono) and period pieces (jidai mono) within a single play. Danjūrō II performed Sukeroku for the third and last time in 1749 at the age of sixty-two. For that performance the original *itchū bushi* accompaniment, a Kyoto musical style with a dignified and elegant melodic line, was changed to *katō bushi*, a type of music especially popular among wealthy Edo townspeople who were fans of kabuki and Danjūrō. Katō bushi also has an elegant vocal line but uses a stronger shamisen accompaniment.

A variety of new musical styles emerged in Edo kabuki along with the development of dance plays (*shosa goto*), which in the first half of the eighteenth century were the specialty of onnagata and in the second half were written for male roles as well. *Nagauta*, now considered kabuki music par excellence, was created in the Osaka area, where it was used mostly in teahouses and private homes. In Edo, however, it became an essential part of kabuki music. *Bungo bushi*, a style created by the chanter Miyakoji Bungonojō (ca. 1660–1740), who moved to Edo in 1739, was used for passionate and suggestive love-suicide pieces. Indeed, this style of music achieved such great popularity that it was banned by censorious government authorities. Bungonojō's tradition spawned other styles as well, including *tokiwazu* and *kiyomoto*, both of which continue to be used today, especially for dance pieces. Some of the dance plays, like the example in this anthology, *A Maiden at Dōjōji* (Musume Dōjōji), were derived from noh but became so imbued with the characteristics of kabuki that they are now considered an essential part of that theater.

The 1796 move from Osaka to Edo by the playwright Namiki Gohei I (1747–1808) marks the triumph of Edo as the theatrical center. In Edo, Gohei introduced some of Osaka's more successful dramaturgical practices. For example, he encouraged programs made up of two separate pieces, a period piece and a domestic piece, rather than continuing the earlier practice of combining the two modes. He himself is credited with more than 110 plays of both types.

Tsuruya Namboku IV (1755–1829), one of the greatest kabuki playwrights, was born in Edo, the son of a dyer. Although he became an apprentice playwright when he was twenty-one, he is best known for the domestic plays he wrote after he turned fifty. His *Osome and Hisamatsu* (Osome Hisamatsu ukina no yomiuri, 1813) includes seven roles for the same actor, which makes it a popular showpiece for versatile actors such as the current Ichikawa Ennosuke (b. 1939). The open eroticism of Namboku's *Scarlet Princess of Edo* (Sakura-hime Azuma Bunshō, 1817) harks back to early plays like *Narukami*, and his best-known work, *Yotsuya Ghost Stories* (Tōkaidō Yotsuya kaidan; partially translated in part 3), with its skillful blend of the supernatural and the quotidian, portrays the world of petty villains and corrupt samurai as well as the wretched lot of women. Namboku's depictions of the lower strata of society led to the growth of a new genre called "raw-life pieces" (*kizewa mono*). Plays of this type, which combined the sentimental, the grizzly, and the grotesque, influenced popular novels of the time.

During the first few decades of the nineteenth century, kabuki and kabuki-related arts prospered. Dance plays derived from noh and kyōgen (*matsubamme mono*) were particularly popular in this period. The first such piece, *The Subscription List* (Kanjinchō), based on the noh play *Ataka*, premiered in 1840 and is still one of the most popular plays in the repertoire. The cast of eleven, headed by Danjūrō VII in 1840, includes no female roles. Unlike earlier borrowings from noh, which were completely redone as kabuki (such as *A Maiden at Dōjōji*), the matsubamme mono adapted elements of noh performance as well as the story. They borrowed the music, costumes, props, and the pine-tree background, considered an audacious act when noh was the preserve of the samurai class. *Henge mono* (transformation piece), another dance genre, also reached the height of its popularity in the early nineteenth century. In these pieces the leading dancer changed costume and character from three to as many as twelve times. *Rokkasen* (Six saints of poetry) is the only one of these dances performed in its entirety today, but parts of other henge mono, such as *Fuji musume* (Wisteria maiden), remain popular.

The publication of illustrated kabuki playbooks designed for reading and of woodblock prints depicting actors and scenes from plays prospered in the early 1800s, and kabuki-style dances (*buyō*) were regularly performed in teahouses and at private homes by both male and female dancers. Kabuki also flourished outside the major urban centers; permanent and semipermanent stages were built in villages and religious centers throughout Japan. Traveling groups of actors (and puppeteers) performed on these stages, and local amateurs produced their own plays. Rural performances proliferated when the government banned farmers from attending urban theaters. The popularity of kabuki became so broad-based that the government threatened to ban it totally, a threat it fortunately did not carry out. In 1842, however, the authorities forced theaters in Edo to move from the center of town to the outskirts near the Yoshiwara pleasure district, proscribed all performances within the precincts of shrines and temples, and prohibited the publication of theater-related woodblock prints. Individual actors were also punished for breaking the very restrictive laws that governed their lives: Onoe Baikō was manacled for appearing without a sedge hat, Nakamura Utaemon was jailed for going to a sumo match, and Ichikawa Danjūrō VII (1791–1859) was exiled for his opulent lifestyle (Shively 1978:44).

Despite the overwhelming popularity of kabuki after the mid-eighteenth century and the government's censorship of theater in general, the puppet theater managed to survive. Sometime in the 1780s a puppeteer from the Inland Sea island of Awaji, Masai Kahei (d. 1810), better known by his stage name Bunrakuken, took his troupe to Osaka and began performing on the riverbanks. His skill revived interest in the puppet theater, and in 1811 his daughter and her husband were allowed to set up a theater at the Inari Shrine. The troupe prospered there until the edicts of 1842 forced it to close. Fortunately, the ban on theaters at religious institutions was lifted the following year (after its promulgator died), and the puppet theater continued performing at the shrine until 1872, when it moved to the western part of Osaka and was named the Bunraku Theater (Bunraku-za) after the troupe's founder. The theater was so successful that *bunraku* became widely used as a generic term for Japanese puppets; it is used today in the name of the National Bunraku Theater (Kokuritsu bunraku gekijō) in Osaka.

Although noh and kyōgen were largely the preserve of the warrior class during the Tokugawa era, there were some opportunities for others to attend performances. Selected commoners were admitted to some of the ceremonial performances sponsored by the shogun and the feudal lords. For example, the farmers of Kurokawa, who trace their still-active tradition of amateur noh back to the fifteenth century, saw noh at the Tsurugaoka castle of the Sakai family. Subscription performances open to the public for a fee were also held occasionally, more frequently in Osaka than elsewhere, and now and then the government sponsored large public performances by members of the five official schools. Records of such performances in 1750 and in 1848 show that approximately four thousand people attended each day for fifteen days (Omote and Amano 1987:153). Contemporary accounts reveal that it was difficult to hear or see the performers, that some of the audience drank or slept, and that the kyōgen pieces were more popular than the noh plays. Small groups of independent noh and kyōgen performers roamed the countryside, playing in empty lots or temple grounds, and occasionally attracting enough notice to arouse the ire of the five government-supported schools of noh actors. The chanting of noh texts was a popular pastime and spread beyond the warrior class to the public at large. Small sections of plays (ko-utai) were even included in the textbooks used by the temple schools. Publishing chantbooks (utaibon) was a profitable business, and some performers were even able to earn their living by giving chanting lessons to townspeople.

As the Tokugawa period drew to a close, the last great kabuki playwright, Kawatake Mokuami (1816–1893), portrayed life in his native Edo. Continuing in the tradition of Namboku, Mokuami wrote raw-life pieces (kizewa mono) about murderers, thieves, and lowlifes, including the famous Benten the Thief (Benten kozō, 1862; excerpted in part 3) and The Love of Izayoi and Seishin (Izayoi Seishin, 1859). His plays are often unwieldy, but individual acts, especially extortion and murder scenes, are extremely effective and still very popular. They, too, encountered bouts of official censorship, such as the 1866 edict that forbade excessive realism in the portrayal of thieves and prostitutes to avoid tempting people to enter these professions. Mokuami also adapted some plays from the noh theater, most notably Tsuchigumo (The monstrous spider) and Momijigari (Hunting for autumn leaves; the names of the kabuki pieces and the noh plays are the same).

The opening of Japan to the West in the mid-nineteenth century and the establishment of a new form of government after 1868 brought changes to all forms of traditional Japanese theater. Noh and kyōgen, which had depended on the patronage of the defunct Tokugawa shogunate, were the most radically affected. Most actors entered new professions. Despite the overwhelming craze for new and foreign things, however, one stubborn actor, Umewaka Minoru I (1828–1909) was determined to preserve noh and was able to convince another actor, Hōshō Kurō XVI (1837–1917), to join him in his struggle.

Foreign relations contributed to their eventual success. In 1869 the Duke of Edinburgh had to be entertained, and even though noh was out of favor, it was deemed the only form dignified enough for the occasion. When Iwakura Tomomi (1825–1883) led a delegation of high-ranking government officials to the West in 1871, he saw similarities between noh and opera, the theatrical form most often used to entertain state dignitaries. Consequently, in 1876 Iwakura entertained the imperial family with noh performances by both Umewaka and Hōshō, and thereafter the imperial family, especially the Meiji emperor's mother Eishō (1833–1897), began to patronize noh. The first head of state (actually former head) ever to visit Japan, U.S. president Ulysses S. Grant, arrived in 1879 and was entertained with performances of both noh and kyōgen. Grant reportedly admired the noh and urged that it be preserved. As a result Iwakura established the Noh Society (Nōgakusha), which built the first permanent noh stage for the general public at Shiba Park in Tokyo. It opened to great acclaim in 1881, and its success helped ensure the viability of noh in the modern world.

The puppet theater was able to thrive in the early Meiji period thanks to several excellent performers, including Toyozawa Dampei (1827–1898), one of the greatest shamisen players of all times and co-composer with his wife of the popular play *The Miracle of the Tsubosaka Kannon* (Tsubosaka Kannon reigenki; part 3), and the puppeteer Yoshida Tamazō I (1828–1905), who introduced many new puppet techniques. There was also a resurgence of popular female chanters, who had been relegated to amateur status but who now reappeared in the theaters for a brief period. The poor management of the Bunraku Theater, which housed the major troupe, led to its sale to the Shochiku Company in 1909. Then the theater building burned down in 1926, destroying most of the valuable old puppets. Dedicated and talented performers continued to struggle, but it was an uphill battle until the 1930s when the government began to encourage bunraku as a traditional Japanese art.

For kabuki, the end of the Tokugawa rule meant a reduction in government restrictions and a rise in the official status of the actors from outcasts to ordinary citizens. A modern kabuki theater was constructed in the heart of Tokyo in 1872 (the Morita-za), and the following year the metropolitan government licensed ten theaters—there had been only three during most of the Tokugawa period. In 1887 the emperor went to see a kabuki play, a historical first, and other members of the upper classes followed suit. A concerted effort was made to "modernize" kabuki. The theater buildings adapted more Western features: the original Kabuki-za (1889) had a Western-style exterior, and the Teikoku-gekijō (Imperial theater), which opened in 1911, was Japan's first purely Western-style theater.

New types of plays were also created. Ichikawa Danjūrō IX (1838–1903) produced living history plays (*katsureki geki*), which emphasized historical accuracy and often dealt with the recent past, and his rival Onoe Kikugorō V (1844–1903) produced "clipped-hair" pieces (*zangiri mono*), domestic pieces depicting contemporary men who had cut off their now forbidden topknots and wore Western clothes. Plays of both sorts were written by Mokuami, who also wrote for the third of the great Meiji kabuki actors Ichikawa Sadanji I (1842–1904). These plays, however, were still steeped in the old traditions and soon came to seem old-fashioned.

A somewhat different attempt to modernize kabuki and compete with the influx of Western plays resulted in "new kabuki" (*shin kabuki*), written by such scholars and litterateurs as Tsubouchi Shōyō (1859–1935), Mori Ōgai (1862–1922), and Okamoto Kidō (1827–1939), the most successful writer in this genre. Composed according to modern European dramaturgical norms, these plays were performed in kabuki style, often by Ichikawa Sadanji II (1880–1940), who in 1910 also revived some of the old Eighteen Kabuki of the Ichikawa family (*kabuki jūhachiban*), including *Narukami*. The efforts to make kabuki into a "modern" theater were, fortunately, unsuccessful.

When it became clear that other styles of theater could better present twentieth-century life onstage, kabuki returned to a more traditional repertory. Although many more "new" plays have become established in kabuki than in the other traditional theaters, the older plays remain the perennial favorites.

World War II left the theater world in disarray: the destruction of Osaka and Tokyo severely damaged or leveled most of the theater buildings, and poverty reduced the audience to a handful. In addition, censorship was reversed. The Occupation authorities prohibited the very classics that were almost the only plays allowed during the war. *Chūshingura*, for example, was alleged to glorify the feudal mentality that had led to war. The traditional theaters were thus slow to regain their audiences, but by the mid-1960s they were nearly back to their prewar levels.

In the 1960s, when the Japanese economy was expanding rapidly, the government once again began to support the arts seriously. Perhaps, like the shogun Yoshimitsu in the fourteenth century, the government felt a need to prove (this time in an international context) that Japan also had a culture.

Whatever the motivation, the policy continues to benefit the traditional performing arts: the government selects performers to name as Intangible Cultural Assets or National Living Treasures and awards them stipends; it encourages and underwrites foreign tours, supports international conferences of theater scholars, and, most important, builds and maintains new facilities. The National Theater (Kokuritsu gekijō) opened in Tokyo in November 1966. Its large auditorium seats 1,746 spectators and is used chiefly for kabuki; a smaller theater holds 630 and is equipped for puppet plays and other traditional forms, such as buyō (kabuki dance). In September 1983, the National Noh Theater (Kokuritsu nōgakudō), seating 591 people, opened in Tokyo, and the following April the National Bunraku Theater (Kokuritsu bunraku gekijō) was inaugurated in Osaka. These national theaters are more than performance places; they provide research facilities, archives, training schools, and opportunities for performers to revive older works and to create new ones. Their existence helps ensure the vitality of traditional theater in Japan today.

General Characteristics

It is impossible to generalize accurately about theatrical forms as diverse as noh, kyōgen, kabuki, and the puppet theater. But because these genres share the same historical background and a relatively isolated geographical context, it is instructive to try. In attempting to isolate and describe some of the characteristics shared by these genres, I usually have refrained from making comparisons with other types of theater, but the informed reader will discover many; none of the attributes discussed is unique to Japanese theater. Nevertheless, the particular ways in which these characteristics have been combined and emphasized in Japan's performing arts may be what makes its theatrical tradition distinctive.

The Text Speaks Itself

The scripts of Japanese traditional theater are not solely, or even primarily, concerned with reproducing ordinary dialogue. That is, in addition to dialogue, they also include descriptions of and commentary on the setting, the stage actions, and the characters. The lines may be in poetry or metered prose and may be sung, chanted, or spoken, often with patterned intonation. The words uttered by a particular actor are not limited to lines that his character might "logically" or "naturally" speak; that is, the actor is not restricted to remaining "in character." Moreover, a chanter or chorus may recite large parts of a play, including the first-person utterances of the characters, in which case the reciter(s) may momentarily take on the voice of one or another character. These reciters, however, are never personified storytellers; the noh chorus is not a group of townspeople commenting or elaborating on the action, and the chanter in the puppet theater is not a garrulous, happy, wise, or foolish old man offering his own perspective on events. Rather, they are stage figures voicing the text,[3] a text that is not limited to creating naturalistic characters or sustaining fixed points of view.

This aspect of theater is related in part to one characteristic of Japanese prose style, the fluidity of its narrative stance, in which the text flows from one subject position to another without necessarily naming either the speaker or the subject of a "sentence." This is possible because of the structure of Japanese grammar: verbs or adjectives may stand alone as complete expressions; the same marker (generally *to* or *tote*) may indicate thoughts, speech, or intention; and singular or plural markers are not required. Consequently, distinguishing between direct and indirect speech or between thoughts and spoken expressions is often impossible, as is identifying the narrator, pinning down precisely who is making a statement.

This fluid narrative stance is exploited in both verbal and visual enactments of theatrical texts. Moments occur in all types of theater when the text speaks without apparently being spoken; that is, the words are voiced by the performers, but no character or clearly defined narrator is speaking them. Released from the limitations of direct mime and defined narrative voice, playwrights and/or actors can manipulate the presentation of the text for aesthetic effects and practical purposes. Important words can be put into the mouth of a major stage figure even if they do not logically belong to the character he is portraying. Likewise, an image or metaphor can be highlighted by having a stage figure step out of character to create it. On the other hand, the words of the character may be given to the chorus or chanters to exploit the magnification of multiple voices or to relieve the actor from speaking when he is involved in dance or other strenuous stage business. The enunciation of a single thought may be divided between two or more stage figures or spoken by them in unison. Let us turn to a few specific examples.

Instead of always assigning appropriate lines to the individual actors representing particular characters, noh, kyōgen, and kabuki regularly have stage figures speaking in unison or dividing lines among them. In kabuki this technique is called "pass-along dialogue" (*watari serifu*). The following example is from the end of *Saint Narukami* (translated in part 1), when a group of monks identify the source of Narukami's downfall:

3. There is an important difference in visual presentation here: the members of the noh chorus maintain immobile positions and expressionless faces while the *jōruri* chanter employs exaggerated facial expressions to help emphasize the sense of the text.

THIRD MONK:
She is Lady Taema of the Clouds,
FOURTH MONK:
most beautiful lady of the Court,
WHITE CLOUD:
by the emperor's command, come to seduce
MONKS IN UNISON:
our master!

In this case, the sharing of lines serves to emphasize the words, to identify the nemesis.

A similar sharing of lines with a more complex effect occurs in the following passage (*kakeai*) from the noh play *Yamamba* (translated in part 2):

TSURE:
Yet I do fear, old woman,
the ebony gloom from which emerges
a figure with speech that's human, but
SHITE:
with a thicket of snowy brambles for hair,
TSURE:
with eyes that sparkle like stars,
SHITE:
and a face that's
TSURE:
painted red—
SHITE:
a demon gargoyle crouching at the eaves—*looks up to right*
TSURE:
this apparition, perceived for the first time tonight,
SHITE:
to what does it compare?
TOGETHER:
The demon of the ancient tale, who . . .

The two players—the main actor (shite) plays Yamamba (a supernatural old woman who lives in the mountains) and the companion actor (*tsure*) represents a woman who makes her livelihood performing a dance about Yamamba—are not carrying on a normal conversation. Rather, they are describing Yamamba, but in effect they are describing themselves. One of the metaphors used to describe the demon is that of a red-faced gargoyle, an image emphasized by the actor's pointing as though there were a real gargoyle onstage. Furthermore, the mask of the shite, which represents the face of Yamamba, is usually not red at all.[4] The text paints a picture different from that presented onstage.

A final example of the complex manner in which a text may be expressed comes

---

4. Only the Kongō school of actors uses a reddish mask, a practice that seems to be inspired by this passage.

from the noh play *Tadanori*. Like the play *Atsumori* (translated in part 2), this piece is about the ghost of a warrior who, toward the end of the play, enacts the last moments of his former life. The main actor (shite), costumed as Tadanori, mimes his final battle while the chorus describes it from a third-person position that uses honorifics to refer to Tadanori. After a retainer of his enemy Rokuyata has sliced off Tadanori's right arm, the shite raises his left hand in prayer, leaving his right arm dangling down at his side. At this point the following rather extraordinary sequence occurs:

FIGURE 1.6. Toward the end of the noh play *Tadanori*, the actor's left arm represents Tadanori praying; then his right arm depicts Rokuyata drawing his sword and cutting off Tadanori's head. Dropping the tip of the raised fan to the back suggests the beheading. The musicians and kōken are wearing crested kimono and hakama. (Photo courtesy of Monica Bethe.)

CHORUS: Rokuyata unsheathes his sword

The shite uses his right hand (no longer representing Tadanori's cut-off arm) to draw his sword—suggested by a closed fan.

and cuts off Tadanori's head

The shite raises his fan and lets the tip drop toward his head as he looks down [figure 1.6].

SHITE: Rokuyata ponders

The shite looks thoughtful.

CHORUS: How sad, when I look at his corpse

The shite stands and looks down as though viewing the corpse.

At the beginning of this passage, the shite is performing the actions of Tadanori, and at the end, those of Rokuyata. His right arm changes its stance before the rest of his body does, and the single line he speaks is in the third person, describing what his body is enacting. When the chorus takes up the chant again, it speaks from Rokuyata's point of view, using humble verb forms. The actor's words and movements clearly exceed the confines of the character whose costume he wears, and the chorus shares in the creation of the characters.

Flexibility of Time and Space

Theatrical time and space are manipulated quite differently in the various genres, but in all cases they are fluid and malleable. The action of the plays easily leaves the dramatic present and readily overflows the confines of the physical stage. Theatrical time may be contracted or expanded to match plot requirements or aesthetic values, and a given locale may disappear as quickly as it is invoked.

FIGURE 1.7. Wanting to escape from his exile on Devil Island, Shunkan finds the ocean approaching in the form of a ground cloth pulled along the rampway. The slats in the back walls are the facade of the music room (*geza*). (Photo by Aoki Shinji.)

Noh and kyōgen do not utilize sets; instead, a scene is created by verbal description, movements, and a few props, leaving much to the audience's imagination. In the first act of the noh play *Izutsu* (translated in part 2), a lonely evening at Ariwara Temple is evoked through poetic description, which is enhanced by the presence of a simple stage prop—a bamboo frame with pampas grass attached. During the opening passage the prop represents a grave mound covered with grasses, but later in the play it suggests both a well and a clump of pampas grass (see figures 2.12 and 2.16). In the kyōgen play *The Snail* (part 2), a dense thicket is conjured up by announcing its presence, by miming the pushing aside of brambles and stepping over underbrush, and by uttering exaggerated sounds of effort ("*ei, ei yatto na*"). The mountain priest and the servant Tarō each employ these means of defining the thicket when they enter, yet when they leave, there is no sign of any obstacles. An imaginary scene is created and then erased, simply by ignoring its existence.

In all theatrical genres, offstage areas often are temporarily incorporated into the setting. In the noh play *Atsumori* (part 2), the main actor rushes to the front of the stage, raises his fan, and looks out over the heads of the audience at the ships at sea (see figure 2.10B); and in a noh play entitled *Tōru*, the actor dips his buckets over the front edge of the stage to draw water from an imaginary pond. Likewise, the frequent use of the kabuki rampway (hanamichi) incorporates the entire auditorium into the set, particularly when two rampways are used for simultaneous entrances (see figure 1.13). In *Shunkan at Devil Island*, the single rampway is converted into an ocean by running a blue ground cloth along it (figure 1.7), and when the actors look out over the audience at an approaching ship, the entire auditorium becomes the sea. In earlier performance practice, a boat moved across the back of the auditorium; now the performers watch an imaginary vessel following its progress around 180 degrees until a small boat actually appears moving across the back of the stage. Finally, the prow of an enormous ship is rolled onstage from stage left (figure 1.8).[5] The imaginary remainder of the ship draws offstage space into the setting as characters appear to move around on board.

Theatrical time is as pliant as theatrical space. A journey may be signified by a few formulaic movements, or both time and place may be transformed by a turn of the actor's head. For instance, when the noh warrior Atsumori catches sight of the

5. This example also illustrates a technique for portraying perspective: a small stage figure is replaced by a large one, or vice versa. The difference in size between the two boats may be so exaggerated that it evokes laughter. This is a typical bit of kabuki self-reflectivity—the performance laughs at itself.

secondary actor portraying his former enemy turned monk, the past becomes the dramatic present (see figure 2.11). A kabuki actor breaches the boundaries of the dramatic present by referring to himself or other actors by their own names or by noting the popularity of the play in which he is starring. Moments of stillness in noh (when, for example, the woman in *Izutsu* stares into the well) and formal poses (*mie*) in the kabuki theater stop the flow of time, perhaps analogous to close-up shots. In kabuki and puppet plays, slow-motion actions are used to indicate darkness, particularly during fights at night. Fight scenes may also fragment time visually. For instance, simultaneous duels are presented sequentially as though a camera were switching shots from one pair to another. This same technique is effectively employed to depict traumatic events: when a severed head is presented for inspection, for example, the head is uncovered, and then the important characters react to the revelation one by one. Theatrical time is expanded to allow the audience to understand more fully the significance of the event.

FIGURE 1.8. In *Shunkan at Devil Island*, perspective is represented by having a small ship move across the horizon and then rolling the prow of a large ship onstage. The disparity in sizes may also add a humorous touch to the performance. (Photo by Aoki Shinji.)

Centrality of Form

Mime in Japanese theater is mediated by form. Movements, text, costumes, and music all are valued for their formal beauty as well as for their expressive effectiveness. An old man is created not by directly imitating all the details of his decrepitude, but by selecting the essential characteristics of age and presenting them in a stylized and aesthetically pleasing manner. This practice is related to the poetic concept of essential characteristics (*hon'i*), which Zeami and other playwrights adapted to theatrical purposes. Selected elements of expression gradually evolved into the fixed performance patterns (*kata* and *furi*) that are the building blocks of all theatrical genres. The expression of weeping is a good example. In noh this is rendered by tilting the upper body forward slightly, slowly raising the left hand with fingers extended up to eye level and then lowering it again (see figure 2.28). This graceful pattern (*shiori*) may be performed standing or sitting and is intensified by repetition or by using both hands. It suggests the concealing of tearful eyes. The other genres employ similar stylized gestures. In the puppet theater, the weeping

FIGURE 1.9. An *ushiro-buri* (turning to the rear) in the kabuki play A *Maiden at Dōjōji*. The long sleeves of the kimono (*furisode*) and the ends of the obi (*furisage*) are wrapped around the dancer's arms. This movement pattern was developed in the puppet theater and adapted by kabuki. (Photo by Aoki Shinji.)

pattern may be intensified by having a shaking puppet bite her sleeve (the edge of the raised sleeve is caught on a special needle, called *kuchibari*, "at the side of the lips") to represent the stifling of her tears.

Not all movement patterns have this kind of referential meaning; some were developed basically for the beauty of their forms. For example, to show off an attractive kimono, a pattern called "turning to the rear" (*ushiro-buri*) was developed in the puppet theater and copied in kabuki. The female figure's back is turned to the audience; the body bends slightly so that the full line of the kimono is revealed; the sleeves may be spread; and the head turned to look over the shoulder at the audience (figure 1.9). This elegant movement has no direct connection with the text but is included and appreciated for its formal beauty. It is also an example of the various types of movements that interrupt narrative time.

Stylized patterns occur in all the theatrical arts. Instrumental music consists of fixed patterns that are basically abstract, although the manner of their execution contributes to the meaning of the performance. In noh, for example, drummers accompany their drumming with vocal calls (*kakegoe*), and the style of these calls is varied to match the mood and action of a specific play. The intense, eerie calls used in *Dōjōji* create an effect quite different from that of the softer sounds produced for *Izutsu*, even though the drummers may be voicing the same syllables on the same beats. Kabuki music uses instrumental patterns to evoke aspects of a scene such as the sounds of waves (*nami no oto*), the falling of snow (*yuki no oto*), or the clash of battle (*tōyose*). These highly conventionalized patterns are recognized through widespread use rather than more literal mimesis.

Likewise, props, costumes, masks, makeup, and puppet heads all are highly stylized, with the same or similar items appearing many times in different contexts. The puppet head *musume* (young girl), for example, is used for the Kannon in *The Miracle of the Tsubosaka Kannon* and the dancer in A *Maiden at Dōjōji*. The altar in *Kamo* and the well frame in *Izutsu* are variations of the same form, and the women characters in the kyōgen plays "*Sickley*" *Stomach* and *Kanaoka* wear the same basic costume. In fact, all genres use a limited number of basic forms over and over again, but with such variation in speed, timing, intensity, design, or color and in such different contexts that the untrained audience is unaware of the repetition.

This emphasis on stylized forms has particularly important ramifications for training performers and producing plays. The implications for training are, simply put, that mastery of form is fundamental. A young player learns by imitating his teacher—questions about the meaning of a piece or even of specific words are not relevant at this point. A traditional Japanese actor is perhaps better compared with a musician than with a Western actor; that is, only after he has memorized every movement and every sound of a piece does he consider questions of interpretation. All performers are well trained. Traditionally they begin as young children and learn their roles individually with their teachers—group rehearsal time is minimal. In noh and kyōgen, there is a preperformance gathering (*mōshiawase*), but the players only discuss the piece and run through tricky or unusual sections. Puppeteers also learn their roles with their individual teachers; the three operators begin to work together and with the musicians only at dress rehearsal. Kabuki players devote more time to rehearsals, scheduling several the week before a program opens. Not surprisingly, more thorough rehearsals are needed for new or rarely performed plays than for old favorites. Even new plays, however, can be prepared quickly because they, too, are built around traditional stylized forms.

Two productions of a noh or kyōgen play by actors of the same school are almost identical, and even the variations among performers of different schools are relatively minor. Again, the musical analogy works best: one attends two different performances of a Mozart quartet or a noh play by Zeami expecting to experience the same basic forms, but in different renditions. Although puppet and kabuki productions show more variety, most of the traditional plays were codified long ago. Somewhere along the way a great performer created a set of effective forms (kata) that have come to define a particular role. In recent years, thanks partly to the efforts of the national theaters, a considerable number of old plays have been revived in all genres. When only the words have survived, performance patterns are adapted from similar contexts in plays from the active repertory. Performers may experiment with new forms for a while, but then they too become part of the tradition.

Emphasis on form diminishes interest in verisimilitude. The attention given to formal beauty in the creation of some movement patterns is apparent in other areas as well. In the kabuki play *Saint Narukami,* for example, Black Cloud uses a small bottle and cup he had concealed on his person to serve White Cloud some sake. Later, when Saint Narukami serves sake to Taema, he takes out a cup twenty inches across and a large wooden casket and says, "The little monks thought they could hide these from me by the waterfall, but I saw them." Black Cloud's simple utensils would not suit the more elegant seduction scene, and no voice of realism demands that the same utensils be used. Similarly, the outrageous costume worn by the main character in the play *Shibaraku* has nothing to do with realism, but it creates wonderful visual effects.

Theatricalization of the Mechanics of Theater

Traditional Japanese theater's lack of interest in verisimilitude is reflected not only in its emphasis on form and formal beauty but also in its incorporation into the show of the mechanics of theatrical production. Most notably, the majority of the musicians—the music room (*geza*) players are the major exception—perform onstage, in full view of the audience. Appropriately costumed, with their postures and movements dictated by convention, these performers become an important part of the visual as well as the aural show (see figures 2.12 and 3.94).

Other people are onstage but not as part of the scene; they are considered "invisible." The most prominent of these invisible figures are the puppeteers. That the audience can become involved with a three-quarter life-size doll when it is surrounded by three manipulators seems incredible, but anyone who has attended a puppet performance knows how soon the puppeteers fade from sight. As mentioned earlier, this was not always so. In the early days of the puppet theater, the puppeteers held the one-person puppets over their heads while they themselves were shielded by a curtain, which also hid the chanter and shamisen player from view. Donald Keene suggests that as the dolls themselves became more lifelike and the scripts more realistic, these steps were deliberately taken to maintain the balance between realism and nonrealism, a balance that Chikamatsu emphasized in his writings (Keene 1990:141).

Attendants regularly enter and exit the stage during performances. In noh the two stage attendants (*kōken*) for the shite kneel at backstage right whenever the shite is onstage (see figure 2.8). These attendants have vital roles. The older one is usually of equal or senior status to the shite and is responsible generally for the performance. He serves as the prompter, speaking the next lines from memory should an actor forget, and as an understudy, ready to step in and take over should an actor become disabled. The kōken's responsibilities also include bringing out and retrieving props, helping with onstage costume changes, and rearranging any disheveled costume parts while the actor continues to perform. Attendants to the drummers also enter the stage (usually during the kyōgen interlude) to deliver a hip drum (*ōtsuzumi*) with freshly dried skins or to perform other chores. Some kabuki stage attendants—dressed as the noh attendants are in kimono and *hakama* (dark, divided skirts)—are onstage during danced portions of the plays to aid the performer (see figure 3.94). Most attendants in kabuki, however, are dressed from head to toe in black (much as the puppeteers are) and serve a multitude of functions. The *kyōgen kata* serves as the prompter and plays the hand-held, wooden clackers (*hyōshigi* or *ki*), whose sound announces the opening and closing of the main curtain (see figure 3.4). Other black-clad attendants (*kurogo*, literally "black dress") scurry about delivering and retrieving props and costume pieces. These attendants, usually young actors who also serve as understudies, remain "invisible" by switching to white costumes during snow scenes. Stagehands, also dressed in black, adjust sets as necessary, especially when the stage revolves. The attendants in the puppet theater scamper around the legs of the puppeteers, usually hidden in large part by the low, front partition.

In kabuki, and to a lesser extent in the puppet theater, curtains and stage machinery are openly manipulated as part of the visual picture. Lifts and traps transport props and performers from below the stage to high above it. The top portions of flats fall forward to create new scenes; doors open onto smaller doors to create perspective; and the stage revolves in full view of the audience. In addition to the main curtain, which is pulled aside, drop curtains may keep the set or a group of musicians temporarily concealed to heighten expectation (figure 1.10), and small curtains carried by stage attendants are used to hide a "corpse" as he walks off stage or to delay an important entrance. The skill with which these mechanics are performed is meant to be appreciated as part of the show.

The transformation of stage figures, at the heart of much Japanese theater, may take place onstage, often with rapid changes of costume, make-up, and masks or puppet heads accompanied by abrupt shifts in music and dance styles. The puppet character Sugawara no Michizane and the kabuki character Saint Narukami both make dramatic transformations on-stage into thunder gods, and the young woman in the noh *Dōjōji* metamorphoses into a demon inside the bell

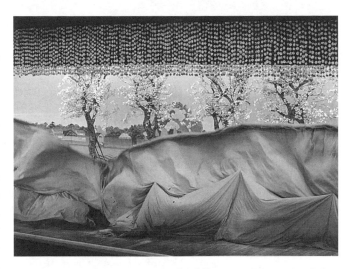

FIGURE 1.10. A drop curtain (*donchō*) falls to reveal the set in a kabuki production. Stage hands (visible as bumps under the curtain) carry it offstage. (Photo by Aoki Shinji.)

prop. The bell conceals the shite from the eyes of the audience, but everyone is aware of the difficulty of the costume change being made in dark, cramped quarters. The numerous costume changes in the kabuki play *Musume Dōjōji* have become an aesthetic end in themselves. In some kabuki plays, such as *Yotsuya Ghost Stories*, the transformation trope is reversed: the character being presented is not transformed; rather, a single actor plays several characters, switching rapidly from one to another. He is applauded for doing so skillfully and quickly.

Intensity of Intertextuality

Originality as it is prized in twentieth-century America is not of great significance in Japanese art in general. Instead, copying, alluding to, manipulating, and varying the familiar is generally accorded high aesthetic value. In Japanese theater, most plots are based on earlier texts. These may be literary, historical, or religious works or accounts of a current event (a suicide or revenge killing, perhaps). Zeami advocated using an earlier text (*honsetsu*), although he allowed the possibility of producing a successful made-up play (*tsukuri noh*) by using a famous locale as the setting and incorporating poems about that place into the script. Kyōgen plays are exceptional. Although they draw on earlier materials, their plots usually have no identifiable sources. Instead, they explore quotidian crises through the creation of fictional characters.

The art of allusion is highly developed in the Japanese literary tradition and is freely used in theater. Noh, for example, often makes use of multiple, related allusions by stringing them together in sequences, as occurs in the list of rivers in *Kamo* or of bells in *Miidera*. Allusions from various sources may be combined to create an effect or make a point. Through a skillful use of allusion, Zeami relates the young warrior Atsumori to the courtier and poet Ariwara no Yukihira (818–893) and the shining prince of *The Tale of Genji*. His success is attested to in the puppet play *Ichinotani*, which draws on the noh play in the Suma Bay scene and goes on to claim that Atsumori is the son of an emperor! Noh also often fragments an old poem, introducing and repeating individual images and phrases until it re-creates the whole with expanded meaning. In *Izutsu*, two poems are treated in this manner. The first is a "passage poem" about Tatsuta Mountain, which originally concerned Ariwara no Narihira's travels to meet his lover but which, by the end of act 1, has come to suggest the passage of his wife's ghost back to earth. The second is the poem about the well, the prop and imagistic center of the play. The first phrases of this poem, *tsutsu izutsu ni*, are repeated so many times that they achieve mantric intensity, and the well itself becomes a mirror of the past and of self-awareness.

Kyōgen treats noh texts parodically. In addition to humorous allusions to specific noh plays (for some good examples, see *The Cicada* and *Mushrooms* in part 2), kyōgen parodies the characters and the general plots of noh. For instance, the thunderbolt in *Kaminari* is a kyōgen version of a noh deity, and the presentation of mountain priests in kyōgen, though based on real-life figures, is mediated by their treatment in noh. The humor of the failed exorcism in *The Mushrooms* is increased by an awareness of the noh models, such as the one in *Dōjōji*. *Kanaoka* is clearly a takeoff on crazed-person plays such as *Miidera*. Although in this kyōgen a man is befuddled by longing, in noh it is usually women who are driven "crazy" by love. The main point of *The Cicada*—and other kyōgen dance plays (*maikyōgen*) in which fauna, flora, or lowly humans return as ghosts to reenact their deaths—is, of course, to spoof the warrior plays of noh, such as *Atsumori*.

The puppet and kabuki theaters directly allude to noh and kyōgen plays (Chikamatsu's works include more than ninety such references) and often recycle their stories, dances, and music. In addition, they exploit prior texts through the use of conventionalized "worlds" (sekai), discussed earlier. Because censorship prohibited direct reference to many types of current events, the plays were recast into an early setting, and the actions were attributed to well-known historical or literary figures. The resulting plays rewrote history freely and often anachronistically. The pleasure quarters depicted in the "Teahouse scene" of *Chūshingura*, for example, are clearly from the seventeenth century, not the fourteenth-century world of Kō no Moronao that the play purports to present. These worlds became highly conventionalized. Handbooks, such as the authoritative *Classification of Worlds* (Sekai kōmoku; published sometime before 1791), provided playwrights with a setting and characters to which the audience could easily relate.

In short, traditional Japanese theater is a theater of fluid transformations in which time, space, character, and action are often fragmented and then recombined in new contexts. The lack of concern for verisimilitude allows theatrically effective devices to be exploited freely and stage mechanics to be revealed to the audience. Earlier texts are constantly reused but are often broken up and reintegrated with new meanings or interspersed with other texts, old or new. Earle Ernst probably best summed up these characteristics when he described kabuki as presentational rather than representational theater: "In the representational theater every effort is made to convince the audience that the stage is not a stage and that the actor is not an actor" (1956:19). In presentational theater, however, the actor presents his character on an acting platform, and the audience enjoys the performance for the play they know that it is. Although all Japanese traditional theater is presentational and the major genres share the characteristics discussed here to a greater or lesser extent, the differences among the performance traditions are significant. The following section and the introductions to parts 2 and 3 describe more fully the elements of each genre, and the translations present concrete examples.

The Stages

The stage on which noh and kyōgen are currently performed is a small architectural gem with an austere beauty that is never compromised by sets. It is a raised and roofed structure with a square performing space approximate-

FIGURE 1.11. The stage for noh and kyōgen. The bridgeway (*hashigakari*) at the left leads to the curtained exit (*agemaku*) and is lined with three pines; only the first pine is visible here. An epiphany pine (*yōgōmatsu*) is painted on the back wall, and bamboo are painted around the small door (*kirido*) at stage left that is used by the chorus and stage attendants. The stage is always empty when the audience enters the performance space. (Photo by Monica Bethe.)

ly nineteen feet by nineteen feet, surrounded by a small area for the musicians, another at stage left for the chorus, and a bridgeway (*hashigakari*) that serves as a secondary performing area leading from backstage right to a curtained exit into the dressing rooms (figure 1.11). The stage was once a separate structure, with the audience seated in the surrounding garden or in a facing building, but the modern stage is more commonly a roofed structure within a larger auditorium. The floor is constructed of highly polished wooden boards, with ceramic jars strategically placed underneath to add resonance to the stamps of the stocking-footed actors, and pillars at each corner and along the bridgeway. The back wall of the stage proper is decorated with a large, painted pine tree, and three small pines line the front of the bridgeway. There is a tiny door (*kirido*) at the rear of stage left for inconspicuous entrances and exits, which most often is used by the chorus and stage attendants, but characters who have been killed also exit there. The wall around this door is decorated with painted bamboo. The audience is seated, nowadays usually in chairs, in a semicircle from the front of the bridgeway around to far stage left.

Three types of actors participate in a noh play. The most numerous are shite actors who function as the main performer (called shite), companion actors (tsure), the chorus (*jiutai*), stage attendants (kōken), and child actors (kokata). *Waki* actors perform the secondary role (waki) and serve as companions to the waki (*wakizure*); kyōgen actors function as minor characters in noh plays and present the interludes between acts (*aikyōgen*), as well as performing independent kyōgen plays. In addition, there are four types of musicians, all of whom appear on the stage: the flutist, two hand drummers who play the larger, hip drum (ōtsuzumi or *ōkawa*) and the

FIGURE 1.12. The noh instrumentalists playing entrance music: the stick drum (*taiko*), the hip drum (*ōtsuzumi*), the shoulder drum (*kotsuzumi*), and the flute (*nōkan*). Compare the pine on this back wall with that in figure 1.11. (Photo by Karen Brazell.)

smaller, shoulder drum (*kotsuzumi*), and a stick drummer who plays the taiko (figure 1.12).

Noh plays rarely focus on character development or dramatic conflict; rather, they explore an emotion (love, anguish, longing, regret, resentment), celebrate deities, poetry, longevity, fertility, or harmony, or exorcise external or internal ghosts and demons. The action is expressed through a stream of associated images and danced movement. Act 1 generally introduces a narrative—the establishment of a shrine, the death of a warrior, the loss of a loved one—and act 2 presents some portion or result of that story in song and dance.[6] A single player, normally the shite, usually performs most of the action and is the visual center of interest. He is garbed in a large, brightly colored costume and a carved, wooden mask, both of which may be of museum quality. The shite, however, is always surrounded by supporting performers, a large number for such a small stage, and it is the interaction among the entire ensemble that creates the power and the beauty of the performance.

Kyōgen plays are performed between noh plays, which they complement in many respects. Whereas a noh play requires at least thirteen participants (three actors, six members of the chorus, three musicians, and a stage attendant), two players are sufficient for many kyōgen plays: a shite and a second actor, usually labeled *ado*. The characters that these actors portray are ordinary, even lowly, beings. Visually, kyōgen is more austere than noh: large props are rare, and the costumes are less voluminous, more somber, and less richly textured than noh garments. Masks are worn infrequently. When musicians are needed, both the instrumentalists and a chorus of four to six members sit along the back of the stage. The mood of kyōgen plays is generally light and humorous, and a delicate balance is maintained between simplification and exaggeration.[7] A long journey may be accomplished in a few steps, yet a moment of laughter may be so prolonged and overplayed that the audience cannot help but laugh at the laughing. In kyōgen an actor's personality and face (or at least the persona and stage face) are much more accessible to the audience than they are in noh; hence the actor's art seems more individualized and intimate.

Kabuki theaters have relatively wide stages (about ninety feet across) and rather shallow auditoriums (about sixty feet deep). Hence even in a large theater (the

6. One subgroup of the category of living-character plays (*genzai nō*) does depict direct conflict. Good examples are plays about the Soga brothers translated by Kominz 1995.

7. A few kyōgen plays are not humorous at all but are poignant vignettes of human suffering. The "blind men" plays, such as *Kawakami*, are good examples.

Kabuki-za seats 2,600 and the National Theater 1,746), no viewer is far from the action, although one may be rather high above it in the top balcony of the Kabuki-za, where connoisseurs mix with people who purchase tickets by the act. There is a raised rampway (hanamichi), about five feet wide, which runs from the right part of the stage to the back of the auditorium where a curtain is hung, and for some performances a second hanamichi is temporarily placed at stage left (figure 1.13). Until the early twentieth century, a forestage projected out into the audience, providing a prominent acting area, but Western influence pushed the whole stage back behind a proscenium arch.

Kabuki sets, often opulently decorated, are not meant to create illusionary places but instead serve as decorative backdrops against which brightly costumed actors perform. Sophisticated stage traps (seri)—on both the seven-three spot of the hanamichi (three-sevenths of the way from the stage) and the stage proper—and a revolving stage are used to move scenery, actors, and props (figure 1.14).

The stage is often populated with a great many figures (see, for example, figure 3.94). The heroes of aragoto-style plays and the courtesans of domestic pieces are larger than life: their elabo-

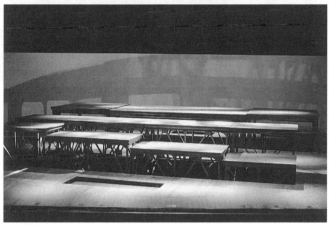

FIGURE 1.13. The National Theater (*Kokuritsu gekijo*) with two rampways (*hanamichi*). The closer one is temporary, set up as needed. The boats are being pushed by stage assistants in black (*kurogo*), and the musicians are lined up on stage. (Photo by Aoki Shinji.)

FIGURE 1.14. The complex series of lifts (*seri*) on the revolving stage in the National Theater, on which actors, props, or sets can be raised or lowered. (Photo by Aoki Shinji.)

rate costumes and wigs may weigh fifty or sixty pounds, and their faces are painted flat white or marked with stylized lines. They may be accompanied by a group of similarly dressed servants, warriors, or monks who act as an ensemble, and as many as thirty chanters and musicians may be seated along the back of the stage. At other times, a pair of lovers is alone on the stage, or a single figure may enter or exit slowly down the rampway while an instrument or two plays from a concealed music room at stage right (geza) or stage left (chobo). Variety is valued, as are rapid changes of pace and scene.

The puppet stage is traditionally about thirty-six feet wide and fifteen feet high, although the stage at the National Bunraku Theater in Osaka is somewhat wider. Its depth of about twenty-four feet is divided into sections by three partitions (*tesuri*)

FIGURE 1.15. The puppet theater chanter and shamisen player sit on an auxiliary stage jutting out into the auditorium at stage left. There is a revolving platform in the middle of the auxiliary stage that allows the performers to be changed smoothly. (Photo by Barbara C. Adachi.)

of different heights that run the width of the stage, concealing the puppeteers' lower bodies and serving as a "floor" or "ground" on which the puppets appear to walk or sit. The area immediately behind the first partition (a black, ten-inch-high wall) contains footlights and the curtain. Behind the second partition (nineteen inches above the forestage and usually painted a neutral color) is the major performing area, approximately seven feet deep with a floor recessed fourteen inches below stage level. This area, called *funazoko* (ship's bottom), runs the entire width of the stage and has curtained exits at both sides (Adachi 1985:175). The rear area contains the major set, sometimes simply a painted flat but often an interior space. In the latter case, the third partition (thirty-three inches high) is designed as the base of the building, and the puppets appear to be moving or sitting on tatami mats. Exits may be made from either side or at the back. Because of the number of people who must move around (each major puppet has three manipulators), stage props are relatively few, and furnishings, such as chests or scrolls, are often painted on the backdrop. Essential large props (gates, bridges, trees) may be wheeled in and out as needed. A boat, for example, is made from a flat on wheels and is pushed along by the puppeteers, who walk behind it (see figure 3.9).

Players in a small music room (geza) concealed by a bamboo blind above the exit at stage right produce offstage music and limited sound effects. An auxiliary stage jutting out into the auditorium at stage left has a small, revolving platform on which the chanter and shamisen player sit, the chanter closer to the stage (figure 1.15). A rampway (hanamichi) through the audience at stage right, borrowed from the kabuki theater, is used only occasionally for dramatic exits and even less frequently for entrances.

When a performance is in progress, it is immediately apparent that there are two centers of interest, the movements of the puppets and the sounds produced by the chanter and the shamisen. The power of the music may draw one's attention to the auxiliary stage, where the chanter and the shamisen player are a pleasure to observe. Inevitably, however, the viewer turns to watch the dolls come to life with delicate and graceful movements or exaggerated bombastic gestures. As Barbara Adachi describes it:

> The puppets gradually assume life-size proportions. No longer do the faces seem small and immobile as they turn this way and that, glancing at each other, then away. The faces of the principal puppeteers are ciphers: neutral, immobile elements present onstage only to be ignored. The assistants are no more obtrusive than shadows. One postpones the question of how the illusions are created as one enjoys watching the lovers in animated conversation, noting only in passing that the unmasked puppeteer's hand is visible beneath that of the doll's. (1985:28)

Illusion is at the heart of all theater. Although the stages of the traditional Japanese theaters do not attempt to represent realistic or naturalistic characters or places, they do effectively draw the audience into the dramatic action, the illusion created onstage. The gasp of horror of parents being shown the severed head of their son is no less real because the performers are puppets. One weeps as a young woman grieves over her lover's death, forgetting momentarily that the "woman" is a male noh actor singing in a masculine voice and with coarse hands shielding his eyes. The gall of servants deliberately destroying their master's treasures is astonishing, even though the treasures are conjured up only through movements and sounds. And the appealing, feminine grace of an onnagata may arouse envy in the hearts of the female spectators.

Four Figures of the Thunder God:
Examples of the Four Major Genres

Storm gods have raged and romped through the literature and art of Japan since at least the autumn of 463, when Emperor Yūraku is said to have ordered the capture of the deity of Mount Miwa. Presented with an enormous serpent roaring thunderously and flashing flames, the terrified emperor renamed the deity "thunder" (*ikazuchi*, meaning "powerful, fearsome thing") and returned it to the mountain. Later retellings of this tale transformed the great serpent into dragon gods, traditional dispensers of rain. Other tales recount how vengeful spirits of the dead transform themselves into thunder gods and strike down their enemies with bolts of lightning. Conversely, thunder is sometimes depicted in a benign anthropomorphic form—most often with an arc of drums around his head and a drum stick in his hand and paired with a wind deity.

All types of Japanese theaters have made use of the figure of thunder, so here, to introduce the four major genres, are selections from four plays featuring thunder gods. These pieces are not textually related; but they simply share the figure of a thunder god, be he ferocious, funny, friendly, or frightened. Each play also involves

FIGURE 1.16. Four theatrical figures of the thunder god. The noh deity in *Kamo* (top left) has cloud circles, hexagons, and bold diagonals (lightning) in his costume design. The strips of paper attached to the purification wand (*gohei*) also suggest lightning. The kyōgen costume for *Kaminari* (top right) is a simplified version of the noh apparel. The drum (*taiko*) at the actor's waist is "struck" with the closed fan to indicate thunder. In the kabuki play *Saint Narukami* (bottom left), the thunder god holds a *vajra* (a ritual object in esoteric Buddhism); his makeup is in the bold aragoto style, and his outer robe has flame designs. In *Sugawara and the Secrets of Calligraphy* (bottom right), the puppet representing the thunder god ascends a cliff where he waves a white paper over his head and poses fiercely. (Top two photos: Courtesy of the Noh Research Archive of Musashino Women's College; bottom left: photo by Aoki Shinji; bottom right: photo by Barbara C. Adachi.)

physical transformation, and each depicts a thunderstorm. The nature of the transformations and the techniques used to present the storms illustrate basic characteristics of the theatrical forms (figure 1.16).

In the noh play *Kamo*, a play retaining traces of noh's religious origins, the thunder god in his benign aspect sends timely rains to nourish crops. In the first act of the play, a young woman relates one version of the legend of the thunder god (*wake-ikazuchi*) worshiped at the Kamo shrines in northern Kyoto: a woman drawing water from a river scoops up an arrow in her bucket and later gives birth to the thunder god's son. The recitation of this tale is followed by a poetic enumeration of rivers and streams—an incantation to water, which contributes to the ritual effect of the play. Then the maiden draws water to offer to the deity and to purify herself. In act 2, the mother goddess appears, performs a dance, and dips her sleeve in the river, precipitating the arrival of the thunder god. The original act of scooping up the arrow is thus enacted in two forms as the old tale is retold and the thunder god's theophany is re-created. After majestically announcing himself, the thunder god dances up a storm for the benefit of the land and the reign of its lord—a virtuous reign is reflected in a bountiful harvest. Indeed, early versions of *Kamo* might have been employed as ritual rain dances in services requesting rain or celebrating its arrival.

The kyōgen play *Thunderbolt* (Kaminari, literally "the deity who roars") also presents a theophany, but sacrality is not central here. Thunderbolt falls from heaven, injuring his hip, and is cured by a frightened country quack with an oversized needle. The deity pays the doctor with a promise of eight hundred years of beneficial rain; then he storms back to heaven, once again terrifying the apprehensive quack. In typical kyōgen fashion, this piece spoofs doctors and deities, fear of storms, and fear of needles. The august deity of *Kamo* is clearly brought down to earth.

The kabuki play *Saint Narukami and the God Fudō* illustrates how the powers of transformation attained through ascetic practices can be used for evil as well as for good. A powerful monk quells a thunderstorm and receives the name "roaring deity" (*naru-kami*) from a grateful emperor. After the emperor refuses Narukami's request that a temple be built in his honor, the "saint" captures the dragon gods and locks them in a cave, causing a severe drought. In the act of the play translated here, a beautiful woman sent by the emperor gets Narukami drunk, seduces him, and releases the rain gods. To wreak his revenge, Narukami transforms himself into a thunder deity. The seduction scene blends comedy—resulting mostly from the antics of the disciples   and eroticism, a combination typical of early kabuki. In the midst of the seduction scene, Narukami relates the story that is the model for this play, showing that he is aware of the dangers of succumbing to sake and sex. No amount of intellectualization, however, can compensate for the power of lust.

The transformation of the exiled courtier Sugawara no Michizane into a thunder god is presented in the first, brief excerpt from act 4 of the puppet play *Sugawara and the Secrets of Calligraphy*. Sugawara undergoes the transformation in order to return to the capital and prevent his enemy Fujiwara no Shihei from usurping the throne. Act 5 of the play recounts his success in that endeavor. By means of a thunderstorm, which kills his two henchmen, the traitor Shihei is prevented from assassinating Sugawara's son. As Shihei flees to an altar for protection, snakes emerge from his ears and turn into the ghosts of two of Sugawara's loyal retainers, who reveal Shihei's treasonous intentions and kill him. The emperor thereupon reinstates the Sugawara family and orders the building of Kitano Shrine in Kyoto to honor Sugawara as a divine protector of the imperial realm. The play thus ends, as the noh *Kamo* began, with the story of the origins of a shrine.

The depiction of the thunderstorm in the kyōgen play is a model of simplicity produced by the appearance, words, and movements of the two players. Wearing a fierce *buaku* mask, a red demon hairpiece, and ō thick, boldly patterned kimono, Thunderbolt enters beating a drum at his waist and crying *"Pikkari, gwarari, gwarari, pikkari, gwarari, gwarari, gwarari, gwarari, don don don"*—the sounds for lightning and thunder. Onomatopoeia are the typical means of creating sound effects in kyōgen. The characters' reactions also are a means of portraying events. Here the doctor covers his ears and flees from the thunder god, shouting a parodic spell ("Mulberry, mulberry," *kuwabara, kuwabara*) against the lightning as he races away.

In the noh play, the storm is visually represented by motifs in the shite's costume—clouds, zigzags, and/or dragons—and by the zigzag shape of the paper dangling from the purification wand the shite brandishes, as well as by his movements onstage. Dance movements emphasize verbal descriptions as the dancer leaps up and then falls to his knees, his sleeve tossed over his head, as "bolts of lightning" strike. At the words "claps of thunder carry rain, falling footsteps far, *horo horo horo horo*, and near *todoro todoro*, stamping feet resound, drums of thundering god," the dancer's numerous stamps resound to the chant. The mention of drums draws the viewer's attention to the actual drums producing standard rhythmic patterns behind the dancer. Thus the thunder resounds in the descriptive text and the onomatopoeia (divided between the shite and the chorus), the sight and sound of the dancer's stamps, and the drumbeats. This is a typical noh presentation: onstage music, movements, costume, and words work together to create the scene.

The storm in the kabuki selection is first produced with sound effects and stage movements without verbal description. Concealed drums and a flute produce thunder and rain motifs as the seductress Taema cuts the sacred ropes and frees the dragon gods—costumed actors who climb up a waterfall and disappear. As in kyōgen, the characters' reactions are important to the presentation: the woman stumbles, falls, and looks fearful; and a crowd of monks, entering along the two rampways through the audience, hold up their sleeves to protect their faces from the driving rain. Only then do they describe the storm in shared lines:

WHITE CLOUD: And so the rains
MONKS: come pouring down,
BLACK CLOUD: lightning and thunder
MONKS: flash and roar.

The words are accompanied by the large drum (*ōdaiko*) beating sound-of-rain patterns (*ame no oto*), and stylized bolts of white lightning appear overhead. The storm fills the eyes and the ears of the audience.

In the puppet piece, the chanter first describes a storm to sound effects provided by music-room drums. Then, as Shihei and his companions attempt to kill

Sugawara's son, gongs join the drums to underscore the text: "Wind and rain descend, and bolts of lightning blaze across the firmament, while claps of monstrous thunder rend heaven and earth—Crack! Bang! Rumble! BOOM!!!" Then the storm turns murderous: "Above his head a wheel of fire appears to descend, and Mareyo's body is enveloped in the searing flames." The puppet collapses as the drums and gongs play on. A serpentine storm emblem appears over Shihei's head as he cowers before the altar, and "from each of his ears appear small snakes." The snakes, analogous to the dragon gods in the kabuki play, are held on long poles by stage assistants. The depiction of the storm in the puppet play depends more on textual description than does the kabuki version, which relies more on gestures and stage effects.

A human character is transformed into a thunder deity in three of these plays. The kyōgen play *Thunderbolt* does not involve a physical transformation, although there is a transfer of fear from doctor to deity and back again as power shifts between the characters. In the noh play *Kamo*, the physical transformations (costume changes) occur offstage between the acts. In act 1, the thunder god is represented by an arrow, and the woman is a maiden; in act 2, the female character is the mother goddess, and the thunder god appears in his "true" form. In the kabuki play, Narukami's transformation is an onstage spectacle. First the Saint, who has been sleeping in a grotto, raises his head to reveal a change of makeup and wig; then the outer layer of his costume is stripped away twice, each time revealing a more vivid lightning design on the kimono beneath. As Narukami declares, "I shall become a living thunder god," he hurls accordion-pleated sutras, which unfold to each side of him like lightning bolts. Fierce poses to shamisen and drum music emphasize his transfiguration. The transformation of Sugawara in the bunraku play involves a change of puppet heads. When the puppet presenting Sugawara reenters in act 5, it has a different, fiercer head, but the full effect of this substitution is not readily apparent, for the face may be partially covered with a white cloth, and the hair is tied back until it is time for Sugawara to turn into a thunder god. Then the cloth is removed, the hair is loosened, and several layers of kimono are peeled back, one after the other. The puppet's vigorous movements, accompanied by drums, gongs, and clappers, emphasize the transformation, which culminates in a change of sets—the temple becomes a cliff covered with swirling gray and black clouds. Sugawara mounts the cliff, waves a piece of white paper attached to a stick, and strikes a fierce pose.

These four selections can serve as an introduction to the diversity and range of traditional Japanese theater and its performance practices. Each is typical of its genre, and at least parts of all the plays are regularly performed in Japan today.

Kamo

A deity noh play attributed to Zenchiku
(1405–1470?)

Translated by Monica Bethe

Deity plays (*waki nō*), the first of the five traditional categories of noh, are auspicious, celebratory pieces; they exalt the land and its rulers, anticipate or give thanks for a fruitful harvest, and extol the virtues of shrines, deities, sacred objects, and rituals. A passage from the deity play *Takasago*, which celebrates peace, the rulers, poetry, and conjugal love, is chanted at many weddings today. The forty deity plays currently performed present a wide cast of supernatural characters, including the goddess Benzaiten and a dragon deity (*Chikubushima*), the Queen Mother of the West (*Seiōbō*), the Sun Goddess (*Ema*), a mountain deity (*Yōrō*), and the spirit of an old pine tree (*Oimatsu*), as well as a thunder god (*Kamo*).

Kamo celebrates fertility, peace, the ruling class, and the deities of the shrines. The Upper and Lower Kamo Shrines predate the 794 transfer of the capital to Kyoto (then called Heiankyō); in fact, the imperial court petitioned their tutelary deities for permission to relocate. The principal deity worshiped at the Kamo shrines is the thunder god, who, according to the version of the origin tale (*engi*) used in this play, had a son by a woman of the Hata clan. Zeami credits the illustrious progenitor of the Hata clan, Kawakatsu (seventh century, also pronounced Kōkatsu), with creating the theatrical forms leading to noh, and Zeami's nephew, Komparu Zenchiku, the probable author of this play, claims descent from Kawakatsu. A Hōshō actor starred in the play's first known performance in Nara in 1515, when it headed a seventeen-play program in celebration of rain (*ama-yorokobi nō*). Two other plays included in this volume, *Atsumori* and *Yamamba*, were also performed on that occasion.

The white-feathered arrow (*shiraha no ya*), central to the story of the Kamo thunder god, is an important image in the play. An actual arrow is attached to a square frame prop representing an altar[1] and is identified with the thunder god by a young woman (played by the shite) (figure 1.17). Later manipulations of the arrow image hint

---

1. The play was originally called *Yatate Kamo* (Kamo of the standing arrow).

at some of the underlying politics of noh in the medieval period, when the warrior class wielded power in the name of a figurehead emperor. The playwright, dependent on shogunal patronage, carefully links the warriors to the deities through puns involving the white-feathered arrow. For example, *shira* is read as "not know" (*shirazu*), "white bow" (*shira mayumi*), "make known" (*shirase*), and "white feather" (*shiraha*); and *ya* (arrow) is embedded in two words, "brave" (*yatake*) and "eight hundred thousand" (*yaoyorozu*). The dense passage in which these puns occur may be paraphrased as "we common folk don't know the secrets of the gods as well as you brave men of the white bow and arrow do; may the white-feathered arrow make known your rule for eight hundred thousand ages." This is clearly good politics as well as effective theater.

Such elaborate wordplay, suggesting a belief in the efficacy of language, occurs throughout the text. Like many other plays, including *Miidera* presented in part 2, *Kamo* incorporates a poetic list of things (*mono no tsukushi*), here a catalog of rivers, full of puns on names and allusions to prior texts. This list is part of a larger meditation on the purifying powers of water, in which physical and spiritual aspects are unified through wordplay: pure waters purify the heart; clear water clarifies the mind; and the act of drawing water draws one closer to the divine spirit.

FIGURE 1.17. The arrow prop in *Kamo*. A bamboo frame wrapped with long strips of white cloth forms the base of the altar and supports a large, white-feathered arrow, a pivotal image in act 1. The small exit (*kirido*) is visible behind the flutist. (Photo by Monica Bethe.)

Kamo is a colorful play, full of variety. The two simply clad young women of act 1 are replaced by the dignified mother goddess and the powerful thunder god in act 2, and the kyōgen interlude features the friendly and vivacious deity of a subsidiary shrine. These figures sing and dance in various performance styles. The music, which Monica Bethe describes with particular care, includes five types of entrance and exit music and accompaniments for three different dances.

One unusual aspect of this play is its allocation of roles. The shite plays the young woman in act 1 and the thunder god in act 2. The logic of the plot would seem to demand that the actor playing the young woman in act 1 play the mother goddess in act 2, leaving the portrayal of the thunder god (represented in act 1 by the arrow) to another actor. Indeed, the piece may once have been played in that way, but current performance practice challenges the main actor to portray both a gentle, young woman and a vigorous deity. A few other plays, such as the popular *Funa Benkei*, provide similar opportunities.

Although the kyōgen interlude most commonly performed is translated here, the now independent kyōgen piece entitled *Onda* (Sacred paddies) or *Taue* (Rice planting) was once regularly used as the interlude. Today it appears only in variant performances (*kogaki*). *Onda* is based on rice-planting rituals commonly performed throughout Japan (see figure 1.3). A priest from the Kamo Shrine summons four maidens to join him in rituals to ensure a good harvest. They sing humorous and witty rice-planting songs (*taueuta*), and the priest dances with a hoe, miming the planting of rice seedlings.

Bethe's translation is based mainly on the text of *Kamo* found in Yokomichi and Omote 1963, although she also referred to Itō 1986, Koyama 1975, Sanari 1931, and Kanze and Kita school chantbooks. Her descriptions of stage business and music derive from a 1980 performance by Takabayashi Kōji of the Kita school. The play is in the repertories of all five schools and is performed often.

CHARACTERS

SHITE: in act 1, a young woman; in act 2, the thunder god, Wake-ikazuchi
TSURE: in act 1, a young woman; in act 2, the mother goddess
WAKI: a Shinto priest
WAKIZURE: three other priests
AIKYŌGEN: deity of a subsidiary shrine at Kamo

MUSICIANS

Chorus of eight to ten members
A flute and two hand drums for act 1; a stick drum adds its beat in the exit music
for act 1 and during act 2

ACT 1

After the musicians take their places at the back of the stage and the chorus members sit at stage left, two attendants carry in a square frame with an upright arrow attached to it and place the prop at center front.

Shin no shidai entrance music   *The two hand drummers play formal entrance music, with the flute adding embellishments. When the music quickens, the waki and wakizure, dressed as Shinto priests, walk down the bridgeway to the front of the stage. The wakizure stand at stage right, facing front, and the waki is at stage left, facing back.*

Shidai   *The priests turn to face one another and sing this metered song in the dynamic mode (tsuyogin or gōgin), keeping their rhythms congruent (hyōshi au) with those of the drum accompaniment. The flute embellishes the last line, and the instruments continue to play briefly after the last repetition of the lines.*

WAKI AND WAKIZURE:
> Clear and pure the spring we seek,
> clear and pure the spring we seek,
> traveling to the shrine of Kamo.

Jitori

CHORUS (*In a lower-pitched murmur*):
> Clear and pure the spring we seek,
> traveling to the shrine of Kamo.

As the instrumental music concludes this shidai segment, the waki faces back, circles, and then takes two steps forward and two steps back. The wakizure kneel in place.

Nanori   *Faces front to speak without instrumental music [figure 1.18].*

WAKI: I am a priest serving the deity of Muro in Banshu.[2] Although the god of my

---

2. A Kamo shrine in the town of Mitsu in present-day Hyōgo Prefecture (formerly Harima). The deity is Wake-ikazuchi, the thunder god (literally, splitting thunder).

FIGURE 1.18. The *Kamo* waki portrays a Shinto priest. His round-necked cloak (*kariginu*) and white divided skirts (*ōkuchi*) suggest traditional Heian-period court styles, simplified versions of which are still worn by shrine priests. He wears a court cap (*eboshi*). The chorus wears crested ·kimono and hakama. (Photo by Karen Brazell.)

> shrine and the god of the Kamo Shrine in the capital are one and the same, I have yet to make a pilgrimage there, so now I am off to the capital to visit the Kamo Shrine.

During a drum interlude, the waki steps forward, bringing his arms together to the front; then he steps to the side; and finally he faces the wakizure, who have stood up to face him.

Ageuta *A travel song in the dynamic mode, sung with its rhythms congruent with those of the drum accompaniment.*

WAKI AND WAKIZURE:
> On the Harima coast
> over the harbor at Muro day breaks,

Instrumental interlude (uchikiri): *the waki faces back and then front.*

> on the Harima coast
> over the harbor at Muro dawn opens,
> as we set off in dark-dyed traveling cloaks.
> On foot we pass Shikama and with
> boats follow distant
> rising clouds up to the moon-famed capital,
> where in the shade of the mountain
> we arrive at Kamo Shrine,

The waki steps forward, rises on his toes, and then steps back and forward again.

we arrive at Kamo Shrine.

Flute and drum music end the passage. The waki faces front; the wakizure face the chorus.

Tsukizerifu   *Spoken without instrumental music.*
    In our haste we've arrived quickly at the shrine of Kamo. On that riverbank over there stands a new altar holding white cloth streamers and a white-feathered arrow. If someone comes along, I'll ask about it.

The waki and wakizure face each other, then go to the waki spot and sit.

Shin no issei entrance music   *The two hand drummers take turns playing sparse beats preceded by long, drawn-out calls. The flute adds decorative embellishments to this slow, stately entrance music that calls forth the main actors. The third flute passage is a signal for the entrance of the shite and tsure, both dressed as local women and carrying buckets. The tsure stops at the first pine, the shite at the third.*

Issei   *The shite and tsure face each other and sing in the dynamic mode in non-congruent (hyōshi awazu) rhythm to quiet drum accompaniment. The flute enters toward the end.*

SHITE AND TSURE:
    Sacred stream:
    waters pure clear the mind
    and flow toward the
    Kamo riverbank, which
    we too approach.
TSURE (*Faces front*):
    When with clear conscience humans pray,
SHITE AND TSURE (*Face each other*):
    it is the god of Tadasu[3] who guides them down the path.

Ashirai   *The tsure and shite advance to the stage proper accompanied by free-flowing drum music. The tsure goes to center stage, and the shite stands at the shite spot, both facing forward.*

Sashi   *This is recited in noncongruent rhythm to a drum accompaniment; the flute enters at the end.*

SHITE:
    Half gone, the late summer moon shedding its light.
    Soon autumn will be upon the River of Purification.
SHITE AND TSURE (*Facing each other*):
    A breeze blows cool over evening waves.
    The heart clears; the clear water in our pails
    reveals a visage.

---

3. Tadasu is the name of the woods in the Lower Kamo Shrine. A homonym means "to correct or set right."

Though not of high lineage
we travel to the abode of the exalted gods
our hearts as unclouded as this site.

Sageuta *Drums play softly to congruent song rhythms.*

SHITE AND TSURE:
Before this god we offer our vows;
let us draw the sacred water.

Ageuta *The drums continue to play, with the flute adding embellishments.*

Sacred stream
rippling in the cool of summer shade.

Drum interlude; the waki turns to face the shite.

Through the treetops of Tadasu
echo the calls of the *hototogisu*[4]
luring us to linger,
but a sudden shower
clouds the twilight rays.
Cool eddies at the river bend
cool shade so refreshing
we would be drawn to it
even if we were not here to draw water;
we would be drawn to it
even if we were not here to draw water;

As the segment ends, the shite goes to center stage, the tsure to the corner.

Kakeai *Without instrumental music. The waki stands and addresses the women.*

WAKI: Hello there. I have something to ask of you women drawing water.
SHITE: What is it you would like to ask? Yours is not a familiar face around here. Where do you come from?
WAKI: You miss nothing, do you? We are priests serving the deity of Muro in Banshu. This is our first visit to this shrine. Over on that riverbank (*looks at the stage prop*) is a new altar holding white streamers and a white-feathered arrow. It appears most sacred. What does it signify?
SHITE: So you are visitors from Muro, are you? This arrow (*faces front*) is both the receptacle of the divine essence and the sacred treasure of this shrine. It is a most holy arrow. (*Faces the waki*) Wouldn't you like to pay homage to it? (*Faces front.*)
WAKI: Ah, it is indeed most worthy. And now, there must be many secrets concerning this shrine. Won't you tell me some of the details of the story behind the arrow?
SHITE: One does not discuss the gods and their doings openly, but even so (*faces the waki*), I will give you a general account of the story.

4. The *hototogisu* is a bird in the cuckoo family. It appears frequently in Japanese literary works and has connotations similar to those of the nightingale in European literature.

Katari   Spoken without instrumental accompaniment. The shite stands at center stage facing front.

SHITE: Of old in the hamlet of Kamo, there lived a person known as the "woman of the Hata clan." Morning and evening she came to this riverside and drew water to dedicate to the god. One day a white-feathered arrow came floating down the stream and lodged in her pail. She scooped it up, brought it home, and stuck it in the eaves of her hut. Then unexpectedly, she became pregnant and bore a son. When the boy was three, people gathered in a circle to ask who his father was. He pointed to this arrow. The arrow turned into thundering lightning, rose into the heavens, and became a deity. This is the origin of the god Splitting Thunder (*faces the waki*).

Kakeai   Sung noncongruently in the dynamic mode without accompaniment.

TSURE:
The mother also became a goddess, and
the three are enshrined in the three Kamo shrines.[5]
SHITE:
The awesome truth of this tale
is beyond the comprehension
SHITE AND TSURE:
of humble folk like us. Still it appears
the white-feathered arrow heralded
brave warriors whose might will reign
till the end of time. The white feathers
record for generations to come the age
of the bow and the brush.[6]

Kakeai   Sung in the dynamic mode to a drum accompaniment.

WAKI:
I am very glad to hear this.
However, that arrow was of the past.
Why is this one of the degenerate present
still revered as divine?
SHITE (*Speaks*):
A good question. But there is
no difference between the two; each thing
WAKI:
has its essence: the clear and the muddy,
SHITE (*Sings in the dynamic mode*)·
both flow in the same

5. Wake-ikazuchi is enshrined at the Upper Kamo Shrine (Kamigamo); the mother at the Lower Shrine (Shimogamo); and the child (known as Ōyamagui) at the Matsuo Shrine in western Kyoto.
6. This intricate, obscure passage indeed shrouds the ways of the gods from open view. The multiple levels of interlacing poetic imagery are open to a number of interpretations. See the introduction to this play for a brief discussion of some of the associations and wordplay.

WAKI:

Kamo River, whose name also changes:

SHITE:

its lower reaches are known as White River,

WAKI:

its upper reaches as Kamo River,

SHITE:

and along the way

WAKI:

other names such as

Ageuta *During this passage, the chorus's first song, the tsure goes to sit in front of the chorus; the waki returns to his seat; and the shite circles the stage, ending in front of the stick drum player. The drums play with flute embellishments, and the singing style changes to the melodic mode* (yowagin *or* wagin). *The song and drum rhythms are congruent.*

CHORUS:

"Stone River and
Rapid Stream, so clear

Drum interlude with flute.

Rapid Stream, so clear
the moon's radiance seeks out its flow."[7]
Clean or muddy,
the river remains the same.
Consider the implications,
and you will ask no more
of old or new. Years pass
as quickly as an arrow.
The past, though remembered, does not return;
so also the water flowing
past, like our offering,
is ever renewed.

Sageuta *The shite faces the tsure and takes one step; drums play.*

CHORUS:

Now, let us draw water
now, let us draw water.

Drum interlude.

Rongi *The shite faces front. The song continues in the melodic mode, its rhythms congruent with those of the drums playing softly in the background.*

CHORUS:

How drawing water

---

7. Poem 1894 in the *Shinkokinshū* by Kamo no Chōmei. An allusion to his famous prose work, the *Hōjōki*, is made at the end of this passage. His father was a priest at the Lower Kamo Shrine.

cleanses the spirit!
What is it like, then,
the river's source?

SHITE:

What is it like?
Pushing past rocks and pine roots,
then rushing out in sparkling white cataracts,
echoes the Kibune River.

Faces front.

CHORUS:

The Ōi River appears to be dry
after a windblown rain of autumn leaves."[8]

SHITE:

At the foot of Storm Mountain, the Tonase
rapids race by, high famed

Looks into the distance.

CHORUS:

"Water here to draw at Clear Falls
means snow has left the high peaks."

The shite turns to face the bridgeway.

SHITE:

As we await the dawn,
let's draw water.

The shite faces front and steps forward.

CHORUS:

"Inviolate the booming falls of Otowa"

SHITE:

froth forth like snow white locks to

CHORUS (*The shite goes forward to center front [figure 1.19]*):

crown our heads, our pails too

SHITE (*Steps back*):

reveal our fate

CHORUS (*The shite circles right to the shite spot*):

to grow old, as we all know we must,
as surely as the sun will set.
This day too illumines the reality of dreams.

The shite faces the waki.

Shifting light reflected

---

8. This poetic list of rivers contains allusions to poems by Fujiwara no Sadayori (d. 1045; poem 365 in the *Goshūishū*), Saigyō (1118–1190; poem 27 in the *Shinkokinshū*), and Mibu no Tadamine (868–965; poem 928 in the *Kokinshū*), respectively. Here the playwright has indulged in a bit of poetic license. The Ōi River is not a section of the Kamo River; rather, it flows through the foothills of Arashiyama to the west of Kyoto.

FIGURE 1.19. This young woman, the shite in act 1 of *Kamo*, wears a brocade robe (*karaori*) loosely crossed over the chest and snugly wrapped around the hips in the straight style (*kinagashi*). The young woman mask (*ko-omote*) covers her brocade headband (*kazuraobi*). She carries a bucket of water for an offering. (Photo by Karen Brazell.)

in unclouded water to scoop up
for the bounteous deity and

The shite goes to the front of the altar and kneels, lifts her arms in prayer, stands, turns, and goes to center back, where she kneels to pray again.

draw near the divine spirit,
draw near the divine spirit.

Kakeai   *Spoken.*

WAKI: That is truly a marvelous story. But who are you that you can relate such things so explicitly?

SHITE (*Kneels at center stage; an attendant takes away the pails*):
Must you still ask who I am?

Sings in the dynamic mode with noncongruent rhythms.

Do you still not know? If you serve the god,
if you have come to see the god,
then to tell you to do homage to the divine essence
of Kamo who protects the land
I have appeared.

Ageuta   *Sung in the dynamic mode with congruent rhythms. During this passage the stick drummer prepares his instrument and sets it in place. The shite faces forward, in a kneeling position, then turns toward the waki.*

Ashamed am I, should I reveal
Ashamed am I, should I reveal
my true form

The shite stands.

too plainly would I be seen
in the coming dawn.
At least I shall withhold my name—

Goes to the shite spot.

great as that of the god

Goes toward the waki, points, and spreads her arms.

of the white bow and arrow,

Looks at the waki from center stage, then goes to the corner.

she declares and fades away

Goes to the shite spot.

into the fluttering streamers
and is gone, invisible, the god
now is gone.

The stick drum begins to beat during this last line.

Raijo exit music   *The shite slowly exits down the bridgeway to solemn music played by the flute and drums. The long, drawn-out drummers' calls and the protracted beats of the two hand drums are joined by the more insistent beats of the stick drum. Tension and expectation hover in the suspended notes of this exit music. The tsure follows the shite down the bridgeway and exits.*

Interlude

Massha raijo entrance music   *The stage attendant takes away the prop, and the music changes to a lighter, faster tempo, heralding the entrance of the masked kyō-gen actor, dressed as the deity of a subsidiary shrine. He stops at the shite spot and points forward with his fan.*

Katari   *Recited in the kyōgen style without instrumental accompaniment.*

KYŌGEN: I am a god of a subsidiary shrine serving the deity of Kamo. Many pilgrims come to this shrine because the Great Deity, exalted among the gods and spirits, embodies the miraculous virtue of the Imperial Palace.[9] Let me tell you some of the legends connected with this place.

Once long ago, a person known simply as the "daughter of the Hata clan" lived in the village of Kamo. Every morning and evening she would go to the Kamo River to pray and draw water for the gods. One day a white-feathered arrow came skimming along the surface of the water. It floated straight into

9. The Kamo Shrine was an imperial shrine, and its high priestess was chosen from the imperial family.

FIGURE 1.20. A subsidiary deity of Kamo Shrine (*aikyōgen*) does a lively, light-footed dance, which matches the humor in his wrinkled, bearded *noborihige* mask. The plain color of his cloak (*mizugoromo*) is offset by the brilliance of his tall hat (*zukin*). (Photo by Karen Brazell.)

her pail, so she took it home and stuck it into the eaves of her hut. A while later the woman discovered she was pregnant. After ten months of suffering, the umbilical cord was cut, and a jewel-like boy was born.

When the boy was three, the villagers asked who his father was. He pointed to the arrow in the eaves and said, "That's my father." Instantly the arrow turned into lightning and rose to the heavens. This, in other words, was the god Splitting Thunder. The mother and son also became deities, whose miraculous virtue extends even to you who serve the deity of Muro in Banshu *(goes to center stage and kneels; speaks to the waki)*. The deity is delighted that you have come on a pilgrimage to this shrine and has already revealed to you the water-drawing scene from the past. He then withdrew, wanting to present you with a miracle as well. I have come from a subsidiary shrine to amuse you with a dance while you wait.

Having got this far, I might as well get on and perform my piece *(stands and goes to the shite spot)*. Ha ha, they were delighted. I said it all in good cheer and must have done all right. They smiled. Quick, quick, better begin. *(He goes to center back, pushes up his sleeves, and begins to chant.)* A time of great celebration.

Sandan no mai   *To light-spirited, medium-tempo music, the kyōgen player dances around the stage, marking the corners and stamping periodically [figure 1.20]. This is a light-hearted kyōgen version of the medium-tempo dance* (chū no mai) *that the heavenly woman will perform in act 2. The kyōgen ends his dance at the shite spot. The drums continue playing to the kyōgen's noncongruent song.*

> Indeed most auspicious, most auspicious.
> At exactly the right instant
> a subsidiary god like me came along
> to amuse the guests.
> Now this little god,
> now this little god,
> will retire to the main shrine.

He stamps and exits down the bridgeway to drum accompaniment.

ACT 2

Deha entrance music *The music changes pace again as the stick drummer plays a series of beats with high arm movements. This lively yet elegant entrance music is played by all three drums, and the flute summons forth the tsure, costumed as the mother goddess. The tsure comes down the bridgeway and stops at the shite spot to sing. All sung portions of this act are in the dynamic mode.*

Unnamed segment *Facing front, the tsure sings in noncongruent rhythm to background drums.*

TSURE:
> These are blessed times!
> As the goddess of this place, I
> extend my love to the broad world,
> even to the lowliest.
> Treating all as my children,
> I lavish divine care,
> protecting the unclouded reign.

The tsure goes to center stage and turns to face the waki.

CHORUS:
> Yes, I shall stand guard, I shall,
> for our sovcreign's blessings are at hand

TSURE:
> now this very moment—the time has come.

She closes her fan and circles right to center back.

CHORUS:
> When creatures call and deities respond,
> then before our very eyes
> the resplendent gods appear,
> gracefully bedecked with jewels.
> O wonder and delight!

The tsure bows with fists together in front of her face.

Tennyo no mai *The mother goddess dances a graceful, medium-tempo dance in three parts to the accompaniment of the three drums and the flute playing repetitive patterns [figure 1.21]. During the dance, which lasts five minutes, she reopens her fan.*

Noriji *Sung in congruent rhythm with a steady beat (ōnori) to repeating drum patterns.*

CHORUS:
> Rows of Kamo hills, mirrored
> waves in pure waters,
> rows of Kamo hills, mirrored
> waves in pure waters,

The tsure goes to center front and kneels.

FIGURE 1.21. The mother goddess performs a heavenly maiden dance (*tennyo no mai*). She wears broad divided skirts (*ōkuchii*) and a gauze-weave cloak (*chō-ken*), shown here with the sleeve flipped over the arm. Her *zōonna* mask has a distilled elegance reserved for celestial beings and is topped with a heavenly crown (*tengan*). (Photo by Karen Brazell.)

> reflecting green
> onto her sleeves

Looks at her left sleeve.

> dipped to absorb the cool,
> fresh
> refreshing waters

Mimes, with fan motion, pouring water on her sleeve [figure 1.22].

> wetting skirts,
> when suddenly

Noncongruent; gradually gaining speed.

> mountains, rivers,
> blossoms, trees,

She stands, circles to the back, and holds her fan high.

> quiver and quake before
> our very eyes
> as the thunder god ap-
> pears in sacred form!

The tsure goes to the waki spot and kneels; the waki and wakizure all move farther toward the back of the stage.

Hayabue entrance music *A brisk, energetic flute melody and rapid drumbeats herald the thunder god, Wake-ikazuchi. Flashing gold from mask and garments, he rushes in, holding in his right hand a purification wand with streaming white paper strips. He stops at the shite spot.*

Unnamed segment *Sung forcefully to noncongruent drum accompaniment.*

SHITE:
> Here am I—
> guardian of the capital,
> protector of the way of lord and subject,[10]
> Wake-ikazuchi, the thunder god.

Noriji *In a pulsating song to repeating drum patterns, the shite stamps.*

CHORUS:
> I become a heavenly being
> soaring through the skies

10. There is a pun on the name Wake-ikazuchi in which *wake* is taken to mean "distinguish [the ways of the sovereign and his subjects]." In Japan's feudal system, the subject owed supreme loyalty to his lord, who in turn was obliged to sustain his subjects.

The shite flips his sleeve and goes to the waki spot.

SHITE:

> or take on an earthly shape—to save
> sentient beings,

He points to the audience with his wand, then goes to center back.

CHORUS:

> modulating radiance, mingling with the
> dust,[11]
> to save sentient beings—
> a miraculous event!

The shite stamps.

Maibataraki *While the three drums beat energetically and the flute plays a spirited tune, the shite swiftly circles the stage, kneeling at times and flashing his wand [figure 1.23 and see figure 1.16].*

Noriji *The shite goes to the corner and, with his sleeve over head, looks into the distance. The song pulsates, with cyclical drum patterns.*

SHITE:

> in the season for wind and rain,

CHORUS (*The shite zigzags around the stage*):

> in that season, from a cloudy abode

SHITE:

> thunder splits clouds and mists

CHORUS (*The shite points and then jumps to a kneeling position with his sleeve over his head*):

> sending bolts of lightning
> to alight on dewy seedlings;

SHITE (*Stands*):

> lodging briefly; claps of thunder

CHORUS (*The shite twirls to the front and poses with his left hand placed over the outstretched wand*):

> carry rain, falling footsteps

SHITE (*Stamps sixteen times*):

> far, *horo horo*

CHORUS:

> *horo horo*

FIGURE 1.22 The mother goddess mimes dipping water from the Kamo River onto her sleeve. The double-width gauze sleeves of her *chōken* cloak enlarge the simple movements. Long hair (*kurotare*) hangs down her back. (Photo by Karen Brazell.)

---

11. The concept of *wakōdōjin*: deities take on mundane forms in order to relate to earthly beings and enlighten them.

FIGURE 1.23. The thunder god's flashy costume and quick movements represent a storm. The bulging-eyed gold mask (ōtobide) sparks out from behind a long and bushy red headpiece, and the stiff divided skirts (hangiri) are woven of damask with large patterns in gold or silver. His purification wand flashes like lightning as he dances. Compare the costume in figure 1.16. (Photo by Karen Brazell.)

and near, *todoro todoro,*
  stamping feet resound,

The shite dances around the stage with broad gestures.

drums of thundering god. In time will come
  the ripening of grains in a protected land,
  a peaceful reign, this god's virtues his majesty reveal.

The shite's swirling leap ends in a kneeling position. He points to the tsure as she exits.

Toward Tadasu woods the mother goddess

The shite stands and, following the tsure, goes to the shite spot.

flies away; she flies away.

The shite kneels and, flipping first one sleeve and then the other, goes to center front, then circles left to

the shite spot.

Rising to follow, the god of thunder pierces[12] clouds and mist
this god too ascends the heavenly path;

Swinging the wand, the shite goes down the bridgeway to the third pine.

this god too ascends the heavenly path;

The shite stamps, throws his wand over his shoulder, and, with a swirling leap, exits.

rises to the heavens and disappears.

After the waki and the wakizure exit up the bridgeway, the instrumentalists follow, and the chorus exits through the small door at upstage left.

---

12. Another pun on the thunder god's name, Wake-ikazuchi: *wake* can mean "to split."

Thunderbolt (Kaminari)

A kyōgen play

Translated by Royall Tyler

In this kyōgen play, the awesome thunder god of noh is presented as a frightening thunderbolt, who is himself easily frightened. The piece is categorized as a demon play (*oni kyōgen*), but kyōgen demons are never really dangerous. In *Kubihiki* (Neck-pulling), for example, a father demon tries to teach his daughter how to eat a human, unsuccessfully; in *Setsubun* (A demon in love), a woman realizes that a male demon is as easy to outwit as a male human; and in *Asahina*, Emma, the keeper of hell, finds himself assisting the warrior Asahina up to heaven rather than hurrying him down to damnation. These demons, like the thunderbolt, are supernatural beings brought down to earth.

Thunderbolt reveals a humanlike fear of the doctor's needle and is easily conned into believing in the efficacy of the quack's cures; yet his power continues to awe the doctor. Hence the two are able to negotiate payment for services rendered. Then the brief interaction ends as it began, with the thunderbolt roaring around the stage expressing his explosive nature, as the doctor flees mouthing his pseudocharm, "Mulberry! Mulberry!" The many onomatopoeic words, which Royall Tyler has translated into contemporary American equivalents, give the play the feel of a modern comic strip or animated film, which is perhaps an apt analogy for kyōgen in the medieval period.

The props and mask used in this play are unusual and constitute part of the fun. To cure the thunderbolt, the doctor uses an oversized needle that he pounds in with a mallet—everyone's nightmare of going to the doctor. Thunder is produced not only by onomatopoeia but also by the small drum and drumsticks the thunderbolt carries and beats as he enters. The thunderbolt's mask is a special one, used only for this play and for *Buaku*, a play in which a servant disguises himself as a ghost to frighten his master.

This translation is based on the Yamamoto Azuma text of the Ōkura school in Koyama 1961, and it was originally published in Tyler 1978a. Both the Izumi and the Ōkura schools of kyōgen performers include this play in their active repertoires.

CHARACTERS

SHITE: Thunderbolt

ADO: A doctor, who has a needle and a mallet stuck in his waistband

MUSICIANS

Chorus of four or five performers
Noh flute and two hand drums

A Play in One Act

Shidai entrance music   *Doctor walks down the bridgeway to the music of the drums and flute and stands at the shite spot.*

Shidai   *Sung facing the pine tree on the back wall.*

DOCTOR:

> He has no remedies,
> the country quack,
> he has no remedies,
> the country quack
> just trusts yellow bark
> to see him through.

> (*Faces front*) I'm a doctor and I live in the capital. What with all the slick competition in town these days . . . Oh, they've got some fancy titles, too, those fellows, like surgeon general and whatnot! A good old country quack like me can hardly scare up a patient, even to check a measly pulse. It's rough, I tell you. But from what I hear, out east they're desperate for doctors. So I think I'll just head out east myself and find me some work. Well, it's time to ease on along (*starts walking around the stage*). Goodness, I really hate to leave our lovely capital for the wilds of the east, but there it is, I've no choice. I've got to make a living. Anyway, if I strike it rich, I'll come right back to the capital (*stops at center stage*). Well, what do you know? Here I am at a wide, wide moor. I've no idea what this moor could be called. Oh-oh, now what? All of a sudden the sky's clouded up and it's thundering. I'd rather not hang around. Better head for a village (*starts toward the bridgeway*). I just hope it doesn't thunder too loud before I get there! Oh dear, I don't like this at all!

THUNDERBOLT (*Enters banging on his drum [see figure 1.16]*): Zap, zap, wham, wham, bang!

DOCTOR (*Meeting him on the bridgeway, yells a spell against lightning*): Help! Mulberry, mulberry (*flees*)!

THUNDERBOLT (*Chasing the doctor around the stage*): Zap, zap, wham, wham, bang, bang, bang, kaboom! (*Drops to boards at center stage while the doctor cowers at the waki spot*) Ouch! Ouch! Ow! Owowow! (*Manages to sit up*)

There I was today, having a wonderful time crackling and banging around the sky, when suddenly I stepped through a gap in the cloud, tumbled here to earth, and got a terrible whack on the butt. Hmm, there's no tree around here to help me back on my feet. (*Glances toward the waki spot*) Say, there's some creature! Hey! Hey! Hey, you! You over there!

DOCTOR: YESSIR!

THUNDERBOLT: What *are* you, anyway?

DOCTOR: A doctor, sir.

THUNDERBOLT: You're what? A dock burr?

DOCTOR: That's right, sir.

THUNDERBOLT: Dock burrs can't talk!

DOCTOR: No, no, sir, I said doctor. My business is making sick humans well.

THUNDERBOLT: You're a doctor, you say? And your business is making sick humans well?

DOCTOR: That's correct, sir.

THUNDERBOLT: Well, I'll have you know I'm a Thunderbolt!

DOCTOR: Yes sir!

THUNDERBOLT: There I was today, having a wonderful time crackling and banging around the sky, when suddenly I stepped through a gap in the clouds, fell here to earth, and got a terrible whack on the butt. If you're really a doctor, get busy and fix my butt!

DOCTOR: I'd be honored, sir, but you see, it's human ailments I cure. I've never worked on a distinguished Thunderbolt. Please allow me to forgo the privilege.

THUNDERBOLT: Why, you pipsqueak, what's the big difference between humans and thunderbolts? How dare you refuse to cure me? Any more talk like that and I'll tear you limb from limb!

DOCTOR: Oh no, no sir! I'll cure you! I'll cure you!

THUNDERBOLT: Then hop to it.

DOCTOR: First, sir, I'll check your pulse.

THUNDERBOLT: My pulse?

DOCTOR: For a human, sir, we check the pulse at either wrist. But for a distinguished Thunderbolt, we make what's known as a head pulse check.

THUNDERBOLT: My, my! You really know your stuff, don't you!

DOCTOR: Yes sir!

THUNDERBOLT: Then make it snappy!

DOCTOR: By all means, sir! (*Goes behind Thunderbolt and twists his head around and round [figure 1.24].*)

THUNDERBOLT: What are you up to?

DOCTOR (*Returns to the waki spot*): I checked it, sir.

THUNDERBOLT: Well? What did you find?

DOCTOR: Distinguished Thunderbolt, you appear to be suffering from dysphoria.

THUNDERBOLT: Whew, you're fantastic! I'm suffering from dysphoria, huh?

DOCTOR: Precisely, sir. If we were at my office now, I could give you medicine for it, but out here in the middle of nowhere I'll have to try acupuncture.

THUNDERBOLT: Acupuncture?

FIGURE 1.24. The doctor twists Thunderbolt's neck to check his "head pulse." The doctor wears a plaid cap (*zukin*) and kimono (*noshime*), a haori and patterned hakama, and Thunderbolt wears a thunder god mask and a red headpiece (*kashira*). (Courtesy of the Noh Research Archive of Musashino Women's College.)

DOCTOR: Just a moment, sir. I'll show you. (*Takes a needle and mallet from his waistband*) Here's the needle, sir.

THUNDERBOLT: What do you do with *that*?

DOCTOR: I insert it, sir, into the seat of the pain.

THUNDERBOLT: You mean you're actually going to stick that thing into me?

DOCTOR: Certainly, sir. I insert it even into humans. For a distinguished Thunderbolt to refuse the operation would make him a bit of a coward.

THUNDERBOLT: Impossible! Humans let you do *that*?

DOCTOR: Indeed they do, sir.

THUNDERBOLT: Well if *they* do, then a Thunderbolt's going to have to let you do it, too. All right, go ahead. Stick the needle in.

DOCTOR: As you wish, sir. But first, sir, please lie down.

THUNDERBOLT: Fine. (*Lies down facing stage right*) Puff, grunt, groan.

DOCTOR: Pardon me, sir, but is this the spot?

THUNDERBOLT: Right, that's the spot.

DOCTOR: Then I'll proceed with the insertion, sir.

THUNDERBOLT: Do it! Do it!

DOCTOR (*Applying the needle to Thunderbolt's backside and whacking it with the mallet [figure 1.25]*): Clang!

THUNDERBOLT: Ouch!

DOCTOR: Clang!

THUNDERBOLT: Ouch!

DOCTOR: Now, sir, you *must* be careful not to move, or the needle will go in crooked. Clang, clang, clang, clang!

THUNDERBOLT: Ouch, ouch, ouch, ouch! Quick, take it out! Take it out!

DOCTOR: Gladly, sir (*with the needle, he returns to the waki spot*). There you are, it's all over!

THUNDERBOLT: It's all over?

DOCTOR: Yes sir.

THUNDERBOLT (*Sits up*): Why, that's wonderful! But this spot still hurts. This time I want you to stick it in here.

DOCTOR: By all means, sir. Please lie down again.

THUNDERBOLT: Fine. (*Lies down*) Puff, grunt, groan.

DOCTOR: Very good, sir. Is this the spot?

THUNDERBOLT: Right, that's the spot.

DOCTOR: Then, sir, I'll proceed with the insertion (*stage business as before*). Clang!

THUNDERBOLT: Ouch!

DOCTOR: Clang!

THUNDERBOLT: Ouch!

DOCTOR: Sir, *please* try not to move! Clang, clang, clang, clang!

THUNDERBOLT: Ouch, ouch, ouch, ouch! Quick, take it out! Take it out!

DOCTOR: Pleased to do so, sir (*returns to the waki spot as before*). There you are, it's out!

THUNDERBOLT: It's out, you say?

DOCTOR: Absolutely, sir. (*Thunderbolt sits up.*) How do you feel?

THUNDERBOLT: First-rate! Just take my arm while I try to stand.

DOCTOR: Very good, sir. Let's see you stand up (*goes to Thunderbolt*).

THUNDERBOLT: Upsidaisy! (*stands*).

DOCTOR (*Returns to the waki spot*): Now then, sir, are you all right?

THUNDERBOLT: I tell you, you're quite a doctor. Why, I feel as fit as a fiddle! Well, it's back up again into the sky with me (*starts toward the corner*).

DOCTOR (*Rushes after him and grabs his sleeve*): Sir, sir, please wait a moment!

THUNDERBOLT (*At the corner*): Wait? What do you mean?

DOCTOR (*Returns to the waki spot*): Please let me have my fee before you go.

THUNDERBOLT: Your fee?

DOCTOR: You see, sir, each time I treat a human patient, the patient pays me. Distinguished Thunderbolt, please pay me too!

FIGURE 1.25. The doctor pounds the "needle" into Thunderbolt with a mallet. (Courtesy of the Noh Research Archive of Musashino Women's College.)

THUNDERBOLT: I see what you mean. But I'm afraid I fell here so suddenly, I didn't bring a thing with me. Still, you're welcome to my drumsticks.

DOCTOR: I'm afraid they're no use to me, sir. Do give me something else.

THUNDERBOLT: Then take my drum.

DOCTOR: Sir, I'm not a child. What would I do with a thing like that? Please let me have something else.

THUNDERBOLT: Goodness, what a problem! Tell me where you live, then, and I'll drop back down to pay you later.

DOCTOR: I'm afraid that's impossible, sir. I must have my fee *now*.

THUNDERBOLT: Dear me, this really is a pickle. How in the world am I to pay you? Aha, I know! All humans have their wishes and desires. You *must* have wishes too.

DOCTOR: Now that you mention it, sir, I do have a little wish.

THUNDERBOLT: What is it, then? Tell me!

DOCTOR: They say a distinguished Thunderbolt can do as he pleases with wind and rain. Is that true?

THUNDERBOLT: Yes, that's right, I can do with them as I please.

DOCTOR: Well, sir, you see, droughts and floods keep coming along and giving us humans a very hard time. You could keep an eye on the floods and droughts and make sure they don't happen any more.

THUNDERBOLT: Fair enough. But how long am I supposed to keep it up?

DOCTOR: Forever, sir, if you'll be so kind.

THUNDERBOLT: No, no, I'd never be done then. How about if I keep a whole year free of floods and droughts?

DOCTOR: Why, sir, a year or two's hardly longer than a dream! See to it there are no droughts or floods for a thousand million years!

THUNDERBOLT: Oh no, I'd never get to the end of a thousand million years. Ah, I know! This Thunderbolt's got a brilliant idea! I'll keep floods and droughts away for eight hundred years!

DOCTOR: That's very generous of you, sir.

THUNDERBOLT: And just for you, I'll see you get to be surgeon general.

DOCTOR: Oh, sir, that *would* be wonderful!

THUNDERBOLT: Then I'll just sing the whole thing and get back on up to the sky. You go over there and listen.

DOCTOR (*Sitting at the waki spot*): Gladly, sir.

THUNDERBOLT (*At center back he sings and begins to dance*): Come rain, come shine

CHORUS (*Having entered a while ago through the little door at backstage left, the chorus picks up the song as the shite dances*):
Come rain, come shine,
eight hundred years
will pass unmarred
by flood or drought!
Why, you're an avatar
of Yakushi in person!
Mighty physician
who heals dysphoria,
you're surgeon general now!
cries Thunderbolt
and there he goes,
Up, up, and away,
and there he goes,
Up, up, and away!

THUNDERBOLT (*Chasing doctor around the stage*): Zap, zap, wham, wham, bang, bang, bang, kaboom!

DOCTOR: Ow! Mulberry, mulberry!

Doctor rushes out down the bridgeway ahead of Thunderbolt. The chorus exits through a side door.

Saint Narukami

A kabuki scene from
Narukami Fudō Kitayama zakura
by Tsuuchi Hanjūrō, Yasuda Abun, and
Nakada Mansuke

Translated by James R. Brandon

The tale of a powerful ascetic who, having locked up the rain gods and caused a drought, has his powers destroyed by a beautiful woman is familiar to audiences throughout Asia. In Japan, popular versions are found in the *Taiheiki* (chapter 37) and the *Konjaku monogatari* (book 5, tale 4), as well as in the noh play *Ikkaku sennin* (One-horned wizard). In the noh play, the king of India dispatches a beautiful woman to the horned wizard's lair, where, after enticing him to drink, she begins to dance. The wizard joins her dance until he collapses, and the dragon gods, played by child actors, are able to escape from the cave (a stage prop), taunt the wizard—whose spiritual powers have waned because of his indulgences—and cause the rains to fall. In the kabuki play *Saint Narukami*, the noh dance is replaced by a long seduction scene, and the saint, angered at being outwitted, turns into a thunder god and vows to revenge himself on the woman.

The first kabuki version of the Narukami story was composed and performed in 1684 by Ichikawa Danjūrō I, the actor credited with creating the bravura style (aragoto) of acting. Danjūrō made the woman Taema's seduction of Narukami the focus of his piece and created the characters White Cloud and Black Cloud. In addition to producing other versions of this play, Danjūrō also created a play featuring the fierce deity Fudō. James R. Brandon (1975:10–11) recounts how, in 1742, sixty years after the first production of *Narukami*, Danjūrō II was hired at a lavish salary to perform for a season in Osaka and display his family's bravura style.

Because his first performance was only a modest success and his second was a failure, the actor suggested a Narukami play for his third production. This play, put together under the direction of the stage manager Sadoshima Chōgorō, combined early Narukami and Fudō plays with a new piece entitled *Whisker Tweezers* (Kenuki) which featured the use of magnets, something of a novelty at the time. Danjūrō II played the lead character in each of the three stories. These disparate subjects were combined into a four-act period piece (jidai mono) by setting them in the world (sekai) of the Heian court, specifically in the time of Fujiwara Mototsune (836–891), the first of the powerful Fujiwara regents. Mototsune's regency was plagued by natural catastrophes, and he was known for his support of incantations and rites to placate angry ghosts. This was an apt setting for the Narukami story. The 1742 production, entitled *Saint Narukami and the God Fudō* (Narukami Fudō Kitayama zakura), was enormously successful, running for 170 days and inspiring a similar piece in Kyoto as soon as it closed.

The tendency toward fragmentation led to the breakdown of this longer work into its constituent parts. Ichikawa Danjūrō VII (1791–1859) included *Narukami*, *Fudō*, and *Kenuki* as separate items in his *Eighteen Kabuki Plays* (Kabuki jūhachiban), a collection that stresses the aragoto-style acting of the Danjūrō line. During the nineteenth century, however, all three plays fell from favor and were not performed for a half-century or more until Ichikawa Sadanji II (1880–1940) revived each of them between 1909 and 1911, basing his revivals on the 1742 text.

In 1967 the National Theater in Tokyo produced the full-length play (*tōshi kyōgen*) of 1742 but omitted the death of Narukami at the hands of Danjō. James Brandon translated all four acts of the 1967 production (1975). The version of the *Saint Narukami* scene presented here was abridged by the editor.

This scene reveals little of the puppet theater influence that became prevalent after the mid-eighteenth century. Although *ōzatsuma* narrative music is played briefly at Narukami's entrance and exit, it is largely a dialogue piece, and its bawdy humor and eroticism—much of which vanished with censorious authorities' increasing demands for "seriousness"—are typical of early kabuki. The piece is about seduction at many levels, including the seduction of the audience to the belief baldly stated in the opening lines: "*Saint Narukami* is a great play!" This bit of self-promotion is repeated when the actor inserts his own name in the script. The performance makes effective use of two rampways through the audience. It also contains one of the most erotic love scenes remaining in kabuki; a dramatic transformation of the saint into the thunder god; an excellent example of stylized, ensemble fighting; and a spectacular exit down the main rampway. This is quintessential kabuki.

CHARACTERS

SAINT NARUKAMI
WHITE CLOUD AND BLACK CLOUD: his disciples
TAEMA: a court lady
Other priests

MUSICIANS

Music-room (geza) musicians
An ōzatsuma chanter and a shamisen player on stage

ACT 3, Scene 2

Saint Narukami Scene (a grotto on North Mountain)

A curtain painted to represent the rock face of a mountain hides the main stage. Fast drum patterns (hayatsuzumi) *are played by the small drums and flute in the music room at stage right. The young monks White Cloud and Black Cloud enter, one by each of the two raised rampways through the audience. They are dressed in white kimono covered in front by black aprons. Their heads are shaved, and they carry black rosaries. They trot on comically, talking as they go, their hands tucked up in their sleeves to ward off the mountain cold.*

WHITE CLOUD: Have you heard? Have you heard?
BLACK CLOUD: I've heard. I've heard.
WHITE CLOUD: Have you heard?
BLACK CLOUD: I've heard.

They continue this exchange until they meet in front of the curtain center stage. The music ends.

WHITE CLOUD (*Delighted to see his friend*): What have you heard?
BLACK CLOUD (*Foolishly*): Everyone in Edo saying *Saint Narukami and the God Fudō* is a great play!
WHITE CLOUD: Donkey. Not that. I mean, Are people talking about our Master Narukami's secret rites?
BLACK CLOUD (*Blankly*): I haven't heard a thing.
WHITE CLOUD (*Disgusted*): You haven't? What he does is remarkable. Listen.

The shamisen play delicate, spring flower–viewing patterns (haru wa hanami) *in the background.*

> The emperor denied Saint Narukami's request that to him a temple be ordained; so, furious, he embarked upon austerities that have captured and bound the dragon gods of rain in all the universe until not a drop of rain could fall. One hundred days have passed since the last single drop of rain has been seen. The land shrivels from dryness.

BLACK CLOUD: It's fine if you like your humidity low, but it must be hard for a farmer to stick his rice in the ground.

WHITE CLOUD: It's awe inspiring to imagine Master's power.

BLACK CLOUD: It's the emperor's own fault. He told a fib.

WHITE CLOUD (*Scandalized*): Sh! Being Master Narukami's disciple is a great honor. He is the needle; we are the thread (*mimes threading a needle*).

BLACK CLOUD: Well, I'm worn to a frazzle—up the mountain every morning to help Master with his austerities, down the mountain to sleep. Three miles each way, and it's cold up here.

WHITE CLOUD (*Severely*): If Master freezes, we freeze to death with him. That's what spiritual discipline means.

BLACK CLOUD: My legs have gone numb with the climbing, up and down, up and down.

WHITE CLOUD: I'm tired too, but I don't complain about it. You're a perfect dummy.

BLACK CLOUD (*Snickering*): If my tongue went numb, I'd be a dumb dummy.

WHITE CLOUD: That would be a blessed relief.

BLACK CLOUD (*Slyly*): I've got medicine here that will take off the chill. You'll feel fit as a fiddle fast. How about a sip?

WHITE CLOUD: Is it good? I might try a drop.

BLACK CLOUD: It's the No-Death-No-Pain-Cures-a-Thousand-Complaints-Pharmaceutical-Preparation.

WHITE CLOUD: Well, where is it?

BLACK CLOUD: So precious I wouldn't dream of carrying it up my sleeve or in my sash. I'll open the gates and bring it out (*gestures*).

WHITE CLOUD: Gates? You're going all the way down to the temple for it? There's no storehouse here.

BLACK CLOUD (*Grinning*): Yes there is. To groin a phrase, the medicine is up my crotch. Isn't that a perfect hiding place for something precious? Besides, crotch heat will hold the medicine at just the right temperature for drinking (*produces a small bottle of rice wine from between his legs*). Here (*takes a wine cup from his sleeve*). And here (*offers them*). Here you are.

WHITE CLOUD: Dissolute, defiled, corrupted, filthy, worldly, dirty monk!

BLACK CLOUD: It's just a little wine.

WHITE CLOUD: Lord Buddha has enjoined murder, theft, lust, lies, and drunkenness. In the midst of our Master Narukami's strict meditation, do you dare break the Buddha's commandment?

BLACK CLOUD: It keeps off the dampness.

WHITE CLOUD (*Chuckling in spite of himself*): So it does.

BLACK CLOUD: Since my elder objects, however, I'll smash this bottle to bits on the rock (*raises the bottle over his head*).

WHITE CLOUD: No, no! What a sacrilege it would be to waste Lord Buddha's bounty, for is not rice, multiplied a thousand times ten thousand grains, nature's source of sake? It would be better, if we must eliminate the sake, to do so by drinking it! Perhaps I'll have a sip.

FIGURE 1.26. In *Saint Narukami*, the two priests Black Cloud and White Cloud, carrying sake and an octopus, argue in front of a drop curtain as it begins to fall. They wear bald-head, bonze wigs (*bōzu katsura*), and White Cloud has his rosary (*juzu*) around his right arm. (Photo by Aoki Shinji.)

Black Cloud pours a cup. White Cloud downs it and sighs. The music stops.

    Ah. You know, when I toss off a cup like that, I feel as if I was being born in Buddha's promised paradise. I'll pour for you.

BLACK CLOUD (*Drinks*): Hmm, very good. But there's nothing to go with it.

WHITE CLOUD: Yes there is, yes there is (*brings out a dried octopus from between his legs*). I knew we'd get famished. I brought an—

BLACK CLOUD: —octopus! A monk who'd eat flesh is depraved. Every servant of the Buddha takes a nip now and then, but eating meat in Master Narukami's place of meditation? I'll tell him.

WHITE CLOUD: You wouldn't.

BLACK CLOUD: Just see if I don't (*snatches the octopus*). Master! Master! White Cloud's eating octopus!

WHITE CLOUD (*Snatches the bottle*): Black Cloud's drinking wine! Master Narukami! [figure 1.26]

BLACK CLOUD: White Cloud smells of fish!

White Cloud raps Black Cloud sharply on the head with his knuckles. At one loud clack of the clapper, the curtain drops to the floor and is whisked away by the stage assistants. A sign reads "North Mountain Grotto Scene." It is the retreat of Narukami, a Buddhist saint whose name means Thunderbolt. Towering gray and black rock cliffs hem in the scene. At stage right, rocks ascend to a natural platform that looks out onto a waterfall plunging from above into a gorge below. A ritual straw rope, tied with sacred white papers, spans the waterfall. At stage left, a small, rustic pavilion roofed with thatch stands on a rock outcropping. The large drum (ōdaiko) booms out mountain storm patterns (yama oroshi). The two monks kneel on either side of a small flight of steps leading up to the pavilion and piously take out rosaries. Stage assistants remove a blue-and-white-striped curtain by the proscenium arch at stage left to reveal an ōzatsuma singer and a shamisen player seated on a dais.

ŌZATSUMA CHANTER *(Sings very slowly, in elaborate style, to deep shamisen music)*:
In the meantime, the great Saint Narukami,
blocks the flight of dragon gods and goddesses,
confining the earth's rain.
Going deep into the mountains,
he undergoes strict austerities,
before Buddha's altar.

During the song Narukami enters on the rampway, sunk in meditation. He wears a thick silver gray kimono and holds a large Buddhist rosary; his hair, uncut for three months, reaches his shoulders. He stops at the seven-three position (shichi-san) and turns toward the audience.

NARUKAMI *(In a rumbling voice)*: Hm. Leaves are blown by the wind; in all things there is cause.

The ozatsuma chanter plays rapidly as Narukami crosses ponderously to the platform. He kneels, facing the waterfall, and clasps his hands in prayer.

At this waterfall's rock-crushing stream,
human impurity washed away,
I bend my spirit to achieve perfect meditation.

He rings a prayer bell. The curtain covering the ōzatsuma musicians is replaced. The large drum beats steady, suspenseful waterfall patterns (taki no oto). A bell is heard from the end of the rampway.

CHORUS *(Sings off stage right to shamisen accompaniment)*:
Hail, great Guardian God Fudō.
Hail, great Guardian God Fudō.

The sound of a prayer bell mingles with the repeated prayer to Fudō and insistent drum beating. The rampway curtain opens, and Taema enters, dressed in an elegant red kimono patterned with spring flowers. The kimono is pulled off the right shoulder, showing an inner kimono. A black robe is folded over her arm. Although she strikes a prayer bell, her walk is languorous and extremely sensual. Taema pivots in a circle at the seven-three position, looking around. She sees the waterfall and then Narukami. She poses. The music ends. Taema assumes a deliberately provocative pose and calls out in a pathetic voice.

TAEMA: Help me, great Guardian God Fudō. Help me, great Guardian God Fudō.

She pauses to see what effect this will have. Narukami turns toward the front, still kneeling. His head is bowed, his eyes half closed. Still in meditation, Narukami is scarcely aware of his surroundings. A stage assistant hurries onto the rampway with a tall black stool for Taema to sit on. She hands him the prayer bell and hammer. Widely spaced beats of the small drum are heard, first near and then far away, playing mountain echo patterns (kodama), and the shamisen gently play the same melody.

NARUKAMI (*In a rumbling voice*): In the mountain is total silence, not a bird calls. Strange. Then why do I hear the sound of prayers to Buddha at this remote waterfall, deep in the mountains, where a human footstep is rare? . . .

Narukami awakens his disciples, who have dozed off, and sends them to investigate the "woeful voice invoking Buddha's name." After a bit of humorous quarreling, they sight her, compare her beauty with that of a top-ranking kabuki actor (jōjōkichi), and begin arguing whether she is an angel or a dragon princess. Narukami decides to investigate himself.

Noh drums play single rhythm patterns (itchō) as Narukami rises and looks toward Taema. He rests his hand on a pillar of the pavilion and calls.

You there! You there! (*No response*) I don't understand. Standing before the craggy waterfall, having passed over a mountain trail difficult even for beasts of prey or birds, seems to be an aristocratic female form. How uncanny. (*Sternly*) What are you?

TAEMA (*Helplessly*): I, sir?
WHITE CLOUD AND BLACK CLOUD (*Simpering, mimicking her*): I, sir?
NARUKAMI: Silence.
WHITE CLOUD AND BLACK CLOUD: Yes, Master.
NARUKAMI (*Firmly*): I am speaking to you.
TAEMA (*Lowers her head pathetically*): I am a woman living at the foot of the distant mountain, who has been parted from her dearest husband, sir.
NARUKAMI: Parted from your husband?
TAEMA (*Pretending to weep*): Yes, Your Reverence.
NARUKAMI: Parted and living, or parted in death?
TAEMA: Ah! This is the seventh day of the seventh week.
NARUKAMI (*Somberly*): The forty-ninth day of death?[1]
TAEMA: Yes, Your Reverence.
NARUKAMI (*Raising the rosary to his forehead*): "Namu Amida Butsu." Buddha the merciful, all hail; Buddha the merciful, all hail.

Mountain echo drum patterns create a lonely mood. Taema looks bashfully at Narukami and then holds out the black robe for him to see.

Waka

TAEMA:
Though once a keepsake,
you are now an enemy
I must abandon;

---

1. The day on which a Buddhist memorial service is held for the dead.

can I then perhaps begin
to hope for forgetfulness?"[2]

And so I had thought to wash from this rough robe the dust of carnal
life, yet the drought is everywhere; wells are dry, streams have stopped. I had
heard of a waterfall in the venerable mountain where, in spite of the drought,
water miraculously never ceases flowing. I only wish to cleanse away past
carnal memories, so I can begin life anew (*glances innocently at Narukami*).
Enchanting husband (*looks at the robe and pretends to weep*), I miss you so.
Can you guess what thought fills my heart?

*Narukami does not understand what is happening, but he cannot take his eyes
from her.*

NARUKAMI: What a pitiful tale. It would appear you were close to him during
your marriage?

TAEMA (*Provocatively*):
He and I were very close.
In heaven, like two proverbial birds,
sharing one eye and one wing—inseparable.
On earth, two trees with branches intertwined.[3]

(*Smiles secretly*) When I think back on it, so many interesting things
occurred.

NARUKAMI (*Piously*): The road to salvation begins from carnal desire. Each word
exchanged with this woman is ordained by karma. Repent your unforgivable
sins for his sake in the next life. I will hear your confession!

*He grasps the rosary in both hands and gazes intently at her. She meets his gaze,
then modestly looks away.*

TAEMA: If I speak, it would lighten the pain in my heart. (*Delicately touches her
breast and looks at him*) Should I speak?

NARUKAMI: Speak! Speak!

TAEMA (*Rising briskly*): Very well, I shall speak. And yet it is so very far from here
to where you are, the words I speak will not reach you in these echoing mountains. (*Pouting*) I want to be near your side when I tell my story.

NARUKAMI (*Catching his breath*): True. Your voice mingles with the water's roar
and is hard to hear. You shall approach. (*Makes a sweeping gesture for her to
approach*) Come near! Come near!

TAEMA: Then I will come close to Your Reverence's side.

*The large drum beats steady waterfall patterns. She moves quickly toward Narukami,
as her stage assistant takes away the stool and hand properties. White Cloud and
Black Cloud run to stop her, clucking and waving their arms [figure 1.27].*

BLACK CLOUD: You mustn't, you mustn't.

WHITE CLOUD: By our master's orders women are forbidden—

2. An anonymous poem (*Kokinshū*, poem 746). It also is alluded to in the noh *Matsukaze* and the
kyōgen *Pillow Mania*.

3. Lines from the Chinese poet Po Chü-i's poem "Everlasting Sorrow."

FIGURE 1.27. White Cloud, holding his rosary in both hands, positions himself between Taema and his master, who stands in the pavilion where he had been praying. Narukami's large, wadded obi is tied in the *tombo-musubi* style for aragoto roles. (Photo by Aoki Shinji.)

BLACK CLOUD: —within seven miles.[4]

WHITE CLOUD AND BLACK CLOUD: Within seven miles you cannot go.

TAEMA (*Seeming to be bewildered*): My, you say such strange things.

NARUKAMI (*Considers*): They are right to say them. No woman may approach my seat of meditation. Hm. You shall sit with my monks close by on either side and speak. Speak!

TAEMA: Very well, Your Reverence. I will tell my story here.

She gestures magnanimously for them to sit. Covering their faces to hide their embarrassment, they kneel. Purposely delaying her story, she turns upstage while a stage attendant, dressed in formal kimono and outer garb, takes her sandals and the black robe. She turns coquettishly to the monks.

My two monks, will you listen, too?

NARUKAMI (*Impatiently*): If they do, will you speak?

WHITE CLOUD AND BLACK CLOUD: We will, we will.

The monks put away their rosaries and look at her expectantly.

Shikata-banashi *Taema kneels between them and takes out a small black fan, partially covering her face with it. She poses alluringly. Shamisen play love music patterns* (chigusa), *and tinkling bells join in. She hesitantly tells them her story,*

4. A Buddhist holy place was to be kept undefiled for seven miles in four directions.

with a great deal of seemingly innocent, but suggestive, pantomime, as if Narukami were not there.

TAEMA: I am embarrassed to say it, but I fell passionately in love with my lord not very long ago. It was in the middle of March last year. I had gone cherry-blossom viewing at Kiyomizu Temple, when a young lord, scarcely more than twenty, suddenly appeared outside our canopy and peeked in at me, sitting inside our silken walls (*miming the action*). How can I describe his nobility, his sweetness, in words? (*Behind the fan*) Instantly, I knew this young lord was to be my beloved.

WHITE CLOUD (*Openmouthed*): Though you'd never seen him before?

TAEMA: Ah, his sweetness was such that, truly, from the nape of my neck (*showing the nape of her neck, she leans toward him*)—

WHITE CLOUD: —a shudder?

TAEMA: —a tremor went through my body.

BLACK CLOUD: You quivered?

TAEMA: I trembled. I turned hot (*fans herself, then hugs her breasts*). I turned cold.

WHITE CLOUD: Oh! I can't bear it!

The monks hug their chests, imagining the scene.

TAEMA: Then this young noble began to tease. First he seemed to be gazing at my face from afar, then he was not (*pretends to pout, puts her fan away*). My lord then took a fold of letter paper from his breast, dipped a writing brush in black ink, and quickly composed a poem, which he ordered my serving maid to deliver.

Dipping her finger in ink, she mimes writing on the closed fan and then "reads" from it.

Waka

> "Still yearning to see
> one whom I have not really
> seen nor have not seen—"[5]

WHITE CLOUD:

> "Still yearning to see

BLACK CLOUD:

> one whom I have not really

WHITE CLOUD AND BLACK CLOUD:

> seen nor have not seen—"

TAEMA: Ah! How did the last half of his poem go?

As she had hoped, Narukami's interest is aroused. He looks at her for the first time during the story. The music stops.

TAEMA (*Pretending to think*):

> "Still yearning to see

5. First part of the *Kokinshū*'s poem 476 by the famous poet and lover, Ariwara no Narihira (833–880). Any educated Japanese person could be expected to know this poem.

> one whom I have not really
> seen nor have not seen—

NARUKAMI (*Pleased with himself*):

> —can I live this way today,
> idly passing the time,"
> is the last half of the poem, is it not?

Taema claps her hand to her breast and looks at him as if he had said the most clever thing in the world.

TAEMA: Oh! That is absolutely right!

The ambiguity of her response does not escape Narukami. He gasps.

NARUKAMI (*Thickly*): And then? And then? What? What!

With a flourish, he pulls a small writing table before him, plants his elbows on it, rests his chin in his hands, and poses in a mie, gazing fixedly at her. He holds the pose as she continues. The shamisen change to faster autumn grasses patterns (nanakusa). The tempo of the story increases.

TAEMA: That night, when others were asleep, I rose and found myself being guided, alone, to the middle of Saga Plain, where, I found, he lived.

WHITE CLOUD AND BLACK CLOUD: Brave lady, brave lady!

TAEMA (*Drawing back in fright*): But then I came to a broad river.

WHITE CLOUD: Naturally, naturally. The Big Dam River. The Cinnamon Tree River.

BLACK CLOUD (*Snickering*): A famous river.

TAEMA: Of course I wanted to cross, but there was no bridge, no ferry (*mimes searching helplessly, then slaps her thigh in resolve*). Since there was no other way, I fixed my courage and crossed the river at night by the light of the stars. As a woman, I did a dauntless thing. Without thinking, I took my skirt—

She rises. Ostensibly turning away from the monks but actually turning toward Narukami, she delicately lifts the hem of her kimono to show a few inches of ankle. He starts and gazes in fascination, pushing the table away and grasping the rosary in both hands for support. She turns away as if embarrassed.

WHITE CLOUD AND BLACK CLOUD: —and edged it up? You edged it up?

TAEMA: Not edged at all. I grasped it firmly and lifted it, entering the middle of the stream.

Lifting her kimono skirt with a jerk, as if by accident she opens the front of the kimono in Narukami's direction. He grasps the rosary harder. Taema and the monks now speak with obvious double meaning.

WHITE CLOUD AND BLACK CLOUD: Brrr? Wasn't it cold?

TAEMA: Without a qualm, I splashed in. Splash, splash.

She raises her kimono and shows her leg at each step as she wades seductively through the river. The monks raise their kimonos and in turn mimic her. They parade in a circle.

WHITE CLOUD: Splash, splash.

BLACK CLOUD: Splash, splash.

All three wade in unison, the monks simpering and giggling. The water gets deeper, their steps slower.

ALL: Splash, splash, splash. Splash. Splash.

WHITE CLOUD (*As if in ecstasy, waggling his hips*): Oh! Deep! Deep!

BLACK CLOUD (*On tiptoe*): I can't reach the bottom!

TAEMA (*Adjusts her skirt and kneels*): In time I reached the bank.

WHITE CLOUD (*Sitting and grinning fatuously*): Oh, damp, damp!

The monks wring out their kimono bottoms. She poses and speaks with deliberate intonation, so that Narukami cannot misunderstand her meaning.

TAEMA: Although in the past I had disliked the slightest moistness caused by dew or love, now I pushed aside the short grass surrounding the small house in which my lord dwelled.

WHITE CLOUD AND BLACK CLOUD (*Weakly*): Did you reach your destination?

TAEMA: When I quickly pushed open his rough gate and instantly entered, my lord said, "Ah! You have come" (*places her hand on White Cloud's thigh*). He took my hand (*takes Black Cloud's hand*) and led me straight to bed (*looks down modestly*).

WHITE CLOUD (*Falling backward*): Rapture! I melt!

BLACK CLOUD (*Holding his hands over his lap*): I don't know about you, but I'm as stiff as a log!

TAEMA (*Demurely*): We exchanged intimate stories. We burned incense, and we drank sake. We hugged and tumbled, tumbled and hugged. Becoming unruly in our passion, we ended having a lover's quarrel. (*Miming both lovers*) "Oh, stop it." "What if I don't?" "I'll pinch you" (*pinches White Cloud*). "I'll hit you." "Just try it once." "Well, I will," I said, and hit my lord on the head.

She slaps their bald heads. They hold their heads and wail.

WHITE CLOUD AND BLACK CLOUD: Wah! Wah!

NARUKAMI (*Entranced, he rises and poses with one foot on the top step*): And then. And then. Yes, what then?

TAEMA (*Rising on her knees, miming*): Very soon our quarrel grew heated. "I'll leave." "No, you will not leave." "I shall if I want," I said as I rose to go. He grasped my sleeve. "You are too heartless," he said. "Try to stop me if you want; I must leave." "No, stay." "Good-bye." I pulled my sleeve and broke away.

Narukami is pulled, like the lover, toward Taema; he takes two steps forward, sways, and, to loud mountain storm and two-beat clapper patterns (batan tsuke), falls down the steps unconscious. He lies huddled on the ground. The monks rush to either side of him [figure 1.28].

WHITE CLOUD: Master! Master!

BLACK CLOUD: Master has fainted!

WHITE CLOUD AND BLACK CLOUD (*Waving their arms helplessly*): Master, Master!

TAEMA (*Innocently*): Dear Reverend.

FIGURE 1.28. Taema's erotic story has become too much for Saint Narukami, who falls to the ground. Black Cloud and White Cloud rush up to help him. The topknot of Taema's wig is draped over a drum-shaped ornament (*fukiwa-mage*), with an elaborate flower comb (*hanagushi*) in front of it. (Photo by Aoki Shinji.)

The monks lift Narukami to a sitting position. Taema hesitates, then rushes to the waterfall, as the large drum loudly beats waterfall patterns.

WHITE CLOUD (*On Narukami's right*): Ah! His whole body—
BLACK CLOUD (*On his left*): has grown cold.

Taema mimes dipping up water with her long kimono sleeve. She rises to bring it to Narukami, but it spills. She puts her face into the water, rises, and hurries to Narukami. She kneels beside him and, placing her lips against his, gives him the water. She massages his breast gently. The monks gasp. Feigning embarrassment, she backs away and kneels with her face to the ground. The music stops.

TAEMA (*Softly*): My saint, my saint.
NARUKAMI (*Suddenly opens his eyes, his face unbelieving*): Companion monks?
WHITE CLOUD: Praise to Buddha!
BLACK CLOUD: Master has revived.
NARUKAMI: Something not of priestly nature has occurred. Engrossed without knowing it by the woman's tale, I fell unconscious from my seat of meditation.

Yet, even though my senses had fled, I think I felt a cool drop of water enter my mouth and revive me.

TAEMA (*Modestly*): Yes, it happened. From my mouth to yours, I transferred water from the stream.

NARUKAMI (*Looks wonderingly at her*): Eh? Was the one who placed a drop of cool water on my lips you?

TAEMA (*Bowing*): Yes, Your Reverence.

NARUKAMI: And the one who pressed their flesh to mine to warm my breast was you?

TAEMA (*Bowing*): Yes, Your Reverence.

NARUKAMI (*Considering*): Hm.

Suddenly he leaps to his feet and strikes her to the ground. The drum loudly beats mountain storm patterns.

Monks, watch her!

Narukami swiftly returns to the pavilion. He turns and glares savagely at her. The monks drop to their knees facing Taema.

Ah! Dangerous female!

The music changes to moistness patterns (miuki sanjū) played by the shamisen. Narukami speaks rapidly, rhythmically, with great force.

In ancient times there was a priest in India from Benaras called the Holy One-Horned Wizard.[6] Such was his wizardry that he rode the clouds, he walked on water, until the day the dragon gods of rain deluged the ground with endless downpour, when unthinkingly the holy hermit slipped and fell into a valley far below. Enraged, he cursed all the dragon gods living between the heavens and the seas, saying, "You caused the rain that caused the muddy earth to cast me down." With angry eyes the size of wagon wheels, the holy wizard imprisoned all offending gods of rain. (*Slowly*) He sealed them in a rock cave made magically inviolate by holy prayers hung upon a sacred rope. Drought seized the world; fields whirled with dust; everywhere the people suffered. Then the emperor of that time conceived a plan by which the power of this wizard would be destroyed. He called into his presence that lady of the court most perfect in countenance, Lady Sendara, and said to her, "Go to the grotto where the hermit dwells and, with your sensual charms, seduce this man so that rain will fall." Vowing this, she sought him out, bewitched him with her sexual charms, and broke his secret spells. (*More and more rapidly*) Black clouds filled the sky; rains deluged the land in torrents day and night until, moistened, trees, grass, and the five grains came alive again. That silk-gowned woman drowned in lust a wizard of such power as he! Confess it, woman! Like her you are ordered by the emperor to disrupt my meditation!

Music fades to silence.

6. This account is almost identical to that in chapter 37 of the *Taiheiki* and is undoubtedly from that source. The story is also dramatized in the noh play *Ikkaku sennin* (One-horned wizard).

Well? Answer in absolute truth, or on this spot you shall be ripped to pieces and flung away! Well? Well? Speak!

He glares at her, plants his right foot on the top step, whirls the rosary over his head in his left hand, and poses in a fierce mie pose to three-beat clapper patterns (battari tsuke).

TAEMA: Your suspicions overwhelm me. In truth, it was my fondest dream to become Your Reverence's disciple, but you allowed no one to approach. Then, distracted by your presence, I told you of my intimate affairs. Now, since you doubt me, it is useless to go on living. (*Weeps pathetically, then suddenly rises and gestures distractedly toward the waterfall*) I shall sink myself in the pool of the waterfall! May death vindicate my intentions! Yes!

The drum loudly beats waterfall patterns. Dramatically pressing her hands to her breast, she rushes toward the falls.

NARUKAMI: Stop her, monks!
WHITE CLOUD AND BLACK CLOUD: Yes, Master! Wait, please! Please, lady!

They seize her by the arms at the brink of the falls and bring her back.

TAEMA (*Helplessly*): No, no. Let me go. Please let me die.

She falls to her knees struggling as they continue to hold her arms. The waterfall patterns fade away. Narukami stands struck with admiration.

NARUKAMI: What impetuosity. In spite of once having sinned, your face radiates your true character. Admirable. (*Gravely*) You must not die, for salvation does not lie in death.
TAEMA (*Meekly*): Yet, though I live—
NARUKAMI: Become a nun. Become a priestess.
TAEMA: Eh?

She breaks away from the monks. They kneel to her right.

NARUKAMI (*Warming to the subject*): Narukami will administer your tonsure. You will become a disciple of Buddha. Monks, go down the mountain. Bring a razor and comb for the tonsure, and return.
WHITE CLOUD (*Rhythmically*): But when we vanish, the master—
BLACK CLOUD: and that woman—
BOTH: will be alone together!
NARUKAMI: What?

White Cloud and Black Cloud laugh and point accusingly at Narukami. They wave good-bye and dance off down the rampway as the audience applauds.

NARUKAMI: Foolish fellows! Detestable pair!

Taema looks coyly up at him and bows very slowly.

TAEMA: And now, my teacher?
NARUKAMI: Already you call me teacher. If I am your teacher, you must become my pupil. Maintain a pure heart, and soon you will be ordained a nun.

TAEMA (*Drawing back*): When they return with the razor, will you cut off all my hair?

NARUKAMI: You'll have a clean-shaven pate before you know it!

She cries piteously. He looks bewildered.

Why do you cry?

TAEMA (*Weakly, between sobs*): When I think that my black hair, each strand of which I have smoothed a thousand times, is to be cut and thrown away.

NARUKAMI (*Touched*): You weep in sorrow?

TAEMA: I do.

Turning away, as if weeping, she thinks. Suddenly she rises on her knees and presses her fingers to her breast. She gasps and cries out in pain. She does this several times as the large drum beats ominous mountain storm patterns.

Ahh! Ahh! Ahhhh!

NARUKAMI: What is it? What is the matter?

TAEMA: The sorrow I feel has brought on a spasm. Ahhhh!

She gasps pitifully, and her body weaves from side to side. He stands helplessly beside her.

NARUKAMI: How dreadful. We don't have medicine. Ah! I could massage your back.

TAEMA: I am too much trouble, dear Master (*she has another spasm*).

NARUKAMI (*Righteously*): In case of sickness all barriers are cast aside. Here, now. Here, now.

With naive self-righteousness he stands behind her and very properly rubs her shoulders. The drumming stops. Her cries subside. Silence.

TAEMA (*Tiny, innocent voice*): There is pain in my abdomen.

Nureba

NARUKAMI: Ah, the source of pain must be in the pit of your solar plexus. I have the power to cure spasms by the laying on of hands. Here, now. Here, now.

As before, he approaches his task with utmost seriousness. He kneels, placing his left hand on her shoulder, and deliberately inserts his right hand into the breast of her kimono. He rubs a moment, then stops [figure 1.29].

Does that feel good? Am I reaching the seat of your distress?

Share

TAEMA (*Innocently leans against him*): Your kind hands touch my heart.

NARUKAMI (*Rubbing*): There, there. Is that better? Is it better?

His hand goes deeper inside her kimono. Suddenly he starts, and falls back. He stands in amazement.

TAEMA (*Meekly*): What have you done?

NARUKAMI: My, my hand touched a wonderful thing.

TAEMA (*Innocently*): And what was that?

FIGURE 1.29. In perhaps the sexiest nureba scene in kabuki today, Saint Narukami puts his hand inside Taema's kimono to relieve the pain in her abdomen. Taema's eyebrows are partially hidden by the purple cloth (*bōshi*) placed under her wig. (Photo by Aoki Shinji.)

NARUKAMI: For the first time since I was born, my hand has been inside a woman's kimono. There, on the middle of your chest, my hand touched something soft, like two pillows hanging down with little hand pulls on the front.

TAEMA (*Chiding*): And you are called teacher? (*Hides her face as if embarrassed*) They are breasts, Your Reverence.

NARUKAMI (*Genuinely surprised*): Breasts? Is that so? The breasts to which I was indebted when as a child, I gratefully drank my mother's milk? What is a monk, that he forgets such a thing as breasts? (*Strikes his head in wonder*) I am dull, like a block of wood.

TAEMA: Such purity is laudable, Master.

NARUKAMI: And now I shall discover the source of your illness.

No longer serious, he shows innocent delight in what he has discovered. She rises on her knees to be more accessible. He stands behind her, with feet planted widely apart, his hand in her kimono. He rubs with broad gestures, his face shining with joy. Their bodies sway from side to side.

Here now, here now. Ah, yes. Yes! Here are the breasts! How round and plump they are. (*Hand goes lower*) Beneath them lies the stomach, cramped before, it now lies soft to my touch. (*Hand goes lower*) Next we reach the navel, Divine Seat of Life, Heaven's Center. (*Hand goes lower*) Below Heaven's Center, the Sea of Seducing Vapors. (*Hand goes lower*) Below the Sea of Seducing Vapors, Buddha's Pure Paradise! (*Holds her tightly*) Is my touch pleasing?

They pose in silence. Narukami's facial expression gradually changes, showing his rising excitement and lust. Still feigning innocence, Taema slowly looks up until she meets his gaze.

TAEMA (*In a scarcely audible voice*): Master, no more.

With a choked cry he rubs her deliriously.

NARUKAMI: Ahhh! I adore you! I worship you! My hope of teaching Buddha's Highest Paradise is gone. Only let me dwell in the bottom of the lowest level of heaven.

He embraces her in both arms. She escapes, and they both fall back onto the ground.

TAEMA (*Feigning surprise*): Master. My saint. What are you?

He faces her on all fours, pleading. His voice is slow, harsh, almost unrecognizable.

NARUKAMI: Would you say I am mad?

TAEMA (*Carefully*): This is not your true nature.

NARUKAMI: Would you say Buddha is offended?

TAEMA: You are a saintly monk who could not offend Buddha.

He rushes to her, seizes her arm, and shakes it violently. She pulls away. He towers over her [figure 1.30].

NARUKAMI: I am damned! I am damned! Still living but fallen into hell! Though damned, though sinking, what do I care! What do I care! Buddha himself was

FIGURE 1.30. Taema cowers before Narukami as he presses his affection for her. She rises to her knees, revealing the beauty of her long sleeves. The outer gown with padded hems has been removed from her right arm. (Photo by Aoki Shinji.)

first a mortal. He had a wife as Prince Shitta, he had children. Say yes! Say yes to me!

He advances; she edges away trembling.

Refuse me, and I shall transform myself on this very spot into a devil! I shall devour that beautiful throat and carry you into hell with me!

She buries her face in her kimono sleeve with a little cry. His face is tortured. His voice is terrible.

Woman! Well? Well? What is your answer?!

Kuriage

TAEMA (*Pretending fear but actually toying with him*): My dear saint.
NARUKAMI (*Pressing*): Do not refuse me!
TAEMA: Your Reverence.
NARUKAMI (*Voice rising to a scream*): Do not refuse me!
TAEMA (*Prolonging his agony as long as she can before speaking*): Yes, my teacher.
NARUKAMI: Ahhh!

He collapses to the floor in relief. His lust evaporates, and once more he is the naive and happy monk.

TAEMA (*Chiding*): Who ever walked the path of love with such a face as yours? It was frightening.

NARUKAMI: But, but will you?

TAEMA (*Sweetly*): If you want, I will.

NARUKAMI (*Like an eager child*): Death will be painless! To paradise! Come, come!

He rises gleefully and takes her hand, pointing to the pavilion. Pretending coyness, she pulls him back. He kneels beside her.

TAEMA: You're in such a hurry. Tell me, dear teacher, are you determined to make me your wife?

NARUKAMI: There is a rule for marriage: plunge headlong into the pool.

TAEMA: Come now, do wait a bit. If you want to marry me, I will, but a monk for a husband is hateful (*she turns away pouting*).

NARUKAMI (*Jovially*): They say a monk is good medicine for beriberi.

TAEMA: Will you quit the priesthood if I ask?

NARUKAMI: I'll do it this minute.

TAEMA: You'll become a man?

NARUKAMI: And fix my hair in the latest fashion.

TAEMA (*Wheedling*): Will you, honestly?

NARUKAMI: I swear by the founder of Buddhism!

He holds up the rosary to his forehead. She flounces.

TAEMA: That oath stinks of Buddha. And your noble name too, "Saint" Narukami.

NARUKAMI: Now, now, I can change the name.

TAEMA: Change it? To?

NARUKAMI (*Slaps down the rosary and poses proudly*): The lecher, Ichikawa Danjūrō.[7]

She smiles, and he laughs heartily at himself. The audience applauds.

TAEMA (*Modestly*): We will be a loving couple.

He takes both her hands and rises.

Share

NARUKAMI: Come, come let us began our play!

The audience laughs at the pun.

TAEMA (*Shaking him off*): Again, you want to rush so. Before we become a couple, I want to drink our betrothal cup of wine.

NARUKAMI (*Agreeably*): We will, we will. We'll drink the cup. We have wine.

TAEMA (*Surprised*): Eh?

NARUKAMI: And we have a sake cup.

A bell tolls in the distance. The shamisen play the bell melody (kin aikata) in the background. Narukami crosses to the rocks by the pavilion and receives from a formally dressed stage attendant a red-lacquered "cup," almost twenty inches across, and a wooden cask of wine. Chuckling, he shows them to her.

---

7. Ichikawa Danjūrō Sukebei. Sukebei (lecher) sounds like a proper name, since both parts, *suke* and *bei*, are often used in names. Ichikawa Danjūrō I created this role, which has been played by generations of his similarly named descendants. Other actors would insert their own name here.

The little monks thought they could hide these from me by the waterfall, but I saw them.

He sits and pours her a cup of sake. Daintily she drinks the wine in three sips, as prescribed in the wedding ritual, then passes the cup to him. She picks up the cask, but he will not let her pour.

NARUKAMI: No, no.

TAEMA (*Hurt*): Why not?

NARUKAMI (*Embarrassed, blurts it out*): I haven't touched a drop in my life. I even hate cucumbers pickled in wine.

TAEMA: It may have been all very well to abstain before, but when you take a wife, it is proper that you should drink . . .

She persuades him to drink an enormous cupful.

TAEMA: How do you feel?

NARUKAMI: For the first time since I was born, I have drunk sake. My stomach has turned upside down. (*He shivers and hugs himself*) I'm cold.

She moves behind him and provocatively puts her arms around his shoulders. She convinces him to accept another cup of sake. She leans forward on her knees to pour. Suddenly she pulls back in fright.

TAEMA: Ahhh!

NARUKAMI: What is it?

TAEMA (*Hands to her breast*): In the middle of the cup is a snake!

NARUKAMI (*Laughing*): What silliness. There is nothing.

TAEMA: There is.

NARUKAMI: Here. Look. (*Looks and is startled*) Ah, I see. It's not a snake. That is the sacred rope. See.

He stamps forward with his left foot and brings the cup near her. He points into the cup and then at the rope across the waterfall. With a great show of fear, she looks first into the cup and then up at the straw rope.

TAEMA: Indeed, it is a sacred rope.

NARUKAMI (*Laughing heartily*): Ha, ha, ha! You are a timid one!

TAEMA (*Casually*): What kind of rope is it?

NARUKAMI (*Proudly*): That is a miraculous rope.

TAEMA: Oh. And why?

NARUKAMI: A secret too precious to be spoken to anyone!

TAEMA (*Submissively*): Ah.

She backs away, as if accepting his refusal, but from time to time, she glances surreptitiously at the rope. He lifts and drains the enormous cup. Her display of timidity has made him feel masterful, and he abandons caution. He poses. A distant temple bell tolls. The shamisen play the bell melody softly in the background.

NARUKAMI: I nurse a hatred for the emperor and have imprisoned all the dragon gods of the world in this grotto. (*The bell tolls*) Hung with secret prayers, the sacred rope binds them. (*Puts the cup down and on one elbow, feeling the effects of the wine, confides in her*) Cut the rope, and the escaping dragon gods will bring down floods and torrents of rain. Ha, ha, ha!

He falls over, laughing loudly. The bell tolls. He faces her on all fours.

Absolutely, do not speak of this.

TAEMA: If the rope is cut, will rain fall? How remarkable. Should I—

She looks at the rope and almost rushes to it. The bell tolls. She catches herself and quickly picks up the wine cask.

pour more wine? Come.

She overcomes his feeble protests and pours a full cup of wine. He gulps it down and sits in a blissful daze.

NARUKAMI: Come.

TAEMA: Yes.

Waka   *Sung from the music room to shamisen accompaniment to indicate the passing of time as Narukami leads Taema up the steps to the pavilion.*

CHORUS:
    No sooner used to,
    our evening's rain of pleasure,
    when the dawn of morning comes;
    the sleeves of your sleeping robe,
    dampened in the morning mist.

Taema poses by the pillar, looking at the sacred rope. Narukami draws her into his arms, and they sink to the floor of the pavilion before the altar. He places a hand on her thigh. She leans against his chest. The blinds are lowered, hiding them. A stage assistant clears away the cask and wine cup. The music ends.

TAEMA (*From inside the blind*): Master. Wake up. Please, Master. Wake up, wake up.

Her voice trails off. She knows he will not wake. A side blind is partially raised. The large drum beats waterfall patterns in a steady rhythm, gradually rising in a crescendo throughout Taema's scene. She slips out and rushes down to center stage. She kneels, facing the pavilion, and bows contritely.

Forgive me, Narukami. I have been wicked. I did not want your fall, but it was our most gracious emperor's command. As I promised, I will break the spell.

The shamisen and small drums play fast rock step patterns (ishidan). Taema quails when she sees how high the rocks are, but she tries to climb the steep rock steps to the waterfall, to scattered two-beat clapper patterns. Her long court robe hinders her, and she trips again and again on the slippery rocks. Slowly she pulls herself up, using a creeping vine for support. At the top she poses to the roar of the large drum and three-beat clapper patterns. She kneels, takes a bundle from her sash, and unwraps a short dagger. She clasps her hands together in prayer. The music stops.

Believing in the Three Treasures of Buddha and pressing my head to the ground, I pray to the Twelve Heavenly Generals, the Twenty-Five

FIGURE 1.31. Taema takes out a dagger, preparing to cut the sacred rope that is restraining the dragon gods of rain. (Photo by Aoki Shinji.)

Bodhisattvas, and the Eight Great Dragon Kings, let rain fall.[8] Believing in the Three Treasures of Buddha, I press my head to the ground.

The waterfall drum patterns swell. Taema rushes forward to cut the rope with her dagger, but the icy spray drives her back [figure 1.31]. Again and again she tries. At last she forces her way up to the rope and cuts it through, to three-beat clapper patterns. The flute and stick drum burst into quick flute patterns (hayabue), and the large drum plays rain patterns (ame no [oto]). She falls back in fright as the dragon gods, one after the other, escape up the falls. In the next instant, lightning flashes, and there is a roar of thunder. To continuous-beat clapper patterns (bata-bata tsuke), Taema flees onto the rampway. She stumbles and falls at the seven-three position. Silence. She turns back and looks fearfully at the pavilion. The music resumes. She rises, pivots completely to show her beauty, and, to deliberate continuous-beat clapper patterns, moves elegantly down the runway and off. Stylized lightning bolts appear overhead. The large drum plays thunder patterns (kaminari oto), and the clapper plays loud continuous-beat patterns. White Cloud and Black Cloud lead a dozen white-clad monks onto the two runways. They fold their arms in their sleeves and try to protect their faces from the pouring rain. They call out as they run.

MONKS: Master! Saint Narukami!

8. The Three Treasures (*sambō*) are the Buddha, the Dharma or the law, and the Sangha or the Buddhist priesthood; the Twelve Heavenly Generals (*jūni-shinshō*) guard the Buddha Yakushi and fulfill the wishes of those who call his name; the Twenty-Five Bodhisattvas (*nijūgo bosatsu*) protect aspirants to Amida's Pure Land; and the Eight Great Dragon Kings (*hachidai ryūō*) appear in the Lotus Sutra.

The blinds of the pavilion are raised. In the dim light of the storm, we can make out only that Narukami is on his hands and knees and that his head is down. White Cloud and Black Cloud hurry up to the steps to greet him. The others remain at stage right.

WHITE CLOUD (*Relieved*): Ah, Master, here you are. Here you are. Agh! He smells!
BLACK CLOUD (*Covering his nose*): He's been drinking wine!
MONKS: Ahh! Master!

They all notice the dangling ends of the rope. They gape and tremble.

WHITE CLOUD: Our Narukami's secret spell has been broken!
BLACK CLOUD: The sacred rope is cut, the dragon gods—
MONKS: have escaped and gone!
WHITE CLOUD: And so the rains—
MONKS: come pouring down!

The large drum furiously beats rain patterns. The monks tremble and hug themselves.

BLACK CLOUD: Lightning and thunder—
MONKS: flash and roar!

Lightning flashes, and the swelling thunder patterns of the large drum terrify the monks, who fall to their knees.

Buddha save us! Buddha save us!

The sound rouses Narukami. He moves, but his face cannot be seen.

NARUKAMI (*In a fearsome, demonic voice*): What? It is raining!

The roar of thunder patterns. Lightning flashes.

NARUKAMI: Why does the rain pour (*rain patterns*)? Why does the thunder roar (*thunder patterns and lightning*)?

Watari-zerifu

WHITE CLOUD (*Rising*): Because, dear Master, you were ruined by a woman just now.
BLACK CLOUD: We asked her name and where she fled.
THIRD MONK: She is Lady Taema of the Clouds—
FOURTH MONK: the most beautiful lady of the court—
WHITE CLOUD: by the emperor's command, come to seduce
MONKS: our master!
NARUKAMI (*In a terrible voice*): Ehhh? The woman came to destroy my power? Aghhh!

He lifts his head slowly during the speech. His face is transformed: bold black and dark blue lines painted around his mouth and eyes show hatred and power. His head is topped with a great bush of black hair. With a cry, he rips his rosary in two. He cocks his head, plants his right foot on the top step, flings his arms wide, and stands in a furious mie pose, to three-beat clapper patterns. The monks fall to the ground. The shamisen again play moistness patterns in the background. As Narukami speaks, two monks and a stage assistant help him slip off his kimono top, revealing a white kimono with a jagged silver design representing lightning [figure 1.32].

FIGURE 1.32. Saint Narukami becomes a thunder god. At the upper left, Narukami stands in his pavilion, early in the scene. Following this, a bamboo blind temporarily covered his pavilion, enabling the change of makeup and wig revealed in the upper right picture. A stage assistant then pulls down the top of his white kimono, revealing another kimono beneath it with a flame design (lower left). The assistant holds up the dropped top half of his kimono for this wrap-around-the-pillar pose (*hashira-maki*) performed before the fight scene with the monks. (Photos by Aoki Shinji.)

FIGURE 1.33. Saint Narukami, transformed into a thunder god, hurls sutras to his right and left like bolts of lightning. The stage assistant again holds up the top of his kimono to give his figure more bulk. (Photo by Aoki Shinji.)

> For each inch of good a foot of evil blocks our way! (*Throws down the rosary*) The secret spells are shattered! I have transgressed Buddha's laws and incurred Buddha's wrath! So be it then. I shall become a living thunder god and pursue you, woman, to the ends of the earth! Hah, hah! How easy it will be!

He rises up majestically, towering over White Cloud and Black Cloud. He hurls one sutra to the right, another to the left. They are accordion folded and flutter open into long streamers [figure 1.33]. Again the monks fall. Narukami stands in a ferocious pose. The small curtain at stage left drops to show the ōzatsuma chanter and the shamisen player.

ŌZATSUMA CHANTER (*Accompanied by the shamisen*):
> Spirit of Thunder and Lightning, Narukami,
> concentrating mind and spirit, to search out,
> to approach and overtake her.

White Cloud and Black Cloud seize Narukami's arms and pull him first one way and then the other. With a powerful gesture, he throws them off; they fall, pulling out basting threads in his sleeves, and a stage assistant pulls down his silver and white kimono top to reveal beneath it a third kimono, silver with a brilliant design of orange and yellow leaping flames representing the power of lightning. The two terrified monks leap down from the pavilion to the ground below. Narukami rips a sutra in half and throws both halves to the monks. Each holds an end as Narukami poses to three-beat clapper patterns.

Narukami leaps from the platform onto the main stage and starts out in pursuit of Taema. The monks try to stop him, but they are no match for the thunder god. A stylized group battle scene is performed to ōzatsuma chanting and music by the shami-

FIGURE 1.34. Having overcome the monks, Narukami leaps up the rampway in a tobi roppō exit. Behind him are the monks fallen on their backs and two pairs of ōzatsuma chanters and shamisen players seated on a platform at stage left. (Photo by Aoki Shinji.)

sen, drums, and flute. During the fight Narukami performs two wrap-around-the-pillar poses [hashira-maki; see figure 1.32] and then takes the diamond scepter from the altar and brandishes it [see figure 1.16]. At one point he puts it into his mouth and is lifted up on the backs of three of the monks as the others pose around them. Finally, Narukami easily moves through the monks and rushes onto the rampway.

At the seven-three position, Narukami turns back and glares at the monks. They fall to the ground, shielding their faces. A sharp clacker beat. Narukami faces the audience. Swelling clapper beats [uchiage tsuke] gradually rise to a crescendo, fade away, and then swell again as Narukami raises his arms high over his head, crosses his eyes, and strikes a mie pose to three-beat clapper patterns and loud beats of the large drum.

Hikkomi *Narukami begins a powerful stylized exit. Glaring fiercely, he pulls back one step, draws himself up, and leaps forward onto the left leg [figure 1.34].*

Leaping exit *The music changes to leaping exit patterns [tobi roppō] played by the large drum, stick drum, and flute. Narukami holds the pose a long moment, then again pulls back, draws himself up, and leaps forward onto his right leg. With his arms powerfully thrusting forward, he leaps—at first slowly and with great deliberation and then gradually faster and faster—down the rampway and out of sight to the sound of thundering drums and continuous-beat clapper patterns. The audience applauds. The curtain is pulled closed to beats of the clacker.*

Mount Tempai and Tumult in the Palace

A puppet piece from *Sugawara denjū tenarai kagami* by Takeda Izumo II, Namiki Senryū, and Miyoshi Shōraku

Translated by Stanleigh H. Jones, Jr.

Sugawara no Michizane (845–903) is Japan's preeminent example of an angry ghost wreaking havoc on the world. The historic Michizane was exiled to Kyushu in 901 on the basis of accusations by his political rivals, led by Fujiwara Shihei. After Michizane died in exile, the mysterious deaths of several of his enemies and some unusual catastrophes led many people to believe that Michizane's angry ghost was at work, and every effort was made to pacify his spirit. He was ultimately deified as Temman Tenjin, and shrines to him (called *temmangū*) were established throughout the country. Kitano Temmangū in Kyoto, the most important of these, is still a flourishing institution where throngs of visitors view the spring profusion of blossoming plums (Michizane's favorite tree), and apprehensive students and their parents pray for success on school entrance exams (Michizane was a scholar of renown). He is also revered as the deity of calligraphy. The ox who faithfully transported him to Kyushu is represented at his shrines, usually as a statue that worshipers rub to cure their own afflictions.

An encounter between the priest Hosshō and Sugawara Michizane's ghost is recorded in chapter 12 of the *Taiheiki* and in *Kitano tenjin engi* (The origins of the Kitano deity) and is dramatized in the noh play *Raiden*. In act 1 of *Raiden*, the ghost of Sugawara appears to Hosshō, who is praying at the Enryaku Temple on Mount Hiei, expresses his resentment at the false accusations that led to his exile, and then goes on a rampage, defiling the altar until he is quieted by a *mudra* (sacred hand signal) that Hosshō performs. In act 2, Sugawara appears at the imperial palace as a thunder god and struggles with Hosshō until he is deified as Temman Tenjin. The last act of *Sugawara and the Secrets of Calligraphy* draws on this noh play.

The sections of the puppet play translated here depict Sugawara's transformation into a thunder god and his storming of the palace. These are not the most popular parts of the play; the last act is rarely performed in the puppet theater and never in the kabuki version. They are, however, representative of some of the virtues of puppets. What more effective format than puppets could portray the lopping off of a head with a branch of plum blossoms, the ascension to heaven of an angry spirit, lightning killing humans, the ghostly flailing of an enemy with cherry-branch whips, and the stabbing of a corpse by a princess?

Sugawara was the first of the three great masterpieces that Izumo II, Senryū, and Shōraku composed as a team. The other two are *Yoshitsune sembon zakura* and *Chū-shingura*, scenes from which are translated in part 3. The inspiration for *Sugawara* is said to have been the birth of triplets to a family in the Temma section of Osaka, a well-publicized event. The triplets in the play—three sons of Sugawara's retainer Shiradayū, named Plum, Cherry, and Pine—serve Sugawara, Prince Tokiyo, and Minister Shihei, respectively. When Shihei becomes Sugawara's active enemy, his retainer Matsuōmaru (Pine) is estranged from his brothers. The tension caused by divided loyalties is at the heart of the play and is most dramatically expressed in the "Tearing Apart the Carriage" (Kuramabiki) scene in which the three men literally pull apart the carriage in which Shihei is riding. The puppet rendition of this scene was influenced by kabuki performance techniques. The "Village School" (Terakoya) scene portrays Matsuōmaru's inner struggles and his sacrifice of his own son for Michizane's. He then has to misidentify the head to please his master, Shihei. That scene is considered one of the best examples of the art of both the puppet and the kabuki theaters.

When this puppet play was first performed, at the Takemoto Theater in Osaka in 1746, the famous puppeteer Yoshida Bunzaburō operated the puppets for Suga-wara, Shiradayū, and Chiyo, the wife of Matsuōmaru. The production ran for eight months. The next year an Edo production played for more than 120 days to an audience that included many calligraphy teachers, and kabuki versions were staged in both Kyoto and Edo. A performance of almost the full play at the National Theater in Tokyo in 1972 provided the opportunity for Stanleigh H. Jones, Jr. to prepare a translation of the entire play, from which this excerpt was taken (Jones 1985). The editor modified and expanded the stage directions using the National Theater video of that 1972 performance. All of the text is voiced by the chanter, and so the name of the character assumed to be talking is given in brackets.

CHARACTERS

SUGAWARA NO MICHIZANE: minister of the right, also known as Kan Shōjō
LADY KARIYA: Sugawara's adopted daughter
KAN SHŪSAI: Sugawara's young son
SHIRADAYŪ: Sugawara's retainer and the father of triplets
UMEŌMARU (PLUM): Sugawara's retainer
SAKURAMARU (CHERRY): Tokiyo's retainer, appears as a ghost with his wife, Yae
MATSUŌMARU (PINE): Shihei's retainer, appears only in the final tableau
FUJIWARA NO SHIHEI: minister of the left, who wants to become the emperor
WASHIZUKA HEIMA: Shihei's retainer
MIYOSHI NO KIYOTSURA: Shihei's retainer
MAREYO: Sugawara's calligraphy disciple, who sides with Shihei
HOSSHŌ: a well-known Buddhist priest
COURTIERS
PRINCE TOKIYO: younger brother of the emperor
HANGANDAI TERUKUNI: Sugawara's escort

MUSICIANS

A gidayū shamisen and a chanter on their auxiliary stage at stage left
Drums, gongs, and sound effects in the music room (geza) at stage right

---

ACT 4, Scene 1

Mount Tempai

It is the middle of the second month of the year 903. The scene is the Anraku Temple in the countryside near Dazaifu in Kyushu, Lord Sugawara's place of exile. To emphasize the hardship and melancholy of his exile, the puppet head for Sugawara differs from that used in earlier scenes. Previously, the head was the rather rotund Kōmei, with its gentle, noble features, whereas here the leaner and more angular Shōjō head is used. In the first part of this scene, Sugawara reminisces about a plum tree he had in Kyoto, and the tree magically appears in full bloom on the temple grounds. As Sugawara and his retainer Shiradayū are enjoying it [figure 1.35], one of Shiradayū's triplets, Umeōmaru (Plum), appears with a captive, Shihei's retainer Heima, who confesses.

[HEIMA]: My Lord Shihei has his eyes upon the throne, and he ordered me to take the head of the troublesome Lord Sugawara and return with it to the capital. With Lord Sugawara as his scapegoat, he is going to make his move. He'll engineer an incident for his great ambitions, dispose of the emperor, the prince, and the retired sovereign one after the other, and seize power in a single swoop. And for me (*brightening somewhat*), there was to be the joy of becoming a fine lord. (*Gloomily*) Now my flight of happiness has gone off

FIGURE 1.35. Sugawara (Kan Shōjō) and his retainer Shiradayū are at the Anraku Temple in Dazaifu, Kyushu. Sugawara appeared in earlier scenes with the noble Kōmei head (figure 3.1) but now has the stronger Shōjō head. His legs are cloth covered, his outer robe has padded hems, and he holds a spread-tip fan. His aged retainer, Shiradayū, dressed in a simpler costume, also has an eponymous head. (Photo by Aoki Shinji.)

FIGURE 1.36. Hearing of the treachery going on back at the court, Sugawara grows angry. His hair is loosened, and he shakes his head to spread it out. The cherry blossom motif in his costume reflects the cherry tree blooming overhead. (Photo by Aoki Shinji.)

course, and I find myself most shamefully trussed up. (*Whimperingly*) Please—untie me quickly.

CHANTER:
> As the treacheries of Shihei
> fall one by one upon his ears,
> Lord Sugawara's countenance
> alters suddenly.

Sugawara stands, and the bench he was sitting on is taken away. His hair is untied, and he shakes it so that it spreads out [figure 1.36].

> He stares with bloodshot eyes,
> his eyebrows rise in rage!
> Toward the capital he directs a
>   withering glare,
> and rises up as one gone mad!
> Shiradayū looks on amazed.

[SHIRADAYŪ] (*To Sugawara*): Why, you've known about that conspiracy of Shihei's all along. And yet, as though somehow or other you've just heard about it, your face is more furious than I have ever seen it. You may glare from here, but it won't reach to the capital.

During this speech, the upper part of Sugawara's robe is folded down, revealing a white silk undergarment beneath [figure 1.37].

CHANTER:
> The old man frets
> and shows an anxious face.

[SUGAWARA]: Umeōmaru, Shiradayū! Hear me, both of you! So dire is Lord Shihei's treasonous plot it cannot go unchallenged. I have received no pardon, so I cannot return to the capital. Yet the emperor is in danger, unaware of the traitor who aspires to the throne. My loyalty to his majesty rots away uselessly here in exile. My mortal self has been falsely accused of a crime, but after I am dead I will be free to do as I must! My spirit will return to the imperial capital and serve as a protector of the emperor. Now, before your very eyes, as a token of this my prayer, that I swear to heaven—

CHANTER:
> and from the white blossomed plum

that stands before their very eyes
he snaps a young bough.

The puppet's back is turned to the audience; a branch of cherry is broken off and put in its hand. There is a musical interlude before Sugawara strikes with the branch.

[SUGAWARA]: As a first step in exterminating these fawning villains in league with the imperial traitor, see this!

CHANTER:

With the branch he strikes,
and Heima's head goes flying,

When Sugawara strikes Heima with the branch of blossoms, the puppet falls over backward, and a head attached to a pole flies through the air [figure 1.38].

flung away as are the blossoms
from the branch of the flying
plum,
blossoms showering in waves
like the tempering ripple
on the edge of a well-forged
sword—
yet in Michizane's hand a sword
of plum,
renowned far more than a genuine
blade.
Shiradayū and his son
can only cringe in fear.

FIGURE 1.37. The top layers of Sugawara's gown are folded down by the puppeteers as Sugawara continues to be transformed into a ferocious deity. The white underkimono is of the type worn by people about to commit suicide. (Photo by Aoki Shinji.)

FIGURE 1.38. After Sugawara strikes the treacherous Heima with a branch of cherry blossoms, the puppet head falls off to the back. (Photo by Aoki Shinji.)

[SUGAWARA] (*Holding the branch, which has lost all its blossoms, he gestures in large movements*): Yaaa! Hear me, both of you! You have heard of this terrible danger. Now go without a moment's delay to the capital and report to the emperor about Shihei's evil designs. I will go to the summit of this Mount Tempai to which I raise my eyes, and there for three days and three nights will I bend my mind to the most austere of disciplines. I swear an oath to Bonten, to Taishakuten, and King Emma,[1] and my ghost will become chief of the 168,000 rumbling thunders that reverberate through the heavens.

---

1. Bonten, or Brahma, the supreme creator in Brahmanism, often appears in Buddhist legend with Taishakuten, or Indra, a Vedic deity. Emma is the lord of the world of the dead.

A white mask that has (in some performances) inconspicuously covered the lower part of Sugawara's face is now pulled away, revealing more dramatic eyes; more deeply colored lines around the eyes, nose, and mouth; and a gray hue on the cheeks. This generally more forceful countenance is also enhanced by the loosening of previously tied-back shocks of hair.

[SUGAWARA] *(Moving with many angry gestures and tossing about his long hair):*
I will gather my stalwarts, move upon the capital, and smash the traitorous wretches! This is our final meeting in the present life. Now, go!

CHANTER:
Together with his voice
a raging wind blows up, blows up,

Sugawara throws down the branch, and his body is waved up and down to strong drum accompaniment.

smashing roof tiles of the main hall.
From the priests' quarters and the abbot's cell
blinds and doors fly off
like so many leaves.
Great trees and the flying plum,
flowers and sand in the courtyard
blow violently about.

The drums beat rapidly as the theater lights grow ominously dim.

Shiradayū, Umeōmaru, the priest,
all gaze on dumbfounded.

[SHIRADAYŪ AND UMEŌMARU]: Even if your prayers to the gods are answered, how much grief it will bring to Lady Sugawara and the young master for you to throw away your precious life before its time. Put such thoughts from your mind, we beg you!

CHANTER:
Shiradayū and Umeōmaru seize his sleeve,
but left and right he sends them flying

The puppets approach him one at a time and are pushed and kicked away. The vigorous action of the remainder of the scene is accompanied by drums, gongs, and clappers.

[SUGAWARA]: You, priest. I pray you, make no great effort to stop me! Now, by the grace of the gods, I will show you the miracle of changing my very form to that of a thunder god!

CHANTER:
Taking the scattered flowers
and placing them in his mouth,
he faces toward the heaven
and spews them out—

Sugawara faces the tree, takes some blossoms, and then would-be flames come out of the puppet's mouth.

FIGURE 1.39. Sugawara, transformed into a thunder god, mounts a craggy peak. Whirling a white paper over his head several times (see figure 1.16), he strikes a fierce pose. (Photo by Barbara C. Adachi.)

> white blossoms of the plum!
> The whirling petals turn to flames

Sugawara, flailing and leaping, exits at stage left, followed by the others. The drums play while the cherry tree is taken away, and the flat that had the temple painted on its front falls forward, revealing a rocky cliff painted on its back. The flats that had formed a fence around the temple also fall forward and reveal rocks. A curtain of swirling gray and black clouds falls behind the cliff. Stagehands dressed in black adjust the sets. Mounting a platform behind the rocks, Sugawara sits on the peak holding a strip of white paper on a stick. He whirls it overhead several times and strikes a fierce pose as the chanter sings the following line [figure 1.39].

> as far off to the sky he goes,
> his flight into an unknown realm
> both strange and fearsome.

The curtain is drawn closed, to beats of the wooden clackers.

ACT 5, Scene 1

Tumult in the Palace

The scene is a large room inside the imperial palace in Kyoto. Across the top of the stage hangs the upper paneling of the room, decorated with white cloud patterns against a gold background. The lower center panels, painted with a large stylized pine tree, are drawn apart, revealing a gold and white wall beyond. At the center stands a Buddhist altar of black lacquer ornamented with gold fittings, a pair of gold vases holding golden lotuses, and a black and gold lectern, behind which sits the Buddhist priest Hosshō. Below the altar, a raised black and gold balustrade runs across the stage, broken at the center by three black steps. The forestage represents the palace garden.

CHANTER:

Time shifts,
and already it is late
in the sixth, the rainless, month
in the imperial palace,
tranquil beneath clear skies.
Yet regularly every day
lightning sweeps the heavens

The stage is dim, drums roll, and lightning flashes.

and violent thunder rolls.
Unwonted these endless
convulsions of the firmament.
Responding to envoys
thrice sent with imperial commands,
the high priest Hosshō
has appeared at the palace

More rolling drums.

that he might offer prayers
to ensure the emperor's safety
and turn away the thunder's roar.
Within the palace itself
an altar has been raised,
ringed with sacred hangings,
the dais set with cryptic devices
of the mysterious rites,
and there prays Priest Hosshō.
Surely divine safeguard
will come of all these litanies.
As emissary of the former Emperor Uda—
retired and priestly sovereign—
Hangandai Terukuni makes his entry,
accompanied by Prince Tokiyo,
the Lady Kariya, and young Kan Shūsai.
At the south stairway of the palace
they present themselves.

They enter from stage left [figure 1.40].

From his altar, Hosshō
descends and offers greetings.

[HOSSHŌ]: Ah, most fortunate you
have come.
CHANTER:
As he takes the prince's hand
and leads him to the seat of
honor,
Terukuni bows in reverence.
[TERUKUNI]: His Holiness the retired
emperor has commanded me to
come and inquire if Your Reverence has, on an occasion of the
emperor's good spirits, reported to
him the matter discussed earlier
of Kan Shūsai's succession as
head of the Sugawara house.
CHANTER:
As he speaks, Prince Tokiyo too
turns to Priest Hosshō.

FIGURE 1.40. Priest Hosshō, dressed in the red robes of a high-ranking priest, descends from his altar to greet Prince Tokiyo and the others. (Photo by Aoki Shinji.)

[TOKIYO]: These natural calamities of late, as I think about them, must surely be
the work of the ghost of Lord Sugawara, aggrieved over the baseless charges
brought against him. If this spirit is to be quieted, then as the retired emperor
has said, Kan Shūsai should be pardoned of any transgressions against the
emperor, and the house of Sugawara should be reinstated. If done, this would
dispel the spirit's bitterness and would be most conducive to the happiness of
the country and the people. We beg Your Reverence most earnestly to convey
this to His Majesty. And I would appreciate your offering my apologies to His
Majesty for the displeasure caused him by the groundless rumors about myself.
CHANTER:
He speaks with great deference.
[HOSSHŌ]: Just as you say, these unseasonal happenings are surely due to the
lingering rancor of Lord Sugawara. For some time, his lordship was my
disciple in the faith. I will most gladly recommend to the emperor that
Kan Shūsai's succession to the Sugawara house will pacify the spirit's wrath.
Let this be conveyed by Terukuni to the palace of the retired emperor. The
rest of you, please come with me.
CHANTER:
They accompany the priest inside.
Terukuni is overjoyed.

All but Terukuni exit stage left.

[TERUKUNI]: I must go at once to the retired emperor and report to him that His
Reverence has promised to sponsor our request.
CHANTER:
In high spirits
he returns the way he came.

FIGURE 1.41. Shihei, wearing a court cap (*kammuri*), holds the boy Kan Shūsai as his retainers Mareyo and Kiyotsura are killed by the elements in the blurs of activity to the right. (Photo by Aoki Shinji.)

CHANTER:

His fierce eyes search everywhere.
Now unaware his enemy lies in wait,
in comes Kan Shūsai.

Kan Shūsai enters from stage left.

[KAN SHŪSAI]: Has Terukuni returned?
[SHIHEI]: There he is!
CHANTER:

At Shihei's bellow,
abruptly Mareyo runs forward,
grabs Kan Shūsai by the arm,
and twists him to the floor.
Shihei roars with evil laughter.

[SHIHEI]: You're little more than a fly right now, but if I spare you, you will later become my adversary. (*To Kiyotsura and Mareyo*) Here, you two. Leave the imp Kan Shūsai to me. Bring Prince Tokiyo and Lady Kariya here!

Kan Shūsai is put in Shihei's arms, and he sits at stage center [figure 1.41].

CHANTER:

Kiyotsura and Mareyo
acknowledge the command,

They begin to move toward stage left.

but as they are about to enter
the palace's inner precincts,
suddenly the limpid sky
swarms with turbulent clouds,

Terukuni exits downstage left. Shihei enters from stage right, accompanied by Mareyo and Kiyotsura.

Now, Minister Shihei
is staggered to learn,
that into the palace secretly
have come
Prince Tokiyo and the Sugawara
children.

[SHIHEI] (*Shouting*): Mareyo! Kiyotsura! Follow them quickly! I can see beyond into the emperor's chambers. They are Shihei's mortal enemies. Cut them down one and all! I shall exile the emperor and the retired sovereign, and I myself will ascend the imperial throne! After them, Kiyotsura, Mareyo!

Gongs, rolling and tapping drums.

> wind and rain descend,
> and bolts of lightning
> blaze across the firmament,
> while claps of monstrous thunder
> rend heaven and earth—
> Crack! Bang! Rumble! BOOM!!
> Kiyotsura, Mareyo quaver with terror,
> panic racks their bodies,
> they pale with fright
> and seek escape this way and that.
> Great Minister Shihei stands
> unflinching in the tumult.

[SHIHEI]: Agh! You sniveling cowards! Let the thunder roll, let the lightning fall!
> I'll trample beneath my feet and snuff out both thunder god and lightning fire!

CHANTER:
> Beneath his arm he grips Kan Shūsai,
> and standing upright glares back at the sky.

Shihei holds Kan Shūsai around the neck with his left arm. Mareyo and Kiyotsura cower at his left and right.

> The thunder echoes on and snarls,
> and in the lightning flash and tremors of the earth

Lightning is seen in flashes on the backdrop and overhead.

> Mareyo feels more dead than of the living.
> As he leans over the bottom of the stairs,
> above his head a wheel of fire
> appears to descend, and Mareyo's body
> is enveloped in the searing flames.

Mareyo falls down on his face and then drops behind the low wall.

> This chastening from heaven before one's very eyes
> is vengeance exacted by Lord Sugawara.
> Indeed, for Mareyo, an end so well deserved
> Yet this too fails to daunt
> the sturdy spirit of Shihei.

[SHIHEI]: Miyoshi no Kiyotsura! Where are you? No god of thunder can defy me!
> Come here if you are afraid.

CHANTER:
> His voice gives Kiyotsura heart;
> he approaches his master's side.
> In a twinkling, Kiyotsura too
> is struck down by a lightning shaft,

Pounding drums and gongs sound as Kiyotsura falls over backward and out of sight.

> and on the spot the breath is severed from him.

> At the deaths of his two minions,
> old though he may be, yet now,
> Shihei shrinks back, knees atremble.
> The captive Kan Shūsai
> slips from his grasp and flees
> into concealment.

Shihei falls over; Kan Shūsai escapes and exits off to stage left.

[SHIHEI]: Now I can rely only on the Law of Buddha.

CHANTER:

> He dashes up to the altar, and
> covering his face with both hands,
> cowers down before it,

Shihei tries to get to the altar but falls back and ends up with his head toward the audience, his face to the floor. Two snakes held up from below by the puppeteers wiggle out of his ears and move around.

> as from each of his ears appear
> small snakes but one foot long.

Shihei looks at the snakes and falls over backward. The snakes (now attached to sticks) crawl over his body.

> He writhes and falls upon his back.
> Backward pitches his head,
> and the two snakes slide away,
> entering, it seems, the sacred hangings
> that adorn the altar.
> But then from the altar appear the forms
> of Sakuramaru and his wife,[2]
> shades no longer of this world.
> Like shadows they rise
> abruptly from the sacred place.

The drums beat rapidly. The lights dim, and two white-clad ghosts bathed in a greenish glow rise to each side of Shihei.

[SAKURAMARU] *(The drums continue as he speaks slowly)*: Oooh, the anger, the rancor! Because of you, Lord Sugawara was most foully slandered, and of a tormented heart did he die in Tsukushi. Unable to dispel the bitterness, he became the flames of the thunder god who booms through the murky skies. (*Speaking in a louder, more impassioned voice*) As the red-blooming cherry, the *sakura*, scatters its blossoms, I, Sakuramaru, will tear you apart! Here, come here!

CHANTER:

> He grips Shihei's head
> and seeks to drag him off.

---

2. The deaths of Sakuramaru and his wife, Yae, are described in earlier sections of the play. Sakuramaru committed suicide to atone for his inadvertent part in bringing scandal to Lord Sugawara's house; Yae died defending Lady Sugawara from an attack by Shihei's retainers.

Startled by the sounds,
into the palace runs Priest
    Hosshō.

*Hosshō enters from stage left and
heads toward the beleaguered Shihei
[figure 1.42].*

He sees the ghosts before him,
vividly, as the night-blooming
    cherry.
To drive the spirits away, he prays,
rubbing his rosary, endlessly
    reciting
a spell recondite to the goddess
    Kannon,
deity of a thousand arms.
Shihei stands dazed, not knowing
if the scene be dream or
    substance.
But clouds and mist stand between him
and the phantoms' malevolent obsession.
Their forms are visible,
but hands can touch them not.
Shihei tries to escape, but quickly
there before him, blocking flight,
stand Yae and Sakuramaru.

Rapid drumbeats.

FIGURE 1.42. Hosshō rushes in to help Shihei, who is being attacked by the ghosts of Yae and Sakuramaru. The priest does not yet realize that Shihei is the villain. (Photo by Aoki Shinji.)

[YAE]: Cut down by the sword, I departed this world, whence my body has, by the tormenting flames of hell, been seared red as the carmine cherry. This old man may pray as he will, yet will my loathing pursue you ever. You cannot get away. You will not escape![3]

CHANTER:
Like the hounds of passion,
though driven off,
yet they return again.

[HOSSHŌ]: See how I will make these spirits of the dead depart.

CHANTER:
He rubs his rosary,
rubs away, and chants his prayers,
but the wraiths speak back.

[SAKURAMARU]: No, no, no! Invoke your litanies as you will; we shall make him suffer with us the agonies of the damned!

CHANTER:
They advance;

3. This speech contains several puns on the names of different varieties of cherry blossoms.

the priest prays,
and as he casts his spells,
their forms shift in and out of view.
Slowly, as the petals fall
from the late-blooming cherry,
slowly the spirits disperse.
The approach of chafing beads
seems to fill them with dread—
most eerie the powers of his prayers.
If the priest is in the main palace,
the forms of the ghostly pair
are in the empress's apartments.
Should Priest Hosshō shift there,
the specters appear
in the emperor's quarters.
If to these quarters moves the priest,
then to the Pear Chamber, the Plum Room,
the Bedchamber, the daytime lodgings—
now losing one another,
now coming together.
Priest Hosshō recites his prayers;
the angry wraiths refuse to leave
as they struggle against their exorcist.
At length, brought to his knees by prayer,
Sakuramaru shouts out.

[SAKURAMARU]: Enough! Wait, reverend priest! I cannot fathom your protection
of Shihei, who unjustly accused Lord Sugawara of crimes and who plots to
usurp the throne. Do you lend your might to an imperial foe?

CHANTER:
At these words, Priest Hosshō
stands astonished.

[HOSSHŌ]: What! I did not know that he was such a rebel against the crown.
What sacrilege to have profaned my rosary for him!

CHANTER:
He leaves his place of prayer
and goes within.

Hosshō exits stage left.

Now Shihei, fearful of the apparitions,
tries to flee to the Waiting Chamber,
only to be stopped by the ghosts,
who seize his topknot
and drag him back.

[SAKURAMARU]: Now shall we do with you as we wish! You will accompany us
on the pitch black road to death!

The drums roll as the ghosts attack Shihei with branches of cherry blossoms.

CHANTER:
Waving aloft their whips
made of cherry branches,
they drive Shihei before them,
drive and pursue him.

The gate slides apart at stage right, allowing the puppeteers to get to the lower level and lay Shihei down in the garden.

Lashed and lashed without mercy,
Shihei falls senseless,
like an empty cicada husk,

Intermittent drumbeats.

bereft of life.

[SAKURAMARU]:
Now the rancor has been dispelled.

CHANTER:
The phantoms kick Shihei's corpse
into the palace garden.
Then joyously their forms
dissolve away,
waning as a flower fades,
till they are seen no more.

The ghosts drop their branches and drop down out of sight behind the fence.

Now is laid to rest
the spirit of Lord Sugawara.
The heavens clear,

The lights come up again.

and the great wheel of the sun
shines forth in all its brilliance.
Watching the spectacle,
Kan Shūsai and Lady Kariya
quickly run to the garden.

Kan Shūsai and Lady Kariya enter from stage left.

[KARIYA]: No escape for you, enemy of my father!

Lady Kariya slaps the body, and it moves [figure 1.43].

CHANTER:
From her breast she draws
a dagger saved for this occasion.

[KARIYA]: Know you, this is the sword of my hatred!

CHANTER:
Through and through

FIGURE 1.43. Lady Kariya and Kan Shūsai peer down at the body of their enemy Shihei, and then they stab him to death. Lady Kariya is dressed in a costume similar to that of Sendan in *Saint Narukami*. Shūsai has a child's head and wears a brocade coat with a stand-up collar (*omigoromo*). (Photo by Aoki Shinji.)

she stabs him again and again.
Now indeed is the time
for her rejoicing!
Now, anxious for the safety
of the prince and Lady Kariya
and young Kan Shūsai,
Matsuōmaru appears at the
    palace,
joined by Terukuni.

Matsuōmaru and Terukuni enter from stage left.[4]

Returned from Dazaifu,
Shiradayū and Umeōmaru, too,
present themselves in attendance.
At the stairway's foot.

Shiradayū and Umeōmaru enter from stage left.
As they hear in full
the tale of how the wrathful
    ghosts

of Sakuramaru and Yae
brought to light the evil of Shihei,
the hearts of all soar up in joy.
Rejoicing with them, Priest Hosshō comes forth,
leading in the prince.

Hosshō and Prince Tokiyo enter from stage left.

[HOSSHŌ]: In accordance with all your desires, there has been an imperial proclamation that Kan Shūsai be permitted to succeed as head of the house of Sugawara. On Lord Sugawara is conferred the Senior First Court Rank. A shrine is to be erected in his honor at the equestrian grounds of the palace guards of the Right, and he is to be worshiped as the All-Honored Heaven-Filling Deva King, divine protector of the imperial palace.

CHANTER:
He speaks the words
and all join in the jubilation.
Hearing the echoes of that happy time,
one thinks upon that grove
of a thousand pines at Kitano,[5]
the noble shrine, glorious forever,

4. Or the play may end more simply with only Tokiyo and Hosshō returning to the stage.
5. The pine grove is generally dated from 947 when the Kitano Shrine was established. However, legend has it that on the night of Michizane's death in Dazaifu, several thousand pines suddenly grew up overnight in the area northeast of the Kitano Shrine in Kyoto. The place-name Sembon (Thousand trees) still designates the district.

a palace lasting full a thousand,
nay, ten thousand years—
its curtains of brocade,
finest crystal pillars,
crossbeams wrought in agate,
standing joists of emerald.
All these, with corridor and worship hall,
remain for view today,
vividly recalling that time of long ago.
Known throughout the capital
as Kitano—"North Moor";
in Naniwa,[6] called Temman—
"Heaven-Filling Shrine"—
the virtue and auspicious augury
of its noble god
gives divine assistance to our brush,
as briefly we recount the annals of this shrine,
unrivaled in its glory.
Here in Japan, where passed to generations
are Sugawara's secrets of the brush,
before that lofty majesty,
even now one stands in awe.

The curtain closes to beats of the clackers.

6. Naniwa is an old name for Osaka.

PART 2

The Noh and Kyōgen Theaters

Elements of
Performance

Noh and kyōgen belong to a single per-
formance tradition, although they enact radically dissimilar types of texts. The same
musicians, using different styles, perform in both genres, and kyōgen actors have
roles in most noh plays. Noh actors, however, have nothing to do with kyōgen, a
practice that reveals the perceived hierarchy. Noh, as the "serious" art, has always
considered itself, and has generally been considered, superior to the comic kyōgen—a prejudice against comedy that is certainly not uncommon in the history of
world theater. In this introduction to part 2, I describe the two genres together, emphasizing the similarities in their performance practices. The translated plays reveal
their differences.

The two genres share the same stage, and their plays are usually presented in a
single program, which, in its fullest form, includes the ceremonial piece *Okina* (see
the introduction to *Sambasō* in part 3), five noh plays, and four kyōgen plays. At the
beginning of each year, the various noh and kyōgen schools cooperate to present a
full program, which requires about ten hours to perform. Most programs today,
however, are much shorter. Regular monthly performances by schools, or sub-
groups thereof, present two or three noh, a kyōgen or two, and some danced sections from noh plays (*shimai*). These are usually scheduled on Saturday or Sunday
afternoons and last four to five hours. Weekday-evening programs may consist of
only a single noh or a few kyōgen.

Approximately seventy active noh stages exist in nineteen Japanese prefectures,
twenty-six of which are in Tokyo, nine in Osaka, and seven in Kyoto. The six smallest theaters seat fewer than fifty people, with the dozen largest having capacities of
five hundred or more. In addition to professional noh and kyōgen performances, the
stages are used for training, rehearsals, and amateur recitals, but rarely for other
types of theatrical performances. Noh and kyōgen plays are often presented in other

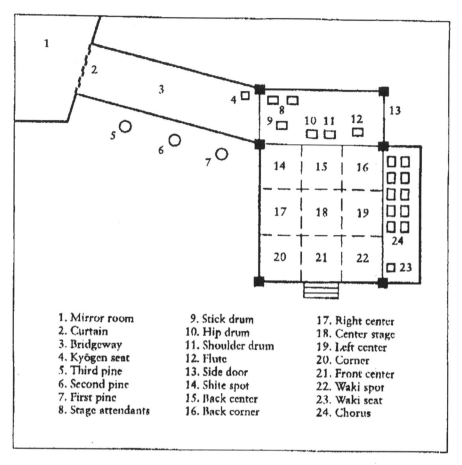

1. Mirror room
2. Curtain
3. Bridgeway
4. Kyōgen seat
5. Third pine
6. Second pine
7. First pine
8. Stage attendants

9. Stick drum
10. Hip drum
11. Shoulder drum
12. Flute
13. Side door
14. Shite spot
15. Back center
16. Back corner

17. Right center
18. Center stage
19. Left center
20. Corner
21. Front center
22. Waki spot
23. Waki seat
24. Chorus

FIGURE 2.1. Diagram of the noh stage. For a photograph of the stage see figure 1.11. (Illustration by Arnie Olds.)

spaces as well, such as Western-style theaters and temple or shrine structures, including temporary stages erected for festivals (figures 2.1, 2.2).

Performers are grouped into schools (ryū) by specialty. Actors are divided into kyōgen actors (two schools), waki actors (three schools), and shite actors (five schools). The musicians include three schools of flutists, four of shoulder drummers, five of hip drummers, and two of stick drummers. Together these schools claim approximately fifteen hundred members: slightly more than one thousand shite actors, fewer than one hundred kyōgen actors, about sixty waki actors, and around fifty players of each instrument. These numbers include many who are not full professionals, such as young performers still in training, advanced amateurs, and those who are licensed to teach an aspect of noh, such as chanting, but who do not perform in professional programs. There are approximately five hundred active, fully professional performers, but few of them are able to make a living solely by performing. Most also give paid lessons to amateurs and to the children of other performers. Since 1947, women have had the legal right to perform professionally with men, and they are included among the members of the schools. In practice, however, coed casts are infrequently found in some schools and never in others. Women are more likely to perform in all-female groups or as amateurs. They also serve as licensed teachers of noh song and dance.

Professional performers generally undergo intensive training from childhood through early adulthood, and the discipline and control they develop are widely admired by their Western counterparts. Even today the theatrical professions are largely hereditary, with fathers (or surrogate fathers) teaching youngsters, and the head of the school or subgroup taking over for the final years of apprenticeship. Training is through imitation and memorization. No discrete physical or mental exercises or techniques are practiced—no musical scales, elocution lessons, or physical arts—rather, sections from plays are learned as performance pieces. Most performers study more than one art, and almost all of them practice chanting as well as one or more instruments. Hence a young actor may learn, for example, to sing and dance the last scene of *Kamo* from his father and to play the stick drum and flute parts in his instrumental lessons. Young actors appear onstage in child roles: the noh play *Miidera* has a small but sensitive part for a boy, and the child who appears in the kyōgen *Mushrooms* as the tiniest fungus contributes much to the humor of the play (both plays are translated in this book).

FIGURE 2.2. Takigi (bonfire) noh performed at the site of the gate to Kōfukuji in Nara. The waki (top), a traveling monk, enters down a makeshift bridgeway at the rear of the stage. The shite dances in act 2 of *Yuki* (Snow). The temporary stage is marked off as sacred space by the folded strips of hanging paper. (Photos by Karen Brazell.)

Flute and drums accompany all noh plays and those kyōgen with instrumental music, such as *Thunderbolt*, *Kanaoka*, and *The Cicada* (figure 2.3). The flute (*nōkan*) is a transverse instrument made of strips of bamboo. It is unusual in that overblowing produces intervals of less than a complete octave, and the tonal system varies from one flute to another. Rather than harmonize with the human voice, the flute provides melodic embellishments to sung sections and joins the drums in instrumental passages for entrances, exits, and dances. The two hand-held drums, the shoulder drum (kotsuzumi) and the hip drum (ōtsuzumi or ōkawa), are played as a pair; the hip drum is generally more active in the first half of a measure, the shoulder drum in the second half. Interesting exceptions are the *rambyōshi* dance in the noh play *Dōjōji*, in which the dancer performs to a shoulder-drum solo, and a version of

FIGURE 2.3. The instruments used in noh and kyōgen: stick drum (*taiko*) on stand, hip drum (*ōtsuzumi* or *ōkawa*) assembled, shoulder drum (*kotsuzumi*) disassembled, and flute. (Photo by Karen Brazell.)

Okina, in which three dancers perform to the beats of three shoulder drums. The shoulder drum produces four distinct, relatively soft and resonant pitches, and the slightly larger hip drum produces a dry crack that varies only in the intensity with which the drum is struck and the amount of resonance permitted. The stick drum (*taiko*) is played with two lightweight wooden sticks about an inch in diameter. This drum is sounded on the half-beats, establishing a strong pulse that dominates the music. For this reason, the stick drum is used in only about half the plays and then only for the later parts.

The drummers use their voices as well as their instruments to contribute to the aural impact of the performance. Their calls (kakegoe) of *yo, ho, yoi,* and *iya* generally sound eerie to the untrained Western ear, but the quality of these sounds (loud, quiet, urgent, lulling, gentle, or vigorous) helps establish the mood of a particular piece, and their precise placement in the drum patterns is an important means of controlling the rhythm. The musicians are also part of the visual picture. They sit in full view of the audience, their posture, movements, and garments strictly regulated by convention. In noh the musicians enter first, walking along the upstage edge of the bridgeway, and leave only after the actors have exited. In kyōgen they enter the stage only when they have a part to perform.

Another group of onstage performers is the chorus. For noh plays, the chorus usually consists of eight to ten shite actors, who enter and exit through the little door at backstage left (kirido). They come onstage after the instrumentalists have entered and exit last. When a chorus is used in kyōgen plays, it is composed of four or five kyōgen actors, who kneel at the back of the stage. Neither chorus represents characters of its own; rather, it impersonally voices the text, shifting easily from speaking in the equivalent of an effaced third-person narrator to chanting the words of the main character in the first person. The leader of the chorus, who sits in the middle of the back row in noh, is an important force in integrating the aural elements of the performance.

Because the stage is decorated only with the painted pine on the back wall, the bamboo on the stage-left wall, and an occasional simple prop, costumes and masks provide most of the color and visual beauty. They also indicate the age, gender, social status, and nature of the characters. Central to the costuming of a noh figure is the mask, a piece of beautifully carved sculpture with almost a life of its own (figure 2.4). In noh plays, adult shite actors are masked except when they play ordinary, living male characters, such as the secondary characters (tsure) in *Shunkan* or the grass cutters in *Atsumori*. Waki actors, who never wear masks, only play living male characters and, like other unmasked noh performers, keep their features immobile.

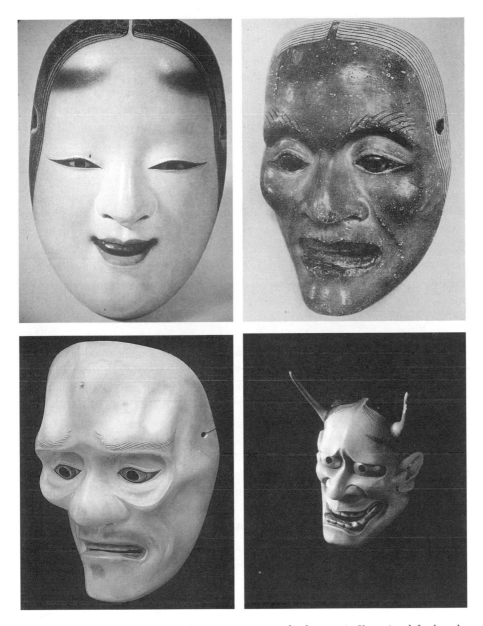

FIGURE 2.4. Noh masks: ko-omote for young women, as for the tsure in *Kamo* (top left: photo by Monica Bethe); Yamamba mask (top right: photo by Monica Bethe); Shunkan mask (bottom left: courtesy of Michelle Li); *hannya* mask for jealous women, as in *Dōjōji* (bottom right: photo by Karen Brazell).

Kyōgen actors, on the other hand, perform most of their roles without masks, using stylized expressions to create stage personae. The few masks used in kyōgen, such as the *buaku* mask for *Thunderbolt* and the bearded *noborihige* for the subsidiary deity in the aikyōgen of *Kamo*, have exaggerated features. The expressions on noh masks range from the serene young woman's mask (*ko-omote*) used in act 1 of *Kamo*, which takes on a cheerful or sad expression as it is carefully raised and lowered, to the fierce deity mask (*ōtobide*) of the thunder god in act 2, which has an exaggerated expression that comes to life most vividly when the head is moved quickly from left to right. A few noh plays, such as *Shunkan* and *Yamamba*, use masks designed for specific characters; most others use generic masks.

The art of costuming, like most arts in noh and kyōgen, consists of varying a relatively small number of forms. The basic garment for characters of both sexes is similar to the modern kimono: a narrow-sleeved,[1] full-length gown made of plain, striped, or plaid material (*noshime*) for male characters and a similar garment appliquéd with gold or silver foil (*surihaku*) or with foil and embroidery (*nuihaku*) for females.[2] Kyōgen female characters wear an embroidered nuihaku by itself, and a few noh characters, such as the female demon in *Dōjōji*, may appear in only these two undergarments: a foiled kimono with its bottom half covered by a folded-down embroidered kimono. Most noh characters also wear an outer garment. The colorful brocade robe (*karaori*), intricately woven with weft floats on a twill ground, is used mostly for women's roles and may be worn in various ways. Both male and female characters may wear a three-quarter-length, light silk or gauze cloak with broad sleeves, such as the versatile travel cloak (*mizugoromo*), the hunting cloak (*kariginu*), and the dancing cloak (*chōken*).

For a fuller stage figure, both male and female characters don divided skirts with stiffened backs and pleated fronts, made of either a plain-colored material (*ōkuchi*) or a satin weave with bold gold or silver weft patterning (*hangiri*). These are usually worn by the shite or a waki playing a high-ranking priest. Other performers wear variations of the soft, pleated trousers called hakama, still part of traditional Japanese dress. Standard, ankle-length hakama are worn by musicians for regular performances (instrumentalists and chorus members always wear similar costumes), and long hakama (*nagabakama*) and matching stiff vests are worn for the most formal occasions. Hakama are generally reserved for male characters and normally are not used for shite roles in noh, although the female demon in *Dōjōji* may wear a long hakama over a scaled kimono. Kyōgen players wear short or long hakama, often with bold geometric designs, or a special type of breeches with leggings (*kukuri-hakama*).

Other costume pieces include wigs, headpieces, hoods, caps, headbands, belts, aprons, and stoles, all used in highly stylized and conventional ways. Masks are worn with wigs, ranging from the tightly tied-back wig (*kazura*) for a woman to the mop of cascading red, white, or black "hair" (*kashira*) for an active deity. Court caps or crowns often top the wig: the woman in *Izutsu* dons her lover's court cap; the thunder god in *Kamo* wears a black crown, the mother deity, an elaborate headpiece. Costume pieces are not always used realistically. Female characters in kyōgen, for example, are not masked; rather, their heads are wrapped in strips of white cloth that hang down on each side of the head, framing the male face (*binan*). In noh the brocade headbands

---

1. Narrow sleeves are made of one width of material, approximately the width necessary to cover an arm from shoulder to wrist, and are sewn up halfway along the outer edge to leave a rather narrow armhole. Wide sleeves are made of one and a half or two widths of material and are not sewn together at the outer edge, only attached at the bottom.

2. To find illustrations of these costume pieces, consult the glossary at the back of this book. Items are listed by their Japanese names.

(*kazura obi*) for women are worn under the mask, presumably to avoid detracting from its beauty; warriors wear their white headbands in a more realistic fashion over the mask (compare figures 2.10 and 2.18).

Noh costuming includes symbolic elements. A female character who appears with the right sleeve of her robe slipped off, revealing the underkimono, is probably deranged, although working or fighting characters—such as the boat woman in the play *Eguchi* and the warrior Atsumori (see figures 2.6 and 2.10)—may also appear in this way. A brocade robe containing red indicates that the wearer is young, and the color of the neckband on a woman's inner kimono reflects her social status. Designs may suggest the nature of the character being portrayed: thus, the undergarment of a passionate woman who turns into a serpent often has a diamond, fishscale design; the costume for a thunder god may include clouds and zigzag lightning patterns; Yamamba's costume often has clouds to represent illusion and circles to suggest the wheel of fate.

Props are of two kinds: large stage props, which, with one or two exceptions (for example, the bell in *Dōjōji*),

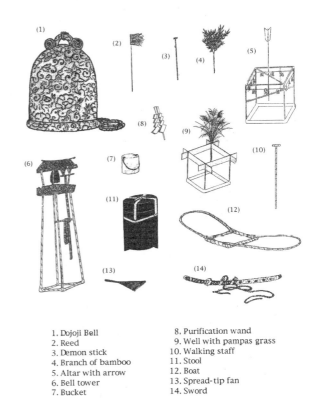

1. Dojoji Bell
2. Reed
3. Demon stick
4. Branch of bamboo
5. Altar with arrow
6. Bell tower
7. Bucket
8. Purification wand
9. Well with pampas grass
10. Walking staff
11. Stool
12. Boat
13. Spread-tip fan
14. Sword

FIGURE 2.5. Noh props. (Illustration by Mien Wong, based on Fukami 1933.)

are constructed anew for each performance, and small, hand-held props, which are stored between uses (figure 2.5). All performers carry fans: the instrumentalists and chorus members place theirs on the stage or hold them in fixed positions while performing. Actors generally carry fans with spread tips (*chūkei*) whose designs, in addition to being aesthetically pleasing, also indicate the nature of the characters. A defeated warrior, for example, carries a fan with a red sun over waves. These fans are used to express an enormous array of actions, from the blowing of the wind to the serving of sake. When hand props are no longer needed, the actor drops them, and they are immediately retrieved by a stage attendant; there is no need to invent a "butler" to remove them realistically. The hand props used in the plays in this anthology illustrate the wide variety that are available: Buddhist rosaries, pails, bundles of grass, paintbrushes, a branch, demon stick, sword, sickle, walking stick, conch shell, mallet, and a needle.

Stage props—carried onstage by one or more attendants before the act in which they are needed—usually are simple frameworks, merely suggesting the object they

FIGURE 2.6. Two types of boat props used in noh. At the top the aikyōgen carries in the simplest boat frame for the play *Funa Benkei*; this prop is also used in *Shunkan*. (Photo by Karen Brazell.) The more elaborate boat frame at the bottom is used in the play *Eguchi*. One woman, at the left, has the right sleeve of her outer robe slipped off to indicate that she is working (poling the boat). The woman at the right wears her kimono (*karaori*) in the straight style (*kinagashi*), and the shite in the middle wears broad divided skirts beneath her brocade kimono worn tucked up (*tsubouchi* style). (Photo by Tanaka Masao.)

represent (figure 2.6). The altar with the arrow attached in *Kamo* and the similarly constructed well frame with pampas grass in *Izutsu* are two examples (compare figures 1.17 and 2.12). Other props, such as the boat in *Shunkan* and the bell in *Miidera*, are manipulated by the actors. Some large props are also used to conceal an actor, as the bell does in *Dōjōji*. Because kyōgen actors create settings through explicit mime, they rarely use stage props, and none occur in the plays in this anthology. A large, round lacquered container with a lid (*shōgi* or *kazura oke*) falls somewhere between the categories of hand prop and stage prop and serves several practical functions: it is used as a seat for the actor in the mirror room or in the center of the stage, and especially in kyōgen, it serves as a useful container for sake or for the "delicious poison" in the play of that name. The lid may be used as a large cup.

Song and dance, the two arts (*nikyoku*) of noh, are used to bring the material elements and the text to life, to create the living tapestry that is the performance. The texts of plays are chanted or sung (it is difficult to decide which English word best describes voice production here) in three basic styles: intoned speech (*kotoba*) and two modes of singing—melodic song (*yowagin* or *wagin*) and dynamic song (*tsuyogin* or *gōgin*). The most prosaic parts of noh and the majority of kyōgen lines are intoned with a full voice in stylized patterns, rendered somewhat differently by shite, waki, and kyōgen actors. The chorus never uses intoned speech. The melodic mode is used for soft passages expressing elegance, sensitivity, and suffering. It has a musical scale composed of three base pitches a perfect fourth apart and sounds vaguely like Gregorian chanting. Dynamic song is used to express excitement, courage, or solemnity. It has no definite scale; rather, certain sounds swell in heavy vibrato, with the "melody" consisting of adding force to the breath to raise the pitch and suddenly withdrawing the force to lower it. The drums may accompany either mode. Sometimes the song matches the rhythms of the drums (hyōshi au, congruent rhythm), and at other times it does not (hyōshi awazu, noncongruent rhythm). The flute embell-ishes the melody line but never harmonizes with the vocal line, and the chorus sings only in unison. Some noh plays, like the woman play *Izutsu* or the demon play *Ya-mamba*, use a single mode, but most use both in various combinations. *Shunkan* alternates between the two modes, depending on the subject, whereas in *Miidera* the waki uses dynamic song, and the distraught mother, melodic song.

Although some kyōgen plays are performed entirely in kyōgen-style intoned speech, more than 60 percent include sung portions. In addition to styles based on noh chanting, kyōgen has adapted various other song types from medieval and Edo-period popular music, such as the bounce-back-again doll (*okiagari koboshi*) song in *Two Daimyō* and the snail song in *The Snail*. Some sung passages in kyōgen are accompanied by instruments, the same drums and flute used in noh. The rhythmic patterns, however, are unique to kyōgen. The shite's entrance scene in *Kanaoka* is a good example of kyōgen adaptations of noh music.

Zeami defined three basic modes of dance (*santai*): the aged (*rōtai*), the femi-nine (*nyotai*), and the martial (*guntai*), terms that are still used to describe noh dance today. In *Kamo*, the celestial mother dances in the feminine mode and the thunder god in the martial mode, and the style used to present the old, demonic woman called Yamamba combines all three. These modes are not strictly typed by gender. The feminine mode suggests a sensitivity to beauty and emotion that is part of the masculine as well as the feminine ideal, and the martial mode suggests a supernatural, demonic quality as well as aggressive masculinity. *Atsumori* is danced in the feminine mode to melodic chanting in the lyrical *kuse* scene, which de-scribes the suffering of the Heike clan, and in the martial mode to dynamic chant-ing in the final scene, depicting Atsumori's death.

An entire play is choreographed and performed in dancelike movements, al-though certain sections typically have more movement than others. Many of these sections are learned and performed as independent dance pieces (shimai). Exam-ples from the plays in this anthology include the bell scene in *Miidera* (*kane no dan*); the segments labeled kuse in *Yamamba* and *Atsumori*, describing the nature of Yamamba and the Heike's sojourn at Suma; and the last sections (*kiri*) of *Atsu-mori* and *Kamo*, which depict a battle and a storm, respectively. All these are dances to song.[3] Kyōgen actors may also use a distinctive form called little dance (*komai*), which the characters typically perform for one another, as is beautifully exemplified in the aikyōgen dance in *Miidera*.

Other dances, including both long dances (mai) and action pieces (*hataraki*), are performed to instrumental music without song. The many named variations of mai share the same basic choreography but are danced in different styles, to differ-ent tempi and instrumentations. The quiet dance (*jo no mai*) in *Izutsu* lasts about fifteen minutes, whereas the fast dance (*kyū no mai*) in *Dōjōji*, with almost the same choreography and instrumentation, takes only four or five minutes. In all cases, the dancer performs to repetitive flute phrases joined by two or three drums, depending on the context. Action pieces have a shorter, less complex musical structure and

---

3. In a complete noh play, instruments accompany the song, but in a shimai performance, only vocal music is used.

usually express an action or emotion. For example, a *kakeri* dance expresses anguish in both the noh play *Miidera* and the kyōgen *Kanaoka*. The hataraki in *Kamo* portrays the power of a thunderstorm; the stroll (*tachimawari*) in *Yamamba* depicts the weight of a burden; and the *notto* in *Dōjōji* represents part of an exorcism.

Noh performance is best explained as a system of highly conventionalized, interlocking parts. The rules developed over the centuries may be reinterpreted somewhat, but they are seldom blatantly broken. Each production of a play is basically the same, and the accepted variations (kogaki) are themselves standardized and even named. Because there is no director to impose a "new" interpretation, the actors control the production. The creativity of noh performers is more comparable to that of musicians than to Western-style actors. What is performed is established by tradition; creativity is expressed through the "how" of the performance, the life the performers breathe into the forms they have received from their teachers. The performance results not from weeks of rehearsals, but from long years of intensive training, during which each performer masters his own role and becomes acquainted with the roles of all the other players. For most performances a single preparatory gathering (mōshiawase) is sufficient. At that time the actor taking the shite role discusses his interpretation of the play and asks the group to rehearse complicated passages.

In addition, a noh performance is a once-in-a-lifetime event. Unlike kabuki, the puppet theater, and most Western theatrical productions, a particular group of performers assembles to produce a given play only once. A single performance without a full dress rehearsal means that no player can predict exactly how the others will perform. The tension created by this sense of uncertainty is an important source of creativity. On foreign tours this once-in-a-lifetime aspect of noh aesthetics must sometimes be disregarded for practical reasons, much to the dismay of the performers, who point out that the variety of foreign performance conditions may create an analogous type of creative tension.

Noh and kyōgen are repertory theaters, a label with somewhat different connotations in Japan than in the West. The repertoire consists of a set number of plays that vary slightly from school to school, although each genre has a core of commonly performed works. Currently there are just over 250 kyōgen plays and just under 250 different noh plays in the repertories of the various schools. The number does not remain static for long, because old plays that have survived only as written texts may be revived and reenter the repertories, and unpopular plays may be dropped. There also is considerable interest among some performers, scholars, and others, including non-Japanese, in creating "new" or "modern" noh and kyōgen plays. These may be performed on noh stages and may use professional performers, but they are not considered part of the traditional repertoire.

Both noh and kyōgen plays are grouped in categories based largely on the nature of the main character. Since the late seventeenth century, noh plays have been divided into five groups, with one play from each group included in a full program. The conventional order of performance is (1) deity plays; (2) ghost-of-warrior plays; (3) woman plays; (4) miscellaneous plays, including living-person and crazed-person plays; and (5) demon plays. The following translations of noh also are arranged in this way, although the deity play *Kamo* appeared in part 1. The categories of kyōgen plays are not as clearly delineated and are not as closely related to performance order. The general categories include daimyō plays, servant plays featuring Tarō Kaja, demon and mountain priest plays, women and bridegroom plays, priest and blind people plays, and a miscellaneous category that includes some direct parodies of noh.

The play scripts translated in this anthology are written in various combinations of prose and poetry and in different levels of language from different historical periods. Kyōgen texts are mainly prose and are relatively colloquial, although the language is that of the seventeenth and eighteenth centuries, not that of contemporary Japan. The scripts also include, however, many repetitive and formulaic lines, poems and songs, formal prayers, elaborate puns, and onomatopoeic expressions. The overall tone is more intimate and informal than that of noh, yet kyōgen language is highly patterned and no longer colloquial. The translations attempt (in various ways) to capture aspects of this tone.

Noh texts are quite different. In most plays a single "character" (sometimes it is more an emotion than a character) is predominant, and all the players work together to create that being or feeling. Consequently, although the waki and kyōgen roles in noh sometimes have names (often they are simply labeled traveling priests or villagers), they rarely have fully individualized voices. The lines they speak are often formulaic, and the content of their speeches is generally predictable: the waki describes a journey, and the kyōgen explains the "story." In fact, many texts, especially chantbooks, leave out most of the kyōgen parts and the more formulaic lines of the waki. Some of the waki's lines and most of the shite's and chorus's lines are poetic: they are metered (sometimes loosely, other times more strictly) and often do not make grammatical sense. Instead, images and allusions are strung together with repetitions, puns, and other types of wordplay. Noh playwrights, especially Zeami, were familiar with the poetic practices of their time and took full advantage of them. Because literary Japanese does not necessarily identify the speaker or subject or distinguish between male and female, present and past, thoughts and speech, singular and plural, or first, second, and third person, the translator into English is forced to make distinctions and supply details not provided in the original. Clearly then, two translations of a single play might be quite different and yet both be "accurate."

The translations in this anthology attempt to reflect the poetic structure of noh rather than to live up to Western expectations of character differentiation or to be more semantically clear than the originals. Generally they attribute lines to the roles (for example, the shite and waki) rather than to the characters that these actors sometimes represent, and they take full advantage of enjambment, both to keep the stream of images flowing and to force the type of rereading that Japanese wordplay creates. In addition, a considerable amount of performance information is included to aid readers interested in theater to visualize what is happening onstage. Finally, these translations are meant to be read slowly; a noh play in print may cover only a half-dozen pages, but in performance it fills one to two hours.

Atsumori

A warrior play by Zeami (1363–1443)

Translated by Karen Brazell

The story of Taira Atsumori, a youthful warrior killed during the battles between the Heike (or Taira) and the Genji (Minamoto) in the twelfth century, has been retold in numerous genres over the centuries: medieval biwa players recited the *The Tale of the Heike* version of his life; noh and kōwaka actors selected and revised elements of the tale to suit their own aesthetic and political purposes; and playwrights for the puppets and kabuki radically recontextualized the story to meet the expectations of Edo-period audiences. Noh, kōwaka, and kabuki versions of Atsumori's death are presented in this anthology to illustrate how the different genres mold their materials to accomplish their goals.

Zeami's noh play *Atsumori* emphasizes both the tragic end of the aristocratic Taira clan, reduced to living as humble seafolk, and the accomplishments of the young Atsumori, renowned as both a musician and a brave warrior. (Another noh play, *Ikuta Atsumori* by Komparu Zempō [1454–1532?], has the ghost of Atsumori appear to his son and describe his suffering after death.) As a child, Zeami received the patronage of the highest-ranking warrior of the time, the shogun Ashikaga Yoshimitsu, and the tutelage of a major poet, Nijō Yoshimoto, so it is not surprising that his works promote the medieval concept of *bumbu*, the combination of artistic and martial skills that came to be the mark of the ideal warrior.

In this play, Atsumori is depicted as an accomplished flutist and is compared, through skillful allusions, with the ninth-century poet Ariwara no Yukihira and the fictional Prince Genji, both of whom were exiled at Suma, the setting of the noh play. In addition, the play enhances the stature of the lower classes (explicitly of grass cutters but implicitly of lowly actors as well) by arguing that they too have artistic talents. An effective parallel is drawn between the grass cutters in act 1 and the Taira clansmen in act 2. The play advocates a social message—don't envy your superiors or despise your inferiors, for in this topsy-turvy world, those at the top may end up at the bottom, and vice versa—and the Buddhist concept of nondualism—opposites are equivalents; enemies indeed are friends.

Atsumori is the most elegant of the sixteen works currently included in the small category of ghost-of-warrior plays (*shura mono*). It includes three danced sections: the kuse, sung in the melodic mode and danced in the feminine mode, combines grace with melancholy; the dance to instrumental music (either a medium-tempo dance or a male dance, depending on the school of the shite) expresses vitality tempered by refinement; and the final dance, performed in the martial mode to dynamic song, portrays battle, death, and the resolution of fate in a forceful, rhythmic manner. The stick drum is not used for this play.

Most of the plays in the warrior category feature men who lost their lives in the Gempei wars in the twelfth century. Only a few are about victors—*Yashima* is a good example. Among the defeated-warrior plays, *Tadanori* is similar in theme and setting to *Atsumori*. *Ebira* depicts the suffering of a deceased warrior in the realm of the *ashura*, where ghosts are condemned to constant battle. *Sanemori* reveals the pride of an old man going off to battle; *Tomoe* stars a female warrior; and *Kiyotsune* explores misunderstandings between a warrior and his wife. The category is small but significant, for it both reflects and helps define the image of the warrior that was so important to medieval Japan.

This translation and many of the notes are based on Yokomichi and Omote 1960, and the stage directions reflect Kita school practices. The aikyōgen text is from Sanari 1931. Zeami drew on *The Tale of the Heike* for the basic story and incorporated many images from *The Tale of Genji*, as filtered through the waka and renga traditions.

CHARACTERS

SHITE: in act 1, a grass cutter without a mask; in act 2, the ghost of Atsumori
TSURE: two or three other maskless grass cutters
WAKI: Renshō (or Rensei), the priestly name of Kumagae (or Kumagai) no Jirō
 Naozane, the man who killed Atsumori in battle
AI: a local man

MUSICIANS

Chorus of eight or ten members
A flute and two hand drums

ACT 1

Shidai entrance music *To the music of the hand drums and the flute, the waki,
dressed as a priest, enters the bridgeway and moves slowly to the shite spot.*

Shidai *Congruent song in the melodic mode with sparse drum accompaniment;
the waki faces the pine tree painted on the back wall of the stage.*

WAKI:
 Awake to awareness, the world's but a dream,
 awake to awareness, the world's but a dream,
 one may cast it aside—is this what is Real?[1]

Jitori *Chanted quietly and pitched low, in noncongruent rhythm.*

CHORUS:
 Awake to awareness, the world's but a dream,
 one may cast it aside—is this what is Real?

Nanori *Intoned speech with no accompaniment; the waki faces front.*

WAKI: I am Kumagae no Jirō Naozane, a resident of Musashi, who has renounced
 this world and taken the priestly name Renshō. I did this because of the deep
 remorse I felt at having killed Atsumori. Now I am going to Ichinotani to pray
 for the repose of his soul.[2]

Ageuta *He continues to face front, to melodic song congruent with drum
accompaniment.*

WAKI:
 Departing the capital as clouds part

Brief instrumental interlude (uchikiri).

 departing the capital as clouds part,

---

1. The confusion between dream and reality (*yume* and *utsutsu*) is a common metaphor for the illusory and transient nature of this life. Here, in the thematic opening song (shidai), the waki questions whether simply taking religious vows is enough to allow one to attain enlightenment.
2. Ichinotani is the place on the Japan Sea near Suma where Kumagae killed Atsumori. It is located in present-day Kobe.

FIGURE 2.7. Three grass cutters (the shite is at the right) enter in act 1 of *Atsumori*. Their costumes are the same combination of garments (*mizugoromo* over *ōkuchi* and *noshime*) but are of different colors and surface designs. (Courtesy of the Noh Research Archive of Musashino Women's College.)

> the moon too travels southward,
> a small wheel rolling toward
> Yodo; Yamazaki soon passed;

Brief instrumental interlude.

> then the ponds of Koya, Ikuta River,

Takes a few steps to indicate travel.

> Suma Bay, where "waves surge beside us";[3]
> at Ichinotani I have arrived,

Takes a few steps to indicate his arrival.

> I have arrived at Ichinotani

Tsukizerifu   *Intoned speech without accompaniment, the waki still facing front.*

WAKI: How quickly I've reached Ichinotani in the province of Tsu. Scenes from the past come to mind as if present. (*Hands together in a prayer gesture*) Hail, Amida Buddha. (*Turns slightly to the right*) What's that? I hear the sound of a flute coming from that high meadow. (*Faces front*) I think I'll wait for the flutist and ask him to tell me something about this place.

Shidai entrance music   *The shite and two or three tsure costumed as humble grass cutters enter along the bridgeway. They are unmasked, and each carries a bamboo pole with grass attached. They proceed to the front of the stage and form two lines [figure 2.7].*

3. This is the first of many phrases in this play taken from the "Suma" chapter of *The Tale of Genji*.

FIGURE 2.8. The grass cutter (*shite*) holding his bundle of grass (*hasami kusa*). Compare this costume (*mizugoromo* over *noshime*) with the skirted one depicted in figure 2.7. The ends of his narrow obi (*koshi obi*) hang down in front. The stage attendant (*kōken*) is seated at the back of the stage. (Courtesy of the Noh Research Archive of Musashino Women's College.)

Shidai   *The shite and tsure face each other and sing the following melodic song to sparse, congruent drum accompaniment.*

SHITE and TSURE:
> The grass cutter's flute adds its
>   voice,
> the grass cutter's flute adds its
>   voice
> to the wind blowing over the
>   meadows.

Sashi   *The shite faces front, to non-congruent, melodic song [figure 2.8].*

SHITE:
> The "man who cuts grass
>   on that hill"[4] makes his way
>   through the fields
> in the gathering dusk; it's time to
>   go home.

SHITE and TSURE (*Facing each other again*):
> Was his way home, too, beside the
>   Suma Sea?
> How limited the path we tread
> entering the hills, returning to
>   the shore;
> how miserable the lowly lives
>   we lead.

Brief instrumental interlude.

Sageuta   *Continuing to face each other.*

SHITE and TSURE:
> "If anyone should ask after me,
> my reply would speak of lonely grief

Brief instrumental interlude.

Ageuta
> here at Suma Bay
> where brine drips from seaweed."[5]
> Should anyone learn who I am,

4. A line from the *Shūishū*, poem 567, by Hitomaro, in which the speaker asks that the grass not be cut, so that it can serve as feed for the horse of an expected lover. Another version of the poem appears in the *Manyōshū* as poem 1291.
5. A variation on poem 962 in the *Kokinshū*, by Ariwara no Yukihira.

Brief instrumental interlude.

>should anyone learn who I am,
>then I, too, would have a friend.
>Such wretched seafolk we've become that
>"even dear ones are grown estranged."[6]

Brief instrumental interlude.

>We live our lives, such as they are,
>yielding to misery, we exhaust our days,

The shite goes to the shite spot while the tsure line up in front of the chorus.

>yielding to misery, we exhaust our days.

Mondō   *The waki stands at the waki spot, faces the shite, and speaks.*

WAKI: Hello there! There's something I'd like to ask you grass cutters.

SHITE: Are you speaking to us? What is it you want?

WAKI: Was one of you playing the flute just now?

SHITE: Yes. One of us was playing.

WAKI: It was exquisite! And all the more exquisite because such music is not expected from men in your position.

SHITE: You say it's unexpected from men in our position. People should neither envy superiors nor despise inferiors, or so it is said.

TSURE (*Chanting*):
>"Foresters' songs, shepherds' pipes"[7] is a set phrase;
>grass cutters' flutes and woodsmen's songs

SHITE and TSURE:
>are well-known topics in poetry;
>bamboo flutes have widespread fame.
>Do not think it strange.

Kakeai   *Congruent song in the melodic mode to quiet drum accompaniment.*

WAKI:
>Indeed there is sense in what you say.
>Those "foresters' songs and shepherds' pipes"

SHITE:
>are the flutes of grass cutters

WAKI:
>and the songs of woodsmen

---

6. An allusion to the Japanese preface to the *Kokinshū*, which states that even close friends desert those who fall in status.

7. A phrase from a Chinese poem by Ki no Seimei that appears as poem 559 in the *Wakan rōeishū*: "When the sun sets on mountain roads/the sounds of foresters' songs (*shōka*) and shepherds' pipes (*bokuteki*) fill the ear./When the birds return to valley nests,/the tints of bamboo smoke and pine mist obstruct the vision." The sinicized terms *shōka* and *bokuteki* are replaced in the next line in the play with the Japanese terms *ashikari no fue* (grass cutters' flutes) and *kikori no uta* (woodsmen's songs).

SHITE:

"passing through this bitter world, a melody"[8]

WAKI:

to sing

SHITE:

to dance,

WAKI:

to blow,

SHITE:

to play.

Brief instrumental interlude.

Ageuta   *Melodic song in a higher pitch.*

CHORUS:

We lead our lives

The shite faces front and spreads his arms.

guided by discerning hearts that fancy,

Brief instrumental interlude; the waki sits at the waki spot.

guided by discerning hearts that fancy
bamboo flutes: Tender Branch, Broken Cicada,
such names as these are numerous.[9]

The shite moves forward slightly.

The flute the grass cutter plays
also has a name:
know it as Green Leaf.
At water's edge near Sumiyoshi

The shite circles the stage to the left, and the three tsure quietly exit up the bridgeway.

one would find Korean flutes;[10]
here at Suma one might say
seafolk play Charred Stick,
seafolk play Charred Stick.[11]

Kakeai   *Intoned speech, no accompaniment.*

8. This phrase, *ukiyo o wataru hitofushi*, was used in the kusemai *Saikoku kudari*, composed by a poet known as Tamarin, to describe the songs of female entertainers. *Atsumori* borrows other phrases from this kusemai.

9. Flutes and other valuable instruments were often named. According to *The Tale of the Heike*, Tender Branch (*saeda*) was the name of the flute Atsumori carried with him to his death; however, other sources claim that the flute was called Green Leaf (*aoba*).

10. Sumiyoshi, in present-day Osaka, was a port frequented by ships from Korea. "Korean" flutes (*koma-fue*) are used in court music (*gagaku*).

11. *Taki-sashi*. The Suma seafolk burned firewood to boil down brine for salt. There is a reference in book 10 of the *Jikkinshō*, a thirteenth-century anthology of tales, to a flute called Charred Head (*kashira-taki*).

WAKI (*Speaking to the shite from the waki spot*): How strange. All the other grass cutters have left, yet you remain. Why is that?

SHITE: Even you ask why? Drawn by the power of your voice above the evening waves, I have come to request ten Hail Amidas. Say them for me, please.

WAKI: Ten Hail Amidas is an easy thing to grant. For whom should I pray?

SHITE: To be honest, I am related to Atsumori.

WAKI: You're related, you say? How nostalgic that makes me,

SHITE: he says, putting his palms together (*clasps his rosary between his hands*), Hail, Amida Buddha.

SHITE (*The shite kneels, and they chant together*): "Should I attain enlightenment, no being in all the world

WAKI: who calls my name shall be cast aside."[12]

Uta   *The shite looks at the waki and lowers his hands.*

CHORUS:
Please cast me not aside.
Though a single cry should suffice,
each day, each night, you pray.
How fortunate I am, my name

Looking down, he stands and then goes toward the shite spot.

unspoken, yet clear, at dawn and at dusk too
you hold services for the soul of one

He turns and looks intently at the waki.

whose name is mine, he says

At the shite spot, he circles right.

as his figure fades from sight,

Facing front, he spreads his arms to indicate his disappearance.

as his figure fades from sight.

He walks quietly up the bridgeway and out under the raised curtain.

Kyōgen Interlude

Mondō   *The aikyōgen, who has entered inconspicuously and seated himself at the kyōgen spot at the back of the bridgeway, now rises and moves to the shite spot.*

AI: I am a person who lives at Suma Bay. Today I've come to amuse myself by watching the boats go by. Hm! There's a priest I've never seen before. Where are you from?

WAKI: I'm a priest from the capital. Do you live nearby?

AI: Yes, indeed I do.

WAKI: Then please come over here. I've something I'd like to ask you.

AI (*Goes to center stage and sits*): Certainly. What is it you want to know?

12. Based on a passage in the *Kammuryōjukyō*, a basic sutra of Pure Land Buddhism that describes meditations centering on Amida.

WAKI: It's a bit unusual. I've heard that this is the harbor where the battle between the Heike and the Genji was fought. Could you please tell me what you know about the death of the Heike nobleman Atsumori?

AI: That's certainly an unexpected request. Those of us who live around here don't know much about such things; however, since you've come out of your way to inquire, what can I do? I don't really know much, but I'll tell what I've heard.

WAKI: Thank you.

Katari   *In stylized speech, facing the audience.*

AI: Sometime in the autumn of Jūei 2 [1183] when the Heike were forced from the capital by Kiso Yoshinaka, they retreated to this spot. However, the Genji, dividing their sixty thousand cavalry into two groups, attacked fiercely from both left and right. The Heike fled, scattering here and there. Among them was the young Atsumori, son of Tsunemori, chief of the Office of Palace Repairs. Atsumori had reached the shore, intending to board a ship, only to realize that he had left his precious flute, known as Little Branch, in the main camp. Not wanting it to fall into enemy hands, he went back to fetch it.

Upon retrieving his flute, Atsumori raced again to the shore, only to discover that all the boats, the imperial barque and the troopships, had already put out to sea. Atsumori's horse was strong, so he urged it into the sea. Just then, however, a resident of Musashi Province, Kumagae no Jirō Naozane, beckoned Atsumori with his fan, and he turned back to face this enemy. They fought in the waves, then grappled on the shore, finally falling from their horses. Kumagae, who was unusually strong, managed to come out on top and was about to cut off Atsumori's head when he glimpsed the face beneath the helmet. He saw the powdered brow and blackened teeth of a youth of fifteen or sixteen.

"A pity! What an elegant warrior. If only I could spare him." He looked around. Doi and Kajiwara were fast approaching with a dozen other warriors.

"I would like to spare you," he explained, "however, as you can see, a group of my allies is almost upon us. I will kill you and then pray for your soul." Thus he took Atsumori's head.

Examining the corpse, he found a flute in a brocade bag. When he made his presentation before the general, people remarked on how cultivated the dead man must have been. Even among the nobility, few would concern themselves with a flute in such a crisis. The victors' armored sleeves were dampened by their tears. Eventually the youth was identified as Atsumori, the young son of Tsunemori.

Kumagae is said to have retired from the world to pray for Atsumori's enlightenment. Since he didn't spare Atsumori when he might have, this seems like a pack of lies to me. If that Kumagae should come here, we would kill him to prove our loyalty to Atsumori.

That's about all that I've heard. Why do you ask me about it? It seems a bit strange.

WAKI: You were kind to tell me this tale. Why should I conceal anything? I was Kumagae no Jirō Naozane. Now I have become a priest and taken the name Renshō. I have come here to pray for the repose of Atsumori's soul.

AI: What! You're that lord Kumagae? Unwittingly I've told you these things. Please forgive me. A force for good is said to be a force for evil too. Maybe it works both ways. I hope that you will pray for Atsumori's soul.

WAKI: Don't be upset. I have come only to pray for his soul. I would like to remain a while and read some efficacious sutras. I shall pray diligently.

AI: If that's the case, I can give you lodging.

WAKI: Thank you. That would be helpful.

AI: At your service.

He goes to the kyōgen spot and sits. After the shite has made his entrance, the kyōgen walks quietly up the bridgeway.

ACT 2

Machiutai *Chanted in the melodic mode as he kneels at the waki spot.*

WAKI:

Spreading dew-drenched grass to make a bed,

Brief instrumental interlude.

spreading dew-drenched grass to make a bed,
now that the sun has set and night fallen
I'll pray to Amida that Atsumori
may yet achieve enlightenment, that he
may yet achieve enlightenment, I'll pray.

Issei entrance music *The shite, now costumed as the warrior Atsumori, enters to instrumental music.*

Ge no ei *Standing at the shite spot facing front.*

SHITE:

"Back and forth to Awaji plovers
fly; their cries awaken one
who guards the pass at Suma."[13]
What is your name?

Kakeai *Sung with the shite standing at the shite spot and the waki sitting at the waki spot.*

SHITE:

Look here, Renshō,
Atsumori has arrived.

WAKI:

How very strange!
Beating on the gong, performing holy rites,
I have not had a moment to doze, and yet
Atsumori appears before me.
Surely this must be a dream.

13. This passage draws on poem 270 in the *Kinyōshū*, by Minamoto Kanemasa (fl. early twelfth century). In the "Suma" chapter of *The Tale of Genji*, the exiled hero also is awakened by the cries of plovers. Here the sound of plovers is a metaphor for the voice of the praying priest.

FIGURE 2.9. The ghost of the warrior Atsumori sits on a stool (*shōgi*) to tell his confessional tale. To faciliate arm movements the right sleeve of the outer robe (*chōken*) is removed and rolled up in back (*katanugi*) to reveal the sleeve of the underkimono (*atsuita*). He wears a white headband (*hachimaki*) over his mask (*jūroku*). Compare the designs on this costume with those used in the following illustrations. (Courtesy of the Noh Research Archive of Musashino Women's College.)

SHITE:

> Why need it be a dream?
> To clear the karma left from this waking
>   world
> I make my appearance here.

WAKI:

> This can't be. It's said,
> "A single Hail Amida erases countless sins."
> I've offered ceaseless prayers
> to clear away all sinful hindrances.
> What karma can remain from this rough
>   sea of life,

SHITE:

> so deep my sins, please wash them away,

WAKI:

> and in doing so, my own salvation seek.

SHITE:

> Your prayers affecting both our future
>   lives—

WAKI:

> once enemies

SHITE:

> now instead

WAKI:

> in Buddha's Law

SHITE:

> made friends (*takes a step toward the waki*).

Uta   *The shite spreads his arms facing front; the melodic song is congruent with the accompanying drum rhythms.*

CHORUS:

> Now I see!
> "Cast aside an evil friend,

The shite points at the waki with his left hand and moves toward him.

> beckon near a enemy who's good";

The shite flips his sleeve over his left arm and stares intently at the waki.

> that refers to you!
> How fortunate, how very fortunate!

Changing the mood, the shite circles left to the shite spot.

> And now, with my confessional tale
> let us while the night away,

At the shite spot, he turns to face the waki.

let us while the night away.

Kuri *The shite goes to center stage and sits on a stool provided by the stage attendant. The song is noncongruent and elaborately embellished [figure 2.9].*

Spring blossoms mounting tips of trees
inspire ascent toward enlightenment;
the autumn moon sinking to ocean's depths
symbolizes grace descending to mankind.

Sashi *All remain seated.*

SHITE:

Even though the clan put forth new sprouts,
kinsmen branching out in all directions,

CHORUS:

"our glory was that of the short-lived rose of sharon "[14]
How difficult to find encouragement toward good—
good hard flintstones engender sparks
whose lights are gone before one knew they were—
the lives of humans flash by like this.

SHITE:

Yet those high up inflict pain on people down below;
those living lives of luxury are unaware of arrogance.

Brief instrumental interlude.

Kuse *The shite stands and dances during the following segment sung in the melodic mode, congruent with the drum accompaniment. The flute enters midway.*

CHORUS:

It happened that the Heike
ruled the world some twenty years,
truly a fleeting generation,[15]
passed in the space of a dream.
"That famous autumn, leaves"[16]

Moves forward slightly.

lured by "winds from the four directions,"[17]
scattered here and there in leaflike

14. Based on a couplet by Po Chü-i included in the *Wakan rōeishū* as poem 291: "The pine has a thousand years, yet in the end it dies;/the rose of sharon a single day, to enjoy its glory."

15. The Nagato version of *The Tale of the Heike* states: "A generation (*hito mukushi*) used to last thirty three years, but now it's only twenty-one." It was twenty-three years from the first Heike uprising of 1160 until the Heike fled the capital in 1183.

16. Based on the Kakuichi version of *The Tale of the Heike*, book 7, "Now it was clear to every eye that adversity and happiness follow the same path, that prosperity and decline are as a turn of the hand. Who could help feeling pity? Once, in Hōgen, they had flourished like springtime blossoms; now, in Juei, they fell like autumn leaves" (McCullough 1988:246).

17. This phrase and eight others in the kuse were listed in an early handbook by Yoshimoto Nijō (1320–1388) as appropriate phrases (*yoriai*) from the "suma" chapter of *The Tale of Genji* to use in linked verse (Goff 1991:64–66; Wada 1976:5). The kuse also borrows from the kusemai *Saikoku kudari.*

Moves his fan in a sweeping gesture and looks to the right.

> boats bobbing on the waves, we sleep,
> not even in our dreams returning home—
> "caged birds longing for cloudy realms,

Goes toward the corner.

> ranks of homing geese broken, scattered,"[18]
> uncertain skies, aimless travel gowns tied

Looks up at the sky and circles left.

> and layered sunsets, moonrises, months, a year
> journeys by, returns to spring
> here at Ichinotani secluded for a while

Moves from the back to center stage.

> here at Suma Shore we live.

SHITE:

> From the hills behind, winds roar down

Opens his fan and raises it before his face.

CHORUS:

> to coastal fields keenly cold
> our boats draw up, no day or night without

Moves forward.

> the cries of plovers,
> our sleeves too

Twirls his sleeve over his arm to make a pillow and kneels.

> dampened by the waves that
> drench our rocky pillows,
> in seaside shacks we huddle together

Stands and goes to the corner.

> befriended only by Suma folk—
> bent like wind-bent pines on the strands

Circles left to the shite spot.

> of evening smoke rising from the fires—

Waving his fan in his left hand, the shite moves forward.

> brushwood, it's called,

Holding out his fan parallel to the floor.

18. Based on book 10 of the Kakuichi version of *The Tale of the Heike*, where the phrases refer to a Heike clansman, Shigehira, who was captured by the Genji: "Must not his thoughts, fretful as a caged bird longing for the clouds, find themselves afloat on the southern seas a thousand leagues distant? Must not his feelings, sad as those of a homing goose lost from its fellows" (McCullough 1988:331).

this stuff piled up to sleep upon.

Goes to the corner.

Our worries, too, pile up in rustic Suma,
where we're forced to play out our lives

Pointing his fan to the right, he looks up.

becoming simple Suma folk—

Circles to the left.

such is our clan's fate; how forlorn we are!

Stops at backstage center.

Kakeai   *The chanting changes from the melodic to the dynamic mode.*

SHITE:
And then, on the night of the sixth day of the second month,
Tsunemori, my father, gathered us together
to enjoy ourselves with song and dance.

WAKI:
And your entertainment that night,
the elegant flute music from your encampment,
was clearly heard by us on the opposing side.[19]

SHITE:
It was indeed Atsumori,
awaiting the end, his bamboo flute

WAKI:
accompanying a variety of

SHITE:
ballads and songs,

WAKI:
many voices

Issei   *The shite circles right to the shite spot.*

CHORUS:
arise, creating steady cadences.

Chū no mai or otoko-mai   *The shite performs a sprightly yet elegant dance to the music of the flute and hand drums. This dance, unusual in a warrior play, emphasizes Atsumori's artistic sensitivity. The context also foregrounds the flute music, which is the normal accompaniment to the dance [figure 2.10, left].*

SHITE *(Standing at the shite spot, he raises his fan [figure 2.10, right]):*
And so it is,
the royal barque sets forth

Brief instrumental interlude.

19. This statement and the following description of Atsumori's death are based on the account given in *The Tale of the Heike* (McCullough 1988:315–17).

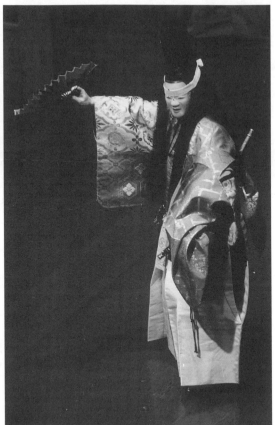

FIGURE 2.10. During the first part of a long dance (*chū-no-mai*), the shite performs with his spread-tip fan (*chūkei*) closed. It is opened after the introductory segment of the dance, as in the photo on the left. In the right photo, the ghost of Atsumori uses his open fan to emphasize looking out to sea at the departing ships. (Courtesy of the Noh Research Archive of Musashino Women's College.)

Noriji *The dynamic song becomes strongly rhythmical; it is congruent with the steady beats of the drums.*

CHORUS:
    and all the members of the clan

The shite stamps his feet.

    board their ships to sail.

Making a sweeping point with his fan, he turns to the right.

    Not wanting to be late

Goes to the front of the stage.

    Atsumori races to the shore;
    the royal barque and troopships, too,
    have already put out to sea.

Raises his fan over his head and looks out into the distance.

SHITE (*noncongruent*): It's hopeless! Reining in his horse

Mimes pulling on the reins with his left hand.

    amidst the breakers, he stands bewildered.

Waves his fan in a figure-eight pattern to indicate agitation.

Chūnoriji   *The dynamic song is congruent with half-beat drum rhythms.*

CHORUS:
    At that very moment

The shite stamps his feet.

    from behind comes

He turns and faces the bridgeway.

    Kumagae no Jirō Naozane.
    "Don't flee!"

Hurries to the shite spot.

    he shouts and charges.
    Atsumori too

Moves quickly to center front.

    turns about his horse, and

Reins in his horse and races backstage.

    in the breakers they draw swords

Mimes drawing a sword (represented by his fan) and goes to the corner.[20]

    and exchange blows, twice, thrice,

Strikes with his fan.

    they are seen to strike;
    on horseback they grapple,

Wraps his arms around himself.

    then fall onto the wave-swept shore,

Twirls around and kneels.

    one atop the other; finally
    struck down, Atsumori dies;

Points his fan at his head and looks down.

    the wheel of fate turns, and they meet.

20. In the Kanze school, the shite throws down his fan and draws his sword here.
21. The *ren* of the priest's name is written with the character for lotus.

FIGURE 2.11. The ghost of Atsumori draws his sword to attack the waki, whom he recognizes as his former enemy, Kumagae. Here the fan represents a shield, and its design, a red sun amid waves, is emblematic of a defeated warrior (*make-shura*). (Courtesy of the Noh Research Archive of Musashino Women's College.)

Stands, goes to center back, and draws sword [figure 2.11].

"The enemy's right here!"

Hurries toward the waki at the waki spot.

he cries and is about to strike.

Raises his sword to strike.

Returning good for evil,

Kneels.

the priest performs services and prays

Stands and returns to backstage.

that in the end they will be reborn together

Spreads his arms, moves toward the waki again, and drops his sword.

on a single lotus petal,

Circles to the corner.

and Renshō the priest[21] is an enemy no more.

Returns to the shite spot.

Please pray for my soul,

Makes a prayer gesture toward the waki.

please pray for my soul.

Turns to face the bridgeway and performs closing stamps; then exits slowly.

Izutsu

A woman play by Zeami (1363–1443)

Translated by Karen Brazell

Zeami labeled *Izutsu* a play of the highest flower (*joka*), and his artistic heir, Zenchiku (1405–1470), acclaimed it a piece of sublime elegance (*yūgen*). In its performance aspects, the play is a model of simplicity. There are only the three basic roles—a shite, a waki, and an aikyōgen. The structure is regular, and all the sung passages are in the melodic mode. The single stage prop is a square bamboo frame with a plume of pampas grass attached, similar in design to the frame used in *Kamo*, although in that play the structure represented an altar topped with an arrow. Act 1 of *Izutsu* includes little movement, and act 2 contains a slow and elegant dance to instrumental music (jo no mai) and a final dance to song (kiri), both performed in the feminine mode. The stick drum is not used.

What is complex about this play, and what gives it its depths of feeling and beauty, is the subject matter and the poetic language. The play is "about" Ariwara no Narihira, perhaps Japan's best-known poet and lover, yet he does not appear directly on the stage; rather, the play evokes memories of him. The seed for the play comes from *The Tales of Ise* (Ise monogatari), an important collection of brief narratives providing a context for one or more poems. First compiled in the tenth century, *Ise monogatari* was often rewritten and reinterpreted during the Heian and medieval periods. Since many of the poems in the collection are attributed to Narihira, he was soon identified as the "man of old," the otherwise unnamed hero of most of the *Tales*' episodes.

The story of *Izutsu* is based on section 23 of *The Tales of Ise*, with additional references to sections 17 and 24. Medieval commentators identified the woman in each of these previously unrelated episodes as the daughter of Ki no Aritsune, even though Narihira was only ten years younger than Aritsune, and hence an unlikely childhood playmate of his daughter. In the play, the ghost of Ki no Aritsune's daughter returns to earth and recalls this medieval version of her life with Narihira.

The play is about love, memory, and poetry. Narihira exists in name only; his fame and his poetry are all that remain. Aritsune's daughter is still attached to her love for Narihira, and this attachment causes her ghost to return to the site of her life and to revive her memories. The daughter is a complex figure. As is usual in ghost plays, the main character in act 1 is an ordinary person, here a young woman who sometimes carries a branch of leaves, suggesting that she is obsessed with love—as is the mother in *Miidera*—or possessed by the spirit of a lover. In this case, both conditions seem to coexist in understated form. In act 2 the woman reappears wearing the court cap and gown of Narihira. When she looks into the well in the climactic moment of the play, she sees not herself but her lover, Narihira. A similar phenomenon occurs in other woman plays. In *Kakitsubata*, for example, a single stage figure embodies two lovers and the spirit of the iris (*kakitsubata*) that is emblematic of their love; in *Matsukaze*, a woman is so obsessed with her lover—this time Narihira's relative Yukihira—that she imagines his presence in a pine tree.

Izutsu exemplifies the ideal female character that Zeami describes in his *Sandō* (The three paths, ca. 1421) when, in discussing an elegant woman possessed, he writes:

> In these and like situations there is a seed for the blossoming of sublime, mysterious beauty (*yūgen*). It is a seed more rare than the one that, as the old poem says, "combines the scent of plum and the blossom of cherry and sets them to bloom on a willow branch." (translated by Hare 1986:132)

Zeami labeled all plays featuring women as plays in the feminine mode (*nyotai*). Today, plays about female deities are included in the first category (deity plays), and crazed-woman plays are placed in the fourth category. Other woman plays make up the third category, called "wig pieces" (*kazura mono*). *Izutsu* is often cited as the best and the most representative of these plays, although in earlier times it appears to have been performed more like a fourth-category, crazed-person play. The amateur noh performer and scholar Shimotsuma Shōshin (1551–1616) noted that the play sometimes included a kakeri, a dance used to express deranged or excited states of mind.

As should already be apparent, *Izutsu* is rich in multiple meanings, with almost everything seen in more than one way. The stage prop is a good example. Verbal description and deictic movements transform it several times in the course of the play. It is a well in the temple grounds that reflects the purifying light of the moon and from which a young woman draws offertory water; it is the tomb of Narihira, with the clump of pampas grass marking his remains; it is the historical well around which the children played and the pampas grass behind which Narihira hid to spy on his wife; and it is a mirror reflecting the woman's memories. The name of the play, *Izutsu*, means a well with a wooden frame. The word is repeated several times in the play until finally the repetitions take on a mantric force—*tsutsu izutsu, tsutsu izutsu, izutsu ni*—translated here, in an attempt to retain the sound values, as "the wooden water well, the wooden water well has a wall which." The translation also attempts to reflect some of the other poetic qualities of the original text, especially its frequent linkage of images through wordplay and repetition rather than syntax. This stream-of-imagery style is characteristic of plays by Zeami and some of his contemporaries.

The translation and stage directions are based on the text found in Yokomichi and Omote 1960, although information from the Kanze school chantbook (1972) and Itō 1983 has also been included. The kyōgen interlude is from Sanari 1931.

SHITE: in act 1, a village woman; in act 2, the ghost of Ki no Aritsune's daughter
WAKI: a traveling priest
AI: a local man

MUSICIANS

A chorus of eight to ten members
A flute and two hand drums

ACT 1

*The stage attendants enter carrying a square bamboo frame wrapped in white cloth
with plume of pampas grass attached to the top, and they place it at front stage center.*

Nanori flute music *The waki enters down the bridgeway and stands at the
shite spot.*

Nanori *Facing forward, the waki speaks without musical accompaniment.*

WAKI: I am a priest traveling around the country. I've been visiting the famous
temples of the southern capital, and now I've decided to travel to Hatsuse.
(*Looks toward the prop*) I inquired about this temple and was told it's called
Ariwara Temple.[1] I think I'll go inside and look around (*goes to center stage*).

Sashi *Facing forward, he chants.*
Hmm, this Ariwara Temple must be in the place called Isonokami, where in
ancient times Narihira and Ki no Aritsune's daughter lived as man and wife.
When winds rise in the offing, white-
capped waves surge high as Mount Tatsuta.
That poem was probably composed right here.

Uta *The waki kneels [figure 2.12].*
Inquiring about remains of tales of old, I learn
this Narihira had a friend, Ki no Aritsune—
always constant in this inconstant world[2]—
whose daughter Narihira wed; I'll pray for the couple,

Rubs his rosary beads between his palms.

whose daughter he wed; I'll pray for the couple.

He goes to the waki spot and sits.

---

1. The southern capital is Nara; Hatsuse, a temple in modern Nara Prefecture, is now more commonly known as Hasedera, and Ariwara Temple, in the present Tenri City, was in ruins in medieval times. In poem 2606 of the *Gyokuyōshū* (an imperial anthology compiled in 1313), Kyōgoku Tameko expresses her grief at the sight of its ruins: "Only the form remains, a relic of days long gone; seeing Ariwara's traces makes me yearn for the past."

2. *Aritsune* literally means "is constant" and hence is used to contrast with "inconstant or transient world" (*tsunenaki yo*). *Tsunenaki* may also refer to the fact that Aritsune is no more.

FIGURE 2.12. The waki kneels in front of the "tomb" to pray (gasshō). He wears a priest's hood (sumibōshi). The position of the chorus members' fans indicates that they are not yet participating in the performance. All the musicians wear stiff, broad-shouldered vests (kataginu) with matching hakama (kamishimo), an indication that this is an important performance. (Courtesy of the Noh Research Archive of Musashino Women's College.)

Shidai entrance music   *The shite enters holding a rosary, a pail, and sometimes a branch of leaves and walks very quietly down the bridgeway [figure 2.13].*

Shidai   *The shite stands at the shite spot and faces the painted pine on the back wall during this melodic song, which is congruent with the accompanying drumbeats.*

SHITE:

Each dawn, I draw hallowed water,
each dawn, I draw hallowed water,
may the pure moon purify my heart.

Jitori   *Low-pitched noncongruent chant.*

Each dawn, I draw hallowed water,
may the pure moon purify my heart.

Sashi   *He faces front.*

Everywhere
autumn nights are lonely, still
more so in this aged temple where people rarely call;
the wind blowing through garden pines deepens the night,
the moon, aslant the eaves where grasses—
forget-me-nots, how-long-ivy, hidden-longing-leaves—[3]

3. The names of these plants (*wasure-gusa*, *itsumade-gusa*, and *shinobu-gusa*)—though translated here as a separate line—are embedded as puns in the next four lines of this long poetic sentence.

FIGURE 2.13. The striped curtain (*agemaku*) at the end of the bridgeway is pushed up with bamboo poles to allow the actors to enter. Here the shite in *Izutsu*, a young village woman dressed in a kimono, is carrying a pail and a rosary. (Photo by Monica Bethe.)

    call to mind a past now forgotten and gone;
    how long shall I endure, longings hidden,
    awaiting nothing? Truly, everything leaves
    memory to people in this mortal world;
    in everything his memory still remains.

Brief instrumental interlude.

Sageuta

    Ceaselessly, with single-minded trust
    in the cord the Buddha's hand extends,[4]
    I pray, guide me, voice of Sacred Law,

Brief instrumental interlude

Ageuta

    the divine vow to illuminate delusion,

Brief instrumental interlude.

    the divine vow to illuminate delusion
    revealed in the light of the dawn moon
    headed toward the western hills,

4. A cord was often attached to the hand of a statue of Amida Buddha. By grasping it, a dying person could concentrate on the Buddha and be drawn safely to the Pure Land. Amida vowed to save all living beings.

FIGURE 2.14. The shite stands at the shite spot and addresses the waki seated at the waki spot in act 1 of *Izutsu*. In this production the instrumentalists and chorus wear hakama and kimono, a less formal costume than that shown in figure 2.12, and the pampas grass is attached to the side of the well frame at stage left. (Photo by Monica Bethe.)

Looks far off to the west.

> yet brightening the entire autumn sky;
> the only sound, the voice of pines

Listens intently.

> swept by winds as stormy and uncertain

Faces front.

> as this world of dream-deluded minds;

He kneels, puts down the branch, and rubs the rosary.

> what sound will bring awakening?
> what sound will bring awakening?

Brief instrumental interlude during which the stage attendant removes the branch; the shite stands at the shite spot [figure 2.14].

Mondō   *The waki remains seated at the waki spot, turns to face the shite, and speaks.*

WAKI: As I pause at this temple to purify my heart, an attractive woman draws water from the wooden well in the garden and puts it with some flowers on that tomb as though she were making an offering. Miss, may I ask who you are?

SHITE *(Remains standing and turns toward the waki)*: I'm just someone who lives in the neighborhood. Ariwara no Narihira, for whom this temple was founded, left a name for himself in this world. Perhaps this shadowy tomb (*looks down at the prop*) marks his remains. I don't know much about it, but I make offerings of flowers and water and pray on his behalf.

WAKI:

> Yes indeed, this Narihira is a well-known figure; however,
> since all that remains is an old tale
> from a time now very long ago,
> the fact that you, a woman,
> offer prayers for the soul
> of Ariwara no Narihira

Changes from speaking to the melodic mode.

> suggests some kind of a relationship.

SHITE *(Speaking):*

> You ask about a relationship?
> Even in his own time Narihira
> was referred to as a "man of old,"[5]
> and now his world is much more distant;
> there can be no relationship or link.

WAKI *(Chanting in the melodic mode):*

> What you say makes sense and yet
> here, this ancient relic of olden times,

SHITE:

> its master now long gone, Narihira's[6]

WAKI:

> trace still lingers, his reputation

SHITE:

> flourishes in a world of tales

WAKI:

> told even now;

SHITE:

> this "man of old" (*takes a step toward the waki*),

Ageuta   *The shite faces front.*

CHORUS:

> his name alone abides in
> Ariwara Temple's aging remains,

Brief instrumental interlude.

> Ariwara Temple remains grow old

Looks at the grave mound.

> just as a pine and grasses grow upon the tomb,

Moves forward slightly.

---

5. The hero of *The Tales of Ise*, popularly identified as Narihira, was called "man of old" (*mukashi otoko*).

6. Puns on names continue: here the *nari* of Narihira is also read "becomes [distant]," and in the first chorus line below the *ari* of Ariwara is also read "is," translated as "abides."

>   this indeed is that, trace of the departed —
>   a clump of pampas grass sending forth its plumes,

Stares intently at the pampas grass.

>   revealing what, recalling when?

Thinks deeply.

>   Lush grow the grasses and
>   deep the dew that falls on this aging tomb —
>   is it real, the past I yearn for,

Circles the stage to the left.

>   its trace creates this melancholy scene,
>   its trace creates this melancholy scene.

The shite stops at the shite spot and faces the waki. During this chorus the aikyōgen has come quietly down the bridgeway and seated himself at the kyōgen spot.

WAKI (*Speaking*): And now please tell me tales of Narihira.

Kuri   *The shite goes to center stage and kneels, and the chorus sings in the melodic mode.*

CHORUS:

>   Long ago the middle captain Ariwara
>   spent years here in "Isonokami,
>   an ancient village flowers" in spring,[7]
>   in autumn the moon is clear.

Sashi   *All remain seated.*

SHITE:

>   It was then he pledged himself to Ki no Aritsune's daughter,
>   and although the couple's love was far from shallow,

CHORUS:

>   there was in Takayasu village in the province of Kawachi
>   another woman, and he secretly trod
>   a duplicitous path. His wife recited:

SHITE:

>   "When winds rise in the offing, white-
>   capped waves surge high as Mount Tatsuta;

CHORUS:

>   does midnight find my lord traveling alone?"
>   Hearing her concern for him
>   and his furtive, nocturnal trips,
>   he let his other amour subside.

SHITE:

>   Truly, poetry conveys compassion,
>   reveals a heart bubbling over with love.

7. An allusion to poem 870 of the *Kokinshū*, by Furu no Imamichi: "Since the sun's rays can penetrate its thickets, in Isonokami, that ancient village, flowers blossom." This poem celebrates the promotion of a man in retreat at Isonokami, which is "ancient" because it served as the capital in the fifth century.

Kuse   *All remain seated as this passage is sung in congruent rhythm with the hand drums. The flute enters midway.*

> Long ago in this very province
> two families dwelt side by side;
> in front of their gates was a wooden
> well, around which their young children
> played, conspiring in friendly ways,
> peering at their reflections in the water mirror,
> heads together, sleeves o'erlaid,

Brief instrumental interlude.

> bosom friends, hearts fathomless as the water
> reflecting them and suns and moons passing by,
> as days and months piled up until
> they became bashful young adults, shyly
> aware of each other's presence.
> Then that sincere young man[8]
> strung together dewlike pearls of words
> to reveal the passion of his heart in bloom.

SHITE:

> "The wooden water well
> has a wall which measures my height;

CHORUS:

> it seems I have grown up since I last saw you, my love."
> When he composed and sent this,
> she replied: "We used to compare
> the length of our hair, now mine hangs low,
> if not for you, my dear, for whom shall I tie it up?"
> Was it because they exchanged these poems,
> that "the woman of the wooden well" became a name

The shite looks at the waki.

> bestowed upon Aritsune's daughter?

Brief instrumental interlude.

Rongi   *All remain seated.*

CHORUS:

> That is indeed a venerable old tale
> as tantalizing as your mysterious presence.
> Please reveal your name!

SHITE:

> In truth, the love gowns I wear are
> Ki no Aritsune's daughter's—no!
> I don't know; "white-capped waves surge high as Mount Tatsuta"
> as I mingle with the dark of night.

8. Another appellation used for the hero in *The Tales of Ise*.

CHORUS:

How very strange! On Tatsuta Mountain
amid the colors of autumn leaves emerges

SHITE:

Ki no Aritsune's daughter,[9] also

CHORUS:

known as the woman of the wooden well.

SHITE:

Reticent though I am to admit it, I am she.

CHORUS:

Long as strands entwined in sacred ropes

The shite stands and moves quietly to the shite spot.

were the years that bound their lives together
in a pledge made here by the wooden well, where
into the shadow of the well wall she disappears,

Facing front, she spreads her arms to indicate her disappearance.

into the well wall's shadow, she disappears.

The shite exits down the bridgeway and through the curtain.

Kyōgen Interlude

AI *(Moving from the kyōgen spot to the shite spot):* I am a resident of Ichinomoto in Yamato Province. I often go to Ariwara Temple to pray, and I think I'll go there today, too. *(Looks at the waki)* Now there's a priest I haven't seen around here before. Perhaps he's traveling and has just dropped by to rest.

WAKI: I'm a priest with no fixed abode. Do you live around here?

AI: Yes, I do.

WAKI: Then could you please come over here? I have something I'd like to ask you.

AI: Certainly, sir. *(Goes to center stage and kneels)* What is it you'd like to ask me? [figure 2.15]

WAKI: This is probably an unusual request, but there must be some stories about the late Narihira and Ki no Aritsune's daughter. Could you please tell them to me?

AI: This is indeed a surprising request. Even though I live around here, I don't know very much about that. However, since it would seem strange not to respond at all to the request of someone I've just met, I'll tell you what I've heard.

WAKI: I would appreciate it.

Katari

AI: Well, it is said that the gentleman known as Ariwara no Narihira was the youngest son of Prince Abo, who resided here at Ariwara Temple. When Narihira was a child, he played with a friend, the daughter of Ki no Aritsune.

9. In this passage Ki no Aritsune's daughter becomes one with the imagery, through puns on her name: *ki*, which earlier was read to mean "wear [love gowns]," may be read here as both "tree" and "yellow (leaves)."

They would stand beside this very well, amusing themselves by peering at their reflections in the water. When they became young adults, they grew bashful and stopped meeting so freely. Finally, Narihira wrote a love letter to the girl. It included the following poem:

> The wooden water well
> has a wall which
> measures my height;
> it seems I have grown up
> since I last saw you, my love.

She replied:

> We used to compare
> the length of our hair,
> mine now hangs low,
> if not for you, my lord,
> for whom shall I tie it up?

Before long, they married and forged a deep bond, it is said. Sometime later Narihira took up with a woman in the village of Takayasu and visited there often. His wife showed no signs of jealousy. She would send him off so cheerfully that Narihira began to suspect that she had another lover. One night, pretending to leave for Kawachi, he instead hid behind a clump of pampas grass in the garden and spied on her. His wife seemed more beautiful than usual as she lit some incense, offered up some flowers, and then came out on the veranda. Looking off in the distance toward Takayasu, she composed a poem:

FIGURE 2.15. The aikyōgen kneels at center stage to deliver his katari. His vest (kataginu) is the kyōgen version of that worn by the musicians in figure 2.12. The patterned material creates a less formal effect. (Courtesy of the Noh Research Archive of Musashino Women's College.)

> When winds blow in the offing
> white-capped waves surge
> high as Mount Tatsuta.
> Does midnight find
> my lord traveling alone?

With a worried air she went inside. On seeing this, Narihira realized that she was not duplicitous, and, it is said, he stopped visiting Kawachi. Sometime later, both Narihira and his wife died. This temple was built for their remains and is called Ariwara Temple. This is as much as I know about the situation. What caused you to ask me about it? It seems rather strange.

WAKI: You have been kind to tell me this tale. I had no particular reason to ask. But before you arrived, a woman appeared from somewhere, prepared flowers, burned some incense, and prayed at this tomb. When I questioned her, she told me about Narihira and Ki no Aritsune's daughter. She related much the same story you just told me. Then she hinted that she was somehow connected to the daughter, and she disappeared from sight over by that well.

AI: I suspect that the spirit of Aritsune's daughter appeared to you. You should stay here a while and pray for the couple's souls.

WAKI: That's a good idea. I will stay a while, recite some felicitous sutras, and pray for them.

AI: Let me know if I can be of any help during your visit.

WAKI: Thank you. I will.

AI: Anytime, please do.

The aikyōgen stands and returns to the kyōgen spot. During the next section, he quietly exits up the bridgeway.

ACT 2

Ageuta   *The waki sits at the waki spot while the following is chanted in the melodic mode.*

WAKI:

It is growing late
at Ariwara Temple, the moon tonight,

Brief instrumental interlude.

at Ariwara Temple, the moon tonight
returns the past; I turn my gown over[10]
to await a dream, arm pillowing my head
I lie down on this verdant bed,
I lie down on this bed of moss.

Sashi   *The shite enters down the bridgeway, now wearing the cap and gown of Ariwara no Narihira over her kimono. She stops at the shite spot facing front and sings in noncongruent rhythm.*

SHITE:

"They've earned a name
for fickleness, these cherry blossoms,
yet they await a man who hasn't come in months."[11]
It was I who composed these words

10. Sleeping with one's robe turned inside out was thought to bring dreams of a lover. The robes of Buddhist priests were called "moss robes" (*koke goromo*), probably because of their color.

11. A poem from section 17 of *The Tales of Ise*, in which a lady, identified in medieval times as Aritsune's daughter, chides her lover for neglecting her.

Turns to face the waki.

> and hence was called "the woman who waits."[12]
> Since our long-ago days at the wooden well,
> "the years have flown like fleeting arrows,"[13]
> and now he's gone, my Narihira, whose
> keepsake cloak I wrap around myself

Holds out her left arm and looks at her sleeve.

Issei

> and reticently

Faces front.

> reflect the man of old in dance:

CHORUS:
> blossoming sleeves, flakes of whirling snow.

Jonomai

The shite performs a slow and stately dance to the music of the flute and drums. The dance is most often in four movements.

Waka   *The shite stops at the shite spot and raises her fan before her face.*

SHITE:
> Coming here,
> to revive the past at Ariwara Temple,

CHORUS *Chanted in a steady-beat rhythm (ōnori):*
> where reflected clearly in the well,
> a moon so radiant,
> a moon so radiant.

Wakauke   *While singing in a noncongruent melodic song, the shite moves forward and circles left to back center stage.*

SHITE:
> "There is not a moon, is there,
> is it the spring of old?"[14] He wrote that
> once, but when was it?

Noriji   *Chanting in the melodic mode to a steady beat (ōnori).*

SHITE:
> The wooden water well

Goes toward the prop.

---

12. This label is applied to her in medieval commentaries such as the *Wakachikenshū*.

13. A reference to section 24 of *The Tales of Ise*, in which a husband goes to the capital, leaving his wife behind. After three years, she agrees to marry another man, but on the eve of the ceremony the husband returns. When he wishes her well in a poem using the words quoted here, she realizes she still loves him and chases after him. Unable to overtake him, she dies. Medieval commentators identify Aritsune's daughter with this woman.

14. This alludes to Ariwara's famous poem: "There's not a moon, is there? This spring is not the spring of old, is it? Am I myself, the only thing remaining as before," included in the *Kokinshū* as poem 747.

FIGURE 2.16. At the climatic movement of the play, the shite pushes aside the pampas grass with her fan and stares into the well water, seeing both herself and her loved one. She wears a chōken, a young woman's mask (*wakaonna*), and a court cap (*eboshi*). (Courtesy of Eileen Katō.)

CHORUS:
"The wooden water well
has a wall that
SHITE:
measures my height;

Raises her open fan.

CHORUS:
it seems I have grown,
SHITE:
indeed I've grown up!"[15]

Deep in thought, she spreads her arms.

CHORUS:
Thus we saw each other, he,

Goes to the corner.

the man of old,

Raises her fan and points to her cap.

his court cap and gown

Moves in a large circle to center back.

now conceal the woman,
it is indeed a man—
the image of Narihira

Goes to the prop and pushes aside the pampas grass with her fan [figure 2.16].

Uta   *There is a climactic moment of no action as the shite looks intently into the well. When the chanting resumes, it is in the softer hiranori style, which continues to the end.*

SHITE:
seeing it, I yearn,
CHORUS:
'tis my own self, yet I yearn.

Backs up, suppressing tears.

SHITE:
The form of a departed lover's ghost:

Circles right to the left of the shite spot.

"a withered flower

15. The sound "oi" may mean both "grow" and "grow old," and commentators differ over which meaning is operative here.

FIGURE 2.17. In the most frequently used ending of noh plays, the shite goes to the shite spot and stamps twice (*tome-byōshi*) before exiting up the bridgeway. (Photo by Monica Bethe.)

Shrinks down to a kneeling position.

   color faded, only its fragrance

Rises slowly to a standing position.

   remains"[16] at Ariwara
   Temple, the bell tolls faintly

Listens intently and stamps her feet.

   dawn at the ancient temple,

Looks up toward the east.

   pine winds tear plantain-leaf-

Pointing with her fan, she goes to the shite spot.

   frail dream, too, breaks awake,

Stamps.

   the dream breaks to dawn.

The shite spreads her arms, faces front, and performs the closing stamps (tome-byōshi), then exits slowly up the bridgeway [figure 2.17].

16. In the preface to the *Kokinshū*, Narihira's poetry is critiqued as expressing "too much feeling with too few words, like a withered flower whose color has faded while its scent remains." The word for color, *iro,* can also mean "form" (the form of the ghost fades away) and "passion," attachment to which must fade if one is to attain enlightenment.

Miidera

A fourth-category crazed-person play

Translated by Eileen Katō

Crazed-person plays (*kyōran mono*) feature characters who have become deranged or distraught through the loss of a loved one and who express their frenzied state through song and dance. Some of the earliest crazed-person plays were about men (*otoko monogurui*), but crazed-woman plays (*kyōjo mono*) became more common and make up about three-quarters of the total today. These women are obsessed with the loss of a son or a lover. Because few of the characters have names or histories known to the audience, the emphasis is on a place and/or an object. The bell in *Miidera* (Mii Temple) is a good example, as are the blossoms in *Sakuragawa* (Cherry Blossom River) and the basket in *Hanagatami* (The flower basket). Crazed men include a husband separated from his wife (*Ashikari*) and fathers separated from their sons (*Kōya monogurui* and *Utaura*). Typically, the plays have happy endings: the separated pair is usually reunited. *Sumidagawa* (Sumida River), the play that inspired Benjamin Britten and William Plomer to compose *Curlew River*, is a sad exception: the mother finds her young son's tomb.

Structurally, crazed-person plays have several things in common. When the plays are in two acts, the first act is usually a brief description of the circumstances behind the shite's wanderings. Actors other than the shite—for example, the tsure, kokata, and aikyōgen—often have expanded roles, and a variety of dances are used. Many of the plays, like *Miidera*, include a kakeri dance to instrumental music. The dance's erratic rhythms suggest the character's state of mind, as does the bamboo branch (an emblem of derangement) that the character often carries. Several plays also contain a special dance to song (dan no uta), which frequently focuses on a prop. *Miidera*, for example, has a bell dance (*kane no dan*); *Ashikari*, a hat dance (*kasa no dan*); and *Sakuragawa*, a net dance (*ami no dan*).

One of the attractive aspects of *Miidera* is the active role of the two aikyōgen in the play itself, rather than in a separate kyōgen interlude. In act 1 the *adoai* (the secondary kyōgen role) interprets the mother's dream for her. Then, at the beginning of act 2 (there is no interlude between the acts, since the shite does not reenter immediately), the chief priest (waki), who is caring for the child Semmitsu, orders the temple servant (the *omoai*, or primary kyōgen role) to entertain the boy. The kyōgen obliges by performing a song and dance (komai), the words of which list various types of children's toys. Such performances are rare within a noh play, as is the humor that the kyōgen continues to introduce in his active role. First, he conspires to let the woman into the temple against the priest's orders, a motif repeated in *Dōjōji* (translated in this book). Later, he strikes the temple bell and permits the mother to strike it as well. This type of expanded kyōgen role, found also in *Dōjōji* and *Ōeyama*, clearly foreshadows the use of multiple characters in puppet and kabuki plays.

The bell plays an important role in *Miidera* as both a stage prop and a poetic image. The Miidera bell is one of the "Eight Famous Views of Lake Biwa" (Ōmi hakkei); several other views are also mentioned in the play. When the mother enters in act 2 and expresses her distraught state of mind, the bell quickly becomes the focal point of her desire, her poetry, and her movements. When she rings it herself, she achieves inner peace and sits down in the moonlight to await the dawn. The play continues with a meditation on bells, one of the more beautiful and evocative lists of things (mono no tsukushi) in noh, sensitively translated here by Eileen Katō. The interweaving of the images of moon and bell provide much of the lyric beauty of this play.

No one is sure who composed this popular play. *Discussions About Sarugaku* (Sarugakudangi, 1430), a record of Zeami's comments on noh compiled by his son Motoyoshi, mentions a play about a bell (*Kane no nō*) that may have been an early version of *Miidera*. That reference criticizes On'ami's (1398–1467; Zeami's nephew) use of the bell prop in a performance before the shogun, Yoshinori. The first reference to a play named *Miidera* is from 1456, and the first known performance took place on the fourth day of the fourth month of 1464. The play has been performed regularly since by all five schools. For her translation, Katō consulted various chant-books and annotated Japanese texts, including Itō 1988 and Koyama et al. 1973, both of which provide the aikyōgen parts as well as useful annotations.

FIGURE 2.18. The mother in act 1 of *Miidera*, wearing a middle-aged woman's mask (*fukai*), kneels in prayer at Kiyomizu Temple. (Courtesy of the Noh Research Archive of Musashino Women's College.)

CHARACTERS

SHITE: the mother of Semmitsu
KOKATA: the child Semmitsu
WAKI: the chief priest of the Miidera
WAKIZURE: two other priests from the temple
OMOAI: a temple servant
ADOAI: a person living outside the gates of Kiyomizu Temple

MUSICIANS

Chorus of eight to ten members
A flute and two hand drums

ACT 1

The musicians and chorus enter and take their places. The shite enters without musical accompaniment, wearing the mask for middle-aged women (fukai) and carrying a Buddhist rosary in her right hand. She proceeds to the center front stage, kneels, and joins her hands in an attitude of devout prayer [figure 2.18].

Sashi   *Sung in the melodic mode with noncongruent drum accompaniment beginning halfway through the segment.*

SHITE:

Praise and glory be forever
to Kannon the All-Merciful,[1]
who vowed in her compassion
she would surely hear
the prayer of anyone
who called her Blessed Name,
whether in silence or aloud,
even one time in true and simple faith.

Lowers her hands.

Then all the more is she now bound to listen
to the prayer of such as me,
who has spent days

1. A promise attributed especially to the Kannon of Kiyomizu Temple in Kyoto. This Kannon of a Thousand Arms actually has only forty arms, each with an eye in the palm. Kannon is the Bodhisattva Avalokiteśvara and, in India, is worshiped as a male bodhisattva. In China this deity gradually took on female attributes, a trend that continued in Japan, although the figure remains androgynous.

and piled up lonely nights
in suppliant plea:
so thinks my heart in sorrow.

Sageuta   *The rhythms become congruent, and the flute plays briefly midway through this and the following segments.*

SHITE:

Oh! have mercy now upon me!
What will become of the beloved child I long for?
What will become of the beloved child I long for?

Ageuta

If even an old withered tree;
if even an old withered tree
can hope to flower once more
by grace of Kannon,[2]
then surely not in vain do I now hope
to see again my sweet green sapling:
I believe that I will meet my child once more.

The shite dozes off briefly.

Unnamed segment   *Waking up.*

SHITE:

Oh joy and gratitude!
When I fell asleep a while,
I was granted in my dream
a happy oracle.
There is a holy man who comes to me now and then
with words of comfort;
I hope he'll come again,
and I will tell him of my dream.

During the preceding segment, the adoai has entered quietly and gone to the kyōgen spot behind the first pine. When this passage is finished, the shite rises and goes quietly to the shite spot.

Nori   *Spoken without instrumental accompaniment, standing at the first pine and facing front.*

ADOAI: I, who have come before you here, am a man who lives by the gate of the Kiyomizu Temple. A woman came here some time ago to do a special course of worship at the temple, and I helped her find lodgings. It now must be about time for her to be leaving the temple. I think I'll go to meet her on her way back (*he turns to face the shite*).

Mondō

There she is already. Madam, it is I, the man who arranged your lodgings.

2. From the dharani of Kannon of the Thousand Arms. A dharani is roughly equivalent to the "efficacious prayers" of Christianity, credited with quasi-magical powers.

I have come out to meet you. Would you please sit down? I have something to say to you.

He places a stool for her at center stage, and then he goes to the corner and sits.

Did you by chance see a dream or receive an oracle while you were at your devotions? I am a reader of dreams, and I ply my trade here by the gate of the Kiyomizu Temple. If you have had a dream, please tell me, and let me interpret it for you.

SHITE: Just now, while I was dozing, I was blessed with a wonderful dream.

ADOAI: Well, what kind of dream was it?

SHITE: I was told that if I wished to see my child, I should go to Miidera Temple in the province of Ōmi.

ADOAI: This is indeed a most auspicious dream. It means that you will find the one you seek. Ō means "to meet" and *mi* means "to see," so your dream means that you will find your child in Miidera Temple in the country of Ōmi. Indeed, you will probably never again have such an auspicious dream. I think you should not delay but should go at once to Miidera.

SHITE: And what way should I take to Miidera?

ADOAI: It's a long, hard way. You must take the high road through the hills, and when you see Lake Biwa on the other side, you will soon reach Miidera.

SHITE *(Sung in the melodic mode)*: Ah! how happy am I at your reading of my dream! Now as the oracle has bid, I shall set out at once for Miidera.

She rises and exits up the bridgeway. The adoai takes the stool and follows her off.

ACT 2

The stage attendants bring in a frame bell tower and stand it in the corner.

Shidai entrance music   *As the flute and drums play rather briskly, the child Semmitsu (kokata), the chief priest of the Miidera (waki), and two attendant priests (wakizure) enter down the bridgeway and onto the stage. The omoai follows them and sits at the kyōgen spot.*

Shidai   *Sung in the dynamic mode with the priests and the kokata standing in rows at front stage facing each other. The drums play congruent rhythms.*

WAKI AND WAKIZURE:
 We wait for night to fall
 this middle night of autumn,
 we wait for night to fall,
 our hearts all given to
 our longing for the moon.

Nanori   *Intoned speech without accompaniment, with the waki and kokata facing front.*

WAKI: I am the chief priest of Miidera Temple in Ōmi Province. This little boy here begged me so earnestly to take him as my disciple that, unworthy as I am, I was finally forced to give in to his pleas. Because tonight, the fifteenth

of the eighth month, is the night of the bright harvest moon, I will take this
child with all the others out to the garden by the lecture hall to see the moon.

Ageuta

*They turn to face each other, singing in a dynamic mode with congruent drums and
a flute passage in the middle.*

WAKI AND WAKIZURE:
"This night's bright moon
is famed as pure and peerless,"[3]
and hearts can hardly wait for night to fall.
Old loving friends
and strangers but now met
are all at one and spend the waiting hours
in prayers and wishes for a cloudless sky,
commending to the day's light
this night's moon bright fame.

They go and sit in a line in front of the chorus.

Unnamed segment   *Intoned speech.*

OMOAI *(Leaves the kyogen spot and enters the stage proper):* Well now, well now,
let me see! What'll I say? Hmm! How about this? Isn't this a grand bright
moon? You always come out to see the famous harvest moon, but there never
was a moon as bright and shiny as tonight's. Let me say that much to start
off with.

Mondō   *He goes and sits at center stage.*

Beg pardon, Your Reverence, I have a word to say. Ahem! Every year you
come out to see the famous harvest moon, but there never was a moon as
bright and shiny as tonight's.
WAKI: Indeed, it is just as you say. Never have I seen a moon as lovely as tonight's.
Furthermore, tonight I have brought this child along. Can you sing something? Oh, anything will do—just to amuse him, for he is a sad little fellow.
OMOAI: Yes, well, I'll see what I can do. How about this?

Komai   *He dances and clowns around while singing in the dynamic mode without
instrumental accompaniment [figure 2.19].*

Oh! I have something for you,
and it's something nice and small—
a doll with a papier-mâché face,
or a boy doll in ceramic
that's all smooth and shiny bright,
with a wee tiny topknot
and a sassy grassy knot
and a Yamashina knot,
and a paper windmill spinning,

---

3. A renga link by Nijō Yoshimoto in the *Tsukubashū*.

FIGURE 2.19 The omoai kyōgen dances (*komai*) to entertain the child Semmitsu in *Miidera*. The musicians do not accompany the song for this dance. (Photo by Monica Bethe.)

and the gourd that gives lodging
to the sparrow from the hills
always busy hunting chestnuts
with his flighty sparrow friends,
and the little dog that wags his head
all striped like a wild tiger,
and the priest that won't lie down,
and the one that plays the drum,
a throwing ball, a bouncing ball,
and, last, a little arrow.

He stops dancing and goes to the shite spot, where he peers into the distance toward the curtain and begins a conversation with an unseen interlocutor.

Mondō *Intoned speech without accompaniment.*

OMOAI: What's all that fuss and commotion over there? What's that you say? There's a madwoman and she's great fun, is that it?—Well now, there's something that would really amuse the kid. I think I'll tell the fellows over there to let her into the temple garden, and we'll have fun with her. But first of all, I'll have to ask the priest in charge.
    (To one of the wakizure): Your Reverence! Your Reverence! Sir!
WAKIZURE: Well, what is it?
OMOAI: Well, it's like this, Your Reverence. They tell me there's a very interesting sort of crazy woman over there. Shall I tell them to let her into the garden, and we'll amuse the kid making fun of her? Or do you have some better idea yourself? Well, how about it, sir?

WAKIZURE: No, absolutely not. It is strictly forbidden to bring any such person, and particularly a woman, into the temple garden.

OMOAI: Ah, but sir, there's no harm at all in it.

WAKIZURE: I say no. She may not be brought in. I strictly forbid it.

OMOAI: But Reverend Sir! Reverend Sir! Your Reverence! Sir! Ah, it's no good! Making such a big thing out of nothing! Not a bit of harm in the world in it, and "I strictly forbid it," says he! Old spoilsport! No wonder nobody likes that priest, and that's the truth, but true or not, what that old priest says goes, so we can forget about putting the crazy woman on show. Hey, you over there! D'you hear me? Your madwoman is not wanted here! Strictly forbidden, no less! What's that you say? Yeah! When the fit is on her, she is great fun to watch! Now there's something that I want to see. Yes, and I'm going to see it, too. Let that priest say what he likes! What do I care? My mind's made up. I'll tell you what we'll do. You pretend to be driving away the madwoman over there, but what you'll really be doing is making sure you open up a way for her to get back here and come in. You make sure she gets in! D'you hear?

He goes and sits in front of the flutist.

Issei entrance music *The drum and flute play in noncongruent rhythms with a sense of urgency as the shite (mother) enters down the bridgeway. She holds a bamboo branch (sasa) over one shoulder, an indication that the character is mentally deranged.*

Sashi *She stands at the first pine, singing melodic song to noncongruent drum patterns [figure 2.20].*

SHITE:
  I have come through the Shiga Pass
  sung in the poem:
  "If these were snowflakes
  Ah! how many times would I
  have brushed my sleeves off!
  But this is a petal storm."[4]
  I gaze far out across the lake

She looks at the lake.

  where mirrored in bright waters
  soars the topless Hill of Hiei,

She looks up.

  an Eagle's Peak[5] with crest unseen,
  and I now see it there before my eyes
  and may revere it.

She joins her hands in prayer.

---

4. The Shiga Pass is on Mount Nyoi between Kyoto and Lake Biwa. The source of the poem has not been identified.
5. The "original" Eagle's Peak, Gridhrakuta, is where Buddha preached the Lotus Sutra. Enryakuji, a temple on Mount Hiei, is considered the "Japanese" Gridhrakuta.

FIGURE 2.20. The crazed mother enters the bridgeway and stops at the first pine. The branch of bamboo grass, emblematic of her frenzied state of mind, is behind the tree, and the tip of her fan sticks out from the fold of her kimono. The sleeves of her outer robe (*mizugoromo*) are tucked up at the shoulders. (Courtesy of Eileen Katō.)

Am I not blessed indeed?

(*Spoken*): My face may look as if I were a normal, feeling person, but I am mad, and in my case this is most natural. Even the birds and beasts (looks up to the right) know how to cherish their own offspring,

so all the more must I, a human mother,

Turns toward the front and resumes singing in the melodic mode.

grieve and mourn distraught
when the child I love
and raised with tender care
is taken from me,

Issei *Standing at the shite spot, she sings in the melodic mode to noncongruent drumbeats.*

CHORUS:
and nowhere is a thread that leads to him.
Ah! this indeed stirs madness in the heart.

Kakeri *The shite circles the stage in a brief dance to noncongruent flute and drum accompaniment, whose uneven rhythms express the unstable state of her mind.*

SHITE (*Standing at the shite spot*):
If I go my way

caring not at all to see
Miyako's autumn,

Dan no uta *The shite dances to melodic song congruent with drum accompaniment; the flute joins midway.*

CHORUS:
will not people sneer and say,
I "must be used to living
in a homeland without" a moon.[6]
But from my native village

6. Alludes to poem 31 in the *Kokinshū*, by Lady Ise: "The wild geese fly away/caring not at all to see/the mists of springtime./They must be used to living/in a homeland without flowers."

let the flowers of spring
and the russet leaves of fall

She goes to the front center.

and the snow and moon and all things pass away.
If only my lost child were there again,
I could be happy in my country home.
Ah! let me go home again,

She circles back to the shite spot.

Ah! let me go home again.
When I turn around on the road that leads back home,

She turns to face front and looks intently.

there, washed by shoreline ripples,
stands the famous lone pine tree
of Shiga's Karasaki.[7]
Its leaves remind me of my child
still in his young green years;

Looks at a pine along the bridgeway.

I shall question the keen wind
that's blowing through it.
That wind that shakes the pines!

Stamps several times.

I do not mind it now,
but if it were to blow in spring
when cherries are in blossom
in Flower-Garden Village,[8]
I would go swiftly by!

She makes a small circle.

Keening through the cedars
terrible the wind, and desolate

Goes to the left center.

is autumn by the lake,
to Miidera I have come,
already I am arrived at Miidera.

She returns to the shite spot.

Kakeai *The shite moves to left center and sings in the melodic mode. The waki sings in the dynamic mode to noncongruent drum accompaniment from the waki spot.*

---

7. Like the Chinese, the Japanese had a fondness for collections of views. This was one of the "Eight Famous Views of Lake Biwa" (Ōmi hakkei). An ancient tree still attracts tourists there.

8. Emperor Tenji's Hanazono Garden. The rough wind that may scatter the blossoms evokes the mother's fear of all that may threaten the life of her child.

WAKI:

> "The moon's great laurel tree bears fruit
> on the fifteenth eve."[9]
> Our hearts drawn by the glory of this moon,
> we sit beneath the garden trees.

SHITE *(Faces front)*:

> "I watch the lovely moonrise of this fifteenth night,
> my heart with yours, old friend, two thousand miles away."[10]
> "A bright flawless moon
> clear mirrored in still waters—
> Ah yes! I count and
> it is the mid-hour of night,
> the middle night of autumn."[11]
> Even the places
> that the moon shines down on and the hour
> lend it loveliness.

Ageuta   *A slow and quiet melodic song with congruent drums; the flute joins midway.*

CHORUS:

> "The mountain moon-bright
> winds stirring the lake waters
> smell of chill fall showers,"[12]

The shite stamps.

> smell of chill fall showers.
> And faintly now
> Awazu Never-Meeting Forest[13]
> looming into view;

The shite goes to center stage.

> and far across the great lake's vast expanse,

Moves forward.

> in the dim distance stands out clear
> Kagamiyama—Mirror Mountain—
> washed in moonlight.

Looks up.

> At Yamada and Yabase[14]

Moves the bamboo branch in a sweeping point.

---

9. From a poem by the T'ang poet Li Chiao.

10. Lines by the Chinese poet Po Chü-i, anthologized as poem 242 in the *Wakan rōeishū*.

11. *Shūishū*, poem 1001, by Minamoto no Shitago (911–983), with the last line slightly revised.

12. Nijō no Yoshimoto's (1320–1388) opening verse for a renga called *Ishiyama hyakuin* (1385).

13. This pine forest—especially when dimly seen through mists or gathering twilight—was counted as another of the Eight Views of Lake Biwa. *Awazu* also means "not meet."

14. Boats sailing on the evening lake at these places were yet another of the Eight Views.

though no traveler crosses
at this late night hour,

Lowers the branch and stamps.

lured on by the lovely moon

Looks around.

the ferrymen want to row out,
the ferrymen want to row out.

*Holding the bamboo in her left hand, the shite
goes to the first pine.*

Shaberi   *Intoned speech without
accompaniment.*

OMOAI *(Goes to the shite spot)*: Good Heavens!
The festival saké must have gone to my
head. I'm so befuddled I near forgot to ring
the midnight bell. I'd better hurry up and
strike it right away; there's no doubt about it
but this is a great bell. They have a saying,
"The Tōdaiji bell for size, the Byōdōin's for
shape, and the Miidera's for sound," so this
is one of the three best bells in all the land.
Well then, let me up and at it.

*He goes to center stage and mimes striking the
bell [figure 2.21].*

Heave, heave ho and a ding dong dohnng
Heave, heave ho and a ding dong dohnng
Heave, heave ho and a ding dong dohnng

Mondō   *Hearing the sound of the bell, the shite
comes onto the stage proper and strikes the
aikyōgen with her bamboo.*

OMOAI: A bee's stinging me!
SHITE: Let me strike the bell, too.
OMOAI: Oh no, no. This bell is not a bell that people can strike.
SHITE: Who can strike the bell then, if people can't?
OMOAI: I have the right to strike the bell, because this temple's Bell Bonze Beetle
is none other than myself.[15] *(The aikyōgen goes and sits in front of flute.)*

Unnamed segment   *Combines intoned speech and song without instrumental
accompaniment.*

SHITE:
How lovely sounds that bell!

FIGURE 2.21. The omoai mimes ringing the temple bell.
He wears a servant's cap (*zukin*), a gauze travel robe (*mizu-goromo*) over a kimono, and kyōgen trousers with leggings
(*kukuri-hakama*). (Courtesy of the Noh Research Archive
of Musashino Women's College.)

15. *Kane tsuku tsuku hōshi. Tsuku* means "to strike the bell" (*kane*), and *hōshi* is "bonze" or "priest,"
but *tsukutsukubōshi* is also the name for a kind of cicada.

at home how often did I listen to
the temple bell of Kiyomi![16]
I remember an old poem,
"Where the lake waves lap,
age-old Miidera's bell
tolls out as ever.
But it rings no note that will
bring back again the old days."[17]
Indeed, this is the very bell

She looks at the bell.

that Hidesato brought back
from the dragon's palace.[18]
The young daughter of the dragon
attained Buddhahood.
I too must sound that bell
she once heard toll
and trust that she will help me.

Shidai *Sung in the dynamic mode congruent to drum accompaniment.*

CHORUS:
The pure cold moonlight lays,
the pure cold moonlight lays
a frost on earth tonight;
the bell will ring out loud and clear

Looking up at the bell.

through such a moon frost.[19]

Mondō *The shite drops her bamboo branch, takes out her fan, and moves toward the bell.*

OMOAI *(To the waki):* Your Reverence. It's that madwoman. She says she's going to strike the bell. I couldn't help it, sir.
WAKI: I understand.

The omoai exits through the small door at stage right.

WAKI *(Rising to face the shite):* Now! Now! Wait a moment! How dare you strike the bell? You, a madwoman. Get away from there quickly!

16. We learn later in the play that she is from a place called Kiyomi no Seki in Suruga Province (now part of Shizuoka Prefecture).

17. This poem has been attributed to a Kamakura-period poet named Teien, who was a monk at Miidera.

18. Hidesato was a tenth-century warrior who helped put down the famous Masakado rebellion. The *Taiheiki* (book 15) describes how Hidesato visited the underwater palace of the dragon king and received the Miidera bell. In principle, only beings born as men can hope to attain Buddhahood, but exceptions like this female dragon give hope to women that if they are reborn as males, they can be saved.

19. This conventional fusion of moonlight and frost derives from Chinese poetic tradition, especially from T'ang poets such as Li Po and Po Chü-i.

SHITE: "Climbed Yu Kung's bell tower in the night"[20] goes the poem by a poet who was deeply moved by the moon. And I, in the same way, would like to ring the bell. Oh, please, let me do it!

WAKI: Those are the words of a poet of olden times and have nothing to do with your case. It is unthinkable for me to allow a madwoman to ring the temple bell.

[Katari] *Spoken predominantly in intoned speech, with drum accompaniment midway.*

SHITE: Please! Do not forbid me to ring the bell on such a moonlit night as this just because I am out of my mind. There was a poet who began a quatrain

> Slowly, slowly from the sea-cape climbing sky,
> softly, softly cleaving the cloud ways high.[21]

but he couldn't find the right words for the second couplet. Then when he was again gazing on the harvest moon, suddenly his mind grew clear, and in that moment of light, he wrote

> The full bright moon a flawless round tonight,
> and all the earth lies washed in that pure light.

The poem finished, his wits were awhirl in an ecstasy of joy, and climbing into a high bell tower, he began to ring the bell. And when the astonished people began to upbraid him and ask what the meaning of this was, he said that poetry and the moon had troubled his wits.

Kane no dan *Sung in the melodic mode with congruent drums, with the flute playing for last two lines. This "bell scene" is unique to Miidera.*

> If moonlight's loveliness
> could even set a sage's wits astray,
> why should you blame
> a pitiful crazed creature such as me?

She joins her palms in supplication toward the waki.

CHORUS: Please, good people, let me ring the bell!

The waki goes and sits, signifying acquiescence

> The bell awakens us
> out of the dream of human passions,
> in its slow pure tones
> ring truths of Holy Law.
> When the vesper bell is tolled,

---

20. A line from poem 374 in the *Wakan rōeishū* by Hsieh Kuan: "From Liu Wang's garden at the dawn/I saw the clustered hills snow piled./Climbed Yu Kung's bell tower in the night/and saw a thousand moonlit miles." Yu Kung was a poet and singer of the Han dynasty whose name was associated with the expression of emotion. *The Tale of the Heike* (book 3, chap. 11) claims, "When Yu Kung sang his songs, he stirred the very dust of the rafters. The man of real feeling cannot fail to awaken a deep response."

21. There is some doubt about the authorship of this poem, but commentators think it may be by the T'ang poet Chia Tao.

SHITE:

It echoes "Nothing is here to stay."

CHORUS:

When the late-night bell resounds,

The shite circles the stage.

SHITE:

it echoes "All things born must die."

CHORUS:

What echo does the matin bell ring out?

She circles at center back stage.

SHITE:

"When what must pass has ceased to be."

CHORUS:

What does the tolling curfew tell?

SHITE:

"Then is the bliss

CHORUS:

of nothingness."[22]

The shite goes to the bell tower and gazes up at the bell.

And so the bell rings, teaching Holy Law.
As the pure moon waxes full,
it brings to light

She picks up the bell rope [figure 2.22].

the hundred and eight passions,
and shows up the illusions

She pulls the rope twice to sound the bell.

of this world of dream.

Once again she sounds the bell.

Oh listen, now I toll the midnight bell
and suddenly feel cleared of the dark clouds
of the five limitations
that a woman bears,[23]
and so am at peace within myself,

She drops the rope and goes to center stage.

my gaze upon the moon,

22. All four quoted phrases occur consecutively in the Nirvana Sutra. The passage in the noh was a popular chant once as familiar to the Japanese as "Oranges and lemons say the bells of St. Clemens" is to the English.

23. Mentioned in Devadatta section of the Lotus Sutra. A woman cannot be (1) a Brahma king, (2) Indra, (3) the king of Hell who sits in the judgment seat, (4) a king who turns the wheel of the law—that is, an ideal ruler in this world—or (5) a Buddha, because a woman's basic nature is, according to Buddhism, the very opposite of what these should be.

FIGURE 2.22 In *Miidera*, the mother "rings" the bell by holding a long ribbon attached to a tiny bell. Japanese temple bells are actually rung by pulling a rope attached to a horizontally hung log and making the log strike the outside of a large bell. (Photo by Monica Bethe.)

She sits down.

> the light of perfect truth,
> I wait for day to break.

Kuri *Ornate melodic song in noncongruent rhythm to drum accompaniment. The flute plays during the first and last lines.*

> "Bell voices of the lasting Pleasure Palace
> peal muffled through the flowers and die away,

SHITE:

> the greening willows by the Lake of Dragons,

CHORUS:

> grown wet, glow all the greener in the rain."[24]

Sashi *Melodic song to instrumental accompaniment.*

SHITE:

> Although here in our land too
> the poets down the ages
> have left woods of word-leaves about bells.[25]

CHORUS:

> "Hark how the far-famed

24. Another poem by Li Chiao, poem 81 in the *Wakan rōeishū*.
25. "Woods" (*lin*) is often used in Chinese to refer to collections of verses. "Word-leaf woods" in Japanese denotes waka poems.

bell of Onoe rings out
in Takasago!
Through the dawn, that clear note tells
chill autumn frosts have fallen."[26]
Hatsusedera hid in cloudy hills,
Naniwadera far away,[27]

SHITE:

and oh, so many ancient temples
all around our land
long known for their pure bell tones

CHORUS:

sounding out down the ages
the unchanging Holy Law.

Kuse   *Melodic song congruent with the drums; the flute enters midway.*

"I climb high up to
a hill temple, and I see
in the spring twilight,
while the curfew tolls their knell,
the cherry blossoms falling."[28]
Ah! why does spring so fast
go from us like a dream
and leave us lonely?
The matin bell rings all too soon
for lovers who must part,
but there is yet another poem that says:
"Listening to the bell
ring out the lonely night hours
while I wait in vain,
I think the cock less cruel
that crows to part fond lovers!"[29]
So sang poets for whom bells
tolled out the course of true love—
and when the old lie sleepless all the night,
unable even in a dream
to live once more the days of youth,
their old eyes blinded by the lone heart's tears,
the bell will ring out the night hours

She stares at the bell.

and stir them to a sorrow that is like no other

26. A poem by Ōe no Masafusa anthologized in the *Senzaishū*.
27. Hatsusedera is also written Hasedera; Naniwadera refers to the Shittenōji in Osaka.
28. Poem 116 from the *Shinkokinshū*, by priest Nōin (988–1052). The play changes "mountain village" to "temple." Also quoted in *Dōjōji*.
29. Lady Kojiju's poem, number 1191 in the *Shinkokinshū*.

Looks down.

while they lie there longing for the dawn.[30]

SHITE (*She stands and holds her opened fan in front of her face*):
"The moon is going down, a crow cries out,
sharp frost fills air, and fishing fires burn low;
hark there, the tolling of the midnight bell

She moves to the front of the stage.

comes to the traveler where his boat lies moored."[31]

She looks down at the boat.

How desolate the traveler's troubled sleep

Circles left.

out on the sea roads in a rocking boat,
while from the reed-mat roofing overhead,
the rain drips, drips, drips down!
But on the level lake tonight

She goes to the corner, raises her fan, and looks out in the distance.

the winds and waves are still,

Circles the stage.

all through the quiet autumn night
the moon shines clear,
and clear too rings out far and wide
the bell of Miidera.

At the shite spot, she looks up at the bell.

Mondō   *Intoned speech without accompaniment.*

SEMMITSU (*Still seated, she faces the waki*): I would like to make a request
of you.
WAKI: What is it?
SEMMITSU: Would you please ask this madwoman what country and (*faces the
shite*) what village she is from?
WAKI: How strange that you should want to ask such a thing! But it is easily
done, and I will ask her as you wish. (*Stands*) Ho there, you madwoman!
Tell us where your native home is.
SHITE (*To the waki*): I come from Kiyomi Barrier down in Suruga country.
SEMMITSU: What was that? Did she not say she is from Kiyomi Barrier?

30. This seems to contain an echo of Po Chü-i's "Song of Everlasting Sorrow," in which the aged
and sleepless emperor, unable to see his lost love Yang Kuei-fei even in his dreams, lies desperately alone
listening to "the slow sad watches of the night/tolled out by bell and drum."
31. A considerably adapted version of a famous poem by Chang Chi of T'ang, called "Mooring a
Boat at Night by Maple Bridge": "The moon is going down, somewhere a crow cries out,/sharp frost fills
air, the torchlight flickers low,/hark! while the wanderer's boat is moored, from depths of night/the bell
of Hanshan Temple there outside Soochow!"

SHITE *(Turns to Semmitsu)*: Why! What is this? The boy who spoke those words is surely my son Semmitsu.

WAKI: Now wait a moment! This madwoman is talking foolishness, proof indeed that she is not in her right mind.

SHITE:
No, this is no folly.
I may have gone out of my mind
because my child was lost,
but now that he is found once more
why should I still be mad?
This surely is my own dear son.

She makes as if to approach her son.

WAKIZURE: Now you, get away from here, you mad creature!

He pushes her away. She seems to stagger back, pauses, and sits dejected. The priests sit.

SEMMITSU: Oh, pity! pity! Do not strike her so!

WAKI: I can see in your face the distress you do not speak. Now tell me about it, and tell us who you are.

Kudoki

SEMMITSU: Yes. Why should I hide it any longer? I am from Kiyomi Barrier in Suruga, but I fell into the hands of slavers and later came to live in Miidera.
I never dreamt
that my poor mother had gone mad
for love of me
or that she wandered seeking me
so far from home.

SHITE:
The sorrow of being parted
from my little one
was all that caused my madness,
and now great is my joy
that we are met again,
and yet I am afraid
that straightway claiming him
as my lost child

Sageuta

may shame him in the eyes of men,
but when a woman wanders in her mind
from mother love,
she knows no shame,
nor can she heed the eyes of others (*weeps*).

Rongi   *Melodic song congruent with the drums.*

CHORUS:

    How movingly she speaks!
    There may be times
    when one must hide from prying eyes,
    but in the bliss of such reunion,
    you may give yourself to joy.

The waki helps the child stand up.

SHITE:

    My joy is great,

The shite looks intently at the child.

    yet great too is my shame
    that all could see me in my wretched state;
    my eyes brim over with unbidden tears
        (*weeps*).
    Shame Forest drops will fall in spite of
        me![32]

CHORUS:

    It was so hard to find her son,
    for seldom do a parted child and parent
    live to meet again,
    but for these two, the hard-won bond
    was not fated yet to end.[33]

SHITE:

    The days of loss were many
    and the nights,

CHORUS:

    and now tonight
    you chance to come to Miidera

SHITE:

    and here find my son.

CHORUS:

    What brought it all about?
    It was the bell

The shite rises, goes to Semmitsu, and puts her hand on his shoulder [figure 2.23].

    that tolled a tale of madness,
    and the uproar revealed all.
    Although for lovers it may be
    the hateful "parting bell,"

FIGURE 2.23. The mother puts her hand on her son Semmitsu's shoulder and looks up at the bell that united them. (Courtesy of the Noh Research Archive of Musashino Women's College.)

32. *Hazukashi no mori* is the Hazukashi Forest, but *hazukashi* also means "shame," and *mori*, "dripping" or "dropping."

33. In Buddhist belief, because one has only a slight chance of being born a human being, the chance of any two humans being reborn into a parent-child bond is even less likely. These chances have to be merited in a previous existence.

The shite looks at the bell.

> here for this mother and her child
> it rang reunion.
> Oh, night of joyful meeting!
> Oh, happy, happy pealing of the bell!

Kiri *Melodic song congruent with the drums, with the flute playing during the last two lines.*

> And then together they set out for home;

The shite guides the child to the shite spot.

> and then together they set out for home,
> and lived there happy ever after,
> their house long blessed with joy and fortune.
> Oh, virtue of the love that binds child and parent!
> Oh, virtue of the love that binds child and parent!

The shite stamps twice at the shite spot and exits after the child. Others quietly follow up the bridgeway.

Shunkan

A fourth-category play about human emotions

Translated by Eileen Katō

The story of Shunkan, like that of Atsu-
mori, comes from *The Tale of the Heike* and is popular in various theatrical forms
(see *Shunkan on Devil Island* in part 3). Unlike Atsumori, Shunkan is presented in
noh as a living person. Because Shunkan's suffering is so intense, however, a special
mask was created for this role (see figure 2.4), even though most living middle-aged
male characters are played bare faced (*hitamen*). The mask is worn with one of
three head coverings: a peaked head covering often used by religious figures (*sumibōshi*), a draped hood (*hana bōshi*), or a large black headpiece (*kurogashira*). The
tsure play the two men who were exiled with Shunkan: Yasuyori, costumed as a
priest, and Naritsune, dressed as an ordinary man in a travel cloak.

Shunkan is categorized as a "human feeling" play (*ninjō mono*), along with
other heartrending pieces such as *Kagekiyo* and *Hachi no ki*. The crux of the action
of *Shunkan* is revealed in the waki's initial announcement that he is going to deliver a pardon to two men, Yasuyori and Naritsune. The audience, familiar with the
tale, are aware that there are three exiles. Only two of them, however, have been
conducting religious practices on Devil Island. Shunkan, when he appears after his
two fellow exiles have described their devotions, sings of the sad fate that has over-
taken them, offers "wine" to his friends, and then celebrates the wine as a Taoist
elixir of life. This expression of the solace of friendship intensifies the tragedy that
befalls Shunkan when he is deserted at the end of the play. The range of Shunkan's
emotions are expressed through song and a few effective gestures. There is no formal dance.

The boat that appears in *Shunkan* is an often-used prop, a simple bamboo frame
wrapped in white cloth to which an object indicating the boat's specific function,
such as a fishing torch or a bundle of brushwood, may be attached (figure 2.24). In
Shunkan, the boat may be unembellished, or as indicated in Eileen Katō's translation, it may have a large rope attached. Some actors, and the translator, feel that an

FIGURE 2.24. This 1899 illustration of *Shunkan* shows Naritsune wearing a black headpiece (*kashira*), Yasuyori, and the messenger (the waki, dressed in *suō*) in the boat prop, with Shunkan grieving at being left behind. The boatman is seated behind the prop. (Photo by Karen Brazell.)

imaginary rope is more evocative. The manipulation of the prop emphasizes noh's lack of regard for realism. When everyone has disembarked, the kyōgen representing the boatman may lean the prop against the back wall of the bridgeway until it is needed again (see figure 2.28). Then when the three more important characters enter the prop, the boatman remains seated in his spot behind the prop—there is no room for a fourth person in the boat, even the boatman. To sail away, the three men step out of the boat and walk up the bridgeway; the aikyōgen picks up the boat and follows them out.

It is not clear who wrote *Shunkan*. Early attributions to Zeami are no longer considered valid. Some scholars attribute the play to Zenchiku, whereas others believe that Zeami's son Motomasa (d. 1432) is the playwright. All five schools perform this play. The Kita school version is known as *Devil Island* (Kikaigashima). Katō's translation draws most frequently on the texts and notes in Yokomichi and Omote 1963 and Itō 1986. A videocassette of the late Kanze Hisao's performance of *Shunkan* has been issued by VHS Victor (VGT 164).

CHARACTERS

SHITE: Shunkan, a member of the Minamoto clan (the Genji), who was the chief administrator of Hosshō Temple before being exiled for his involvement in a plot against the Heike

TSURE: Captain Naritsune, an exile and a member of the Fujiwara family, who married Taira no Kiyomori's niece

TSURE: a monk justice of the peace, Taira no Yasuyori, an exile

AI: a boatman

WAKI: a messenger, one of Taira no Kiyomori's men

MUSICIANS

Chorus of eight to twelve members
A flute and two hand drums

A Play in One Act

Nanori entrance music   *To the music of the flute, the waki enters, followed by the aikyōgen. The waki has a letter scroll tucked into the breast of his kimono. He stops at the shite spot, with the aikyōgen standing just behind him.*

Nanori   *Spoken without music, facing front.*

WAKI: I am a man in the prime minister's service.[1] Since prayers and propitiations are now being offered for the imperial consort's safe delivery, a special act of amnesty has been proclaimed, extending to all in banishment throughout the provinces of the realm and to the exiles banished to Devil Island.[2] Captain Naritsune, the governor of Tamba, and Monk Justice Taira no Yasuyori have been granted pardon. I have been appointed bearer of the documents of pardon and am now hurrying to the island.

Mondō   *The waki goes to center stage and faces the aikyōgen.*

WAKI: Ho! Is there anyone there?
AI: Here I am, sir.
WAKI: I must go to Devil Island. Make ready a boat at once.
AI: At your service, sir (*both exit up the bridgeway*).

Shidai entrance music   *The two tsure, Naritsune and Yasuyori, come onstage.*

---

1. Taira no Kiyomori, the head of the Heike or the Taira clan. His daughter, the imperial consort—best known by the religious name of Kenreimon'in—was pregnant with the future emperor Antoku, who drowned at age seven when the Heike were defeated at Dannoura in 1185. She had a difficult pregnancy, and soothsayers maintained that she was pursued by ghosts of Kiyomori's victims, both living and dead, including the living ghosts of the exiles on Devil Island. These reasons were behind the decision to grant them an amnesty.

2. Kikai-ga-shima, a sulfurous island off the coast of Satsuma on the southern tip of Kyushu. It is also called Sulfur Island (Iōgashima, not to be confused with Iwojima).

Neither wears a mask. Yasuyori wears a religious headdress and carries a Buddhist rosary. They move toward stage front.

Shidai   *Sung in the melodic mode facing each other.*

BOTH TSURE:

> On Sulfur Island we have made three shrines;
> on Sulfur Island we have made three shrines
> to pray to the gods of Kumano of the three holy hills:[3]
> will they not hear our threefold rising prayer?

CHORUS (*In a low mumble*):

> To pray to the gods of Kumano of the three holy hills:
> will they not hear our threefold rising prayer?

Nanori zashi   *They turn to face front.*

BOTH:

> We are two of the exiles on Devil Island
> in the Bay of Satsuma off Kyushu.

NARITSUNE:

> Captain Naritsune of Tamba,

YASUYORI:

> Monk Justice Taira no Yasuyori, the lay priest,

BOTH:

> and now we've come to this.

Sashi

> When we lived in Kyoto, we made a vow
> to make thirty-three pilgrimages to Kumano.
> Before we had made even half,
> we were sent into banishment,
> our vow still unfulfilled,
> much to our distress.
> Now we beg the gods of Kumano
> to come to us on this island.
> We have set up token replicas
> of the ninety-nine shrine stations
> along the way from Kyoto
> to Kumano's inmost sanctuary.

Sageuta

> So we carry out our pilgrim's vow
> offering *nusa* streamers[4]
> at each shrine along the way.

---

3. Kumano, an important religious complex on the Kii peninsula south of Kyoto, has three major shrines: the "original" shrine (*hongū*) in the mountains, the "new" shrine (*shingū*) on a river near the coast, and Nachi waterfall halfway between. This is a striking example of Japanese syncretism: these men are Buddhists, but their prayers are to Shinto deities.

4. The ritual Shinto offering of zigzag streamers made of white rice paper or silk.

Ageuta

> We are far here from Kumano
> but our shrines house the same gods.
> We are far here from Kumano
> but our shrines house the same gods.
> "By Kumano Bay
> thrive the double sand flowers"[5]
> but not manifold
> the sand flowers of these shores,
> single and thin
> as our frayed, faded hempen clothes
> that must serve, too, for pilgrim robes.
> We gather up white sand for rice libation,
> and wave the white sand flowers
> for purification wands,
> and so we walk our pilgrim's pathway to the gods,
> we walk our pilgrim's pathway to the gods.

They both go and sit in front of the chorus.

Issei entrance music   *As the flute and drums play, the shite, representing Shunkan, comes on, carrying a pail, and stops at the first pine. He wears the special Shunkan mask and is dressed partly as an eminent religious figure and partly as a poor fisherman wearing a straw apron. He carries a small bucket.*

Issei   *He sings in the noncongruent dynamic mode, standing at the first pine facing front.*

SHITE:

> While still alive upon this earth
> I've fallen into hell:
> Now I am warden
> of this Devil Island.
> "Out of a dark way

Sashi

> into a way still darker"[6] have I come.
> "The bright jade moon-hare sleeps by day
> in barren mica lands,
> the golden sun-crow roosts by night
> upon a bare black branch."[7]

---

5. This is an allusion to poem 496 in the *Manyōshū*, by Hitomaro: "By Kumano Bay/thrive the double sand flowers—/no less manifold/are my heart's piled-up longings/but I can never meet you."

6. This alludes to the so-called death poem of Izumi Shikibu. It is found in her personal anthology (*Izumi Shikibushū*, poem 66) as well as in the *Shūishū* (1342). The entire poem reads: "Out of a dark way/into a way still darker/I now have to go/shine your far-off light on me/oh moon on the mountain rim." The allusion also harks back to the parable of the Magic City in the Lotus Sutra.

7. Obviously a quotation, most probably from Chinese sources but not identified. These figures fallen from former glory seem well suited to the character of Shunkan, a Tendai priest of esoteric Buddhism.

"The cicada of fall clings to a withered tree
and sings his death song,
and he no more turns his head."[8]
Ah! All of them show forth the fate of Shunkan.

He goes onstage to the shite spot.

Mondō   *The tsure stand and face the shite. They speak.*

YASUYORI: Hey there! Is that you, Shunkan? What brings you out here?

SHITE: Ah! How quickly you recognized me! I came out to meet you homing
pilgrims with some wine to cheer you on the way back.[9]

YASUYORI: Did you say wine? Can the nectar of the bamboo leaf[10] be found
anywhere on such an island? I'll draw near to have a look. (*Approaches the
shite and peers into the pail.*) Why! This is water! (*Returns to his place in front
of the chorus.*)

SHITE: What you say may well be true, and yet, and yet, our word *wine* was first
used to refer to an elixir that had seemed to be water. So this, too, may be
taken for rare wine.

BOTH:
Truly, truly, what you say has reason in it.
The time of year is the ninth month,

SHITE:
the day the ninth, the Double Feast.[11]

BOTH:
The place a pathway in the hills

SHITE:
along a valley stream.

ALL THREE:
P'eng Tsu knew its hidden powers:[12]
he took the water from a deep ravine
and lived seven hundred years or more

The tsure sit in front of the chorus.

Ageuta   *The shite kneels in front of the tsure and uses his fan to mime pouring
the wine.*

CHORUS:
after he drank it.
The chrysanthemum water
to its lowest depths was white silk pure,

The shite goes to center stage and sits.

---

8. Japanese scholars trace this to a work called the *Baika mujinzō*.

9. It was the custom to meet pilgrims returning from Kumano with food and drink.

10. Bamboo leaf (*chikuyō*) is a commonly used medieval expression for wine.

11. The feast of the chrysanthemum and friendship. Old friends made every effort to reunite on that
day. The Taoist elixir of life was a legendary brew made of the trickling dewdrops from chrysanthemum
petals.

12. A Taoist immortal known as Hōso in Japanese.

cleansing the heart clear to the core,
and proved a life elixir.
The chrysanthemum water
was a life elixir, this we know,
yet fail to plumb its secret.
"His white silken robe
drenched with the chrysanthemum dew
along the hill path,
dried in what seemed a twinkling,
yet it was a thousand years."[13]
But oh! to me
the moment is a thousand years!
How long, how much longer must we stay here
in this dreadful place?
The spring goes from us
and the summer grows apace,

He stands and goes to the shite spot carrying a bucket.

the autumn deepens
and the winter comes,
but here we know it
only by the colors of

Turns to face front, looking up at the treetops.

the changing trees and grasses.
Ah! how we long for the dear days gone by!
And all we see serves to awaken thoughts of them.

Lowers his mask.

Uta   *The shite and the tsure face each other.*

CHORUS:

When I lived in Kyoto,
Hosshōji and Hōjōji were as Indra's Palace:[14]
there sweet pleasures bloomed
like flowers of spring,
but now all, all is changed;
in the sere autumn of my years
I rot here withering away
through the five deadly failings.[15]
The leaves the trees let fall

13. Poem 273 in the *Kokinshū*, by Priest Sosei. It refers to the P'eng Tsu story.

14. Shunkan was the administrator of Hosshōji, a temple founded by Emperor Shirakawa in 1073 and, in its heyday in the late eleventh century, had as its abbots princes of the blood. Hōjōji, founded by Fujiwara no Michinaga in 1022, was another of the most prestigious and most richly endowed temples in Kyoto. Indra's Palace is in the Buddhist Paradise, a place of endless pleasure and delight.

15. The five stages of corruption and decay through which celestial beings had to pass at the end of their long heavenly lives. The nobles of Kyoto were "people who live above the clouds" (*kumo no uebito*), and their fall from grace was often described in terms usually applied to fallen angels.

FIGURE 2.25. Shunkan, wearing the peaked head covering used by religous figures (*sumibōshi*) and a fisherman's apron, catches falling leaves in his fan. (Courtesy of Eileen Katō.)

FIGURE 2.26. A messenger from the capital (the *waki*) brings a pardon from the capital for two of the three exiles on Devil Island. In this performance Shunkan wears a black headpiece (*kashira*). (Courtesy of the Noh Research Archive of Musashino Women's College.)

The shite steps forward and holds out his fan in his left hand as though to catch the leaves [figure 2.25].

> here do for wine cups,
> the only wine a valley stream,

Kneels and looks to the left at the flowing stream.

> and flowing with it streams of
>   tears
> rise from a stricken heart
> that knows no end to sorrow.

He stands, goes to sit in front of the drums, and puts down his bucket and fan for a stage attendant to remove.

Issei entrance music *While the flute and drums play, the aikyōgen brings out a framework boat prop and sets it down on the bridgeway. He stands in it with an oar in his hand. The waki enters and steps into the boat with the aikyōgen.*

Issei *Sung in the dynamic mode.*

WAKI:

> As the ship speeds on
> with a fair wind behind her,
> bounding o'er the main,
> joy must fill the manly hearts
> of her gallant sailors.

Mondō *Spoken.*

AI: Others may boast of manly hearts, but not me. That Devil Island is a terrible place. Oh! But here it is already: we have reached Devil Island. Now you had better go and look for the exiles.

WAKI: I will do that right away. (*He steps out of the prop, which the aikyōgen then leans up against the back wall of the bridgeway. The waki removes the letter scroll from his garment and brandishes it high as he calls*): Ahoy there, exiles of this island, where are you [figure 2.26]?

Advances toward them.

I have come from Kyoto with a letter of pardon.

Goes to the corner and faces the shite.

Come quickly and look at it.

The shite approaches, and the waki gives the letter to him.

Here it is.

SHITE: Oh, joy and gratitude! Here, you, Yasuyori, please read it out to us. (*Shunkan hands the letter to Yasuyori, who goes to center stage, sits down, unrolls the scroll, and reads it* [figure 2.27].)

YASUYORI: "On this occasion of offering state prayers and propitiations for Her Imperial Majesty's safe delivery, a special amnesty has been declared, extending to all who have been banished. The exiles of Devil Island, Captain Naritsune, governor of Tamba, and Monk Justice Taira no Yasuyori, are hereby granted pardon."

SHITE (*Looks intently at Yasuyori*): How is it you have missed the name of Shunkan?

YASUYORI: If only your name were here! But take a look at the letter of pardon for yourself (*gives the letter to Shunkan and goes to sit in front of the chorus*).

SHITE (*Scans the letter searchingly for a long moment and then turns to face the waki*): Then it must be the letter writer's mistake.

WAKI: No. My instructions in the capital were to return with Yasuyori and Naritsune. My orders clearly said that Shunkan was to be left behind alone on this island.

Kudoki-guri

SHITE:
But how can it be so?

FIGURE 2.27. Yasuyori reads the pardon delivered by the messenger to an attentive Shunkan. (Photo by Karen Brazell.)

FIGURE 2.28. When he cannot find his name on the pardon, Shunkan weeps (*shiori*). The aikyōgen has leaned the boat prop with its black rope up against the wall until it is needed again. (Photo by Karen Brazell.)

Was not the crime the same,
the place of banishment the same?
And so should be the pardon.
Why should I alone
be dropped out of salvation's net
to fall quite down into hell's lowest depths?

The shite holds the letter in his right hand and uses his left to indicate weeping [figure 2.28].

Kudoki

All this time have not the three of us
endured together in this place,
and now must I stay on alone
along the fearsome craggy shores
of this wild awful island—
seaweed not wanted by the homing fishermen
cast out upon the waves
and left to sink or swim?
But how could any man
endure a life so lonely?
I know that crying is no use
but like the forlorn plover by the shore
I cannot help but cry.
Oh! what a wretched state! (*Weeps.*)

Kuse   *The waki goes to sit in front of the stage attendant; the shite remains seated.*

CHORUS:
When the unhappy heart weeps for the times,
the very flowers shed tears;
when loving friends are torn apart,
even the birds will cry for sorrow![16]
I hear that from old
this place was called Devil Island
and is full of fiends;
surely the place is a hell on earth,
but is there even here a fiend so foul
he cannot feel my sorrow?
Is it not written,
"Man's sorrow has the power to stir
all heaven and earth
and all the gods and demons"?[17]
Hear how the island's birds and beasts cry out (*weeps*).
Are they not moved because I suffer?

16. Adapted from Tu Fu's "A View of Spring."
17. From the Chinese preface to the *Kokinshū* by Ki no Yoshimochi.

SHITE:
> Such pain is all too much to bear!

CHORUS:
> Still hoping against hope,
> again he takes the scroll (*opens the scroll*)
> he has already seen,
> opens it out and there
> goes over every word

Carefully reads the scroll.

> once more and still once more,
> his eyes dart hither, thither, everywhere.
> Yet though he looks and looks
> the only names he can see written there
> are Naritsune and Yasuyori.
> But might it not be on the wrapper?

Turns over the scroll and examines the back.

> He turns the cover back and front
> and looks and looks again,
> but there is nothing:
> no word reads Prelate,
> no letters there spell Shunkan.

He folds the scroll in two and holds it with his left hand.

> Is all this a dream?

He slaps his knee and rises.

> Oh if it is, let me wake up!

Goes to center stage, throws down the scroll, and puts his hands together in supplication.

> Let me wake out of it!

The shite sits in an attitude of great dejection in front of the drummers.

> But it is real, and he weeps and wails;
> and beats the ground in helpless rage,
> Oh! Shunkan's state is pitiful to see.

Naritsune picks up the letter, rolls it up, and puts it in his bosom. The aikyōgen places the boat prop on the floor and brings the mooring rope as far as the front of the drummers. The waki steps into the boat.

Kakeai   *Sung in a dynamic mode.*

WAKI:
> Come! We must not waste time.
> Naritsune and Yasuyori, would you please
> get on board immediately?

BOTH *(Singing in a melodic mode)*:
> So it has to be,

They stand and go to the boat.

> and we must board the boat now
> shaking off the anguish of another.

SHITE *(Standing)*: The prelate, saying that he too wants to board the boat, clutches Yasuyori by the sleeve *(grabs Yasuyori's sleeve)*.

WAKI *(Singing in a dynamic mode)*: The prelate shall not be taken aboard. My orders are to leave him.

SHITE *(Trying to approach the boat; speaking)*: Have you no pity! Do you forget that official duty can have a place for human feelings? Have mercy and at least take me to the other shore *(looks toward the curtain)*.

WAKI *(Naritsune steps into the boat. The waki removes the right sleeve of his outer garment and brandishes his oar. The following is in a dynamic mode)*:
> The boatman knows no pity but lifts his oar to strike.

The shite releases Yasuyori's sleeve, and he too steps into the boat.

SHITE *(Goes to center stage and takes hold of the rope. Sings in the melodic mode)*:
> Now the wretched Shunkan
> grips the mooring rope
> and hangs on for dear life

Switches to the dynamic mode.

> as he tries to hold back the boat

WAKI *(Releases the rope from the boat and speaks)*:
> but the sailors cut the hawser and push out into the deep.

SHITE *(Still holding the rope, he collapses to his knees and sings in the melodic mode)*:
> Quite helpless now,
> Shunkan wrings his hands and cries out
> *(dynamic mode)* Ship ahoy!

WAKI:
> He shouts ahoy but can't be let on board.

SHITE *(Melodic mode)*:
> Now all is lost

Ageuta *The rhythms become congruent.*

CHORUS:
> and all his strength is gone:
> he drags himself up to the sea's edge,
> lies down prostrate on the sands,
> and sobs aloud.

The shite makes a weeping gesture with both hands.

> No greater than my sorrow

was the pain that broke the heart
of Lady Sayo at Matsura![18]

Rongi *The waki and two tsure are
standing in the boat looking toward
Shunkan, who is sitting at center stage
in a dejected posture [figure 2.29].*

ALL THREE:

Oh! how we feel for you!
When we get home to Kyoto,
we will plead for you,
and you will soon come home.
Do not be faint of heart, just wait
a while,

SHITE:

"Wait a while and you'll
come home to Kyoto,"
say the voices coming faint from
far away,
and faint his hope,
but Shunkan there cast down
beneath the shoreline pines
stifles his sobs
and bends his ear to listen.

Assumes an attitude of intense listening.

THREE:

Can he hear our call
across the evening tides?
Joining our voices,
we will plead for Shunkan.

SHITE:

You will plead and soon

THREE:

Oh! without fail
he will return to Kyoto.

SHITE (*Rising higher on his knees*):

Oh! do you really mean it?

THREE:

Yes, yes, of course we mean it.

SHITE:

I beg it of you.
I am counting on you.

FIGURE 2.29. Shunkan watches dejectedly as his two companions, Naritsune and Yasuyori, head for home. (Photo by Karen Brazell.)

18. Lady Sayo stood on a hill looking out to sea and waving her scarf in farewell to her love Otomo no Sadehiko, who had been sent off on an expedition to Korea. Legend says that she turned to stone and is still standing there.

CHORUS:
"Wait a while, oh! wait a while,"
say the far voices growing fainter,
as the human forms grow dim
and now the billows of the offshore
blot them out.

The waki and two tsure quietly exit up the bridgeway, and the aikyōgen carries the boat off the bridgeway. Shunkan is left all alone, looking after them.

The far, faint voices die away,

The shite rises, goes to the shite spot, and looks off toward the curtain.

and boat and men are seen no more;
gone, gone without a trace

He turns slightly to his left and weeps.

and seen no more.

A moment of silence, then Shunkan exits.[19]

19. The full pathos of the ending can be felt by readers who know—as the Japanese can be expected to—that Naritsune and Yasuyori will reconsider and not risk Kiyomori's further displeasure by interceding for Shunkan. The once exalted prelate is doomed to die in the following year, in a scarcely human state of appalling wretchedness and neglect.

Dōjōji

A fourth-category play of attachment

Translated by Donald Keene

One of the more spectacular plays in the noh repertory, *Dōjōji* enacts what is possibly the best-known tale in Japan. The theme is misogynistic and reflects a widely held belief that hell hath no fury like a woman scorned. In this case, she is scorned by a monk. As in *Miidera*, the woman seeks to enter a temple and is admitted contrary to priestly orders. Whereas in *Miidera*, the mother achieves peace of mind and reunion with her son, the woman in *Dōjōji* turns into a fire-breathing serpent whom the priests are able to evict but are unable, or perhaps unwilling, to enlighten. It has not always been so. An earlier noh version of the story called *Kanemaki* (Coiling around a bell), recently revived after years outside the repertory, includes a much longer discussion of religion by the woman and ends with her achieving release from her passionate attachment. Although *Kanemaki* is sometimes attributed to Kanze Kojirō Nobumitsu (1435–1516), there is no hard evidence for this attribution and no indication of who was responsible for converting it to *Dōjōji*. Both plays were performed during the sixteenth century, but *Dōjōji* became the preferred version.

Dōjōji is technically difficult and serves as a kind of rite of passage to full professional status for the actor playing the shite role. Permission from the head of his school is required for an actor to debut in this role. The two most demanding aspects of the play, the rambyōshi dance and the leap into the bell, were added during the process of transformation from *Kanemaki* to *Dōjōji*. The rambyōshi, a dance that probably predates noh, was sometimes performed by shirabyōshi, the type of dancer who appears in act 1 of the noh play. Dancing a rambyōshi in *Dōjōji* used to be a specialty of the Komparu school (other schools included the dance in different plays), but now it is performed by all schools only in this play. The rambyōshi is danced to a shoulder drum solo. As the drummer produces a series of piercing, drawn-out calls, each followed by a drumbeat and a long pause, the dancer bends from the waist, lifts and turns her toe, raises her leg, stamps to the drumbeat, and then remains still in the silence before the next call. The dancer traces triangles on the stage, matching the serpentine triangles in her costume and suggesting the climb up the stairs of the bell tower. The increasing tension as the two performers repeatedly strain to match the movements, drum beats, and drummer's cries creates a near hypnotic trance, broken only when the rambyōshi comes to a sudden end and a quick dance (kyū no mai) to the flute and all three drums begins.

At the climax of her dance, the dancer knocks off her tall cap and stands under the large bell prop with her hands raised. As the bell falls, she leaps into the air, and for a brief moment, there is only space between the rim of the descending bell and the floor. Within the dark confines of the bell, the actor must change his costume, mask, and wig without the usual assistance from stage attendants. By the end of the kyōgen interlude, he must have hung the discarded costume parts on the pegs in the bell and be in position, kneeling with his head covered by his robe and facing front. This is no easy task.

Dōjōji is usually labeled an exorcism piece (*inori mono*) and is grouped with two other plays about scorned women seeking revenge: *Aoi no Ue*, in which an ignored woman kills her lover's wife, and *Kanawa*, in which an abandoned wife attempts to kill her husband and his new wife. A broader category called *shūnen mono* (resentful attachment pieces) adds *Koi no omoni* (The heavy burden of love) and *Aya no Tsuzumi* (The damask drum)—two noh versions of the same story in which a man resents harsh treatment at the hands of a higher-class woman—and *Kinuta*, which features a lonely wife whose resentment causes her to suffer in hell. These plays are related to another group, *shūshin mono* (devoted attachment pieces), in which the main character longs for a loved one or for life in general, as in *Kayoi Komachi* and *Motomezuka*.

Donald Keene's translation of *Dōjōji* was first published in his *Twenty Plays of the Nō Theater* (1970). The Japanese text in Yokomichi and Omote 1963 describes several variations of the work. The editor made some changes in the translation (such as adding technical terms and expanding the stage directions) to follow the conventions used in this anthology and to reflect a specific performance of the play, that by Izumi Yoshio in December 1980.

CHARACTERS

SHITE: in act 1, a dancer; in act 2,
   a woman serpent
WAKI: the abbot of Dōjōji
WAKIZURE: two priests of the temple
OMOAI: a temple servant
ADOAI: another temple servant

MUSICIANS

Chorus of eight to ten members
A flute, two hand drums, and a
   stick drum

FIGURE 2.30. *Dōjōji* requires an unusually large number of stage attendants to carry the bell down the bridgeway and hang it from the hook in
the middle of the stage roof. (Photo by Monica Bethe.)

ACT 1

*The stage attendants carry in a large bell prop and hang it from a hook in the
center of the stage ceiling.[1] Extra stage attendants remain in the left upstage corner
of the stage to manipulate the bell later [figure 2.30].*

Nanori flute entrance music   *As the flute plays, the waki (abbot) enters, followed
by the two The stage attendants carry in a large bell prop and hang it from a hook
in the center of the stage wakizure (priests) and the two temple servants (aikyōgen).
The waki goes to center stage, and the others kneel on the bridgeway.*

Nanori   *Spoken, facing front.*

WAKI: I am the abbot of Dōjōji, a temple in the province of Kii. For many years,
   no bell has hung in the belfry tower of the temple, and for a good reason. I
   have decided lately to restore the ancient custom, and at my order a new bell
   has been cast. In the calendar, today is a day of good omen. I have ordered
   that the bell be raised into the tower and that there be a service of dedication.

The waki sits at the waki spot, and the two wakizure sit upstage of the waki.

Mondō   *The waki calls toward the bridgeway.*

   Servant!
WAKI: Have you already raised the bell?
OMOAI (*Approaching the waki, he kneels*): Yes sir, the bell is raised. Please see for
   yourself.
WAKI: Then we will hold the dedication service today. For certain reasons best
   known to me, women are not to be admitted to the courtyard where the
   ceremonies are held. Make sure that everyone understands this.
OMOAI: Your orders shall be obeyed.

He goes to the shite position and faces forward.

---

1. In *shimogakari* schools, the priests (waki and wakizure) enter first and order the servants (aikyōgen) to get the bell. They make a humorous scene out of carrying the bell in and raising it (see Keene
1970:241–42).

Fure

> Listen, you people! The new bell of the Dōjōji is to be dedicated today. All who wish to attend the ceremony are welcome. However, for reasons known only to himself, the abbot has ordered that women not be allowed inside the courtyard where the service will take place. Take care that you all obey his orders!

He walks to the spot in front of the flute player and kneels.

Shū no shidai   *The shite enters to quietly ominous instrumental music. She wears the middle-aged woman's mask (fukai), a long wig, a brocade outer robe, an inner kimono with a fish-scale pattern, and a crested garment tied around her waist. She stops at the shite spot.*

Shidai   *Sung in the dynamic mode as she faces the rear.*

SHITE:

> My sin, my guilt, will melt away,
> my sin, my guilt, will melt away,
> I will go to the service for the bell.

Nanori   *(Spoken as she faces forward)*

> I am a dancer who lives in a remote village of this province of Kii. I have heard that a bell is to be dedicated at the Dōjōji, and so I am hurrying there now, in hopes of improving my chances of salvation.

Ageuta   *Sung in the melodic mode to congruent rhythms of the drums.*

> The moon will soon be sinking;

Instrumental interlude.

> the moon will soon be sinking;
> as I pass the groves of little pines
> the rising tide weaves veils of mist around them,
> but look—can it be my heart's impatience?—

She takes a few steps to the right, then returns to her original position. This indicates that she has reached the temple.

> Dusk has not yet fallen, the sun's still high,[2]
> but I have already arrived;
> I am here at the temple of Dōjōji.

She faces forward.

Tsukizerifu   *(Spoken)*

> My journey has been swift,
>   and now I have reached the temple.
> I shall go at once to watch the ceremony.

---

2. There is a play here on the name of the river Hitaka (sun high), on whose banks the Dōjōji is located.

Mondō *She moves toward the center of the stage. The omoai rises and moves toward the front of the stage [figure 2.31].*

OMOAI: Stop! You can't go into the courtyard. Women aren't allowed. Go away immediately.

SHITE: I am a shirabyōshi dancer who lives nearby, and I am to perform at the dedication of the bell. Please let me see the ceremony.

OMOAI: A dancer? That's right, I suppose she doesn't count as an ordinary woman.[3] *(To the shite)* Very well, I'll let you into the courtyard on my own, but in return you must dance for me. *(He goes in front of the flute player, picks up a tall court cap lying on the stage, and brings it to the shite)* Here, take this hat. It just happened to be around. Put it on, and let's see you dance.

SHITE: With pleasure. I'll dance for you as best I can.

FIGURE 2.31. The omoai, a temple servant dressed in mizugoromo, kukuri-hakama, and a zukin, addresses the shite, a dancer wearing a *shakumi* mask, warning her not to enter the temple grounds. The adoai is seated at the kyōgen spot. (Photo by Monica Bethe.)

Monogi ashirai *To instrumental music, the shite goes to the stage attendants' position to alter her costume, and the omoai returns to the kyōgen spot on the bridgeway and sits beside the adoai. The attendants help the shite put on the tall cap.*

Ashirai *The shite goes to the first pine and stares up at the bell. The taiko drum begins a solo passage, rapidly increasing the tempo, and she moves back onto the stage to the increased tempo of the drums. She stops at the shite spot.*

[Unnamed] *She stands just upstage of the corner.*

SHITE: How happy you have made me! I will dance for you! *(She describes her actions)* Borrowing for a moment a courtier's hat and puts it on her head. Her feet already stamp the rhythm.

Shidai *(Sung in the melodic mode)*

Apart from cherry blossoms,
there are only the pines,
apart from cherry blossoms,
there are only the pines.

---

3. Many texts have a section here in which the servant asks the priest for permission for the woman to enter. Although permission is denied, he allows her to enter anyway, because he wants to see her dance. This is usually omitted in current performance practice. *Kanemaki* has a long passage in which the dancer reveals her reasons for wishing to enter the temple grounds and the depth of her religious understanding.

FIGURE 2.32. The bell has been raised and the shite has donned a tall lacquered hat (*eboshi*) to prepare for the rambyōshi dance, performed to solo shoulder drum accompaniment. The foot movements and posture are unlike those in a regular noh dance. The hip drummer in the top photo is in a resting position; in the bottom photo he has returned to his stool in preparation for the next segment. (Photos by Monica Bethe.)

When the darkness starts to fall
the temple bell will resound.[4]

Rambyōshi *The shite dances to the shoulder drummer's piercing calls, drumbeats, and long pauses. She lifts the hem of her robe a little with her left hand and lifts and stamps her feet as if she were climbing step by step up to the bell. The drumbeats and the dancer's movements are matched, and they are repeated many times, with increasing tension [figure 2.32].*

Rambyōshi utai *Sung in the dynamic mode as the shite continues to dance.*

SHITE:

> Prince Michinari, at the imperial
>> command,
> first raised these sacred walls,
> and because the temple was his
>> work,
> Tachibana no Michinari,
> they called it Dōjōji.[5]

The shite stamps numerous times.

Waka *Sung in the dynamic mode, to noncongruent rhythms.*

CHORUS: To a temple in the
mountains

Kyū no mai *The shite performs a rapid dance to the feverish music of the flute and the three drums.*

Waka *Standing at the shite spot, she holds her open fan in front of her face.*

SHITE:

Now, on this evening in spring,
I have come, I have seen

4. *Kanemaki* includes a kuse scene here detailing the temple's founding.
5. The characters for Michinari may also be pronounced *dōjō*.

CHORUS *(Sung in the dynamic mode to a strong, steady beat [ōnori] as the shite waves her fan to the left and right)*:

> the blossoms scattered with the evening bell;
> the blossoms scatter, the blossoms fall.

Noriji *The singing and dancing continue quickly and rhythmically.*

SHITE:

> And all the while,
> and all the while,

Faces forward.

> at temples everywhere across the land

CHORUS:

> the sinking moon strikes the bell.

The shite moves forward and looks up.

> The birds sing, and frost and snow fill the sky;
> soon the swelling tide will recede.
> The peaceful fishers will show their lights

She stamps, then makes a circle and goes to the corner.

> in villages along the riverbanks—
> and if the watchers sleep when danger threatens,
> I'll not let my chances pass me by!

The servants have become hypnotized by the rhythm of the dance. The dancer looks at the waki and the priests.

CHORUS:

> Up to the bell she stealthily creeps
> Pretending to go on with her dance.

She holds up her fan and looks at the bell.

> She starts to strike it!

She swings the fan back and forth like a bell hammer.

> This loathsome bell, now I remember it!

She unfastens the cord of her hat, then strikes the hat from her hand with a blow of her fan. She stands under the bell.

> Placing her hand on the dragon-head boss,[6]
> she seems to fly upward into the bell.

The dancer rests her hand on the edge of the bell, then leaps up into it. At the same moment the stage assistant loosens the rope and drops the bell over her [figure 2.33].

> She wraps the bell around her,
> she has disappeared.

6. A metal ornament in the shape of a dragon's head on the bell.

FIGURE 2.33. The dancer stands under the bell, touching the inside of the rim; she jumps up as it falls, leaving an empty space between the bell and the floor. (Photos by Monica Bethe.)

Kyōgen Interlude

Mondō *The aikyōgen, who have been drowsing, hypnotized by the dance, wake up, startled by the noise of the bell falling. The omoai tumbles in confusion on the stage, and the adoai falls on the bridgeway.*

BOTH *(Variously)*: Ho! Hi! What was that frightful noise? That awful crashing racket? I'm so frightened, I don't know what I'm doing.

OMOAI: That certainly was a terrible crash. I wonder where the other fellow went. (*He sees the adoai*) Hey there, are you all right?

ADOAI: How about you?

OMOAI: I still don't know.

ADOAI: No wonder. We got so carried away by her dance, we dozed off. Then came that awful bang. What do you think that was?

OMOAI: Do you suppose it was thunder? If it was thunder, there should have been some sort of warning—a little clap or two before the big one. Strange, very strange.

ADOAI: Yes, you're right. Whatever it was, the earth shook something terrible.

OMOAI: I don't think it was an earth-quake. Look—come over here. (*He discovers the bell and claps his hands in recognition*) Here's what made the noise.

ADOAI: You're right!

OMOAI: I hung it up very carefully, but the loop must've snapped. How else could it have fallen?

ADOAI: No. Look. The loop's all right. Nothing's broken. It's certainly a mystery. (*He touches the bell*) Oww! This bell is scorching hot!

OMOAI: Why should falling make it hot? (*He too touches the bell*) Oww! Boiling hot!

ADOAI: It's a problem, all right. What do you suppose it can mean? It's beyond me. Well, we'd better report what's happened. We can't leave things this way.

OMOAI: That's a good idea. Too bad if the abbot heard about it from anyone but us! We've got to do something. But I don't think I should be the one to tell. You tell him.

ADOAI: Telling him is no problem, but it would look peculiar if I went. You tell him—you were left in charge.

OMOAI: That's what makes it so hard! You tell him, please (*he pushes the adoai forward*).

ADOAI: No, it's not my business to tell him. You tell him. Hurry! (*He pushes the omoai.*)

OMOAI: Please, I beg of you, as a favor. You tell him.

ADOAI: Why should I? You tell him. I don't know anything about it.

The adoai leaves, and the omoai watches him go.

OMOAI: He's gone! Now I have no choice. I'll have to tell the abbot, and it's going to get me into trouble. Well, I'll get it over with. (*He goes up to the waki*) It fell down.

WAKI: What fell down?

OMOAI: The bell. It fell from the belfry.

WAKI: What? Our bell? From the belfry?

OMOAI: Yes, Master.

WAKI: What caused it?

OMOAI: I fastened it very carefully, but all the same it fell down. Ah! That reminds me. There was a dancer here a little while ago. She said she lives nearby and asked me to let her into the courtyard to see the dedication of the bell. Of course I told her that it wasn't allowed, but she said she wasn't an ordinary woman and that she was going to offer a dance. So I let her in. I wonder if she had something to do with this?

WAKI: You idiot! What a stupid thing to do! I knew this would happen. That's why I forbade you strictly to allow any women in here! You blundering fool!

OMOAI: Ahhhh (*bows to the ground*).

WAKI: I suppose I must go now and take a look.

OMOAI: Yes, Master. Please hurry. Help! Help!

He exits up the bridgeway, still crying for help.

WAKI (*To the wakizure*): Priests, come with me.

They stand up and go over to the bell.

Do you know why I gave the order that no woman was to be permitted to enter the temple during the dedication of the bell?

WAKIZURE: No, Master. We have no idea.

WAKI: Then I will tell you.

WAKIZURE: Yes, please tell us the whole story.

Katari *Spoken, with the waki at the waki spot facing front and the wakizure standing upstage of him.*

WAKI: Many years ago there lived in this region a man who was the steward of the manor of Manago, and he had an only daughter. In those days, too, there was a certain yamabushi priest who came here every year from the northern provinces on his way to worship at the shrine of Kumano, and he would always stay with this same steward. The priest never forgot to bring charming little presents for the steward's daughter, and the steward, who doted on the girl, as a joke once told her (*faces the wakizure*), "Some day that priest will be your husband, and you will be his wife!" (*Faces front*) In her childish innocence the girl thought he was speaking the truth, and for months and years she waited.

Time passed, and once again the priest came to the landlord's house. Late one night, after everyone else was asleep, the girl went to his bedroom and chided him, "Do you intend to leave me here forever? (*Faces the wakizure*) Claim me soon as your wife."

(*Faces front again*) Amazed to hear these words, the priest turned away the girl with a joking answer. That night he crept out into the darkness and came to this temple, imploring us to hide him. But having nowhere else we could hide him, we lowered the bell (*looks up at the bell*) and hid him inside.

(*Faces the wakizure*) Soon the girl followed (*faces forward*), swearing she would never let him go (*takes three swift steps forward*). At that time the river Hitaka was swollen to a furious flood, and the girl could not cross over. She ran up and down the bank (*looks left and right*), wild with rage, until at last her jealous fury turned her into a venomous snake (*three steps back*), and she easily swam across the river.

The serpent glided here, to the temple of Dōjōji, and searched here and there (*moves forward and looks left and right, then looks suddenly at the bell*) until her suspicions were aroused by the lowered bell (*stares at the bell*). Taking the metal loop between her teeth, she coiled herself around the bell in seven coils. Then, breathing smoke and flames, she lashed the bell with her tail. At once the bronze grew hot, boiling hot (*faces front and claps his hands together*), and the monk, hidden inside, was roasted alive. (*To the priests*) Isn't that a horrible story?

Mondō

WAKIZURE: Unspeakable! The worst I have ever heard!

WAKI: I have felt her jealous ghost around here, and I feared she might bring some harm to our new bell. All our austerities and penances have been for strength in this moment. Pray with all your hearts. Let us try to raise the bell again.

WAKIZURE: We will, Master.

ACT 2

Notto *The waki and wakizure put their fans in their waistbands and take out their Buddhist rosaries. As the instruments begin playing forcefully, they approach the bell [figure 2.34].*

FIGURE 2.34. The priests rub their rosaries and pray to raise the bell. The shite has changed his mask and costume in the dark interior of the bell without the aid of stage attendants. (Photo by Monica Bethe.)

Unnamed *Sung in the dynamic mode.*

WAKI:

Though the waters of Hitaka River seethe and dry up,
though the sands of its shores run out,
can the sacred strength of our holy order fail?

They pray, their rosaries clasped in their hands.

WAKIZURE:

All raise their voices together:[7]

WAKI:

to the East, the Guardian King, Conqueror of the Three Realms;

WAKIZURE:

to the South, the Guardian King, Conqueror of the Demons;

Their hands remaining together in prayer, they stare at the bell.

WAKI:

to the West, the Guardian King, Conqueror of Evil Serpents and Dragons;

WAKIZURE:

to the North, the Guardian King, Conqueror of Frightful Monsters;

WAKI:

and you in the Center, Messenger of the Sun, All-Holy Immovable One,

7. The following passage is a prayer much favored by yamabushi priests for invoking the five *myōō*, or rajas, the messengers of Vairocana's wrath against evil spirits.

ALL THREE (*Holding their rosaries between the palms of their upraised hands, they*
rub them together furiously at each of the following lines):
Will you make the bell move?
Show us the power of your avenging noose!
Namaku samanda basarada
senda makaroshana sowataya
un tarata kamman
"I dedicate myself to the universal diamond,
may this raging fury be destroyed!"[8]
"He who harkens to My Law shall gain enlightenment,
he who knows My Heart will be a Buddha in this flesh."
Now that we have prayed
for the serpent's salvation,
what rancor could it bear us?
As the moon at daybreak

WAKI:
strikes the hanging bell—

Noriji   *Chanted to a steady beat as the priests rub their rosaries.*

CHORUS:
Look! Look! It moves!
Pray with all your hearts!
Pray to raise the bell!

The stage attendants raise the bell a little as the shite shakes it from within.

Here the priests, joining hands,
invoke the sacred spell of the Thousand-Handed One,

The priests back up, slowly rubbing their beads.

the Song of Salvation of the Guardian King,
the Immovable One, the Flaming One.
Black smoke rises from their frantic prayers,

Frantically rubbing their rosaries.

and as they pray,
and as they pray,
though no one strikes the bell,
it sounds!

The shite inside the bell strikes cymbals.

Though no one tugs the rope, the bell begins to dance!

The stage attendants raise the bell up higher, and the shite shakes it.

Soon it rises to the belfry tower,
look! A serpent form emerges!

---

8. This is the mantra of Fudō, the Immovable One, and the following quotation is part of the vow
of Fudō.

Inori *The attendants lift the bell completely. The shite is kneeling, face to the floor, with her brocade robe covering her head. She rises, lowering the robe behind her to reveal her transformation into a demonic figure [figure 2.35]. The flute and drums play strong rhythms as she stands, wraps the robe around her, and tries to drive away the waki. The waki and wakizure pray, trying to subdue her. The shite is driven onto the bridgeway, where she drops her outer robe. Then she is forced back as far as the curtain, only to turn on the waki again, this time making him withdraw. She stands with her back to the shite pillar, throws one arm around it, pauses, and then invades the stage again. She tries to pull down the bell, but the waki forces her to the ground with the power of his rosary. The demon rises again, and during the following passage sung by the chorus, she and the waki struggle.*

Chūnoriji *Chanted in half-beat rhythm as the instruments play loudly. The shite advances and falls back as the waki rubs his beads [figure 2.36].*

FIGURE 2.35. When the bell is raised, the dancer has been transformed into a demonic figure. As she stands, she wraps a robe around her, later shedding it as a serpent would shed its skin. She wears long red hakama, a *hannya* mask, and a red headpiece (*kashira*) and carries a demon's mallet. (Courtesy of Eileen Katō.)

CHORUS:
　　Humbly we ask the help of the Green-Bodied,
　　the Green Dragon of the East,[9]
　　humbly we ask the help of the White-Bodied,
　　the White Dragon of the West;
　　humbly we ask the help of the Yellow-Bodied,
　　the Yellow Dragon of the Center,
　　all ye countless dragon kings of the three thousand worlds;
　　have mercy, hear our prayers!
　　If now you show your mercy, your benevolence,
　　what refuge can the serpent find?
　　And as we pray,
　　defeated by our prayers,
　　behold the serpent fall!

She staggers back under the pressure of the waki's prayers and drops to the ground.

9. This begins the invocation to the five dragon kings, only three of which are included in the play.

Again she springs to her feet,
the breath she vomits at the bell
has turned to raging flames.

She rises and rushes to the bridgeway.

Her body burns in her own fire.
she leaps into the river pool,

She rushes through the curtain.

into the waves of the river Hitaka,
and there she vanishes.
The priests, their prayers granted,
return to the temple,
return to the temple.

*The waki performs the closing stamps
at the shite spot and exits up the
bridgeway, followed by the wakizure.*

FIGURE 2.36. The demon fights against the priests, in a group (*inori*) and then against the waki alone. In the picture at the top, she wears a bold robe wrapped around her hips (*koshimaki*) rather than long hakama. In both cases the upper kimono (*surihaku*) has triangles to suggest the scales of a serpent. (Top: courtesy of the Noh Research Archive of Musashino Women's College; bottom: photo by Monica Bethe.)

Yamamba

A demon play, usually attributed to Zeami

Translated by Monica Bethe and Karen Brazell

Legends about a mysterious old woman (*uba*) living in the mountains (*yama*) have circulated in Japan since early times and form part of the background of *Yamamba*. The mountain woman depicted in the play, like the aggregate of the legends, is an enigma: she is, simultaneously, a benevolent demon, a supernatural human, and an enlightened being tormented by delusive attachments. In short, she seems to be an impossible bundle of contradictions until one understands a major point of the play: "good and evil are not two; right and wrong are the same." This concept of nondualism, popular in medieval Japan, is also developed in the play *Eguchi*, in which a lowly female entertainer is revealed to be an incarnation of a deity. In *Yamamba*, the nature of identity is more complex, largely because of the presence of an entertainer called Hyakuma Yamamba (the tsure), who makes her living performing a song and dance (kusemai) about Yamamba. Reality and its imitation, truth and delusion, human life, nature and art intermingle as the "real" Yamamba appears to entertain the entertainer with the true form of her dance.

The ambiguities of Yamamba's nature are expressed through all aspects of the performance. The text, which describes both her enlightened acts and her tormented sufferings, is sung entirely in the dynamic mode, usually reserved for males or strong deities, and is danced in a mixed style that reflects Yamamba's age, gender, and superhuman qualities. Her worldly travels are enacted in the dance to song in the kuse scene, and the weight of the spiritual burden she carries is expressed in the slow movements of the dance to instrumental music (a tachimawari), emphasized by the addition of the stick drum. In the final dance, when Yamamba is transformed into a mountain demon, the tempo quickens noticeably for the last few moments of the performance.

The costume for Yamamba is always bulky with bold patterns. There is, however, considerable variety among Yamamba masks: the Kanze school version depicts a relatively gentle old woman, but with gold eyes and with teeth revealed; the Kongō school version is painted vermilion and has deep wrinkles on the forehead and cheeks; and an extreme version belonging to the Umewaka family is more like a serpent mask with ears, sunken eye sockets, and an open mouth revealing both teeth and gums (figure 2.37). The mask may be worn with a standard old woman's wig, tied at the nape of the neck, or with the large white headpiece used in the variant performance (*shirogashira kogaki*) presented here.

Conversations About Sarugaku (Sarugaku dangi, 1430) mentions a *Yamamba* performance by Zeami for the shogun Ashikaga Yoshimochi (r. 1394–1423). In the period before 1600, it was presented more times than any other noh play in this anthology (Nose 1938), and it remains popular today. Scholars generally attribute the play to Zeami, who insisted that demons (*oni*) could be ferocious in their form as long as they had human hearts and that the style of their presentation should reveal delicacy within strength (Rimer and Yamazaki 1984:157). Fifth-category, or demon, plays feature a wide range of characters—generally supernatural beings but not necessarily demonic or even fierce. *Tōru*, for example, presents the ghost of an aristocrat celebrating his life on earth. On the other hand, the shite in act 2 of *Funa Benkei* is the avenging ghost of a warrior who is exorcised in the play. Other "demons" include, in *Nue*, the spirit of a fantastic bird and, in *Raiden*, the ghost of Sugawara Michizane, whom we encountered in part 1 as a thunder god.

Bethe and Brazell's translation of *Yamamba* derives from work they began in their earlier studies of performance aspects of noh (1978 and 1982). The text generally follows the Japanese version in Koyama et al. 1975 and Sanari 1931, both of which give full aikyōgen parts, although the translators also referred to Itō 1988 and Yokomichi and Omote 1963.

FIGURE 2.37. This fairly strong version of the Yamamba mask goes well with a large, white headpiece (*shirogashira*). Its open mouth reveals two rows of teeth, and its round eyeballs are gold. Compare this with the gentler mask in figure 2.4. (Photo by Tanaka Masao.)

CHARACTERS

SHITE: in act 1, an old woman; in act 2, Yamamba
TSURE: a dancer called Hyakuma Yamamba
WAKI: her chief attendant
WAKIZURE: other attendants
AI: a local man

MUSICIANS

Chorus of eight to ten members
A flute and two drums; the stick drum enters at the end of the kuse in act 2

ACT 1

Shidai entrance music   *High sharp notes of the flute signal the hand drums to play measured beats punctuated by full drummers' calls. When the flute plays for the third time, the tsure (Hyakuma Yamamba) and her retinue of men from the capital, the waki and the wakizure, enter down the bridgeway and take their places in two rows left and right of center stage. The aikyōgen follows and sits at the kyōgen spot.*

Shidai *The waki, wakizure, and tsure face one another as they sing this formal song.*

TOGETHER:
> Seeking the radiance of beneficent light
> seeking the radiance of beneficent light
> we venture to the Buddha's temple.[1]

Nanori *The waki faces front to speak.*

WAKI: We live in the capital, and the lady with us is an entertainer known to one and all as Hyakuma Yamamba. The neighborhood kids call her that because she performs a song she composed about Yamamba making her mountain rounds.[2] Hyakuma decided to make a pilgrimage to the Temple of Good Light, Zenkōji, and she asked us to accompany her. We are now on our way to Zenkōji in Shinano Province.

Sashi *Facing one another they sing this noncongruent song (awazu) describing the places they pass.*

WAKI AND WAKIZURE:
> With the capital behind us, ripples run along
> Shiga's shore, where we boat across the lake burdened
> by yearnings and follow rough roads to Arachi,
> gemlike dew drops on our sleeves at Tamae, whose
> suspension bridge we traverse, then lengthy Koshi roads,
> trudging anxiously onward, farther and farther.[3]

Instrumental interlude (uchikiri).

Ageuta *Congruent travel song. The hand drums mark the beat quietly, and the flute bridges the break between the first two lines and embellishes the last.*

> Waving stands of treetops, tides at Shiokoshi,

Instrumental interlude.

> waving stands of treetops, tides at Shiokoshi,
> the pines of Ataka shrouded in evening smoke that
> lingers as do sins in our sad lives, only severed

---

1. This is a play on the name Zenkōji, "good light temple." "Beneficent light" (*yoki hikari*) suggests the temple's name.

2. A kusemai, a medieval dance-to-song entertainment performed by female dancers. The noh play *Hyakuman* features a kusemai dancer of that name, which may have inspired the character Hyakuma Yamamba.

3. This passage is filled with poetic wordplay: ripples are an epithet (*makura kotoba*) for Shiga; *kogaru* can mean "to row a boat" and "to worry or yearn"; Arachi is a homonym for "rough roads"; and Tamae means Jewel Inlet. They are traveling northeast through the provinces bordering the Japan Sea. The Koshi road passes through three provinces, each using in their names the character pronounced either *koshi* or *echi*: Echizen, Etchū, and Echigo.

by Amida's sword, honed sharp as Tonami peak[4]
on whose cloudy paths we hasten through three
provinces and, in a remote village, ask our
whereabouts; far, distant from the capital,
we have arrived at Boundary River,

Drum interlude (uchikiri).

we have arrived at Boundary River.

The tsure goes and sits at the waki spot, and the wakizure sit in a row in front of the chorus. The waki goes to the shite spot.

Tsukizerifu   *The waki faces front to speak, without instrumentation.*

WAKI: We have traveled quickly and already reached Boundary River between Etchū and Echigo Provinces. From here, the roads diverge. I shall seek directions from a local person. (*To the tsure*) Please remain here awhile.

Mondō   *Speech.*

WAKI: Is there anyone around from Boundary River?
AI (*Stands at the kyōgen spot*): What is it you want, a native of Boundary River?
WAKI: We come from the capital. Could you tell us how to get to Zenkōji?
AI: Certainly. There are several paths from here to Zenkōji: the upper way, the lower way, and Agero Pass. Agero Pass is the path Amida himself takes as he descends to receive souls. Following this path is an initiation into the secrets of Buddhahood, but it is perilously steep and you seem to be accompanying a well-born lady. The road is impossible for a litter.
WAKI: Thank you for your kind explanation. I will consult with my mistress. Please wait here a moment. *The aikyōgen sits.*

Mondō   *The waki goes to stage center, faces the tsure, and kneels.*

WAKI: When I asked about the road to Zenkōji, I was told that there are several ways to go. Among them, the Agero Pass is compared to walking with Amida, his Pure Land in your heart. However, it is too perilous for a litter.
TSURE (*Remains seated*): The Western Pure Land is usually said to be a hundred thousand leagues away. If Agero Pass is the direct route to Amida's welcome, then that is the path we must follow. This is, after all, a pilgrimage. We will leave the litter here and proceed on foot as befits a true pilgrim. Please guide me.
WAKI: I shall do what I can.

The waki stands, goes to the shite spot, and calls the ai again. The ai stands [figure 2.38].

WAKI: Where is the man I spoke with before?

AI: I am here.

---

4. The dense wordplay continues: *namitatsu* refers both to "standing in a row" and "waves rising"; Tsurugi no Tonami, a place-name, incorporates a sword (*tsurugi*) and a whetstone (the character used to write *To*). Amida's sword refers to lines in a hymn by a priest named Zendō: "Amida's name is a sharp sword; call on it once and all transgressions are cut away."

FIGURE 2.38. Hyakuma's retainer (the waki, dressed in a *suō*, ordinary male attire) asks a local man (aikyōgen, wearing *naga-kamishimo* over a striped *noshime*) the way to the Temple of Light (Zenkōji). (Photo by Karen Brazell.)

WAKI: I have consulted my mistress. We will leave the litter here and proceed by foot. Would you be our guide?

AI: Willingly, but other responsibilities make it impossible right now.

WAKI: If there is any way at all you can arrange it, I implore you to be our guide.

AI: Well, if you insist, I'll put off my other business and lead you. Let's get started quickly.

WAKI: Thank you. We are ready.

The waki turns to face the tsure, who stands, as do the wakizure. The waki joins them in the front of the chorus, and the ai goes to the shite spot.

Mondō   *Speech.*

AI: As you can see, the way is even more perilous than I indicated.

WAKI: It's actually more difficult than I expected.

AI: A litter would be out of the question. (*Looks up at the sky*) What's this? It seems to be getting dark already (*looks toward the waki*).

WAKI: You're right. The sun has set too quickly. Is there some place to stay around here?

AI: No, there's no place at all.

WAKI (*Faces front*): How very strange! It's the middle of the day, no time for the sun to go down, yet suddenly it's getting dark. What shall we do?

Mondō   *The shite speaks from behind the curtain at the end of the bridgeway.*

SHITE: Hello there, hellooo. I will give you lodgings.

AI (*To the waki*): She's offering you a place to stay.

The ai returns to the kyōgen spot.

SHITE (*Entering down the bridgeway*): Mount Agero is far from human habitation. The day is over, so why not spend the night in my thatched hut?

The shite stops at the third pine and faces the waki, who moves to stage center.

WAKI: What good fortune. We will gratefully stay with you.

The shite enters the stage proper and kneels at center stage. Meanwhile the tsure, waki, and wakizure sit in a row from the waki spot along the front of the chorus. This indicates that they have entered the house.

Mondō   *The shite begins to sing slowly, but in a determined fashion in non-congruent rhythm.*

SHITE: I have a special reason for offering you lodgings tonight. (*Switches to speech*) Please sing the song about Yamamba for me. I have wanted to hear it for a long time, and you can imagine what a treasured memory it would be for a country person like myself. (*Faces front and switches to song*) This is the reason I made the sun go down and offered you a place to stay. (*Faces the tsure*) Come, you must sing for me.

WAKI (*To the shite, in speech*): Your request is most unexpected. Whom do you think you are addressing with your appeal for the song of Yamamba?

SHITE (*Turning to the waki, in a somewhat forceful speech*): What are you trying to hide? Isn't it true that the entertainer you accompany is the well-known Hyakuma Yamamba? Now then, the opening lines of the song runs something like this (*faces front*):

Dragging good and evil, Yamamba
makes her mountain rounds.

So fascinating. (*Raises her head after a thoughtful moment*) This woman takes her name from the kusemai (*turns to the waki*), but does she have any idea what the true Yamamba is like?

WAKI: Judging from the kusemai, Yamamba is a demoness dwelling in the mountains.

SHITE (*As if talking to herself*): Isn't a demoness a female demon? (*Lifting her head definitively*) Well, whether demon or human, if you're talking about (*turning to the waki*) a woman who lives in the mountains, doesn't that fit my situation?

Singing, turning to the front.

For years you have given form to sheaves of words,
yet no longer than the dew lies on the grass
does your heart concern itself with what you sing.

Speaking, facing the tsure.

I have come to express my resentment.

Singing, facing front.

You have attained the highest level of your art;
your reputation blossoms, a "wondrous flower of earthly splendor."[5]
Isn't it all because of this single piece?
Since that is the case, you should pray for me.
Let the vibrant strains of your music
and dance serve as a Buddhist sacrament
for then I, too, will escape from transmigration
and return to the blessed state of enlightenment.[6]

Sageuta *Sung deliberately to congruent drums in the background.*

5. Zeami uses this phrase in the *Fushikaden* (Omote and Katō 1974:46; Rimer and Yamazaki 1984:42).

6. There is probably a play here on the sounds *kishō*, which can mean "demonic nature" or "return to (enlightened) nature." In the Buddhism advocated here, enlightenment is inherent; one has only to recognize it. The idea was widely held in the medieval period that song and dance, as well as other arts, could function as a means to salvation.

SHITE (*Looking up*):
> My resentment echoes through the night
> mountains; beasts and birds add their cries,
> lifting their voices to Agero's Yamamba;[7]

Speaking heavily, she turns to the tsure.

> whose fiendish wraith has come before you now.

Kakeai   *The pace accelerates.*

TSURE (*To the shite*):
> What strange things I am hearing!
> You say the true Yamamba has come here?

SHITE (*Facing the tsure and speaking deliberately*):
> In the course of my mountain rounds
> today I have come here especially
> that I might ascertain the merits of my name.
> Please sing your song and thus dispel
> my illusory attachments

TSURE (*Sings quickly, to noncongruent drums*) Under these circumstances, I fear to refuse. Who knows what harm would come to me? She chooses a scale appropriate to the time and season, and strikes the beat—

SHITE (*Speaking roughly*): Just a moment, please. (*Lifts her head*) If you're willing to perform, wait for the night to deepen and sing in the moonlight, then I will appear in my true form.

She begins to rise, then kneels, and sings ponderously.

> Indeed, the faint evening moon already glimmers,

Ageuta   *Sung with new feeling to congruent drums.*

SHITE (*Rising to look at the western sky*):
> and not only that, but
> deep in the mountains, as though to hasten darkness

CHORUS:
> deep in the mountains, as though to hasten darkness
> clouds converge; concentrate your heart on them,

The shite stands.

> sing the song of Yamamba (*turns to the tsure*),
> the whole night through,
> and I will reveal my form,
> sleeve to sleeve will I

Points with her left hand to the tsure and looks.

> trace out your dance with you,
> she says, or seems to, and then

---

7. Another passage centered on wordplay: *urami o iuyama* contains both "to speak resentment" and "evening mountain"; and *koe o agero yamauba* contains "raise voices," "Mount Agero," and "mountain hag."

She circles to the shite spot, circles, and looks down.

> like a flame flickering out, she disappears;
> like a flame flickering out, she disappears.

The shite exits up the bridgeway.

Kyōgen Interlude

AI *(He stands and goes to the shite spot)*: Just as I suspected. It's light again. That was really strange. I knew it shouldn't have gotten dark yet. There's the sun still high in the sky. I have never experienced anything like this. It's very odd.

Mondō *Goes to stage center, faces the waki, and kneels.*

AI: What do you think? It's gotten light again.

WAKI: Yes, that was bizarre.

AI: I knew it wasn't time for dusk to fall, and now suddenly the sun is high in the sky again, bright as can be. When it first got dark, I thought I'd made a mistake and should have put you up at Boundary River. I'm relieved it's light again.

WAKI: Is this normal in the mountains? And tell me, who in fact is this Yamamba?

AI: It is not at all normal. I live close to the heart of the mountains, and I've never experienced anything like this before. As you're aware, Boundary River is near the mountains; still I don't know much about that mountain crone, Yamamba. But I could tell you one or two tales I've heard from others.

Katari

> They say that Yamamba is a conglomerate of many things. First, it is said that her head is a crocodile gong worn out from hanging too long at an old shrine and discarded when the shrine was rebuilt.

WAKI: Why a crocodile gong?

AI: Well, the crocodile gong, as you must know, got its name because of its gaping mouth. The gong's mouth became Yamamba's mouth; acorns became her eyes; a walnut her nose; mushrooms her ears; and vines her hair. Her body, they say, is most odd. The resin from many pines on a large mountain oozed together in a single mass, and when a strong wind blew, it rolled over and over until it collided with the crocodile gong I just mentioned, and the two became one and kept rolling, and the more it rolled, the more dust and debris stuck on it, making it bigger and bigger until it got to be what we know as Yamamba, the mountain crone. And that's how it must have been.

WAKI: That's rather difficult to believe.

AI: Well, that's the way I heard it, but I don't know how true it is. On the other hand, people also say that a hatch from some fortifications deep in the mountains became Yamamba.

WAKI: What do you mean?

AI: Well, once an enormous gate house was built and then left to rot without any repairs. The longer it was left, the more it rotted, until all that remained was the hatch. Moss covered it, and somehow some eyes, a nose, a mouth, ears, hands, and legs all attached themselves to it, and Yamamba came into being. That's what they say, and that must be the way it was.

WAKI: That doesn't sound very likely either.

AI: But that's why they call her a mountain hatch.

WAKI: You must mean mountain hag, not mountain hatch.[8]

AI: I guess I haven't been making sense, have I? A man from the capital like you can probably explain it much more logically. Ah, I forgot, there is one more thing they say became Yamamba. What was it now? Ah yes, an old field potato.

WAKI: Why is that?

AI: Well, when it rains day and night, there is always a landslide somewhere in the mountains. At the head of one such slide, the top of an old field potato lay exposed. It was soaked by rain and dew, and its hair—you know that potatoes sprout what are called whiskers, don't you—well, its hair turned white. The potato itself became a body, and bit by bit, eyes, mouth, ears, nose, feet, and hands appeared, and soon it became Yamamba, born of the mountain. That must be how it was.

WAKI: Most unlikely.

AI: That won't do either? I'm sure that's how the story goes, though it is a bit far-fetched for a potato to turn into Yamamba.

Mondō

Whatever the stories, I can't say I really know what Yamamba is. Now, what I would like to know is who that lady over there is.

WAKI: Why, that is the dancer Hyakuma Yamamba.

AI: Is that so? Now I understand why that woman who was here said that if the lady sings the piece about Yamamba, the real Yamamba will appear. I advise you to have her sing immediately. Then you can verify what Yamamba is like with your very own eyes.

WAKI: That's probably a good idea.

The ai returns to the kyōgen seat. He exits inconspicuously up the bridgeway during the next section.

ACT 2

[Unnamed] *Noncongruent song.*

TSURE *(Kneeling at the waki spot):*
    This is too mysterious to believe:
    that demoness cannot be real, and yet
    do I dare deny her request, she wonders and waits as

Ageuta *Hand drums play congruently with the song.*

WAKI AND WAKIZURE:

    wind in the pines joined by the flute;

Instrumental interlude.

8. The Japanese wordplay is *kido,* "wooden door," for *kijo,* "demon woman."

wind in the pines joined by the flute
reverberate, limpid and clear, across
the valley where from winding river waters
poets' hands seize goblets[9] moonlit,
clear voices deep in the mountains;
clear voices deep in the mountains.

Issei *The hand drums play with gathering momentum, punctuated by awesome calls from the drummers. Strains of flute music call forth the figure of Yamamba. Using a thick walking stick, she approaches ominously along the bridgeway and stops at the first pine.*

SHITE *(Facing front, she sings with restrained vigor):*
    Awesome, the deep ravines,
    Awesome, the deep ravines.

Sashi *Noncongruent song, very intense.*

    In graveyards, beating their own bones, fiendish wraiths
    groan, bemoaning their deeds from former lives.
    In cemeteries, offering flowers, angelic spirits
    rejoice in the good rewards of enlightened acts.

Takes two steps forward and sings insistently.

    No! Good and evil are not two.
    What is there to bemoan? (*Turns right*) What to rejoice in?

Facing front, sings deliberately.

    In this world, a myriad entities appear before the eyes:

With both hands on the walking stick in front of her, she looks up and out.

    rushing rivers descending far,
    craggy peaks soaring high.

Kuri *An ornate song with an elaborate flute cadence.*

    Mountains beyond mountains,
    whose skill sculpted those azure cliffs?
    Waters beyond waters,
    in whose house were their jade colors dyed?[10]

During a drum interlude, the shite goes to the shite spot.

Kakeai *The tsure faces the shite during a quiet song.*

TSURE:
    How fearsome! From moonless forest depths
    and mountain shade appears a strange, unearthly form.

---

9. At poetry gatherings beside meandering streams (*kyokusui no en*), the poets were supposed to complete a poem before a saké cup floated past their positions on the stream. They would then take the cup and drink from it.

10. This is from a poem in Chinese by Ōe no Sumiakira (d. 950), which is poem 1013 in the *Wakan rōeishū*.

FIGURE 2.39. The shite raises a hand to indicate Yamamba's hair: "a thicket of snowy brambles." The design in the outer robe (*atsuita*) combines the scales of a serpent or demon with wheels of fortune. (Photo by Tanaka Masao.)

Could this be that mountain
   crone, Yamamba?
SHITE (*Deliberate speech*):
   From words that sprouted forth
      before
   and by this shape, you should
      know me.
   Do not be afraid of me!
TSURE (*Singing*):
   Yet I do fear, old woman,
   the ebony gloom from which
      emerges
   a shape with speech that's human,
SHITE:
   a thicket of snowy brambles for
      hair [figure 2.39],
TSURE:
   with eyes that sparkle like stars,
SHITE:
   and a face that's
TSURE:
   painted red —
SHITE:

a demon gargoyle crouching at the eaves —

Looks up to the right.

TSURE:

this apparition, perceived for the first time tonight,

SHITE:

to what does it compare?

TOGETHER:

The demon of the ancient tale, who

Ageuta   *Congruent hand drum accompaniment.*

CHORUS:

devoured a maiden in a single gulp one rainy night,
devoured a maiden in a single gulp one rainy night
as thunder clapped with a fearsome roar

The shite advances.

that night, after the maiden had asked

Series of stamps.

"What are these? Pearls?"[11]

11. In *Ise monogatari*, episode 6, a lady asks her lover what the dew is just before she is devoured by a demon during a storm. In his grief the lover wishes he could have vanished as easily as the dew and his love (McCullough 1968:73).

She spreads her arms and steps back during the drum interlude.

    Should that be my fate? To become the subject of

Circles left with charged feeling.

    a woeful tale told throughout the world—how shameful!

She stops at the shite spot and faces the tsure.

    a woeful tale told throughout the world—how shameful!

Facing front, she looks down; the flute plays plaintively.

Kakeai   *Spoken deliberately with the tsure kneeling at the waki spot and the shite standing at the shite spot.*

SHITE:
    The poet refused to trade a spring night
    for a thousand pieces of gold, so greatly he loved
    the fragrance of the flowers, the light of the moon.[12]
    Nor would I exchange this precious night,
    when my cherished desire to meet this very person
    and hear her single song will be fulfilled.
    Quickly, I beg you, sing quickly!

TSURE:
    I can find no words to refuse
    in the silence of these mountain depths,

SHITE:
    a warbler bursts into song, flaps its wings,

Flaps her arms together.

TSURE:
    drums of cascading waves,

SHITE:
    sleeves of shimmering white,

Looks at her left sleeve.

TSURE:
    swirls of snow from blossoming trees.

SHITE:
    Is there anything

TSURE:
    not encompassed in Buddhist Law?[13]

Shidai   *The hand drums play formal, intermeshing patterns. The shite stands at the shite spot.*

CHORUS:
    good and evil dragging, Yamamba

---

12. A poem by Su Shih (1036–1101) that is often quoted in noh and elsewhere.
13. Embedded in this passage is the name *Naniwa*, a place famous for reeds; *yoshi* and *ashi*, words that can also be read as "good" and "bad." *Ashi* is then reread with *biki* as "foot-dragging."

dragging good and evil, Yamamba
makes her mountain rounds in pain;
dragging good and evil, Yamamba
makes her mountain rounds in pain.

The shite turns her back to the audience, gives her staff to the stage attendant, and takes out her fan. She turns and goes to center stage, where she sits on a stool that the stage attendant placed there.

Kuri *Hand drums play continuous beats, and the flute adds elaborate embellishments at the end. This is ornately sung with momentum.*

SHITE:

Mountains are said to rise from dust piled up
till, hung with clouds, a thousand rows of peaks;

CHORUS:

oceans swell from dewdrops trickling off the moss
till, on boundless seas, countless billows surge.

Sashi *The drums beat noncongruently in the background. The song has a weighted flow.*

SHITE:

Vast and empty valley voice
reverberates through treetops, echoes
awaken ears to voiceless sound.[14]

CHORUS *(Sung more lightly)*:

Oh, that valley where voices find no echo—
that wished-for place, could this be it?[15]

SHITE *(Slowly and fully)*:

Especially in the landscape of my lofty home:
mountains soaring high, oceans near;
valleys dipping deep, waters far.

CHORUS *(Quickened pace)*:

Before, in brimming waters of the sea
the moon shines down the light of Truth.
Behind, in towering peaks of pine,
the wind wrecks dreams of constant bliss.[16]

SHITE *(More heavily)*:

From decaying bulrush whips, sparks of fireflies disappear;

14. In the *Chuang Tzu*, the man of kingly virtue "sees in the darkest dark, hears where there is no sound. In the midst of darkness, he alone sees the dawn; in the midst of the soundless, he alone hears harmony" (Watson 1968:128).

15. In a Buddhist text known as the *Seven Women Sutra* (Shichinyo kyō), the deity Taishaku (Indra) offers to fulfill the desires of seven women. They reveal their spiritual attainments and confound Taishaku by requesting such things as a shadowless precipice, an echoless valley, and a rootless tree. These images are widely used metaphors for enlightenment.

16. These and the following two lines appear in book 10 of the *Gempei seisuiki*. They are found written on a sliding screen in the hut where the father of Yasuyori, one of the three exiles in *Shunkan on Devil Island* (translated in part 3), had retired and died. They describe part of the landscape of Amida's descent to earth to greet the souls of the dead.

deepening moss deadens drums till
even birds are not alarmed.[17]

The shite faces Hyakuma.

So it has been said.

Faces front again.

Kuse *The hand drums urge on the narrative,
marking the formal division of the segment with
special patterns. The flute embellishes set spots.*

CHORUS:
Surrounded by trees near and far,
unsure of directions deep in the
    mountains,
faint and forlorn, a small bird cries out[18]
how unearthly a sound
the ringing of a woodsman's ax only
makes the mountain stillness greater.[19]
Sacred peaks soaring

She turns right and looks up.

suggest ascent to enlightenment:
lightless valleys deep

Faces front.

betoken grace descending to mankind

Turns right and stamps.

even to the center of the earth.[20]

*She swings her arm so that her fan points down;
she looks down and stamps [figure 2.40].
During the drum interlude, the shite stands.*

And then there is Yamamba:
birthplace unknown, lodgings uncertain,

Stamps, then moves forward and points.

wandering with clouds and streams,
no mountain depths unreachable.

17. From a Chinese couplet (*Wakan rōeishū*, poem 663), which depicts an ideal realm where government and punishment (whips) are unnecessary.

18. A slight variation of poem 29 of the *Kokinshū* (McCullough 1985:19).

19. Lines from a poem by the renowned Chinese poet Tu Fu (712–770).

20. According to Buddhist cosmology, the earth is supported by four disks. The earth disk is supported by the golden disk (*konrinzai*, translated here as the "center of the earth"). Underneath are the water and wind disks.

FIGURE 2.40. Two versions of the gesture emphasizing that grace descends "even to the center of the earth." The shite is sitting on a stool, actually a round lacquer box. The costumes are the same pieces (*atsuita* and *hangiri*) with different designs. (Photos by Tanaka Masao.)

SHITE *(Opens her fan and sings with strength):*
Certainly she cannot be human.
CHORUS:
With shifting form, like drifting clouds,

The shite goes to the left and stamps.

temporarily transforming self,

Goes right and then to downstage center.

by attachment transfigured, a she-demon
appears before our eyes; however,
when right and wrong are seen as one,[21]
form itself is emptiness, and likewise[22]

Goes to the corner, circles, and then circles left to upstage center.

Buddhism entails worldliness;
passions imply enlightenment,
buddhas, living creatures,

Points her sweeping fan to the right to indicate the audience.

living creatures, Yamamba:

Waves her arm to indicate herself.

"willows are green,
blossoms crimson," colors diverse.[23]

Spreads her arms, moves backward, and stamps. The feeling changes, and the pace speeds up.

Then, too, she sports with humans:

Stamps and zigzags across the stage to the corner.

sometimes when a woodsman rests
beside a mountain path beneath the blossoms,[24]
she shoulders his heavy burden and,

Kneels, placing her fan near her shoulder [figure 2.41].

with the moon, comes out the mountain

Looks up at the moon and stands.

going with him to the village below.

21. This phrase is half of a well-known couplet: "good and evil are not two; wrong and right are one" (*zennaku funi, jashō ichinyo*). Yamamba quoted the first phrase when she entered at the beginning of this act.

22. "Form itself is emptiness; emptiness itself is form" (*shiki sokuze kū; kū sokuze shiki*) is an often quoted phrase from the *Heart Sutra* (Hannya kyō).

23. The phrase "Willows are green, blossoms crimson" is often used in Buddhist discourse to show that natural phenomena are emptiness; things simply are. *Iroiro* can mean various colors or simply various or diverse. The character for *iro* also designates passion and phenomenon or form (usually read *shiki* in this case, as in the previous note). Noh often exploits all three levels of meaning.

24. Ōtomo no Kuronushi's poetry is described in the preface to the *Kokinshū* as being poor in form, like "a mountain man carrying a load of wood resting in the shade of the blossoms."

She gazes toward the bridge, then goes to the shite spot and faces front.

> At other times, where weaving girls
> work looms, she enters the window,

Advances and then steps in with high stamps.

> a warbler in willows winding threads,

Points high.

> or she places herself in spinning sheds
> to help humans, and yet

Circles left to the flute, then goes to center stage.

> women whisper—it is

Turns to the left, right, and front.

> an invisible demon they see.[25]

Spreads her arms as she moves backward, stamps.

SHITE (*In a weighted voice*):
> This sad world, an empty husk or battered cloak

CHORUS (*The tempo picks up*):
> whose unbrushed sleeves hold frost

Zigzags to downstage center.

> buried by the cold night moon.
> When wearied beaters pause to rest,
> a thousand, ten thousand, voices[26]

Stamps.

> burst from the fulling block:

Flaps her arms together.

> It is Yamamba's doing!

Looks at Hyakuma and circles left to the shite spot.

> Return to the capital;
> tell the world these tales.

She points from her chest to Hyakuma, pauses, and resumes more slowly.

> But think! Is this still delusion?

Pointing, she goes to the corner and extends her fan.

> Brush it all away, everything, for
> dragging good and evil, Yamamba

FIGURE 2.41. Miming with an open fan (top), Yamamba "shoulders the heavy burden" of a woodsman. In the tachimawari dance, she performs a similar movement pattern using a staff (*tsue*) to suggest that she is burdened by her unenlightened state. (Photos by Tanaka Masao.)

25. The preface to the *Kokinshū* asserts that poetry "stirs the feelings of deities and demons invisible to the eye."
26. A well-known line by Po Chü-i (772–846), poem 345 in the *Wakan rōei shū*.

Circles left to upstage center.

makes her mountain rounds (*slows*) in pain.

Turns to the left, right, and front.

SHITE (*Sung with full embellishment, with the noncongruent stick drum intensifying the beat*):
   Foot-dragging

CHORUS:
   mountain rounds.

Drum interlude. The shite goes to the shite spot. Facing the rear, she gets her walking stick from the stage attendant and then turns to face forward.

Tachimawari   *To slow, weighted beats of the three drums and long drawn-out notes on the flute, the shite paces around the stage leaning on her staff. At center stage, she kneels and lays the stick across her shoulder as though shouldering a heavy burden [see figure 2.41]. She rises and returns to the shite spot.*

SHITE (*Deliberately, to noncongruent drums*):
   To shelter under a single tree, draw water from a single stream,
      these acts cause links in other lives; much stronger our bond
      for you sing my name, wandering round this sad world,

Faces the waki.

   a single song: foolish words, fancy phrases
      lead straight to praising Buddha's way!

Kneels and looks down.

   How I regret that now

Noriji   *The drums, led by the repeated patterns of the stick drum, set a pulsing beat. The song matches the whole beats.*

SHITE:
   I must take my leave and return to the mountains.

CHORUS:
   In spring, waiting for the treetops to bloom,

SHITE:
   I seek out the blossoms, making my mountain rounds.

Goes to the bridgeway behind the third pine.

CHORUS:
   In autumn, seeking the radiant light,

She faces front, lifts her hair from in front of her eyes, and looks up.

SHITE:
   I go to moon-viewing spots, making my mountain rounds.

Goes to the corner, makes a small circle, and looks up.

CHORUS:
   In winter's crisp cold, when storm clouds gather,

SHITE:

I summon forth snow, making my mountain rounds.

Circles left to upstage center.

CHORUS:

Around and around

She drops her stick and makes a small circle.

CHORUS:

bound to fate, clouds of delusion,

She takes off her outer robe and pulls it over her head with both hands.

SHITE:

like bits of dust, mount up to become Yamamba,

She crouches low and then stands, slowly raising her robe high over her head with outspread arms. She then drops her robe, and a stage attendant retrieves it.[27]

CHORUS *(The pace quickens dramatically)*:

a demoness in form. "Look, look!"

Zigzags to downstage center.

she soars up peaks, resounds down valleys.

She leaps up and lands in a kneeling position, raising her fan high and looking down.

Until now she was here, or so it seemed,

Stands and moves backward, stamping.

mountain after mountain, making mountain rounds,

She goes up the bridgeway, stops in front of the curtain, and circles.

her destination never to be known.

Closing stamps.

27. This use of the robe occurs in the "white headpiece" variation (*shirogashira kogaki*) of the play. In the standard performance, the sense of a growing mass is created more subtly by stretching the body and raising and spreading the arms.

Two Daimyō
(Futari daimyō)

A daimyō play

Translated by Richard McKinnon

Daimyō, literally "big name," is the appellation used for members of the warrior class who controlled large (*dai*) parcels of land (*myōden*, "land in the name of"). Although by the seventeenth century, the term referred to only 260 or 270 families, the daimyō depicted in kyōgen are far less lordly. They often are, as in this play, not only lacking in the accoutrements of grandeur but wanting in finesse and intelligence as well. This play is often cited as an example of the "lower classes overpowering the upper classes" (*gekokujō*), a concept used, perhaps too freely, to describe medieval Japan. Plays such as this one do make it clear, however, that censorship did not forbid poking fun at the daimyō class.

The insertion of a mime within the central mime of the play itself—a play within a play as it were—is a common technique in kyōgen. In *Two Daimyō*, when a passerby is goaded into carrying a warrior's sword, he uses the sword to force the warrior and his companion to entertain him (and the audience) by mimicking dogs, cocks, and, finally, armless weighted dolls that spring up each time they are knocked over. Similarly, in the play *The Persimmon Priest* (Kaki yamabushi), an orchard owner, sighting a mountain priest in his persimmon tree, makes him howl like a dog, scratch himself and chatter like a monkey, and, finally, fly like a bird. As might be expected, the once arrogant priest ends up on the ground with a hurt hip.

Another common practice in kyōgen is the recycling of successful plots. For example, in the play *Seaweed Seller* (Kobu uri), a seaweed merchant forced to carry a daimyō's sword uses it to compel the warrior to sell his seaweed, hawking the produce first by chanting in the style of the Heike storytellers and then by singing and dancing. Like the man in *Two Daimyō*, the seaweed merchant runs off with the swords. The two swords of the samurai (one long, one short) were more than weapons of defense; by the Tokugawa period they were emblems of class, and nonsamurai were not permitted to own them.

Two Daimyō develops a kind of communal "rapture" (the term is from Berberich 1989), which also is created in *The Snail* (also translated in this book). The two daimyō and the messenger become so engrossed in their singing and miming that they temporarily forget about everything else; the messenger, however, realizing his advantage, runs off with the daimyōs' swords and clothes.

This translation of the Izumi school text was originally published in Richard McKinnon's anthology *Selected Plays of Kyōgen* (1968). An annotated Japanese text is available in Koyama 1960.

CHARACTERS

SHITE: daimyō 1
ADO: daimyō 2
KOADO: messenger (in the Ōkura school this character is a passerby)

MUSICIANS

None

A Play in One Act

*Daimyō 1 enters carrying a sword and goes to the shite spot. Daimyō 2 follows him
and sits at the rear of the stage.*

DAIMYŌ 1: I am a daimyō of distinction. It is such a lovely day that I plan to go on
an outing. I have a good friend whom I promised to invite along when I go. I'll
call for him on the way. I should get started. (*Moves forward*) I certainly hope
he is at home. If he is, I'm sure he will join me. (*Circles the stage to indicate
travel*) Ah, here I am already. I will call on him. Hello. Is anyone home?

DAIMYŌ 2 (*Standing*): Somebody's at the gate. (*Goes to the waki spot*) Who is it?

DAIMYŌ 1: It is I.

DAIMYŌ 2: Oh, you. What brings you here?

DAIMYŌ 1: It's such a lovely day. I thought I'd go on an outing. I promised to
invite you when I went, so I stopped by to see if you'd like to come along. Will
you join me?

DAIMYŌ 2: Fortunately, I'm not doing anything today. I'd be happy to accompany
you.

DAIMYŌ 1: Let's go then.

DAIMYŌ 2: Very well.

DAIMYŌ 1: Let's be on our way.

DAIMYŌ 2: All right.

*The two, more or less in single file, circle the stage in a slowly paced movement
using the entire width of the stage. The movement is more in a triangular pattern,
with variations woven into each triangle. They stop now and then. The dialogue is
continuous throughout the action.*

DAIMYŌ 1: I sent all my servants out on errands. This is why I'm carrying my ceremonial sword.

DAIMYŌ 2: You should've told me sooner. I would've had one of my servants carry
it for you.

DAIMYŌ 1: It's no trouble. If someone suitable comes along, I'll have him carry it.

DAIMYŌ 2: An excellent thought.

DAIMYŌ 1: Well, here we are, out in the fields.

DAIMYŌ 2: Yes, indeed.

DAIMYŌ 1: There's something wonderful about the fresh green fields of spring.

DAIMYŌ 2: Once you know what it's like out here, you simply can't sit around the house.

DAIMYŌ 1 (*Stops at center stage*): How about stopping here for a while?

DAIMYŌ 2 (*At the shite spot*): Fine. (*They both go to the waki spot and sit.*)

MESSENGER (*Enters down the bridgeway and stops at the shite spot*): I'm on an urgent errand to the other side of the mountain. I'm in a hurry. Master's orders are the master's orders. Day after day, it goes on like this.

DAIMYŌ 1: There comes a good prospect. I'll speak to him.

DAIMYŌ 2: Good idea! (*Both stand.*)

DAIMYŌ 1: Can I speak to you for a minute?

MESSENGER: Me?

DAIMYŌ 1: Where are you from, and where are you going?

MESSENGER: I'm on an urgent errand to the other side of the mountain.

DAIMYŌ 1: I stopped you to ask if you would accompany us.

MESSENGER: I see you're persons of high rank. It wouldn't be appropriate for me to accompany you. If you'll excuse me, I'll be on my way.

DAIMYŌ 1: Wait! Some people make suitable company, some don't. Please join us.

MESSENGER: You really mean it?

DAIMYŌ 1: Yes, I insist.

MESSENGER: In that case, I will.

DAIMYŌ 1: You lead the way.

MESSENGER: No, you.

DAIMYŌ 1 (*Turning to Daimyō 2*): Why don't you lead the way?

DAIMYŌ 2: No, you go first.

DAIMYŌ 1: In that case, I will.

DAIMYŌ 2: Excellent.

DAIMYŌ 1 (*Turning to the messenger*): Shall we go?

MESSENGER: All right.

DAIMYŌ 1: I'm delighted that you so readily agreed to accompany us.

MESSENGER: I'm not suitable company, but I agreed to join you, since you insisted.

DAIMYŌ 1: By the way, I have a small favor to ask. I realize I'm being awfully friendly, when I've only just met you. But would you mind?

MESSENGER: If it's something I can do, I'll be glad to do it.

DAIMYŌ 1: It is something you can do. Will you do it?

MESSENGER: In that case, I will.

DAIMYŌ 1: I'm delighted to hear you say that. Thank you.

MESSENGER: This is awkward. You thank me even before you tell me what you want me to do. Tell me what you want me to do. Tell me what it is, first.

DAIMYŌ 1: I thanked you, remember.

MESSENGER: Yes, sir.

DAIMYŌ 1: Well, the favor I'm asking you is this. I have many servants, but I sent them all out on errands. This is why I'm carrying this sword myself. I'd like you to carry it for me.

MESSENGER: But I've never seen such a beautiful sword, much less carried one. Please don't ask me to.

DAIMYŌ 1: Don't call it a beautiful sword; it's embarrassing. It's only a cheap sword. Do carry it for me.

MESSENGER: I wish you'd allow me to refuse.

DAIMYŌ 1: What? You insist on refusing?

MESSENGER: Yes.

DAIMYŌ 1: What do you mean? After you made me, mind you, a member of the samurai class, thank you, you now dare say that you won't carry it? (*He grasps the hilt of his sword.*)

MESSENGER (*Falls to one knee and holds out his hands*): Wait! [figure 2.42]

DAIMYŌ 2 (*Turning to Daimyō 1*): Now, don't be hasty.

DAIMYŌ 1 (*To the messenger*): What do you mean, "wait"?

MESSENGER: I'll carry it for you.

DAIMYŌ 1: But you said you wouldn't.

MESSENGER: I will.

DAIMYŌ 2: He said he'd carry it for you.

DAIMYŌ 1: You will? (*Releases his hold on the sword.*)

MESSENGER: Yes, sir.

DAIMYŌ 1 (*Laughs happily*): I was only joking. Don't worry. Here, carry it for me.

MESSENGER: The way you joke is frightening.

DAIMYŌ 1: Here, hold it for me.

MESSENGER: Very well (*takes the sword from Daimyō 1 with his left hand*).

DAIMYŌ 1: Carry it in your right hand.

MESSENGER: Aren't I supposed to carry swords like this in my left hand?

DAIMYŌ 1: No, you carry your own sword in your left hand, but your master's in your right. So carry it in your right hand.

MESSENGER: But I'm not in your service.

DAIMYŌ 1: I know you aren't. But since I asked you, do it my way and use your right hand.

MESSENGER (*Switching the sword to his right hand*): Is this the proper way?

DAIMYŌ 1: Exactly. In fact, you look most impressive.

MESSENGER: Not really. Since I'm carrying your sword, call me as you would your own servant. I'll respond accordingly.

DAIMYŌ 1: That's very nice of you. My servant is called Tarō. So I'll call Tarō, and you answer.

MESSENGER: All right.

DAIMYŌ 1 (*To Daimyō 2*): You can call him by that name, too.

DAIMYŌ 2: Fine.

DAIMYŌ 1 (*Calling in a highly formal and declamatory style*): Tarō!

MESSENGER (*The response is equally formal*): Yes, sir.

DAIMYŌ 2: Tarō!

MESSENGER: Yes, sir.

BOTH: Stick close to us! (*They look at each other and laugh.*)

DAIMYŌ 1: We've found a most suitable person.

DAIMYŌ 2: We have, indeed.

MESSENGER *(To himself)*: Disgusting! I'll fix them. *(He prepares for action by taking his right arm out of his vest)* Scoundrels! I'll take care of you.

He unsheathes the sword and holds it with both hands over his head facing the daimyō.

DAIMYŌ 1: What are you doing?

MESSENGER: You made sport of me, didn't you? How'd you like this? Just one stroke and you're dead.

DAIMYŌ 1: Hold it! Hold it!

MESSENGER: Hold what?

DAIMYŌ 1: It's all because I had you hold the sword. Just hand it back to me.

MESSENGER *(Brandishes the sword)*: What do you mean, "hand it back"?

DAIMYŌ 1: Watch out!

MESSENGER: You there!

DAIMYŌ 1: What?

MESSENGER: Hand over the sword you're wearing at your side.

DAIMYŌ 1: A samurai never lets go of the sword he wears. You insolent creature!

MESSENGER: If you don't hand it over, I'll cut you down.

DAIMYŌ 1: All right. All right. I'll give it to you.

MESSENGER: Quick!

DAIMYŌ 1: Here.

He holds out the sword to the messenger with the sheath end toward him.

MESSENGER: Hand it over with the hilt end toward me.

DAIMYŌ 1: Well if you don't like the way I do it, I won't give it to you.

MESSENGER: You won't, huh? *(He brandishes the sword.)*

DAIMYŌ 1: I will, I will!

DAIMYŌ 2: Hurry! Give it to him!

DAIMYŌ 1: All right. Here!

MESSENGER *(He gestures to cut off the daimyō's arm)*: There!

DAIMYŌ 1: Watch out!

MESSENGER *(Turning to the second daimyō)*: Give me yours, too.

DAIMYŌ 2: All right. Here!

MESSENGER *(Gestures to cut off Daimyō 2's arm)*: There!

DAIMYŌ 2: Watch out!

MESSENGER: Both of you, hand over your clothes, all of them.

DAIMYŌ 1: We'd be a sight if we did. Spare us that.

MESSENGER: You won't hand them over, huh? *(He brandishes the sword.)*

DAIMYŌ 1: I will, I will!

FIGURE 2.42. In the kyōgen *Two Daimyō*, both the messenger (left) and Daimyō 2 (middle) are worried when Daimyo 1 threatens to draw his sword. (Courtesy of the Noh Research Archive of Musashino Women's College.)

FIGURE 2.43. Having stolen the daimyō's sword and robes, the messenger threatens him. (Courtesy of the Noh Research Archive of Musashino Women's College.)

MESSENGER: Quick!

DAIMYŌ 1: How terrible!

MESSENGER: You're taking too much time.

DAIMYŌ 2: Hurry up. Give them to him.

DAIMYŌ 1: All right. Here.

MESSENGER (*Again gestures to cut off Daimyō 1's arm*): There! [figure 2.43]

DAIMYŌ 1: Watch out!

MESSENGER (*Turning to the second daimyō*): You give me yours, too.

DAIMYŌ 2: I was all set to give them to you.

MESSENGER: That's the spirit. Let me have them.

As the second daimyō presents his clothes, the messenger threatens to cut his arms off.

DAIMYŌ 2: Watch out!

MESSENGER (*Laughs uproariously*): My, my, do you look funny! Why, you look just like a pair of dogs on their haunches. Come on out here and imitate a dogfight.

DAIMYŌ 1: You're treating the samurai like beasts, are you? Absolutely not!

MESSENGER: If you won't do it, I'll finish you with one blow.

DAIMYŌ 1: We will, we will.

MESSENGER: Quick!

DAIMYŌ 2: Will you give us back our swords if we do it?

MESSENGER: Do it first.

DAIMYŌ 1 (*To the second daimyō*): Won't you join me down here?

DAIMYŌ 2: All right.

The two get down in crouching positions and move about as they growl and bark [figure 2.44].

BOTH: Bow-wow! Bow-wow, wooow! (*The messenger laughs with delight.*) Now give us back our swords. Give us back our swords (*they reach out in anticipation*).

MESSENGER: What? You want them back? (*Again he pretends to cut off their arms.*)

BOTH: Watch out! (*They return to where they were before*).

MESSENGER (*Eyeing them with amusement*): The hats you have on look like cockscombs. Now, imitate a cockfight!

DAIMYŌ 1: If we do, will you return our swords?

DAIMYŌ 2: Give us back our clothes.

MESSENGER: Do it first.

DAIMYŌ 1: Won't you join me down here again?

DAIMYŌ 2: All right.

TWO DAIMYŌ | 233

They face each other, standing, open their fans, and as they move in circular patterns, they go through the motions of moving their arms, simulating the flutter of wings. They let out cries of cocks fighting.

BOTH: Ku-u, ku-u, ku-u, ko-ke-i, ko-kei-i. (*The messenger laughs in obvious enjoyment.*) Give us back our things, give us back our things (*they reach out their arms*).

MESSENGER: What? You want your things back? (*He again pretends to cut off their arms.*)

BOTH: Watch out! Watch out!

They return to where they were before and fold their arms.

MESSENGER: This time I want you to imitate the bounce-back-again dolls that are popular in Kyoto.

DAIMYŌ 1: But I don't know how.

MESSENGER: I'll show you how.

BOTH: All right.

MESSENGER (*Sings as he shows them how to move rhythmically*):
The bounce-back-again doll, the tumbling doll
that's popular in Kyoto,
takes one look at a handsome young man
and easily takes a tumble.
Isn't that so?
That is so.
That is, that is, that is so.

FIGURE 2.44. The messenger forces the daimyō to move around the stage like dogs and bark. (Courtesy of the Noh Research Archive of Musashino Women's College.)

Now sing along as you move, and make it interesting!

DAIMYŌ 1: Be sure to give us back our swords this time!

DAIMYŌ 2: Give us back our clothes.

MESSENGER: Do it first.

DAIMYŌ 1 (*To the second daimyō*): You know how to do it?

DAIMYŌ 2: Pretty much.

DAIMYŌ 1: Join me out here.

DAIMYŌ 2: All right.

BOTH:
The bounce-back-again doll, the tumbling doll
that's popular in Kyoto,
takes one look at a handsome young man
and easily takes a tumble.
Isn't that so?

That is so.

That is, that is, that is so.

This is repeated over and over. Starting from a kneeling position with their arms folded, the daimyō sway, weave, and roll over to the rhythm of the song. As they continue, they become completely absorbed in what they are they doing and start to enjoy themselves. The messenger also joins in the merrymaking and dances with them as he beats out the rhythm with his fan.

MESSENGER: That's enough. That's enough.

BOTH: What do you mean, "enough"?

MESSENGER: I made you do all sorts of things. But as for your swords and clothes, I won't give them back to you.

DAIMYŌ 1: Give them back to us!

MESSENGER *(Pretending to hand them over)* You want these?

BOTH: We do!

MESSENGER: Can't be done! Can't be done!

BOTH: Give them back to us!

MESSENGER: Can't be done! Can't be done!

He turns and runs off up the bridgeway.

BOTH: You won't get away with this. You won't get away with this!

They run off stage after him.

The Delicious Poison (Busu)

A Tarō Kaja play

Translated by Don Kenny

Tarō Kaja ("first servant") is a kyōgen character par excellence. He and his master are all the characters necessary for a play, but he often appears in tandem with his fellow servant Jirō Kaja ("second servant"). Sometimes Tarō Kaja is clever enough to outwit his master verbally or physically, but at other times his ignorance leads him astray. In Tarō Kaja, or "servant," plays (also called *shōmyō*, "small landholder" pieces), the shite plays Tarō Kaja. In other pieces, such as the Yamabushi piece *The Snail*, Tarō Kaja is played by the ado. Unlike the waki role in most noh plays, however, secondary roles in kyōgen are often secondary in name only, with the interactions among the characters usually the basis of the humor.

The plot of *The Delicious Poison* is similar to that of *Tied to a Stick* (Bōshibari), in which a master attempts to safeguard his saké in his absence. In *Tied to a Stick*, physical rather than psychological restraints are used. These two popular plays best represent kyōgen's version of master–servant conflict. The plots in several other plays featuring Tarō Kaja involve a task that the servant is ordered to perform: in *The Inherited Cramp* (Shibiri) he attempts to get out of a shopping expedition by claiming to have cramps, and in *Three Poles* (Sambon no hashira), Tarō Kaja and his fellow servants figure out how two men can carry three poles.

The stage business used in *The Delicious Poison* is particularly effective. The servants repeatedly fan the air to prevent the "poison" from affecting them: as they advance toward and then retreat from the barrel, one of them waves his fan horizontally, the other, vertically. Tarō Kaja's "death," the eating of the sugar, the destruction of the master's treasures, and the sobs of "regret" all are enacted with the lavish use of onomatopoeia. The climax of the play is a song describing the servants' "attempted suicide." These characters clearly deserve to be chased off the stage, but one is inclined to hope that they escape severe punishment.

Unlike most kyōgen plays, *The Delicious Poison* has an identifiable literary source: a story in *Shasekishū*, a thirteenth-century collection of tales (*setsuwa*) compiled by the monk Mujū. Don Kenny's translation is from a performance script of Nomura Mansaku (b. 1931) of the Izumi school. The translation was originally published in Kenny's 1989 anthology *The Kyōgen Book*. An annotated Japanese text from the Ōkura school is available in Koyama 1960.

Don Kenny translates kyōgen plays as performance scripts for English productions, specifically those of the Kenny and Ogawa Kyōgen Players. He attempts to reflect and replicate the archaic style and stylization of the original texts by avoiding overtly colloquial English (especially phrases with regional or historical connotations) and by translating literally many of the idioms (most of which do not exist in modern Japanese) rather than replacing them with more common English phrases of similar meaning. He transliterates purely onomatopoeic sounds directly into the Roman alphabet.

CHARACTERS

SHITE: Tarō Kaja
ADO: master
KOADO: Jirō Kaja

MUSICIANS

None

A Play in One Act

The master, Tarō Kaja, and Jirō Kaja enter down the bridgeway. The servants sit at the rear of the stage, and the master goes to the shite spot.

MASTER: I am a resident of this neighborhood. Today I have a matter to attend to, for which I must travel beyond the mountain. I will call my two servants and order them to watch the house while I am gone. Tarō Kaja, are you there? *(He goes to the waki spot.)*

TARŌ KAJA *(Standing)*: Here!

MASTER: There you are.

TARŌ KAJA: At your service, sir.

MASTER: You came quickly. First call Jirō Kaja.

TARŌ KAJA: As you say, sir. *(To Jirō Kaja)* Here, here, Jirō Kaja! You are summoned.

JIRŌ KAJA *(Standing)*: You say I'm summoned?

TARŌ KAJA: And you must come quickly.

JIRŌ KAJA: With all my heart. *(To the master)* Jirō Kaja is at your service, sir.

MASTER: You came quite quickly. The matter I have called you here about is of no great import. Today I have a matter to attend to, for which I must travel beyond the mountain. Both of you must stay and watch the house.

TARŌ KAJA: As you say, sir. But one of the two of us. . . *(To Jirō Kaja)* Right, Jirō Kaja?

JIRŌ KAJA: Oh, oh!

BOTH: . . .will be most happy to attend you.

MASTER: No, no. Today I have a particular reason for not requiring an attendant. Both of you must stay here and watch the house with care.

TARŌ KAJA: If that is the case

BOTH: We will do as you say, sir.

MASTER: Wait right there for a moment.

BOTH: With all our hearts.

The master takes a large cylindrical lacquerware container, which a stage attendant has put at the rear of the stage, and places it on the floor at center front.

MASTER: Listen well! Over there is a poison called Busu. Prepare your hearts for that!

TARŌ KAJA: Since there is another person here, we both will be happy to attend you.[1]

MASTER: What did you think I said?

TARŌ KAJA: Did you not say that over there is a person called Busu?

MASTER: No, no, that's not right at all. It is a poison called Busu. It is so very fatal that if you are even struck by a breeze that happens to blow across it, you will fall dead upon the spot. So keep your wits about you, and watch it with great care.

JIRŌ KAJA: I have an urgent question, sir. If it is so very fatal, how can it be handled?

MASTER: There is a special incantation that is used.

TARŌ KAJA: Something of that sort

BOTH: would certainly be needed.

MASTER: I will presently return.

TARŌ KAJA: Indeed, we urge you to return

BOTH: as quickly as you can.

MASTER: With all my heart.

He goes to the bridgeway and exits.

TARŌ KAJA: He is gone.

JIRŌ KAJA: He is gone, indeed.

TARŌ KAJA: First let us sit down.

JIRŌ KAJA: With all my heart. (*They sit, one on each side of the container.*)

TARŌ KAJA: Now just what do you think? Whenever I attend him, you are always left to watch the house. And whenever you attend him, I am always left to watch the house. For us to be left together to watch the house today is a most unusual thing.

JIRŌ KAJA: As you say, it is a most unusual thing, indeed.

TARŌ KAJA: Today let us pass the time in pleasant conversation.

JIRŌ KAJA: That is a fine idea. (*Suddenly striking the floor with his hands and running to the first pine*) Watch out!

TARŌ KAJA (*Following Jirō Kaja*): What happened?

JIRŌ KAJA: A breeze blew this way from across the Busu.

TARŌ KAJA: It's a good thing you noticed. I didn't notice a thing.

JIRŌ KAJA: Well, I must say you are not very observant.

TARŌ KAJA: We should not have been so close to it. Let's sit farther away to talk.

JIRŌ KAJA: That is a fine idea. (*They sit farther back from the container.*)

TARŌ KAJA: Tell me now, have you ever seen this thing called a Busu?

JIRŌ KAJA: I have never seen one.

TARŌ KAJA: I have never seen one, either. Since we're watching the house today, this is a very fine chance. I would like to take a quick peek. What do you think?

JIRŌ KAJA: What are you talking about? What good would it do us to look at such an awful fatal poison?

1. In Japanese he mishears *rusu* (a person who remains behind) for *busu*.

TARŌ KAJA: The way things stand with us, we may find ourselves in a most awkward position. If someone or other should come up and say to me, "Tarō Kaja, I hear that there is a thing called Busu at your place. What sort of thing is it?" How can I possibly answer that there is indeed such a thing at our place but that I have no idea what it may be. Our master's absence is a fine chance. Let's open it and take a quick peek.

JIRŌ KAJA: All you say may well be true, but how can you even think of taking a peek at such a fatal poison that if you are even struck by a breeze that happens to blow across it, you will fall dead on the spot?

TARŌ KAJA: I have thought of a fine way to get around that.

JIRŌ KAJA: What is it?

TARŌ KAJA: Since all we must do is avoid being struck by a breeze that happens to blow across it, all we need do is fan with all our might and take a peek while we are fanning.

JIRŌ KAJA: I cannot agree to this.

TARŌ KAJA: You must not talk that way. Just come help me fan.

JIRŌ KAJA: I will fan if you insist I fan, ah, but it makes my skin creep.

They take out their fans, open them, and fan vigorously as they approach the Busu container.

TARŌ KAJA: Come, come! Fan, fan!

JIRO KAJA: I'm fanning, I'm fanning!

TARŌ KAJA: Fan, fan!

JIRŌ KAJA: I'm fanning, I'm fanning!

TARŌ KAJA: Fan, fan!

JIRŌ KAJA: I'm fanning, I'm fanning!

TARŌ KAJA *(Untying the string of the Busu container, he runs back to the bridgeway)*: Watch out!

JIRŌ KAJA *(Following him)*: What happened?

TARŌ KAJA: Now I got the string untied. You go take off the lid.

JIRŌ KAJA: No, no, never. I do not wish to go near such an awful fatal poison.

TARŌ KAJA: If that is the case, I will go again. So come help me fan.

JIRŌ KAJA: With all my heart.

They fan again as they approach the Busu container.

TARŌ KAJA: Fan, fan!

JIRŌ KAJA: I'm fanning, I'm fanning!

TARŌ KAJA: Fan, fan!

JIRŌ KAJA: I'm fanning, I'm fanning!

TARŌ KAJA: Fan, fan!

JIRŌ KAJA: I'm fanning, I'm fanning!

TARŌ KAJA *(Taking off the lid, he runs back to the bridgeway)*: Watch out!

JIRŌ KAJA *(Following him)*: What happened?

TARŌ KAJA: Now I took off the lid [figure 2.45]. If it were alive, it would surely jump right out. It must not be alive, as it has not jumped out yet.

JIRŌ KAJA: No, they always say that the most deceptive ones always sit quiet. So you must keep your wits about you.

FIGURE 2.45. Tarō Kaja and Jirō Kaja continue fanning to keep the delicious poison's fumes away as Tarō Kaja removes the lid from the lacquer container (*shōgi*). (Courtesy of Don Kenny.)

TARŌ KAJA: Let's go take a look.
JIRŌ KAJA: Are you going again?

They fan once more as they approach the Busu container.

TARŌ KAJA: Come, come! Fan, fan!
JIRŌ KAJA: I'm fanning, I'm fanning!
TARŌ KAJA: Fan, fan!
JIRŌ KAJA: I'm fanning, I'm fanning!
TARŌ KAJA *(Stopping and facing Jirō Kaja)*: Are you going to fan or not?!
JIRŌ KAJA: I am fanning!
TARŌ KAJA *(Beginning to fan again)*: Come, come! Fan, fan!
JIRŌ KAJA: I'm fanning, I'm fanning!
TARŌ KAJA: Fan, fan!
JIRŌ KAJA: I'm fanning, I'm fanning!

TARŌ KAJA *(Looking into the Busu container)*: Fan, fan!
JIRŌ KAJA: I'm fanning, I'm fanning!
TARŌ KAJA *(Running to the bridgeway)*: Watch out! I saw it, I saw it!
JIRŌ KAJA *(Following him)*: What is it?
TARŌ KAJA: I don't know just what it is, but it looks like a big black sticky lump, and it looks very good to eat. (*He closes his fan and sticks it in his waistband.*)
JIRŌ KAJA: What are you talking about? How can such an awful fatal poison be any good to eat? (*He closes his fan and sticks it in his waistband.*)
TARŌ KAJA: I would like to take a bite. What do you think?
JIRŌ KAJA: Have you lost your wits completely?
TARŌ KAJA: No, my wits I have not lost, but it seems as though that Busu has possessed me, as I want to eat it more and more. I'll just go take a quick bite (*starts toward the Busu container*).
JIRŌ KAJA *(Running after him and catching hold of his sleeve)*: Oh wait! Please wait!
TARŌ KAJA: Wait for what?
JIRŌ KAJA: As long as I am here, I will not let you go.
TARŌ KAJA: You must not talk like that, and my sleeve, you must let go.
JIRŌ KAJA: No, no, never! Let go your sleeve I'll not!
TARŌ KAJA: Let go, let go!
JIRŌ KAJA: I'll not, I'll not!
TARŌ KAJA *(Singing, he pulls his sleeve loose from Jirō Kaja's grasp and moves toward the Busu container, taking out his folded fan)*:
From sleeves all wet with fresh dew,
I brush tears of parting.
Busu pulls me to its side,
and I must follow.

Tarō Kaja kneels by the Busu container. He begins scooping out the Busu with his fan and eating it.

JIRŌ KAJA *(Watching Tarō from the bridge-way)*: Oh, oh, he has started eating it. If only he is not struck dead!

TARŌ KAJA *(Suddenly dropping to the floor with his hand to his head as though he is in a dead faint)*: Aaagh!

TARŌ KAJA: It looks like he has been struck dead. *(Rushing to Tarō Kaja and pounding him on the back)* Here, here, Tarō Kaja! What's happened, what's happened?!

TARŌ KAJA: Who is it?

JIRŌ KAJA: It's Jirō Kaja! What's happened?

TARŌ KAJA *(Getting to his feet)*: It's sugar!

JIRŌ KAJA: You say it's sugar?

TARŌ KAJA: Just taste it and see.

JIRŌ KAJA: Let me see, let me see! *(He scoops up some Busu and eats it.)* Truly, it is sugar.

TARŌ KAJA: He told us it was Busu and a fatal poison just to keep us from eating it!

JIRŌ KAJA: It is just as you say.

TARŌ KAJA *(Taking the container to one side, he begins eating)*: Oh, how delicious it is! I have never tasted anything so good before [figure 2.46].

FIGURE 2.46. Tarō Kaja uses his fan to eat the poison. (Courtesy of Don Kenny.)

JIRŌ KAJA *(Sneaking the container away while Tarō Kaja is busy eating, he takes it to the other side of the stage and begins eating)*: Oh, how delicious it is! I have never tasted anything so good before!

TARŌ KAJA *(Stealing it back and eating)*: I cannot stop eating it!

JIRŌ KAJA *(Stealing it back and eating)*: The more I eat, the more I like it!

TARŌ KAJA *(Stealing it back and eating)*: I have never tasted anything so good before!

Jirō Kaja picks up the lid of the container, moves to Tarō Kaja's side, and begins scooping the lid full. Tarō Kaja simultaneously scoops back into the container.

JIRŌ KAJA: Don't eat it all yourself. Let me have some, too!

TARŌ KAJA: Divide it fairly, divide it fairly!

JIRŌ KAJA: With all my heart!

They equalize their shares. Jirō Kaja goes back to his side of the stage with the lid. Both eat until the Busu is all gone, exclaiming joyfully with each spoonful.

TARŌ KAJA: I've never tasted anything so good!

JIRŌ KAJA: Oh, how delicious it is!

TARŌ KAJA: The more I eat, the more I like it!

JIRŌ KAJA: I can't stop eating it!

TARŌ KAJA: Oh, how delicious it is!

JIRŌ KAJA: I've never tasted anything so good!

TARŌ KAJA: I can't stop eating it!

JIRŌ KAJA: The more I eat, the more I like it!

TARŌ KAJA (*Hitting the bottom of the container with his fan*): Ho! It is all gone!

JIRŌ KAJA (*Also hitting the bottom*): Mine is all gone, too.

They put their fans back in their waistbands and stand; Tarō Kaja goes to the waki spot, and Jirō Kaja goes to the shite spot.

TARŌ KAJA: Oh, you've done it now!

JIRŌ KAJA: Done what?

TARŌ KAJA: He told us it was Busu and a fatal poison just to keep us from eating it. And now you have eaten it all up. As soon as he comes back, I'll tell him everything right off.

JIRŌ KAJA: Well, you certainly have no sense of justice! Was it not I who warned you against eating it for that very same reason, and you who untied the string and began to eat it first? I no longer care what happens to you! As soon as he comes back, I'll tell him everything right off.

TARŌ KAJA: Here, here! I was only joking.

JIRŌ KAJA: So what will be our excuse?

TARŌ KAJA: Tear that hanging scroll to pieces.

JIRŌ KAJA: If I tear it to pieces, will we have an excuse?

TARŌ KAJA: Oh, oh, we will have an excuse! Tear it quickly!

JIRŌ KAJA: If that is the case, I will tear it.

TARŌ KAJA: Tear it, tear it!

JIRŌ KAJA: With all my heart. (*He mimes grabbing hold of the hanging scroll and tearing it to pieces*) Zarari! Zarari! Now I've torn it.

TARŌ KAJA: Oh, you've done it now!

JIRŌ KAJA: Done what?

TARŌ KAJA: This Busu was only sugar. You could order as much as you liked right now, and you would have no trouble getting as much of the same as you might want, but that hanging scroll was a painting of Kannon Buddha by the great Priest Mokkei, most highly treasured by our master. And now you have torn it to pieces. As soon as he comes back, I'll tell him everything right off.

JIRŌ KAJA: Your sense of justice gets worse and worse! I tore it only because you said that tearing it would give us an excuse. I no longer care what happens to you. As soon as he comes back, I'll tell him everything right off.

TARŌ KAJA: Oh, here, here! I was only joking again.

JIRŌ KAJA: Well, I must say, your joking knows no end. So what will be our excuse?

TARŌ KAJA: Break that Mount Temmoku tea bowl and the stand it's sitting on.

JIRŌ KAJA: You just want me to break it so you can torment me once more.

TARŌ KAJA: Oh, no! This time I will help.

JIRŌ KAJA: You say you'll help?

TARŌ KAJA: Most certainly.

JIRŌ KAJA: Then I will break it. Here, here! Take hold, take hold!

TARŌ KAJA: With all my heart.

They go to the corner of the stage, face each other, and mime grasping opposite sides of the tea bowl stand and lifting it [figure 2.47].

JIRŌ KAJA: Ready?

TARŌ KAJA: Ready!

They throw the stand and tea bowl to the ground.

JIRŌ KAJA: Garari!

TARŌ KAJA: Chin!

JIRŌ KAJA: There are more now!

TARŌ KAJA: It's smashed to pieces! (*Both laugh loudly.*)

FIGURE 2.47. The two servants lift the imaginary tea bowl stand and drop it to the ground, destroying the valuable bowl. (Courtesy of Don Kenny.)

Tarō Kaja goes to the shite spot, and Jirō Kaja goes to the waki spot.

JIRŌ KAJA: So what will be our excuse?

TARŌ KAJA: As soon as he comes back, we must cry.

JIRŌ KAJA: If we cry, will we have an excuse?

TARŌ KAJA: Just leave the rest to me. Now let us sit down here.

JIRŌ KAJA: With all my heart. (*They sit at center stage, facing front.*)

MASTER (*He enters and moves to the first pine*): I have just now come back home. No doubt my servants are eagerly awaiting my return. Here, here! I'm back home now, I'm back home now!

TARŌ KAJA (*To Jirō Kaja*): There! He's come back now. Cry, cry!

Tarō Kaja and Jirō Kaja cover their eyes with both hands and cry.

MASTER: What is the matter here? Suddenly you're all in tears. Tell me what happened!

TARŌ KAJA: Jirō Kaja, you tell.

JIRŌ KAJA: Tarō Kaja, you tell.

MASTER: You've got me worried. Tell me what happened!

TARŌ KAJA: If that is the case, this is how it was. In order not to fall asleep while watching the house, I began a round of sumo wrestling with Jirō Kaja. As Jirō Kaja is better at sumo, he quickly grabbed my thigh and tried to throw me over. To keep my balance, I grabbed ahold of your hanging scroll. Before we knew what happened,

TARŌ KAJA: It was torn in two. (*They cry again.*)

MASTER: What is this? My treasured hanging scroll you have torn in two?!

JIRŌ KAJA: The rebound threw me back, and I fell right on top of your Mount Tenmoku tea bowl. Before we knew what happened,

BOTH: it was smashed to pieces (*they cry*).

MASTER: Even my Mount Tenmoku tea bowl you have smashed to pieces? I'll have your necks for this!

TARŌ KAJA: After we destroyed all your treasures, we were sure that you would have our necks for it. So we decided to die by eating the Busu. We ate until it was all gone, but. . . . Right, Jirō Kaja?

JIRŌ KAJA: Oh, oh!

BOTH: . . . we are still alive (*they cry*).

MASTER: By the three treasures! Even my Busu you have eaten up. Before long, you will drop dead on this very spot!

TARŌ KAJA (*Singing*):

First we took one great big bite,
but we were still alive.

JIRŌ KAJA (*Singing*):

Next we both took one more big bite,

TARŌ KAJA:

three bites and then four bites,

JIRŌ KAJA:

five bites and then six bites
we took more bites than ten

BOTH:

we ate and ate until there was
not a single bite left.
Life that never dies
is the greatest treasure we own.
Oh, how strong is the life we have
within our bodies.

MASTER (*Speaking during the last part of the preceding song*): Oh, I must say, how angry I am! (*Striking Tarō Kaja and Jirō Kaja on the shoulder with his fan*) You hateful rascal! You hateful rascal!

BOTH (*Getting to their feet and running up the bridgeway*): Ah, please forgive us!

MASTER (*Chasing them*): What do you mean, "Forgive us"? You lazy rascals, you will not get away.

BOTH: Oh, forgive us, please forgive us!

MASTER: I'll catch you yet! I'll catch you yet!

BOTH: Oh, forgive us, please forgive us! (*They exit.*)

MASTER: I'll catch you yet, I'll catch you yet! (*He chases them off.*)

Mushrooms (Kusabira)

A yamabushi play

Translated by Carolyn Anne Morley

Yamabushi, mountain priests or ascetics, were common figures in medieval Japan in both the natural and the artistic landscape. They roamed the countryside performing austere ascetic practices, their spiritual effectiveness dependent on their ascetic prowess. Among the many powers they were reputed to have were the abilities to exorcise evil spirits, to make themselves invisible, and to pray birds out of the sky—all tasks they attempt in kyōgen plays in this anthology. Mountain priests appear as characters in most genres of medieval literature, sometimes as awesome personages and sometimes as figures of fun. In kyōgen, they tend to be failures. Of the nine plays featuring yamabushi, they are successful in only two: *The Snail* and *The Lunch Box Thief* (Tsuto yamabushi). *Mushrooms* is a typical example of this failure.

Mushrooms do not usually inhabit the stage, but their lowly nature makes them a perfect foil for the impotent yamabushi, a parody of the powerful figure who appears in the noh plays to which this text alludes. In those plays, the yamabushi exorcises avenging ghosts and frightens fierce warriors. Here, however, a proliferation of fungi defeats the priest, as each of his prayers calls forth yet more mushrooms. Although mushrooms are the lowliest of the creatures to defeat the yamabushi, he is also done in by a crab in *The Crab* (Kani yamabushi) and comes under the spell of an owl in *The Owl* (Fukuro yamabushi).

The variety and movements of the mushrooms popping up all over the stage with their conical hats and strange masks provide much of the humor in this piece. In the Izumi school's performance practice, there is a single young woman mushroom among the males, whereas the Ōkura school favors a cast of female mushrooms (played by male actors, of course). Often, one or more of the mushrooms is a child actor, small enough to stand amid all the adult actors who move about in squatting positions. As many as twelve mushrooms may crowd the stage at one time.

Other edibles appear in kyōgen: in one play (*Konomi arasoi*), fruits led by a tangerine and vegetables led by an eggplant (or a chestnut) engage in battle; in another (*Tokoro*), the spirit of a field potato sings about its torture and death at the hands of humans. More elegant plants grace the noh stage: the spirit of the cherry blossoms (*Saigyō zakura*), an iris (*Kakitsubata*), and pine trees (*Takasago*).

The text of *Mushrooms* that Carolyn Morley used for her translation was written for actors of the Izumi school in the mid-nineteenth century and contains interesting notes of advice to the actors by the play's editor, Yoshida Koichi. His notes are enclosed in brackets. *Mushrooms* also appears with translations of eight other yamabushi plays in Morley's *Transformation, Miracles, and Mischief* (1993).

CHARACTERS

CHARACTERS

SHITE: a mountain priest (yamabushi)
ADO: a man from the neighborhood
ADO: up to twelve mushrooms

MUSICIANS

None

The princess mushroom wears an *oto* mask (the comical, round-faced mask of a young girl), and the demon mushroom wears a fierce buaku mask and carries an umbrella. The others may wear a *kentoku* mask (pop eyes, prominent teeth), an *usofuki* mask (pop eyes and a whistling mouth), or a noborihige mask (flat nose, wrinkles, and beard). They all wear hats of various sizes and shapes.

[Note to the actors:

1. All the mushrooms are masked, but their bodies should be devoid of expression. The expression is in the hats. The mushrooms should pick a spot and crouch there with their backs erect. When they enter and leave the stage, they should maintain this posture, bending only from the knees and walking in a squatting position.

2. When there are more mushrooms than masks, a scarf may be used instead.

3. All the mushrooms tuck their hands into their sleeves and clutch them to their chests or fold them over their chests (the demon mushroom is the exception).]

A Play in One Act

The matsutake mushroom enters[1] and plants himself, crouching at center stage. The man (ado) enters and stands at the shite spot.

MAN: I live in the neighborhood. For some reason, this year for the first time, mushrooms have popped up in my garden. No matter how many times I pull them out, by the next morning they're right back where they were. I've never seen anything like it. There's a powerful mountain priest not far from here. I think I'll ask him to cast a spell for me and see if that gets rid of them. It's a puzzle all right. But if he'd just cast a spell, then we'd know what was going on.

He circles the stage and stops at the shite spot.

Ah! I've only just left home, and here I am already. I'll announce myself.

He goes to the first pine and drops to one knee facing the curtain. The mountain priest enters, lifting his legs high as if climbing a mountain and marches down the bridgeway while reciting in the dynamic mode.[2]

---

1. [Note to the actors: The mushrooms should shuffle onstage without wobbling. Crouch, but keep your back erect and clutch your sleeves to your chests.]

2. [Note to the actor: If the bridgeway is short, you may start your recitation from the curtain. Otherwise, use your discretion.]

FIGURE 2.48. A man, kneeling at right, has entreated a yamabushi (mountain priest) to come to his garden and rid it of mushrooms. The round cap (*tokin*), white pompoms on his chest (*sasakake*), and Buddhist rosary are emblems of a mountain priest. For this performance, a noh-style stage has been laid out on top of a proscenium stage. (Courtesy of the Noh Research Archive of Musashino Women's College.)

MOUNTAIN PRIEST:
Before the window of the nine
    realms of the senses,
on a pallet of the ten vehicles of
    the law,
sprinkled with the holy waters
    of yoga

Changes to the spoken style.

cleansed by the moon of three
    mysteries,[3]
who goes there?

MAN *(Leaps forward, lunging at the priest)*: It's me!

MOUNTAIN PRIEST *(Falls on his seat)*: Hey you! I didn't know who it was, flying up in my face like that. What do you want?

MAN: It's just that for some reason, this year for the first time, mushrooms have been popping up in my garden. No matter how many times I pull them up, by the next morning they're right back where they were. I've tried everything, and I still can't get rid of them. It's really weird. I'd be very grateful if you'd come and cast a spell [figure 2.48].

MOUNTAIN PRIEST: Well, well, so that's the trouble. I've never heard of anything like that before. Of course, mushrooms do spring up, but it's odd that they should keep coming back after you pull them out.

MAN: Exactly. That's why I felt it was out of the ordinary, and so naturally I came to you.

MOUNTAIN PRIEST: I'm engaged in some special austerities at the moment, so I really shouldn't go anywhere. But for you, I'll do it.

MAN: Now that is kind of you. Could you come right away?

MOUNTAIN PRIEST: Of course, let's go.

MAN: In that case, after you, sir.

MOUNTAIN PRIEST: You go first and lead the way.

MAN: Shall I then?

MOUNTAIN PRIEST: Yes, yes, go on.

MAN: In that case, I'll lead the way. Please follow me.

MOUNTAIN PRIEST: Of course.

3. Taken from the noh play *Aoi no ue*, in which it is recited by a powerful ascetic. The following meeting of the man and the mountain priest is a parody of the meeting between the aikyōgen messenger from the court and the ascetic (the waki) in the noh play.

[Note to the actor: The copying of the *Aoi no Ue* greeting scene is not a traditional device. It seems to have been a sudden inspiration, although this parody is now an accepted technique. Since it is rather discourteous to the noh waki, the dynamic mode of chanting may be eliminated.]

The man from the neighborhood goes first and circles the stage, stopping at the shite spot. The mountain priest follows, passing the man at the shite spot and stopping on the bridgeway at the first pine.

MAN *(Circling the stage)*: I'm so glad you could come right away today.

MOUNTAIN PRIEST *(Following the man)*: As I said, I shouldn't go out at all, but for you I've made this exception.

MAN: I really appreciate it. Here we are already.

MOUNTAIN PRIEST: This is the place then?

MAN: Please go ahead.

They exchange places. The priest goes to the shite spot, and the man goes to the first pine on the bridgeway. They turn and face each other.

MOUNTAIN PRIEST: Now, where is this mushroom?

MAN: There it is.

He points out the mushroom crouched at the center stage rear.

MOUNTAIN PRIEST: Wow! Is that it?

MAN: Yes, sir.

MOUNTAIN PRIEST: Indeed! I've seen mushrooms in my day, but never one that big.

MAN: It's really creepy.

MOUNTAIN PRIEST: Not at all. There's nothing creepy about it. This is a matsutake mushroom.

MAN: Excuse me, sir. You say this is a matsutake?

MOUNTAIN PRIEST: That's right.

MAN: If you say so. It seems awfully big for a matsutake.

MOUNTAIN PRIEST: So, you've never had this happen before?

MAN: Oh no. I've never even heard of anything like it before. I know it looks bad; that's why I'm so uneasy.

MOUNTAIN PRIEST: Nothing to worry about. I'll get rid of it with one spell.

MAN: Thank you, sir.

Incantation   *Sung in the noh-style dynamic mode.*

MOUNTAIN PRIEST:
A *tokin* is a foot-long piece of cloth
dyed black, folded in pleats
and popped on the bean,
therefore it's called a tokin.[4]

MAN: Ah ha.

MOUNTAIN PRIEST *(Resumes chanting)*:
Irataka prayer beads, these are not.[5]

4. This is a parody of the mountain priest's incantation recited by Benkei in the noh play *Ataka*, which begins: "A mountain priest is one who follows in the path of the great ascetic En and models himself after the visage of Fudō myōō. A tokin represents the crown of the five wisdoms and is pleated in the twelve karmic ties and worn on the head."

5. *Irataka* beads are a kind of rosary used by the mountain priests when performing incantations or exorcisms. They are made from a collection of animal bones and teeth and the like.

Examines the beads of his rosary.

> I string together any old beads and call them irataka.
> If I offer a prayer,

Begins to rub his beads and sings in the noh style.

> how can a miracle fail to occur?
> Boron, boron, boron, boron.[6]

He stops rubbing his beads and turns to the mushroom, which faces forward and begins to quiver.

MAN: Excuse me, sir. It's moving.

MOUNTAIN PRIEST: A miracle!

MAN: Yes indeed, sir.

MOUNTAIN PRIEST: It will be gone soon.

MAN: Excellent, sir.

MOUNTAIN PRIEST *(Facing the mushroom)*: Boron, boron.

MAN *(Watches a second mushroom shuffle in from the little door at back stage left)*: Oh, how awful! Oh sir! Sir!

MOUNTAIN PRIEST: Well, what is it?

MAN *(Pointing)*: Another big one has sprung up over there!

MOUNTAIN PRIEST: Indeed it has! It looks like a *shiitake* mushroom.

MAN: Quick! Pray it away.

MOUNTAIN PRIEST: Yes, of course. I'll show you how it's done.

MAN: Please!

Incantation   *Sung in the noh-style dynamic mode.*

MOUNTAIN PRIEST:

> Under the bridge the irises bloom;
> who planted the irises,
> who planted the irises?[7]

Two more mushrooms pop through the little door at back stage left (kirido).

MAN: Oh, sir! Sir!

MOUNTAIN PRIEST: What? What is it?

MAN: Look at that! They're springing up here, there, and everywhere.

MOUNTAIN PRIEST: What? More have come up? Oh! This one's a *reishi* mushroom.[8]

MAN: Really? A reishi?

MOUNTAIN PRIEST: Yes, we ought to celebrate!

MAN: Well, whatever it is, they're multiplying!

MOUNTAIN PRIEST: Oh, that's to be expected. Didn't you say that you've pulled

---

6. *Boron* often appears in mountain priests' incantations in kyōgen and appears to be a reduction of a mantra to the universal Buddha, Dainichi Nyorai: *On abiraunken bazara datoban.*

7. A Kamakura-period children's song, sometimes followed by a children's counting song. Children's songs are presumably used here to parody the mountain priests.

8. The *reishi* is also known as the "ten-thousand-year mushroom" (*mannen take*) and therefore is probably a symbol of longevity.

them up again and again but they kept coming back? With my extraordinary powers, I'll make them all pop up. There are already so many up, I doubt there could be any more. Now then, since I've prayed them all up, I'll now pray them away. You ought to have more faith.

MAN: Certainly, sir.

Incantation *Sung in the noh-style dynamic mode.*

MOUNTAIN PRIEST:

I'll pray that the Fierce Guardian
    King[9]
lassos them in his holy rope.
How can a miracle fail to occur?
Boron, boron, boron, boron.

FIGURE 2.49. The more the yamabushi prays, the more mushrooms appear. To the left is the princess mushroom wearing a comical female mask (*oto*) and white cloth to represent hair (*binan*). In this performance on a traditional stage, the exorcist is costumed as a Buddhist priest rather than as a yamabushi. (Courtesy of the Noh Research Archive of Musashino Women's College.)

As he prays, two or three more mushrooms hop out from the little door at backstage right.

MAN: Excuse me, sir. Another whole crowd has popped up.

MOUNTAIN PRIEST: Look at that! A bunch of them have sprung up. This must be a *princess* mushroom. (*Wanders around looking at the mushrooms as they shuffle around the stage. He appears concerned [figure 2.49].*) What a sight!

MAN: Uh . . . sir?

MOUNTAIN PRIEST: Huh?

MAN: What's going on here, anyway?

MOUNTAIN PRIEST (*Looks hopeless*): Nothing to worry about. Things always multiply before they disappear. Relax.

MAN (*Trembling*): Well, I don't know about that. Just get rid of them.

MOUNTAIN PRIEST: You're right.

He prays alternately at one mushroom and then another. The demon mushroom, who has entered silently onto the bridgeway, crouches behind the first pine. The priest keeps on praying without noticing him [figure 2.50].

MAN (*Startled as he notices the demon mushroom*): Sir, sir!

MOUNTAIN PRIEST (*Ignoring him*): Boron, boron.

MAN (*Louder*): Wait a moment, sir!

MOUNTAIN PRIEST: Well, what now?

MAN: Forget about those. Will you take a look at this one! You prayed up a really big one this time.

MOUNTAIN PRIEST (*Spots it and is discouraged but still tries to keep up a good*

9. Fudō myōō, the guardian deity of the mountain priests. He is one of the fierce, bright kings who protect the Buddha, Dainichi Nyorai.

FIGURE 2.50. The yamabushi continues with his prayers over the quivering mushrooms as the demon mushroom enters the stage from the bridgeway with an umbrella around his head. (Courtesy of the Noh Research Archive of Musashino Women's College.)

front): Oh! Well! This is truly miraculous! That must be a giant demon mushroom. It hasn't opened yet, but when it does, it will really be something to see.

MAN: They keep multiplying. It's driving me crazy. Until now I've always thought of you as a living Fudō. I believed you could solve any problem. But today, when I call on you, your prayers are useless. My entire garden is filled with mushrooms. If I'd never summoned you, things wouldn't be this bad!

MOUNTAIN PRIEST: What?! That's simply nonsense. Why, with my extraordinary powers, I can pray the ocean dry. I can pray a mountain to the ground. But these mushrooms now . . . hmm. Clearing them out is really going to be difficult. I wonder what I can do?

MAN: It's that stupidity of yours that has gotten us into this. I don't care how you do it, but pray them away. Quick!

MOUNTAIN PRIEST: Humph. Fool! As if babbling away like that is any help. (*Speaking in a determined manner*) All right, I'll make the sign of the eggplant this time.[10] In one swoop I'll wipe out all of these mushrooms.

MAN: Do as you like. Just get on with it.

Facing front, the priest makes an eggplant sign, then claps his hands suddenly, and the mushrooms begin to quiver. Only the demon mushroom remains as he was.

MOUNTAIN PRIEST: A miracle!

MAN: Hurry up! Pray, pray!

Incantation *The mushrooms quiver. Repulsed by the sight of them, the priest faces front and prays but is unable to resist glancing backward at the mushrooms. He sings in the noh-style dynamic mode.*

MOUNTAIN PRIEST:

No matter how many mushrooms there may be,
when I perform the sign of the eggplant,
and offer a prayer,
how can they fail to disappear?
Boron, boron, boron.

10. [Note to the actor: make up some *mudra* for the eggplant. It's best done very surreptitiously.]
Mudras (*ketsujin*) were secret hand signs of esoteric Buddhism and were used by mountain priests in exorcisms.

He glances here and there at the mushrooms. Most of them move in to surround the man from the neighborhood, but one or two head for the mountain priest.

MAN *(Surrounded and scared)*: What should I do?

He tries to get away, but they come even closer. The mushrooms that encircled the mountain priest come too.

Sir, sir! The mushrooms are all over me!

MOUNTAIN PRIEST: Stand perfectly still.

Chants intently while turning in one direction and then another.

Boron, boron, boron.

The mushrooms become more tenacious in their pursuit of the frightened man.

MAN: Hurry! Pray them away! Please!

He flees to the bridgeway with the mushrooms quivering around him. At the first pine, the man finally extricates himself.

Help! I'm scared! I'm scared!

He flees down the bridgeway with the mushrooms in hot pursuit.

MOUNTAIN PRIEST *(Facing his fleeing neighbor, he tries to stop him by praying)*: Stand perfectly still!

Follows the man to the shite spot and gazes after him as he exits, pursued by the mushrooms.

Hey, hey! What's this? Hey, hey! This won't do. He's already gone. Now I am in a fix. I'm all on my own. At least I've gotten rid of most of the mushrooms. *(Spots the demon mushroom)* Oh well, I'm getting out of here, too.

Glancing fearfully behind him, he tries to slip past the demon mushroom along the bridgeway. The demon suddenly opens his umbrella, blocking the way. Surprised, the priest retreats to the main stage, looking alarmed, repulsed, and frightened. He peers at the mushroom from behind the shite pillar.

He's moving! I can't take much more of this. I'll make the sign of the eggplant again and get rid of him.

He turns to the mushroom, makes the eggplant sign, and claps his hands.

Incantation   *Sung in a noh-style dynamic chant.*

MOUNTAIN PRIEST:
No matter how evil a demon mushroom you are,
when the mountain priest, the living body of the Buddha,
makes the sign of the eggplant and prays,
how can a miracle fail to occur?
Boron, boron, boron, boron.

During the prayer, the mushroom enters the stage and faces the priest.

I make the sign of the eggplant.
Boron, boron . . .

The priest continues to pray, backing up as he does so. When he reaches the bridge-way, the mushroom tries to close the umbrella over him. The priest falls backward on his seat.

> I make the sign of the eggplant,
> the sign of the eggplant.

He rises as he prays. The mushroom again attempts to catch him in the umbrella.

> Help! Nothing works! Help! Help!

He runs down the bridgeway and exits with the mushroom in pursuit.

[Notes to the actor:

1. This ending is very important and should be carefully timed and acted.

2. Alternative ending: The demon mushroom is not used. When the man is chased offstage, half the mushrooms remain on stage; continue as follows:

MOUNTAIN PRIEST: This won't do. He's fled. My, my! This is terrible. Now, I'll pray the rest of you away. (*They all begin to quiver, and the priest is left standing there. Revolted by them, he makes the sign of the eggplant*) Boron, boron. (*As he prays, the mushrooms surround him. He heads for the shite spot as he makes the eggplant sign*) Boron, boron. (*Again and again he prays, and finally at the first pine on the bridgeway, he stops*) I can't bear it. Leave me alone! (*He flees, followed immediately by the silent mushrooms chasing him offstage.*)

3. In the old days, the play ended with a *shagiri* flute melody, and there were other alternative endings, but that was the old style. I'm not at all sure how they would work today.]

The Snail (Kagyū)

A yamabushi and Tarō Kaja play

Translated by Don Kenny

As it is now performed, *The Snail* features two of kyōgen's most popular characters, the yamabushi and Tarō Kaja. The yamabushi toys with Tarō Kaja and escapes unscathed, but only here and in *The Lunch Box Thief* (Tsuto yamabushi) is he so fortunate. In the latter play, a thief attempts to blame a yamabushi for the disappearance of a woodsman's lunch but is caught by the power of the priest's prayers and is finally forced to confess.

The action of *The Snail* centers on two devices often used in kyōgen. The first involves a misunderstanding: a servant or acolyte, told to get something for his master, arrives with the wrong object, usually because some shyster—in this case a yamabushi—takes advantage of his ignorance. Often the misunderstanding revolves around a pun. For example, in *Wakame* an acolyte comes home with a young woman (*wakame*) rather than the seaweed (also *wakame*, but written with different characters) that the head priest had asked him to get. Similarly, in *Kane no ne*, an acolyte checks out the "sounds of bells" rather than the "price of gold" (both pronounced *kane no ne*), and in *Haridako* a drum (*hariduiko*) is purchased instead of "dried octopus" (*haridako*). The master generally describes the attributes of the desired object, so the shyster must be able to relate them to the object he is attempting to fob off on the unsuspecting servant. For example, like seaweed, a young woman can be said to have good color, be from Ise, and be salty (when she cries salty tears); and a thick skin can refer to both an octopus and a drum. *The Snail* plays on the shared attributes of yamabushi and snails!

The second theatrical device in this play is one used in a somewhat simpler form in the play *Two Daimyō*: the repetitious use of song and dance to draw the characters and the audience into communal rapture or euphoria. The careful, detailed stage directions in Don Kenny's translation show how this is accomplished. Once the yamabushi gets Tarō Kaja involved in singing and dancing the snail song, the performance becomes contagious. The master gets caught up in the joy of performing, and so does the audience. In a production in Ithaca, New York, in 1987, Nomura Mansaku performed the play with its alternative ending—the three characters dance down the bridgeway, singing and dancing together—and the English-speaking audience filed out of the auditorium for the intermission repeating *Den den mushi mushi* ("Come out, come out, you slimy snail").

Don Kenny's translation of the Izumi school text (Nomura 1929) was originally published in the *Asian Theater Journal* in 1986. The stage directions were checked against a videotape of a Nomura family performance at the Kanze Noh Theater in Tokyo on November 16, 1982. The editor revised the terminology of the stage directions in keeping with the conventions used in this anthology and added notes. An Ōkura school text is available in Koyama 1961.

CHARACTERS

SHITE: a warrior priest (yamabushi)[1]
ADO: master[2]
KOADO: Tarō Kaja

MUSICIANS

None

FIGURE 2.51. The yamabushi (warrior priest) in *The Snail*. The pom-poms on his chest (*sasakake*), the round hat (*tokin*), and the high-stepping walk are all typical of the yamabushi, who also carries a rosary. (Courtesy of Don Kenny.)

A Play in One Act

The warrior priest enters down the bridgeway.[3] He stops at the shite spot facing front, then turns to face upstage left, and takes four steps [figure 2.51]. In the meantime, the stage attendant enters through the small door [kirido] upstage left, crosses to the stage attendant spot, and sits on his knees facing front.

WARRIOR PRIEST *(Singing):*
Descending Mounts Omine and Kazuraki,
I return to my own mountain home.
STAGE ATTENDANT *(Singing):*
My mountain home.

The warrior priest returns to the shite spot and faces front.

WARRIOR PRIEST *(Speaking):* I am a warrior priest from Mount Haguro in the Land of Dewa. I have completed my ascetic training on the sacred Mounts Omine and Kazuraki and am now heading toward home. *(Begins his trip)* I must hurry on my way. Truly, the life of a warrior priest is one of great penance. He must sleep in the fields and on mountains, with only rocks and trees to pillow his head. But this strict ascetic self-mortification endows us with such great and wonderful powers *(ending his trip upstage right and facing*

1. Yamabushi is translated elsewhere as "mountain priest" or "mountain ascetic." Don Kenny uses the term "warrior priest" in his performance scripts to evoke the fierceness of the yamabushi, who were sometimes armed, as well as the bluster and braggadocio of the kyōgen character. For further information about Kenny's translation style, see the introduction to *The Delicious Poison*.

2. In a late Edo-period Izumi school text (*Kumogata bon*), the two ado represent a father and son (Morley 1993:181).

3. An alternative performance practice has the shidai entrance music played by the flute and two drums. In that case, the first lines are sung as a shidai.

FIGURE 2.52. Sent out to find a snail to cure his master's grandfather, Tarō Kaja pushes aside the brush to enter a thicket. The same movement kata was performed by the Yamabushi earlier. (Courtesy of Don Kenny.)

front) that we can instantly (*looking upward to his left*) pray any bird (*looking upward to his right*) that happens to fly overhead (*stamping once with his right foot and at the same time moving his head sharply downward to look at the floor in front of him*) to the ground, with the greatest of ease. (*Returns to normal posture*) Well, I set out so early this morning that I find I am quite sleepy now. I would like to take a little nap before I continue on my way. (*Makes a small trip ending upstage right facing downstage left*) And fortunately, here is a thicket. First l will step inside. (*Crosses to center stage, mimes pushing the brush apart, and takes one large step forward over the underbrush*) Ei, ei, yatto-na. Well now, what a big, wide thicket this is. (*Crosses downstage left*) I'll just lie down right here. (*Puts his conch shell on the floor and lies down next to it facing offstage left with his hand toward the audience*) Ei, ei, ei. Oh, how comfortable. How very comfortable I am.

The master and Tarō Kaja enter down the bridgeway. The master stops at the shite spot, and Tarō Kaja goes to the rear of the stage and sits.

MASTER (*Entering down the bridgeway*): I have a grandfather who has lived a long and happy life. They say that if he is given a snail, he will live even longer. I will call my servant Tarō Kaja and give him a job to do. (*Crossing to the waki spot and turning to face Tarō Kaja*) Tarō Kaja, are you there?

TARŌ KAJA (*Goes to the shite spot and faces his master*): Here.

MASTER: There you are.

TARŌ KAJA (*Bowing*): At your service, sir.

MASTER: You came quite quickly. The matter I have called you here about is of no great import. Don't you agree that there is no one so fortunate as my grandfather?

TARŌ KAJA: It is just as you say, sir. He is (*bowing*) a most fortunate grandfather, indeed.

MASTER: Concerning which, they say that if he is given a snail, he will live even longer. Although I realize it is a great imposition, I order you to go out right now and catch a snail.

TARŌ KAJA (*Bowing*): As you say, sir, but I have no idea (*facing front*) what sort of thing a snail may be. And I also have no idea (*facing his master*) where one may be found. I humbly beg you (*bowing*) to allow me not to go.

MASTER: They are found in thickets in great numbers.

TARŌ KAJA: You say they are found in thickets in great numbers?

MASTER (*Both face front*): To begin with, they have black heads; they carry a shell on their hips; and sometimes (*facing Tarō Kaja*) they show their horns.

TARŌ KAJA (*Facing his master*): You say they show their horns?

MASTER: And I hear that the older ones often grow as big as a person. I order you to do your best to catch the best snail you can find.

FIGURE 2.53. Once inside the thicket, Tarō Kaja backs into a sleeping yamabushi. He wears a typical Tarō Kaja costume, a plaid noshime and patterned hakama under an unmatched vest of kataginu. The master, out of the action, sits quietly in the background, and the yamabushi's conch shell lies on the floor. (Courtesy of Don Kenny.)

TARŌ KAJA: On that score, I assure you, you have no need for concern.

MASTER: Go quickly and hurry back.

TARŌ KAJA: Ha.

MASTER (*Taking one step forward*): Ei.

TARŌ KAJA (*Bowing*): Ha.

Tarō Kaja bows. The master pivots to his left, crosses upstage left, and sits on both knees facing front. This position indicates that he is no longer involved in the action on the stage. Tarō Kaja takes one step forward, returns to the shite spot, and faces front. This sequence of movements is a set pattern that always indicates a change of scene.

TARŌ KAJA: I have been given a most urgent task. (*Beginning his trip*) I must hurry on my way. Truly, there is no one so fortunate as my master's grandfather. (*Circles the stage, stops at the shite spot facing front, and takes one step backward*) Well, here I am at a thicket already. First I will step inside. (*Crosses to center stage, mimes pushing the brush apart [figure 2.52], and takes one large step forward over the underbrush. These movements are identical to the movements performed by the warrior priest when he entered the same thicket earlier*) Ei, ei, yatto-na. (*Facing left and then right, looking here and there*) Well now, what a big, wide thicket this is. But I have no idea where this thing called a snail may be. (*Crossing downstage right*) My master said that, to begin with, they have black heads; they carry a shell on their hip; and sometimes they show their horns. (*Turning this way and that in his search, Tarō Kaja finally backs into the sleeping warrior priest [figure 2.53]. He turns to look at the warrior priest and crosses hurriedly to the shite spot and looks aside*) Something with a black head is sleeping over there. First I will wake it up and question it.

(Crosses over to the warrior priest, kneels on his right knee beside him, and shakes his shoulder twice) Here, here. Wake up. Wake up, I say.

WARRIOR PRIEST *(Stirring in his sleep):* Mm, mm, mm.

TARŌ KAJA *(Shaking the warrior priest's shoulder twice more):* Wake up. Wake up, I say.

Tarō Kaja crosses to the shite spot and faces the warrior priest.

WARRIOR PRIEST *(Stretching as he awakens):* Mm, mm, mm, mm, mm. *(Getting to his feet and facing front)* How well I slept. How well I slept. I had myself a very good nap. *(Turns toward Tarō Kaja)* Oh, are you the one who woke me up?

TARŌ KAJA: I am, indeed.

WARRIOR PRIEST: And what is it you want of me?

TARŌ KAJA: Although I realize how rude it may seem *(taking one step forward)*, are you not perhaps one who is known as Master Snail?

WARRIOR PRIEST: What's this? *(Taking one step back)* You ask me if I am a snail?

TARŌ KAJA: I do, indeed.

WARRIOR PRIEST *(Taking one step forward):* And why do you ask me that?

TARŌ KAJA *(Taking one step back):* I have heard *(both face front)* that the thing they call a snail has a black head. *(Facing the warrior priest)* When I saw you, I noticed that your head was black. Thus I wondered if you might not be *(bowing)* Master Snail himself.

WARRIOR PRIEST *(Facing Tarō Kaja):* What's that you say? Since my head is black, you wonder if I might not be a snail?

TARŌ KAJA *(Bowing):* I do, indeed.

WARRIOR PRIEST *(Taking one step forward):* Wait right here for a minute.

TARŌ KAJA: With all my heart. *(Faces front.)*

WARRIOR PRIEST *(Looks aside, takes two steps forward, raises his right arm to cover his face, and laughs heartily):* What is this? He finds a warrior priest and asks if he is a snail. He seems a fool, indeed. I'll just give him a good ribbing for his trouble. *(Faces Tarō Kaja)* Here, here. *(Tarō Kaja looks at the warrior priest)* You are a happy man. *(Takes one step forward)* I am a snail.

TARŌ KAJA: In that case, I am a happy man. But they say that a snail carries a shell on its hip. *(Taking one step forward)* Do you have a shell?

WARRIOR PRIEST *(Taking one step back):* So you want to see my shell?

TARŌ KAJA: I want to see it.

WARRIOR PRIEST: I will show it to you. *(Takes one step forward)* Wait right there for a minute.

TARŌ KAJA: With all my heart.

Tarō Kaja faces front, and the warrior priest turns to face downstage left, where he put his conch shell on the ground when he went to sleep, picks the conch shell up in both hands, turns toward Tarō Kaja, and takes one step toward him with each repetition of the following line:

WARRIOR PRIEST: There it is.

(Tarō Kaja looks at the warrior priest)

There it is. There it is. There it is. (*The warrior priest stamps his right foot and strikes a pose with his face turned forward and his conch shell thrust out to his right side.*) Is it not a fine shell?

TARŌ KAJA (*Takes a small step to his right and bends down to look at the conch shell*): It is a fine shell, indeed. (*Taking a small step backward, still facing the warrior priest*) They also say that you sometimes show your horns. Do you have horns?

The warrior priest crosses downstage left and puts the conch shell back on the floor where it was before. The stage attendant comes out to take the conch shell away.

WARRIOR PRIEST (*Facing Tarō Kaja*): You say (*taking one step back*) you want to see my horns?

TARŌ KAJA: Most certainly.

WARRIOR PRIEST (*Takes one step forward*): Wait right here for a minute.

TARŌ KAJA: With all my heart. (*Faces front.*)

WARRIOR PRIEST (*Looks aside and takes one step forward*): What is this? He has me stuck on these horns. (*Thinking*) I wonder what I should do. (*Looks at the pompoms on his neckpiece, first left and then right, nods, and turns back to Tarō Kaja*) Here, here. (*Tarō Kaja looks at the warrior priest.*) I will show you my horns (*Taking one step forward*), but you must never tell anyone you saw them.

TARŌ KAJA: No, never. I will never tell anyone I saw them.

WARRIOR PRIEST (*Pointing toward the corner with his chin*): Then come all the way over here.

TARŌ KAJA: With all my heart.

Tarō Kaja crosses over to the corner and faces the warrior priest, who turns his back to Tarō Kaja, grasps his pompom neckpiece with both hands, and raises it up to his ears in such a way that one pair of pompoms shows over his shoulders.

WARRIOR PRIEST: Here they come. Here they come. Here they come.

TARŌ KAJA (*Crosses to the shite spot and faces the warrior priest*): Truly, you have shown your horns. You are without any doubt Master Snail himself.

WARRIOR PRIEST (*Readjusts his costume, turns to face Tarō Kaja, and takes one step forward*): And what might you want of a snail?

TARŌ KAJA: I was just about to tell you. (*Both face front*) My master has a grandfather who has lived a long and happy life. They say that if he is given a snail, he will live even longer. (*Facing the warrior priest*) This is why I have come looking for a snail. I humbly beg you to come along with me.

WARRIOR PRIEST (*Looking at Tarō Kaja*): I would like to go with you, indeed, but these days snails have become so popular with grandfathers that I have no free time at all. (*Faces front*) Thus I cannot go with you.

TARŌ KAJA: This is indeed a shame, as I was so very happy to have found you. I humbly beg you to cancel your previous promises (*taking one step forward*) and come along with me.

WARRIOR PRIEST (*Looking at Tarō Kaja*): Well, if you insist, I will go, but I will not go on my own feet. (*Takes one step forward and raises his arms*) You must carry me on your back.

TARŌ KAJA *(Taking one step back)*: As I am very weak, I humbly beg you to come *(bowing)* walking on your own feet.

WARRIOR PRIEST *(Facing downstage left)*: No, no, I will not just walk. If that is the case *(facing Tarō Kaja)*, you must join me in a song and dance as we go along.

TARŌ KAJA: Is it difficult to do?

WARRIOR PRIEST: It is not at all difficult. This is how it goes.

TARŌ KAJA: How does it go?

WARRIOR PRIEST: It is not at all difficult. This is how it goes.

TARŌ KAJA: How does it go?

WARRIOR PRIEST *(Both face front)*: You just sing *(still speaking)*:

> Whether it rains
> or whether the wind blows,
> if you don't come out,
> I'll break your shell.[4]

Facing each other.

> Then I sing

The warrior priest faces downstage left, and Tarō Kaja faces front, still speaking.

> Come out, slimy snailie,
> come out, slimy snailie,
> come out, you slimy snail.[5]

Facing each other.

> And we'll have ourselves a fine time dancing as we go.

TARŌ KAJA *(Taking one step back)*: Well, then, first I'll see if I can say it.

WARRIOR PRIEST: Come, come. Try to say it. *(Both face front.)*

TARŌ KAJA *(Speaking)*:

> Whether it rains
> or whether the wind blows,
> if you don't come out,
> I'll break your shell.

They face each other.

> How was that?

WARRIOR PRIEST: That's it, that's it. *(Taking one step forward)* Now let us sing and dance it.

TARŌ KAJA: With all my heart.

Both face front. Tarō Kaja takes his fan from his sash and holds it in his right hand,

---

4. Songs about a snail have long been popular in Japan. The following version appears in the twelfth-century *Ryōjin hishō* as song 408: "Dance, dance, little snail!/If you don't dance,/I'll have the pony and the calf kick you/and trample you all to pieces./If you dance beautifully,/I'll let you play in the flower garden."

5. In Japanese the refrain is a repetition of *den den mushi mushi. Dendenmushi* is one word for snail, which suggests *deyo deyo,* "come out, come out."

resting the end in his left hand while
he sings the verse.

TARŌ KAJA:

> Whether it rains
> or whether the wind blows,
> if you don't come out,
> I'll break your shell;
> if you don't come out,
> I'll break your shell.

The warrior priest nods in approval
and sings the refrain while dancing in
circling movements [figure 2.54].

WARRIOR PRIEST:

> Come out, slimy snailie,
> come out, slimy snailie,
> come out, you slimy snail.

FIGURE 2.54. Tarō Kaja and the yamabushi repeat the "slimy snail" song and dance numerous times, varying it slightly with each repetition. (Courtesy of Don Kenny.)

The warrior priest ends with a stamp of
his right foot and turns toward Tarō Kaja. Tarō Kaja faces the warrior priest, and
they sing and dance the verse together, lifting their legs alternately on the upbeats.
Tarō Kaja also taps the palm of his left hand with his fan on each upbeat.

BOTH:

> Whether it rains
> or whether the wind blows,
> if you don't come out,
> I'll break your shell;
> if you don't come out,
> I'll break your shell.

Both face front. The warrior priest sings the refrain while doing a stamping dance.

WARRIOR PRIEST:

> Come out, slimy snailie.
> Come out, slimy snailie.
> Come out, you slimy snail.

The third time through, they face each other, and Tarō Kaja taps the palm of his
left hand with his fan on each upbeat as they sing and dance the verse together,
once more lifting their legs alternately on the upbeats.

BOTH:

> Whether it rains
> or whether the wind blows,
> if you don't come out,
> I'll break your shell;
> if you don't come out,
> I'll break your shell.

Both face front. The warrior priest sings the refrain while doing a squatting and leaping dance.

WARRIOR PRIEST:

Come out, slimy snailie,
come out, slimy snailie,
come out, you slimy snail.

The singing and dancing become more intense, and the rhythm gradually becomes faster as they continue to sing and dance a total of eight times. The movements are the same for the verse throughout, but the refrain varies with each repetition. The fourth time, after the verse, the warrior priest does a hopping dance while singing the refrain. The fifth time, after the verse, both sing the refrain while hopping on one foot to exchange positions, ending with the warrior priest at the shite spot and Tarō Kaja at the waki spot. The sixth time, after the verse, the warrior priest sings the refrain while doing a circling dance similar to the one he did the first time. The seventh time, after the verse, both sing the refrain while hopping on one foot to exchange positions once more, ending with the warrior priest back at the waki spot and Tarō Kaja at the shite spot. The eighth time, after the verse, the warrior priest does a stamping and whirling dance. The master, who has been sitting upstage left, rises to his feet and crosses the upstage area to the bridgeway. He stops at the first pine and faces front.

MASTER: I sent my servant Tarō Kaja out to catch a snail some time ago. He is so late that I have decided to go out and look for him. (*Crosses upstage to the right behind Tarō Kaja*) What is this? Here, here, Tarō Kaja.

TARŌ KAJA (*Facing his master*): Huh? It's you, sir.

MASTER: What are you up to?

TARŌ KAJA: I am escorting Master Snail.

WARRIOR PRIEST (*Crosses over to Tarō Kaja and tugs at his sleeve*): Hey, hey. Are you going to sing and dance or not? Are you going to sing and dance?

TARŌ KAJA (*Facing the warrior priest*): With all my heart.

The warrior priest and Tarō Kaja begin the song and dance for the ninth time. During this and the following repetitions of the verse, the warrior priest encourages Tarō Kaja from time to time with "That's it. That's it!"

MASTER (*Crosses to the first pine on the bridgeway and faces front*): What is this? It looks like he has lost his mind. (*Crosses to behind Tarō Kaja*) Tarō Kaja. Tarō Kaja. Hey, Tarō Kaja. (*Tarō Kaja turns toward his master.*) You are a fool. That is a warrior priest.

TARŌ KAJA: You say he's a warrior priest?

WARRIOR PRIEST (*Crosses to behind Tarō Kaja and tugs at his sleeve*): Hey. Are you going to sing and dance or not? Are you going to sing and dance?

TARŌ KAJA (*Facing the warrior priest*): He says you are a warrior priest.

WARRIOR PRIEST (*Taking one step back*): What a rude idea. How could I be a warrior priest? The older ones often grow as big as a person.

TARŌ KAJA: Oh, that's right.

WARRIOR PRIEST (*Singing*): You slimy snail . . .

The warrior priest draws Tarō Kaja back into their tenth repetition of the song and dance. The master crosses to the first pine and faces front.

BOTH:
> Whether it rains
> or whether the wind blows,
> if you don't come out,
> I'll break your shell;
> if you don't come out,
> I'll break your shell.

Tarō Kaja faces front while the warrior priest goes on singing and dancing the refrain until the master interrupts.

WARRIOR PRIEST:
> Come out, slimy snailie.
> Come out, slimy snailie.
> Come out, you slimy snail.

MASTER: I must say, what a vexing thing this is. (*Crosses to behind Tarō Kaja*) Tarō Kaja. Tarō Kaja. Hey, Tarō Kaja.

TARŌ KAJA (*Facing his master*): Huh?

MASTER: Get a hold of yourself. That is a warrior priest, and a phony one at that.

TARŌ KAJA: So you say it really is a warrior priest?

MASTER: It most certainly is a warrior priest.

WARRIOR PRIEST (*Crosses to behind Tarō Kaja and tugs at his sleeve*): Hey. Are you going to sing and dance or not? Are you going to sing and dance?

TARŌ KAJA (*Stamping with his right foot and raising his right arm to point with his fan at the warrior priest*): Hey, you rascal.

WARRIOR PRIEST (*Takes one step back and brings down his left foot with a loud stamp*): What?

TARŌ KAJA: He says you are a warrior priest, and a phony one at that.

The warrior priest stamps with his right foot and thrusts his right arm toward Tarō Kaja's face. They begin singing the refrain and dancing. They do a one-foot hop dance during which they reverse positions once again, ending with Tarō Kaja at the waki spot and the warrior priest at the shite spot.

BOTH:
> Come out, slimy snailie,
> come out, slimy snailie,
> come out, you slimy snail.

MASTER (*Crosses to the first pine and faces front*): Well, I must say, what a vexing thing this is.

The master crosses to Tarō Kaja. Simultaneously, the warrior priest moves to center stage right and faces front.[6]

---

6. Another ending omits what follows and instead has the master unintentionally get caught up in the hypnotic rhythms and repetitions of the song and dance. He gradually joins the others in circling the stage and follows them off, singing and dancing up the bridgeway.

WARRIOR PRIEST (*Laughs loudly*): I'll rib them a little more.

The warrior priest takes his rosary out of his bosom, swings it sharply left and then right. He opens his arms straight out to both sides, brings them together in front still extended, and pulls his hands toward his face, bending his knees and lowering his head at the same time. This semisquatting position renders him invisible to the other characters.

MASTER (*Crosses downstage left to behind Tarō Kaja*): Tarō Kaja. Tarō Kaja. (*Tugging at Tarō Kaja's sleeve*) Hey, Tarō Kaja. (*Tarō Kaja turns to his master*) I order you to get ahold of yourself. That is a warrior priest and a phony one at that.

TARŌ KAJA: So you say he really is a phony?

MASTER: Catch him and thrash him right now.

TARŌ KAJA: With all my heart.

MASTER (*Facing the corner, he raises his right arm to point with his fan and takes several steps*): You are a hateful rascal.

TARŌ KAJA (*Also facing the corner, he raises his right arm to point with his fan and takes several steps*): You are a hateful rascal.

MASTER (*Both the master and Tarō Kaja look left*): Huh? He has gone away somewhere.

TARŌ KAJA (*Both the master and Tarō Kaja look right*): He has gone away somewhere.

The warrior priest crosses to the waki spot and thrusts his left arm toward the faces of the master and Tarō Kaja, making himself visible to them once more. They throw up their arms and fall over backward, exclaiming in unison, "Aaaaaah." The warrior priest laughs loudly as he turns and runs off the stage and up the bridgeway, shouting repeatedly.

WARRIOR PRIEST: You fools. You fools.

MASTER (*Getting to his feet and looking toward the vanishing warrior priest*): Where do you think you're going?

TARŌ KAJA (*Getting to his feet and looking after the vanishing warrior priest*): There he goes.

MASTER (*To Tarō Kaja*): Catch him quickly.

TARŌ KAJA (*To his master*): Catch him quickly, sir.

They raise their right arms to shoulder height to point with their fans and chase after the warrior priest, Tarō Kaja behind his master, shouting repeatedly in unison.

BOTH: We'll catch you yet. We'll catch you yet.

WARRIOR PRIEST: You fools. You fools.

They exit under the lifted curtain.

BOTH: We'll catch you yet. We'll catch you yet.

The "Sickley" Stomach (Kamabara)

A woman play

Translated by Ayako Kano

Woman plays in noh feature a female character and explore her emotions and behavior, at least as they were conceived — and usually idealized — by male playwrights and actors. In kyōgen, woman plays include a female character, but the action generally centers on her relationship with a man or even, as is the case here, on the man himself. The shite almost always plays a male character. In two plays that do have female shite roles, *Bikusada* (The aged nun and Bikusada) and *Iori no ume* (The plum blossom hut), they play aged nuns. The latter play is unique in that all the characters are female — played, of course, by male actors. Although the female character is normally played as a secondary role (by an ado), she often ends up "triumphant," having outwitted or otherwise overcome the male figure. Many of the most humorous plays include marital conflicts. In premodern Japan it was simple for a husband to divorce his wife, yet in such kyōgen as *Hikkuri* (Caught in a sack) and *Inabado* (The drunken wife), the women devise means of keeping their men.

The "Sickley" Stomach is about a marital dispute, but most of the action centers on the husband and his attempt to commit suicide. The title is a pun, deftly transformed by Ayako Kano: *kama* means "sickle," and *bara* is "stomach" and part of the compound *harakiri*, the vulgar word for describing the Japanese method of suicide by cutting open one's abdomen. There is also an echo of Kamakura, the country's military center from 1186 to 1333. It is unclear when this title was given to the play; earlier versions of the play were simply called *Hara kirazu* (Not cutting one's abdomen).

The heart of this play is a parody of ritual suicide presented in the husband's long soliloquy and enhanced by exaggerated bits of mime. Since he is not a member of the warrior class and has no access to a sword, the husband attempts to commit suicide with a sickle. But he lacks the samurai valor so elegized in puppet and kabuki plays, in which even a lowly retainer like Kampei in *Chūshingura* manages to redeem himself by committing suicide. The husband also lacks a witness to his deed; he cannot even summon a grass cutter to his side. Finally, therefore, he gives up.

The version of the play translated here by Ayako Kano is that currently performed by the Ōkura school. It is based on the Yamamoto Azuma text found in Koyama 1961. This version ends where it begins, with the wife hounding the husband. Another version, now used by the Izumi school and translated by Richard McKinnon (1968), ends with the husband deciding to postpone his suicide attempt and to go back to work. The wife does not reappear on the stage.

CHARACTERS

SHITE: a man named Tarō (not meant to be identified with Tarō Kaja)
ADO: his wife
KOADO: a mediator

MUSICIANS

None

A Play in One Act

Foot stamps are heard behind the curtain, accompanied by a woman's angry voice. The curtain is raised, and Tarō appears on the bridgeway pursued by his wife, who brandishes a pole with a sickle tied to it.

WIFE: Hey, you hateful man, you! You may want to escape, but I won't let you get away with this, I'll hack you to pieces!

TARŌ: Good heavens, what's happening? Oh, please forgive me! What are you doing? Isn't somebody here? Help, help, help, help, help! Oh no, oh no!

Followed by his wife, Tarō makes one circuit of the stage. He goes up the bridgeway to the first pine, but she remains on the stage.

MEDIATOR *(Appearing on the bridgeway after the couple)*: Well now, this is awful. I wonder what happened. *(Walks onto the stage and restrains the woman)* Whoa, whoa, wait a second, wait a second [figure 2.55].

WIFE: Out of my way! I'll hack him to pieces!

MEDIATOR: Hold on a minute. There'll be no reckless behavior while I'm here. Now, first tell me what's the matter.

WIFE *(Going to center stage)*: OK, but listen to me! That man has made all three realms of the world his home![1] He stays out day and night; he even makes me repair the holes in the roof! He came home today—a rare occasion indeed—so I told him to go to the mountains and cut wood, but he makes all kinds of excuses and just won't go. A man like that is not worth keeping alive. Now please get out of my way. I'll hack him to pieces and then kill myself! *(Tries to get at Tarō.)*

MEDIATOR: Whoa, whoa, now, now, wait a second.

TARŌ *(At the first pine)*: Oh, please stop her, stop her!

MEDIATOR *(To wife)*: I'll talk to him and give him a good scolding. You wait here.

WIFE: Be sure you give him a good scolding.

MEDIATOR: At your service, ma'am. *(Going toward the bridgeway)* Hey Tarō!

TARŌ: I'm so ashamed.

1. The three realms in Buddhism are the worlds of desire, form, and formlessness, but the expression came to mean the entire world. Tarō is accused of roaming about in the world, forgetting his own home.

FIGURE 2.55. The mediator in *The "Sickley" Stomach* attempts to disarm the wife, who has been threatening her husband with a sickle tied to a stick. The wife wears a small-sleeved kimono and the white headdress (*binan*) used for female characters in kyōgen. (Courtesy of the Noh Research Archive of Musashino Women's College.)

MEDIATOR: You say you're ashamed! Your wife has just told me everything, and she's right. You're an absolute disgrace!

TARŌ: But wait! If you only listened to her, of course she's right. I stayed away day and night because I care so much about my home and family. I have patrons[2] in various places, and when I go anywhere, they say to me, "Hello, Tarō. Nice of you to drop by. Spend the night; stay tomorrow, too." I can't visit one place and not another, so I end up putting off coming home from day to day. Today I had the rare opportunity to come home, and before I could even settle down, she was after me to go into the mountains to cut wood. I didn't even refuse to go. I said I would go after I had rested for a while, but she is such an impatient woman, she comes after me with a pole like that and makes me run for my life. Anyway, all I have to do is go into the mountains, and all will be well. Would you please bring me that sickle and carrying pole?

MEDIATOR: You will go to the mountains then?

TARŌ: Yes, indeed.

MEDIATOR: In that case, I'll bring you the tools. Wait here.

TARŌ: Ha.

MEDIATOR (*Returning to the shite spot*): There now, I've told him what you said and have given him a good scolding. He says he'll go to the mountains. Give him the sickle and pole.

WIFE: You mean he says he'll go to the mountains?

MEDIATOR: Yes, he does.

WIFE: As long as he goes to the mountains, all will be well. Would you mind giving him these? (*Hands over the pole with the sickle attached.*)

MEDIATOR: At your service, ma'am. (*Takes the pole and goes to the end of the bridgeway*) There now, take this and go quickly to the mountains.

TARŌ: I'm very much indebted to you. (*Takes the pole*) Well, you really appeared at a fortunate moment today. I would have been hacked to pieces by that woman if you hadn't come.

MEDIATOR: It was indeed a close call. Now Tarō, listen well. Time and again you and your wife have quarreled. It has gotten so that all the people in our town and friends in other towns point their fingers at you and laugh. Today I came

2. *Danna* is a term originally used by Buddhist priests to refer to patrons who contribute money and goods. It came to mean patrons of business as well.

to settle things between you, but if you quarrel again in the future, I won't come, so be warned.

TARŌ: I promise I will never, ever quarrel with her again.

WIFE (*At the shite spot*): Hey you hateful man. You're still not going to the mountains?!

TARŌ: Oh, such impatience! I was just about to leave for the mountains, wasn't I?

MEDIATOR (*Turning toward the woman*): There, there. Why don't you go into the house and get some rest?

WIFE: If you say so, sir.

MEDIATOR (*To Tarō*): Tarō, you'd better hurry up and go to the mountains.

TARŌ: Please get some rest yourself, sir.

MEDIATOR: I shall. (*He follows the wife up the bridgeway and exits.*)

TARŌ (*Goes to the shite spot*): Oh dear, oh dear. That was a dangerous moment. If our mediator had not come, I would have been hacked to pieces by that woman. By heaven's grace, my life was saved. Now I'd better hurry to the mountains.

He starts walking, with the pole over his shoulder.

Indeed, there must be married couples in this world that get along well; no woman could be as shrewish as my own wife.[3] What have I done to deserve being married to such a woman, I wonder? It must have been a match made in my previous life.

He circles the stage and stops again at the shite spot.

Let's see now, what did the mediator say? "Time and again you and your wife have quarreled." "It has gotten so that all the people in our town and friends in other towns point their fingers at you and laugh. Today I came to settle things between you, but if you quarrel again in the future, I won't come to help you." If we ever quarrel again and if he won't come to my rescue, I'll eventually be hacked to death by that woman. It would be too sad to be born a man and be hacked to death by a woman, but what can I do?

Ponders.

Oh, look, there's a gorge. I'll go jump off the cliff and kill myself. (*Goes to stage front*) Hmm, on second thought . . . (*Reconsidering, he returns to the shite spot*) If I kill myself by jumping into this gorge, people will say that Tarō, harried and hounded by his old lady, went to the mountains to cut wood and killed himself by jumping into a gorge. I'd be a laughingstock even after my death. I must think of a courageous way to die that will leave me with an honorable name.

Thinking, he glances at the sickle.

Aha! I have a sickle. That gives me a great idea! I'll commit ritual disembowelment using this sickle, as befits a peasant like myself.[4] (*Puts down the pole and*

3. The Japanese adjective is *wawashii*, which is often translated as "loudmouthed."

4. To commit *harakiri* using a sword was a privilege of the warrior class. A peasant might choose a more humble instrument.

FIGURE 2.56. The husband, Tarō, attempts to commit suicide in the mountains. He has failed at cutting open his stomach, so he contemplates cutting his neck. (Courtesy of the Noh Research Archive of Musashino Women's College.)

unties the sickle) It is said, "A man with guts his stomach cuts." Lately I've been thinking I should cut wood; I've been planning to cut wood, I even sharpened my sickle in preparation for cutting wood, but I must have sharpened it on an unlucky day. It's not wood but my own stomach that I'll end up cutting. (*Holding the sickle in his hand, he walks to center stage*) Let me see now, I've never committed disembowelment before. How should I go about it? Well, hmm, there can't be anything very difficult about it. To disembowel oneself, one must first strip the upper body like this (*sits and removes the upper half of his garment*),[5] then hold the sickle like this (*stands and mimes the following*), then plunge it into the left side, and pull, pull, pull with all my might to the right side. Then my intestines will glob, glob, glob out, and I'll get dizzy, dizzy, dizzy, and then I'll die just like that. That's a courageous way to die. But first I must proclaim this before I die.

Standing at the shite spot, he calls toward the curtain.

Hi ho, hear ye, hear ye, all people of this town and friends in other towns. So you all point your fingers, do you, and laugh at this Tarō, who constantly quarrels with his wife? Well, Tarō can no longer defend his honor as a man, and so he will hereby commit sickle suicide. Won't someone come and watch me perform this feat? Is there no one in the mountains? (*Faces forward*) Ha, I guess it's too early in the day. No one's around. Oops, while I say this, time goes by. I must hurry and commit sickle suicide. (*Goes to front center*) Now, my end is here. Eeeyaa, ay! (*Puts the sickle to his stomach*) Ouch, ouch, ouch, ouch! (*Throws the sickle aside and holds his stomach*) Wow, that was painful, but I wonder if I even made a wound? No, it didn't even make a scratch. Oh, ouch, ouch, ouch. (*Looks at the sickle, laughs, and picks it up*) Well, no wonder it hurts. If one touches a tender spot with such a sharp thing, it ought to hurt. It could prove to be difficult cutting my stomach like this. What should I do?

Thinks.

Ho, ho, this time I'll put the sickle around my neck (*mimes this and the following actions*), and pull and yank forward with all my might. Then my

5. Only the vest is removed by actors of the Ōkura school. In the Izumi school, the top of the striped robe is pulled off and tucked into the belt.

head will plop to the ground, and I'll die just like that. Indeed, that's an unusual way to die. I'll commit sickle slashing this time. But first I have to proclaim anew before I die [figure 2.56].

Goes to the edge of the bridgeway and calls toward the curtain.

Hear ye, hear ye, this Tarō has slightly modified his intentions and has now decided to commit something called sickle beheading. This is a most unusual way to die. Come and watch me perform this feat. Are there no grass cutters around? (*Turns to the front*) What a shame, today of all days, no one seems to be in the mountains. Oops, while I say this, time goes by. (*Goes to center stage*) Now I shall commit sickle beheading. I can't just yank like that. I'll count to three and pull on the third count. (*Puts the sickle around his neck*) Eeyaa, ay. That's one. Eeeyaa, ay. That's two. Now this is the last. Eeeyaa ay, ay, ay, ay, ay.

He tries to pull on the sickle but cannot do it. He removes it from around his neck, sits down, and laughs.

I wanted to pull, I tried to pull, but this arm is too cowardly and just won't pull. It looks like sickle beheading is impossible, too. I must think of some way to die without using my arms.

Thinks.

Hi ho. I have a great idea. This time, I'll plunge the sickle thus into the bush. (*Puts the sickle on the floor near the waki spot and turns toward the bridgeway*) Then I'll run from all the way back there to all the way down here (*looks at the sickle*) and somersault two or three times onto that sickle, and I'll die just like that. That's a better way, since I don't have to use my arms. All right, I'll quickly make a run for it. (*Goes to the first pine and looks toward the sickle*) The direction is right on. Now this is really the end. Eeeyaa, run, run, run, run. (*Runs toward the sickle, stops in front of it, and laughs*) Ah, that was close, that was dangerous. Indeed, I wanted to somersault, I tried to somersault, but when I saw that sickle sickly shining like that, I was just too scared to do it. That's because my eyes had cold feet. This time I'll run with my eyes closed. But I must first proclaim the correction before I die.

Goes to the shite spot and turns toward the curtain.

Hi ho out there. This Tarō has changed his mind again. This time I will kill myself by performing what is called a "sickley"-sprinting-sightless-suicide. This is an extremely courageous and unusual way to die. Won't anybody come and see me perform the feat? Tell the women to come, too. Is there no one in the mountains? Are there no grass cutters here? (*Turns toward the audience*) Well, I don't understand this. Today of all days, no one is in the mountains. I don't understand this at all. I wish I could show someone my courageous manner of dying. Oops, while I say this, time goes by. I'll quickly perform my sickly-sprinting-sightless-suicide. (*Goes to the first pine*) Now, this is truly the end. Eeeyaaa!

He covers his eyes with both hands and runs toward the sickle but opens his eyes and stops in front of it. He laughs.

Oh dear, when I thought I got close to the sickle, my eyes goggled wide open before I knew, and I just couldn't somersault. If things go on like this, I'm going to have a hard time killing myself. What should I do?

Thinks.

Oh, yes, yes. I have indeed lost my mind. If I go into the mountains, cut wood, return home, and humor my old lady, I don't even need to die. By heaven's grace, my life is saved. Let's see, let's see, let's pack the sickle and rush off to the mountains. (*Sits at the shite spot*) Today, by heaven's grace, my life was saved. (*Ties the sickle back on the pole.*)

WIFE (*Appears on the bridgeway and speaks at the first pine. She has heard of Tarō's suicide attempts*): What, what? Is that true now, is that right? Dear, dear, how distressing. I wonder where my husband is.

TARŌ (*Hastily untying the sickle from the pole again as his wife appears on the bridgeway*): Oh, no. That's the voice of my old lady. Now, this is the end. (*Goes to center stage and puts the sickle to his stomach*) Eeeyaa!

WIFE (*Entering the stage proper and approaching Tarō*): Oh no! What's going on? Dear, dear, what are you doing? Please stop and change your mind. (*Clings to him.*)

TARŌ: Who's there? Who is it?

WIFE: It's me, it's me.

TARŌ: Who's me? My old lady?

WIFE: Yes, yes, it's me.

TARŌ: Did you come to watch me commit suicide? Let me go. I'll cut my stomach open and whack you with my guts.

WIFE: No. Oh dear, oh dear. Please wait a minute. Why would I come to watch you commit suicide? I heard that you were going to cut your stomach, and I dropped everything to hurry here as fast as I could. I admit that everything was my fault, so please forgive me and change your mind.

TARŌ: Listen to me, wife. Time and again you have hounded me, making all the people of our town and friends in other towns point their fingers at me and laugh. Therefore, Tarō can no longer defend his manly honor, and therefore he will commit sickle suicide. I'll whack you with my guts.

WIFE: Wait a moment, please. I will never ever hound you again, so please forgive me and change your mind.

TARŌ: You may say that now, but I know you'll hound me again when we return home. This is something a real man has decided to do. I absolutely must commit suicide.

WIFE: How awful, how awful. Please forgive me and change your mind.

TARŌ: No, no! I absolutely must commit suicide.

They struggle with each other [figure 2.57].

WIFE: Then you won't change your mind, no matter how much I ask you to?

TARŌ: I have committed myself. How can I not do it?

WIFE: Well then, I have no choice. Please divorce me.

TARŌ (*Goes to the waki spot*): What did you say? Divorce you?

WIFE (*Goes to the shite spot*): Yes indeed.

TARŌ: What would you want to do with a divorce?

WIFE: Stop and think about it for a minute. Could I go on living as your wife, having made you cut your stomach? I'd have to fling myself into a gorge or something to kill myself. (*Weeps.*)

TARŌ: Well, well. That would really be a shame. Now then, I might consider changing my mind. But will you promise not ever to hound me again?

WIFE: No matter what happens, I'll never hound you again.

TARŌ: In that case, I'll change my mind.

WIFE: Thank goodness, I'm certainly happy to hear that.

TARŌ: Now, I have a little proposal to make to you.

WIFE: What could that be?

TARŌ: It's just this. To tell you the truth, I really wanted to commit suicide, so I tried this and that, but I was too much of a coward and just couldn't do it. Now you, on the other hand, just now said that you would jump into a gorge to kill yourself.

FIGURE 2.57. The woman attempts to take away the sickle from her husband. (Courtesy of the Noh Research Archive of Musashino Women's College.)

If you care so little about your life, would you mind taking my place and cutting your stomach with this sickle? (*Slides the sickle on the floor toward her and runs off toward the bridgeway.*)

WIFE (*Picks up the sickle*): Ah, my guts are boiling. Will you never stop uttering such nonsense?! What am I going to do with you! Hey, catch that hateful man. You won't get away with this! You won't get away with this! (*Runs up the bridgeway after Tarō.*)

TARŌ: Forgive me, forgive me! (*Exits.*)

WIFE: You won't get away with this! You won't get away with this! (*Exits chasing Tarō.*)

Kanaoka

A crazed-person play

Translated by Carolyn Haynes

This is a play of bittersweet humor, a gentle depiction of human foibles, in which farcical elements give way to a warm humanity. *Kanaoka* does not stand alone in this respect, however; some of the blind-person plays, such as *Kawakami* (translated as "Sight gained and lost"), delve even further into pathos. In this kyōgen, the painter Kanaoka is obsessed with a lady he met only briefly, much as the mother in *Miidera* was crazed by obsessive longing for her child. But *Kanaoka* is not so much a parody of the noh as a kyōgen treatment of a similar theme. A more parodic treatment of the obsessed-person theme is found in *Makura monogurui* (Pillow mania), which comically depicts an old man in love with a young girl. *Hōshigahaha* (The baby's mother) similarly portrays a man who recklessly divorced his wife and wants her back.

As Carolyn Haynes's translation reveals, *Kanaoka* is more nohlike in its structure than are the previous kyōgen plays. It uses a chorus, flute, and two drums, and dance is central. The shite first reveals his madness in a kyōgen version of the noh kakeri dance, and then he continues to dance as he sings of his obsession. Another kakeri occurs toward the end of the play, when the dance incorporates painting the wife's face in a farcically serious attempt to make her resemble the woman who infatuates him. This dance is technically difficult: the dancer must hold two long brushes, wet with real paint, in one hand. The emotional import of the dance, the despair of the painter's unattainable love, also is difficult to convey. When the dance ends and the song resumes, the mood changes: the husband grows angry at his impossible task, his own artistic failure, and his wife's lack of beauty. His movements and the singing speed up and become more dramatic. The intensity of this struggle dissolves into slapstick as he pushes his wife off her stool and she chases him offstage in a typical kyōgen ending.

The ending may be conventional, but the subject matter is not; the play, like *Yamamba*, explores the nature and potential of art, albeit in an unconventional and humorous manner. Along with *The "Sickley" Stomach*, *Kanaoka* is categorized as a woman play, but again, the emphasis is almost entirely on the man. Even though the wife is sympathetic to her husband's plight, he fails at what, in hindsight, was an impossible task.

Although texts of this play exist in the Ōkura school and the now defunct Sagi school versions, *Kanaoka* remains in the active repertory only in the Izumi school, which counts it as one of its major works (*daikyoku*), along with *Hanago* and *Tsuri-gitsune* (Fox trapping). Carolyn Haynes's detailed movement descriptions are based on a videotaped performance by Izumi Motohide, broadcast on NHK on November 3, 1975. The translation is based on the Izumi text found in Nonomura and Andō 1931.

CHARACTERS

SHITE: Kanaoka, a painter
ADO: his wife

MUSICIANS

Chorus of four or five members
A noh flute and two hand drums

A Play in One Act

The instrumentalists enter from the little door at backstage right and sit at the back of the stage, with the drummers facing the flutist. A chorus of four or five enter and sit behind the musicians. The ado, costumed as a woman, enters the bridgeway and goes to the shite spot.

WIFE: I am the wife of the painter Kanaoka. My husband went off suddenly some ten days ago and hasn't returned yet. When I ask about him, people tell me he's lost his senses and is wandering madly around the outskirts of the capital. Today I'm going to try to find him. (*Circles stage as she talks*) What a fix this is! He's always so sensible—what could possibly have driven him mad? People will surely gossip. I certainly hope I can get him to come home with me today. Well, here I am at Kiyomizu already. I'll wait for him here (*sits down in front of the flutist*).

Issei entrance music   *The shite enters to instrumental music and stands at the first pine. He carries a branch of bamboo in his right hand, balanced on his right shoulder. He points with his left hand and calls out toward stage front.*

SHITE: "Hey, you children over there, what are you laughing at? (*Lowers his left hand*) What's that?"[1]
You think my madness strange?

Facing front, the shite slowly sings the following in the melodic mode without accompaniment.

> "How cruel they are!
> The branch was still just now,
> but beckoned by the wind (*looks right*)
> a single leaf will fall.

Looks down, watching the falling leaf.

> My mind for once was calm,

Lowers the branch of bamboo.

> but then they called me mad
> and lo, my distracted heart

---

1. This line is taken from the noh play *Semimaru*.

Crosses rapidly to the corner.

CHORUS:

runs wild"[2] (*circles left to backstage center*).

Kakeri *The shite dances to flute music.[3] He stamps slowly ten times, then circles the stage, first right and then left, with slow, melancholy movements. The pace quickens as he crosses the stage again and hurries to the first pine on the bridgeway, where he comes to an abrupt halt. He returns to center stage and points toward the waki spot. The slow, deliberate movements of this dance reflect the anguish of searching for a loved one. The measured pace is punctuated by the vigorous flips necessary to straighten the trailing legs of the long trousers at each change of direction.*

SHITE: Ohh, that lady over there! I'd surely like to see under your veil! What?
Again they laugh, calling me mad!

Singing very slowly.

"In the Blossom Capital's crisscross weave,

Faces front.

if there's a street you've never seen,

Slowly pivots left.

just ask, and you won't lose your way.

Crosses slowly to the bridgeway.

But oh, the road of love!
You may think you know it well,
but you could lose your wits!"[4]

Faces front at the first pine.

"Love, oh love,
do not forsake me
halfway to love!"[5]
"The winds of love blow

He holds his left sleeve in front of his body to protect himself from the winds.

twining my sleeves about me.

Flips his left sleeve over his arm.

Oh, how heavy are my sleeves,

Returns his sleeve to its normal position.

how weighty the winds of love!"

---

2. Quoted, with minor alterations, from the noh play *Hanjo.*

3. Usually both drums and the flute play for this dance.

4. This section consists of several popular songs strung together. This one is song 18 in the *Kanginshū* (Hoff 1978). "Crisscross weave" is a translation of *tatenuki*, a weaving term referring to the warp and woof of fabric, here used as a metaphor for the grid of streets.

5. Probably a popular song, although of uncertain origin. It occurs in other noh and kyōgen plays, often paired with the song that follows it here, *Kanginshū* poem 72.

Raises the bamboo grass and drops it back on his shoulder, crouching slightly as if under its weight. Speaks the next line.

Oh, her lovely face!

Lowers the bamboo and looks toward the curtain. Sings again.

"What spring was it that first I saw,

Goes rapidly to the second pine.

that first I loved her?

Returns to the first pine.

Never shall I forget—

Makes a circlet to the left.

that feast of blossoms!"[6]
"Beneath the cherry trees

Stamps and goes to the shite spot; the pace quickens.

at Kiyomizu, at Kiyomizu,
I trysted with a lovely youth.
Oh, you mustn't kiss just once,

Opens his arms wide and brings them together while moving toward center stage.

and you mustn't kiss just twice!

He makes circlets, flaps his arms together again, and goes to the corner.

How wretched, wretched I am!"[7]

Backs up to the shite spot, drops the bamboo branch, sits, and weeps.

WIFE (*Moves forward to the waki spot and addresses her husband*): This is madness, just madness! Tell me what this is all about, right now!

SHITE (*Looks up*): Is that you, wife? What are you doing here?

He takes out his fan and stands. A stage attendant removes the branch.

WIFE: You've been gone for more than ten days. People said you'd lost your senses and were wandering around the outskirts of the capital. *That's* why I came looking for you. What is it that's driven you mad?

SHITE: Now, now, you're speaking recklessly. I haven't lost my wits. Don't act so crazy!

WIFE: Look at you! Wandering around all disheveled like this. Isn't that madness?

SHITE: Hmm, it's that obvious, is it? But you won't like it when you hear what this is about, I warn you.

WIFE: Now, now, you're my husband—I won't make a fuss, even if it's something I don't want to hear. Please just tell me.

SHITE: Well, if you insist, I'll tell you. But don't get angry when you hear it.

6. A song (*kouta*) also used in the kyōgen *Hanago*. The "feast of blossoms" (*hana no en*) is a poetic term for conjugal felicity.

7. There are no other occurrences of this song, but it is presumed to be a contemporary kouta.

WIFE: Why ever should I get angry? Just tell me what it is.

SHITE (*Both face front*): Well, some time ago I went to the palace, where I'd been summoned to do some paintings. I was commanded to paint scenes of the four seasons on the sliding doors of the dressing room. "At once," I said, and I set to work, exhausting every secret of my art to paint beautiful scenes in the tradition of my ancestors. When I'd finished, a number of women in gorgeous robes, looking like so many poppies in a vase, crowded in to see my work. They all were incomparably beautiful. Then one of the ladies—she couldn't have been more than twenty years old, a true beauty—approached me (*turns slightly toward his wife*).

WIFE: This will never do. This will never do.

SHITE: Remember, don't get angry!

WIFE: Don't worry; go on.

SHITE (*Faces front*): Oh! Her expression was so gentle, so elegant! How can I describe it? Her hair like a cloud, her face, a blossom.[8] I never saw the Chinese beauties Yang Kuei-Fei or Empress Li,[9] but even the celestial maidens in my paintings couldn't compare with her! (*Vigorously shaking his head*) Oh, I thought, what a beautiful lady! And I was gazing at her shyly when she held out a white fan and said, "Would you draw something on this?" (*Holds out his fan, handle first*) I was so happy, overcome by her generosity. Right then and there (*opens his fan and holds it vertically*), in a light ink wash, I drew autumn grasses in a field on the front (*switches his fan to his left hand*), and on the other side, I made a quick sketch of a Chinese scene. (*Gazes at his fan, then closes it*) I dashed these off, then handed the sketch back to her. But I couldn't contain myself, and as I handed back the fan (*holds out his fan, handle first*), I squeezed her hand. (*Lowers his right hand quickly and reaches forward as if grasping with his left hand*) She glanced at me and laughed. Dawn or dusk, sleeping or waking, I cannot forget how beautiful she looked as she laughed. This is what has driven me mad! (*Builds up to exaggerated weeping. His sobbing and his wife's cry of anger overlap.*)

WIFE: Ohhh, I'm furious! Just furious! Has there ever been anything so preposterous—ever?!

SHITE (*Faces her*): You see? You made me tell you something you wouldn't like, and now you're angry.

WIFE: No, no, I'm not angry. Calm down and listen to me. Women make themselves beautiful with makeup—especially a lady like that, with her tooth-black, rouge, and powder, her hairpieces and gorgeous robes.[10] Of course you think her incomparable. I'll bet if I dressed up like that, I'd be just as pretty as that lady.

SHITE: Don't be absurd! Even if you applied makeup for three days and nights, you wouldn't come close.

8. A line used in various noh plays including *Yōkihi*, whose main character is Yang Kuei-fei (715–756), consort of the Chinese emperor Hsüan Tsung (r. 713–756).

9. Empress Li was consort to Emperor Wu (r. 140–86 B.C.).

10. A similar list of women's cosmetics appears in the kyōgen *Kagami otoko* (The mirror).

FIGURE 2.58. The wife in *Kanaoka* is ready to have her face painted by her husband. She is sitting on the round lacquered cask (*shōgi*) used in both noh and kyōgen. The husband wears a brightly designed gown over patterned hakama, and the wife has on a typical kyōgen woman's kimono and white headdress (*binan*). (Courtesy of the Noh Research Archive of Musashino Women's College.)

WIFE: Well then, I have an idea. Thank heavens you're such a good artist. Why don't you just paint my face to look like what you want?

SHITE: Now that's an idea. I paint Chinese trees and grasses when I've never seen them. This plan is a bit like that situation—even easier, in fact, for I certainly remember what she looked like. All right, let me get my tools, the heirlooms passed down from my ancestors. Then, entrusting everything to my brushes, I'll try to paint her likeness. To start with, sit over here.

WIFE: Certainly.

She sits on a lacquered barrel that the stage attendant has placed in front of the drummers. The attendant hands the shite a paint box and two long brushes.

SHITE: This is a very interesting plan of yours! First I'll dissolve the glue in a spiral shell.

He places the paint box in front of her. The following lines are sung in the melodic mode.

WIFE: Then he opens the box [figure 2.58].

SHITE: And now I'll begin to paint.

He crosses to the shite spot, holding both paintbrushes in his right hand.

Kakeri   *Danced to the noncongruent rhythms of the drums and flute. He begins with a series of stamps and circlets that end in a formal obeisance, going down on one knee and lowering his head. He approaches his wife twice, each time drawing a white circle with a red center on one of her cheeks. As he completes each circle, he goes to the front of the stage, the first time to the corner and the second to the waki spot, turns slowly to look back at the woman, and registers seeing her with an exaggerated start followed by a slow, disappointed shake of his head. He then goes to the shite spot, turns left and right circling his fan, and stamps.*

SHITE: And now I'll begin to paint.

He goes to the corner. The dance movements switch to the martial style, and the chanting, to the dynamic mode.

CHORUS:
   He dabs with rouge and white powder,

He approaches the woman and points at her.

but the base is dark as mountain crows.

He backs up, looks sharply left, right, left, right, and center.

People will only laugh!

He backs up to the shite spot, spreads his arms, and brings them together sharply.

SHITE:
   Still hoping to make her resemble the
      other

Goes to the corner.

CHORUS:
   he approaches once again.

Goes to the woman, kneels, and paints a red streak across her chin and a white streak on her nose [figure 2.59].

   Her blossom red lips, her gentle
      silhouette—

Stands.

   yet no matter what he does,

Stamps.

   this face will never match
   his beloved's countenance,
   will never match his beloved's
      countenance.

He circles to the shite spot, circles his arm, and throws down his brushes.

   She's a fox spirit in disguise!

Pushes the woman off her seat.

WIFE: What? Ohh, I'm furious! Just furious!
SHITE: Now wait a minute!
WIFE: What do you mean, "wait"?
SHITE: With a face as swarthy as yours, no matter how I paint it, it'll never match hers.
WIFE: What? Ohh, I'm furious! Just furious!
SHITE: Forgive me! Forgive me!

These last two lines are repeated several times as the woman chases her husband up the bridgeway and offstage.

FIGURE 2.59. Having decorated his wife's cheeks with red spots surrounded with white circles, the husband paints her chin, holding two different-colored brushes in one hand. (Courtesy of the Noh Research Archive of Musashino Women's College.)

The Cicada (Semi)

A parody of a noh ghost play

Translated by Carolyn Haynes

A small group of kyōgen plays (*mai kyō-gen*, or "dance kyōgen") are direct parodies of noh ghost plays. In noh, it is usually the ghost of a well-known warrior or a talented or beautiful woman who comes to life on stage, whereas in kyōgen the human ghosts are more lowly: an unskilled umbrella maker (*Yūzen*), a pushy flutist (*Rakuami*), and an overworked teahouse proprietor (*Tsūen*). Another group of kyōgen ghosts are innocent victims of thoughtless slaughter: a field potato (*Tokoro*) and an octopus (*Tako*), as well as the cicada of this play.

In addition to spotlighting incongruous heroes, these plays create humor by parodying the language, structure, and performance practices of noh. One of them, *Tsūen*, contains an almost line-by-line parody of the battle scene from the noh warrior play *Yorimasa*. The warrior Yorimasa fought against overwhelming odds, and then, when defeat was certain, he took his own life. The tea master Tsūen, overcome by the crush of too many customers on the occasion of the dedication of a new bridge at Uji, whisks himself away from life. The setting for both plays is Uji, famous for its tea. The flora and fauna plays burlesque the noh warrior plays more generally, although the torments suffered by the kyōgen heroes are worse than those encountered by any warrior in battle: the octopus is caught, scrubbed, skinned, cut up, dried, and salted; the potato is dug up, boiled, peeled, mashed, and eaten, but at least he is eaten by a Buddhist priest and thus eventually escapes from hell. The cicada is crushed to bits by crows and suffers in a hell designed especially for him before he is ultimately saved.

These plays are filled with puns—not the elegant wordplay of the classical poetic tradition and noh, but more down-to-earth puns on everyday words. Kyōgen allusions are equally playful and humble: hanging bridges are related to buckwheat noodles hanging out to dry. In her translation, Carolyn Haynes skillfully transposes many of the wordplays into English puns and offers explanations of others. Her translation is based on the Izumi text found in Nonomura and Andō 1931, and the performance notes are taken from Nonomura 1935. The Ōkura school no longer performs this piece.

SHITE: the ghost of a cicada
WAKI: a traveling priest
AI: a local man

MUSICIANS

Chorus with four or five members
A flute and two hand drums

A Play in One Act

The chorus and instrumentalists enter and take their places in two lines along the rear of the stage, with the chorus in the back.

Shidai entrance music   *To simple, muted instrumental music, the waki enters down the bridgeway wearing a travel cloak over a plain kimono, with his trousers wrapped and tucked into gaiters. He has on a monk's headdress and carries a rosary.*

Shidai   *He stops at the shite spot and faces back.*

WAKI:

> I wander about, I know not where,
> I wander about, I know not where,
> whatever will become of me?

(Faces front): I'm a wandering monk. I've never been to Zenkōji[1] in Shinano Province, so I've made up my mind to go there now.

Michiyuki   In Shinano
> famous bridges hang between high peaks.
> Famous, too, the noodles that hang[2]
> in disarray at Sarashina,
> where the moon lingers over Mount Asama.

Slowly goes forward a few steps.

> Near or far,
> I never know where I'll lodge.[3]

Returns to the shite spot.

---

1. An important temple in present-day Nagano City, this is also the destination of the dancer in the noh play *Yamamba*.

2. A pun on *soba*, "peaks/buckwheat noodles"; the latter are a specialty of Sarashina, mentioned later. They are hung to dry.

3. This passage plays on a famous poem by Ariwara Narihira (825–880), from *The Tales of Ise*, episode 8; it also appears in the *Shinkokinshū* as poem 903 and is alluded to in the noh *Kakitsubata*: "Can there be any, near or far,/who fail to marvel at the sight/of the smoke that rises/from Asama peak in Shinano?"

But here I am at the village of Agematsu. I've come so fast, here I am already at Agematsu. Here's a nice pine tree—a fine-looking, lush old tree—

Looks toward the center front.

I think I'll rest under it for a while.[4] (*Advances to center front*) But what's this? There's a slip of paper with a poem hung on it for some reason.

"Dewdrops on a cicada's wing
lie hidden among the trees.
So, too, the tear-drenched sleeves
of my secret, secret longing."[5]

Well! This poem seems to be a special eulogy composed a long time ago for a cicada shell. There must be a story behind this; I think I'll ask someone about it.

Goes to the bridgeway and calls out.

Hello, is anyone around?

AI (*Entered earlier, now stands at the first pine*): Who's calling?

WAKI: I'd like to ask about this interesting poem on this pine tree. There must be a story behind it—please tell me what you know.

AI: Well, every summer there are a lot of cicadas on this grove of pine trees, and people gather to listen to them, singing songs and reciting verses and having a good time. Last summer a big cicada lit on this branch, but then birds swooped down and snatched it up. The people thought it quite pitiful, and ever since then they have hung up poems to commemorate it. Even now, some thoughtful person has come and left a poem. Even though you have only a fleeting connection to the cicada, Your Reverence, do please say a prayer for it before you continue on your way.

WAKI: I'm very grateful to you for telling me all this. I'll go over and pray for it before I go on.

AI: If I can be of any further service, don't hesitate to ask.

WAKI: Thank you, I will.

AI: At your service.

He retires to the kyōgen spot and exits through a small door at stage right when the shite enters.

WAKI (*Goes to center front and kneels*): How pitiful, the fleeting existence of a summer cicada! Its life a dewdrop; it knows neither spring nor fall—its world is like a brief dream. "Have faith in the Three Treasures, the Three Treasures."[6]

He goes to the waki spot and kneels.

Issei entrance music   *The shite enters to simple drum and flute music. He is wearing a travel cloak with the sleeves tacked up, a long black wig, and a usofuki*

---

4. The pine tree is usually not represented on stage.

5. A slight variation on a poem by Lady Ise, quoted in *The Tale of Genji*'s "Utsusemi" chapter.

6. *Namu kyara tannō toraya*, a Buddhist invocation. The Three Treasures are the Buddha, the Buddhist law, and the Buddhist clergy.

FIGURE 2.60. The shite in *The Cicada* wears an usofuki mask with a black kashira wig and a gauze travel gown (*mizugoromo*) over a dark kimono. (Photo by Yoshikoshi Ken.)

mask with a puckered mouth.

Issei *The shite goes to the shite spot and sings.*

SHITE:

"Beneath a tree, the empty shell
of a cicada who's shed its skin.

If only I might see once more
the vanished lady herself!"[7]

WAKI: How strange! Beside my pillow, where I've barely laid my head,
something appears, yet it's certainly not a person. What manner of being are
you?

SHITE:

I am the ghost of the cicada. (*Faces the waki*):
In gratitude for your prayers, I have appeared to you.

WAKI: So the ghost of the cicada has appeared! I must expound the Law for you—
it does not differentiate between human and creature. We will transform the
retribution for your evil deeds in life. Tell me in detail of your sins—they will
dissolve in confession.

SHITE:

Yes, I'll tell you about the inescapable torments I suffer.
A flock of crows
spread their wings at dusk,

Stamps.

CHORUS:

a flock of crows
spread their wings at dusk,
and swooped down faster than a kite.

Goes to center front and jumps.

One grabbed me, crying,
"I'll crush you whole!"

Strikes his left hand twice with his closed fan.

He opened his filthy maw
and crushed me to bits.
My fellow cicadas

Opens his fan and circles to center back and kneels [figure 2.60].

hid among leaves or fled to rotten trees,
and there wasn't a soul to help me,

Circles rapidly to the shite spot and kneels.

there wasn't a soul to help me.

Covers his face with his fan.

SHITE:

And now, to speak of my torments in hell,

Stands and stamps.

7. Another poem from the "Utsusemi" chapter of *The Tale of Genji*. In the original tale, Genji sends
this poem to a lady who had defended her virtue by fleeing precipitously, leaving a robe behind, when
Genji entered her bedroom. Genji compares her robe, which he has taken as a memento, to the empty
shell of a cicada.

CHORUS:

and now, to speak of my torments in hell:
as was my way in the world of the living,

Goes to center front with sweeping movements of both arms.

I light on treetops, but now

Returns to center back.

their branches turn to swords
and tear through my body.

Jumps.

I fly into the air, but fierce black
mountain spiders have spread their webs

Stamps and goes to the corner.

wide across the entire expanse,
and I'm caught in a net of a thousand ropes

Puts his hands on his shoulders.

wrapped round and round,

Spins to the left two or three times.

round and round and round.

Spins to the right three times, moving upstage.

And, when the sun goes down,[8]

Sits at the shite spot.

I'm dinner for a horned owl
—oh, the misery!
This is the retribution for my sins,
this agony, night and noon.

Points to the waki and kneels.

But now, oh priest, I'll be your disciple.

Bows.

Thus surely I'll be freed from this cycle
and attain Buddhahood.
So saying, he takes the tonsure,

He removes his wig and drops it at center front.

accepts the Five Precepts,[9]

Goes to the waki spot.

---

8. *Kurureba*, an extension of the preceding onomatopoeia, *kururi kururi kuru kuru kuru*, "round and round," and so on.

9. The five injunctions followed by lay priests: prohibitions against killing, stealing, adultery, falsehood, and drinking.

and, donning a robe
light as a cicada's wing,[10]

He stamps twice, circles right, and kneels.

is transformed into Bonze Bug.[11]

He turns left, then right, and circles with his fan to indicate closure and exits up the bridgeway.

10. *Semi no hagoromo*, literally, "cicada-wing robe," an extremely lightweight summer robe.
11. A pun on *tsukutsuku bōshi*, a kind of cicada (whose name is said to represent its voice), and *hōshi*, "priest." The same pun is used in the noh play *Miidera*.

Other Performance Traditions

Kurokawa noh, Mibu kyōgen, and Kōwaka

Performance traditions related to noh and kyōgen have appeared over the centuries in many parts of Japan, and some remain active today. Perhaps the two best known are Kurokawa noh and Mibu kyōgen. Kurokawa village in Yamagata Prefecture in the mountains of northeastern Japan celebrates its annual festival, the Ōgi Matsuri, in early February at the local Kasuga Shrine and in traditional farmhouses. The festival includes performances of noh and kyōgen by local residents. Legend has it that a member of the imperial family—some suggest Prince Ogawa (1414–1433), the third son of Emperor Gokomatsu (r. 1392–1412)—moved to Kurokawa and was responsible for bringing noh to the area. More likely, noh and kyōgen performances began in the village at the end of the fifteenth or the beginning of the sixteenth century. Semiprofessional noh performers (te sarugaku) probably visited the area; some farmers were able to visit Kyoto and see noh performed there, and others attended performances in the castle of the Sakai daimyō during the Tokugawa period.

Today, approximately 150 people—from young boys to great-grandfathers—are divided into two groups, known as *kamiza* and *shimoza* (upper and lower troupes). They perform noh and kyōgen with song and dance styles somewhat different from those of professional performers. All the noh plays translated in this anthology except *Miidera* are included in modern lists of the Kurokawa repertoire, which contains more than two hundred (Martzel 1982:176–178). Many fewer plays, however, have been performed in recent years, among which is the perennial favorite *Dōjōji* (performed by the kamiza) and a version of the older, related play *Kanemaki* (performed by the shimoza). *Sambasō* and kyōgen plays such as *The Delicious Poison* also are performed (figure 2.61).

The Mibu Temple in Kyoto traces its performance tradition back to Kamakura-period *dainembutsu* (great-name invocation) religious rites. Mibu kyōgen, presented every April, are masked mimes performed without words to the accompaniment of a drum, flute, and gong. Tradition relates how the abbot Engaku attracted such large crowds that his voice could not be heard by all, so he used gestures instead of words. The subjects of early plays may have been religious, but the current repertoire of thirty plays owes much to noh and kyōgen. The plays may be categorized as ceremonial, domestic battle, and demon- or monster-subjugating pieces. The most important ceremonial piece, *Hōraku-wari* (Breaking the pottery), is the opening play in each day's program. The pottery consists of clay plates, on each of which is written a donor's name and age. In the course of the performance, the plates are dropped from the second-floor stage and broken, symbolizing the dropping off of misfortune from the donors. The broken pieces may then be used as charms to protect the purity of water. In the play in which this is done, a seller of drums occupies a spot under a sign saying that the first merchant to set up shop here will not have to pay taxes. A pottery merchant attempts to usurp the place. Eventually the drum merchant breaks all the plates and wins the tax exemption. Monster-subjugating plays include a version of the ubiquitous *Dōjōji* as well as the popular *Tsuchigumo* (Earth spider), also based on a noh play. In the latter, the space between the building with the stage and the one where the audience sits is put to spectacular use as the threads of the spider web that the monster tosses out fly through the air (figure 2.62).

Several theatrical genres, popular in the medieval period, have since disappeared. Kusemai—elements of which

FIGURE 2.61. Kurokawa noh has its own version of *Okina*. Top: Okina, with distinctive white strips hanging down from the hat, is performed by a kamiza player. The back wall lists donations made to the shrine. Bottom: Sambasō, performed by a shimoza player, dances with his bells as the audience surrounds the stage. Compare the Awaji puppet *Sambasō* in figure 3.48. (Top: photo by Kurosaki Akira; bottom: courtesy of the Noh Research Archive of Musashino Women's College.)

FIGURE 2.62. At Mibu Temple, in *Tsuchigumo*, based on the noh play of the same name, the spider throws his web from the stage across to the separate building where the audience sits. (Courtesy of the Noh Research Archive of Musashino Women's College.)

were incorporated into noh by Kanna-mi—is known today only through a few independent texts that were probably influenced by noh. Another genre, an outgrowth of kusemai that gained great popularity among the warrior class, is known as *kōwaka* or *kōwaka-mai* (kōwaka dance). A troupe of kōwaka performers, presumably male and apparently from Echizen in Kyushu, was active in Kyoto in the fifteenth century. They are mentioned in extant texts as early as 1442, and the names of their pieces were even recorded in 1498. Oda Nobunaga (1534–1582), the first of the three great leaders to emerge in the sixteenth century, was an amateur performer and an ardent supporter of kōwaka, and the art became a serious rival of noh.

Unfortunately, the performance practices of kōwaka are almost entirely lost. We do not know, and probably never will know, how much more movement was involved. Because the performance was labeled *mai*, some type of dance was likely performed to long, recited narratives, mostly about the Gempei wars of the twelfth century. A small group of performers in Ōe village, in Kyushu, continues to perform eight of these pieces, their performances consisting of chanting with only a few, conventionalized movements.

Fortunately, the fifty surviving kōwaka texts give us a good idea of the content of this genre. Several of the texts cover the same materials, and even have the same names as noh plays, such as *Atsumori*—excerpts from which are translated here—*Yashima*, *Eboshi ori*, and *Chōryō*. Although kōwaka dance traditions may have been related to those of noh, the texts are more clearly in the tradition of narrative recitation and are a clear precursor of puppet and kabuki plays.

Atsumori

Translated by James T. Araki

[James T. Araki's translation of *Atsumori*
is taken from his full-length study of the genre (1964). The text is in narrative form,
with no indication of individual speakers. This piece is not one of those still performed in Ōe village. The following translation was abridged by the editor.]

To begin, on the occasion of the battle of Ichinotani, the Heike lost all sixteen
of their samurai commanders. Among them, the one who especially inspired sad reflections was Atsumori, who was the son of Tsunemori, the younger brother of the
nation's overseer, Kiyomori.[1] Indeed, he inspired sad reflections. His attire on that
day was of greater resplendence than usual.[2] Atsumori accompanied Emperor
Antoku down to the beach together with members of his clan, but he left his transverse flute made of Chinese bamboo in the Inner Palace—a mishap that augured
his expiring fortune.[3] Had he gone on, forsaking the flute, the matter would have
been of little consequence. Yet he reasoned that to leave the flute behind would be
a discredit to the clan, a folly in a young courtier. So he went back to retrieve it, but
by the time he returned, the great vessels had pushed out far to sea. Ah, how piteous,
Atsumori! He fled in the direction of Shioya.

Just at this moment, Kumagae no Jirō Naozane, a resident of Musashi Province,
came riding along the surf. Although he had led the charge this time at Ichinotani,
he was most chagrined that he had not achieved any noteworthy feat. "The glory

1. Taira no Kiyomori (1118–1181) was the head of the Taira clan at its height and prime minister of the
country. He is commonly known in literature under the sobriquet "nation's overseer" (*sōkoku*).
2. A lengthy description of the costume is omitted here.
3. The clan took the young Emperor Antoku (1178–1185), Kiyomori's grandson, with them on their
flight from the capital. The Inner Palace refers to the emperor's living quarters at Ichinotani.

that could be mine," he thought, "if only a worthy foe would pass by, so that I could press up to him and grapple with him, to take him alive." When he saw Atsumori, he was delighted indeed.

"You, in flight over there! I take it that you are a worthy commander of the Heike! Come back and let us contend! Who is this warrior who speaks thus, you would say? I am a resident of the province of Musashi, the banner head for the Shi band of warriors, Kumagae no Jirō Naozane! As a foe, I am a worthy one! Would you wrongly show your enemy the tasseled cord and reverse plate of your armor? Come back! Come back!" And Kumagae pursued Atsumori.

Ah, how piteous, Atsumori! Hearing that it was Kumagae, he knew that he could not escape, but he fled, letting his steed run of its own will.

Just at that moment, Atsumori glanced out toward the sea and saw a great vessel afloat very close to shore. Thinking that he would signal the vessel to come in so that he might board it, he pulled out from his waist a fan emblazoned with a crimson disk and waved it toward the vessel out at sea, signaling to it. Lord Kadowaki[4] looked to those in the vessel. "If it is Atsumori, take this vessel near and rescue him."

The water master and helmsman complied. They reset their oars and the tiller and attempted to take the vessel toward the surf. But on this day the waves were again surging. The wind was furious, and the waves coiled like mighty serpents. Buffeted by the enfolding waves, the great vessel moved forward gradually but seemed unable to draw closer to shore. Atsumori observed this and decided instead to swim his horse to the vessel that he might board it. He hung on tightly to the horse's reins and rode into the sea, but he could barely stay above the water as his horse swam. How piteous, Atsumori! Had he been a seasoned warrior, he would have ridden down on the croup, calling out to the horse from time to time; his horse—a superb specimen—would have reached the great vessel far out at sea with little difficulty. "Above all, I must not be separated from my horse," he reasoned—a tragic folly of an inexperienced warrior. The horse—superb specimen though it was—was buffeted by the enfolding waves and appeared to be failing. And Kumagae saw this.

"Foolhardy Heike!" he shouted. "The great vessel out at sea is drifting farther away. And with the sea so tempestuous and the wind so violent, what can you do? Come back and let us fight. It shall not be otherwise, for I will send forth an arrow." He fitted an arrow into his bow and drew it slowly. And Atsumori saw this.

"If a rusty arrow should perchance find its mark in me, this would be a disgrace to the clan," he reasoned. He pulled the reins and turned his horse around. As they reached the shallows, the steed pranced, kicking up beads of water. Atsumori fitted a hollow-pointed arrow with dyed feathers into his bow, and he recited the following:

> The catalpa bow:
> when you nock an arrow
> and draw it back,
> so you know, my lord,
> how to slacken the pull?

4. Taira no Norimori (1129–1189), a younger brother and a favorite of Kiyomori.

Now Kumagae, too, was a bow handler with a prudent mind, and he was touched. He kicked away his stirrups and returned the following poem:

> In target practice
> the "A" arrow missed,
> so I had thought;
> but a voice called "A hit!"
> and so I halted.[5]

He recited it and awaited Atsumori.

Now Atsumori threw his bow and arrow aside and drew his sword. "Take this!" he cried, and he struck. Kumagae parried lightly, regained his stance, and struck back hard. They struck hard at each other—two blows, three blows. Since the contest would not be decided in this way, they threw their weapons aside so that they could come closer and grapple. They pulled each other by the armor sleeves, came to tight grips, and plunged to the ground between their horses.

Ah, how piteous, Atsumori! Though his heart was bold and courageous, he was no match for the seasoned warrior Kumagae, who easily pinned him down. Kumagae tore off Atsumori's helmet and threw it aside; he drew a blade from his waist and was about to take Atsumori's head. But he felt it odd that the resistance should be so frail, and he looked downward to behold the countenance of his foe. The face was lightly powdered, the teeth dyed black, the eyebrows drawn thickly; he was unmistakably a person of palace rank, his age perhaps fourteen or fifteen. Because he looked so pitiable, Kumagae slackened his hold.

"To speak the truth, courtier," he asked, "are you the noble scion of what personage of the Heike? Speak your name."

Ah, how piteous, Atsumori! Pinned by the seasoned warrior Kumagae and breathing with great agony, he spoke:

"Truly, I had heard that you, Kumagae, were renowned in the ways of both the literati and the samurai. Why, then, do you say things that do not accord with the laws of battle? I am a subject of the emperor of the subcelestial realm; I am one who frequents the room of the dwellers above the clouds,[6] one who is accomplished in the ways of poetry and music. In the two or three years since we left the imperial capital amid emotions of yearning, the fortune of our clan having expired, I have come to know roughly the code of the samurai's daring. I have learned that one speaks his name during the thick of battles as warriors swarm toward one another's positions; that warriors bearing quivers announce their names by calling out, "I am so and so of such and such a province"; and that they fight to the finish using weapons or by grappling. But here I lie pinned by my foe. I have never before heard of a code that tells one to speak his name while looking up at his adversary from below. Ah, I understand, Kumagae. You want me to speak my name so that you can take my head to show to your master, Yoshi-

---

5. The target tender's call to indicate a hit is "ya," a hailing word homonymous with the word meaning "arrow." Kumagae is acknowledging Atsumori's response to his challenge.

6. A room in the imperial palace to which higher-ranking courtiers had access, described earlier as those of "palace rank" (*tenjōbito*).

tsune.[7] That is well and good, not a thing unknown in this world. Take my head, then, and show it to your master, Yoshitsune; perhaps he will recognize it. Should he not recognize it, then show it to Kaba no Kanja.[8] Should Kaba no Kanja not recognize it, then turn it toward the Heike captives—there should be many—let them see it, and then inquire of them. Should they not recognize it, then consider it the head of a person of no renown whatever and leave it in the grass. After you have thrown it away, it will concern you no more, Kumagae."

Kumagae heard him. "How well you know the code of the samurai's daring, courtier. We are the sorrowful ones of this world. When we comply with our lord's wishes and endeavor to advance ourselves, we dispute with our parents, war against our sons, and only create wrongs that we did not foresee. This is the custom among the samurai. The pleasure of entertaining a guest for half a day under the blossoms or a friend for an evening while viewing the moon; the enjoyment of the clear wind, of the moon viewed from a tower, of the scattering of blossoms, of the falling of leaves—all are decreed, they say, by a marvelous fate that is not the result of our present life. Although there were many men in this battle, it was I, Kumagae, whom you encountered. Accept this as a fate ordained in a previous life, and speak your name. Though I shall take your head, I will pray for your soul in the afterworld. This I will do in my faithfulness to serve you."

Atsumori heard this. "I did not think I would speak my name, but your concern for my life in the afterworld has so gladdened me that I shall speak my name for you to hear. For whom do you take me? I am the third son of Kadowaki no Tsunemori, who is the younger brother of the venerated Jōkai.[9] I am still without office; I am Atsumori; my age is sixteen. This is my first time in battle. That is all you need to know. Take my head quickly, Kumagae!"

Kumagae heard him. "Then you, courtier, are a descendant of Emperor Kammu?[10] And your age is sixteen? My heir Kojirō is sixteen years of age. You both are the same age. The worthless Kojirō is homely and dark-skinned, and I regard him an unfeeling eastern barbarian; but when I think that he is my own I am moved to pity. Ah, how merciless I have been! At the front gate of Ichinotani this morning, an arrow released by the foe Marei caught Kojirō in the left upper arm. When he turned to me and said, "Pull out the arrow for me,' I wanted to ask him whether the wound was painful or slight. As a bow handler of great renown, I thought that I dare not let either friend or foe hear me utter such a tender inquiry. I glared at him and said, "What an unworthy one you are, Kojirō! If that arm is seriously wounded, then stay and put the blade to your belly. If it is only a slight wound, then seek out the foe and die fighting. Make our fort your pillow in death and disgrace not the name

---

7. Minamoto no Yoshitsune (1159–1189) was one of the leaders of the Genji uprising against Heike dominance. His elder brother Yoritomo (1147–1199) later had him killed and went on to become the military ruler of the country. It is Yoshitsune, however, who had captured the hearts of the Japanese and is celebrated in numerous stories and plays.

8. A popular sobriquet for Minamoto no Noriyori, an elder brother of Yoshitsune.

9. The Buddhist name that Kiyomori acquired when he took the tonsure in 1168.

10. The main branch of the Heike was descended from the second son of Emperor Kammu (737–806). Descendants of three other of his sons were also included in the clan.

of the Shi band." He understood this and cast one longing glance toward me before running off into the enemy position.

"I know not of his fate since then. Should I, Kumagae, be suffered to live on and return to the province of Musashi and meet Kojirō's mother? How his thin-haired mother will grieve when I tell her that he was slain. And how Tsunemori, too, must be grieving, having left this youthful lord of blooming fairness alone at the water's edge." . . .

"Though I may receive a prize for having taken the head of this lord, would it keep a thousand years? Would I live a myriad years? Let me spare this lord so that it will be told though all the ages to come." Thus did he ponder.

"Listen, Atsumori. Tell those of the Heike that you grappled at the water's edge with one known as Kumagae of Musashi but were spared because you reminded him of his own son, Kojirō."

He helped him up, brushed away the dust on his suit of armor, and lifted him onto his horse. Naozane, too, mounted his horse. After they had ridden some five *chō* westward, he glanced back and saw some commanders of the Genji from Omi Province at the head of five hundred horsemen riding in pursuit of them. He scanned the direction of his bow hand and saw Narita and Hirayama positioned there. From his steed-hand side, Lord Dohi with seven riders came in pursuit. Watching them from the hill above was the Genji scion Yoshitsune, with Musashibō Benkei and others in close attendance.[11]

"Kumagae was wrestling with a foe but has spared him," they all clamored. "This looks like treason. If Kumagae has treasonable intent, slay him too!" And they vied with one another to pursue him.

If this lord in his plight were compared to things in nature, he would be like a bird in a cage or an ice fish caught in the barrier net. There was no escape. "Rather than let him perish at the hands of others, I, Naozane, would see him killed by my own hand, for I shall pray for his soul in the afterworld." He again grasped Atsumori, and they plunged to the ground. How piteous! He struck off Atsumori's head quickly and held it high. And a ferocious demon though he was, Kumagae wept helplessly.

[The preceding is about 40 percent of the narrative, which goes on to relate how, when searching the corpse of Atsumori, Kumagae discovers a flute and a scroll with a long poem that Atsumori had written expressing his feelings for a girl he had courted briefly before he fled the capital. Kumagae took Atsumori's head, the flute, and the scroll to his leader Yoshitsune and had the rest of Atsumori's remains returned to the Heike. He also wrote a letter to the family describing his sorrow at Atsumori's death and his intention to pray for his soul and received a response from Atsumori's father, Tsunemori. Returning to the capital, Kumagae secretly stole Atsumori's head from the prison gate where it was on display and had it cremated during a memorial service. He then became a monk with the name Renshō. One

11. Of these Genji warriors (the text lists more), Hirayama appears in the kabuki story of Atsumori, and Musashibō Benkei, Yoshitsune's loyal retainer, is a theatrical favorite.

day he set out on a journey to Mount Kōya on the Kii peninsula. After a leisurely trip, he arrived at the mountain cloister, where he deposited Atsumori's ashes and built himself a hermitage, where he died at the age of eighty-three. The piece ends with the following lines describing Kumagae]:

He was mighty in wickedness but equally strong in goodness—a man renowned in the ways of both the literati and the samurai. We know not of the houses of China, but in Japan—and there is no one who feels otherwise—there was no warrior as worthy as he.

PART 3

The Puppet and Kabuki Theaters

Elements of Performance

Interaction between the puppet and kabuki theaters is almost as old as the genres themselves. Both evolved in the seventeenth century, struggled to cope with strict government regulations and financial and social restraints, and competed for the same urban audiences. This rivalry led to extensive borrowing: as each genre produced new texts and invented new techniques, the other adapted them to suit its own needs. For example, kabuki, whose initial subject matter was daily life in the pleasure quarters, staged a love suicide (*shinju mono*) between a courtesan and her patron in 1683. The topic immediately became popular in kabuki, and Chikamatsu Monzaemon adapted it to his puppet plays, creating masterpieces such as *Love Suicides at Sonesaki* and *Love Suicides at Ten no Amijima*, which were then revised for the kabuki stage. Rivalry with kabuki probably spurred on the puppet theater to develop elaborate, three-man puppets capable of enacting more lifelike movements. In turn, the kabuki actors copied some of the dolls' movements when they adapted puppet plays and music (gidayū). As a result of centuries of such interaction, the two theaters—one starring puppets, the other humans—share a large number of texts, performance practices, and music.

Since the last of its rivals closed in 1914, the Bunraku Troupe of Osaka has been the major professional group of puppeteers in Japan, and the term *bunraku* has become synonymous with puppet theater. Other troupes and traditions, however, are also active. In 1987 the Hyōgo prefectural government built a new puppet theater on the southern tip of the island of Awaji, located south of Osaka Bay in the Inland Sea, which now supports a professional troupe that performs chiefly for tourists. Scores of small semiprofessional or amateur groups—some deriving from the Awaji–Bunraku tradition, and others quite independent—are active elsewhere in Japan.

The Bunraku Troupe, housed since 1984 in the National Bunraku Theater (Kokusai bunraku gekijō) in Osaka, consists of approximately thirty chanters, twenty shamisen players, and forty puppeteers, plus backstage musicians, costumers, and

FIGURE 3.1. A three-man puppet dressed for the character of Michizane in the play *Sugawara and the Secrets of Calligraphy*. His karaginu robe is closed with a koshi obi, with its broad ends hanging down. The male puppets have feet, whereas most female puppets are legless; the puppeteer manipulates the bottom of the skirt to indicate leg movements. This puppet head (*kōmei*) has movable eyes and is used for noble characters. (Photos by Aoki Shinji.)

other professionals. Each year it presents five runs of fifteen to twenty days each in Osaka (in January, April, July, August, and October), four fifteen-day runs at the National Theater in Tokyo (February, May, September, and December), annual performances in Kyoto and Yokohama, and as many as sixty performances on the road in Japan. In addition, every few years the troupe makes a foreign tour.[1]

Although father-to-son transmission has always been less common in the puppet theater than in the other traditional performing arts, many performers are still trained in the traditional manner, studying from childhood to become puppeteers, shamisen players, or chanters. Others, however, enter the profession in their late teens or early twenties through a two-year training course established in 1972 by the Bunraku Association, a group founded with government support in 1963 to preserve the art form. By May 1997, this course had produced thirty-six performers: six chanters, ten shamisen players, and twenty puppeteers.[2] When a performer becomes a professional, he takes one of the eight traditional family names (two for chanters and three each for shamisen players and puppeteers) and is given a stage name, which may change during the course of his career.

1. For a detailed and moving description of the troupe and its work, see Adachi 1985.
2. Figures provided by the National Bunraku Theater.

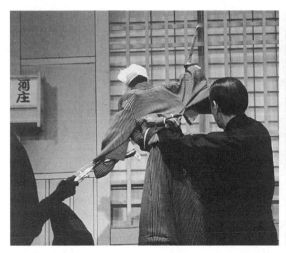

FIGURE 3.2. Manipulation of a three-man puppet. The head puppeteer (unhooded) uses his left hand to control the doll's head and his right for its right arm. The second puppeteer holds a long toggle-pole in his own right hand to move the doll's left hand, and he manipulates props with his left hand. In the photograph on the right, the "prop" is a head. The third man manipulates the feet. In the photograph on the left the puppeteers spread out to give the audience a view of the doll. Only the cap of the third puppeteer is visible. (Left: photo by Barbara C. Adachi; right: photo by Aoki Shinji.)

The puppeteers train individually rather than as a team. Each operator first learns to manipulate the doll's feet, an art that traditionally required ten years to master, and then to manipulate the left hand. Finally, after long years of experience, he earns the position of head puppeteer and begins to specialize in either male or female puppets. In his first appearances as head puppeteer, a more experienced operator may support him by serving as the left-arm operator. During any performance, the head puppeteer may work with more than one set of assistants, with the more experienced performers, of course, assigned the major roles.

Bunraku puppets range from two and one-half to almost five feet tall, weigh from eight to fifty pounds, and may have movable mouths, eyes, eyebrows, wrists, or fingers (figure 3.1). Three operators (ningyō zukai) are required to manipulate each major puppet. The head puppeteer inserts his left arm into the doll's trunk to control the head and uses his right hand to maneuver the puppet's right arm. He controls the movable joints with toggles. With his right hand, the second operator manipulates a fifteen-inch-long wooden rod with cords attached to the puppet's left arm. The third, junior manipulator works the puppet's feet or, in the case of most female dolls, the hem of the kimono, to simulate leg movements. He also stamps his own feet for sound effects. The second operator uses his left hand to manage the hand props, generally handed to him by a stage attendant (figure 3.2). The puppeteers generally insert their own hands through the doll's sleeves to grasp and maneuver these props (see figure 3.21). One-man puppets (*tsume*) are used for minor roles such as the Chinese soldiers in *Coxinga* (see figure 3.14) and the fox in the *Yoshitsune* travel scene (see figure 3.34).

The main puppeteer usually wears a formal kimono and hakama, although for certain scenes, such as the Hirado Beach scene in *Coxinga* (see figure 3.7), he dresses like the two other operators, entirely in black with a hood covering his head and face. The various families of puppeteers wear differently shaped hoods: the Kiritake puppeteers wear flat-topped hoods, and the Yoshida and Toyomatsu wear pointed ones. High wooden clogs wrapped in straw give the main operator the height to manipulate the puppet's head and also enable him to move quietly; the other puppeteers wear flat straw sandals.

The puppet for a specific character is assembled out of reusable parts: a frame for the trunk, a head, hands, feet, and an elaborate costume. The parts are highly specialized; for example, there are nine major types of hands, with another twenty-four available for special needs. The hands range from those in which fingers, knuckles, and the wrist can move independently to those with only wrist movement. Forty types of heads are in general use, plus thirty special ones. The National Bunraku Theater owns more than three hundred individual heads, and some puppeteers have smaller collections. The heads are broadly categorized by sex, age, and nature (such as good, evil, and comic) and may be used for various characters. The Young Woman's head (musume) with immobile features, for example, is used for Okaru in *Chūshingura*, Shizuka in *Yoshitsune*, and the Kannon in *Tsubosaka*. The Genta head (named after a young but accomplished warrior), which usually has moving eyes and eyebrows, is used for Kampei in *Chūshingura*, Tadanobu in *Yoshitsune*, and, in a special variation with smallpox scars on it, for Sawaichi in *Tsubosaka*. The most important male head in bunraku, called Bunshichi after a character in *Otokodate itsutsu karigane* (1745), expresses courage and a powerful, secret grief. This head is used for Matsuōmaru in *Sugawara* and Kumagai in *Ichinotani*. A version in which the mouth as well as the eyeballs and eyebrows move is used for the evil Prime Minister Shihei in *Sugawara*. The effect of the heads varies considerably with the type of wig and other headgear worn with them.

Specialists in heads, wigs, costumes, and props (which include headgear and footgear) create and maintain the puppets' parts; specific puppets, however, are assembled by the puppeteers themselves. Once the head has been selected, the wig master creates the appropriate hairdo. The costume director and seamstress prepare a costume, made primarily of silk, but sometimes cotton, velvet, and brocade. Each puppeteer has his own set of puppet frames of different sizes and shapes to suit the various characters and the manipulator's personal preferences. He carefully sews the costume pieces, given to him by the costume director, around this framework to create the gentle curves of a courtesan or the larger bulk of a warrior. He then attaches the arms and head and gives the doll to the junior operator, who attaches the legs and sews on leggings or split-toe socks. The propman provides the footgear and headgear, and the puppet is ready to go onstage.

As is true in noh and kyōgen, the puppet theater employs a fixed number of movement patterns. The forty-odd basic patterns are of two types. *Furi* evoke human movements such as sitting, running, crying, panting, or smoking; and *kata* are poses that accent the beauty of a woman's kimono (for example, the ushiroburi in figure 1.9) or reveal a man's intense emotion. Some of these movements were created for the puppets and subsequently were adopted by kabuki actors, whereas others are based on noh and kyōgen movements or were adapted from kabuki.

In addition to the puppeteers, chanters (*tayū*) and shamisen players (*shamisen hiki*) assist in bringing the puppets to life. For most scenes, one chanter and one shamisen player sit on an auxiliary stage that projects into the auditorium at stage left (see figure 1.15). Generally, a pair plays for a single scene in a period piece and an act in a domestic piece, both of which last from a few minutes to nearly two hours. The center of the auxiliary stage then revolves, and another pair takes over. A chanter changes his voice to produce each major role and attempts to express the essence of character in a stylized manner that both mimes and exaggerates natural speech. The words of the characters are usually produced in speechlike patterns (kotoba) and descriptive passages are sung (*ji*), but a intermediate mode of recitation (*iro*) also exists, and the transitions between dialogue and narrative are far from clear-cut. The chanter's face is highly expressive, and his delivery is often exaggerated, especially in long crescendos of sobbing or laughter. Certain scenes, for example, the travel scene in *Yoshitsune*, use several chanters and shamisen players. Multiple chanters may narrate in unison or divide the script by roles (kakeai). The latter practice, which gives each of the major characters a unique voice and a more distinct personality, may well have been inspired by kabuki.

The gidayū shamisen (or samisen) used in the puppet theater is the largest of three common types of this instrument. Its three strings are made of braided silk and are plucked with a large ivory plectrum to produce strong, incisive sounds. The music consists mostly of set phrases, with chords and single notes commenting on the recited passages, and more sustained, melodic passages accompanying the songs and dances and serving as preludes to the acts or as transitions between movements or narrative sections. The shamisen music establishes the mood or atmosphere, underlines and decorates the narrator's expressions, and regulates and accents the puppets' movements. In addition, the shamisen player produces various vocalizations to direct the tempo of the entire production and to increase or ease the dramatic tension. The partnership between a shamisen player and a chanter is intimate and usually long-lasting. After years of playing together, each can immediately sense the other's mood. The older member of the pair serves as mentor to the younger, who in turn later takes on a younger partner to guide.

Another group of performers are the "offstage" musicians who perform in the small music room (geza) at stage right over that exit. A bamboo blind conceals the musicians from the audience but enables them to see the stage. The room contains a variety of drums, flutes, whistles, gongs, bells, various stringed instruments, and three or four musicians, who sometimes add their own voices to the sounds of their instruments. These performers create sound effects as required by the text: pitched battles and raging storms, the gentle patter of rain or the gurgle of a creek, the cries of birds, insects, and babies. More important than accurate imitation is the creation of the proper mood for a scene. The deep tolling of a temple bell, for example, is often used to indicate the loneliness of a quiet evening. Much of the activity in the music room occurs at the beginning of an act, just before the curtain opens; then, for long sections of dialogue, the room may be deserted.

FIGURE 3.3. Kabuki instrumentalists (*narimono*) playing in the music room (*geza*). A stick drum (*taiko*, at left) and a flute are also used in noh; the large drum (*ōdaiko*, at right) is unique to kabuki. (Photo by Aoki Shinji.)

The music room plays a more important role in kabuki than in the puppet theater. In the kabuki theater, it is at stage level and contains two types of musicians: the general instrumentalists (*narimono-shi* or *hayashi-kata*), who play percussion and wind instruments adapted from noh, religious, and folk music, and the nagauta performers, shamisen players, and chanters. Nagauta music, played on the smallest shamisen, is the music most closely associated with kabuki. Another typical kabuki instrument is the large drum (*ōdaiko*), which beats out a dozen or more atmospheric patterns, including the sound of wind, water, rain, waterfalls, waves, and snow, as well as special patterns for the entrance of ghosts, villains, and other character types (figure 3.3). In general, geza music (*geza ongaku*), which is used in all kabuki plays, creates atmosphere, defines character, accompanies dances, produces sound effects, and heightens tension. In many "pure" kabuki plays, such as *Yotsuya Ghost Stories* and *Benten the Thief*, all the music is produced in the music room, except for that of the sounds of the wooden clappers (described later).

Dance plays use large, onstage orchestras, called *debayashi* when the music is in the nagauta style and *degatari* when other styles are employed. In *The Maiden at Dōjōji*, for example, as many as ten nagauta shamisen players, ten chanters, and eight noh-style flutists and drummers sit on a two-tiered platform along the back of the stage, with the shamisen players (stage right) and the chanters (stage left) seated on the upper level and the drummers and flutists below. The color of the stand and the patterns in the players' costumes match the backdrop (see figure 3.94). The same type of platform may also be placed at either stage right or stage left or be divided in two, with half the musicians on either side, and the music played may be in other styles such as Kiyomoto or Tokiwazu, both of which employ medium-size shamisens.

Plays derived from the puppet theater also use Gidayū music (gidayū-bushi, also known as Takemoto music, both names being from the famous chanter Takemoto Gidayū). The gidayū shamisen and chanters (jointly called *chobo* in kabuki) are usually seated at stage left, either on a raised platform on the stage or in a second-story room. Depending on their importance to the scene, they may be revealed to the audience or be hidden from view by a bamboo screen. Sometimes the chanter sings an entire passage while the actor mimes (as in *The Maiden at Dōjōji*). At other times the chanter recites only the descriptive passages, and the actors speak the words attributed to their characters (such as in *Suma Bay*). The nagauta shamisen in the music room may alternate phrases with the gidayū shamisen. Another musical style used for the selections in this anthology is ōzatsuma music. In *Saint Narukami* an ōzatsuma en-

FIGURE 3.4. At the left, the stage manager (*kyōgen kata*) beats a pair of clackers (*hyōshigi* or *ki*) to announce the opening of the curtain. On the right, a specially trained stagehand (*tsuke-uchi*) beats the clappers (*tsuke*) on a wooden board during the performance to emphasize dramatic moments. (Photos by Aoki Shinji.)

semble is seated on a dais located at downstage left (see figure 1.34). They are hidden by a curtain that is removed when they play and then replaced.

Two types of wooden clappers play important roles in both kabuki and the puppet theater. The clackers (ki or hyōshigi) are two rectangular hardwood blocks that are clacked together to signal the opening and closing of the main curtain and to give cues for pending actions to the crew and cast. *Tsuke* is the art of striking two shorter wooden rectangles or clappers on a flat board placed on the floor at stage left. The beating of these clappers emphasizes entrances, exits, running, striking, falling, or fighting, and they also intensify the movements of actors during poses (mie). The clackers' (ki) function is technical, whereas the clappers' (tsuke) is dramatic.[3] Although the sounds from both sets of clappers add to the total aural effects of the performance, the players are not "musicians" but stagehands. The ki is played by the kyōgen kata, who is a general stage manager, and the tsuke is the responsibility of a trained stagehand called a *tsuke-uchi*. Both are clad in black (kurogo) and are visible to the audience at front stage left (figure 3.4).

Important as the music and stage effects are, in kabuki the actor is central. In puppet drama, the puppeteers and musicians work together to convey the text, whereas in kabuki, the musicians, stage effects, and even the text serve to highlight the actor and his art. More than three hundred professional kabuki actors are currently active, performing most often at the two major theaters in Tokyo: the Kabukiza and the

3. For a description of the patterns used by both instruments, see Brandon 1975:351–356.

National Theater (Kokuritsu gekijō). These theaters produce a new program each month in a run of twenty-four or twenty-five days. Other theaters in Tokyo, Osaka, and Kyoto stage fewer performances, and groups of kabuki players also present shows abroad. The actors are divided into two broad groups: those of the first rank (*nadai*), whose names appear prominently in programs and on billboards, and the others (*nadaishita*), whose names are simply listed in the program. Although there are now biennial exams for entrance into the upper level, it is, in practice, difficult to attain that status unless one is born or adopted into a prominent kabuki family.

Traditionally, kabuki actors have specialized in specific roles (*yakugara*), and only a few actors have been able to move successfully beyond their specialization. Early women's and young men's kabuki divided the roles in the same way as noh does into the shite, waki, and tsure parts. But once these two groups were banned from the stage, adult actors began to specialize in either male (*tachiyaku*) or female roles (onnagata). In the Edo period, the latter sometimes even lived as women in their daily life. The number of roles gradually increased, with divisions based on age, the nature of the character, and acting—style as well as gender. Classifications included the bravura-style player (*aragoto-shi*), the power-seeking villain (*jitsuaku*), the soft and somewhat effeminate lead (*pintokona*), the high-ranking courtesan (tayū), and the evil woman (*akuba*). The institutionalization of roles encouraged the codification of makeup, wig, costume, and performance styles and influenced the composition of plays. By the late Edo period, however, this extreme specialization began to disappear, and today actors may still specialize in women's roles, for example, but they are more likely to play a variety of roles. Plays such as *Yotsuya Ghost Stories*, in which one person plays several roles, provide actors with unusual opportunities to demonstrate their versatility.

Onstage there are several ways in which an actor can "advertise" himself as an actor. In some cases, actors refer to themselves or to the play in which they are appearing. In *Saint Narukami*, for example, the young priests exclaim how great the play is, and Saint Narukami mentions his name as an actor when he is flirting with Taema. The same type of exchange occurs in *Hamamatsu-ya*. Visually, actors may identify themselves by putting their family crest in the design on their costumes, a lantern, an umbrella, or some other prop. The chrysanthemum design in Benten's kimono (in *Hamamatsu-ya*), for example, identifies the role with the Kikugoro (*kiku* means chrysanthemum) lineage (see figure 3.88). Towels with the actor's crest on them are distributed to the audience in the dance play *The Maiden at Dōjōji*. The audience responds to the actor as a star by shouting his "shop name" (*yagō*) at appropriate times during the performance. Shop names first appeared in the early Edo period when actors, whose status was too low to permit the use of surnames, adapted a name derived from the businesses in which they participated as sidelines or from places connected with their family. Some forty shop names have been handed down and are currently used by one to a dozen or more actors. The most common names are Otowaya for members of the Onoe and Bandō families, Narikomaya used by some Nakamuras, and Matsushimaya used by some Kataokas.

At prescribed times and on certain formal occasions, the performers address the audience directly. During puppet performances, for example, a black-clad figure announces the names of the chanter, shamisen player, and head puppeteers each time there is a change of players. In kabuki, formal announcements are made when a performance serves as a memorial service for a deceased actor or when an actor is making his first stage appearance, has been promoted to the first rank (nadai), or is receiving a new name. In the last case, a rather elaborate ceremony (*shūmei hiro*) may be held, with all the actors in the performance appearing onstage in formal attire as the newly named actor, costumed in a role related to the name he is assuming, addresses the audience. A successful actor uses a variety of names in the course of his career. He takes his first stage name when he debuts; then as his proficiency develops, he may succeed to names held by his father, elder brother, or master. One of the great modern onnagata, Nakamura Utaemon VI, for example, was born in 1917 as the second son of Utaemon V. He made his debut as Nakamura Kotarō III in 1922 and became Nakamura Fukusuke VI in 1933, Shikan VI in 1941, and Utaemon VI in 1951. Utaemon is the family's highest-ranking name.

Kabuki actors appear onstage elaborately costumed and heavily made up (figure 3.5). The usual makeup for all types of characters, from the beautiful Shizuka in *Yoshitsune* to the thieves in *Benten the Thief*, is a dead white, the color that showed up most effectively before electric lighting. Darker makeup is used for peasant types or for contrast. In the kabuki version of *Shunkan*, for example, Yasuyori, who is more gentle and of higher status than his fellow exiles, wears whiter makeup. (The same distinction is made in the noh version of this play through costuming and in the puppet theater version by using different types of heads.) The most dramatic makeup in kabuki is that used for bold-style acting (aragoto). In this highly stylized and elaborately codified style (kumadori), the veins, sinews, and muscles of the face (and sometimes other parts of the body) are outlined in red, black, or blue. The patterns vary with the nature of the character (compare figures 1.32 and 3.13). If the nature of a single character changes in the course of a play, the actor's makeup is redone: the actor playing Saint Narukami changes his makeup as he transforms

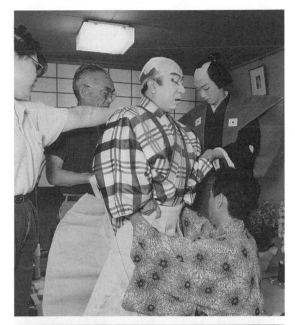

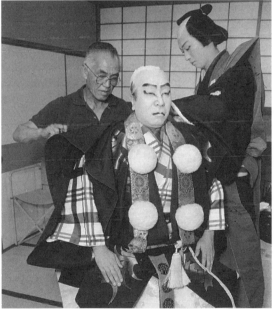

FIGURE 3.5. The kabuki actor Ichikawa Danjūrō IV is costumed as a yamabushi for the role of Benkei in *Kanjinchō*. A pair of light-colored ōkuchi are tied over a plaid noshime. This is covered by a mizugoromo with the shoulders stitched together to shorten the sleeves and overlaid with a sasakake with pompoms. The actor in the kamishimo will be an onstage attendant (*kōken*) during the performance. His costume bears the crest (*mon*) of the Ichikawa Danjūrō line because *Kanjinchō* belongs to that family's famous collection of plays the *Kabuki jūhachiban*. (Photos by Aoki Shinji.)

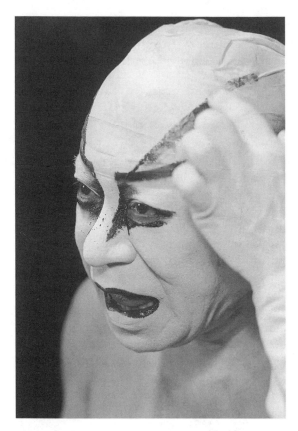

FIGURE 3.6. The actor Nakamura Tomijūrō V redoes his makeup to aragoto style as he changes character from Saint Narukami to the thunder god. A white cap covers the actor's natural hairline. For before and after pictures, see figure 1.32. (Photo by Aoki Shinji.)

from a saint to an avenging thunder god (figure 3.6). But no matter what type of makeup they wear, the actors, especially those in secondary roles, keep their faces expressionless and remain motionless most of the time they are onstage. Consequently, an actor performs before a frieze of statuelike figures, and any change of expression is highly magnified.

The actors maintain a space around themselves that is seldom violated by other actors. Physical contact is rare, the breast-rubbing scene in *Saint Narukami* being an exception. Usually a brief reaching out to touch hands is a sufficient expression of physical attraction. Actors often speak important lines facing the audience and ignore the characters they are supposed to be addressing. This is done even in relatively "realistic" plays such as *Benten the Thief* (see figure 3.89). As a result, the downstage area is the most powerful, and upstaging an actor is impossible. Character tends to be presented in a series of unrelated, detached moments. The brief glimpses of various types of women in the dance play *The Maiden at Dōjōji* are extreme examples. Action revolves around fixed poses, either of an individual in the grip of a strong emotion or of a group of performers. Group tableaux often end an act (see figures 3.14 and 3.101). Ensemble acting is a highly developed technique in that a group of players may perform lines and actions either simultaneously or sequentially. For instance, the fourteen priests in *The Maiden at Dōjōji*, identically clad and beautifully choreographed, contrast visually and psychologically with the lone female figure.

Kabuki and bunraku share a large number of scripts, although the borrowing has been largely unilateral. The kabuki repertoire of slightly more than three hundred plays consists of an almost equal number of dance pieces (shosa goto), plays derived from the puppet theater, and plays originally written for kabuki. The great majority of plays in the bunraku repertory, however, were written originally for the dolls. All the puppet plays in this anthology have kabuki versions, many of them important pieces in that repertoire. *Yotsuya Ghost Stories* and *The Maiden at Dōjōji* have puppet versions, but they are not highly valued.

Plays other than dance pieces are broadly divided into two categories: period pieces (jidai mono) and domestic pieces (sewa mono). The former presents aristocrats and warriors, and the latter, townspeople and lowlifes. *Coxinga*, the most successful of Chikamatsu Monzaemon's period pieces and the only one still regularly performed in both theaters, dramatizes the life of a seventeenth-century man of mixed Chinese and Japanese ancestry. This play, with its international setting, is unusual, however. The twelfth-century civil wars in Japan, from which *Ichinotani* and *Shunkan* draw their characters, are a more common source for period pieces. An important subcategory called *ōchō* or *ōdai mono* features Heian-period courtiers. Both *Narukami* and *Sugawara* are examples. Another subcategory (called *oie mono* or *oie sōdō mono*) dramatizes conflicts among important warrior families of the Tokugawa era but are set in an earlier period to avoid censorship. *Chūshingura* is the prime example. Domestic pieces generally depict contemporary life and range from Chikamatsu Monzaemon's most popular domestic piece, *Amijima*, composed in 1721, to *Tsubosaka*, written in the 1870s. Both *Yotsuya Ghost Stories* and *Benten the Thief* belong to the subcategory of raw domestic pieces (kizewa mono), that deal with lowlife characters. Dance plays (shosa goto), most of which were composed in the nineteenth century for kabuki, derive from various sources, including noh and kyōgen. *The Maiden at Dōjōji*, an early adaptation from noh, is now considered quintessential kabuki.

Although these general categories are useful, they are not exclusive, and the acts or scenes of a long play are sometimes of different types. For example, the travel scene from *Yoshitsune*, a period piece about the twelfth-century battles, is often performed as an independent dance piece in both kabuki and bunraku. Scenes also often belong to identifiable and conventionalized types such as love, suicide, travel, lamentation, extortion, and murder. Examples of all these types of scenes are represented in this anthology. The major type not included is the head inspection scene, which is usually more interesting in production than as text.

Today, both kabuki and puppet theater programs usually consist of a four- to five-hour-long series of acts or scenes from different plays. The Kabukiza in Tokyo and the Osaka National Bunraku Theater offer two such programs each day. The early performance begins at 11:00 A.M. or 12:00 A.M., and the evening one starts between 4:00 P.M. and 5:00 P.M. At the Kabukiza, a seat in the upper balcony can be purchased for a single scene or act. The major theaters have restaurants where the audience flocks to eat preordered meals during the intermission and stands where box lunches can be bought and eaten in the lobby or at one's seat. The biggest theaters offer earphone service in both Japanese or English that introduces the performers, explains the background of the plays, describes the performance practices, and provides modern Japanese or English translations of the words, which are not always intelligible even to native Japanese.

The Battles of Coxinga

Act 2 of *Kokusen'ya kassen*, a period piece by
Chikamatsu Monzaemon

Translated by Donald Keene

This play, one of the puppet theater's greatest successes, opened in the Takemoto Theater in Osaka in the eleventh month of 1715 and ran for seventeen months. In 1716 a kabuki version premiered in Kyoto, and in the following year productions of both versions opened in Osaka and in Edo, thus generating a wave of puppet adaptations to the kabuki stage.

Chikamatsu Monzaemon wrote *Kokusen'ya kassen* a year after the death of his collaborator and mentor, the chanter Takemoto Gidayū. At sixty-one, Chikamatsu, as senior member of a troupe with no star performer, was under pressure to write a play that would enable the Takemoto Theater to survive under its new head, the young Masatayū (1691–1744; later named Harima no Shōjō). Although Chikamatsu had written some period pieces (jidai mono) for the puppets almost thirty years earlier, performance practices had changed. For example, the gradual disappearance of between-the-acts comic interludes usually performed by Noroma-style puppets meant that the plays could be longer, with more characters and complex plots.[1] The presentation of such plays required more frequent rotation of the chanters and shamisen players and sometimes, as in this play, more than one set for a single scene.

With *The Battles of Coxinga*, Chikamatsu successfully met the challenges and opportunities facing him. His story is loosely based on the life of a seventeenth-century man popularly known as Coxinga (Lord of the Imperial Surname; Kuo-hsing-yeh in Chinese, Kokusen'ya in Japanese), who had a Chinese father and a Japanese mother. Coxinga was determined to overthrow the Manchus and restore the Ming rulers to the throne of China. In real life he failed, but in this play he succeeds. In Chikamatsu's dramatic version of this story, one character gouges out his own eye

---

1. Noroma-style puppets, still used on Sado Island, are one-man puppets with simple, folksy heads. See Keene 1965:154, 249.

to prove his loyalty (falsely, it turns out); another sacrifices his infant son; two women are killed by the Manchus; two others commit suicide to aid Coxinga's cause; and many battles are staged, including the one with a tiger in the section translated here. The varied settings include the Chinese court, a deserted beach, and a mountaintop occupied by two immortals from which the heroes escape on a bridge of clouds that miraculously appears and, just as miraculously, disappears when the pursuing Manchus attempt to cross. The puppet head used for Watōnai, the future Coxinga, was created specially for this role. It is called "large Danshichi" (ōdanshichi) and has a moveable mouth, eyebrows, and eyeballs. Kabuki actors use kumadori makeup and bravado style (aragoto) acting to portray Watōnai.

As is evident in Donald Keene's translation, the language ranges from the elegantly poetic to the baldly humorous. Scene 1 includes a poetic catalog, comparable to those found in the noh plays *Kamo* and *Miidera* (also translated in this book), but with erotic overtones. Two chanters and two shamisen players join forces to emphasize this passage musically. The tiger-fighting scene is a theatrical favorite in both bunraku and kabuki. Percussion instruments from the music room and stamps produced by the puppeteers heighten the dramatic action, and the final bestowing of "Japanese" names on the Chinese officials adds a touch of international humor. To the excitement of battle is added the celebration of nationalism and motherhood—his mother's sacred talisman from the Ise Shrine is decisive in the victory. Exoticism, nationalism, danger, deceit, love, loyalty, and humor all combine to make this play a perennial favorite.

Despite its popularity and influence, *Coxinga* was not performed in its entirety for very long. The tendency toward fragmentation has left only acts 2 and 3 in regular production in either bunraku or kabuki today. Fortunately, the entire play can be read in English translation in Keene's collection of Chikamatsu plays (1961), from which this selection has been excerpted. The Japanese text for this play is available in Shuzui and Ōkubo 1959. Keene also wrote a detailed study of the play (1951). Like most Chikamatsu plays, this one contains descriptions of the scenery, the actions, and the characters' emotions. The editor added descriptions of the stage actions not clearly described in the text, which were taken from a videotape of a performance at the National Theater on February 14, 1980.

CHARACTERS

All lines are actually spoken by a chanter, who modifies his voice according to the character he is presenting. To make the text readable and yet remind the reader of the chanter's role, the characters' names have been indicated in square brackets.

WATŌNAI: later known as Coxinga
IKKAN: his father, also called Tei Shiryū Rōikkan
AN TAIJIN: a captain under Ri Tōten
MOTHER OF COXINGA
KOMUTSU: wife of Coxinga
SENDAN: a Chinese princess
AN TAIJIN and other Chinese officers serving as beaters in the tiger hunt

MUSICIANS

Gidayū chanters and shamisen players seated on an auxiliary stage
Music-room instrumentalists

ACT 2, Scene 1

The Beach at Hirado

A blue curtain with wave designs hides the setting even after the main curtain has been pulled aside. Two shamisen and two chanters occupy the supplementary stage at the right of the auditorium. The center pair presents this first section.

CHANTER: The twittering yellow thrush rests on the corner of the mound. If a man fails to rest in the place meant for him, does it mean that he is inferior to this bird?[2]

There lives in the town of Hirado, in the county of Matsura of Hizen Province in Japan, a young man named Watōnai Sankan[3] who earns his living by casting his line and drawing his nets. His wife follows the same fisher's trade and, like the creature *warekara*[4] that lives in the seaweed, she has of herself, without asking a go-between, joined her pillow to a man's. She is blessed with the name Komutsu—"Little Friend"—and lives on friendly terms with the world.

Now the father of this Watōnai was originally not a Japanese. He served as a loyal subject to the great Ming court, where he was known as the Grand Tutor Tei Shiryū. He admonished in vain the foolish emperor and, threatened

2. From *The Great Learning* (Legge 1959:362). The meaning here would seem to be that Watōnai and Ikkan are admirable in that like the yellow bird, they know their proper tasks.

3. This name was invented by Chikamatsu. *Wa* is an ancient name for Japan; *tō* (T'ang in Chinese), the name of a dynasty, was frequently used for China; *nai* means "between." For more historical information on Coxinga, see Keene 1951:44–75.

4. *Warekara* is at once the name of a sea creature, Caprella, and a word meaning "of oneself."

with banishment, fled instead to the Bay of Tsukushi in the Land of the Rising Sun, where he changed his name to Rōikkan. Marrying a woman who lived by the bay, he begot this son to whom he gave the name of Watōnai, with Wa standing for Japan, his mother's birthplace, and Tō for his father's old home.

Twenty and more springs have elapsed since the boy was born, and autumn is now passing, but November is as warm as a second July. Husband and wife go out together in the evening calm, fishing baskets hung from their rakes, to dig clams for their livelihood. They look out over the beach and see the seagulls imprinting their seals in the sand, and the bay plovers clustering on the offshore islets. Watōnai rakes the beach dried by the receding tide, and Komutsu, treading on clams, gathers shells of every kind, indifferent to the water that soaks her skirts. What are the shells that they gather?

The following catalog is performed by all four musicians, sometimes in unison and sometimes in pairs.

Hermit crabs, periwinkles, carpet clams. When the bamboo blind–shell is raised by the salt-blowing shell, I catch a glimpse of a princess-shell and fall in love at first sight. I would like to take my brush and send a letter on a flat-shell. When her red lips-shells part and she smiles-shell, my heart-goes-to-her-shell— ah, what pain-shell! "You draw me to you and I would cling-shell to you, but my love is one-sided as the abalone shell. Oh, cruel one! I could give you a taste of my fist-shell in your monkey-face-shell. Plum blossom-shells, cherry blossom-shells . . ."[5] "Sleeplessly I all alone spend-the-night shell. For whom do I wait-shell? I forget-shell that people-may-see shell, and only dream of how, when lying together in bed-shell, the joys of marriage will sink-shell into our hearts, and we will celebrate-shell with a triumphant peal-shell the happy beginning of our wedded bliss-shell." These were the shells that they gather.

The blue curtain falls to the beat of drums and is dragged offstage, revealing the seashore. Waves are depicted on the lower part of the backdrop and on a ground cloth that covers the stage right area. Watōnai is standing on a rock at stage center looking down at a clam in the waves.

Among the shells is one, a huge clam, with its mouth open to the sun. Unaware that someone stands nearby, ready to capture him, the clam is blowing foamy brine.

[WATŌNAI]: Yes, they say that clams sometimes spew out vapor to form castles.[6] This must be an example.

A puppeteer manipulates a bird on the end of a long pole. The clam is manipulated from below by a puppeteer hidden by the wall [figure 3.7].

CHANTER: As he gazes on in fascination, a shrike flying across the seaweed in quest of food swoops down with a curious flapping of the wings. It spots the clam and approaches with angry beak, intent on snapping up the clam with

5. The catalog of shells is arranged so as to yield a mildly erotic story when the names of the shells are taken into account. The first statement "You draw me . . ." is presumably made by the man, and the second "Sleeplessly . . ." by the woman.

6. One variety of *hameguri* (clam) was said to be a kind of dragon that could emit a vaporous castle.

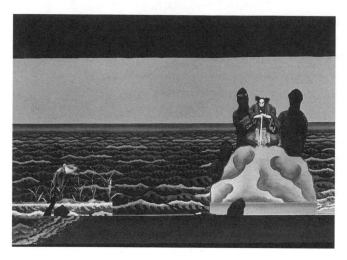

FIGURE 3.7. Watōnai observes the struggle between a clam and a shrike at Hirado Beach in *The Battles of Coxinga*. All the puppeteers are dressed in black and hooded. The shrike is "flying at the end of a long pole," and the clam is provided a bit of ocean by the wave ground cloth covering part of the low wall (*tesuri*), which hides all but the hooded heads of the puppeteers. Coxinga has an Ōdanshichi head with an elaborate hairdo. (Photo by Aoki Shinji.)

one swift peck. Horrid master shrike! Don't you who chant the sutras realize that you break the command against taking life? And see how the clam immodestly gapes, in flagrant violation of the Buddha's injunction![7]

The shrike flies at the clam and pecks furiously, but suddenly the shells clamp onto the shrike's bill and hold it fast. The pleasure drains all at once from the shrike's face. It tugs frantically with its bill. With a flap of the wings, it shakes its head and edges over to the base of a rock, hoping in its bird wisdom to smash the clam. But the clam digs back into the sand, struggling to drag down into a puddle of seawater its prize. The shrike, straining its feathers, flies up a dozen feet, only to fall with the clam's weight. It rises quickly again, to fall just as abruptly. The shrike struggles desperately, beating its wings a hundred times, standing its feathers on end.

Watōnai, absorbed, throws down his rake.

[WATŌNAI]: Extraordinary! I understand now why the priest discovered his true nature in the snow that broke the bamboos—and how, by cutting off his arm, he learned the meaning of the teachings brought by the Master from the West.[8] I have studied at my father's command the Chinese texts of military strategy and examined the principles underlying the success or failure in battle of the great Japanese generals of ancient and modern times. I have devoted my attention to problems in tactics. But only now have I gained sudden enlightenment into the most profound secret of the science, thanks to this battle between a shrike and a clam.

Watōnai gestures with his arms to mime the actions described.

The clam, secure in the hardness of its shells, did not realize that a shrike would attack. The shrike, proud of its sharp beak, did not foresee that the clam would snap shut its mouth. The shells will not let go, and the shrike, straining all its

---

7. The chirps of the shrike were said to resemble the chanting of Buddhist sutras. The clam was violating the command against keeping one's mouth open—that is, looseness of speech.

8. A reference to the story of Hui-k'o (d. 593). When Hui-k'o went to see the great Zen teacher Bodhidharma to ask for instruction, the teacher would not see him. Hui-k'o continued to wait in his garden, even though it was snowing so heavily that the bamboos broke under the weight of the snow. Bodhidharma, moved to pity, asked what he wanted. Hui-k'o asked for instruction but was refused. He thereupon cut off his arm and placed it before the master to prove his sincerity. Chikamatsu has misread this story as an example of sudden enlightenment.

energies to free itself, has no time to look behind it. Nothing could be simpler than for me to seize both of them in one swoop. The hardness of the clam's shells will be of no avail, and the shrike's sharp beak will not frighten me. This is the secret of military tactics to provoke a quarrel between two adversaries and then to catch both when they least expect it. This was in China the strategy behind the vertical and horizontal alliances that the first emperor of the Ch'in used to swallow up the Six Kingdoms.[9] When we read the *Taiheiki*[10] of Japan, it tells how Emperor Godaigo ruled the country laxly, like the clam with its shells open. A shrike named the Lay Priest of Sagami beat his wings in Kamakura; his arrogant beak was sharp. He attacked at Yoshino and Chihaya and forced the clam to blow saltwater, only for his beak to be caught in an attack by the two shells called Kusunoki Masashige and Nitta Yoshisada.[11] Takauji, a master of martial strategy, struck at the shrike and the clam, profiting by their preoccupation, and seized the empty shells and clam together.[12]

I have heard that in the land of my father Ikkan's birth a battle is now raging between China and Tartary, exactly like that between the shrike and clam. If I were to go to China and attack, applying what I have now learned to the present struggle, I am sure that I could swallow up both China and Tartary in one gulp!

CHANTER: He racks his brains with schemes of conquest, not taking his eyes from the shrike and the clam. The determination that stirs in this warrior promises splendid deeds. *The puppet's large arm gestures emphasize the words.* What could be more natural than that this man should cross to China, conquer China and Tartary, and gain glory abroad and at home? This young man is no other than the future Coxinga, prince of Empei.[13]

Komutsu, carrying a rake and a basket, enters from stage left and approaches the clam and bird. Watōnai comes down from the rock and stands beside Komutsu.

[KOMUTSU]: Look! The tide is already coming in. What are you staring at?

CHANTER: She runs up.

[KOMUTSU]: Well! The shrike and the clam are kissing! This is the first I knew they were married. Shame on them—in broad daylight, like dogs! I'll separate them somehow. (*Komutsu puts down her rake and basket to pry the animals apart.*)

CHANTER: She pulls out a hairpin and pries the shells apart. The shrike, delighted, heads for the reeds while the clam buries itself in the sand as the tide flows in.

[WATŌNAI]: It looks like rain. Let's go back.

A boat appears from stage right [figure 3.8].

9. The stratagem was advocated by Chang I, a counselor of the state of Ch'in, and succeeded in winning all China for the ruler of Ch'in.

10. A chronicle written about 1360; translated by McCullough 1959.

11. Kusunoki Masashige (1294–1336) and Nitta Yoshisada (1301–1338) were loyal generals of Emperor Godaigo. They defeated Hōjō Takatoki (the Lay Priest of Sagami) but were ultimately vanquished by Ashikaga Takauji (1305–1358).

12. Not an exact parallel—if the shells are Kusunoki and Nitta, the shrike (Takatoki) is no longer around to be captured by Takauji.

13. Empei is Yen-p'ing in Chinese. Japanese pronunciations of Chinese names are used in play scripts.

FIGURE 3.8. The boat, a painted flat, is rolled on stage, and Sendan and her attendants (one-man puppets) disembark. Komutsu is bewildered by Sendan's boat. The low wall (*tesuri*) serves as the "ground" for the puppets. The costumes in this performance are more lavish than those in figure 3.9. (Photo by Aoki Shinji.)

CHANTER: He happens to glance out at the end of the sandbar and sees a rudderless boat of curious construction drifting toward them.

[WATŌNAI]: That's not a whaling boat. I wonder if it's a Chinese tea boat?

[KOMUTSU]: I have no idea.

The princess, dressed in an elaborate red and gold kimono, rises from the bottom of the boat.

CHANTER: They examine the boat and discover inside a high-born lady of sixteen or more years, who looks like a Chinese. Her face is a lotus blossom, her eyebrows willow leaves. Her sleeves are wet with a tide of tears, and the sea winds have washed the rouge and powder from her face, which is pale and drawn. She is touchingly lovely, like the first flowers of spring wilted by the rain.[14] Komutsu speaks in a whisper.

[KOMUTSU]: She must be a Chinese empress, the kind they draw in pictures, who's had a love affair and been exiled.

[WATŌNAI]: Yes, that's a good guess. I made the mistake of thinking that she might be the ghost of Yang Kuei-fei,[15] and it frightened me. Anyway, she's certainly a lovely girl, isn't she?

[KOMUTSU]: You horrid man! (*She slaps him lightly.*) Do Chinese women attract you? If your father'd stayed all along in China, you'd have been born there too, and you'd be sleeping with a woman like that in your arms. But unluckily for you, you were born in Japan, and you're saddled with a wife like me. (*She slaps him again.*) I feel sorry for you!

[WATŌNAI]: Don't be silly! No matter how pretty a Chinese woman may be, her clothes and the way she does her hair make me think I'm looking at Benzaiten![16] I could never get to sleep with one—I'd feel much too on edge!

CHANTER: He laughs. As they talk, the lady steps on shore and beckons to them.

[SENDAN]: Japanese! Japanese! *Na mu kya ra chon nō to ra ya a ya!*[17]

CHANTER: Komutsu bursts out laughing.

[KOMUTSU]: What sutra is *that*?

CHANTER: She holds her sides with amusement.

---

14. Keene omitted the phrase—not intended by Chikamatsu to be comic—"with a nose and mouth attached."

15. A celebrated Chinese beauty (718–756).

16. A Buddhist goddess of beauty known in Sanskrit as Sarasvati.

17. The words, as used here, have no meaning and merely represent what Chinese sounds like to a Japanese. For the derivation, see Keene 1951:184.

[WATŌNAI]: You mustn't laugh! She said, "Japanese, come here. I have something to request of you."

CHANTER: He brushes Komutsu aside and goes to the lady, who is blinded with tears.

[SENDAN]: Great Ming *chin shin nyō ro.* Sir, *ken ku ru mei ta ka rin kan kyū, sai mō su ga sun hei su ru,* on the other hand, *kon ta ka rin ton na, a ri shi te ken san hai ro. To ra ya a ya, to ra ya a ya.*

CHANTER: These are her only words before she melts in tears again. Komutsu plops down on the beach, convulsed with laughter, unable to endure more. Watōnai, who learned his father's tongue, touches his hands to the ground, and bows his head.

[WATŌNAI]: *U su u su u sa su ha mō, sa ki ga chin bu ri ka ku san kin nai ro. Kin nyō, kin nyō.*

CHANTER: He claps his hands, then takes the lady's hands in his, most intimately. His tears of sympathy suggest that they are old friends. Komutsu, enraged, catches the breast of his kimono.

[KOMUTSU]: See here, you! I don't want to hear any more of your Chinese talk. For all your flirtations, when did you manage to get in touch with her in China? You've extended your operations too far afield! (*Komutsu strikes the ground fiercely.*) And as for you, with your *tora ya a ya,* how dare you go *kinnyō-kinnyō*-ing to my precious husband? I won't give you the chance to taste what a Japanese man is like. Try a taste of this instead!

CHANTER: She brandishes her rake, but Watōnai snatches it away.

[WATŌNAI]: Open your eyes before you start being jealous! This is the Princess Sendan, the younger sister of the emperor of China, my father's former master he has so often told us about. The storms of a revolution have blown her here. We cannot abandon her in this pitiful condition. But if we take her directly home, we'll have to bother with the village headman's permission, and the governor's office is sure to investigate. The best plan is to ask my father's advice. Go home and bring Father here at once. Quickly, before people see!

CHANTER: Komutsu claps her hands.

[KOMUTSU]: The poor dear! I've heard how ladies of noble birth have met with stormy winds even in Japan. How much worse it must be for a princess from China to be brought to such a sorry state! Some deep connection between master and retainer must have guided her boat ashore here, out of all the many harbors. I'll call Father at once. You poor thing, *to ra ya a ya, kin nyō, kin nyō.*

CHANTER: Her eyes fill with tears as she leaves on the road home.

Komutsu exits stage left, and the puppeteers turn their backs to the audience, hiding the puppets from view as a single shamisen and chanter replace the two pairs. During a shamisen interlude, the puppeteers turn around again, and the princess and Watōnai appear to converse as the new chanter continues the narration:

Ikkan and his wife, unaware of what has happened, are walking along the beach on their return from the Sumiyoshi Shrine of Matsura, where they have worshiped following a strange and wonderful dream. *(The two puppets enter from stage left.)* Watōnai calls them to him.

[WATŌNAI]: The Princess Sendan has fled the disorders in China, and her boat has been stranded here. See what a piteous state she is in!

CHANTER: Before he has finished speaking, Ikkan and his wife bow their heads to the ground.

[IKKAN]: I believe that Your Highness may have heard of me. I was formerly known as Tei Shiryū. My present wife and my son are Japanese, but I should not be acting as a loyal subject if I failed to repay old obligations. I am bent with years, but my son is well versed in martial matters, and as you can see, he is of a naturally powerful build. He is bold and invincible, a hero who will restore the dynasty of the great Ming and bring peace to the late emperor in the other world. Please be of good cheer (*he bows low*).

CHANTER: He speaks reassuringly. The princess is moved to tears.

[SENDAN]: Are you indeed the Tei Shiryū of whom I have heard so much? Ri Tōten treacherously allied himself with Tartary. He killed my brother, the emperor, and usurped the country. I, too, would have been killed had it not been for the loyal protection of Go Sankei and his wife. Their efforts have preserved to this day a life that I would not begrudge. I put myself in your hands, helpless and uncertain as the dew.

CHANTER: These are her only words before she melts again in tears. Only because of some lasting connection are these reiterated words of regret over the past exchanged between strangers. Watōnai's mother can hardly wring out her sleeve for the tears.

[MOTHER]: I see now it must have been as a sign that we would hear such tidings that my husband and I had the same revelation in dreams this morning. It plainly foretold that a battle would be waged two thousand leagues from here,[18] followed by a victory in the west. Watōnai, you must interpret this dream and bear it in mind as you strive in loyal service for the success of the imperial cause. What do you say?

CHANTER: Watōnai answers respectfully.

Watōnai is at stage center in front of the rock; the princess is to his right; and his father and mother are to his left. His narrative is chanted quickly with lively shamisen accompaniment.

[WATŌNAI]: A few moments ago on this beach I witnessed an extraordinary encounter between a shrike and a clam. It has enlightened me about the most profound secret of military strategy. The prophecy that victory would come in the west a thousand leagues from here must refer to China, a country situated a thousand leagues over the rough waves to the west of Japan. The ideograph for strategy is written with the symbol for "water" and the symbol for "to leave." (*Watōnai mimes writing the Chinese characters.*) This was clearly a divine message enjoining me to entrust myself to the waters of the rising tide

---

18. The distance between Japan and China is variously estimated at one, two, and three thousand *ri*. To keep the meaning vague, *ri* is translated as "league."

and leave Japanese soil at once. My fortune is the "hexagram of the general." "The general" stands for an army. The hexagram is arranged with the trigram for earth above and that for water below. One yang controls many yin,[19] it says, meaning that I alone shall be a general commanding tens of thousands of troops. (*He makes large, lively gestures.*) I shall leave Japan immediately, on the rising tide indicated by the symbol for water, and push on to Nanking and Peking. I shall join counsel with Go Sankei, if he still survives in this mortal world, and crush the traitorous followers of Ri Tōten. (*His eyebrows are raised, and his arms and legs are moved in large, dynamic gestures.*) Gathering an army around me, I shall counterattack Tartary and twist the Tartars by the pigtails on their shaven pates.[20] I'll behead them all! I'll drive them back, cut them down, and then raise a hymn of victory for the long prosperity of the Ming! These are the plans that fill my soul. They say that "opportunities of time vouchsafed by Heaven are not equal to advantages of situation afforded by the Earth, and advantages of situation afforded by the Earth are not equal to the union arising from the accord of Men."[21] And again, "Good or bad fortune depends on man and not on the stars." I shall set sail without further delay and persuade the barbarians of islands along the way to join my forces. Then I shall do battle in the manner I have planned. To the front! (*He turns and motions to his parents.*)

CHANTER (*Watōnai stands and gestures while the drums emphasize his movements*): In his bold figure they seem to behold the Empress Jingū standing fiercely at the helm as she set off to conquer Korea.[22]

His father is greatly impressed.

[IKKAN]: What noble and promising sentiments! Indeed, the text is true that says that a single flower seed does not rot in the ground but grows at last into a thousand blossoms.[23] You are truly a son of Ikkan! Your mother and I should offer to accompany the princess in the same boat, but if we are too many, we shall attract attention, and there is the danger that we may be arrested at one of the points of shipping control. We shall therefore sail secretly instead from the Bay of Fujitsu.[24] You depart from here and leave the princess at some convenient island on the way. Then change course and catch up with us. They say that the gods dwell in honest heads; a divine wind will surely guide over the sea so loyal a father and son. Let us meet at the Bamboo Forest of a Thousand Leagues, famous throughout China. Wait for us there. Now hasten on your way!

CHANTER: Husband and wife take leave of the princess and set off on their distant journey (*they exit stage left*). Watōnai takes the princess by the hand and leads

19. The seventh hexagram in *I-Ching* (Book of changes). Legge says of it (1882:72): "The conduct of military expedition in a feudal kingdom, and we may say, generally, is denoted by the hexagram Sze." The hexagram has one yang (unbroken) line and five yin (divided) lines.

20. Manchus shaved their heads except for a tuft at the top, which hung down as a pigtail.

21. From *The Book of Mencius*, translated by Legge (1861–72, vol. 1:208).

22. The conquest of Korea by Jingū (also pronounced Jingō) is said to have occurred in the fourth century A.D.

23. From the noh play *Semimaru*.

24. The coast of Fujitsu-gun in the present Saga Prefecture.

FIGURE 3.9. Watōnai attempts to strike Komutsu with an oar; Princess Sendan objects. Nine puppeteers work in a very small space, but their black costumes render them inconspicuous. Watōnai's head puppeteer has thrust his gloved hand through the doll's sleeve to hold the oar. (Photo by Aoki Shinji.)

her aboard the Chinese boat. He is about to push off when his wife runs up, all out of breath. (*Komutsu enters from stage left and runs over to the boat.*) She seizes the hawser.

[KOMUTSU]: Your father and mother weren't home. I thought something funny was up, and I see I was right. You and your father planned this long ago. You sent for a wife from his country, and now the four of you are going off to China with all our property, leaving me behind! This is too brutal of you, too heartless! What did I do to displease you? We promised each other we'd go together not merely to China or Korea but to India or to the ends of the clouds. We were joined by pledges and oaths locked in our hearts, and not by go-betweens or formalities. For the love you once bore me, however weary of me you may have become, take me aboard the boat with you. I won't complain even if you throw me into the waves five or ten leagues from shore and I become food for sharks. Please let me die at my husband's hands, Tōnai.

CHANTER: She beats on the prow, she weeps, she pleads with him, and gives no sign of releasing the hawser.

[WATŌNAI]: Your bawling face will bring me bad luck, just when we're starting on an important mission. Be off—or I'll teach you a lesson!

CHANTER: He menaces her with an oar (*drums emphasize the action [figure 3.9]*). The princess, alarmed, clings to him, but he brushes aside her restraining hand and beats the side of the boat hard enough to break the oar. Komutsu thrusts herself under the blows intended only as a threat.

[KOMUTSU]: Beat me to death—that's all I ask!

CHANTER: She falls on the beach and rolls over in anguish, wailing at the top of her lungs.

[KOMUTSU]: And I still can't die! Very well! My trouble all along has been that I'm too good-natured. I'll throw myself to the bottom of the sea, and my fury will turn into a serpent of jealousy. The love I once bore you will today become hatred! I'll have my revenge!

CHANTER: She picks up some stones and drops them into her hanging sleeves. She starts to climb a cliff over the sea, when Watōnai rushes up after her and takes her in his arms.

[WATŌNAI]: Don't act so rashly! I'm sure now that I can depend on you. (*They sit down to talk.*) I shall leave the princess in your care until the warfare in China ends and peace is restored. It was my intention to leave her here in Japan, but

I had to test you, a woman of low birth, to see if you were worthy. That is why I deliberately acted so cruelly. Now I entrust you with the princess, the equal in importance of all four hundred districts of China—that should prove that your husband's heart has not changed. It will be a hundred times more exacting to serve the princess than to serve your father-in-law or your husband. I ask this most seriously—it is a matter of life and death. When peace is restored in China, I will send a ship for the princess, and I want you to escort her.

CHANTER: Komutsu listens obediently to his soothing words.

[KOMUTSU]: Don't worry about anything here. May all go well with you!

CHANTER: She speaks bravely, but her woman's heart weakens.

[KOMUTSU]: Not even one night together before you leave? What a nightmare separation this is! (*Watōnai puts his arm around Komutsu's shoulder.*)

CHANTER: She clings to her husband's sleeve and weeps aloud, inconsolable. Watōnai, too, is choked with emotion, and his eyes cloud over in sympathy. For a moment, both are torn by conflicting emotions. (*She puts her head in his lap.*)

[WATŌNAI]: We can't keep saying good-bye indefinitely. I must leave you. Farewell! (*He pushes her away and stands.*) Farewell.

CHANTER: He takes his leave. Sendan is also in tears.

Princess Sendan gets out of the boat, and Watōnai gets in.

[SENDAN]: I will await your boat. Then I shall return to my country with your wife. I hope it will come soon.

CHANTER: Watōnai bows in assent; then, still weeping, he pushes off the boat. Komutsu again catches the hawser.

[KOMUTSU]: I have something else to tell you. Wait just a moment.

CHANTER: She stops him.

[WATŌNAI]: Unreasonable woman!

Watōnai takes out his dagger; actually the left-hand manipulator puts it in the puppet's right hand.

CHANTER: He cuts the rope and rows the boat out to the deep. She follows him helplessly until her body is soaked in the waves. (*The wave-patterned ground cloth is moved to the edge of the rock; then both the rock and the cloth move farther to stage left [figure 3.10].*) She can only raise her head and call to the boat, though by now it is too distant for her cries to be heard. She runs back on shore and climbs a stony crag. She watches on tiptoe as the boat moves ever farther out to sea. (*The boat moves off stage left as Komutsu waves from the rock.[25] Sendan stands below rock and weeps.*)

[KOMUTSU]: I feel now like the women for whom they named the Watching Wife Mountain of China and the Scarf-Waving Mountain of Japan.[26] I shall not

25. Poses atop rocks or cliffs are a favorite means of ending a scene. Michizane poses thus at the end of the "Tempai" scene (see figure 1.39), and Shunkan also does at the end of "The Devil Island" scene (see figure 3.68).

26. A legend tells of a woman who climbed a mountain in Anhwei Province in China to watch for her husband's return. She remained there so long that she eventually turned to stone. The "Scarf-Waving Mountain" refers to the wife of Ōtomo no Sadehiko, a fifth-century courtier, who waved to her husband's ship when it left for Korea.

FIGURE 3.10. Komutsu and Sendan grieve as Watōnai leaves. The ground cloth is drawn to the rock and then moves toward stage left with the rock to indicate that the boat is moving away from the women. Compare this with figure 3.7. (Photo by Aoki Shinji.)

move. I shall not leave this spot, though I turn to stone, though I become a part of the mountain.

CHANTER: She assures him of her love, weeping with unstinted tears. They call to each other, but the salt spray hides their figures, and the waves of the open sea interrupt their voices. The seagulls and beach plovers hovering offshore join their cries of sorrow over parting.

The curtain is drawn closed to the clapping of the ki. Lively percussion and flute music plays between the scenes.

Scene 2

The Bamboo Forest of a Thousand Leagues

The main curtain is drawn open to reveal a plain blue drop curtain concealing the set. The shamisen plays a short passage before the chanter begins.

CHANTER: Father and son part, bound for their uncertain destination. Their boats, leaving behind Tsukushi of burning seafire[27] hidden in clouds, meet with a divine wind that carries them through the myriad waves to arrive on the shores of Cathay at one and the same hour. (*The three puppets are brought on from stage right [figure 3.11].*) Tei Shiryū Ikkan, in honor of his homecoming, changes to a costume of Chinese brocade. He turns to his wife and son.

[IKKAN]: This is my native land, but the times have changed, and the dynasty is no longer the same. The entire country, thanks to Ri Tōten's machinations, has been enslaved by the Tartar barbarians. Who of all the friends and family I once knew is left? There is no way to tell. How can I raise a standard for loyal troops to follow when I am not sure where Go Sankei may be, or even if he is still alive? Where shall I find a castle in which to entrench our forces? I know of none.

Ikkan gestures with his right hand as these lines are chanted.

Yet when I departed this country in the fifth year of Tenkei [1625] and crossed the seas to Japan, I left behind in her nurse's sleeve a daughter barely two years old. Her mother died in childbirth, and I, her father, have been separated from her by the broad barrier of the sea. The girl has never known father or mother,

27. *Shiranuhi* (seafire) is used as both an epithet for Tsukushi (Kyushu) and as a pivot word, meaning "unknown" (destination).

and she has grown as plants and trees grow, by the grace of rain and dew. Heaven and Earth have been her parents and her succor. Traveling merchants have told me that she has reached womanhood and become the wife of the lord of a castle, a prince named Gojōgun Kanki. I have no one else to turn to. If only my daughter is willing to help us, out of love for her father, I'm sure that it will be simple to ask Kanki's cooperation. His castle is 180 leagues from here. People will suspect us if we travel together, so I shall journey alone, by a different road.

FIGURE 3.11. Watōnai, his mother, and his father arrive in China. This scene is performed in front of a drop curtain. As is normal for female puppets, the mother has no feet. In honor of his return home, the father has changed to Chinese-style dress, and Coxinga has donned a padded kimono with the anchor robe design (*ikarizuna*) that is related to this role. The head puppeteers are unhooded, and Watōnai's wears tall geta to give the doll added height. (Photo by Aoki Shinji.)

Ikkan turns toward Watōnai.

Watōnai, take your mother. Use your intelligence. If you tell people that you've been shipwrecked from a Japanese fishing vessel, they'll let you stay in their houses. You can catch up later if you fall behind. Ahead of us lies the famous Bamboo Forest of a Thousand Leagues, the haunt of tigers (*stamps for emphasis*). Beyond this huge forest is the Jinyō River, where monkeys live (*gestures with his right hand*). Next you'll see a tall mountain of majestic aspect called the Red Cliff. That was where Su Tung-p'o was exiled in days of old.[28] Wait for me at the Red Cliff, where we will make our future plans.

Father exits stage left, mother and Watōnai, stage right. The curtain falls and is dragged off stage left, revealing a bamboo forest with groupings of rocks. A new shamisen player and chanter appear on the supplementary stage, and their names are announced. Watōnai and his mother enter from stage right during the following passage.

CHANTER: Not knowing which direction to follow, they take the sun shining through the white clouds for their guide and part to east and west. Watōnai, in obedience to his father's instructions, keeps an eye open for houses where he may hide. He steadfastly trudges forward, his mother on his back. He jumps and leaps over unscalable rocks and boulders, the roots of mossy trees, and swift currents, but even though he speeds ahead swift as a bird in flight, China is a land of immense distances, and he wanders into the vast bamboo forest, far from the habitation of men. Watōnai is baffled and bewildered.

[WATŌNAI]: Mother, I can tell by the strain in my legs that we must have come forty or fifty leagues, but we have met neither man nor monkey. The farther we go, the deeper we get in the forest. Ah, I have it! This must be the work of Chinese foxes. They see that we Japanese don't know the way, and they're

---

28. *The Red Cliff* is a prose poem in two parts by Su Tung-p'o (1036–1101). He was exiled to various palaces, but the Red Cliff (in modern Hupei Province) was not one of them.

playing tricks on us. If they want to bewitch us, let them! We have no other inn on our journey—we'll stay wherever they take us, and we'll be glad to share in a dish of rice and red beans!²⁹

CHANTER: He pushes and tramples through the underbrush and tall bamboos, penetrating ever deeper into the forest when—strange to tell—thousands of voices suddenly echo, together with a noise of hand drums and bass drums, bugles and trumpets, coming closer as if in attack (*loud percussion sound effects*).

[WATŌNAI] (*Making large arm and leg movements*): Good heavens! Have they discovered us? Are those the advancing drums of an enemy surrounding us? Or is it the work of foxes?

CHANTER (*The drumming becomes louder and more insistent*): He stands perplexed when a gale all at once arises, blowing fiercely enough to scoop holes in the ground and curl back the bamboo leaves. The bamboo stalks broken by the wind are like swords, and the scene is horrifying beyond description. Watōnai is not in the least perturbed.

[WATŌNAI]: I know what this is—a Chinese tiger hunt. Those gongs and drums were the beaters. These are the hunting grounds of the Thousand Leagues. They say that when a tiger roars, a wind rises. I'm sure that this storm must be the work of some wild beast. Yang Hsiang, one of the twenty-four examples of filial piety, escaped danger from a ferocious tiger because of his devotion to his parents. I am not his equal in piety, but my courage is braced by my loyalty. This will be the first test of my strength since my coming to China. But it would be unmanly to face a tiger with my sword, knowing that the blade is imbued with the strength of the Japanese gods. (*Large arm and leg movements and loud stamps*) I can crush with one blow of my fist an elephant or a demon, let alone a tiger!

CHANTER (*Watōnai pushes his mother behind the trees at stage right and stands facing stage left*): He tucks up his skirts from behind and readies himself. As he stands guard over his mother, he is a sight to inspire terror even in the Indian lion, the king of beasts. (*A tiger jumps out from behind rocks and attacks Watōnai.*) Exactly as he predicted, a raging tiger appears on the heels of the storm. It rubs its muzzle against the base of a ringed bamboo and sharpens its claws on a jutting rock, glaring at the strangers all the while. The tiger snaps its jaws angrily, but Watōnai remains unimpressed. He strikes the tiger with his left hand and fends it off with his right. Watōnai dodges as the tiger attacks with a twisting motion. The tiger falters, and Watōnai nimbly leaps on its back. Now up, now down, they engage in a life-and-death struggle, a test of endurance. Watōnai shouts under the effort, and the tiger, his fur bristling, roars in fury, a noise like mountains crumbling [figure 3.12].

Watōnai's hair is disheveled, and half the tiger's fur has been pulled out. Both are out of breath. When Watōnai clambers onto a boulder to catch his breath, the tiger, exhausted, hangs its head among the rocks. Its heavy panting echoes like a powerful bellows. Watōnai's mother rushes up from her shelter in the bamboo grove.

29. Rice boiled with red beans was believed to be a favorite dish of foxes. Children's stories give accounts of people bewitched by foxes who are treated to this dish.

[MOTHER]: Watōnai! You were born in the Land of the Gods, and you mustn't harm the body, hair, and skin you received from them in a contest with a brute beast. Japan is far away, but the gods dwell in your body. Why shouldn't this sacred charm from the Great Shrine by the Isuzu River[30] be effective now?

CHANTER (*The left-hand puppeteer puts a charm into the puppet's right hand, and she gives it to Watōnai*): She offers him the charm that she wears next to her skin.

[WATŌNAI]: Indeed, it is as you say.

CHANTER: He accepts the charm reverently and points it at the tiger. He lifts the charm, when—what is the mysterious power of the Land of the Gods!—the tiger, the very embodiment of ferocity, suddenly drops its tail, hangs its ears, and draws in its legs timidly. It creeps into a cave in the rocks, trembling with fear. Watōnai, seizing the tiger by the base of its tail, flings it backward and forces it down. When it recoils, he leaps on it and presses it beneath his feet, showing the divine strength of the god Susanoo when he flayed the piebald colt of Heaven.[31] How awe-inspiring is the majestic power of the goddess Amaterasu! [figure 3.13]

FIGURE 3.12. The bunraku and kabuki versions of the tiger attacking Watōnai. (Photos by Aoki Shinji.)

At this moment, five beaters rush on from upstage left. The leader, An Taijin, is operated by three puppeteers; the other four are one-man puppets. The tiger moves to stage right and sits quietly.

[AN TAIJIN]: Where have you come from? Vagabond! How dare you deny me my glory? This tiger is one we've been hunting so that we might offer it to the king of Tartary as a present from our exalted master, the general of the right Ri Tōten. Surrender it at once! If you refuse, you're a dead man! Ho, officers!

CHANTER: Watōnai smiles with pleasure at the mention of Ri Tōten.

[WATŌNAI]: They say that even a devil counts as a human being! You certainly talk the part of a bold man! I was born in great Japan, and you've said one word too many in calling me a vagabond (*he shakes his fist at them*). If you want the tiger so badly, ask your master Ri Tōten or Tokoroten,[32] or whatever

30. The Great Shrine at Ise stands by this river.

31. A reference to the story in the first book of the *Kojiki*, telling how the god Susanoo, to spite his sister Amaterasu, flayed a piebald colt backward and threw it into her halls (Philippi 1968:80).

32. Watōnai is making fun of Ri Tōten's name. *Tokoroten* is a kind of jellied noodle served cold in the summertime.

FIGURE 3.13. The bunraku and kabuki versions of Watōnai's victory over the tiger. Watōnai holds the Ise Shrine charm that he received from his mother. The kabuki actor uses kumadori makeup; the puppet has the strong large Danshichi (ōdanshichi) head. (Photos by Aoki Shinji.)

his name is, to come and beg for it! I have business with him and must see him personally. Otherwise you'll never get your tiger.

CHANTER: He glares at the man.

[AN TAIJIN]: Don't let him say another word! Kill him!

CHANTER: The men all draw their swords.

[WATŌNAI]: I'm ready for you!

CHANTER (*A stage assistant enters to help put the charm around the tiger's neck*): He places the charm on the tiger's head and stations the beast beside his mother. The tiger lies motionless, as though rooted to the spot.

[WATŌNAI]: Now I have nothing to worry about!

CHANTER: He lifts his broad sword and, charging into the throng, slashes his way irresistibly in every direction, rolling the men back. (*Watōnai forces them to retreat at downstage left and follows them offstage.*) An Taijin, the chief of the beaters, counterattacks, leading his officers. (*The beaters reenter at upstage left.*)

[AN TAIJIN]: Kill the old hag, too!

CHANTER: They make a beeline for her with flailing swords, but—a further sign of divine protection—the gods lend their strength to the tiger. It springs up and, quivering, bares its teeth. (*An Taijin throws his sword at the attacking tiger, but it misses and lands harmlessly on the floor. A stage assistant removes it.*) It leaps with a fierce roar at the enemy. An Taijin and the beaters cry, "We're no match for him!" They fling at the tiger their hunting spears, rough lances, and whatever else comes to hand and slash with their swords. The tiger, possessed of divine strength, leaps about at will, snatching their swords in midair with his jaws and dashing them to splinters against the rocks. The glint of the blades scatters like a hail of jewels or slivers of ice.

During the fight, the leader takes the swords of each of the other beaters and throws them ineffectively at the tiger. The tiger attacks one of the officers, mauls him, and throws him behind a rock.

The officers, with no more weapons to wield, are clearly beaten, and they flee in confusion. Watōnai appears behind them (*enters from stage left*). With a shout of "I won't let you go!" he grips An Taijin's neck and lifts him high in the air. He whirls him round and round, then flings him like a ripe persimmon against a rock. An Taijin's body is shattered and he perishes. (*An Taijin's body is thrown down on a rock and then moved out of sight.*) Now if the officers attempt to retreat, they are confronted by the jaws of the ferocious tiger, and if they go forward, Watōnai, bold as a guardian king, menaces them. (*As the officers race around the stage, the fourth man, who had been mauled by the tiger, rejoins them.*)

[OFFICERS]: Forgive us, please. We crave your pardon.

CHANTER: They join their hands in supplication and weep bitterly, their faces pressed to the ground. Watōnai strokes the tiger's head.

[WATŌNAI]: Vile creatures! You who despise the Japanese for coming from a small country—have you learned now the meaning of Japanese prowess, before which even tigers tremble? I am the son of Tei Shiryū, of whom you have no doubt heard. I am the Watōnai who grew up at Hirado in Kyushu. I met there by chance the Princess Sendan, the sister of the late emperor, and I returned to my father's country hoping to restore order and thereby repay the debt of three lifetimes.[33] Join me, if you value your lives. Refuse, and you become food for the tiger! Will it be yes or no?

CHANTER: He presses them for an answer.

[OFFICERS]: Why should we say no? We served the king of Tartary and Ri Tōten only because we feared for our lives. From now on we shall be your followers. We beg your indulgence.

CHANTER: They bow until their noses scrape the ground.

[WATŌNAI]: Hurrah! But if you're to be my men, you'll have to shave your foreheads in the Japanese manner. Once you've had your coming-of-age ceremony, you must change your names. Then you can serve me.

CHANTER: He orders them to remove their short swords—even these can be used in an emergency for razors. His mother helps collect the blades. Together they shave at a breakneck pace the heads lined up before them, not troubling to sprinkle or massage the scalps.

Each mimes shaving two of the beaters. Watōnai uses his long sword, his mother, a short one. Actually, the puppeteers remove the puppets' headbands, which are connected to part of the wigs, leaving a bald space on the front of the head.

The razors slash away with abandon, sometimes going so far that they leave only a fringe of hair on the sides or the crown. The shaving is completed in the flash of an eye, and the victims, despite a couple of desperate strokes of the comb, are left with only an unkempt tangle of hair. Their heads are Japanese, their beards Tartar, and their bodies Chinese. They exchange looks of consternation. Then the shaven heads feel the wind, and soon they have caught cold. (*Lined up at stage left, they rub their bald heads and then begin to sneeze.*) They sneeze again and again, with running noses and tears like driving rain. Mother and son burst out laughing.

[WATŌNAI]: My followers are all matched now! Take new names in the Japanese style, on the order of something-*zaemon* or something-*bei*, or using numbers,

33. A familiar saying had it that the relations between parent and child lasted one lifetime, those between husband and wife two lifetimes, and those between ruler and subject three lifetimes.

FIGURE 3.14. Watōnai, his mother on the tiger, and the beaters with their shaved heads line up for the final pose (*mie*) before the curtain is drawn. One-man puppets are used for the beaters. (Photo by Aoki Shinji.)

from *tarō* and *jirō* all the way to *jūrō*.[34] Put the place you come from at the head of your name. Then form two ranks and start moving.

CHANTER: "Yes, sir" is the reply. The first to set out are Chang-chowzaemon, Cambodiaemon, Luzombei, Tonkimbei, Siamtarō, Champajirō, Chaulshirō, Borneogorō, Unsunrokurō, Sunkichikurō, Moghulzaemon, Jakartabei, Santomehachirō, and Englandbei.[35]

The officers pass by Watōnai one by one to receive their names and then take hold of the rope that a stage assistant has attached around the tiger's neck. As the listing of names continues, mother is put on the tiger's back, and the officers leading the tiger move toward stage right. Once they are strung out in a line, leg movements and rhythmic stamping by the puppeteers indicate forward movement as the chanter continues.

His new followers to the fore, the rear of Watōnai's train is brought up by draft horses and his mother's striped steed. He helps his mother onto the tiger's back and wins a name for filial piety, as soon he will win the country. His fame spreads to both China and Japan, like his legs in the saddle and stirrups when he jumps on the tiger's back; he displays his might to the world for a thousand leagues around.

The puppets are turned to face stage front, and the curtain is pulled shut to beats of the clackers [figure 3.14].

34. Familiar suffixes to Japanese personal names. The eldest son often had a name ending in *tarō* (first son), and subsequent sons might be given names ending in *jirō*, *saburō*, *shirō*, and so forth, standing for second, third, or fourth sons. *Jūrō* would be the tenth son.

35. There is disagreement about some of the place-names given here. Unsun was a game of cards introduced by the Dutch. Sunkichi is unknown.

The Love Suicides at Amijima (Shinjū Ten no Amijima)

A domestic play by Chikamatsu Monzaemon

Translated by Donald Keene

Usually considered Chikamatsu's masterpiece, *The Love Suicides at Amijima* is an excellent example of plays depicting love suicides, a subject prohibited less than two years after the play premiered on January 3, 1721. By the time the ban was lifted, the topic was no longer of great interest to playwrights. Like Chikamatsu's earlier success, *The Love Suicides at Sonezaki* (Sonezaki shinjū, 1703), which popularized the genre in the puppet theater, *Amijima* was based on a real incident, a pair of lovers who killed themselves on the Amijima Daichō Temple grounds in Osaka on November 13, 1720. The puppet play opened not quite two months later. In *Amijima*, Chikamatsu goes well beyond simply staging a current event. The play explores the intricacies of a love triangle by treating the wife, Osan, as a major character. The entangling web of interactions between the wife and the courtesan, Koharu, complicates the plot and adds new depths to a familiar story.

The play contrasts the world of the pleasure quarters with that of domesticity, but the two women, the courtesan and the wife, are probably more alike than their external appearance reveals. The puppet for Osan, the wife, has a mature woman head (*fukeoyama*) and wears an apron over a simple kimono with an overall pattern. Koharu's young woman (musume) head is topped with an elaborate headdress, and she wears a more elegant kimono. Jihei may be played with two heads: the Genta head when he is in the teahouse and the more naive young man's (*wakaotoko*) head when he is at home.

In addition to exploring love and the mutual sense of obligation felt by the characters, *Amijima* presents the possibility of salvation even for such imperfect people. A pun in the name of the play suggests this theme: *Ten no ami* means "net of heaven" and refers, among other things, to the saving net of Amida Buddha, who has vowed to save all living creatures, a vow mentioned in the last lines of the play.

When the couple faces death, they choose not to die as lovers but as two individuals who have accepted the tonsure and entered the way of the Buddha.

Many later versions of this play were written for both the puppets and the kabuki stage. The most successful one was *The Love Suicide of Kamiya Jihei* (Shinjū Kamiya Jihei), produced in Osaka in 1778 by Chikamatsu Hanji and Takeda Bunkichi. The revisions tend to explain every aspect of the action in great detail, some adding new twists to the plot. For example, Osan's little daughter Osue sometimes appears to Koharu and Jihei with a message written on her white underkimono, revealing that mother and daughter have taken religious vows so that the lovers can be together and also that the family's financial problems were not due to Jihei's dissipation in the pleasure quarters but to a loan he made to his father-in-law Gozaemon. However, after a few other improbable events occur, the lovers decide that they must commit suicide despite Osan's sacrifice.

The major parts of all three acts of *The Love Suicides at Amijima* are included in this anthology as an example of a multiact puppet play. It is a tightly constructed piece, especially in comparison to later puppet and kabuki plays. The editor abridged this translation slightly, cutting the first scene and a few short passages with the servant Sangorō and the children. These sections can be found in Donald Keene's *Major Plays of Chikamatsu* (1961), from which this translation is taken. A good Japanese text with some annotations is available in Shigetomo 1958. Chikamatsu's text and the photographs illustrating this selection indicate most of what occurs on the stage. The editor added a few more descriptions of stage action from the video of a performance given at the National Theater in February 1987. That production, which began with Jihei's entrance in the middle of act 1, scene 2, lasted for two hours and forty minutes.

CHARACTERS (all lines are spoken by a chanter)

KAMIYA JIHEI (familiarly abbreviated as Kamiji): a paper merchant
OSAN: Jihei's wife
Other members of Jihei's household: Tama, Osan's maid; two children, Kantaro, a
    son, age six, and Osue, a daughter, age four; Jihei's servant Sangoro
AUNT, Jihei's aunt who is also Osan's mother
GOZAEMON: Osan's father
MAGOEMON (at first disguised as a samurai): Jihei's brother, a flour merchant
KOHARU: a courtesan at the Kinokuni House in Sonezaki, Jihei's lover
TAHEI: a rival for Koharu
PROPRIETRESS of the Kawachi House, which is also called Kawashō
DEMBEI: proprietor of the Yamato House

MUSICIANS

A chanter and a shamisen player seated on the auxiliary stage
Sound effects from the music room

ACT 1

[Scene 1, which is seldom performed, introduces the milieu of the Sonezaki section of the pleasure quarters as Koharu makes her way to the Kawachi Teahouse to
meet a samurai customer. We learn that she is in love with Jihei and that Tahei, a
man she dislikes immensely, wants to buy out her contract. She sees him in the
street and flees.]

Scene 2

The Kawachi House, a Teahouse in Sonezaki

*The curtain opens to reveal the Kawachi House. At stage left is an enclosed room
with a sliding door leading to a center room open in the front. The stage right area
is the street with a curtained entrance to the house, a lantern with the name
Kawashō on it,[1] and a lattice window [figure 3.15].*

CHANTER: Koharu slips away, under cover of the crowd, and hurries into the
    Kawachi House.

*Koharu enters the house through the curtained door at stage right, and the propri-
etress comes in from the sliding door at stage left. They sit to converse.*

[PROPRIETRESS]: Well, well, I hadn't expected you so soon. It's been ages since
    I've even heard your name mentioned. What a rare visitor you are, Koharu!
    And what a long time it's been!
CHANTER: The proprietress greets Koharu cheerfully.

---

1. A contraction of Kawachi House and the owner's name, which begins with the syllable *shō*.

FIGURE 3.15. The kabuki setting for act 1, scene 2, of *The Love Suicides at Amijima* is similar to that used in bunraku. There is no curtained exit at stage right, and the lattice window is replaced with a lattice door through which Jihei (played in the wagoto style) is spying on Koharu and her mysterious samurai customer. Compare this with figure 3.39. (Photo by Aoki Shinji.)

[KOHARU]: Oh—you can be heard as far as the gate. Please don't call me Koharu in such a loud voice. That horrible Ri Tōten[2] is out there. I beg you, keep your voice down.

CHANTER: Were her words overheard? In bursts a party of three men. (*They enter from stage right.*)

[TAHEI]: I must thank you first of all, dear Koharu, for bestowing a new name on me, Ri Tōten. I never was called *that* before. Well, friends, this is the Koharu I've confided to you about—the good-hearted, good-natured, good-in-bed Koharu. Step up and meet the whore who's started all the rivalry! Will I soon be the lucky man and get Koharu for my wife? Or will Kamiya Jihei ransom her?

CHANTER: He swaggers up.

[KOHARU]: I don't want to hear another word. If you think it's such an achievement to start unfounded rumors about someone you don't even know, throw yourself into it, say what you please. But I don't want to hear.

CHANTER: She steps away suddenly, but he sidles up again.

[TAHEI]: You may not want to hear me, but the clink of my gold coins will make you listen! What a lucky girl you are! Just think of all the many men in Temma and the rest of Osaka, you chose Jihei the paper dealer, the father of two children, with his cousin for his wife and his uncle for his father-in-law!

2. The villain of the play *The Battles of Coxinga*.

FIGURE 3.16. Tahei gestures with his pipe as he taunts Koharu. The proprietess is at stage left, and Tahei's friend is at stage right. (Photo by Barbara C. Adachi.)

A man whose business is so tight he's at his wits' end every sixty days merely to pay the wholesalers' bills! Do you think he'll be able to fork over nearly ten *kamme*[3] to ransom you? That reminds me of the mantis who picked a fight with an oncoming cart![4] But look at me—I haven't a wife, a father-in-law, a father, or even an uncle, for that matter. Tahei the Lone Wolf—that's the name I'm known by. I admit that I'm no match for Jihei when it comes to bragging about myself in the Quarter, but when it comes to money, I'm an easy winner. If I pushed with all the strength of my money, who knows what I might conquer? How about it, men? Your customer tonight, I'm sure, is none other than Jihei, but I'm taking over. The Lone Wolf's taking over. Hostess! Bring on the sake! On with the sake!

[PROPRIETRESS]: What are you saying? Her customer tonight is a samurai, and he'll be here any moment. Please amuse yourself elsewhere.

[TAHEI] *(To Koharu):* You may try to avoid me all you please, but some special connection from a former life must have brought us together. I owe everything to that ballad-singing priest—what a wonderful thing the power of prayer is! I think I'll recite a prayer of my own. Here, this ashtray will be my bell, and my pipe the hammer. This is fun [figure 3.16].

Chan Chan Chan Chan Chan.
Ei Ei Ei Ei.
Jihei the paper dealer—
Too much love for Koharu
Has made him a foolscap,

3. This would amount to more than $25,000 in current purchasing power. The price is unusually high; no doubt Tahei is exaggerating.

4. A simile, derived ultimately from ancient Chinese texts, for someone who does not know his own limitations.

He wastepapers sheets of gold
Till his fortune's shredded to confetti
And Jihei himself is like scrap paper
You can't even blow your nose on!
Hail, Hail Amida Buddha!
Namaida Namaida Namaida.

CHANTER: As he prances wildly, roaring his song, a man appears at the gate, so anxious not to be recognized that he wears, even at night, a wicker hat.[5] (*The samurai enters from stage right.*)

[TAHEI]: Well, Toilet Paper's showed up! That's quite a disguise! Why don't you come in, Toilet Paper? If my prayer's frightened you, say a Hail Amida![6] Here, I'll take off your hat!

CHANTER: He drags in the man and examines him. It is the genuine article, a two-sworded samurai, somber in dress and expression, who glares at Tahei through his woven hat, his eyeballs round as gongs. Tahei, unable to utter either a Hail or an Amida, gasps "Haaa!" in dismay, but his face is unflinching.

[TAHEI]: Koharu, I'm a townsman. I've never worn a sword, but I've lots of New Silver[7] at my place, and I think that the glint could twist a mere couple of swords out of joint. Imagine that wretch from the toilet paper shop, with a capital as thin as tissue, trying to compete with the Lone Wolf! That's the height of impertinence! I'll wander down now from Sakura Bridge to Middle Street, and if I meet that Wastepaper along the way, I'll trample him underfoot. Come on, men. (*They exit stage right.*)

CHANTER: Their gestures, at least, have a cavalier assurance as they swagger off, taking up the whole street. The samurai customer patiently endures the fool, indifferent to his remarks because of the surroundings, but every word of gossip about Jihei, whether for good or ill, affects Koharu. She is so depressed that she stands there blankly, unable even to greet her guest.

A maid from the house to which Koharu belongs examines the samurai to make sure he is not Jihei in disguise.

[SAMURAI]: What's the meaning of this? You'd think from the way she appraised my face that I was a tea canister or a porcelain cup! I didn't come here to be trifled with. It's difficult enough for me to leave the residence even by day, and in order to spend a night away I had to ask the senior officer's permission and sign the register. You can see how complicated the regulations make things. But I'm in love, miss, just from hearing about you, and I wanted very badly to spend a night with you. I came here a while ago without an escort and made the arrangements with the teahouse. I had been looking forward to your kind

5. Customers visiting the Quarter by day wear these deep wicker hats (which virtually conceal the face) in order to preserve the secrecy of their visits; but this customer wears a hat even at night, when the darkness normally is sufficient protection.

6. A play on words devolving on the syllables *ami*, part of the name Amida, and on *amigasa*, meaning "woven hat."

7. Good-quality coinage of about 1720. It was necessary to specify the kind of silver one meant because devaluations and revaluations altered the value of coins of nominally the same denomination.

reception, a memory to last me a lifetime, but you haven't so much as smiled at me or said a word of greeting. You keep your head down, as if you were counting money in your lap. Aren't you afraid of getting a stiff neck? Madam— I've never heard the like. Here I come to a teahouse, and I must play the part of a night nurse in a maternity ward!

[PROPRIETRESS]: You're quite right, sir. Your surprise is entirely justified, considering that you don't know the reasons. This girl is deeply in love with a customer named Kamiji. It's been Kamiji today and Kamiji tomorrow, with nobody else allowed a chance at her. That's why all her guests are examined. Koharu naturally is depressed—it's only to be expected. You are annoyed, which is equally to be expected. But speaking as the proprietress here, it seems to me that the essential thing is for you to meet each other halfway and cheer up. Come, have a drink. Act a little more lively, Koharu.

CHANTER: Koharu, without answering, lifts her tear-stained face.

[KOHARU]: Tell me, samurai, they say that if you're going to kill yourself anyway, people who die during the Ten Nights[8] are sure to become Buddhas. Is that really true?

[SAMURAI]: How should I know? Ask the priest at your family temple.

[KOHARU]: Yes, that's right. But there's something I'd like to ask a samurai. If you're committing suicide, it'd be a lot more painful, wouldn't it, to cut your throat rather than hang yourself?

[SAMURAI]: I've never tried cutting my throat to see whether or not it hurt. Please ask more sensible questions. What an unpleasant girl!

CHANTER: Samurai though he is, he looks nonplussed.

[PROPRIETRESS]: Koharu, that's a shocking way to treat a guest the first time you meet him. I'll go and get my husband. We'll have some sake together. That ought to liven things up a bit. (*She exits stage left.*)

CHANTER: The gate she leaves by is illumined by the evening moon low in the sky; the clouds and the passersby in the street have thinned. . . .

Jihei and Koharu have been thwarted in their love, unable to meet. They swore in the last letters they exchanged that if only they could meet, that day would be their last. Night after night Jihei, ready for death, trudges to the Quarter, distracted, as though his soul had left a body consumed by the fires of love [figure 3.17].

At a roadside eating stand he hears people gossiping about Koharu. "She's at the Kawashō with a samurai customer," someone says, and immediately Jihei decides, "It will be tonight."

Jihei enters from stage right, peeks through the curtained entrance to the teahouse, and then goes to the latticed window and peers inside.

CHANTER: He peers through the latticework window and sees a guest in the inside room, his face obscured by a hood. Only the moving chin is visible, and Jihei cannot hear what is said.

[JIHEI]: Poor Koharu! How thin her face is! She keeps it averted from

8. The sixth to the sixteenth nights of the tenth moon when special Buddhist services were conducted in Pure Land temples. It was believed that persons who died then immediately became Buddhas.

FIGURE 3.17. Jihei, searching for Koharu, approaches the Kawashō. He wears a white hand towel (*tenugui*) around his head to suggest that he is avoiding public attention. (Photo by Barbara C. Adachi.)

the lamp. In her heart she's thinking only of me. I'll signal her that I'm here, and we'll run off together. Then which will it be—Umeda or Kitano?[9] Oh—I want to tell her I'm here. I want to call her.

CHANTER: He beckons with his heart, his spirit flies to her, but his body, like a cicada's cast-off shell, clings to the latticework. He weeps with impatience. The guest in the inside room gives a great yawn.

[SAMURAI]: What a bore, playing nursemaid to a prostitute with worries on her mind! The street seems quiet now. Let's go to the end room. We can at least distract ourselves by looking at the lanterns. Come with me.

CHANTER: They go together to the outer room. Jihei, alarmed, squeezes into the patch of shadow under the lattice window. Inside, they do not realize that anyone is eavesdropping.

[SAMURAI]: I've been noticing your behavior and the little things you've said this evening. It's plain to me that you intend a love suicide with Kamiji, or whatever his name is—the man the hostess mentioned. I'm sure I'm right. I realize that no amount of advice or reasoning is likely to penetrate the ears of somebody bewitched by the god of death, but I must say that you're exceedingly foolish. This is only our first meeting, but as a samurai, I can't let you die without trying to save you. I will never reveal to anyone what you tell me. Open your heart without fear.

CHANTER: He whispers these words. She joins her hands and bows.

As they talk, Koharu cleans a pipe, lights it with charcoal from the hibachi, and gives it to the samurai [figure 3.18].

[KOHARU]: I'm extremely grateful. Thank you for your kind words. You were right. I have promised Kamiji to die with him. But we've been completely prevented from meeting by my master, and Jihei, for various reasons, can't ransom me at once. My contracts with my former master[10] and my present one still have five years to run. If somebody else claimed me during that time, it would be a blow to me, of course, but a worse disgrace to Jihei's honor. He suggested that it would be better if we killed ourselves, and I agreed. I was caught by obligations from which I could not withdraw, and I promised him before I knew what I was doing. I said, "We'll watch for a chance, and I'll slip out when you give the signal." "Yes," he said, "slip out somehow." Ever since then I've been leading a life of uncertainty, never knowing from one day to the next when my last hour will come. I have a mother living in a back alley south of here. She has no one but me to depend on, and she does piecework

9. Both places had well-known cemeteries.
10. The master at the bathhouse where Koharu formerly worked.

to eke out a living. I keep thinking that after I'm dead, she'll become a beggar or an outcast and maybe she'll die of starvation. That's the only sad part about dying. I have just this one life. I'm ashamed that you may think me a coldhearted woman, but I must endure the shame. The most important thing is that I don't want to die. I beg you, please help me to stay alive.

CHANTER: As she speaks, the samurai nods thoughtfully. Jihei, crouching outside, hears her words with astonishment; they are so unexpected to his manly heart that he feels like a monkey who has tumbled from a tree. He is frantic with agitation.

[JIHEI] (*To himself*): Then was everything a lie? Ahhh—I'm furious! For two whole years I've been bewitched by that rotten she-fox! Shall I break in and kill her with one blow of my sword? Or shall I satisfy my anger by shaming her to her face?

CHANTER: He gnashes his teeth and weeps in chagrin. Inside the house Koharu speaks through her tears.

[KOHARU]: It's a curious thing to ask, but would you please show the kindness of a samurai and become my customer for the rest of this year and into next spring? Whenever Jihei comes, intent on death, please interfere and force him to postpone his plan. In this way our relations can be broken quite naturally. He won't have to kill himself, and my life also will be saved.—What evil connection from a former existence made us promise to die? How I regret it now!

CHANTER: She weeps, leaning on the samurai's knee [figure 3.19].

[SAMURAI]: Very well, I'll do as you ask. I think I can help you.—But there's a draft blowing. Somebody may be watching.

CHANTER: He slams shut the latticework shōji. Jihei, listening outside, is in a frenzy.

[JIHEI]: Exactly what you'd expect from a whore, a cheap whore! I misjudged her foul nature. She robbed the soul from my body, the thieving harlot! Shall I slash her down or run her through? What am I to do?

CHANTER: The shadows of two profiles fall on the shōji.

[JIHEI]: I'd like to give her a taste of my fist and trample her. What are they chattering about? See how they nod to each other! Now she's bowing to him, whispering and sniveling. I've tried to control myself—I've pressed my chest, I've stroked it—but I can't stand any more. This is too much to endure!

FIGURE 3.18. As they converse, Koharu prepares a pipe for her samurai client (actually Magoemon with a Kōmei head and a hood to disguise his identity). The bottom picture is a kabuki version of the same actions. The doll's obi is tied in the back, whereas in kabuki the obi is tied in the front. The pipe (*kiseru*) is an often used hand prop in both theaters. (Top: photo by Barbara C. Adachi; bottom: photo by Aoki Shinji.)

FIGURE 3.19. Koharu attempts to persuade the samurai to become her customer so that she and Jihei will not be forced to commit suicide. (Photo by Barbara C. Adachi.)

CHANTER: His heart pounds wildly as he unsheathes his dirk, a Magoroku of Seki. "Koharu's side must be here," he judges, and stabs through an opening in the latticework. (*He slides the window open a bit and stabs through it with his sword.*) But Koharu is too far away for his thrust, and though she cries out in terror, she remains unharmed. Her guest instantly leaps at Jihei, grabs his hands, and jerks them through the latticework. With his sword knot he quickly and securely fastens Jihei's hands to the window upright. (*The samurai is working behind the window so that he cannot be clearly seen by Jihei or the audience.*)

[SAMURAI]: Don't make any outcry, Koharu. You are not to look at him.

CHANTER: At this moment the proprietress enters. He exclaims in alarm.

[SAMURAI]: This needn't concern you. Some ruffian ran his sword through the shō-ji, and I've tied his arms to the latticework. I have my own way of dealing with him. Don't untie the cord. If you attract a crowd, the place is sure to be thrown in an uproar. Let's all go inside. Come with me, Koharu. We'll go to bed.

CHANTER: Koharu answers, "Yes," but she recognizes the handle of the dirk, and the memory—if not the blade—transfixes her breast.

[KOHARU]: There're always people doing crazy things in the Quarter when they've had too much to drink. Why don't you let him go without making any trouble? I think that's best, don't you?

[SAMURAI]: Out of the question. Do as I say—inside, all of you. Koharu, come along. (*They exit through the sliding door at stage left.*)

CHANTER: Jihei can still see their shadows even after they enter the inner room, but he is bound to the spot, his hands held in fetters that grip him more tightly as he struggles, his body beset by suffering as he tastes a living shame

FIGURE 3.20. Finding Jihei tied to the window frame, Tahei grabs his obi and unties it. (Photo by Barbara C. Adachi.)

worse than a dog's.[11] More determined than ever to die, he sheds tears of blood, a pitiful sight. Tahei the Lone Wolf returns from his carousing. (*Tahei and a companion enter from stage right.*)

[TAHEI]: That's Jihei standing by the window. I'll give him a tossing.

CHANTER: He catches Jihei by the collar and starts to lift him over his back.

[JIHEI]: Owww!

[TAHEI]: Owww? What kind of weakling are you? Oh, I see—you're tied here. You must've been pulling off a robbery. You dirty pickpocket! You rotten pickpocket! (*He pulls on Jihei's obi, untying it [figure 3.20].*)

CHANTER: He drubs Jihei mercilessly.

[TAHEI]: You burglar! You convict!

CHANTER: He kicks him wildly.

[TAHEI]: Kamiya Jihei's been caught burgling, and they've tied him up!

CHANTER: Passersby and people of the neighborhood, attracted by his shouts, quickly gather. The samurai rushes from the house. (*The samurai, who has removed his hood and jacket, enters through the door at stage left.*)

[SAMURAI]: Who's calling him a burglar? You? Tell me what Jihei's stolen! Out with it!

CHANTER: He seizes Tahei and forces him into the dirt. Tahei rises to his feet only for the samurai to kick him down again and again. He grips Tahei.

[SAMURAI]: Jihei! Trample him to your heart's content!

CHANTER: He pushes Tahei under Jihei's feet. Bound though he is, Jihei stamps

---

11. A proverb of Buddhist origin, "Suffering follows one like a dog," is embedded in the text.

FIGURE 3.21. As he scolds his brother, Magoemon gestures with a fan, which has not been reduced to puppet scale. It is held by the puppeteer, whose hand is slipped through the doll's sleeve. The second puppeteer uses his left hand to hold the sword. (Photo by Barbara C. Adachi.)

furiously over Tahei's face. Tahei, thoroughly trampled and covered with mire, gets to his feet and glares around him.

[TAHEI] *(To the bystanders)*: How could you fools stand there calmly and let him step on me? I've memorized every one of your faces, and I intend to pay you back. Remember that!

CHANTER: He makes his escape, still determined to have the last word. The spectators burst out laughing.

[VOICES]: Listen to him brag, even after he's been trampled on! Let's throw him from the bridge and give him a drink of water! Don't let him get away!

CHANTER: They chase after him. When the crowd has dispersed, the samurai approaches Jihei and unfastens the knots. He shows his face with his hood removed.

[JIHEI]: Magoemon! My brother! How mortifying!

CHANTER: He sinks to the ground and weeps, prostrating himself in the dirt.

[KOHARU] *(Koharu enters from stage left)*: Are you his brother, sir?

CHANTER: Koharu runs to them. Jihei, catching her by the front of the kimono, forces her to the ground.

[JIHEI]: Beast! She-fox! I'd sooner trample on you than on Tahei!

CHANTER: He raises his foot, but Magoemon calls out.

They sit, with Magoemon in the center.

[MAGOEMON]: That's the kind of foolishness responsible for all your trouble. A prostitute's business is to deceive men. Have you just now waked up to that? It's deplorable. You're my younger brother, but you're almost thirty, and you've got a six-year-old boy and a four-year-old girl, Kantarō and Osue. You run a shop with a thirty-six-foot frontage,[12] but you don't seem to realize that your whole fortune's collapsing. (*Magoemon gestures first with a fan and then with his sheathed sword as he scolds his brother [figure 3.21].*) I realized that your marriage couldn't last much longer at this rate. I decided that I'd see with my own eyes what kind of woman Koharu was and work out some sort of solution afterward. I consulted the proprietress here, then came myself to investigate the cause of your sickness. I see now how natural it was that you should desert your wife and children. What a faithful prostitute you discovered! I congratulate you! And here I am, Magoemon the Miller, known far and wide for my paragon of a brother, dressed up like a masquerader at a festival or maybe a lunatic! I put on

12. It was customary to refer to the size of shops by giving their street frontage.

swords for the first time in my life and announced myself, like a bit player in a costume piece, as an officer at a residence. I feel like an absolute idiot with these swords—it's so infuriating—and ridiculous—that it's given me a pain in the chest.

CHANTER: He gnashes his teeth and grimaces, attempting to hide his tears. Koharu, choking the while with emotion, can only say

[KOHARU]: Yes, you're entirely right.

CHANTER: The rest is lost in tears. Jihei pounds the earth with his fist.

[JIHEI]: I was wrong. Forgive me, Magoemon. For three years I've been possessed by that witch. I've neglected my parents, relatives— even my wife and children—and wrecked my fortune, all because I was deceived by Koharu, that sneak thief! I'm utterly mortified. But I'm through with her now, and I'll never set foot here again. Weasel! Vixen! Sneak thief! Here's proof that I've broken with her!

CHANTER: He pulls out the amulet bag that has rested next to his skin.

[JIHEI]: Here are the written oaths we've exchanged, one at the beginning of each month, twenty-nine in all. I return them. This means our love and affection are over. Take them.

CHANTER: He flings the notes at her.

[JIHEI]: Magoemon, collect from her my pledges. Please make sure you get them all. Then burn them with your own hands. (*To Koharu*) Hand them to my brother.

[KOHARU]: As you wish.

FIGURE 3.22. In the kabuki version, Magoemon swears to Koharu that he will not show Osan's letter to anyone. Below, in the bunraku version, Magoemon attempts to keep Jihei from attacking Koharu while indicating to Koharu his understanding of the importance of the letter. (Top: photo by Aoki Shinji; bottom: photo by Barbara C. Adachi.)

CHANTER: In tears, she surrenders the amulet bag. Magoemon opens it.

[MAGOEMON]: One, two, three, four . . . ten . . . twenty-nine. They're all here. There's also a letter from a woman. What's this?

CHANTER: He starts to unfold it.

[KOHARU]: That's an important letter. I can't let you see it.

CHANTER: She clings to Magoemon's arm, but he pushes her away. He holds the letter to the lamplight and examines the address, "To Miss Koharu from Kamiya Osan." As soon as he reads the words, he casually thrusts the letter into his kimono.

[MAGOEMON]: Koharu, a while ago I swore by my good fortune as a samurai, but now Magoemon the Miller swears by his good fortune as a businessman that he will show this letter to no one, not even his wife. I alone will read it, then burn it with the oaths. You can trust me. I will not break this oath [figure 3.22].

[KOHARU]: Thank you. You have saved my honor.

CHANTER: She bursts into tears again.

[JIHEI] (*Laughs contemptuously*): Save your honor! You talk like a human being! (*To Magoemon*) I don't want to see her cursed face another minute. Let's go. No—I can't hold so much resentment and bitterness! I'll kick her one in the face, a memory to treasure for the rest of my life. Excuse me, please.

CHANTER: He strides up to Koharu and stamps on the ground.

[JIHEI]: For three years I've loved you, delighted in you, longed for you, adored you, but today my foot will say my only farewells.

CHANTER: He kicks her sharply on the forehead and bursts into tears. The brothers leave, forlorn figures. Koharu, unhappy woman, raises her voice in lament as she watches them go. Is she faithful or unfaithful? Her true feelings are hidden in the words penned by Jihei's wife, a letter no one has seen. Jihei goes his separate way without learning the truth.

ACT 2, Scene 1

The House and Shop of Kamiya Jihei
Time: Ten days later

The general layout of the stage is similar to that of the earlier scene, but the setting is now a paper merchant's home and shop. The walls are dark, with a curtained door at center back and a chest of drawers with account pads hung above it on the back wall to the right of the door. A stand containing an abacus sits in front of them. There are sliding doors to an enclosed room at stage left, and Jihei sleeps under a futon in the left part of the central room. Osan is seated, looking out the window at the street.

CHANTER: The busy street that runs straight to Tenjin Bridge, named for the god of Temma, bringer of good fortune, is known as the Street Before the Kami, and here a paper shop does business under the name Kamiya Jihei.[13] The paper is honestly sold, the shop well situated; it is a long-established firm, and customers come thick as raindrops. Outside crowds pass in the street, on their way to the Ten Nights service, while inside the husband dozes in the *kotatsu*,[14] shielded from draughts by a screen at his pillow [figure 3.23]. His wife Osan keeps a solitary, anxious watch over the shop and house.

The son Kantarō; the maid Tama, with Osue on her back; and the servant Sangorō return. They interact briefly.

[TAMA]: Oh, I almost forgot to tell you, ma'am, that Mr. Magoemon and his aunt[15] are on their way here from the west.

[OSAN]: Oh dear! I'll have to wake Jihei in that case. (*To Jihei*) Please get up. Mother and Magoemon are coming. They'll be upset again if you let them see you, a businessman, sleeping in the afternoon, with the day as short as it is.

13. Temma Tenjin is Sugawara no Michizane's name as a deity. This is a play on the words *kami* (deity) and *kami* (paper).
14. A source of heat in which a charcoal burner is placed under a low, quilt-covered table.
15. Magoemon's (and Jihei's) aunt, but Osan's mother.

[JIHEI]: All right.

CHANTER: He struggles to a sitting position and, with his abacus in one hand, pulls his account book toward him with the other.

[JIHEI]: Two into ten goes five, three into nine goes three, three into six goes two, seven times eight is fifty-six.

CHANTER: His fifty-six-year-old aunt enters with Magoemon.

[JIHEI]: Magoemon, aunt. How good of you. Please come in. I was in the midst of some urgent calculations. Four nines makes thirty-six *momme*. Three sixes make eighteen *fun*. That's two momme less two fun.[16] Kantarō! Osue! Granny and Uncle have come! Bring the tobacco tray! One times three makes three. Osan, serve the tea!

CHANTER: He jabbers away.

FIGURE 3.23. Act 2 opens with Jihei in bed while his wife, Osan, attends to the shop and their family. (Photo by Barbara C. Adachi.)

[AUNT]: We haven't come for tea or tobacco. Osan, you're young, I know, but you're the mother of two children, and your excessive forbearance does you no credit. A man's dissipation can always be traced to his wife's carelessness. Remember, it's not only the man who's disgraced when he goes bankrupt and his marriage breaks up. You'd do well to take notice of what's going on and assert yourself a bit more.

[MAGOEMON]: It's foolish to hope for any results, aunt. The scoundrel even deceives me, his elder brother. Why should he take to heart criticism from his wife? Jihei—you played me for a fool. After showing me how you returned Koharu's pledges, here you are, not ten days later, redeeming her! What does this mean? I suppose your urgent calculations are of Koharu's debts! I've had enough!

CHANTER: He snatches away the abacus and flings it clattering into the hallway.

[JIHEI]: You're making an enormous fuss without any cause. I haven't crossed the threshold since the last time I saw you, except to go twice to the wholesalers in Imabashi and once to the Tenjin Shrine. I haven't even thought of Koharu, much less redeemed her.

[AUNT]: None of your evasions! Last evening at the Ten Nights service I heard the people in the congregation gossiping. Everybody was talking about the great patron from Temma who'd fallen in love with a prostitute named Koharu from the Kinokuni House in Sonezaki. They said he'd driven away her other guests and was going to ransom her in the next couple of days. There was all kinds of gossip about the abundance of money and fools, even in these days of high prices. My husband Gozaemon has been hearing about Koharu constantly, and he's sure that her great patron from Temma must be you, Jihei. He told me, "He's your nephew, but for me he's a stranger, and my

16. Meaningless calculations. Twenty *fun* made two *momme*.

daughter's happiness is my chief concern. Once he ransoms the prostitute, he'll no doubt sell his wife to a brothel. I intend to take her back before he starts selling her clothes." He was halfway out of the house before I could restrain him. "Don't get so excited. We can settle this calmly. First we must make sure whether or not the rumors are true." That's why Magoemon and I are here now. He was telling me a while ago that the Jihei of today is not the Jihei of yesterday—that you'd broken all connections with Sonezaki and completely reformed. But now I heard that you've had a relapse. What disease can this be? Your father was my brother. When the poor man was on his deathbed, he lifted his head from the pillow and begged me to look after you, as my son-in-law and nephew. I've never forgotten those last words, but your perversity has made a mockery of his request!

CHANTER: She collapses in tears of resentment. Jihei claps his hands in sudden recognition.

[JIHEI]: I have it! The Koharu everybody's gossiping about is the same Koharu, but the great patron who's to redeem her is a different man. The other day, as my brother can tell you, Tahei—they call him the Lone Wolf because he hasn't any family or relations—started a fight and was trampled on. He gets all the money he needs from his hometown, and he's been trying for a long time to redeem Koharu. I've always prevented him, but I'm sure he's decided that now is his chance. I have nothing to do with it.

CHANTER: Osan brightens at his words.

[OSAN]: No matter how forbearing I might be—even if I were an angel—you don't suppose I'd encourage my husband to redeem a prostitute! In this instance, at any rate, there's not a word of untruth in what my husband has said. I'll be a witness to that, Mother.

CHANTER: Husband's and wife's words tally perfectly.

[AUNT]: Then it's true?

CHANTER: The aunt and nephew clap their hands with relief.

[MAGOEMON]: Well, I'm happy it's over, anyway. To make us feel doubly reassured, will you write an affidavit that will dispel any doubts your stubborn uncle may have?

[JIHEI]: Certainly. I'll write a thousand if you like.

[MAGOEMON]: Splendid! I happen to have bought this on the way here.

CHANTER: Magoemon takes from the fold of his kimono a sheet of oath-paper from Kumano, the sacred characters formed by flocks of crows.[17] Instead of vows of eternal love, Jihei now signs under penalty of Heaven's wrath an oath that he will sever all ties and affections with Koharu. "If I should lie, may Bonten and Taishaku above, and the Four Great Kings below afflict me!"[18] So the text runs, and to it is appended the names of many Buddhas and gods. He

17. The charms issued by the Shinto shrine at Kumano, on whose face was printed six Chinese characters, the strokes of which were in the shape of crows. The reverse side of these charms was used for writing oaths.

18. A formal oath. Bonten (Brahma) and Taishaku (Sakra), though Hindu gods, were considered to be protective deities of the Buddhist law. The four Deva kings served under Sakra and also were protectors of Buddhism.

signs his name, Kamiya Jihei, in bold characters, imprints the oath with a seal
of blood, and proffers it.

[OSAN]: It's a great relief to me too. Mother, I have you and Magoemon to thank.
Jihei and I have had two children, but this is his firmest pledge of affection.
I hope you share my joy.

[AUNT]: Indeed we do. I'm sure that Jihei will settle down and his business will
improve, now that he's in this frame of mind. It's been entirely for his sake
and for love of the grandchildren that we've intervened. Come, Magoemon,
let's be on our way. I'm anxious to set my husband's mind at ease. It's become
chilly here. See that the children don't catch cold. This, too, we owe to the
Buddha of the Ten Nights. I'll say a prayer of thanks before I go. Hail,
Amida Buddha!

CHANTER: She leaves, her heart innocent as Buddha's. Jihei is perfunctory even
about seeing them to the door. Hardly have they crossed the threshold than
he slumps down again at the kotatsu. He pulls the checked quilting over
his head.

*The revolving dais on the auxiliary stage turns to bring out a new chanter and
shamisen player.*

[OSAN]: You still haven't forgotten Sonezaki, have you?

CHANTER: She goes up to him in disgust and tears away the quilting. He is
weeping; a waterfall of tears streams along the pillow, deep enough to bear
him afloat. She tugs him upright and props his body against the kotatsu frame.
She stares into his face.

[OSAN]: You're acting outrageously, Jihei. You shouldn't have signed that oath if
you felt so reluctant to leave her. The year before last, on the middle day of
the Boar of the tenth moon,[19] we lit the first fire in the kotatsu and celebrated
by sleeping here together, pillow to pillow. Ever since then—did some demon
or snake creep into my bosom that night?—for two whole years I've been
condemned to keep watch over an empty nest. I thought that tonight at least,
thanks to Mother and Magoemon, we'd share sweet words in bed as husbands
and wives do, but my pleasure didn't last long. How cruel of you, how utterly
heartless! Go ahead, cry your eyes out if you're so attached to her. Your tears
will flow into the Shijimi River, and Koharu, no doubt, will ladle them out
and drink them! You're ignoble, inhuman.

CHANTER: She embraces his knees and throws herself over him, moaning in
supplication. Jihei wipes his eyes.

[JIHEI]: It's not surprising that you can't tell what's in my heart. I have not a shred
of attachment left for that vampire in human skin, but I bear a grudge against
Tahei. He has all the money he wants, no wife or children. He's schemed
again and again to redeem her, but Koharu refused to give in, at least until I
broke with her. She told me time and again, "You have nothing to worry
about. I'll never let myself be redeemed by Tahei, not even if my ties with you

19. It was customary to light the first fire of the winter on this day, which would generally be toward
the end of November in the Western calendar.

FIGURE 3.24. Osan takes her kimono from a chest and piles them on a large cloth for Jihei to pawn. (Photo by Barbara C. Adachi.)

are ended and I can no longer stay by your side. If my master is induced by Tahei's money to deliver me to him, I'll kill myself in a way that'll do you credit!" But think—not ten days have passed since I broke with her, and she's to be redeemed by Tahei! That rotten whore! That animal! No, I haven't a trace of affection left for her, but I can just hear how Tahei will be boasting. He'll spread the word around Osaka that my business has come to a standstill and I'm hard-pressed for money. I'll meet with contemptuous stares from the wholesalers. I'll be dishonored. My heart is broken, and my body burns with shame. What a disgrace! How maddening! I've passed the stage of shedding hot tears, tears of blood, sticky tears—my tears now are of molten iron!

CHANTER: He collapses with weeping. Osan pales with alarm.

[OSAN]: If that's the situation, poor Koharu will surely kill herself.

[JIHEI]: You're too well bred, despite your intelligence, to understand her likes! What makes you suppose that faithless creature would kill herself? Far from it—she's probably taking moxa treatments and medicine to prolong her life!

[OSAN]: No, that's not true. I was determined never to tell you so long as I lived, but I'm afraid of the crime I'd be committing if I concealed the facts and let her die with my knowledge. I will reveal my great secret. There is not a grain of deceit in Koharu. It was I who schemed to end the relations between you. I could see signs that you were drifting toward suicide. I felt so unhappy that I wrote a letter, begging her as one woman to another to break with you, though I knew how painful it would be. I asked her to save your life. The letter must have moved her. She answered that she would give you up, though you were more precious than life itself, because she could not shirk her duty to me. I've kept her letter with me ever since—it's been like a protective charm. Could such a noble-hearted woman violate her promise and brazenly marry Tahei? When a woman—I no less than another—has given herself completely to a man, she does not change. I'm sure she'll kill herself. I'm sure of it. Ahhh— what a dreadful thing to have happened! Save her, please.

CHANTER: Her voice rises in agitation. Her husband is thrown into a turmoil.

[JIHEI]: There was a letter in an unknown woman's hand among the written oaths she surrendered to my brother. It must have been from you. If that's the case, Koharu will surely commit suicide.

[OSAN]: Alas! I'd be failing in the obligations I owe her as another woman if I allowed her to die. Please go to her at once. Don't let her kill herself.

CHANTER: Clinging to her husband, she melts in tears.

[JIHEI]: But what can I possibly do? It'd take half the amount of her ransom in earnest money merely to keep her out of Tahei's clutches. I can't save Koharu's life without administering a dose of 750 momme in New Silver. How could I raise that much money in my present financial straits? Even if I crush my body to powder, where will the money come from?

[OSAN]: Don't exaggerate the difficulties. If that's all you need, it's simple enough.

Osan opens the sliding door at stage left to reveal a large chest of drawers. She removes a small cloth bag from one of the drawers.

CHANTER: She goes to the wardrobe and, opening a small drawer, takes out a bag fastened with cords of twisted silk. She unhesitantly tears it open and throws down a packet that Jihei retrieves.

[JIHEI]: What's this? Money? Four hundred momme in New Silver? How in the world—

CHANTER: He stares astonished at this money he never put there.

[OSAN]: I'll tell you later where this money came from. I've scraped it together to pay the bill for the Iwakuni paper that falls due the day after tomorrow. We'll have to ask Magoemon to help us keep the business from betraying its insolvency. But Koharu comes first. The packet contains 400 momme. That leaves 350 momme to raise.

She spreads out a large cloth and begins piling kimono from the chest on it [figure 3.24].

CHANTER: She unlocks a large drawer. From the wardrobe a Kyoto crepe kimono lined in pale brown, insubstantial as her husband's life that flickers today and may vanish tomorrow; a padded kimono of Osue's, flaming scarlet inside and out—Osan flushes with pain to part with it; Kantarō's sleeveless, unlined jacket—if she pawns this, he'll be cold this winter. Next comes a garment of striped Gunnai silk lined in pale blue and never worn, and then her best formal costume—heavy black silk dyed with her family crest, an ivy leaf in a ring. They say that those joined by marriage ties can even go naked at home, though outside the house, clothes make the man. She snatches up even her husband's finery, a silken cloak, making fifteen articles in all.

[OSAN]: The very least the pawnshop can offer is 350 momme in New Silver.

CHANTER: Her face glows as though she already held the money she needs; she hides in the one bundle her husband's shame and her own obligation and puts in her love besides.

[OSAN]: It doesn't matter if the children and I have nothing to wear. My husband's reputation concerns me more. Ransom Koharu. Save her. Assert your honor before Tahei.

CHANTER: But Jihei's eyes remain downcast all the while, and he is silently weeping.

[JIHEI]: Yes, I can pay the earnest money and keep her out of Tahei's hands. But once I've redeemed her, I'll either have to maintain her in a separate establishment or bring her here. Then what will become of you?

CHANTER: Osan is at a loss to answer.

[OSAN]: Yes, what shall I do? Shall I become your children's nurse or the cook? Or perhaps the retired mistress of the house?

CHANTER: She falls to the floor with a cry of woe.

[JIHEI]: That would be too selfish. I'd be afraid to accept such generosity. Even if the punishment for my crimes against my parents, against Heaven, against the gods and the Buddhas fail to strike me, the punishment for my crimes against my wife alone will be sufficient to destroy all hope for the future life. Forgive me, I beg you.

CHANTER: He joins his hands in tearful entreaty.

[OSAN]: Why should you bow before me? I don't deserve it. I'd be glad to rip the nails from my fingers and toes, to do anything which might serve my husband. I've been pawning my clothes for some time in order to scrape together the money for the paper wholesalers' bills. My wardrobe is empty, but I don't regret it in the least. But it's too late now to talk of such things. Hurry, change your cloak and go to her with a smile.

They both go out through the curtained exit at center back.

CHANTER: He puts on an underkimono of Gunnai silk, a robe of heavy black silk, and a striped cloak. His sash of figured damask holds a dirk of middle length worked in gold. Buddha surely knows that tonight it will be stained with Koharu's blood.

Osan returns and summons the servant, who enters and walks in front of the bundle.

[OSAN]: Sangorō! Come here!

Jihei reenters dressed in a dark kimono with a short, striped jacket over it.

CHANTER: Jihei loads the bundle on the servant's back, intending to take him along. Then he firmly thrusts the wallet next to his skin and starts toward the gate.

[VOICE]: Is Jihei at home?

CHANTER: A man enters, removing his fur cap. They see—good heavens!—that it is Gozaemon.

Gozaemon, Osan's father, enters from stage right and bumps into Sangorō.

[OSAN AND JIHEI]: Ahhh—how fortunate that you should come at this moment!

Gozaemon takes the bundle from Sangorō and enters the room.

CHANTER: Husband and wife are upset and confused. Gozaemon snatches away Sangorō's bundle and sits heavily. His voice is sharp.

[GOZAEMON]: Stay where you are, harlot!—My esteemed son-in-law, what a rare pleasure to see you dressed in your finest attire, with a dirk and a silken cloak! Ahhh—that's how a gentleman of means spends his money! No one would take you for a paper dealer. Are you perchance on your way to the New Quarter? What commendable perseverance! You have no need for your wife, I take it.—Give her a divorce. I've come to take her home with me.

CHANTER: He speaks needles and his voice is bitter. Jihei has not a word to reply.

[OSAN]: How kind of you, Father, to walk here on such a cold day. Do have a cup of tea.

CHANTER: Offering the teacup serves as an excuse for edging closer.

[OSAN]: Mother and Magoemon came here a while ago, and they told my husband how much they disapproved of his visits to the New Quarter. Jihei was in tears and he wrote out an oath swearing he had reformed. He gave it to Mother. Haven't you seen it yet?

[GOZAEMON]: His written oath? Do you mean this?

CHANTER: He takes the paper from his kimono.

[GOZAEMON]: Libertines scatter vows and oaths wherever they go, as if they were monthly statements of accounts. I thought there was something peculiar about this oath, and now that I am here I can see I was right. Do you still swear to Bonten and Taishaku? Instead of such nonsense, write out a bill of divorce!

CHANTER: He rips the oath to shreds and throws down the pieces. Husband and wife exchange looks of alarm, stunned into silence. Jihei touches his hands to the floor and bows his head.

[JIHEI]: Your anger is justified. If I were still my former self, I would try to offer explanations, but today I appeal entirely to your generosity. Please let me stay with Osan. I promise that even if I become a beggar or an outcast and must sustain life with the scraps that fall from other people's chopsticks, I will hold Osan in high honor and protect her from every harsh and bitter experience. I feel so deeply indebted to Osan that I cannot divorce her. You will understand that this is true as time passes and I show you how I apply myself to my work and restore my fortune. Until then, please shut your eyes and allow us to remain together.

CHANTER: Tears of blood stream from his eyes, and his face is pressed to the matting in contrition.

[GOZAEMON]: The wife of an outcast! That's all the worse. Write the bill of divorce at once! I will verify and seal the furniture and clothes Osan brought in her dowry.

CHANTER: He goes to the wardrobe. Osan is alarmed.

[OSAN]: My clothes are all here. There's no need to examine them.

CHANTER: She runs up to forestall him, but Gozaemon pushes her aside and jerks open a drawer.

[GOZAEMON]: What does this mean?

CHANTER: He opens another drawer, but it, too, is empty. He pulls out every last drawer, but not so much as a foot of patchwork cloth is to be seen. He tears open the wicker hampers, long boxes, and clothes chest.

[GOZAEMON]: Stripped bare, are they?

CHANTER: His eyes set in fury. Jihei and Osan huddle under the striped kotatsu quilt, ready to sink into the fire with humiliation.

[GOZAEMON]: This bundle looks suspicious.

CHANTER: He unties the knots and dumps out the contents.

[GOZAEMON]: As I thought! You were sending these to the pawnshop, I take it. Jihei—you'd strip the skin from your wife's and your children's bodies to squander the money on your whore! Dirty thief! You're my wife's nephew, but an utter stranger to me, and I'm under no obligation to suffer for your sake. I'll explain to Magoemon what has happened and ask him to make good whatever inroads you've already made on Osan's belongings. But first, the bill of divorce!

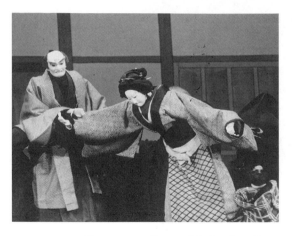

FIGURE 3.25. Gozaemon pulls away his daughter Osan. Her child is at her feet. (Photo by Barbara C. Adachi.)

CHANTER: Even if Jihei could escape through seven padlocked doors, eight thicknesses of chains, and a hundred girdling walls, he could not evade so stringent a demand.

[JIHEI]: I won't use a brush to write the bill of divorce. Here's what I'll do instead! Goodbye, Osan.

CHANTER: He lays his hand on his dirk, but Osan clings to him.

[OSAN]: Father—Jihei admits that he's done wrong, and he's apologized in every way. You press your advantage too hard. Jihei may be a stranger, but his children are your grandchildren. Have you no affection for them? I will not accept a bill of divorce.

CHANTER: She embraces her husband and raises her voice in tears.

[GOZAEMON]: Very well. I won't insist on it. Come with me, woman.

CHANTER: He pulls her to her feet.

[OSAN]: No, I won't go. What bitterness makes you expose to such shame a man and wife who still love each other? I will not suffer it.

CHANTER: She pleads with him, weeping, but he pays her no heed.

[GOZAEMON]: Is there some greater shame? I'll shout it through the town!

CHANTER: He pulls her up, but she shakes free. Caught by the wrist she totters forward when—alas! her toes brush against her sleeping children. They open their eyes [figure 3.25].

[CHILDREN]: Mother dear, why is Grandfather, the bad man, taking you away? Whom will we sleep beside now?

CHANTER: They call out after her.

[OSAN]: My poor dears! You've never spent a night away from Mother's side since you were born. Sleep tonight beside your father. (*To Jihei*) Please don't forget to give the children their tonic before breakfast. Oh, my heart is broken!

CHANTER: These are her parting words. She leaves her children behind, abandoned as in the woods; the twin-trunked bamboo of conjugal love is sundered forever [figure 3.26].

Jihei carries the baby out through curtained exit at back, and the boy follows. Father and Osan exit to stage right. Drums accompany the exit, and the stage darkens.

ACT 3, Scene 1

Sonezaki New Quarter, in front of the Yamato House
Time: That night

The set is changed in darkness without drawing the curtain. Stage right and front is a dark street with a door to the Yamato Teahouse near the center of the stage. As the

FIGURE 3.26. Jihei is left with his children after Osan's father drags her away. In the bunraku version, he picks up the younger one; in kabuki, two older children cling to him. (Left: photo by Barbara C. Adachi; right: photo by Aoki Shinji.)

chanter sings, some palanquin bearers come and go, and a woman briefly comes out of a doorway.

CHANTER: This is Shijimi River, the haunt of love and affection. Its flowing water and the feet of passersby are stilled now at two in the morning, and the full moon shines clear in the sky. Here in the street a dim doorway lantern is marked "Yamatoya Dembei" in a single scrawl. The night watchman's clappers take on a deep cadence as he totters by on uncertain legs. The very thickness of his voice crying, "Beware of fire! Beware of fire!" tells how far advanced the night is. Between two and four, even the teahouse kettle rests; the flame flickering in the low candle stand narrows; and the frost spreads in the cold river-wind of the deepening night. The master's voice breaks the stillness.

Dembei and Jihei come out the door of the Yamato House.

[DEMBEI] (*To Jihei*): It's still the middle of the night. I'll send somebody with you. (*To the servants*) Mr. Jihei is leaving. Wake Koharu. Call her here.
CHANTER: Jihei slides open the side door.
[JIHEI]: No, Dembei, not a word to Koharu. I'll be trapped here till dawn if she hears I'm leaving. That's why I'm letting her sleep and slipping off this way. Wake her up after sunrise and send her back then. I'm returning home now and will leave for Kyoto immediately on business. I have so many engagements that I may not be able to return in time for the interim payment. Please use the money I gave you earlier this evening to clear my account. I'd like you also to send 150 *me* of Old Silver to the Kawashō for the moon-viewing party last month. Please get a receipt. Give Saietsubō[20] from Fukushima one piece of silver as a contribution to the Buddhist altar he's bought, and tell him to use it for a memorial service. Wasn't there something else? Oh yes—give Isoichi a tip of four silver coins. That's the lot. Now you can close up and get

---

20. The name of a male entertainer in the Quarter. Fukushima was west of Sonezaki.

FIGURE 3.27. Jihei sneaks off to the Yamato House to get Koharu. (Photo by Barbara C. Adachi.)

to bed. Good-bye. I'll see you when I return from Kyoto.

CHANTER: Hardly has he taken two or three steps than he turns back.

[JIHEI]: I forgot my dirk. Fetch it for me, won't you? Yes, Dembei, this is one respect in which it's easier being a townsman. If I were a samurai and forgot my sword, I'd probably commit suicide on the spot!

[DEMBEI]: I completely forgot that I was keeping it for you. Yes, here it is.

CHANTER: He gives the dirk to Jihei, who fastens it firmly into his sash.

[JIHEI]: I feel secure as long as I have this. Good night!

CHANTER: He goes off.

[DEMBEI]: Please come back to Osaka soon! Thank you for your patronage!

CHANTER: With this hasty farewell, Dembei rattles the door bolt shut; then not another sound is heard as the silence deepens. Jihei pretends to leave, only to creep back again with stealthy steps.

[There is a brief section, omitted here, in which Magoemon, accompanied by Sangorō and the children, comes in search of his brother. He fears that Jihei will commit suicide but is relieved to learn that Jihei has left and Koharu remains. From the shadows of a doorway Jihei watches them come and go.]

CHANTER: Jihei peers through a crack in the side door of the Yamato House and glimpses a figure [figure 3.27].

[JIHEI]: That's Koharu, isn't it? I'll let her know I'm here.

CHANTER: He clears his throat, their signal. "Ahem, ahem"—the sound blends with the clack of wooden clappers as the watchman comes from the upper street, coughing in the night wind. He hurries on his round of fire warning, "Take care! Beware!" Even this cry has a dismal sound to one in hiding. Jihei, concealing himself like the god of Katsuragi,[21] lets the watchman pass. He sees his chance and rushes to the side door, which softly opens from within.

[JIHEI]: Koharu?

[KOHARU]: Were you waiting? Jihei—I want to leave quickly.

CHANTER: She is all impatience, but the more hastily they open the door, the more likely people will be to hear the casters turning. They lift the door; it gives a moaning that thunders in their ears and in their hearts. Jihei lends a

21. The god was so ashamed of his ugliness that he ventured forth only at night.

hand from the outside, but his fingertips tremble with the trembling of his heart. The door opens a quarter of an inch, a half, an inch—an inch ahead are the tortures of hell, but more than hell itself they fear the guardian demon's eyes. At last the door opens, and with the joy of New Year's morn, Koharu slips out. They catch each other's hands. Shall they go north or south, west or east? Their pounding hearts urge them on, though they know not to what destination. Turning their backs on the moon reflected in the Shijimi River, they hurry eastward as fast as their legs will carry them.

They move back and forth, bumping into each other. Jihei puts his jacket over Koharu's shoulders, and they exit to drum music. The curtain is closed.

Scene 2

The Farewell Journey of Many Bridges

The musicians change; five chanters and five shamisen players sit on the auxiliary stage. When the curtains open, the scene is dark. Two bridge railings stand toward the left and right of the stage. Jihei and Koharu enter from stage right; they both wear scarves on their heads. They move across the stage, over the two bridges, as the chanters sing to shamisen accompaniment.

CHANTERS: Poor creatures, though they would discover today their destiny in the Sutra of Cause and Effect,[22] tomorrow the gossip of the world will scatter like blossoms the scandal of Kamiya Jihei's love suicide, and carved in cherry wood,[23] his story to the last detail will be printed in illustrated sheets. Jihei, led on by the spirit of death—if such there be among the gods—is resigned to this punishment for neglect of his trade. But at times—who could blame him?— his heart is drawn to those he has left behind, and it is hard to keep walking on. Even in the full moon's light, this fifteenth night of the tenth moon, he cannot see his way ahead—a sign perhaps of the darkness in his heart? The frost now falling will melt by dawn, but even more quickly than this symbol of human frailty, the lovers themselves will melt away. What will become of the fragrance that lingered when he held her tenderly at night in their bed-chamber? This bridge, Tenjin Bridge, he has crossed every day, morning and night, gazing at Shijimi River to the west. Long ago, when Tenjin, then called Michizane, was exiled to Tsukushi, his plum tree, following its master, flew in one bound to Dazaifu, and here is Plum-field Bridge. Green Bridge recalls the aged pine that followed later, and Cherry Bridge the tree that withered away in grief over parting. Such are the tales still told, bespeaking the power of a single poem.[24]

---

22. A sacred text of Buddhism (Karma Sutra). Chikamatsu here alludes to the line from that text: "If you wish to know the past cause, look at the present effect; if you wish to know the future effect, look at the present cause."

23. The blocks from which illustrated books were printed were frequently made of cherry wood. The illustrated sheets mentioned here featured current scandals, such as lovers' suicides.

24. The poem by Michizane bewailing the inconstancy of his pine tree. Michizane's exile is also described in the selection from act 4 of *Sugawara and the Secrets of Calligraphy*, translated here.

FIGURE 3.28. As Jihei and Koharu move across the stage and back, the railings move into new configurations to suggest that they are passing over many bridges. (Photo by Barbara C. Adachi.)

As they continue their journey, turning to move from stage left to right, the railings move together, forming a long bridge [figure 3.28].

[JIHEI]: Though born the parishioner of so holy and mighty a god, I shall kill you and then myself. If you ask the cause, it was that I lacked even the wisdom that might fill a tiny Shell Bridge. Our stay in this world has been short as an autumn day. This evening will be the last of your nineteen, of my twenty-eight years. The time has come to cast away our lives. We promised we'd remain together faithfully, till you were an old woman and I an old man, but before we knew each other three full years, we have met this disaster. Look, there is Ōe Bridge. We follow the river from Little Naniwa Bridge to Funairi Bridge. The farther we journey, the closer we approach the road to death.

CHANTERS: He laments. She clings to him.

[KOHARU]: Is this already the road to death?

CHANTERS: Falling tears obscure from each the other's face and threaten to immerse even the Horikawa bridges.

[JIHEI]: A few steps north and I could glimpse my house, but I will not turn back. I will bury in my breast all thoughts of my children's future, all pity for my wife. We cross southward over the river. Why did they call a place with as many buildings as a bridge has piers "Eight Houses"? Hurry, we want to arrive before the downriver boat from Fushimi comes—with what happy couples sleeping aboard! Next is Temma Bridge, a frightening name[25] for us about to depart this world. Here the two streams Yodo and Yamato join in one great river, as fish with water, and as Koharu and I, dying on one blade, will cross together the River of Three Fords.[26] I would like this water for our tomb offering!

[KOHARU]: What have we to grieve about? Though in this world we could not stay together, in the next and through each successive world to come until the end of time, we shall be husband and wife. Every summer for my devotions, I have copied the All-Compassionate and All-Merciful Chapter of the Lotus Sutra, in the hope that we may be reborn on one lotus.

CHANTERS: They cross over Sutra Bridge and reach the opposite shore.[27]

[KOHARU]: If I can save living creatures at will when once I mount a lotus calyx in Paradise and become a Buddha, I want to protect women of my profession, so that never again will there be love suicides.

CHANTERS: This unattainable prayer stems from worldly attachment, but it

25. The characters used for Temma literally mean "demon."
26. A river in the Buddhist underworld that had to be crossed to reach the world of the dead. Mention here is induced arithmetically: one blade plus two people equals three fords.
27. "Opposite shore" suggests the Buddhist term *higan* (nirvana).

touchingly reveals her heart. They cross Onari Bridge. The waters of Noda Creek are shrouded with morning haze; the mountain tips show faintly white.

[JIHEI]: Listen—the voices of the temple bells begin to boom [figure 3.29]. How much farther can we go on this way? We are not fated to live any longer—let us make an end quickly. Come this way.

CHANTERS: Tears are strung with the 108 beads of the rosaries in their hands. They have come now to Amijima, to the Daichō Temple; the overflowing sluice gate of a little stream beside a bamboo thicket will be their place of death.

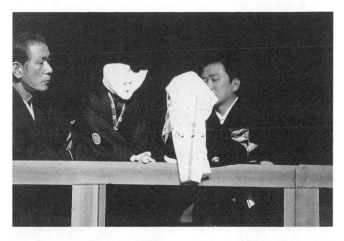

FIGURE 3.29. Koharu and Jihei pause in the middle of a bridge and listen to the temple bells. (Photo by Barbara C. Adachi.)

They exit briefly at stage right and return. The backdrop is lifted to reveal another with an island scene, and some of the bridge railings drop down out of sight.

Scene 3

Amijima

Koharu and Jihei remove their scarves as they cross to center stage.

[JIHEI]: No matter how far we walk, there'll never be a spot marked "For Suicides." Let us kill ourselves here.

CHANTERS: He takes her hand and sits on the ground.

[KOHARU]: Yes, that's true. One place is as good as another to die. But I've been thinking on the way that if they find our dead bodies together, people will say that Koharu and Jihei committed a lovers' suicide. Osan will think then that I treated as mere scrap paper the letter I sent promising her, when she asked me not to kill you, that I would not, and vowing to break all relations. She will be sure that I lured her precious husband into a lovers' suicide. She will despise me as a one-night prostitute, a false woman with no sense of decency. I fear her contempt more than the slander of a thousand or ten thousand strangers. I can imagine how she will resent and envy me. That is the greatest obstacle to my salvation. Kill me here, then choose another spot, far away, for yourself.

CHANTERS: She leans against him. Jihei joins in her tears of pleading.

[JIHEI]: What foolish worries! Osan has been taken back by my father-in-law. I've divorced her. She and I are strangers now. Why should you feel obliged to a divorced woman? You were saying on the way that you and I will be husband and wife through each successive world until the end of time. Who can criticize us, who can be jealous, if we die side by side?

[KOHARU]: But who is responsible for your divorce? You're even less reasonable than I. Do you suppose that our bodies will accompany us to the afterworld?

FIGURE 3.30. In the kabuki version Koharu holds the dirk, which Jihei will use to kill her. (Photo by Aoki Shinji.)

We may die in different places, our bodies may be pecked by kites and crows, but what does it matter as long as our souls are twined together? Take me with you to heaven or to hell!

CHANTERS: She sinks again in tears.

[JIHEI]: You're right. Our bodies are made of earth, water, fire, and wind, and when we die they revert to emptiness. But our souls will not decay, no matter how often reborn. And here's a guarantee that our souls will be married and never part!

CHANTERS: He whips out his dirk and slashes off his black locks at the base of the top knot.

[JIHEI]: Look, Koharu. As long as I had this hair I was Kamiya Jihei, Osan's husband, but cutting it has made me a monk. I have fled the burning house of the three worlds of delusion; I am a priest, unencumbered by wife, children, or worldly possessions. Now that I no longer have a wife named Osan, you owe her no obligations either.

CHANTERS: In tears he flings away the hair.

[KOHARU]: I am happy.

CHANTERS: Koharu takes up the dirk and ruthlessly, unhesitantly, slices through her flowing Shimada coiffure [figure 3.30]. She casts aside the tresses she has so often washed and combed and stroked. How heartbreaking to see their locks tangled with the weeds and midnight frost of this desolate field!

[JIHEI]: We have escaped the inconstant world, a nun and a priest. Our duties as husband and wife belong to our profane past. It would be best to choose quite separate places for our deaths, a mountain for one, the river for the other. We will pretend that the ground above this sluice gate is a mountain. You will die there. I shall hang myself by this stream. The time of our deaths will be the same, but the method and place will differ. In this way we can honor to the end our duty to Osan. Give me your undersash.

CHANTERS: Its fresh violet color and fragrance will be lost in the winds of impermanence; the crinkled silk long enough to wind twice round her body will bind two worlds, this and the next. He firmly fastens one end to the cross-piece of the sluice, then twists the other into a noose for his neck. He will hang for love of his wife like the "pheasant in the hunting grounds."[28]

Koharu watches Jihei prepare for his death. Her eyes swim with tears; her mind is distraught.

[KOHARU]: Is that how you're going to kill yourself? If we are to die apart, I have only a little while longer by your side. Come near me.

CHANTERS: They take each other's hands.

[KOHARU]: It's over in a moment with a sword, but I'm sure you'll suffer. My poor darling!

CHANTERS: She cannot stop the silent tears.

[JIHEI]: Can suicide ever be pleasant, whether by hanging or cutting the throat? You mustn't let worries over trifles disturb the prayers of your last moments. Keep your eyes on the westward-moving moon, and worship it as Amida himself.[29] Concentrate your thoughts on the Western Paradise. If you have any regrets about leaving the world, tell me now, then die.

[KOHARU]: I have none at all, none at all. But I'm sure you must be worried about your children.

[JIHEI]: You make me cry all over again by mentioning them. I can almost see their faces, sleeping peacefully, unaware, poor dears, that their father is about to kill himself. They're the one thing I can't forget.

CHANTERS: He droops to the ground with weeping. The voices of the crows leaving their nests at dawn rival his sobs. Are the crows mourning his fate? The thought brings more tears.

[JIHEI]: Listen to them. The crows have come to guide us to the world of the dead. There's an old saying that every time somebody writes an oath on the back of a Kumano charm, three crows of Kumano die on the holy mountain. The first words we've written each New Year have been vows of love, and how often we've inscribed oaths at the beginning of the month! If each oath has killed three crows, what a multitude must have perished! Their cries have always sounded like "beloved, beloved," but hatred for our crime of taking life makes their voices ring tonight "revenge, revenge!"[30] Whose fault is it that they demand revenge? Because of me, you will die a painful death. Forgive me!

CHANTERS: He takes her in his arms.

[KOHARU]: No, it's my fault!

CHANTERS: They cling to each other, face pressed to face; their side locks, drenched with tears, freeze in the winds blowing over the fields. Behind them echoes the voice of the Daichō Temple.

[JIHEI]: Even the long winter night seems short as our lives.

28. A reference to a poem by Ōtomo no Yakamochi (718–785): "The pheasant foraging in the fields of spring reveals his whereabouts to man as he cries for his mate" (*Shūishū*, poem 21).

29. Amida's paradise lies in the west. The moon is also frequently used as a symbol of Buddhist enlightenment.

30. The cries have always sounded like "*kawai, kawai,*" but now they sound like "*mukui, mukui.*" These Japanese sounds seem more within the range of a crow's articulatory powers than "beloved" and "revenge."

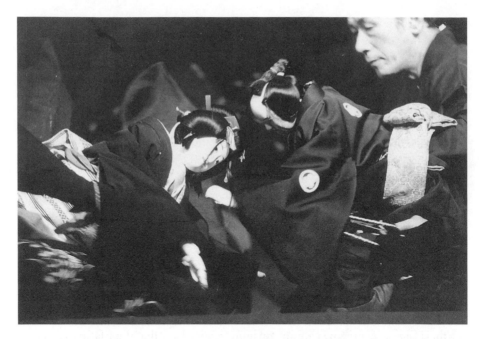

FIGURE 3.31. Jihei makes the dying Koharu comfortable by putting his cloak under her head. The text says he covers her with it, but stage actions often differ slightly from those described in the script. (Photo by Barbara C. Adachi.)

CHANTERS: Dawn is already breaking, and matins can be heard. He draws her to him.

[JIHEI]: The moment has come for our glorious end. Let there be no tears on your face when they find you later.

[KOHARU]: There won't be any.

CHANTERS: She smiles. His hands, numbed by the frost, tremble before the pale vision of her face, and his eyes are first to cloud. He is weeping so profusely that he cannot control the blade.

[KOHARU]: Compose yourself—but be quick!

CHANTERS: Her encouragement lends him strength; the invocations to Amida carried by the wind urge a final prayer. *Namu Amida Butsu.*

Koharu, with her back to the audience, leans into the sword held by Jihei. Chimes sound as it pierces her neck.

He thrusts in the saving sword. Stabbed, she falls backward, despite his staying hand, and struggles in terrible pain. The point of the blade has missed her windpipe, and these are the final tortures before she can die. He writhes with her in agony, then painfully summons his strength again.

He stabs her harder and harder until she falls over backward to strong shamisen accompaniment.

He draws her to him and plunges in his dirk to the hilt. He twists the blade in the wound, and her life fades away like an unfinished dream at dawning. He arranges her corpse head to the north, face to the west, lying on her right side,[31] and throws his cloak over her [figure 3.31]. He turns away at last, unable to exhaust with tears his grief over parting.

Jihei takes Koharu's obi. He goes to the bridge railing and hangs himself with the obi.

He pulls the sash to him and fastens the noose around his neck. The service in the temple has reached the closing section, the prayers for the dead. "Believers and unbelievers will equally share in the divine grace," the voices proclaim, and at the final words Jihei jumps from the sluice gate.

[JIHEI]: May we be reborn on one lotus! Hail Amida Buddha!

CHANTERS: For a few moments he writhes like a gourd swinging in the wind, but gradually the passage of his breath is blocked as are the streams dammed by the sluice gate, where his ties with this life are snapped.

He looks at Koharu, who continues to writhe as he dies.

Fishermen out for the morning catch find the body in their net.[32]

[FISHERMEN]: A dead man! Look, a dead man! Come here, everybody!

CHANTERS: The tale is spread from mouth to mouth. People say that they who are caught in the net of Buddha's vow immediately gain salvation and deliverance, and all who hear the tale of the Love Suicides at Amijima are moved to tears.

31. The dead were arranged in this manner because Shakyamuni Buddha chose this position when he died.

32. "Net" (*ami*) is mentioned because of the connection with fishermen. It is echoed a few lines later in the mention of the name *Ami*jima. The vow of the Buddha to save all living creatures is likened to a net that catches people in its meshes.

The First Note
of Spring

The travel scene (*michiyuki*) from act 4 of
Yoshitsune sembon zakura by Takeda Izumo II,
Miyoshi Shōraku, and Namiki Senryū

Translated by Janet Goff

Yoshitsune sembon zakura (Yoshitsune and
a thousand cherry trees) is a period piece set in the world of the twelfth-century
Gempei wars in which Atsumori died (see *Atsumori* and *Suma Bay* in this book).
Yoshitsune (1158–1189), however, was on the winning side; he was a commander of
the Genji, or Minamoto, forces and the younger, half brother of Yoritomo (1147–
1199), the first Kamakura shogun. In composing this piece the playwrights take great
liberties with history; moreover, many of the characters hide their true identity during much of the play.

The plot begins after the defeat of the Heike, but some of the major Heike generals and the young emperor Antoku who actually died during the wars are resuscitated for the purposes of the play. For example, Tomomori and Koremori first appear
in *Yoshitsune sembon zakura* disguised as a shipping agent and a sushi shop apprentice, respectively—a device similar to one used in noh in which the ghosts of warriors
appear in the first act in the guise of commoners. In act 2 of this play, Tomomori, pretending to be his own ghost, fights Yoshitsune in a scene that echoes the noh play
Funa Benkei. After he is mortally wounded, Tomomori ties himself to an anchor and
jumps into the sea, as he does, albeit less graphically, in the noh play *Ikarikazuki*.
Koremori's story, told in the often-performed sushi shop scene in act 3, involves conflicting loyalties, a head substitution, a wayward son who is revealed on his deathbed
to have been partially good, and an enemy who turns out to be secretly sympathetic—
subplots that recur frequently in successful eighteenth-century plays.

The travel scene in act 4 belongs to a subplot concerning Yoshitsune's mistress,
the shirabyōshi dancer Shizuka, his retainer Tadanobu, a drum, and a fox. The scenes
telling this story are sometimes performed as a set in both bunraku and kabuki under
the title *Kitsune Tadanobu* (Fox Tadanobu). In *Yoshitsune and a Thousand Cherry
Trees*, the scenes are scattered throughout the play. In act 1, which is seldom performed, the retired emperor GoShirakawa bestows on Yoshitsune a hand drum called

Hatsune (First note) as a reward for his services at the battle of Yashima. In act 2, Yoshitsune gives the drum to Shizuka as a keepsake when he parts from her at Inari Shrine, a place closely connected with foxes. An enemy sees Shizuka and is about to carry her off when Tadanobu, one of Yoshitsune's retainers, appears from nowhere and rescues her. The grateful Yoshitsune bestows part of his own name and a suit of armor on Tadanobu and puts Shizuka under his protection. Later in the play, when Yoshitsune is fleeing from Yoritomo, Shizuka and Tadanobu seek him out. Their journey is depicted in the travel scene translated here.

When Shizuka is reunited with Yoshitsune later in act 4, she discovers that another "Tadanobu" is accompanying him. She beats the drum, and her travel companion Tadanobu appears and explains that he is actually a fox whose parents were killed and skins were used in making the drum. The drum is given to the fox as a reward for its services. The fox then saves Yoshitsune from yet another resuscitated Heike warrior, Noritsune, who had killed the real Tadanobu's brother at the battle of Yashima. The fox Tadanobu's exit is sometimes executed with a dramatic bit of stage business: the puppet, the drum, and the main puppeteer fly through the air suspended from a wire, a technique known as *chūnori*. Some kabuki actors, most notably the current Ichikawa Ennosuke, also employ this technique.

"The First Note of Spring" is often cited as the best of all the *michiyuki* (travel scenes) because it incorporates such a rich variety of singing, music, and dance styles. In a charming solo dance at the beginning of the scene, Shizuka uses a fan to mime the actions of several popular Edo-period songs strung together in the text. As she dances, the sleeves of her two outer robes are removed, creating new color combinations. The white fox, represented by a puppet manipulated by a single puppeteer, performs a charming little dance to instrumental music, wiggling its ears, scratching its side, biting its tail, and listening intently to the drum. Tadanobu's true nature as a fox is hinted at by shamisen music suggesting a fox's gait and by the movements of his feet. His attachment to the drum is revealed at the end of the scene. Shizuka and Tadanobu—each manipulated by three puppeteers, the chief of whom appears without a hood—perform several duets, imitating a wild goose and a swallow, miming the lively sword fight between Kagekiyo and Mionoya, and depicting the sad death of Tadanobu's brother.

Yoshitsune sembon zakura, composed by the same trio of playwrights who created *Sugawara and the Secrets of Calligraphy*, was an enormous hit when it was first performed in 1747, the year after *Sugawara* successfully opened. *Yoshitsune* was immediately transferred to the kabuki stage, where it has also been a perennial hit. In kabuki, the travel scene is sometimes performed as a separate dance piece (figure 3.32). Tadanobu rises to the stage through a trap door (*suppon*) to the accompaniment of entrance music (*raijo*) adapted from noh. His is a difficult role, for the performer must act as a retainer yet give suggestions of his fox nature through subtle gestures, a foxlike enunciation of certain words, and reactions to the sound of the drum.

Janet Goff's translation of the puppet version is based on the text in Yūda 1965 and on the commentary in Tsunoda and Uchiyama 1991. Her detailed descriptions of stage business are taken from a videotaped performance at the National Theater on September 26, 1991. For a translation of the complete play, see Jones 1993.

FIGURE 3.32. A kabuki version of the michiyuki scene from *Yoshi-tsune sembon zakura*. Shizuka and Tadanobu have set off on their journey, hats (*kasa*) in their hands. The musicians line the back of the stage, and the chanters are to the right of the shamisen players. (Photo by Aoki Shinji.)

CHARACTERS (both parts are sung by the chanters)

SHIZUKA GOZEN: a shirabyōshi dancer who was the mistress of the twelfth-century hero Minamoto no Yoshitsune

SATŌ TADANOBU: a retainer of Yoshitsune, who is actually a fox

MUSICIANS

Five gidayū chanters and five shamisen players

Drum, percussion, and sound effects from performers in the music room

---

ACT 4

The Travel Scene: The First Note of Spring

A red-and-white-striped curtain hides the stage. Five chanters and five shamisen players sit in a row on a platform in front of the curtain at stage left.

Prelude

CHANTERS:
> Is love
> or loyalty deeper? The depth of love
> cannot be measured, it is so strong.

[SHIZUKA]:
> Entrusted to a loyal and true warrior,
> a sign of Yoshitsune's love,

CHANTERS:
> Shizuka, secretly yearning,
> leaves the capital behind.[1]
> Dressed in lovely but subdued attire,
> she sets forth on a journey
> seeking the whereabouts of Yoshitsune,

[SHIZUKA]:
> who, buffeted by the waves at Naniwa,

1. The names of the characters are woven into the text: "loyal" and "true" are translations of *chū* and *makoto,* which are written with Chinese characters that can also be read *tada* and *nobu.* Shizuka's name is embedded in *shizuka ni shinobu* ("secretly yearning"). In *nari mo Yoshitsune, yoshi* can mean "good," hence "lovely attire."

wandered at sea. Now

CHANTERS:

he is said to be in Yoshino:
the rumor serves as a guide.
Heading for the Yamato trail,

*A shamisen interlude is played as
the curtain drops and is carried away,
revealing the hills of Yoshino covered
with cherry blossoms. Shizuka stands
by a tree at center stage dressed in
travel attire, carrying on her back a
bundle wrapped in a purple cloth and
holding a staff and a large lacquered
hat. Her outer kimono bears an elaborate floral design [figure 3.33].*[2]

FIGURE 3.33. Shizuka as she enters dressed for travel at the beginning of the michiyuki in *Yoshitsune sembon zakura*. This scene is performed with the chief puppeteer unhooded and dressed in kamishimo. Shizuka's costume is similar to the one used in kabuki (see figure 3.32). (Courtesy of the National Bunraku Theater.)

overcome by yearning,
along a faint, unfamiliar
path through thickly covered
    fields,
she parts the young grasses to the left and right.
Startled pheasants, seeking food, rise,
crying *hororo kenken* and beating their wings.
You passionately care for your young;
as I wander lost on the path of love,
how envious I am,

[SHIZUKA]:

how jealous I am.

CHANTERS:

The first wild goose and its mate heading homeward,
their wings outstretched like stiffly pleated trousers,
are better off than I am.
Brushwood is offered

[SHIZUKA]:

at Uga no Mitama Shrine, dedicated to the god of food,[3]
solemn and radiant
in the mist. Mika no Hara field[4]

CHANTERS:

is clearly visible.
The leather covered drum,

2. The September 1991 performance omits the following lines as far as "while forlornly passing Hosono."

3. The messenger of the god of food worshiped at Inari shrines is thought to be a fox.

4. Mika no Hara lies south of Kyoto. The play alludes to *Shinkokinshū*, poem 996, by Fujiwara no Kanesuke (877–933): "Izumi River welling up/in Mika no Hara, divides the field/as it flows along./How could I yearn so for her,/when we have never met?"

received as a keepsake,
is especially charming.
Charming, charming is the bond
the bundle conceals from others' eyes.

[SHIZUKA]:
Like the staff, it provides support

CHANTERS:
while forlornly passing Hosono.
She gazes around

Shizuka looks around.

at the surrounding treetops all lightly tinted.
In Utahime, where a maiden once sang about a plum branch,[5]

As Shizuka faces the rear of the stage, her bundle, staff, and hat are removed.

men's voices are heard in the village:

Shizuka mimes the following words.

"My wife
makes amorous advances.
Sharing a pillow in broad daylight—
who ever heard of such a thing?"[6]

She takes out and partly opens her fan.

Oh, who ever heard of such a thing?
At the droll tune,
people laugh. Even children raised
beneath a thatched roof
play battledore and shuttlecock at the start of spring.

She imitates hitting a shuttlecock.

[SHIZUKA]:
A gaily colored handball

CHANTERS:
bounces once, twice.

Shizuka pretends to bounce a ball.

Attentive ears can also hear
the spring breeze from the east
as it melts last year's ice.

Shamisen interlude   *To drumbeats, Shizuka opens her fan all the way and begins to dance.*

"May our lord prosper ten thousand years,
blessed with eternal youth.

5. *Utahime* literally means "song maiden." *Ume ga e* ("plum blossom") alludes to a song in book 3 of *Matsu no ha* (1703), an anthology of popular songs written for shamisen music.
6. An Edo-period folksong.

Brief shamisen interlude and drumbeats as Shizuka continues to dance.

It is a happy, auspicious sign."[7]
Surely, if the singers are Yamato folk
I can ask where he is hidden.

With her back turned to the audience, the right sleeve of Shizuka's outer robe is removed and tucked into the sash at her back, revealing the sleeve of a red underkimono. She is given a drum and is turned to face stage front.

[SHIZUKA]:
I will play this drum,
CHANTERS:
the first note of spring,[8]
celebrating our lord's prosperity,

Shizuka tightens the drum's strings.

hoping to restore the past again.[9]

The cry of a nightingale is heard offstage.

The nightingale in the valley
utters its first note in spring;
the first-beat drum, the first-beat drum

FIGURE 3.34. As Shizuka mimes drumming, the shamisen music mimics drum sounds. Attracted to the sounds of the drum, the fox (manipulated by a single puppeteer working without a hood) nuzzles up to the back of Shizuka's kimono, spread out to display its beauty. (Courtesy of the National Bunraku Theater.)

The shamisen music imitates Shizuka's playing on the drum. During a shamisen interlude with flute music and drum rolls, a white fox suddenly emerges from stage right and wiggles its ears. It approaches Shizuka, who has turned her back to the audience, and nuzzles her kimono [figure 3.34]. It returns downstage, scratches its head, bites its tail, and wiggles its ears again.

plays a beckoning tune.
The sound beckons!

The fox disappears behind a knoll at stage right. The knoll falls down, revealing Tadanobu in travel attire, with hat in hand and a bundle wrapped in an aqua cloth on his back [figure 3.35].

[TADANOBU]:
Hastening to catch up,
the tardy Tadanobu, dressed for the road,
carries a bundle firmly on his back.

---

7. *Manzai* (ten thousand years), a rustic New Year's entertainment from Yamato (the Nara area), is evoked because of its conventional association with drums. The performers go from house to house singing and dancing to drum accompaniment.

8. The name of the drum, *hatsune*, suggests a nightingale's first song in spring and the first beat of a drum.

9. *Mukashi o ima ni nasu yoshi mogana* echoes the last two lines of a poem by Shizuka in *Gikeiki*, a fifteenth-century tale of Yoshitsune's life: "As humble as Shizuka,/the humble bobbin/spins round and round./I wish I could make the past/return again."

FIGURE 3.35. Tadanobu dressed for travel, his hat in his hand. The puppet has a Genta head, and its robe is decorated with a Genji-wheel pattern. The costume is more lavish than that in the kabuki version (see figure 3.32). (Courtesy of the National Bunraku Theater.)

Along a path through fields and
across the ridges of rice paddies, nimbly,

The shamisen music imitates a fox's gait, and Shizuka plays the drum.

[SHIZUKA]:
   nimbly,

The left sleeve of her outer robe is removed and tucked into the sash at her back.

[TADANOBU]:
   in simple attire, he travels happily along.
   Standing discreetly away from the path,
   he mocks the lady's footsteps;
   "You must have been waiting for a long
      time.
   Fortunately, no one is in sight."
   Removing the general's armor given to him
   by Yoshitsune along with his name,
   Tadanobu reverently bows before it.[10]

The bundle is removed from Tadanobu's back, and the armor is unwrapped and set up on a tree stump. Shizuka places the drum on the armor and then faces stage front, takes out her fan, and dances.

[SHIZUKA]:
   Shizuka places the drum on the armor,
   suggesting Yoshitsune's face.
   Like a rock hidden far from shore,
   unbeknownst to anyone, Yoshitsune
   headed by sea for the western provinces.

Shizuka opens her fan.

   The wind and waves were rough,

She waves the fan in her right hand with downward motions to suggest wind.

   driving the ship into Sumiyoshi Bay.

She throws her fan up in the air, catches it, and poses [figure 3.36].

   Since then, it is said,
   he has been in Yoshino.

She raises her left hand as she circles left. Then lowering the fan, she looks downstage.

[SHIZUKA and TADANOBU]: We will soon be there,

---

10. After Tadanobu rescues Shizuka at the Inari Shrine in act 2, Yoshitsune bestows his armor and part of his name on him. Yoshitsune's gesture is also motivated by his gratitude toward Tadanobu's brother Tsuginobu, who sacrificed his life defending Yoshitsune at the battle of Yashima in 1185.

Facing each other, they stamp their feet and move backward toward stage left and right.

they say, putting away their keepsakes.

The armor and drum are taken away. After the sleeves of Shizuka's red robe are removed, revealing a white underrobe, she dances with Tadanobu during the following song, accompanied by shamisen music and percussion sounds.

CHANTERS:

"A wild goose or a swallow,

They use their sleeves to imitate the birds.

which is more charming?
The swallow raising its young is more charming.
If a wild goose abandoning flowers

They look up.

is a bearer of letters, it may renew old bonds.

Shizuka holds out her left sleeve as though it were a letter.

How true. How true."

Instrumental interlude; they dance briefly to drum beats.

What an entertaining song.

FIGURE 3.36. In the course of this dance, Shizuka throws her fan up, catches it, and poses. The top half of her outer robe has been taken off her arms to reveal an underkimono of a different color and design. The armor that Yoshitsune gave Tadanobu is on the tree stump behind Shizuka. (Courtesy of the National Bunraku Theater.)

Upstage, Shizuka stands with the hem of her sleeve at her mouth; downstage, Tadanobu crouches with his sleeve at his mouth. From the folds of his kimono, Tadanobu takes out a black fan with a red sun on it.

[TADANOBU]:

I received this armor because of
my elder brother Tsuginobu's loyal service.
How well I remember what happened at Dannoura.[11]
At sea, the warships and red banners of the Heike clan;

He points off into the distance with his right hand.

on land, white banners of the Genji warriors.

Extending his right leg, Tadanobu draws his fan toward his left side.

Shamisen interlude   *The sleeves of Tadanobu's outer robe are removed, revealing a*

---

11. In the spring of 1185 the Heike were defeated at the battle of Dannoura; the opposing Genji forces were led by Yoshitsune. The following description of the famous Kagekiyo's fight with the Genji warrior Mionoya at Yashima earlier that year closely follows the account in the noh play *Kagekiyo*, which draws on a story in *The Tale of the Heike* (book 11). The fight is also recounted in the noh play *Yashima*. The first lines of this battle sequence are chanted in a nohlike style.

FIGURE 3.37. Tadanobu and Shizuka miming the fight between Kagekiyo and Mionoya, using their closed fans as weapons. (Courtesy of the National Bunraku Theater.)

red and white underrobe.

"What a great to-do," said a warrior
drawing his halberd firmly

Tadanobu extends his right hand, which holds his fan, and places his left hand on his right arm.

to his side in the evening sunlight.
"I am Akushichibyōe Kagekiyo
of the Heike clan."
Announcing his name he attacks;
announcing his name he attacks.
He slashes to the left and right;
he slashes to the left and right.

Shamisen interlude *Tadanobu circles to the right, stamps his feet, and poses, facing front with his hands held aloft.*

As he slashes to the left and right
[SHIZUKA]:
like a gale sweeping blossoms away,

Shizuka imitates falling petals with her fan as Tadanobu approaches from downstage.

the scruffy soldiers scatter.

Shizuka brushes Tadanobu with her fan, sending him flying downstage, where he poses with his left leg extended and holding up his fan in his right hand. At center stage, Shizuka poses with her fan held aloft in her right hand.

[TADANOBU]:
"What cowards!
Mionoya no Shirō
is here," a warrior announces,
attacking at the water's edge.

Shizuka and Tadanobu face each other, stamp their feet, and bring their closed fans together at center stage [figure 3.37]. The following fight is accompanied by drum beats.

[TOGETHER]:
The deftly handled halberd

They change places, then separate.

sweeps the sword aside. The warriors are
evenly matched. The sound of waves striking the shore
intermingles with the striking of a sword guard.
The blade breaks off.

Miming the effect of a broken sword, they suddenly sit on the ground.

Like the receding tide,

[SHIZUKA]:

    like a returning wild goose,

[TOGETHER]:

    does Mionoya abandon the fight
       at its peak?

    Tucking his halberd beneath his
       arm,

    Kagekiyo seizes the neck guard
    of his opponent's helmet.

*Tadanobu puts his open fan against
the nape of his neck to suggest Mionoya's neck guard; Shizuka, suggesting Kagekiyo's actions, places her fan
on Tadanobu's [figure 3.38].*

FIGURE 3.38. Shizuka uses her fan to mime Kagekiyo's pulling on Mionoya's neckpiece (represented by Tadanobu's fan held behind his back). Tadanobu's outer robe has been lowered from his shoulders, and yet another layer of Shizuka's costume is revealed. (Photo by Aoki Shinji.)

[SHIZUKA]:

    Pulling, Kagekiyo stumbles
       backward;

[TADANOBU]:

    Mionoya's advancing footsteps
       falter.

[TOGETHER]:

    Kagekiyo breaks off the neck guard with a mighty pull;
    with a thud, both fall to the ground.

*Shizuka moves upstage while Tadanobu retreats downstage. Tadanobu sits with
both legs extended, and Shizuka sits holding her fan in front of her legs. During a
brief shamisen interlude, they move their heads from left to right.*

[TADANOBU]:

    What a strong arm, says one;

*Tadanobu holds down his left arm with his right hand. Shizuka closes her fan and
points it at Tadanobu.*

[SHIZUKA]:

    or a strong neck bone, says the other,

[TADANOBU]:

    Ha, ha, ha, ha, ha.

Shizuka opens her fan and holds it in front of her face as she laughs.

[SHIZUKA]:

    Ho, ho, ho, ho, ho.

[TOGETHER]:

    After the laughter, turmoil ensues.

They wave their open fans.

    During the fierce struggle,

[TADANOBU]:

my brother Tsuginobu
rushes to place his horse in front of Yoshitsune's mount

With his fan, he mimes shielding Yoshitsune's horse. Shizuka closes her fan.

to shield our lord from arrows.

[SHIZUKA]:

Oh, oh. I hear that, at that moment,
on the Heike side, the renowned archer

Shizuka imitates shooting an arrow.

Noto no kami Noritsune
drew back his bow with all his might
and let fly an arrow before
he had even finished announcing his name.

[TADANOBU]:

The hateful arrowhead

Tadanobu moves forward, then stamps his feet as he moves backward.

pierces Tsuginobu's breastplate.
Unable to withstand the pain,

Shizuka throws open her fan backward over her shoulder, striking Tadanobu in the chest.

he falls headfirst from his horse.

Tadanobu falls down.

[TOGETHER]:

His sad end earned him fame
as a loyal and true follower.

Tadanobu returns the fan to Shizuka, and both face the rear of the stage and prepare to resume their journey.

The memory drenches my sleeves with tears
as deep as the well of Tsutsui.

Finale

CHANTERS:

Some day my lord's life
will be carefree and as long
as the willow strands of Yagyū in spring.[12]
Surely the bond formed by entwined branches
will never die.
Together
they encourage each other

---

12. Yagyū literally means "willows grow." Entwined branches are a common metaphor for the intimate bond between lovers; here it may also suggest the bond between Yoshitsune and his half brother Yoritomo, who are estranged.

Shizuka goes upstage, and Tadanobu goes downstage.

> as they try to hasten along, yet their progress is slow
> through the hamlet of Kō at Ashiwara Pass;
> not far away on the path through the fields
> are Tsuchida and Mutsuda. The spring breeze

Tadanobu rushes longingly over to the drum tied to Shizuka's back.

> chases a cloud away:

When Shizuka looks back, Tadanobu retreats downstage.

> they have reached the village
> below the hills of cloudlike Yoshino.

Upstage, Shizuka looks back in Tadanobu's direction; downstage, Tadanobu extends his left leg and holds out his hat in his right hand. The curtain is closed to the sound of the wooden clackers and drum.

At the Farmhouse

Act 6 of *Kanadehon chūshingura*, a period piece
by Takeda Izumo II, Miyoshi Shōraku,
and Namiki Senryū

Translated by Donald Keene

The same trio of playwrights who composed *Sugawara and the Secrets of Calligraphy* (1746) and *Yoshitsune and a Thousand Cherry Trees* (1747) also created *Kanadehon chūshingura* (The treasury of loyal retainers, 1748), which is, without doubt, the best-known theatrical work in Japan. The historical event behind the play occurred on January 30, 1703, when the former retainers of the late Lord Asano burst into the mansion of Lord Kira Yoshinaka in Edo and killed him to avenge the death of their master almost two years earlier. Asano, an inexperienced country lord who had not offered the expected bribe to Kira, was goaded by him into drawing his sword in the shogunal palace. For this drastic breach of decorum, Asano had been ordered to commit ritual suicide. Although people of every class cheered the boldness of the retainers' retaliation, the government ruled, after some debate, that it was not a "legal" vendetta and condemned forty-six retainers to ritual suicide less than two months after their deed.

This incident was too newsworthy for dramatists to ignore, and the first kabuki play about it is said to have been written in the same month that Asano drew his sword in the palace! Another version was apparently staged at the Nakamura Theater in Edo two weeks after the loyal warriors were buried; however, it stuck too close to the facts and was forced to close after only three performances. Thereafter, many attempts were made to portray at least some of these events on stage without attracting the ire of the censors, who ardently protected the good name of the major warrior families. An effective way of getting around the censors was to set the play in an earlier period or "world" (sekai), as the most commonly used settings were called. One of the first playwrights to choose the fourteenth-century *taiheiki* world as the setting for this event was Chikamatsu Monzaemon, whose *Goban Taiheiki* of 1706 is the earliest surviving treatment of this material.

After their estates were restored to the Asano family in 1709, the censorship was relaxed, and a kabuki version of the incident entitled *Onikage musashiabuni* ran for

120 days in Osaka and was adapted to the puppet theater to compete with Chikamatsu's play. Both pieces strongly influenced the 1748 production translated here. Although this was followed by many other new versions, it has remained the favorite. A 1766 variation entitled *Taiheiki chūshingura kōshaku*, composed by Chikamatsu Hanji and his associates, influenced later playsk, including *Yotsuya Ghost Stories*, an act of which is translated here. A modern new kabuki (*shinkabuki*) called *Genroku chūshingura* and written by the playwright and scholar Mayama Seika (1878–1948) premiered in 1934 and is still occasionally performed. It is an attempt, not very successful theatrically, to portray more accurately the historical events and the quality of life in the Genroku period (roughly 1680 to 1720).

Chūshingura means "a treasury of loyal retainers," and *kanadehon* refers to a *kana* (Japanese syllabary) copybook. The relationship is made explicit at the end of the play: the forty-seven *kana* syllables stand for the forty-seven loyal retainers, although only forty-six were actually condemned to death. The play handles this discrepancy by having one retainer commit suicide before the vendetta is complete. This character, Hayano Kampei, was created by Namiki Senryū in a 1732 play on the subject. Although Kampei is one of the most lowly of the retainers, act 6, in which he commits suicide, is one of the most important of the play's eleven acts.

Kampei is in attendance on Lord Enya (the fictional character of Lord Asano) on the day he foolishly draws his sword. Instead of remaining with his master, however, Kampei goes outside the gate to dally with his girlfriend, Okaru. After the incident, he recognizes and regrets his negligence and flees with Okaru to her parents' house, where he hopes to figure out how to make amends. (The kabuki versions often add a travel scene [michiyuki] depicting their journey to the country.) Kampei meets with one of the other retainers and is told that he may be permitted to contribute to a "memorial" for their master (a euphemism for the planned vendetta) if he can come up with some money. Thereupon Okaru's father goes to Kyoto and sells his daughter to a brothel owner. On his way home the father is killed and robbed by a rascal, Sadakuro. (Kabuki actors make much of this scene, performing it as an elaborate pantomime.) Also, on his way to his father-in-law's house, Kampei shoots at a wild boar and is startled to discover that he has killed a man instead. Nonetheless, he is not too scrupulous to take the bag of coins he finds on the body, which is where act 6 opens.

The setting for this act is one of the most commonly used designs in both the puppet and the kabuki theaters: a building with one or two rooms at upstage left with an outdoor area to the right. Good use is made of both areas in this act, with its numerous comings and goings. The range of emotions that Kampei expresses is a challenge for performers. As is conventional, Kampei's death is drawn out long enough for numerous revelations to occur. His end in this humble house contrasts with the more formal suicide of his master two acts earlier.

Chūshingura is one of the few puppet–kabuki plays to be produced in large sections (*tōshi*). Occasionally all eleven acts are performed. For a complete translation of this play, see Keene 1971, from which this selection is taken. The editor added some descriptions of stage business from the National Theater's videotape of a performance in 1979.

(all lines are spoken by the chanter)

HAYANO KAMPEI: son-in-law of Yōichibei and a former retainer of Lord Enya,
    who was forced to commit suicide after his dispute with Moronao
OKARU: his wife
GŌEMON and YAGORŌ: two of Lord Enya's forty-seven retainers
Okaru's mother
ICHIMONJIYA: the owner of a brothel
Two palanquin bearers
Three hunters: Yahachi, Roku, and Kakuhei

MUSICIANS

A gidayū chanter and shamisen player, who sit on the auxiliary stage
Instrumentalists in the music room

ACT 6

The Farmhouse Scene

*The names of the chanter and shamisen player, seated on the auxiliary stage, are
announced by a hooded figure who appears in front of the curtain. He also names
the head puppeteers. After a brief shamisen prelude, the curtain opens to reveal the
simple living room of a farmhouse to stage left and the fields outside on stage right.*

CHANTER:
    The dance at Misaki is just at its height,
    Grandpa, won't you go?
    Take old grandma, take her along,
    Grandpa, won't you go?

    This is the song the farmers sing when pounding barley, here at Yamazaki,
    famed in story, where Yōichibei, a small farmer, has his humble cottage. Here,
    too, Hayano Kampei lives the secluded life of a *rōnin* [masterless warrior].

*Okaru enters carrying a towel. She goes to a mirror on a stand at center stage and
dabs at her face and combs her hair. She takes the mirror from the stand to look at
the results.*

    His wife Okaru opens her comb box to tidy her hair disheveled by sleep.
    Dawn is near, but still her husband does not return. To pass the tedious hours
    waiting for him, she combs and binds her locks into a hanging bun. As she
    passes the wet comb of boxwood through her hair, her mind fills with
    thoughts of the unspeakable fate she can reveal to no one. She combs a lovely
    sheen into her tresses, and when she ties them elegantly, such beauty seems
    wasted in a country place.

FIGURE 3.39. In act 6 of *Chūshingura*, Okaru, left, talks with her mother inside their farmhouse. This type of indoor/outdoor setting is often used in bunraku and kabuki. Compare this with figure 3.15. (Photo by Barbara C. Adachi.)

Leaning on a stick, her aged mother comes tottering home along the path through the fields.

[MOTHER] (*Enters through door at stage right and sits to talk with Okaru*): Oh, you've done up your hair, daughter! You've arranged it very nicely [figure 3.39]. (*Okaru finishes with her hair, puts the mirror aside, and turns to her mother. The puppeteer removes the mirror.*) Everywhere you go in the country at this time of year, people are busy harvesting barley. Just now as I passed the bamboo grove, I heard the young men singing the barley pounders' song—"Grandpa, won't you go? Take old grandma, take her along." That reminded me how late the old man is in coming home. I was so worried I went all the way to the end of the village, but it didn't do any good. There wasn't a sign of him.

[OKARU]: Yes. I wonder why he's so late. I'll run out and have a look (*rises and goes toward the door*).

[MOTHER]: No, a young woman should not go outside alone (*Okaru sits down again.*) Why, you never liked walking around the village even when you were a little girl. That's why we sent you into service with Lord Enya. But something must have drawn you back to this out-of-the-way place. I never even see you look bored as long as Kampei is with you.

[OKARU]: That's natural, Mother. It doesn't bother me to live in poverty, let alone in a village, when I'm with the man I love. The Bon Festival[1] will be here soon, and Kampei and I plan to go to see the dancing, just the two of us, the way it goes in the song (*shamisen music*), "Papa, won't you go? Take mama, take her along." I'm sure you remember what it was like when you were young.

---

1. A summer festival for the spirits of the dead. Group dancing usually is a major part of the festivities.

CHANTER: The forthright girl speaks her mind freely, and her spirits seem buoyant (*the puppets gesture as though speaking, and the shamisen stops playing*).

[MOTHER]: You sound cheerful, full of fun, but in your heart, I know—

[OKARU]: No, Mother. I'm resigned to it. I've long since made up my mind to go into service at Gion[2] for my husband's sake. But for Father, at his age, to take all this trouble—

[MOTHER]: You shouldn't say that. Your brother, after all, was a retainer of Lord Enya, though he had only a minor position, so it isn't like taking trouble for a stranger.

CHANTER: As they are talking, along the road, urging his palanquin ahead, comes Ichimonjiya from Gion.

Okaru is combing her mother's hair as Ichimonjiya enters from stage right waving his fan and followed by a palanquin, accompanied by lively shamisen music.

[ICHIMONJIYA]: This is the place.

CHANTER: He calls from the gate as he goes in.

[ICHIMONJIYA]: Is my Yōichibei at home?

Ichimonjiya enters the house and sits near the door. Okaru gives him a handled box with smoking paraphernalia in it.

[MOTHER]: Oh, what a surprise! You've certainly come a long distance! Daughter, bring out the tobacco and offer our guest some tea.

CHANTER: Mother and daughter in a flurry of excitement wait on him. The master of the brothel speaks.

Okaru serves him tea, which he drinks.

[ICHIMONJIYA] *(The music stops)*: It was extremely kind of the old gentleman to have visited my place last night. I trust he returned home safely?

[MOTHER] *(Surprised)*: You mean you haven't brought him back with you? This is strange. Ever since he set out for your place—

[ICHIMONJIYA]: He hasn't come back? How peculiar. I wonder if he strolled past the Inari Shrine and was bewitched by a fox (*half rises and gestures with his fan and pipe*) [figure 3.40].[3] At any rate, we agreed without difficulty, as we had decided when I came here the other day, that your daughter's term of service will be a full five years and that her wages will be one hundred *ryō* in gold. The old gentleman told me he had to deliver the money tonight and begged me in tears to let him sign the bond of service last evening so that he might receive the hundred *ryō* in advance (*mimes writing the receipt*). I agreed to pay him half the sum on signing the bond and the balance on receipt of the girl. In any case, he was overjoyed when I gave him the fifty *ryō*, and he lifted the money to his forehead (*mimes this using his fan*). He was still babbling on when he left; it must have been about ten o'clock. I tried to stop him, saying it was dangerous to walk alone on the road at night

---

2. Gion is the pleasure quarters in Kyoto where Okaru would work as a prostitute.

3. The fox is the messenger of the deities associated with the Inari Shrines. This association also appears in *Yoshitsune and a Thousand Cherry Trees*.

FIGURE 3.40. Ichinomiya, the brothel master (*Matahei* head), describes to Okaru (right: *musume* head) and her mother (*baba* head) his last encounter with Okaru's father. He gestures with a pipe and a small fan. (Photo by Barbara C. Adachi.)

carrying money, but he wouldn't listen to me. He left for home, but I wonder if on the way—

[OKARU]: No, there was nowhere for him to stop, was there, Mother?

[MOTHER]: No, of course not. By all rights he should've come rushing back, all out of breath, eager to get home the first possible moment so he could make us happy by showing us the money. I can't understand it.

[ICHIMONJIYA]: Well, whether you can understand it or not, that's your problem. I intend to deliver the balance of the money and take my new employee with me.

CHANTER: He produces the money (*the puppeteer puts money into the puppet's hand*).

[ICHIMONJIYA] (*Placing the money in front of the women*): Here are the remaining fifty ryō. This makes a total of one hundred ryō. Please take them.

[MOTHER]: But Okaru, I can't let you go, can I, before your father gets back?

[ICHIMONJIYA]: If you keep dawdling, we'll never be finished. Look, this is Yōichibei's seal; there's no disputing it (*unfolds a piece of paper and holds it up*). The bond of service is my witness. I have this day with my money bought the girl's body. One day's delay in delivery means so much loss for me. It looks as if I have no choice but to do it this way.

The two palanquin bearers enter the house and stand at each side of Okaru, accompanied by loud shamisen music.

CHANTER: They seize the girl's arms and drag her to her feet.

[MOTHER]: Wait, I beg you!

FIGURE 3.41. The palanquin (*kago*) bearers wait outside as Ichinomiya, Mother, Okaru, and Kampei (right) discuss the family's situation. (Photo by Barbara C. Adachi.)

She approaches Ichimonjiya and attempts to grab him, but he pushes her aside and goes out the door after the bearers, who are dragging Okaru.

CHANTER: He shakes off the mother's clutching hand, and with brute force, he pushes Okaru into his palanquin. As the bearers lift the shafts, Kampei appears at the gate, gun in hand, wearing his straw raincoat and hat. He boldly strides in.

Kampei enters from stage right and approaches Ichimonjiya, who has moved to the front of the house.

[KAMPEI]: Where are they taking my wife?

[MOTHER]: You've come back in the nick of time, Kampei.

CHANTER: He does not understand his mother's joy.

Kampei, Ichimonjiya, and everyone else enter the house and sit [figure 3.41]. Okaru places a tobacco box in front of Kampei, who smokes during the ensuing conversation.

[KAMPEI]: There's something at the bottom of this. Mother, Okaru, I'd like to know what's going on.

CHANTER: He seats himself squarely in the middle of the room. Ichimonjiya speaks.

[ICHIMONJIYA]: I take it you are my employee's husband. But there's nothing you can do about this. I have it in the bond, signed and sealed by the old man, that "no contravention or interference in the execution of this contract will be permitted even by the husband or fiancé of the employee." I intend to collect my employee now (*flourishes the piece of paper*).

[MOTHER]: You must be wondering what all this means, Kampei. We've heard for a long time from Okaru about how badly you needed money, and we spoke of nothing but of how much we wanted to raise it for you, but we had nowhere to turn for even a copper coin. Then your father suggested that perhaps you had thought of selling your wife to raise the money. Of course, this was most unlikely, but it might be that you felt constrained because of your wife's parents. Your father said, "The best thing would be for me to sell my daughter without telling Kampei. When a samurai is desperate, he'll eventually turn to crime, they say. It's no disgrace to sell his wife—the money is for his lord's sake. If we raise the money and give it to him, I'm sure he won't be angry with us." So yesterday he went to Gion to settle the matter, but he hasn't come home yet. Okaru and I were worrying about him when the gentleman came and said he had given Father half the money last night and would pay the balance now and take Okaru with him. I begged him to wait until we had seen Father, but he wouldn't listen. He was just about to take Okaru away. What shall we do, Kampei?

[KAMPEI]: To begin with, I must tell you how grateful I am for Father's solicitude. But I have had rather a piece of luck myself, which I'll tell you about in a moment, and I'm not turning over my wife until my father gets back.

[ICHIMONJIYA]: Why not?

[KAMPEI]: Well, he is her father and the man who signed the bond. You claim you paid him half the money, fifty ryō in gold, last night. No doubt that's true, but—

[ICHIMONJIYA] (Loudly with broad, angry gestures): Do you realize who I am? I'm Ichimonjiya. I cover the whole Kyoto–Osaka area, and I have enough women in my employ to populate the Island of Dames.[4] Would I say I'd paid him the money if I hadn't? But I have even more positive proof. When I saw your old man wrap up the fifty ryō in his little towel and tuck it into his kimono, I said, "That's dangerous. Put it in this and carry it around your neck." I lent him a wallet made out of striped cloth, the same material as this kimono I'm wearing.

He stands, moves in front of the women to Kampei, and holds out his leg to reveal his underkimono.

He's sure to be coming back soon with the wallet around his neck.

[KAMPEI] (Points and stares at the kimono): What did you say? Did you say the wallet was made from the same striped material as your kimono?

[ICHIMONJIYA]: That's right.

[KAMPEI] (In extreme agitation and disbelief): The exact same striped material?

[ICHIMONJIYA]: What more positive proof could there be?

Kampei drops his pipe into the box and sets it aside to take out a wallet and compare it with the kimono.

CHANTER: Kampei is stunned. He glances cautiously around him, then takes the wallet from his sleeve and compares it with the kimono. Both are of a mixed cotton and silk striped cloth, absolutely identical in pattern.

Ichimonjiya moves backstage and sits; the shamisen plays.

[KAMPEI]: Good heavens! Was the man I shot last night my father-in-law?

CHANTER: A pain shoots through him more severe than if the two bullets had pierced his own breast. His wife, knowing nothing of his anguish, asks—

---

4. Nyogo no shima, a mythical island populated entirely by women.

[OKARU]: Kampei, please don't hesitate so. Make up your mind whether you are going to send me away or not.

[KAMPEI]: Why yes. He's given such convincing proof I don't suppose we have any choice but to let you go, have we?

[OKARU]: Without seeing Father?

[KAMPEI]: I ran into your father briefly this morning. There's no telling when he'll get back.

[OKARU]: Then you saw Father? Why didn't you say so instead of making Mother and me worry?

CHANTER: Ichimonjiya takes advantage of the situation.

[ICHIMONJIYA]: Ask seven times before you suspect a man, they say. Now that we know where the old man is, it's a big load off your minds and mine too. If you still have any complaints to make, whatever they may be, we'll leave them for a court to decide. Anyway, I'm glad everything has been settled. I hope the old folks will pay me a little visit when you worship at Rokujō.[5] (*Stands and goes to Okaru*) Come now, into the palanquin with you.

[OKARU] (*To Ichimonjiya, who goes outside*): Yes, yes. (*Turns to Kampei*) Kampei, I'm going now. From now on it's up to you to look after my old parents, especially Father. He's got a bad complaint. Please take good care of him.

She takes out a handkerchief and weeps, her head near his knees. He puts his arm around her shoulders.

CHANTER: Not having the slightest suspicion that her father is dead, she makes this request, so pathetic, so touching that Kampei wonders whether he shouldn't confess the whole truth. But others are present, so he bears the agony in his heart in silence.

[MOTHER]: I'm sure Kampei would like to take proper leave of you and say goodbye like a husband to his wife. He must be afraid you'll break down.

Okaru wipes her eyes and moves away from Kampei.

[OKARU]: There's no danger of that. I'm leaving my husband, it's true, but I'm selling myself for our master's sake, so I don't feel sad or anything like that. (*Moving toward her mother*) I go in good spirits, Mother. I am only sorry I'm leaving without seeing Father.

[MOTHER]: I'm sure he'll go and visit you as soon as he gets back.

[OKARU]: Take moxa treatment so you don't get sick, and please come see me so I'll know you're all right.

The palanquin bearers enter the house and lead the weeping Okaru toward the door, accompanied by gentle shamisen music.

[MOTHER]: Oh, if you haven't got handkerchiefs or a fan, you'll need them. (*She weeps*) Do you have everything else? Don't rush about too much and hurt yourself.

Okaru leaves the house reluctantly.

5. A reference to Nishi Honganji, a great temple of Shin Buddhism situated at Rokujō, Kyoto.

CHANTER: She fusses over Okaru until the girl is actually inside the palanquin. As they bid each other good-bye, she wonders what ill fate has decreed that a daughter as attractive as the next girl should have to experience such sadness. She clenches her teeth and weeps, and her daughter, clinging to the sides of the palanquin, stifles her sobs, afraid lest her tears be seen or heard.

FIGURE 3.42. The kabuki version of the three hunters entering with the body they have discovered. In kabuki, they carry the body in through the door, but in bunraku, they go to the front of the house and place it on the low wall (*tesuri*) that serves as the floor. (Photo by Aoki Shinji.)

Okaru enters the palanquin, and the bearers carry it off stage right with Ichimonjiya following; drums accompany them. Mother goes out the door and stares after them. The audience applauds them as they exit.

The bearers, indifferent to their grief, lift the chair and hurry down the road. The mother gazes after them.

[MOTHER] (*Going back into the house, she sits beside Kampei*): I'm sure I upset Okaru by saying such foolish things. Kampei, I hope you won't keep fretting over your wife. You'll only make yourself sick. I'm her mother, and you saw how bravely I've resigned myself. I wonder why Father hasn't returned. You said you saw him, didn't you?

[KAMPEI]: That's right.

[MOTHER]: Where was it you met him? And where did he go after he left you?

[KAMPEI]: Let me see. The place where I left him was Toba, I think. Or was it Fushimi or Yodo or perhaps Takeda?

Mother picks up the money that has been on the floor since Ichimonjiya placed it there. The three hunters enter from stage right, two of them carrying a body on a wooden shutter [figure 3.42].

CHANTER: As he speaks this nonsense—whatever comes to his lips—Big-Mouth Yahachi, Roku the Musketeer, and Kakuhei the Badger, three hunters of the vicinity, burst unceremoniously into the room. They bear the body of the old man, covered with a straw raincoat, on a shutter.

[HUNTER A]: I was going home after finishing my hunting for the night when I stumbled across your old man. He's been killed. Me and these other hunters brought him back. (*They remain outside the house.*)

CHANTER: The mother starts in amazement at his words (*she goes to the body and uncovers it [figure 3.43]*).

[MOTHER]: Who did it, Kampei? What monster could have killed him? You must kill the murderer! (*Weeping*) Oh, my husband, my dear husband.

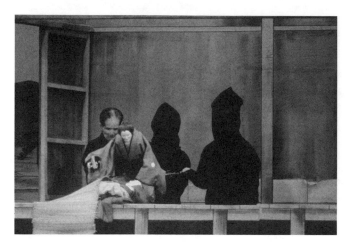

FIGURE 3.43. Mother uncovers the body of her husband (*Takeuji* head), discovered by hunters. (Photo by Barbara C. Adachi.)

CHANTER: She calls and shrieks, but in vain; for her, there are only tears. The huntsmen speak one after the other.

[HUNTER A]: Poor old lady! It must be sad for you.

[HUNTER B]: You should report this to the district office and get them to investigate.

[HUNTER C]: It's a terrible shame.

CHANTER: They go out together, each bound for his own home. The mother, still weeping, moves closer to Kampei.

[MOTHER]: I've fought against the thought you might possibly, conceivably, have anything to do with this, Kampei. But there is one thing I don't understand. I know you used to be a samurai, but still, you should have acted a little more surprised when you saw your father-in-law's dead body. Are you sure you didn't get the money when you met him on the road? What did he say to you? Tell me, please. What does this mean? You don't seem to have an answer, do you? And here's the reason why!

CHANTER: She thrusts her hand into Kampei's kimono and pulls out the wallet.

[MOTHER] (*Holding the wallet in her right hand*): I caught a glimpse of this wallet a while ago. Look! It's stained with blood. You killed your father.

[KAMPEI]: No, you see—

[MOTHER] (*Hitting the floor with the wallet*): What do you mean "you see"? No matter how hard you try to hide the truth, it won't stay hidden. (*She weeps and puts down the wallet*) Heaven will reveal it. You killed your father and robbed him. And for whose sake do you suppose that money was intended? I know what happened. You thought your father, because he was poor, had intercepted half the money he got from selling his daughter and that he would pocket it and not give it to you. So you killed him and took the money for yourself. It makes my blood boil that I was always deceived into supposing, until this very moment, that you were a decent, upright man. You monster! You revolt me so I can't even cry. (*She goes back to the body and talks to it*) Poor Yōichibei. You never realized what a beast you had for a son-in-law. You were so anxious for him to become a samurai again, the way he used to be, that you went running all over Kyoto, a man of your age, not resting even at night, throwing away your own money, and everything you did to help him has harmed yourself. (*Weeps*) Your hand has been bitten by the dog you fed. Who could have imagined you would be killed in such a horrible way? (*She turns to Kampei*) And as for you, you fiend, you serpent! Give me back my husband! Give him back to me alive! (*She picks up the wallet and hits Kampei on the head with it.*)

CHANTER: All restraint and politeness lost, she seizes the man by his topknot and, pulling him down, beats his head against the floor.

She continues to hit him with the wallet and pushes his head to the floor; he struggles against her. Finally, she pulls away, stands, then falls to the floor and weeps.

[MOTHER]: I could hack you to pieces, and still my anger would not be appeased.

CHANTER: She falls prostrate on the floor, still muttering her resentment. Boiling hot sweat pours over Kampei's whole body for the crime he has committed. (*He stands and then bows*) He presses his face into the matting. Now he knows what it is to suffer the wrath of heaven.

FIGURE 3.44. Hara Gōemon and Senzaki Yagorō, two of the loyal retainers, visit the farmhouse, their faces hidden by large wicker hats (*kasa*). (Photo by Barbara C. Adachi.)

Two samurai, their faces hidden by wicker hats, enter at stage right and appear at the door [figure 3.44].

[GŌEMON]: Is Hayano Kampei at home? Hara Gōemon and Senzaki Yagoro would like to see him.

Kampei straightens up, motions his mother to leave through the back center curtained door, goes over to the body, covers it and pushes it to the back wall, goes to the room at stage left to get his sword, and then goes to the door and sits beside it. The shamisen and drum accompany him.

CHANTER: Their visit comes at the worst possible moment, but Kampei goes to meet them, his rudely made sword under his arm.

[KAMPEI]: I am deeply grateful, gentlemen, that you should have condescended to visit such a humble cottage.

CHANTER: He bows his head.

[GŌEMON]: There seems to have been some misfortune in this house.

[KAMPEI]: A minor domestic matter. Please pay no attention to it, but come right in.

[GŌEMON]: Then, with your permission, we shall do so.

They remove their hats, enter the house, and cross in front of Kampei to sit at stage left.

CHANTER: They go straight in and seat themselves. Kampei bows, both his hands on the floor.

[KAMPEI]: I was gravely at fault not to have been present when the terrible misfortune befell our master. I have not a word to say in my defense. But I implore you, gentlemen, to intercede on my behalf so that my offense may be pardoned and I may be permitted to attend with the others of the clan the services on the anniversary of our master's death.

CHANTER: He speaks in terms of humble supplication. Gōemon at once responds.

[GŌEMON]: Yuranosuke was at first most impressed that you, a rōnin of no means, should have offered such a large sum as your contribution for the monument.[6] But then he said, "We are erecting this monument so that we may promote the salvation of our late master. It would not please his spirit if we paid for the monument with money taken from a man who had proved disloyal and faithless to his lordship." The money is therefore being returned, the seal still unbroken.

He moves toward Kampei and puts money on the floor. The back curtain parts slightly to reveal his mother listening.

CHANTER: Yagorō takes the money from his kimono and lays it before Kampei, who is speechless with bewilderment. The mother, still weeping, speaks.

[MOTHER] (*Entering, she sits between Kampei and the samurai and points accusingly at Kampei*): You loathsome villain! Do you know now what a father's vengeance is? (*Bows to Gōemon and Yagorō*) Gentlemen, please listen to me. My husband, old though he was, gave not thought to his own future happiness but sold his daughter for his son-in-law's sake. He was returning with the money he had raised when this monster ambushed him. This is the money he took after killing his father. (*Kampei approaches her, but she pushes him back*) How can such money be of use to you, as long as there is a god in heaven? I'll never believe in the gods or buddhas again if this patricide and vile robber is not punished. (*Weeps*) Strike this unfilial beast and kill him by inches! Ah— I'm seething with rage!

CHANTER: She throws herself down on the floor and weeps. (*She stands, attacks Kampei, then moves back and out through the curtain*) The two men, astonished by her words, draw their swords and close in on Kampei from either side. Yagorō's voice is harsh.

Yagorō goes to stage right waving his sword.

[YAGORŌ]: Kampei, I never suggested you atone for your offense by taking money in such an inhuman, unspeakable way. It would be useless trying to explain to you what it means to be a samurai. You're a double criminal. You've killed your father-in-law—that's the same as a father—and robbed him of his money. You should be skewered on a spear like a string of dumplings, and I intend to do precisely that! (*Kampei moves toward Gōemon at stage left.*)

CHANTER: He glares at Kampei.

[GŌEMON] (*Kampei bows before him, gesturing with his fan as he talks*): The just man takes it as his maxim that no matter how thirsty he may be, he will not drink water from a spring that thieves have drunk from. Did you suppose that the money you took after killing your father-in-law could be spent for

---

6. The retainers are plotting their revenge in secret, so they are pretending to be collecting donations for a monument.

our master's cause? I marvel all the more at Yuranosuke's acumen in spurning your money. He intuitively recognized that the man who offered it was corrupt and disloyal through and through. The unfortunate thing is that word of this will get around, and people may say that Hayano Kampei, a retainer of Enya Hangan, committed a monstrous crime. This will disgrace not only you but our late master. Didn't you realize that? (*He hits Kampei with his fan*) You blockhead! You never used to be so stupid that you couldn't understand something so obvious. What devil has gotten into you?

FIGURE 3.45. Having removed the top of his outer robe, Kampei poses before plunging a dagger into his abdomen. (Photo by Barbara C. Adachi.)

CHANTER (*Chanting quickly to shamisen accompaniment as Kampei performs the actions described*): Tears blur his sharp eyes. Kampei, unable to withstand these arguments and dogged questions, slips his kimono from his shoulders, draws his dagger, and instantly plunges the blade into his abdomen [figure 3.45].

Shamisen music with occasional percussion; Kampei, obviously in pain, gestures broadly as he tells his tale.

[KAMPEI]: I am ashamed to appear before you in these humiliating circumstances. I had made up my mind to commit *seppuku* if you refused my request. I'll tell you everything, since, as you say, the crime of killing my father reflects disgrace on our late master. Please hear me out. Last evening, on my way home after leaving Yagorō, I sighted a wild boar running over the hill in the dusk. I stopped it with two shots. I ran up and searched for it, only to find I had shot not a wild boar but a man. I was dumfounded at my terrible mistake. I felt in his bosom for some medicine, but I discovered instead a wallet containing this money (*reaches out for his wallet*). It was wrong of me, I know, but it seemed like money from heaven, so I rushed off to Yagorō and gave it to him. When I got back home, I learned what had happened. The man I killed was my father-in-law (*looks toward the body*) and the money the price of my wife. Everything I do goes at cross-purposes, like the crossbill's beak. My luck as a samurai seems to have run out. Try to imagine how this fate afflicts me!

CHANTER: Tears of chagrin are in his bloodshot eyes. Yagorō rises as soon as he has heard this account. He lifts the dead body, turns it over, and examines the wounds.

[YAGORŌ]: Gōemon, these look like gunshot wounds, but actually they've been gouged out with a sword. Kampei, you acted too quickly!

FIGURE 3.46. Kampei's suicide (*seppuku*). Top: in the bunraku version, the dying Kampei talks with his mother. Bottom: in the kabuki version, he is about to draw the dagger across his abdomen as Yagorō and Gōemon look on. (Top: photo by Barbara C. Adachi; bottom: photo by Aoki Shinji.)

Mother enters through curtain and sits in front of it. Yagorō covers all of the body but the head.

CHANTER: The wounded man Kampei looks up in surprise, and his mother is amazed. Gōemon has a sudden recollection.

[GŌEMON]: It makes sense now! (*To Yagorō*) You remember that on our way here we saw the dead body of a traveler. When we examined it, we found the man had been killed by a bullet. It was Ono Sadakurō, a ruffian so depraved that even his rapacious old father Kudayū had disowned him and refused even to see him again. I remember hearing that Sadakurō had become a highwayman for want of any other occupation. Undoubtedly it was he who murdered Kampei's father-in-law.

[MOTHER]: You mean it wasn't Kampei who killed my husband?

CHANTER: She clings to the wounded man with a shriek of dismay.

[MOTHER]: Kampei, I bow before you. I entreat you. I made a terrible mistake in abusing you. It was all an old woman's foolishness. Forgive me, please, Kampei, and don't die, don't die (*she puts her hand on his shoulder*).

CHANTER: She weeps, pleading with him. He lifts his head [figure 3.46].

[KAMPEI] (*Pushing her away*): This moment, when my mother's suspicions have been allayed and the blot on my honor removed, will be the remembrance I take with me to the afterworld. I shall catch up with my father-in-law and accompany him to the Mountain of Death and the River of the Three Ways.

CHANTER: He starts to pull the dagger across his belly.

[GŌEMON]: Wait, wait! (*Stops him with hand*) You killed your father-in-law's enemy without even intending to. Doesn't that show your luck as a samurai still holds? Kampei, you have, by the mercy of the god of war, performed a deed of great merit. I have something secret to show you while you still breathe.

CHANTER: He takes out a scroll and quickly unrolls it.

He puts the scroll on the floor in front of Kampei.

[GŌEMON]: Here are the signatures of the men in our league. We have exchanged written oaths to the gods that we will kill Kō no Moronao, our master's enemy.

CHANTER: Kampei, in agony, cannot read through the whole.

[KAMPEI]: Whose names are there?

[GŌEMON]: There are forty-five in all. Now that we have seen your true character, we will add you to our league and make our number forty-six.[7] Take this remembrance with you to the afterworld.

FIGURE 3.47. Kampei, who has used his entrails to make his bloody mark on the oath, looks on as Gōemon (Shūto head) holds up the signed paper. (Photo by Barbara C. Adachi.)

CHANTER: He takes out a writing kit and inscribes Kampei's name.

[GŌEMON]: Seal it with your blood, Kampei (*leans over him*).

[KAMPEI]: I will.

CHANTER: He cuts his belly in a cross and, pulling out his entrails, presses them to the paper.

He mimes taking out his entrails; Gōemon takes his hand and guides it to the paper. Gōemon holds up the scroll, revealing the bloody seal [figure 3.47].

[KAMPEI]: I have sealed the document in my blood. Ahhh, how grateful, how thankful I am! My long-cherished wish has become a reality. Mother, please do not grieve. Father's death and my wife's becoming a prostitute have not been in vain. Offer this money as our contribution to the league.

She takes the money from the floor and puts it in front of Gōemon.

CHANTER: His mother, still weeping, places before the two men the wallet and the packets of money (*bows*).

[MOTHER]: Kampei's soul is in this wallet. Think of it as being my son, and take it with you when you go to kill our enemy.

[GŌEMON]: We will. That would be most appropriate.

CHANTER: Gōemon takes the money.

[GŌEMON]: It occurs to me now that the gold in the striped wallet stands for the rays of purplish gold emanating from the Buddha. May your worthy deeds obtain you Buddha's happiness! (*He puts his hand on Kampei's shoulder.*)

7. There are forty-seven symbols in the Japanese syllabary (*kana*), and there were presumably forty-seven men involved in the vendetta, including an honorary participant. The play, however, is inconsistent in the use of both the names and the numbers of the participants.

[KAMPEI]: Buddha's happiness! I spurn it! I refuse to die, I refuse. My soul shall stay on earth and go with you when you attack.

CHANTER: His voice trembles with agony. His mother is blinded by tears.

[MOTHER]: Kampei, I wish I could let my daughter know this, so she could at least see you before you die.

[KAMPEI]: No, Mother. Tell her, if you wish, of her father's death, but please never reveal that I am dead. My wife was sold for our master's sake, but if she learns of my death and then neglects her service, it would be just the same as if she were disloyal to our master. Leave things as they are. I die content.

CHANTER: He drives the point of his dagger into his throat and falls forward, breathing his last (*the puppet falls forward*).

Mother goes to his right, the samurai to his left.

[MOTHER] (*Mother moves back and forth between the two bodies*): Kampei, are you dead so soon? Is there in all the world another person so unlucky as myself? My husband is dead, and the son-in-law who was my support has gone before me. My beloved daughter is still alive, but we have been torn apart. How can I, an old woman left alone in the world, go on living? Dear husband, Yōichibei, please take me with you.

CHANTER: She flings herself on the body, weeping and wailing, then stands again.

[MOTHER]: Kampei, your mother is going with you.

CHANTER: She clings to him and sinks to the floor. She weeps first over one of the dead, then over the other, until at last she collapses with a shriek, sobbing unrestrainedly, a sight too pitiful to behold. Gōemon rises.

[GŌEMON]: You have every cause to weep, old lady. (*He goes and moves the husband's body back by the wall*) I am sure Yuranosuke will be gratified when I report how Kampei died and when I give him Kampei's contribution. The money represents fifty ryō each for the forty-nine days of prayer for your husband and for your son-in-law, that is a hundred ryō for a hundred days of mourning. (*He puts the money back on the floor.*) Pray for them devoutly. And now farewell, farewell.

CHANTER: Tears are in her eyes as she watches them depart, and tears blur their eyes, too, as they look back, waves of tears that rise between them in this world of sadness.

They go to the door, take their hats, and go outside. They turn to look back at the farmhouse where Mother leans over Kampei. They turn to go as drums and beats of the clackers mark the closing of the curtain.

The Awaji Tradition

Jane Marie Law

The numerous folk varieties of puppets in Japan may not be as polished as their urban cousins, but they certainly have what can be called "performative force." In the words of one of Japan's leading ritual performance and puppetry experts, Nagata Kōkichi, "These puppets are like wild animals. If you restrict them to a stage, it is like putting them in a cage. They lose their innate raw and wild nature."[1] Folk puppets, unlike those of the bunraku stage, find a niche in the world of Japanese theater much closer to the lives of the Japanese people—in rice fields, along fishing docks, on boats, in the entryways to homes, and in the precincts of local shrines. It is hard to imagine a place in Japan that has not served as a temporary stage for a puppet performance.

Nagata Kōkichi's 1983 index of puppetry groups in Japan lists 141 troupes, with a total number of 5,900 carved puppet heads. These troupes are merely those that have survived the demise of folk performances in the postwar period. Although no comprehensive figures exist for the Tokugawa period, it is likely that during that time the number of small troupes performing throughout the countryside was considerable, perhaps even ten times greater. Almost half the manipulated-puppet traditions in Japan claim to have originated in the puppets of Awaji Island. The original theater Bunraku troupe is said to have been named after the Awaji puppeteer Uemura Bunrakuken, and a number of traditions in central and northern Japan claim Awaji puppeteers as their founders.

The Awaji tradition maintained the practice of ritual puppetry alongside the dramatic ballad tradition (jōruri) long after the latter had become more popular. For this reason, it makes an interesting case for studying the development of Japanese theater from its ritual origins. A 1638 text entitled the *Dōkumbō denki* (The legends of Dōkumbō) narrates the mythical "history" of the tradition: a fisherman

---

1. Comment made to Jane Marie Law in December 1988, shortly before Professor Nagata's death.

named Hyakudayū was out at sea one day when suddenly the sky grew dark and lightning flashed all around his tiny boat.[2] Overcome by fear, he saw another boat floating nearby and, looking at it closely, discovered in it a solitary child about twelve years old with a remarkable countenance. As the storm raged about them, the child turned to Hyakudayū and identified himself as the abandoned child of the world-creating pair Izanagi and Izanami: "I am the Leech Child of long ago.[3] Until now, I have been floating on the waves with no hall where I can be worshiped. Build me a worship hall on the shore near Nishinomiya [near modern Kobe]." As he spoke, the storm died down. Hyakudayū realized that he had heard the words of a deity and did as he had been instructed. The worship hall he built in honor of the Leech Child came to be known as Nishinomiya Daimyōjin Ebisu Saburō den. There, a priest by the name of Dōkumbō served the Leech Child faithfully until he died.

After the priest died, the Leech Child had no one to serve him and so grew restless and angry and caused numerous calamities on land and sea. Hyakudayū, the fisherman who had first encountered the deity, learned of these disasters and, following an imperial edict, made a puppet with the face and bearing of the deceased priest Dōkumbō. He manipulated this surrogate in front of the worship hall of the Leech Child in Nishinomiya, and the child deity, satisfied that his faithful servant had returned, ceased making trouble. Hyakudayū then traveled around the country performing appeasement rites with puppets and eventually settled on Awaji in the village of Sanjo, where he married, had a son, and eventually died. This, so the Awaji legend goes, is the origin of deity propitiation rites using puppets. The text concludes with a stern warning concerning the ritual use of puppets: "Notice: This art is for the appeasement of divine spirits. Do not take it lightly. It will weigh heavily on those who do. Those who come after this should be sorely afraid."

The earliest written document describing Awaji puppets dates from 1570 and states that an Awaji puppeteer by the name of Uemura Gennojō had received the "proper edicts" to perform ritual puppetry. Later, the name Awaji was affixed to persons being honored as puppeteers. Although these works, along with the *Dōkumbō denki*, are the earliest records, other types of sources suggest that the use of puppets in magical rites existed on Awaji much earlier.

Awaji puppet performances can be divided into two broad categories according to whether the targeted audience is divine or human. In practice, however, the audience often consists of both deities and humans. Performances intended for deities (*shinji*, "sacred matters") have human beings as "onlookers" and even sponsors. The two examples of these sacred rites in the Awaji tradition are the Sambasō rite, used as a purifying ceremony and invocation of the deity's blessing at events inaugurating something—from new rice-paddy dikes to a marriage—and the Dance of Ebisu,

2. *Dōkumbō denki* is translated in Law 1992. The significance of the name Hyakudayū is controversial. It may refer to a plague spirit, a deity of prostitutes, a child protector deity, the deity of puppeteers, or, as this myth suggests, the historical founder of the Awaji tradition (Law 1993).

3. According to Japanese mythology, these two deities created the Japanese archipelago. Their first attempt at procreation, however, failed, since the woman spoke first. The result was a leech child, which at three years of age could not even walk. They set the child adrift in a reed boat on the waves and, rectifying their ways, proceeded to create the rest of the cosmos (Philippi 1968:47–73).

a lively performance enacting the life and love—namely, sake—of Ebisu, the deity of fishermen and shop owners.

The other category is the large repertoire of dramatic pieces, generally referred to as jōruri, which are, like bunraku plays, divided into period and domestic plays. Currently, the Awaji troupe has more than thirty plays in its active repertoire, although in the last twenty years it has performed more than fifty different pieces. Many of these plays are also performed in the bunraku theater, though with considerable variation in staging technique and puppet manipulation. Unlike the puppets in the ritual plays, which are manipulated by a single unhooded puppeteer, the puppets for the dramatic stage pieces are operated by three puppeteers, usually hooded, following the practices of bunraku.

The Awaji puppets are somewhat larger than their Bunraku cousins. One puppet complete with costume can weigh up to sixty pounds and stand nearly four feet tall. Their larger size reflects the original performance contexts of these puppets: they were often presented to large audiences gathered outdoors. Awaji puppets were "puppets of the road," and their large size was necessary so that they could be easily seen by crowds of people who did not have the luxury of tiered seating.

The contexts for these performances varied. The most popular time was the period immediately following the harvest, when temporary stages (nōgake butai) were built on a newly harvested field or in the precincts of a shrine. Since the hard labor of the year was over, people enjoyed a much-needed rest, and the puppetry festival would last for several days. Each morning, the day began with the performance of the Sambasō rite to invite the deities of the harvest to come and join the day's events and bless the audience. During the day, a full-length play would be performed along with individual famous scenes from several popular plays, such as Tsubosaka reigenki, included here.

During the three centuries that puppetry has been the pride of Awaji, many of the islanders have practiced reciting the pieces as a hobby. Consequently, the audiences on Awaji have been knowledgeable about the nuances of performance, and in the past, many knew the plays by heart. Sometimes they would even call out and correct or chide the chanter if he or she[4] made a mistake. Elderly people on Awaji love to tell the story of a visit to Awaji by a famous chanter from Osaka. Underestimating his audience, he took it easy and gave a mediocre performance. Consequently, he was chased offstage by an angry mob and replaced by an old local farmer who, though an amateur chanter, gave a "far superior performance." Whether or not this anecdote is true, it reflects the Awaji people's pride in their claim to be the "cradle of puppetry." This tradition of jōruri recitation by amateurs is once again becoming popular on Awaji.

It was the custom for people to bring elaborate box lunches to share between acts or plays with others in the audience, as well as with the performers. The ambience of the performance, with the knowledgeable audience and the party atmosphere with lots of sake, created a situation in which, as one old man put it, "You

---

4. At the end of the nineteenth century, female chanters frequently performed with puppet troupes. Unlike the Bunraku troupe, however, the Awaji group continues to encourage women not only as chanters but also as shamisen players and puppeteers. Currently about half of the performers are female.

couldn't tell the difference among the puppets, the performers, the audience, and the deities."

Early in the nineteenth century, during the heyday of Awaji puppetry, eighteen troupes performed on the island and toured Japan. This number had dropped to sixteen by 1907 and six by 1935. At the end of the war, five troupes were struggling to keep afloat. Finally, in the early 1950s, all closed their doors and boxed up their puppets, and the performers found more lucrative work. The demise of Awaji puppetry has had an impact on our understanding of many aspects of this art, such as the religious uses of puppets, the forms for appeasing deities with puppets, and the detailed histories of some of the major troupes on the island.

Today, one professional troupe and numerous amateur groups preserve the art of Awaji puppetry. The tradition has made a remarkable comeback, owing in large part to the efforts of two people, Umazume Masaru, the director of the Awaji Puppet Theater since the early 1960s, and Naniwa Kunie, who became a puppeteer in the early 1940s and performed through the 1980s. They both struggled to form a troupe from the remaining performers, props, puppets, and funds available on the island in the late 1950s. Rare puppets that had not been sold off after the war to buy rice or burned to heat bathwater were donated to the cause, and a few performers found the time to put together performances. They obtained space on the second floor of a gift shop near the harbor in the town of Fukura at the southern tip of Awaji Island, where they performed through 1983, slowly rebuilding the pool of performers.

The much-strengthened troupe now performs in its own modern theater overlooking the Naruto Bridge linking Awaji to Shikoku. The 300-seat theater is part of a cultural center called Naruto Hall, which opened in 1984, having been built with prefectural subsidies and local contributions. Each year the troupe recruits the best puppeteers, chanters, and shamisen players from student puppetry clubs around the island and initiates these new recruits into the lifelong training of the theater. Currently there are more than twenty full-time employees (men and women) in the theater, with the older musicians, chanters, and puppeteers training the younger performers. The national government supports the continuation of this art form by designating the troupe an Important Cultural Treasure and paying the members monthly salaries. The Awaji troupe toured the United States in 1974, Europe in 1978 and 1979, Australia and New Zealand in 1986, and Europe again in 1992. In the fall of 1997, they will again tour the United States. Recently, under Umazume's direction, the group has begun to revive the ritual uses of puppetry, and in 1990, Ebisu performances were presented in their traditional setting—before the worship hall of the Ebisu Shrine with an audience of fishermen. Since 1990, Umazume has convened annual summits to bring together Awaji-lineage puppetry groups from around Japan to revive the art form. In October 1993, the summit focused on the Sambasō performance in which seven puppet versions of the rite were presented.

For the most part, however, what remains is theater and not ritual performance. Even the ritual pieces of Ebisu and Sambasō are usually presented on stages and as "examples" of the history of the tradition; they are performed in ritual contexts only once or twice a year. Selected jōruri pieces are presented daily at the theater, and seasonal puppet festivals with long, varied programs are performed four or five times a year. Each October features a month-long puppetry festival with varied daily performances.

The jōruri plays are decidedly tragic, and Awaji puppetry is often referred to as the "theater of grief." Building on the nuances of the ritual appeasement tradition, the puppets create a geography in which human audiences, like the divine audience of the myth, can come to understand the tragedies of being human. The nearly life-size puppets come, at times, close to being—yet never fully become—the humans they supposedly emulate. The "world set apart," populated with its own ethereal beings, creates a safe space in which to explore the tragedies of separations, broken love affairs, violent deaths, and daily drudgery. When the wooden clackers call the audience to attention, the sharp tones of the shamisen cut through the air, the chanter opens the narration, and the wooden and lacquered beings are brought to life by three puppeteers breathing in unison; the world of magic and power over which the puppets have reigned for centuries is only as far away as the dimly lit stage.

The Song of Sambasō (Sambasō jiutai)

A ritual piece

Translated by Jane Marie Law

The names *Sambasō* and *Okina* refer to a wide range of ritual pieces found in most Japanese performing arts. Where the pieces came from is a matter of controversy. One popular account claims that once, a long time ago, an old man (*okina*) dancing under a pine tree at the Kasuga Shrine in Nara was identified as the local deity. Each year thereafter a human would dance under the same tree during the shrine festival, hoping to be possessed by the deity. The practice is continued today by the head of the Komparu school, who performs the noh version of *Okina* annually under an old and rather decrepit tree. A painting of this "epiphany pine" (*yōgō no matsu*) appears on the back wall of noh stages and is used as the backdrop for the stage version of the puppet piece.

The modern noh *Okina* presents three characters: Okina himself, the most important figure; Senzai, now performed as a young man, although his name means "one thousand years"; and Sambasō, played by a kyōgen actor. *Okina* is performed at the beginning of a full, formal program of five noh and four kyōgen plays, in shorter programs on special occasions, and on ritual occasions such as the annual Kasuga Wakamiya Shrine Festival. The actor playing Okina usually undergoes a ritual purification before the day of the performance, and there is a short ritual in the dressing room immediately before the piece begins. In Kurokawa noh, separate *Okina* and *Sambasō* pieces are performed (see figure 2.61).

Although in early times *Okina/Sambasō* may have been performed by ritual puppeteers as well as actors, both the bunraku and kabuki theaters adapted *Okina* from noh, although they shifted the center of focus from Okina to the Sambasō figure. In the Tokugawa period it was customary in both genres for a Sambasō dance—each theater had its own version—to be performed every day when the theater opened. Since a few earlier arrivals were the only audience, a low-ranking actor performed the dance, and the practice died out at the major theaters toward the end of the nineteenth century, although it is still followed at some regional performances.

Numerous versions of *Sambasō* have been created over the years. A kabuki variant called *Okina watashi* used to be performed at New Year's and on other special occasions, with the stage manager as Okina, his son as Senzai, and the chief actor as Sambasō. The performance was offered as a prayer for peace in the realm, a good harvest, and the prosperity of the theater. A similarly felicitous bunraku piece, *Kotobuki Sambasō*, has two Sambasō roles. In some kabuki plays, Sambasō appeared as a clown or as a puppet manipulated by a stage attendant, and one dance piece (shōsagoto) still performed is commonly called *The Tongue-Sticking-Out Sambasō* (Shitadashi Sambasō), because the dancer does just that in the middle of his performance.

In the ritual puppetry version (*kadozuke*) presented here, Sambasō is central, but the religious rather than the humorous aspect of the figure is emphasized. Jane Marie Law translated the ritual version performed on Awaji called *Okina watari*, *Shiki Sambasō*, or simply *Sambasō*. Itinerant puppeteers, a common feature of the Awaji countryside until the postwar period, presented this rite of purification, sanctification, and blessing during felicitous seasons of the year (rice planting, harvesting, and the new year) and when something needed to be ritually inaugurated (like a wedding, a new home, or the launching of a new or repaired boat). When presented in such a context, one, two, or three ritual spe-

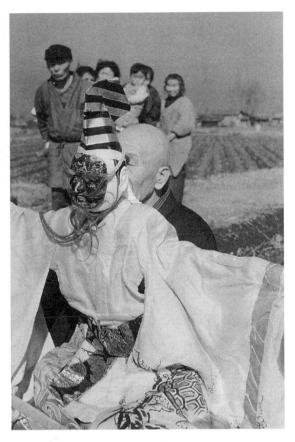

FIGURE 3.48. Passersby stop to watch as an itinerant Awaji puppeteer manipulates Sambasō before a roadside shrine (photo taken circa 1940). The puppet is wearing the black sambasō mask. Compare the Kurokawa noh Sambasō in figure 2.61. (Photo by Fudō Sai'ichi, courtesy of Fudō Bin.)

cialists carry the puppets, flutes, and drums in boxes to shrines or from door to door (figure 3.48). The dolls are one-person puppets (*hitori zukai*), manipulated with the puppeteer's right hand operating the puppet's right hand, and his left hand going through the back of the puppet to manipulate the head and left arm. When not in use, the puppets are placed in a "sleeping" position, face down and bent at the waist in front of the puppeteer. After their final use, the puppeteer returns them to the large box that remains by him throughout the performance.

Although the itinerant version of this rite has largely died out, there now are attempts to revive it, and a stage presentation based on the ritual form is often presented. The following translation compares the two versions. The ritual directions are primary and are based on a film of two aged itinerant puppeteers performing in a private home shortly after World War II. The directions for the stage version, given in brackets, are based on a performance presented by the Awaji Puppet Theater in the summer of 1988. The puppet heads used by the ritual specialists were given to the Awaji Puppet Theater and were used, with fresh new costumes, in the 1988 stage

FIGURE 3.49. An Awaji puppeteer cuts white paper to make gohei, the paper strips used to delineate the sacred space for a ritual puppet performance (photo taken circa 1940). (Photo by Fudō Sai'ichi, courtesy of Fudō Bin.)

presentation. In both cases, two puppeteers work together to manipulate all three dolls, chant the text, and provide flute and drum music. In preparing this translation, Law used the transcription of the aforementioned Awaji performance filmed shortly after World War II and the noh version in Sanari 1931. The section divisions are hers.[1] The piece takes from five to seven minutes to perform.

1. For a detailed discussion of this ritual chant and its magical use of language, see Law 1995.

CHARACTERS (the puppeteers chant the entire text)

OKINA

SENZAI

SAMBASŌ

All three puppets are manipulated by a single puppeteer, except in the dialogue section, in which the drummer-puppeteer manipulates Okina.

MUSICIANS

A flute and a hand-held drum beaten with a stick are played by the two puppeteers who also chant the entire text.

A Ritual Performance

*Two itinerant puppeteers in formal Japanese dress approach a Japanese home. One carries the puppets in a box wrapped in a black cloth slung over his shoulder, and the other has a flute and small drum in a small bag attached to his waist. They arrive in the entryway, bow several times to the woman of the house, and are invited up into the room where the family Shinto altar (*kamidana, *a shelf for the sacred) is located. The hostess brings in a wooden tray holding ritual items such as white paper and a pair of scissors. One puppeteer cuts the paper into zigzag strips (*gohei*), which will demarcate the space as sacred [figure 3.49]. The other puppeteer prepares the puppets, and the householder, a younger woman, and a child sit at the side of the room to watch the ritual. The performance is directed at the sacred forces present in the kamidana. To begin, the puppeteers offer a prayer in front of the kamidana, clapping their hands in unison and then bowing their heads to the tatami mats. The puppeteer, with the puppets in front of him, hereafter called simply the puppeteer, takes out the flute and plays a sharp, quick piece. The other performer, hereafter called the drummer, plays lively rhythms on a hand-held drum beaten with a stick. The cadence is immediately intense, and the melody high pitched.*

[In the staged version, a curtain depicting a stylized pine tree (reminiscent of the noh stage) hangs as a backdrop. A stage attendant places a large black box at center stage.[2] Two puppeteers clad in formal Japanese dress and unhooded enter and sit at center stage behind the box. The performer at stage right plays a few notes on the flute and the other, the "drummer," accompanies him with sharp, single strikes of the drum. The cadence is very slow and dignified.]

The puppeteer puts down the flute and picks up the Okina puppet as the drummer continues to play. The invocation is chanted by both performers, who divide the lines, sometimes overlapping their delivery and sometimes taking turns. Their chant is ritualized and their voices shrill. The drummer continues to play, and the cadence becomes more intense. The cadence calls of "yo, ho o" are inter-

---

2. In more recent performances, the puppeteers carry the all implements on stage with them, in a closer imitation of the kadozuke ritual version.

spersed with the chanting. During the invocation, the puppet bows, spreads out his arms, and then moves in a lively fashion, flipping one sleeve and then the other behind his head.

[On the stage, the drummer recites most of the lines, and the cadence is slower than in the ritual performance. The puppeteer also rises higher on his knees to manipulate the puppet.]

Invocation

[OKINA]:
   Tō tō tarari tarari ra
   tarari agari rarari tō
CHANTER:
   chiriya tarari rari ra
   tarari agari rarari tō[3]
[OKINA]:
   Live a long, long time.[4]
CHANTER:
   We will also serve a thousand autumns
[OKINA]:
   as long as the crane and the turtle live.[5]
CHANTER:
   Let us enjoy good fortune.
[OKINA]:
   Tō tō tarari tarari ra
CHANTER:
   chiriya tarari tarari ra
   tarari agari rarari tō
[OKINA]:
   "The sound of the waterfall,
   the sound of the waterfall,
   even if the sun is shining,
CHANTER:
   will not cease,"[6]
   tō tari ari utō tō tō
   it will not cease,

Okina is put down in the sleeping position beside the box so that he can easily be picked up later.

   tō tarari agari utō tō tō

Senzai is picked up [figure 3.50].

3. The syllables in Japanese have no meaning but reflect a magical use of sound in the chant.
4. This piece is intended as a longevity rite for the sovereign and is written as though addressed to this august person. The blessing extends to all present.
5. The crane was thought to live one thousand years, the turtle, ten thousand years.
6. These are lines from a popular song (imayō) recorded as song 404 in the Ryōjin hishō. In the imayō, the waterfall makes the sound rendered onomatopoetically as tōtae.

Senzai's dance and poetic interlude

[SENZAI]:

> it will not cease;
> *tō tari ari*
> it will go on forever.

Senzai performs a slow dance, waving his sleeves from side to side to purify the space.

[SENZAI]:

> May you live a thousand years.
> A heavenly maiden's robe of
>   feathers.[7]
> Even if the sun is shining,
> the sound of the waterfall will
>   not cease;

CHANTER:

> it will not cease
> *tōtari ari utō tō tō*

FIGURE 3.50. The Awaji Okina puppet has been put down between the puppeteers, ready to be picked up again. Senzai is about to perform, Sambasō remains in the box, and the sacred paper strips (*gohei*) are on the tray. The puppeteer on the right strikes a small hand drum with two sticks. (Photo by Jane Marie Law.)

Senzai is put down in a sleeping position, and Okina is picked up and made to dance slowly.

Okina's dance and poetic interlude

CHANTER:

> *tōtari ari utō tō tō*

[OKINA]:

> "Ah, my lover with the braided hair,
> *ya ton do ya*

CHANTER:

> only a short distance away from me!"[8]
> *yo ton dō ya.*

The drumming continues, and the Okina puppet bows, spreads its arms, then aggressively thrusts forward its right hand, holding a fan, and flips both sleeves behind its head.

[On the stage, the puppet makes similar movements, but both the drum cadences and the puppets' movements are slower and more dignified than in the ritual performance.]

[OKINA]:

> Although we're seated,

---

7. The popular legend of a heavenly maiden in Japan (the subject of the noh play *Hagoromo*) uses a classical Indian notion of time: a *kalpa* is as long as it takes for a heavenly maiden to wear away a gigantic rock if she descends to earth once every one hundred years to brush it with her robe of feathers (*hagoromo*).

8. These lines are from a popular Saibara song ("Agemaki," song 57). A man and woman sleeping a short distance apart toss and turn during the night and eventually roll toward each other. The Saibara includes the syllables *tō tō*.

FIGURE 3.51. Sambasō is being lifted out of the box to perform his dance. A bell rattle (*suzu*) is attached to his right hand. The setting is in front of a worship hall on Awaji (1990). (Photo by Jane Marie Law.)

CHANTER:

let's begin!

[OKINA]:

We have been celebrating a long time,[9]
since the age of the gods

CHANTER:

soyo yari chiya ton dō ya

[OKINA]:

the thousand-year crane sings the
Manzairaku song of longevity,[10]
and the turtle who has lived in the pond
for ten thousand generations
carries heaven, earth, and humankind
on his shell.
The color of the morning sun glistens
in the rustling, spreading sands of the
seashore;
the evening moon floats clearly
in the cool, pure water of the falls.
Peace under heaven! Tranquillity
throughout the land.
This is today's prayer.

Arrival of the sacred

Okina pauses briefly, as though to listen.
[On the stage, the next three lines are skipped.]

CHANTER:

Who are those old men?[11]

Who are they?
Where are they from?

[OKINA]:

Since this dance is for a thousand autumns,
ten thousand years of bliss,[12]
let's do one Manzairaku dance of longevity,
the Dance of Ten Thousand Years.

9. This refers to *The Tales of Ise*, episode 117, in which an emperor encounters the Sumiyoshi deity, who says: "Do you not know of the tie that unites us? Since times as ancient as my sacred fence have I protected you." The Sumiyoshi deities, with whom the imperial line has always been in direct interaction, are being invoked in this rite.

10. *Manzairaku* (Ten-thousand-year music) is the name of a bugaku piece imported from China. It is frequently performed on felicitous occasions.

11. "Old men" refer to Okina and Sambasō, who have been summoned by the music, chanting, and felicitous imagery.

12. *Senshu manzai* (One thousand autumns, ten thousand years) refers to dances performed at the imperial court as a New Year's ritual from the Nara period onward. The form was popularized by medieval itinerant performers called *senshu manzai hōshi*, and their art influenced that of the itinerant puppet tradition.

CHANTER:

    Manzairaku,

[OKINA]:

    Manzairaku,

CHANTER:

    Manzairaku![13]

Trance dance and apotheosis of Sambasō

The puppeteer puts down Okina to his left and picks up Sambasō [figure 3.51]. This puppet has feet (the other two do not), and a rattle made of small bells with streamers attached is inserted into a hole in the puppet's right hand so that when the arm is moved, the rattle sounds. Shaking the rattle purifies the space, and the rattle itself serves as a torimono, an object into which a sacred force will descend. Sambasō's brief dance to drum accompaniment includes his feet stamping to drive out evil and his eyeballs rapidly moving to indicate that he is undergoing a transformation into sacred status.

Humorous interlude

When the trance dance is finished, the puppeteer puts a black mask over the doll's face. The "drummer" sets aside his drum, puts a white mask on Okina's face, and picks him up. The two puppets are manipulated without accompaniment. As the characters converse, the puppets cover their faces with their sleeves [figure 3.52].

[SAMBASŌ]: Oh! Such joy, such joy, such joy! I won't let it slip away![14]

[OKINA]: How felicitous!

[SAMBASŌ]: I will summon that ado actor who takes care of things.[15]

[OKINA]: I came just at the right time.

[SAMBASŌ]: Who's standing there?

[OKINA]: It's that actor you mentioned, the one who takes care of everything.

[SAMBASŌ]: Really!

[OKINA]: You are to dance the felicitous Thousand Autumns and Ten Thousand Years for today's blessing. You, the black-faced old man.

[SAMBASŌ]: This black-faced old man will be happy to dance the felicitous Thousand Autumns and Ten Thousand Years piece for today's blessing. There is nothing I would like to do more! But first, sir, you must return to your seat and settle down.

[UKINA]: After the old man's dance I will be happy to return to my seat. First, perform the dance.

The drummer puts down the Okina doll and picks up his drum to accompany the masked dance of Sambasō, called the bell dance (suzu no dan) in noh. Both the mask and the bell indicate that Sambasō is now fully possessed by sacred forces.

13. In the noh version Okina dances here; he and Senzai then exit.

14. In the noh version, at this point the still unmasked Sambasō performs a dance called *momi no dan*.

15. The ado is a secondary kyōgen actor. In the noh version, Sambasō, played by the primary (omo or shite) kyōgen actor, has this discussion with the secondary (ado) kyōgen actor, who serves as the mask bearer.

FIGURE 3.52. Sambasō (left) and Okina, with their masks on, hold up their sleeves to cover their faces while they talk. The puppeteer on the right has put down his drum to manipulate the Okina puppet. (Photo by Jane Marie Law.)

Words of blessing (masked Sambasō dance)

Sambasō dances frenetically to the following chant. His bell rattle cuts through space and shakes wildly from side to side as he leaps about in the air. The energy intensifies as the performers chant the text, beat the drum, and voice the cadence calls.

[On the stage, Sambasō dances to drum accompaniment. The dance begins slowly and gradually becomes ecstatic. His sleeves fly in every direction, and his feet stamping becomes intense as he shakes his bell rattle rhythmically from side to side and up and down, imitating the sowing of grain and the falling of rain. In addition, the following text is omitted.][16]

CHANTERS:

Oh how grateful we are for this
    manifestation of the deity.
How blissful to give thanks to the deity
    with this sacred rite.[17]
Indeed, at Suminoe we will hear
the clear, lovely voices of many dancing girls.
The blue waves of the ocean[18] there are said
to reflect the shadow of the Sumiyoshi pines.
The way of the kami and the way of our
    sovereign
should lead straight to the capital in
    springtime.
This is the dance called Returning to the Palace.[19]
For the Dance of Ten Thousand Years
we use pure white robes.
Sweeping arms purify you of all evil;
outstretched hands receive longevity and good fortune.
The Dance of a Thousand Autumns caresses the people;

16. This final section, not included in the noh Okina piece, is borrowed from the end of the noh play *Takasago*, in which the lines are divided between the Sumiyoshi deity and the chorus. The "wind in the pines" is understood to be a manifestation of the deity and suggests peace and harmony in the realm.

17. *Kami asobi* (playing with the sacred) refers to the aspect of a *matsuri* (festival) intended to entertain, and thus appease, the deity who has been invoked. It assumes that the deity is a participant in the festivities. In early texts, the term is also synonymous with kagura.

18. *Seigaiha* (Blue waves of the ocean) refers to a bugaku dance performed by two dancers. It is thought to have originated in China and was popular in Japan during the classical period.

19. *Genjōraku* (Going-to-the-castle music) is the name of a bugaku piece, in which a snake is subdued by a person wearing a demon mask.

the Dance of Ten Thousand Years lengthens our days.
We enjoy the voices of the wind in the pines;
we enjoy these gentle voices.

As the chant concludes, the puppet ceases to dance and shakes his bell rattle from side to side to bless the space. The puppet is put into the box on top of the other two puppets. The performers clap their hands together and bow to conclude the rite.

The Miracle of the Tsubosaka Kannon

From *Tsubosaka Kannon reigenki*, by Kako
Chikajo and Toyozawa Dampei II

Translated by Jane Marie Law

An Awaji woman, Kako Chikajo, and her husband, the famous shamisen player Toyozawa Dampei II (1827–1898), composed this play in the 1870s, and Dampei revised it in 1887 with the help of the chanter Takemoto Osumidayū III. That version, which premiered in the Hikoroku Theater in Osaka, became the standard and is still popular in both the puppet and the kabuki theaters. In fact, Osato's lament after the death of her husband is considered an outstanding example of the onnagata's art. The Bunraku troupe presented this play on a 1962 tour of the western United States, and it was performed as kabuki in New York City in 1960. It was a success in both genres.

Although *Tsubosaka* is the newest original play to have earned a place in the traditional puppet repertory (there are later adaptations from kabuki and noh), its themes go back to the genre's beginnings. Miracle tales were popular in medieval narrative and in the seventeenth-century puppet traditions of both the jōruri and the sekkyō bushi types. In 1614 one of the most famous plays performed in both genres, *The Chest Splitting of Amida* (Amida no munewari), was presented before the retired emperor Goyōzei. That six-act play includes many improbable events: Shakyamuni Buddha must call on the help of the devils to conquer a wicked rich couple whose virtuous, yet poor, orphaned children have various dire misadventures, brought to an end only when Amida Buddha offers his own liver (hence "chest splitting") to save the girl.

The Chest Splitting of Amida is no longer performed, but Jane Marie Law suggests that *Tsubosaka* is faithful to the miracle-story genre on a number of counts. First, the plot is so simple, easily discerned, remembered, embroidered, and retold that even a small child can understand it. Second, the level of emotion in the play is extremely high, with a great deal of tear shedding, heated dialogue, and celebration of the pathetic and helpless. Third, the play is heavily moralistic, and goodness is readily recognizable. It provides a basic ethical lesson: good wives are devoted to their husbands, even unto death, and simple faith is rewarded with miracles. Fourth, the play presents didactic Buddhist interpretations of events. And finally, the play teaches that the sufferings of this world are not without their causes in past lives and rewards in this life or the next.

The brevity of the play, the limited number of characters, and the highly emotional content make *The Miracle of the Tsubosaka Kannon* popular with regional puppet theaters throughout Japan. The entire play contains two acts, but only the latter half of the second is regularly performed by the Awaji troupe. The performance time for the typical Awaji presentation is between twenty-seven and thirty-eight minutes. Law's translation is based on the script currently used by the Awaji puppets, and the descriptions of performance are from the Awaji performance video cassette produced by the Kōyōsha Studio. The performance in October 1993 at the Third Annual Puppet Summit and performances regularly staged at the theater are similar to the video.

CHARACTERS (the chanter speaks for both characters)

OSATO: the wife
SAWAICHI: her husband, who is blind

MUSICIANS

One chanter
Two shamisen players, one playing only for the final segment

ACT 2, Scene 2

The Journey to Tsubosaka

[The earlier scenes reveal that Osato, a devoted and pure-hearted woman, has been leaving her house each evening and returning around dawn. Her blind husband, Sawaichi, suspects that she has a lover and confronts her. Her response to his accusations is a mixture of grief and anger. In tears, she confesses to him that she has been going to the Tsubosaka Kannon Temple to pray for the restoration of his sight. Ashamed of having doubted her, Sawaichi asks her forgiveness, and she implores him to go to the temple with her to pray to Kannon. Together the two of them make their way to the Tsubosaka Kannon Temple.]

The main curtain rises to reveal a black-clad, hooded performer, who strikes the clackers, announces the names of the play and the performers, and exits stage right.[1] The backdrop depicts a small temple building on top of a high cliff. The low wall at stage left behind the sunken front performing area represents a lower cliff with a pine tree on it. One chanter and one shamisen player (both women) are seated on the auxiliary stage. There is a brief shamisen prelude.

CHANTER: It has been told of the Kannon of Tsubosaka, that in the fiftieth generation of emperors, when Emperor Kammu[2] was in Nara, he had a very bad eye ailment. The priest who resided there, named Dōki Shōnin, recited prayers for 107 days, and thereupon the emperor's eyes were healed. Now this site is the sixth station on the Saikoku pilgrimage route and is well known among people as a holy place.[3]

Osato enters from stage right with Sawaichi, who supports himself with a large walking stick. They each hold the end of a long white strip of cloth. On one level, this cloth shows that Osato is guiding her blind husband. In the puppet theater, however, the

---

1. At the Awaji Theater overlooking the Naruto Straits, the traditional draw curtain is used only for visiting troupes. When the Awaji troupe performs, they use a drop curtain of elaborate brocade on which are depicted the Naruto Straits, a puppet head, and the mother and daughter from the famous play *Keisei Awa no Naruto* (The tragedy of the Naruto Straits).
2. Kammu was sovereign from 781 to 806.
3. The Saikoku route, one of the most famous pilgrimage routes in Japan, consists of thirty-three temples in which the Bodhisattva Kannon is the central deity. Each temple claims its own Kannon miracle, and this is a summary of the Tsubosaka miracle.

cloth is understood to tie the two characters together at a deep karmic level.[4]

Just as Sawaichi and his wife come near the temple marker on the road, from down the hill is heard the sound of pilgrims singing devotional songs to Kannon.[5]

[OSATO]: Sawaichi, listen. Although a devoted heart is very important, the more depressed you are, the sicker you will become. At a time like this, it will cheer you up to sing some songs you know by heart. Why don't you sing something aloud and not be so serious?

Sawaichi turns his head from side to side as if listening for other people.

[SAWAICHI]: Yes, that is really true. As you say, worrying over things is bad for my eyes. If that is the case, I will think of this as practice. But is anybody watching us?

CHANTER: He begins to sing and mimes playing the shamisen in accompaniment:

[SAWAICHI] *(Singing)*: "Is gloom compassion? Or is compassion gloom?"

CHANTER: He makes the noises to himself of the strumming of the shamisen.

[SAWAICHI] *(Singing)*: "As the dew disappears, my body . . ." (*He begins to dance and loses his balance*) Oops, I tripped! Oh, I forget the next part of that song.

CHANTER *(Laughs)*: The song becomes like the transitory grass on the road, and they climb up to the worship hall of the temple.

FIGURE 3.53. In *The Miracle of the Tsubosaka Kannon*, Osato tells her husband that they have arrived at the Kannon Hall. Sawaichi wears a light blue kimono and has a variation of the Genta head covered with smallpox scars. His eyes are closed to indicate his blindness, and he uses a simple walking stick (*tsue*). Osato's kimono is maroon, and she has a *tsubushi shimada* head. (Courtesy of the Awaji Puppet Theater.)

They continue up the hill, Osato leading her husband by the hand; he gropes with his cane. They stop at center stage, and Osato goes around behind Sawaichi to stand at his right [figure 3.53].

[OSATO]: Sawaichi, we've arrived at the hall of Kannon.

They both sit down, and Osato tucks the cloth into her belt.

[SAWAICHI]: Oh, is this Kannon-sama? (*He puts down his stick to his left*) Oh, how fortunate, how fortunate. (*Folds his hand in prayer*) Namu Amida Butsu. Namu Amida Butsu. Namu Amida Butsu. Namu Amida Butsu.

4. A similarly symbolic white cloth is also held by the mother and daughter in the play *Keisei Awa no Naruto*.

5. *Eika*, a common type of devotional singing. Each bodhisattva has its own song.

FIGURE 3.54. When they arrive at Tsubosaka Temple, where Sawaichi will fast for three days, Osato takes out a hand towel (*tenugui*) to wipe off his face as she comforts him before she returns home. (Courtesy of the Awaji Puppet Theater.)

Osato moves closer to Sawaichi and touches his arm.

[OSATO]: Here! Come over here! Tonight, on this very night, why don't we leisurely sing a devotional song all night long?

Sawaichi moves away a bit, and the two figures, hands folded in prayer, look off toward stage left in the direction of the worship hall.

CHANTER: And the husband and wife's voices are pure as they chant together into the night.

[TOGETHER] *(Singing):*
"The Kannon of Tsubosaka, who builds mountains and fills lakes with water; the sands of the garden become the Pure Land."

Sawaichi turns to Osato.

[SAWAICHI]: Oh! Osato! I thought this was impossible, but anyway, I followed your word and have come this far, but my sight is not being restored.

Osato moves closer to Sawaichi and wipes his face and eyes with a cloth [figure 3.54].

[OSATO]: Oh, you! You're being like that again! Here we go again! It was to this very Kannon on Tsubosaka that Emperor Kammu in the Nara capital prayed when he was suffering from an eye disease. Immediately his eyes were opened. That is the reason I have encouraged you, because really there is no difference between the emperor and us, who are like bugs. Having faith means being patient with a calm and concentrated heart throughout many steps of prayerful supplications. With such faith and Kannon's compassion, anything is possible. But instead of wasting time talking like this, why don't we continue chanting?

CHANTER: Saying this and gathering up their strength,

[SAWAICHI]: I guess you are right. From tonight, I am going to fast here for three days. You go home ahead of me and do your work. (*He gestures to be left alone. She moves slightly away from his side.*) These three days will seal my fate as to whether my eyes will heal or not heal.

[OSATO]: I am so glad you said that. If you feel that way, I'll go on home and get things prepared. (*She starts off, then returns to him*) But Sawaichi, listen. This is a steep mountain road, and if you go to the right, there is a valley of unfathomable depths. So don't go anywhere.

As she speaks, Osato moves back and forth between center stage and Sawaichi, and each time touches his arm as though hesitant to leave him.

[SAWAICHI]: Where would I go? For three days it will be just me and Kannon here.

He pats the ground in front of him.

CHANTER: He laughs, and while laughing, the wife leaves her heart behind in her footsteps, dew gathers and is scattered, and she flutters off, not knowing what kind of parting this is. Sawaichi remains behind alone, and unable to endure his downhearted feelings, he lies down and cries.

Sawaichi embraces his wife gently, and she exits stage right, stumbling and looking back over her shoulder as she departs. Sawaichi stretches out, puts his head on his arm, and sobs.

[SAWAICHI]: I am happy, my wife. More than just nursing me these years and months, you have not resented the poverty and suffering. Moreover, not once did your love grow weary, and to me who cannot see, you have had patient endurance. Even so, without your knowing, I have had all kinds of doubts about you. (*He folds his hands in supplication and looks at the sky*) Forgive me. Forgive me. Having just now parted, in what world should we meet again? I am such a pitiful person.

CHANTER (*Weeping*): He throws himself on the ground and bemoans his failure. After a while, he raises his face.

[SAWAICHI]: I won't let myself be remorseful. Even though for three years, my wife faithfully devoted herself to her prayers, there is no benefit in my living any longer. As it is said, if two people are miserable, let them go separate ways so that at least one of them can make a fortune.[6] So my death can be my reward for you (*weeps and falls forward*). While you are alive, marry into whatever good house you are able. As I learned from you just a little while ago, to the right of the hill there is a valley of unfathomable depths. That will be my final resting place. If I become part of the earth of this sacred place, perhaps in the next life I may be saved. Luckily, night has fallen. While there is no one around, I'll do it. I'll do it.

CHANTER: Saying this, he stands and pulls himself together.

He picks up his cane, stands, and, groping with his cane, makes his way to stage right. The puppeteers then step up to the higher floor level and return toward stage left. They are now behind the low wall, and Sawaichi appears to be climbing the cliff. He stumbles and falls, rises again, then hits his head on the tree. He falls backward and relocates the tree with his cane.

[SAWAICHI]: I hurry to my final moment.

CHANTER: He gropes his way along, tapping his cane forcefully side to side, and finally climbs up to the edge of the cliff. (*Holding onto the tree, he leans forward and waves his cane over the precipice, to be sure that he is at the edge*) He hears the thundering sound of the waters below in the valley, and considering this to be a welcome from Amida, he thrusts his cane into the ground, propels himself forward,

6. A famous proverb. This is the same logic used in the noh play *Ashikari*.

He sticks his cane into the earth, removes his sandals, places them beside the cane, and joins his hands in prayer.

[SAWAICHI]: Namu Amida Butsu,

A drum rolls as the puppeteers throw the puppet over the cliff. It falls onto the sunken floor area, and the stage darkens.

CHANTER: and throws himself to his tragic death. Not knowing what has happened, his wife returns along the path, breathing heavily, her mind preoccupied with worries about her husband. Although she knows this path well, she slips and falls but finally makes her way to the top of the slope.

Osato enters hurriedly from stage right as the stage slowly brightens enough so that her figure can be seen. She runs from left to right in the sunken floor area, calling out his name.

[OSATO]: I can't see him anywhere! Sawaichi! Sawaichi! Sawaichi!

CHANTER: She would ask people if they had seen him, but she hears no voices and sees not even the shadow of a person. She staggers back and forth,

Osato runs back and forth. At stage right she turns her back on the audience and leans back, in the classical posture of female lament in the puppet theater. Her sobs are slow, and she sways back and forth, her form viewed from behind.

[OSATO] *(Turning to face front)*: Sawaichi!

The puppeteers step up to the higher level and move toward stage left, up the cliff.

CHANTER: Running here and there, in the light of the moon, she can see something through the trees. She comes close and recognizes his cane, stuck into the ground. *(She jumps back in surprise as she realizes what this means)* She lets out a cry of grief. Startled, she looks down into the valley and, in the shining moon, recognizes the dead form of her husband.

Holding on to the tree, she peers into the valley. She starts as she sees Sawaichi's body [figure 3.55].

[OSATO]: What shall I do now! How sad!

CHANTER: Crazy with grief, she writhes back and forth. Even if she wished to fly down to him in the valley, she has no wings. She calls out to him, but to no avail. No one answers her but her own echo.

Kudoki   *During this section, Osato removes a pin from her hair, allowing it to fall in a single bound strand behind her back. The puppeteers also remove the sleeves of her outer kimono, revealing a bright red underkimono. She writhes back and forth, turns her back on the audience, and then turns around to face them again. She collapses to her knees, sobs, and pounds the ground, shaking her head so that her hair becomes disheveled. There is a loud shamisen accompaniment.*

[OSATO]: I won't hear of this! *(She pounds her hands on the ground)* I won't hear of this! I just won't hear of this! For all the hardships of these years and months *(covers her mouth with her hair and cries)* unbegrudgingly I bore all the difficulties. With a single heart I petitioned to Kannon that your eyes would soon be healed, that you would be saved. *(She folds her hands in prayer,*

FIGURE 3.55. Holding on to a tree, Osato peers over the cliff and sees her husband's lifeless body. (Courtesy of the Awaji Puppet Theater.)

imitating her own gestures of supplication) I have been praying ceaselessly for this, and on this very day, I am the one who is left behind. What shall I do?

She pounds her hands on the ground. She then cries again into her hair, which she holds in front of her mouth. Sitting up, she continues.

What shall I do? Come to think of it, that song you sang somehow bothered me. It stuck in my heart and made me worry. But now I realize that at that time you had already resolved to die. I didn't know! I didn't know! If I had known it would come to this, I would not have urged you to come here with me. Forgive me, forgive me.

She collapses on the ground and sobs.

I wonder if there is anyone more hopeless than I am? To be separated for eternity from my husband to whom I am wedded in two worlds (*gestures to left and right and then rises slowly*), ah, how miserable![7] Is this grief the result of sins from a previous life? How sorrowful! (*Grabbing the tree, she shakes her head in grief*) From the blind darkness of this world, he has gone on to the dark travels of death. (*She walks about, almost in a daze*) Who will take his hand and keep him from getting lost in that world? (*She collapses and breathes heavily.*)

CHANTER: As she pleads into the silence, her tears of grief make the water rise in the valley of Tsubosaka. Finally, she lifts her tearful face.

[OSATO]: I won't regret. I won't lament. (*She sits up with renewed strength*) Everything has been decided from a previous life. I will join my husband in death. Amida, show us the way as we leave this world.

She joins her hands in prayer and then throws Sawaichi's cane over the cliff. The puppeteers throw the puppet over the cliff, making it appear that she has jumped. As the puppet falls to the sunken floor area, a drum rolls, and the lights go out, leaving the stage in darkness.

CHANTER: As she voices this plea to Amida, she falls into the valley, her last gesture chaste. How piteous!

The time is early February. Near dawn, through an opening in the clouds, a beam of light shines forth. Surrounded by beautiful music, Kannon appears in the temporary form of a gracious and lovely woman.[8] In a delicate voice, the bodhisattva speaks:

The stage lightens slightly, turning the backdrop red, and Kannon slowly arises behind the cliff and beside the tree. A spotlight shines on her. She wears a red and gold kimono, her head and shoulders covered by a gold scarf with a gold headpiece on top. She carries a bouquet of lotus flowers. A bell sounds to signify her manifestation.

[KANNON]: Listen, Sawaichi! Because of events in a previous life, you became blind. However, because of your pressing fate, the chaste heart of your wife, and the merit of her daily prayers, I will extend your lives. Since I have bequeathed this to you, go on the pilgrimage of the thirty-three sites, and in faith, show gratitude for the Buddha's compassion. Sawaichi! Sawaichi! Osato! Osato!

CHANTER: As she proclaims this in a divine voice, she disappears without a trace, and the early morning bells reverberate in four directions. The morning

---

7. A common (and romantic) Buddhist notion was that happily married couples may have been together in previous lives. Osato fears that she and Sawaichi will not be united again in the next life.

8. The text uses the term *jōrō*, the highest-ranking courtesan.

dawns, and as the light breaks in the dark valley, two forms, not knowing if they are in a dream, slowly rise up.

Kannon is lowered again behind the cliff, and the stage goes dark. As it gradually lightens, Osato and Sawaichi are lying in front of the cliff. They rise and rub their eyes. Osato approaches Sawaichi.

[OSATO]: Ah! It's you, Sawaichi! It's you! Your eyes are open!

[SAWAICHI]: OH! It's really true! I can see! I can see! I can see! (*He opens his eyes wide, and the lighting brightens*) This is all due to Kannon! Thank you very much! Thank you! Thank you! Thank you! And, you? Who are you?

[OSATO]: Who do you think I am? I am your wife!

[SAWAICHI]: You are my wife? This is the first time I have seen you. Oh how happy I am! How happy I am! This is indeed something very mysterious. I am sure I fell into the valley, and I thought I was dead. While I didn't know what was happening, Kannon appeared, and she explained everything that happened to me from my previous life.

[OSATO]: Yes, and I followed in your footsteps, and there is no doubt that I, too, fell into the valley. But there is not a single wound on my body, and on top of that, you can see! Are we dreaming?

[SAWAICHI]: If that is the case, then there is not doubt that it was Kannon who directly called me back to life, saying "Sawaichiiiiii! Sawaichiiiiiii!!" Ha ha ha! I am so grateful!

The shamisen plays; they bow to each other and begin to dance.

CHANTER: It is indeed Kannon who saves the lives of this intimate husband and wife. Graciously rewarding them by opening Sawaichi's blind eyes, it is as if his youth has returned to him. Today is a happy day, for he sets aside his cane, and as the dawn breaks, he gives thanks to the gods and buddhas. It is

They turn to face the temple painted on the backdrop. Then the puppeteers remove the sleeves of Sawaichi's outer kimono, revealing a bright red underkimono. The two puppets turn to face the audience again. Osato sits and claps her hands as Sawaichi dances. A second shamisen joins the first. Osato joins Sawaichi in his dance to chanting and shamisen interludes. They move back and forth across the entire stage in cheerful celebration.

Kannon who shows him these myriad things; it is the weight of Kannon's vow that builds mountains and fills lakes with water. Even the sands become the Pure Land, and this revelation is the blessed Dharma.[9]

The dance continues. Osato picks up Sawaichi's cane and hands it to him. He dances with it. Finally Osato sits and spreads her arms wide; Sawaichi holds the cane over his head, and they pose as the singing and shamisen music come to an end and the curtain falls.

---

9. The Pure Land is the realm of the Amida Buddha, who, along with Kannon, is a popular focus of religious devotion in Japan. The Dharma refers to the body of teachings of the Buddha and is one of the "three jewels" of Buddhism: the Buddha, the community of Buddhists, and the Dharma.

KABUKI PLAYS

Shunkan on Devil Island

A kabuki adaptation of a scene from *Heike nyogo no shima*, by Chikamatsu Monzaemon

Translated by Samuel L. Leiter

The noh play *Shunkan* and the puppet–kabuki piece *Shunkan on Devil Island* (Shunkan, or Kikaigashima no ba) draw on the same materials from *The Tale of the Heike*: both open with three exiles describing their lives and close with a depiction of Shunkan's loneliness. The way each play progresses from its beginning to the shared conclusion, however, is strikingly different and reveals much about the two traditions. The noh play isolates Shunkan's emotions, portrays the intensity of his loneliness, and advocates the effectiveness of religious practice. Chikamatsu Monzaemon, in writing the puppet play of which "Shunkan on Devil Island" is but a single act, invented new characters to create romantic interests, conflict (leading to the almost obligatory fight scene), and self-sacrifice, all staple elements of the puppet–kabuki tradition in which love, honor, and sacrifice are the predominant virtues.

The kabuki version of this act, the version translated here, contains clear traces of its noh and puppet antecedents. All three musical traditions are represented. The noh flute and drums accompany Shunkan's entrance, and the gidayū shamisen and chanter sit at stage left to describe and accompany much of the action. In kabuki most of the lines of direct speech are spoken by the actors rather than by the chanter, although as is usual in traditional Japanese theater, the boundaries between direct speech and description are often not clear. Typical kabuki music and sound effects echo forth from the music room (geza). Large drum patterns related to water predominate, with ripple patterns (*sazanami*) accompanying the emotional passages and wave patterns (*namioto*) accenting the entrances, exits, and stage action.

Chikamatsu Monzaemon's puppet play *The Heike and the Isle of Women* (Heike nyogo no shima) was first performed at the Takemoto Theater in Osaka in 1719 and was adapted to the kabuki stage in the following year. In 1759 Ichikawa Danzō III (1709–1772) performed the role of Shunkan so successfully that the scene on Devil

Island—most of act 2 of the five-act play—became an independent and frequently produced number and is now the only part of the original play to be offered regularly. It was taken on tour to the Soviet Union in 1961 and to Western Europe in 1965 and was received enthusiastically in both places.

The text used for this translation is that of the National Theater production found in *Kokuritsu gekijōen taihonshū*, II, and in *Meisaku kabuki zenshū*, I. The description of stage business is derived from a performance at Tokyo's Kabuki Theater in May 1975. Samuel L. Leiter's book *The Art of Kabuki*, in which this translation first appeared, contains extensive descriptions of variant performance practices, some of which are included in the footnotes to this translation.

CHARACTERS

SHUNKAN: an exiled priest
YASUYORI: the exiled lord of Hei
NARITSUNE: the exiled lord of Tamba, a member of the Fujiwara clan
CHIDORI: an island diving girl
SENOO TARŌ KANEYASU: a Heike warrior serving as an imperial envoy
TANZAEMON MOTOYASU: an envoy from Taira Shigemori
Retainers and boatmen

MUSICIANS

A gidayū chanter and a shamisen player seated on a platform at stage left
Music-room (geza) musicians, including noh and nagauta musicians

---

ACT 2

The Scene on Devil Island

After the wooden clackers are struck at quickening intervals for several minutes, the noh flute and drums play issei music. Then a large drum beats wave patterns, and the clackers strike faster and faster as the striped curtain is pulled aside to reveal a light blue drop curtain covering the entire width of the stage. After a brief shamisen passage, the chanter begins his recitative.

CHANTER:
From time immemorial
this island's fearful name
has been Kikaigashima
— Devil Island —
a place where demons live.
It is indeed a hell on earth.

The wave drum patterns sound loudly in the music room. The wooden clacker strikes, and the blue curtain suddenly falls, revealing a spot near the shore on the exiles' island [figure 3.56].

The only things to remind one
of bygone days in the capital
are the sun and moon
shining in the sky.

More wave drum patterns as Shunkan enters slowly from upstage right, his movements suggesting weakness and despondency.[1]

---

1. Some actors prefer to be seated in the hut when the curtain drops, whereas others enter down the rampway or from stage left. A method no longer practiced was to appear from the small elevator trap at stage center.

FIGURE 3.56. The kabuki setting for *Shunkan at Devil Island*. Shunkan's ramshackle hut has a makeshift tripodal fireplace in it. Gray and wave-patterned ground cloths mark land and water. Shunkan enters between the rocks at stage right. (Photo by Aoki Shinji.)

> Shunkan, the exiled priest,
> having exchanged some sulfur
> from the mountaintop
> for a fisherman's meager haul,
> comes stumbling, tottering,
> staggering along
> with his wretched, scraggly walking stick;
> he is surely a sight to be pitied.

Shunkan crosses to the right of the hut, leans his staff there, removes his sandals, enters the hut, and kneels, exhausted. He takes the seaweed from the ring, puts it in an abalone shell that he takes from the wall, and fans the embers beneath the shell with a palm leaf until a red glow appears.[2] He busies himself with his cooking as Yasuyori and Naritsune move down the rampway.[3]

> The same may be said of Yasuyori, lord of Hei,
> bedecked in rotting rags,
> and of Naritsune, lord of Tamba,
> who come walking along the sandy beach.

Naritsune, played in the soft, romantic wagoto style, turns to address his friend [figure 3.57].

NARITSUNE: Lord Yasuyori! I can see Lord Shunkan sitting in his hut.

Yasuyori is less a wagoto type than Naritsune is, although Yasuyori speaks and moves with definite grace and refinement.

YASUYORI: Fortunately, the weather today is fine so we can gather at our ease

2. A long soliloquy in which Shunkan laments his life in exile is usually omitted (as it is here), although the Zenshin troupe has restored it in its production.

3. Two rampways are sometimes used, with Naritsune entering on the permanent one and Yasuyori along the temporary rampway. In this case they engage in a dialogue from the rampways, with Shunkan on the stage, and the words coming from three separated sections of the theater create an interesting effect.

FIGURE 3.57. Yasuyori (left) and Naritsune, dressed in patched kimonos, enter down the rampway to the seven-three position. The trapdoor (*suppon*) can be seen beneath their feet. Naritsune's makeup is lighter than that of his fellow exiles, and his movements are in the soft wagoto style. (Photo by Aoki Shinji.)

NARITSUNE: and seek relief

YASUYORI: from our melancholy burdens.

CHANTER:
    Friends to the waves that
    lap at the lonely house
    are the plovers, circling o'er the crests.

Wave drum patterns. Naritsune and Yasuyori cross to stage right, below the rocks.

NARITSUNE: Fortunately, Lord Shunkan

YASUYORI: may be found

BOTH: at home.

SHUNKAN *(Noticing them)*: Ah! Lord Naritsune! Lord Yasuyori! Welcome. Come, come!

Although glad to see his friends, Shunkan has barely enough strength to rise and greet them.

CHANTER:
    Though his means are scanty,
    his welcome is sincere,
    showing how truly close
    their friendship is.

Naritsune and Yasuyori put their baskets on the ground to the right of the hut, and a stage assistant removes them. Shunkan rises slowly, moves down to the left of the hut, sits, and gestures to them to sit down.

YASUYORI: Well, well! We haven't met together recently, so I hope things are well with you.

NARITSUNE: It's been at least four or five days since we last met; we've missed you a great deal.

SHUNKAN: My friends, Lord Yasuyori and Lord Naritsune, although we usually are together, it has been some time since I heard anything of either of you.

He slowly lifts his right hand to his eyes and mimes weeping.

YASUYORI: It is only natural for you to be upset, but let me explain. Together with Naritsune I have been praying daily to the gods of the three shrines of Kumano and simply have not had time to visit you.

The shamisen in the music room begins to play background music.

NARITSUNE: As Yasuyori has said, we have been praying every day that we may be granted a pardon from the capital that will let us return to our loved ones there.

YASUYORI: Therefore, we have had no occasion to get in touch with you. (*Both bow low*) But leaving that aside, what you still don't know, Lord Shunkan, is that we three friends have recently become four.

SHUNKAN: We've become four? Do you mean another exile from the capital has joined us?

YASUYORI (*Smiling*): No, no! Not at all! Lord Naritsune has fallen in love with a charming island diving girl and has taken her for his wife.

Naritsune makes an expression of bashfulness.

SHUNKAN (*Coming to life a bit*): He has? Wonderful, wonderful! Do you know this is the first time in three years any of us has uttered the word *love*? It also is the first time I've seen a smiling face. It reminds me of the love affair of the fabled Prince Yukihira, who fell in love with a fishergirl at Suma Beach.[4] I myself constantly long for my darling wife, Azumaya, whom I had to leave behind in the capital. Although she is my wife, it is as though she were my lover. So not only is the speaker in love, you see, but so is his listener. I beg you, then, to tell me your story.

CHANTER:

Implored to tell his tale
the Lord of Tamba's face reddens.

NARITSUNE (*Embarrassed*): The three of us share the same lot so there is no reason to conceal anything from one another. Thus I will tell you the story of my love for the humble diving girl, the vessel of all my delights.

CHANTER:

Though it embarrasses me to say

NARITSUNE: the girl I love is named Chidori. She is the daughter of a Kiri Island fisherman and works on the beach wearing a sea-stained robe, gathering in the seawater and drying it for its salt.

CHANTER:

When the tide is right,
she reveals her lovely body

Naritsune mimes the words of the narration. Rising on his right knee, he points off into the distance and slowly folds his arms across his body as if bashfully hiding his nakedness.

NARITSUNE:

as she takes a bucket and scythe

CHANTER:

and plunges into the bottomless depths
to gather many kinds of seaweed,
too busy even to keep her hair back with
a boxwood comb.

Naritsune mimes cutting seaweed and combing his hair.

NARITSUNE: In no time at all, the god of marriage swept down on this very island and caused us to fall in love. We are now living as man and wife in my humble cottage. Chidori has only the deepest feelings of devotion and love for me. She told me, in her charming island accent, that she is overwhelmed with gratitude

4. Ariwara no Yukihira (818–893?) was exiled to Suma, where he is said to have fallen in love. In the noh play *Matsukaze*, two local women love Yukihira.

for having been shown kindness and sympathy, though she is but a poor island girl. I have no family, she said, so I pray that my husband's good friend Yasuyori will be my elder brother and that Lord Shunkan will act as my father. I will be a most devoted daughter and sister in return, she said. As she spoke, the tears falling freely from her eyes, her charm was just like that of a woman from the capital. She begged us to take care of her.

Naritsune bows low, his head near the ground.

CHANTER:
Her words have penetrated to my very soul.
Hearing this tale, Lord Shunkan
is overcome with delight.

SHUNKAN: This is just wonderful! Your love story is fascinating yet tinged with pathos, dazzling yet commendable. Yours is a truly precious love. I want to meet this girl. Shall we go to your hut?

YASUYORI: No, no, that won't be necessary. She's come along with us to your place. Wait a moment.

He rises, crosses to the rampway, and beckons with his right hand. The wave drum patterns begin.

Chidori! Chidori! Please come here! Lord Shunkan wishes to meet you.
Come on over, Chidori! Chidori!

CHIDORI *(From the rear of the rampway)*: Coming![5]

CHANTER:
Chidori responds and comes
running through the weeds
carrying a basket of bamboo.

Chidori runs in along the rampway. Overcome by shyness, she turns around and runs out again. Yasuyori laughs. She soon returns, and this time Yasuyori stops her before she can flee again [figure 3.58]. He takes the rake, places it near one of the rocks, and resumes his former position. Chidori sits between him and Naritsune at right center and bows low.

Her beauty is such that,
though she be clad in rags,
it were as if her garments
were of silk and silver threads.
Why in the world was she born
a lowly maker of salt?

YASUYORI: Allow me to introduce Chidori.

SHUNKAN: I must say I have been quite impressed by all the charming things I've heard about you. You've already met with Yasuyori, I know, and I know also that you wish me to act as your father from this day forward. We three men are already virtually related. Since we are to be parent and child, from now on you are my daughter. If a pardon were to be granted to us, we four would return to

---

5. In the Zenshin troupe's production, male and female actors play Chidori in alternating performances. More conservative troupes do not permit women on stage.

the capital together; you would be acknowledged as the wife of Naritsune, lord of Tamba, and would wear long, trailing, scarlet hakama skirts, like any other noblewoman. But what I find terribly annoying is that even if we were to dig through all the rocks and earth on this island (*he looks around and makes grabbing gestures at the sand*), we would not find one drop of wine or even a cup to drink it from. After all, we should perform the congratulatory wedding rites.

FIGURE 3.58. Chidori enters to Yasuyori's summons. Her bright green kimono has an octopus design, and a seaweed motif decorates her pink obi, which is tied in front. Her wicker basket contains a bamboo tube and an abalone shell. The slatted windows of the music room are visible in the background. (Photo by Aoki Shinji.)

CHIDORI: Dear Lord Shunkan, if a lowly saltmaker like me were to wear long, scarlet skirts, she would surely be punished. (*Bows low quickly*) I am happy enough merely to be married to a gentleman from the capital. A sacred hermit lived for seven hundred years by drinking water in which chrysanthemums were floated.[6] (*Takes a bamboo tube from her basket*) We should follow his example and drink fresh water from an island stream as if it were wine. This abalone shell will serve as a winecup. (*Takes a shell from her basket and holds it out as if it were a cup*) We shall thus be parent and child from this day on. How delightful it will be to call each other "Father" and "Daughter."

She runs over to Shunkan, places the abalone shell and bamboo tube next to him, turns back, almost stumbles into the seated Naritsune, and sits at his right, very bashfully, her hand on his.

CHANTER:
The men all laugh at her
charming island accent.

YASUYORI: Congratulations! Congratulations! (*Rises*) Then I will act as go-between. (*Wave drum patterns during the following*) Naritsune, you must sit in the groom's seat. (*Takes Naritsune to stage left, then crosses to Chidori*) You, Chidori, must take the bridal seat.

Chidori faces upstage, removes her straw apron, and gives it to a stage assistant. Yasuyori takes her to the left, where she sits diagonally upstage of Naritsune.

We will have to skip a lot of the formalities, of course. As the groom's father-in-law, Shunkan, you take the seat of honor.

Yasuyori takes the abalone shell and hands it to Chidori. He mimes pouring water

6. Refers to the legend of Kikujidō, a page to King Mu during the Chou dynasty, who became a hermit after being banished and achieved immortality by drinking dew off chrysanthemums. The story is told in the noh play *Kikujido* and many other classical Japanese works.

FIGURE 3.59. Yasuyori uses a bamboo tube to pour "wine" into Chidori's abalone-shell wine cup, with Naritsune (right) and Shunkan awaiting their turns to drink in celebration of the wedding of Chidori and Naritsune. (Photo by Aoki Shinji.)

from the tube [figure 3.59], and she drinks it bashfully. She hands the cup to Naritsune, who also drinks. Yasuyori then takes the shell to Shunkan and pours for him.

CHANTER:
> The abalone shell is a cup of lapis
> lazuli
> as they pretend to be drinking
> wine.
> The three—no—four friends
> celebrate the nuptials.

Yasuyori gives a stage assistant the bamboo tube and abalone shell.

SHUNKAN: I will whet your appetites.

He nods to each side, picks up the pine branch lying nearby, and dusts it off on his hand and knee.[7]

CHANTER:
> Thoughts of their sulfur-belching island fade
> as their hearts drift to an enchanted world of make-believe.

The following is from a traditional wedding ceremony dance and song performed in noh style. It is derived from the play Shōjō. The movements are stately and ceremonious and the chanting deep and sonorous, although of course, the emaciated Shunkan can barely move or speak with any vigor. He begins to chant as he rises on his right knee, stumbles slightly, and with sliding steps moves slightly downstage.

SHUNKAN:
> They revel in the never-ceasing flow of wine
> from the inexhaustible wine fount.

He holds the branch out to the right, stumbles a step forward, raises the branch high, and then falls down on his back. He laughs delightedly, and the others laugh too and then bow low.

CHANTER:
> They all make merry.

Laughing, Yasuyori happens to look off into the distance.

YASUYORI: My god! There's a large boat out there. I've never seen it before. It's headed in this direction.

Shunkan shields his eyes with both hands as he looks off. All rise on their knees, looking off.

NARITSUNE: Maybe it's another exile.

---

7. Actors use a branch of *yatsude* (eight-fingered plant) or a tattered noh-style fan (*chūkei*) to perform the following dance. The Zenshin troupe replaces this dance with a lively one by Yasuyori using the bamboo tube and abalone shell.

SHUNKAN: No, no! Its sails are spread, and you can clearly see it's a ship from the capital.

YASUYORI: Look, look! It's coming closer and closer!

NARITSUNE: There's no doubt it's an official ship from the capital!

SHUNKAN: It's surely a reception boat!

CHIDORI: Look, look! It's almost here!

They form a tight group, and moving as a unit, they cross near the farthest downstage rock as if looking at the boat [figure 3.60]. They point to it and then go behind the rock and crouch there, out of sight, as a miniature boat moves slowly across the backdrop from right to left.[8] This is accompanied by drum music.

FIGURE 3.60. The three exiles and Chidori join hands as they watch the boat approaching their island. They follow an imaginary boat moving across the back and right side of the auditorium until a "real" boat appears at the back of the stage. (Photo by Aoki Shinji.)

CHANTER:

As they chatter in excitement,
a Kyoto government ship
makes its berth at the shore.

Several seconds after the miniature boat passes off to the left, the prow of a large wooden boat moves onstage from the wings at left. Only the prow is visible, but the impression is of the entire boat's presence [see figure 1.8]. As the boat rolls to a stop, five or six boatmen appear on the prow. One jumps off and ties the ship's thick rope to a rock. Several others lay a gangplank down to a rock and descend. They sit crosslegged at upstage right.

CHANTER:

The boat's anchor is dropped
at the dry and sandy beach.

A VOICE *(Offstage):* We have arrived at Devil Island.

VOICES *(Offstage):* At last!

CHANTER:

The Heike samurai Senoo Tarō Kaneyasu
descends from the boat
and calmly walks along the beach.

Senoo walks down the plank to the shore, followed by four men who stand in a row before the boatmen [figure 3.61].

SENOO *(Bellowing):* Hear ye! Hear ye! Are the exiles Naritsune, lord of Tamba, and Yasuyori, lord of Hei, sent here three years ago, present?

Senoo's four samurai sit on their haunches.

NARITSUNE *(As he appears from behind the rock):* I am Naritsune.

8. A variant no longer used was to have a small boat appear out in the audience, moving along the edge of the balcony seats.

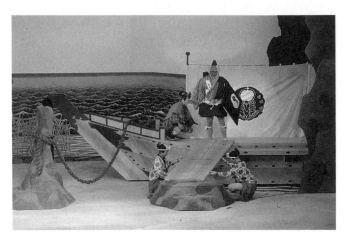

FIGURE 3.61. Senoo prepares to alight, with the pardon tucked into his kimono. He wears the highly stylized costume (*ryūjin-maki*) of a forceful samurai serving as an important envoy and also a curly hair wig (*chirichiri-katsura*) and "queue concealer" (*mage-kakeshi*) hat. Compare the envoy in the noh version in figure 2.26. (Photo by Aoki Shinji.)

YASUYORI (*Emerging in his turn*):
And I am Yasuyori.

SHUNKAN: And I, Shunkan, am here as well.

All bow low.

CHANTER:
They bow formally, their heads low.
Senoo takes a letter of pardon from his breast and reads it with great show of ceremony.

SENOO:
"Because of the recent birth of a son to their revered majesties, the Emperor and Empress,
a general amnesty has been declared throughout the land.
The two exiles to Devil Island, Naritsune, lord of Tamba, and

Yasuyori, lord of Hei,
are hereby ordered to leave their place of exile
and to return to the capital with all due haste!"
You have heard this from the imperial envoy
Senoo Tarō Kaneyasu!

During the reading, Shunkan, not hearing his name, lifts his head and crawls forward a bit.

CHANTER:
Even before the reading is completed,
the two stunned exiles
are groveling with thanks.

SHUNKAN: I beg to ask why the name of Shunkan was omitted from the reading?

SENOO: Be quiet, Shunkan! How dare you accuse a person such as myself of omitting your name? (*Walks heavily toward Shunkan*) If you think there is any other name than the two I read, you can look at this for yourself!

CHANTER:
Senoo thrusts the papers at Shunkan.

SHUNKAN: Let me see!

CHANTER:
Naritsune and Yasuyori also
marvel at this paper as Shunkan
reads it over and over,
this way and that.
Even when he reads the wrapping sheet,
no sign of Shunkan's name or title can be found.

Shunkan puts down the wrapping paper and then reads the sheet with the writing on it. He soon puts this down and lifts the wrapping paper, examining it carefully. He picks up the pardon again, his hand trembling, and holds the papers up to the light [figure 3.62].[9]

SHUNKAN: Nothing. (*Pause*) Nothing. (*Pause*) Nothing, nothing.

He speaks these words faster and faster, his voice fading in a pathetic sob.

CHANTER:
  Shunkan faces Senoo.

Shunkan throws down the papers and holds them there with his right hand as he addresses Senoo. The others all are bowing low.

FIGURE 3.62. Shunkan examines the pardon and its wrapping paper, searching for his name. Compare the noh version in figure 2.27. Chidori remains behind a rock at stage right. (Photo by Aoki Shinji.)

SHUNKAN: I wish to say something to Lord Senoo. Only the names of Naritsune and Yasuyori appear on this official pardon (*points to the names*), but neither my name nor my title is here. Perhaps it is because Lord Kiyomori[10] forgot to add it, or maybe the scribe merely made an error.

SENOO: Shut up, Shunkan! You have been ordered to remain behind alone as the overseer of this island.

SHUNKAN (*Stunned*): What? Overseer of this island?

SENOO: That is the order of Lord Kiyomori!

SHUNKAN: We have committed the same crime and have been exiled to the same place. We should then receive the same pardon!

CHANTER:
  Only two of us have been pardoned
  and I alone have slipped
  through the net of Buddha's grace.
  Even Buddha's great love and mercy are discriminatory!

Shunkan slaps the papers.

SHUNKAN: If I had killed myself long ago, I would not have to face this grief I feel.

Shunkan picks up the pardon from the floor and holds it out to his friends, his hands trembling. He grabs the wrapping paper with his left hand and angrily crushes the papers together into a ball. Senoo comes over and grabs them away from him. He puts them in his kimono sleeve. Shunkan, wailing, lies in a heap on the ground.

CHANTER:
  He loudly bemoans his lengthened life,
  a life of misery and grief.
  A voice is now heard from the boat.

9. This is the high point of Shunkan's role. Actors sometimes play it more simply, looking at the papers and weeping or demanding the wrapping paper separately and carefully comparing the two.

10. Taira no Kiyomori (1118–1181) was the head of the Taira clan during the peak of its domination of Japanese political life in the last decades of the Heian period.

TANZAEMON: Lord Shunkan. Cease your weeping! It is I, Tanzaemon Motoyasu!
CHANTER:
With these words, Tanzaemon now enters.

Wave drum patterns. Tanzaemon walks to the prow of the boat and down the gangplank. He bows to Senoo. Four of his retainers walk in unison to stage left and sit on their right knees.

TANZAEMON: I should have announced it earlier, but I have held back until now so that you may know to your very marrow the beneficence and goodwill of Lord Shigemori, councillor to Lord Kiyomori.[11] Therefore, listen to me carefully.
CHANTER:
From his breast fold
he removes a document.
TANZAEMON:
"Hear ye! Hear ye! Be it known that
Lord Shigemori, keeper of the privy seal,
out of his great compassion
has seen fit to allow the exiled prisoner,
Lord Shunkan, to return as far as Bizen,
though not to the capital itself.
Signed, Noritsune, Governor of Noto,
Nephew to Lord Kiyomori."
CHANTER:
Even before the reading is over—
SHUNKAN *(Joyfully)*: What? All three of us are pardoned?

Shunkan tries to move forward to the left but is too overcome to make any progress. He crawls a step or two, then his friends come to help him, supporting him as, in time to the shamisen, he struggles several steps to Tanzaemon [figure 3.63].

TANZAEMON: Indeed!

He turns the paper so that the exiles can see the writing.

SHUNKAN: Ah! Ah! Ah!
CHANTER:
He scrapes his head against the sand
bowing deeper and deeper,
overcome with tears of joy.

Tanzaemon folds the papers and inserts them in his kimono.

CHANTER:
Tanzaemon faces Senoo.
TANZAEMON: We have no reason to remain here any longer. Let us embark and leave this island quickly.
SENOO: Fortunately the wind is just right.
TANZAEMON: Attention! The guards will please escort the pardoned exiles onto the boat!

11. Shigemori (1137–1179), Kiyomori's son, often attempted to moderate his father's excesses.

BOATMEN: Aye, aye!

TANZAEMON'S RETAINERS: Come now!

ALL THE RETAINERS: To the boat!

Tanzaemon turns to board the boat. The three exiles and Chidori form a line at right center to go on board, Shunkan at the head.

CHANTER:

Exchanging joyful words,
the pardoned company approach
the boarding plank.
But Senoo now raises his voice
to stop them.

As the foursome moves left, Senoo steps in front of them and strikes Shunkan with his fan. Two cracks of

FIGURE 3.63. Shunkan, supported by his friends, moves toward Tanzaemon, who is refined looking in a light blue envoy costume (*ryūjin-maki*) and black lacquered hat (*samurai eboshi*), with light makeup. (Photo by Aoki Shinji.)

the wooden clappers accent the blow, and the line instantly falls in disarray to the ground. Tanzaemon, who had put one foot on the rock under the plank, turns and moves to the right of the gangplank.

SENOO: Hold it, you shabby creatures! (*Addressing Chidori*) If you're seeing some-one off, you can go no farther, since you're not fit to board this boat. You'd better get out of here right now if you know what's good for you!

NARITSUNE: No! It's all right! Leave her alone! During my period of exile I have become greatly indebted to this girl and was recently wed to her. I have made an unbreakable promise to her that if I were allowed to return to the capital, she could return there with me. Please be kind enough to take us with you to the first port of call. We will be eternally indebted to you for this kindness.

SENOO (*Raising his fan threateningly*): Shut up! Shut up! Shut up! The very idea of taking this woman along in addition to you exiles is preposterous! Men! Get rid of this filthy creature!

SENOO'S RETAINERS: Yes, sir!

CHANTER: A jangle of harsh sounds is heard.

Senoo's men cross behind the exiles and form a wall, standing with hands spread apart, fingers splayed, legs wide. Naritsune turns to them with outstretched arms to keep them back and then takes Chidori in his arms.

NARITSUNE: Wait, wait, wait! Wait! Since you refuse to honor my request, I can do nothing. Therefore, you must leave me behind on this island and return to the capital without me. (*Shunkan looks at him*) My friends, Shunkan and Yasuyori, please board the boat.

As he speaks, Chidori wipes away her tears.

SHUNKAN: No, no! We have no intention of leaving this place without you.

YASUYORI: As Shunkan has said, we are one and will return only as one.

SHUNKAN, YASUYORI, and NARITSUNE: We won't go! We won't go! We won't go! (*The four huddle together, bent low, their heads near one another in the "shell" pattern.*)

CHANTER:

They set their resolute wills
against Senoo and Tanzaemon.

TANZAEMON (*Approaching Senoo*): Lord Senoo, don't you see that this sort of action on your part will constitute an impediment to the prayers offered in the name of the imperial infant? Although you won't permit the girl aboard the boat, perhaps a stay here of one or two days will soften your heart, and you will allow everyone to embark. Since this will be an act of charity on your part, it will undoubtedly have a strong effect on the prayers for the emperor's baby.

SENOO (*In disgust*): Aaach! That would be an act of insubordination on the part of an official! I am not happy about the fact that Lord Noto altered our official document of passage so that the number two would be a three, but by whose permission can we further alter it to a four? Until we hand over the exiles to Lord Kiyomori, they are my responsibility. I don't give a damn if they say they won't board! Yai, yai, yai, yai!

He walks to the group and strikes Shunkan lightly on the shoulder with his fan. Shunkan falls forward, and the "shell" breaks to the right, in a line. Senoo stands over Shunkan.

Shunkan, I'll bet you didn't know that Lord Kiyomori had your wife, Azumaya, killed for refusing his advances, did you?

SHUNKAN: Wha . . . ?

SENOO (*Posing menacingly*): Her head was chopped clean off!

SHUNKAN: What are you saying? My wife, Azumaya—I . . .

SENOO (*Violently*): And there's even more to learn! The hated priest Shunkan will be beheaded in the capital like a common criminal. (*Strikes Shunkan sharply on the back of the neck with his fan*) Take these three prisoners and put them in the bottom of the ship. Tie them so they can't move! That's an order!

Everyone rises. The large group of boatmen go off to the left, above the boat.

CHANTER:

The four retainers roughly
thrust Chidori aside.
The pardoned exiles are brusquely
led aboard the ship.

The retainers attempt to lead the exiles to the boat and force Chidori to remain behind.

TANZAEMON: Although I feel great pity for you, young lady, your presence on the boat will simply cause too many problems when we reach the checkpoint for inspection. After we return to the capital, Lord Naritsune will petition for your person, and I am sure a boat will be sent to bring you back. But for now, you simply must be patient.

SENOO: See here, Tanzaemon. We are officials entrusted with the simple task of bringing back these exiles. Even if we should see the suffering and misery of others, we must act as if we were blind and ignorant!

TANZAEMON: That is simply too cruel a way to be.

SENOO: I know neither compassion nor sympathy. Entrusted with an important mission, I may not permit my private feelings to occupy my time. Fast now, make it fast!

CHANTER:
Pressed to embark, the kindly Tanzaemon
resignedly boards the boat.

Chidori breaks loose from her guard and falls at Senoo's side, taking his hand, pleading. He jabs her sharply in the side with his elbow, laughs cruelly, and boards the boat.

Kudoki   *Chidori, who now has the stage to herself, moves in a rhythmic dance mime to the chant and the shamisen music. She struggles slowly to her feet and then falls in a heap before the hut. She rises and falls several times during the following passage, weeping and wiping her tears with her sleeve.*

Left alone, a pitiful figure, on the beach
the friendless Chidori, bewailing her lot,
slowly lifts her tear-stained face.

CHIDORI: A samurai is said to know the meaning of compassion.

CHANTER:
It is a lie! It is a falsehood!

CHIDORI:
There are no devils on Devil Island.

CHANTER:
The devils all are in the capital.
From the very day we first exchanged vows

CHIDORI:
wishing a letter of pardon from Kyoto

CHANTER:
I worshiped the sun and the moon

Chidori makes a praying gesture.

and fervently prayed to the dragon god,
not because I wanted

CHIDORI:
to return with my husband to the capital
to live a life of splendor,
but because I wanted to sleep
with him there at least one night.

CHANTER:
That would have been
my sole delight.

CHIDORI (*Wiping her tears*): You evil devil! You fiend! Will one girl make your flimsy boat too heavy? Have you no eyes to see the misery of others? Have you no ears with which to hear? Hear me! I want to go on board. I want to go!

CHANTER:

She screams and cries,
stamps her feet and rolls in the sand,

Chidori climbs up a small rock and stretches for a glimpse of the passengers.

wailing and weeping shamelessly
regardless of who may be watching.

Chidori gets off the rock and runs around on the shore, seeking a glimpse of Naritsune on the boat. She removes a small towel (tenugui) from her obi and sinks to her knees and weeps, pressing the towel to her face, then tying it around her waist above her obi.

She is a diving girl,
so a one- or two-league swim
is not unthinkable for her.
But even she cannot swim
the hundreds and hundreds of leagues
from here to the capital.

Chidori rises on one knee, her hands outstretched, making light swimming movements. She makes a gesture of counting on the fingers of both hands. She rises, moves about with difficulty, falls against the hut's post, and weeps.

CHIDORI: I will beat my head against this rock and end my life

CHANTER:

dying for Lord Naritsune.

CHIDORI:

Unable to bear parting from my lord,
I will pray to Buddha for salvation.
Dear God, please remember this poor island maid.

She bows low before the hut, faces front, and wipes her tears as the wave drum patterns begin.

CHANTER:

Seeing her about to die, Lord Shunkan cries.

SHUNKAN *(Coming off the boat)*: No, no! Wait, Chidori, wait!

CHANTER:

Stumbling, staggering, Lord Shunkan,
with great difficulty,
leaves the boat and goes to the girl.

Shunkan falls on his way to her, then takes her left hand. She struggles, trying to flee. They sink to their knees.

SHUNKAN *(Desperately)*: Board the boat! Go to the capital! Board the boat and go to Kyoto! I have been told that my darling wife, Azumaya, was slain after refusing Lord Kiyomori's advances. Now that my beloved is gone, what joy can I find in Kyoto where I would have to view the moon and flowers with only myself for company? Rather than face grief again in the capital, I will remain here on the island, and you will board the boat in my place. The number of people listed on the pardon will remain the same, so there will be no trouble at the checkpoint. The envoys will not be doubted. Please board the boat and leave me, Shunkan—who is all alone in the world—here on this island where I will devote myself to Buddha. Please board the boat!

He rises, pulls her a few steps to the left, then they sink to their knees again.

CHANTER:
    His tears flow copiously
    as he takes the girl's hand
    and leads her to the boat.
SHUNKAN: Honored sirs, I beg you to grant my request. Please allow this girl to embark with you.
CHANTER:
    Hearing this humble plea
    Senoo boils over with rage
    and leaps down from the boat.

Wave drum patterns. Senoo, fuming, pushes the couple roughly.

SENOO: No! Never, never! You dumb priest! When did you crawl down there? How dare you ask me to let this girl go on board? What use would the pardon or we envoys be if we merely did as we pleased? Aach! You're too dumb to even understand!
SHUNKAN *(On his knees):* Sa, sa, sa! I, Shunkan, who have nothing left to live for, am asking you to have some pity! Leave me here and take this girl in my place!
SENOO: How dare you? You impudent, conniving priest! Your pleas are useless! If you want to die, you'll have to do it in the capital!
CHANTER:
    He kicks and tramples on the priest.
SHUNKAN: Then no matter what I say
SENOO: I will refuse!

As the wave drum patterns begin, Shunkan starts to crawl on his knees closer to Senoo, as if praying for leniency, his hands pressed together.

SHUNKAN: Even if I beg you
SENOO: Shut your mouth!
SHUNKAN: for compassion!
CHANTER:
    Shunkan stealthily makes his way
    to the side of Senoo, where his
    sword can be reached.
    As quick as lightning
    he pulls it out
    and wounds the startled envoy.

At the moment that Shunkan strikes Senoo's right shoulder with the short sword he has stolen,[12] two seagulls rise from behind the hut and fly off into the upper reaches of the stage. They are rigged on a wire that is almost invisible from the auditorium. Shunkan falls weakly near Chidori. A stage assistant enters to aid Senoo, who has fallen downstage of the rock. Senoo drops his fan and removes his sandals. He sits cross-legged as the assistant removes his outer jacket and drops his overkimono from his shoulders, revealing a yellow underkimono with a piece of red cloth sewn on the right shoulder to signify blood. The assistant removes the black lacquer cap from Senoo's topknot, revealing a bushy white topknot beneath. Senoo places his left hand on his right shoulder as if in pain.

A SENOO RETAINER *(Appearing on the boat):* Hey! The exile is running riot!
ALL ON BOAT: Part them!
CHANTER:
　　Tanzaemon speaks amid the confusion.

Tanzaemon appears on the boat with his retainers, who line up in a row behind him.

TANZAEMON: Hold it! This is strictly their affair. Every detail of this quarrel between the exile and the envoy must be ascertained and reported to the authorities. No one must interfere on either of their behalfs!
SENOO: Wait, wait! What are you saying, Tanzaemon! Why do you side with this criminal and refuse to help me?
TANZAEMON: My duties extend only to the release of the exiles. I have no other duties. I am just a bystander here.[13]
SENOO: Well, let that be an end to it, then.
CHANTER:
　　Senoo, taken by surprise, rights himself
　　and draws his other sword.

Senoo draws his long sword and crawls toward Shunkan.

　　He swings his sword as best he can
　　but staggers like a willow on unsteady legs.

The two opponents cross swords at the center, struggle to their feet, and fall down. They finally manage to rise with locked swords. They fight, and Shunkan falls.

　　Shunkan totters like a withered pine.
　　Pitting all their strength against each other,
　　the two antagonists breathlessly face
　　the moment of truth
　　as they stagger to and fro
　　on the strand.
　　Unable to bear the strain,

---

12. Actors are divided on whether Shunkan should take Senoo's short sword or the long sword.

13. Tanzaemon justifies his actions using the same logic Senoo used earlier in the play. This is an example of ironic parroting (*ōmu*), a conventional device of kabuki actors, but it does not occur in Chikamatsu's original play for puppets.

Chidori, too, strikes out, but Shunkan's angry voice cuts in.

Senoo is about to strike at the fallen man, but Chidori knocks over Senoo with her rake [figure 3.64].[14]

SHUNKAN: Get away! Get away! I'll consider you my enemy if you so much as hand me a stick! If you interfere, I'll never forgive you!

CHANTER:
Startled by his harshness
Chidori withdraws her proffered aid.

Chidori pouts and shuffles away. Once again, Shunkan and Senoo cross swords. Then Chidori interferes and parts them with her rake.

FIGURE 3.64. Coming to Shunkan's aid, Chidori strikes Senoo with her rake. (Photo by Aoki Shinji.)

The weakened priest, bloody, worn from hunger,
slashes out valiantly as he staggers
and falters in the sand.
The heavy sword hangs loosely
in his tired hands.
The flying sand clogs their lungs,
and danger seems an equal threat to both.

Senoo knocks down Shunkan and stands over him, about to kill his adversary.

Finally, Senoo, used to looking down on men
as though he were an eagle,
is felled by a fatal blow

Chidori tosses sand in Senoo's eyes. Blinded, he falters, and the fallen Shunkan thrusts home. Senoo grimaces and then falls slowly backward.

as the pitiless waves
beat here and there
upon the shore.
As Shunkan raises his blade
to give the coup de grâce

TANZAEMON: No! Wait a moment! You have clearly won the battle. It would be a mistake to give him the finishing blow. It would only increase the number of charges against you and invalidate your pardon. It is not worth the trouble.

SHUNKAN: It is all one with me, since I wish to remain on this island.

TANZAEMON: How can I let you? Leaving you behind would simply negate the kindness shown you by Lords Shigemori and Noto. It would also mar the

---

14. In other versions, she throws her apron over Senoo's head, tosses her basket in his face, or bites his hand.

FIGURE 3.65. Shunkan prepares to kill Senoo, an act that will make it impossible for him to return to the capital but will allow Chidori to go in his place. (Photo by Aoki Shinji.)

celebrations for the imperial infant. I would be held responsible for such an offense. Moreover, if we don't have three exiles on board, we will surely have difficulties with the inspectors at the checkpoint.

SHUNKAN: I understand, I understand. But if this girl boards with Yasuyori and Naritsune, there will be no discrepancy in the number of passengers, and you can't possibly have any trouble at the checkpoint. As for receiving the clemency of Lords Shigemori and Noto for my former offense, I will negate it by killing this envoy and thus become guilty of a new offense.

CHANTER:
I will once again become
an exile on Devil Island[15]

SHUNKAN:
and we'll pass beyond the bounds
of the great imperial amnesty.
Not a bit of blame
will fall to you.

He places his left hand on Senoo's breast to steady himself [figure 3.65].

CHANTER:
Making firm his heart,
Shunkan delivers the mortal blow.

SHUNKAN: Senoo! (*Pause*) Take for your sins

CHANTER: my vengeful sword!

Shunkan thrusts the sword into Senoo's throat; Senoo's arms and legs flail up for a moment and then lie still. The wooden clappers accent the movement. Five boatmen enter and remove the body, one taking the sword with him. Shunkan falls to his face weeping. Naritsune and Yasuyori run onstage aboard the boat and kneel at Tanzaemon's left.

All those on board
burst into tears.
Naritsune and Yasuyori
join their hands in prayer.

15. Some actors perform the Kan'u pose here. This pose has Shunkan thrusting the point of his sword into the ground, one foot extended, while gripping his beard in one hand. The pose is named after the famous Chinese general Kuan Yü and is borrowed from the play *The Battles of Coxinga.*

Chidori, hearing and seeing
all that has transpired
is overcome with grief.

CHIDORI:

Husband and wife will be
together in the next world.
Therefore, I will remain alone on
this bitter island, never forgetting
you. But I will not brazenly board
the boat in your stead. Farewell
everyone, farewell!

*She tries to leave, but Shunkan holds
her back. He is on his knees, and she
sinks to her knees beside him.*

SHUNKAN (*Holding her left hand as
she weeps*): Wait a moment!
Listen to me. I have already
passed through the three evil

FIGURE 3.66. Shunkan and Tanzaemon raise their hands in farewell. In this production, the rope is stretched across the stage and then drawn up, reminiscent of the practice in noh. In other performances, it is stowed away immediately. (Photo by Aoki Shinji.)

hells—the hell of hunger, the hell of battle—as you've just seen—and the hell
of brimstone, which is always being burned on this island. I will surely be
given salvation in the next world. The boat in which Shunkan will ride will be
Buddha's noble craft bringing me to the shores of enlightenment.

CHANTER:

I have no desire to take a boat
back to the floating world.

SHUNKAN: Please leave me here and board the boat, quickly, quickly!

CHANTER:

He takes her by the sleeve,
pulls her by the hand,
and puts her on the royal boat.

*Wave drum patterns. Chidori boards the boat and sits between Naritsune and
Yasuyori.*

Naritsune and his bride,
Yasuyori, too,

YASUYORI:

are loath to leave you,

NARITSUNE and YASUYORI:

Lord Shunkan.

TANZAEMON:

Keep up your spirits!

SHUNKAN (*Standing at center stage, weakly*): Farewell!

A boatman appears, unties the rope, and pulls up the gangplank.

CHANTER:

Farewell tears cloud their eyes.

FIGURE 3.67. The waves (ground cloths) pursue Shunkan as he starts to climb the peak. The revolving stage has begun to rotate, moving the rock to the foreground. Compare this with figure 3.56. (Photo by Aoki Shinji.)

The rope is loosened,
and the oars emerge.
On board a fan is raised,
on shore a hand.

Tanzaemon opens his fan and slowly raises it aloft. Shunkan raises his hand in response. Naritsune, Yasuyori, and Chidori weep. The boat slowly begins to move off to the left [figure 3.66].

SHUNKAN: In the next life!
NARITSUNE and YASUYORI: In the next life!
CHANTER:
Their calls grow faint
as a heartless wind
fills out the sails
and pushes the boat
farther and farther
into the offing.

Drum and shamisen music from the music room. Shunkan watches the ship depart, climbing a small rock to see it more clearly.

Soon, the ship is lost to sight.
Only a glimpse of it
can now and then be caught
beyond the rolling waves.
Though he is resolved to stay,
his heart, after all, is just
like yours or mine.

Shunkan goes to the front of the stage, waving and calling, "Farewell, farewell." The gray ground cloth on the rampway is removed, revealing a wave-patterned cloth covering half its length. Shunkan steps onto the rampway, and the wave cloth, pulled by unseen strings, moves toward the stage. When it comes to his feet, Shunkan stops (see figure 1.7). The waves pursue him, chasing him back to the stage where the ground cloths have also been whisked away to reveal waves. The revolving stage begins to move so that the large rock that was upstage right moves into the foreground [figure 3.67].

He climbs up to the highest point on the shore
and, waving, stretches his frame
as tall as he can,
then breaks down, weeping,
in the pure white sand.
Though he burns with longing
and shouts with despair,
not a soul is there to comfort him.

Only the cries of the gulls
and the wild geese flying
    overhead
answer his lonely calls.
His only friends are the *chidori*,
the plovers, which he lures to
    his side.
The tide rushes in to cut him off
    from those
who have left him behind.

*Shunkan struggles up the large rock
as the stage continues to move until
the rock is at stage center. He stumbles but clings to a vine of ivy. He
turns to gaze off into the distance,
holding the ivy over his shoulder,
then pulls himself to the top. He
comes up behind the small pine tree
and strains for a glimpse of the boat
through the branches. But Shunkan
leans too heavily on a branch, and it
suddenly snaps off. He falls forward,
lifts his hands, waves, and calls
"Ahoy! Ahoy!" [figure 3.68]*

His sleeves are drenched
    by his falling tears.

*The rock moves forward, the lights
dim, and Shunkan is in the spotlight.
He stops calling, lowers his hand, and
sinks down. All hope has fled as he
becomes aware of his real loneliness.
The final crack of the wooden clappers sounds. Wave drum patterns combine with the flute's plaintive notes as the
curtain closes.*

FIGURE 3.68. The kabuki and bunraku versions of Shunkan watching
the ship disappear with the other exiles on it. Shunkan is on the top of
the rock, which has now been turned to face the audience. The specialized puppet head is called Shunkan. (Photos by Aoki Shinji.)

Suma Bay

A kabuki adaptation of a scene from act 2 of
Ichinotani futaba gunki by Namiki Senryū

Translated by James R. Brandon

The death of Atsumori, described in *The Tale of the Heike*, is depicted in both noh and kōwaka (see part 2). The noh features the ghost of Atsumori; his killer, Kumagai[1] turned priest, is the agent who allows the ghost to appear and speeds him toward enlightenment. In the kōwaka, Atsumori as a young hero dies bravely in a battle described at some length. The story then shifts to Kumagai and his attempts to atone for killing Atsumori. The emphasis shifts almost entirely to Kumagai in the puppet version, which was adapted for kabuki. Kumagai is now considered one of kabuki's greatest roles: performing it is a landmark in an actor's career.

Namiki Senryū wrote the first three acts of the puppet version of *The Chronicle of the Battle of Ichinotani* (Ichinotani futaba gunki) shortly before his death in 1751. His colleagues wrote two additional acts, enabling the play to open in Osaka at the end of that year. The puppet play ran for twelve months, and a kabuki version was staged in both Edo and Osaka in 1752. Acts 2 and 3, which tell a complete story in themselves, are the only ones usually performed in either genre today. Act 3, "Kumagai's Camp" (Kumagai jinya), is considered one of the great tragic scenes in kabuki.

Nakamura Utaemon III (1778–1838) is credited with creating the definitive kabuki version of Kumagai when he added new performance techniques (*kata*) to his 1831 production, but Ichikawa Danjūrō VII (1791–1859) and Ichikawa Danjūrō IX (1838–1903) created different forms that also are still used. In performing a text similar to the puppet version, kabuki performers have adapted several of the puppets' performance practices. They create perspective, for example, by using small figures (child actors) to present Kumagai and Atsumori fighting in the distance and large figures (adult actors) when they return to the shore (figure 3.69).

1. In the noh and the kōwaka versions, the name is pronounced Kumagae.

Although the question of whom one should consider a friend is common to all the theatrical versions of Atsumori's death, the ramifications of the question are quite different. In the noh play, Kumagai the enemy in battle becomes Renshō the friend in Buddhist law sometime after Atsumori's death. *Ichinotani futaba gunki* adds an entirely new dimension, a complicated web of social relations involving a favorite Tokugawa-period ploy or plot (*shukō*), the substitution of one's own child for a socially "more important" child. Essential to understanding the pathos of the scene translated here is the knowledge that Kumagai has smuggled the real Atsumori off the battlefield and that the "Atsumori" depicted here is his own son Kojirō in disguise. In the following act Kumagai retells the story of Atsumori's death yet again (this time in a seated mime that is one of the highlights of the play) and then shows the head of "Atsumori" to his master, his own wife, and the real Atsumori's mother—all of whom must pretend that things are what they seem. This is more than enough reason for Kumagai to become Renshō the priest.

FIGURE 3.69. To create a sense of perspective, the distant figure (Atsumori in the ocean) is played by a child actor on a small horse, whereas the role of Kumagai, nearer the audience, is played by an adult. Compare figure 3.72. (Photo by Aoki Shinji.)

One of the visual highlights of the Suma Bay scene is the use of horses, each created by two men who provide the four feet. In the kabuki theater, intense emotion is generated by the skilled kabuki actor as he very slowly and silently loads Atsumori's armor and head onto his horse. This section is much briefer in the puppet theater, since it is impossible for a puppet to express so much silent emotion. In both theaters the head is an important prop, one that is cradled but not seen by Atsumori's blind and dying lover Princess Tamaori and tenderly held by Kojirō's father Kumagai.

Japanese texts of the play are available in Atsumi 1928 and Toita 1955. The translator also consulted the annotations in the puppet version in Yūda 1965. The stage directions are primarily from performances at the Kabukiza in February 1967 and the National Theater in February 1968. The editor abbreviated and slightly revised the stage directions. The scene first appeared in Brandon 1975, along with the first scene of act 2 and all of act 3. Act 3 explains the elaborate network of relationships leading to Kumagai's substitution of his own child for Atsumori.

CHARACTERS

CHARACTERS

HIRAYAMA: a Genji warrior
KUMAGAI: commander of the Genji forces
ATSUMORI: commander of the Taira forces (actually Kumagai's son Kojirō
    dressed as Atsumori)
PRINCESS TAMAORI: Atsumori's lover
Soldiers

MUSICIANS

A gidayū chanter and a shamisen player (*chobo*), at stage left, veiled by a
    bamboo screen
Music-room musicians, at stage right, hidden in the geza

ACT 2, Scene 2

Suma Bay

As the large drum plays wave patterns (nami oto), *and small drums and cymbals play
"battle alarm"* (tōyose), *stage assistants place straw, rocks, and clumps of rushes and
grass in front of the curtain to indicate the edge of the sea. The drum music swells and
stops. Silence. The stage is empty. The gidayū shamisen player, seated at stage left on
a second level hidden behind a bamboo blind, begins a plaintive melody.*

CHANTER (*Seated with the shamisen player, singing plaintively*): Yearning for the
    sight of Prince Atsumori, distraught on the beach at Suma Bay—

The large drum plays wave patterns; the hand drums, mountain echo patterns
(kodama). *Princess Tamaori enters along the raised rampway through the audience,
looking pale and distraught and moving lifelessly. She wears a scarlet kimono and
long red skirts. Her kimono is off the right shoulder, indicating her distress. She
carries a spear and trails a purple cloak behind her.*

    —Princess Tamaori, with tear-soaked sleeves, a sharp dagger near her breast,
    wanders here and there in the spring breeze, beneath the hazy moon.
TAMAORI (*Poses at the seven-three position and then moves onto the main stage*):
    Lord Atsumori, where are you, where are you?
CHANTER: She searches about her. Suddenly, the vague form of a man appears
    silhouetted against the early eastern clouds. It is the warrior Hirayama, fleeing
    along a mountain trail that leads to Suma Bay. He sees Princess Tamaori.

Holding a drawn sword, Hirayama rushes on from stage left to fast, continuous (bata-
bata) *clapper beats. The music stops. Seeing the princess, he sheathes his sword.*

HIRAYAMA (*Gloating*): Can it be Princess Tamaori? This is a lucky meeting!

To loud double (batan) *clapper beats, he seizes her by the sleeve [figure 3.70]. Soft
gidayū shamisen music plays.*

From the first, when I fell in love with you at the capital, you dazzled my eyes. Sleeping or awake I could not forget you until, unable to contain myself, I spoke to your father, Tokitada, who promised you to me in marriage. Now, praise the gods, I have you and will make you my wife. Come.

CHANTER (*Singing to a shamisen accompaniment*): Although he takes her hand, she shakes him off.

Hirayama seizes her hand. To sharp double clapper beats, she frees herself and backs away. The gidayū shamisen music continues.

TAMAORI (*Innocently*): Do not speak so. Whether or not my father gave permission, I am pledged to Atsumori unto our second lifetimes.[2] We are searching for each other now. Should he die, I will die with him. Do not interfere.

CHANTER: Turning to go, she is stopped.

Hirayama crudely steps on the hem of her kimono.

FIGURE 3.70. In *Suma Bay*, Princess Tamaori, searching for her lover Atsumori, is accosted by Hirayama. The right sleeves of her outer kimono have been removed to indicate her distraught state of mind. (Photo by Aoki Shinji.)

HIRAYAMA: Ha! Search for Atsumori as much as you want! Look for him at the bottom of the ocean; you won't find where he's gone!

TAMAORI (*Frightened*): Oh, and why?

HIRAYAMA (*Smiling*): Because Atsumori has just been killed by me.

TAMAORI: Ahh! Atsumori killed, you say?

HIRAYAMA: He is.

TAMAORI: Ahhhh! (*She falls back, presses her hand to her breast, and poses.*)

CHANTER (*Quietly, to a shamisen accompaniment*): Delicate, the princess sinks beneath her grief. Unaware of others' eyes, she raises her voice in tearful cries and falls prostrate upon the ground.

Head down, she weeps, then suddenly pulls a small dagger from her obi and rises.

TAMAORI: Prepare yourself, enemy of my husband!

CHANTER (*Rapidly*): When she declares "enemy of my husband," Hirayama seizes her wrist.

She tries to cut Hirayama, striking left and right to double clapper beats, but he easily avoids her weak movements, then seizes her wrist with his left hand and puts his right threateningly on the hilt of his sword. The gidayū shamisen music continues.

HIRAYAMA (*Harshly*): You! Do you try to oppose me? I should show you no

2. The ties between parent and child were commonly believed to last only one lifetime, those between husband and wife, two.

mercy! (*Laughs*) My, the softness of your hand is just what I expected! You misunderstand me, after all. Change your affections completely, yield, and I will cherish you as my wife. Well, Princess? Will you have me? Will you? (*He presses her hand to his cheek, then, moving behind her, tries to press his cheek against hers.*

CHANTER (*To plaintive shamisen music*): Honeyed words, "will you, will you?" draw tears of anger.

TAMAORI (*Breaks away and kneels*): Ahh! To speak of yielding myself to a detestable samurai, who in normal times would not even dare approach me, is revolting. You are loathsome to me!

CHANTER (*To fast shamisen accompaniment*): Again she slashes, but he seizes and holds her fast.

HIRAYAMA (*Matter-of-factly*): So. Will you become my wife?

Kuriage

TAMAORI: Ah . . . ?

HIRAYAMA: Do you hate me?

TAMAORI: Ah . . . ?

BOTH (*Alternately faster and faster until they speak simultaneously*): Ah, ah, ah, ah!

HIRAYAMA: Say you hate me and I'll kill you. Well? Well?

Coldly he throws her to the ground, unsheathes his sword, and poses—his back to the audience, heels together, and sword upraised—in a formal set pose to triple (battari) clapper beats as the shamisen plays plaintively in the background.

TAMAORI (*Weeping*): Kill me if you are such a beast. Oh, is there no one who will slay this person for me?

CHANTER: She is piteous in her agony; Hirayama's strong-willed anger swells up.

HIRAYAMA: Agh, hateful bitch! On top of rejecting me, you spew out insults! It would be intolerable to let you live, watching you bloom for another man. You'll see what my vengeance is for being cruelly tormented!

The large drum plays swelling wave patterns. In desperation Tamaori rises and slashes to double clapper beats.

CHANTER: As the raised sword is plunged through her breast

With a single stroke, Hirayama drives the sword into her body. She gasps and staggers.

a single gasp of agony! From the rear, battle cries!

Shouts mingle with "battle alarm" on the large drum and cymbals. Panic-stricken, Hirayama throws the princess into rushes at the side of the stage and runs onto the rampway to loud double clapper beats. He holds the naked blade of his sword in front of him and assumes a strong pose to triple clapper beats.

Without a backward glance he runs away.

To accelerating drum and clapper beats, Hirayama rushes off. A stage assistant, dressed in black, unobtrusively removes the spear and dagger that Tamaori dropped. The wave patterns swell, and the clackers beat sharply. The wave curtain falls and is whisked away by stage assistants, revealing Suma Bay framed by towering cliffs on either side. Small pine trees, rocks, and clumps of grass edge the water. The deep blue ocean extends as far as the eye can see. The stage is empty.

Issei *Noh-style music with flute and drum accompaniment.*

CHORUS *(from the music room)*: "And then the entire Heike clan rushed to the water's edge just in time to put out to sea: first the emperor's ship and then the ships of warriors soon had sailed far into the distance."³

Shura-ba *Sung to wave patterns and shamisen accompaniment.*

CHANTER: The enemy has slipped away down the road, and Prince Atsumori hurries to inform his father, Tsunemori, who is aboard the emperor's ship.

"Atsumori" moves down the rampway astride his horse. To the accompaniment of the large drum's wave patterns, the noh drums' hurried entrance patterns (kakeiri), and the gidayū shamisen, Atsumori circles the stage looking for his father. The horse, played by two actors, prances and paws the earth. A flotilla of ships appears on the horizon. Atsumori spurs his horse into the water, and the horse, neck outstretched as if swimming, carries its rider through the "ocean" toward the imperial ship and out of sight at stage right. Atsumori, now played by a child actor on a toy horse, reenters swimming toward the boats, giving the impression of being far out to sea.

CHANTER: And from the rear Kumagai Jirō Naozane—
KUMAGAI *(From offstage at the end of rampway)*: Wait! Wait!!

Furious continuous clapper beats announce Kumagai, who enters the rampway on a black horse. Noh drums play "sudden movement" (tsukkake), and cymbals and large drum play "battle alarm."

CHANTER: —shouting loudly and whipping his horse, enters in pursuit!
KUMAGAI *(At the seven-three position)*: Do I see before my eyes an exalted general of the Taira clan? Do you show your heels to an opponent? Come back! I challenge you! Meet Kumagai Jirō Naozane, leader of the samurai of Musashi! Come back! Come, come! *(Roaring)* Fight me! Fight!!
CHANTER *(Singing to the shamisen, drums, and cymbals)*: Raising his fan and opening it, he calls, "Wait for me, wait!"

Kumagai beckons to Atsumori with his fan, painted gold with a rising sun in the center [figure 3.71]. The clapper beats, noh drums, cymbals, and gidayū shamisen reach a crescendo. Kumagai whips his horse across the stage and into the ocean in pursuit of Atsumori and disappears at stage left.

Tate

CHANTER *(Slowly, to a shamisen accompaniment)*: Is not hearing an opponent's challenge a reason to pause? Atsumori reins in his horse. *(Atsumori pauses and faces front)* Kumagai presses forward.

Kumagai reenters, now played by a boy actor on a small horse.

Together they raise their swords high;

3. The words that introduce the final battle scene in the noh play *Atsumori*.

FIGURE 3.71. Kumagai pauses at the seven-three spot, raises his war fan (*jinsen*), and calls to Atsumori, who has ridden his horse into the ocean. He wears full armor (*yoroi*) over a patterned undergarment. (Photo by Aoki Shinji.)

They fight to clapper beats; first one and then the other seeming to prevail [figure 3.72].

the morning sun glints like lightning on their blades. They attack and turn, attack and turn, clang, clang—the sleeves of their armor flutter, flutter in the wind of Suma Bay—flocks of sea plovers, flocks of sea plovers, burst skyward, ebbing, surging, ebbing again—diamond for diamond, dross for dross, a decision is impossible.

KUMAGAI *(Facing front, in a child's high voice)*: Now, let us grapple!

ATSUMORI *(Facing front, in a child's high voice)*: Yes! Let us!

CHANTER *(To a shamisen accompaniment)*: Though astride their horses, they grasp each other and wrestle. Their feet slide from their stirrups, and they fall between the horses.

Loud wave patterns. Throwing their swords down, they grab each other. A sharp beat of the clackers. They pose to triple clapper beats as a blue-wave curtain falls to hide them. The stick drum and flute play fast flute patterns. Atsumori's horse, riderless, prances across the stage and down the rampway to continuous clapper beats. A sharp beat of the clackers. The blue-wave curtain drops to the stage and is whisked away. The scene is the same. The stick drum, flute, and large drum play together (ōdaiko-iri), while the clapper beats swell, fade, and then reach a crescendo (uchiage). Atsumori and Kumagai, now played by adult actors, rise on a lift at center stage hidden by a red cloth held in front of them by two stage assistants. The cloth is taken away, and we see Kumagai holding Atsumori to the ground. They pose to triple clapper beats. The clackers sound the beginning of the action.

CHANTER *(To a shamisen accompaniment)*: In an instant, Kumagai seizes Atsumori and pins him to the ground.

KUMAGAI *(The music ends)*: Your destiny has reached its end. Speak out your name, so its fame will increase my glory. (*Looks intently into Atsumori's eyes*) Have you a final request in this life? Ask and I will not fail to fulfill it.

CHANTER *(To a shamisen accompaniment, slowly and with great emotion)*: He speaks with great courtesy.

Kumagai releases Atsumori, sheathes his sword, and sits on a tree stump at stage right. A stage assistant removes Atsumori's helmet, and he sits cross-legged at center stage.

ATSUMORI *(Gravely)*: You are a generous-spirited and noble warrior, though an enemy. I will count it the greatest honor of my life to be killed in war by one such as you. When I left for the field of battle, I abandoned thoughts of family and of self.

CHANTER (*Slowly, to a shamisen accompaniment*): He has no request for this life, for he knows no existence in it.

ATSUMORI: Yet it is difficult to forget the kindness of my father and mother. They will grieve deeply when they hear I have died in battle. After I am slain, at least do not fail to deliver this body to my father, to assuage their grief. Know that I am—Minister Tsunemori's youngest son—Atsumori!

CHANTER (*Slowly, the shamisen continues*): Pronouncing the name is an agony. Kumagai is not made of wood or stone, and tears stream from his seeing eyes.

Impassive until now, Kumagai drops his head forward and then, with an effort, straightens. He nods resolutely, crosses over to Atsumori, and kneels beside him.

FIGURE 3.72. Atsumori (wearing a helmet) and Kumagai (played by boys) fight in the ocean. In the puppet version, smaller dolls are used to indicate perspective. Compare figure 3.69. (Photo by Aoki Shinji.)

What does he think, raising him up, brushing the dust, brushing it from his armor?

Having brushed the dust off Atsumori, Kumagai hands him his helmet and sword, moves a respectful distance away, and bows deeply to him. The music stops.

KUMAGAI: Your noble mien bears witness that you are the son of Minister Tsunemori. Sparing one person cannot lose our victory. No one is here; make your escape. (*Points down the rampway with his closed fan, then bows deeply*) Quickly, quickly!

CHANTER (*Slowly, to shamisen accompaniment*): "Quickly, quickly," he says. Gracefully, Prince Atsumori— (*The music stops.*)

ATSUMORI (*Gently*): You may help me escape, but the Heike cannot escape destiny. Rather than be dishonored by a common soldier cutting me down at some future time, quickly kill me yourself.

CHANTER (*Very slowly, to shamisen accompaniment*): Facing west, he clasps his hands,

Migawari   *The noh drums play a melancholy mountain echo pattern, distant thunder is heard, and the gidayū shamisen plays quietly in the background. Kumagai rises with great dignity. Atsumori, who is still sitting cross-legged at stage center, removes his armor and swords. He places his helmet on top of the armor and a short dagger directly in front of him. Silence. He folds his arms in prayer.*

closes his eyes and waits.

FIGURE 3.73. Kumagai finds it extremely difficult to kill "Atsumori," who actually is his son Kojirō. Atsumori folds his hand in prayer. In the kabuki version, Kumagai wears straw sandals (*waraji*) with patterned socks (*tabi*), and in the bunraku version, the Kumagai puppet has a Bunshichi head. (Photos by Aoki Shinji.)

A loud chord from the shamisen. Kumagai starts.

KUMAGAI *(In a choked voice):* Prepare yourself.

CHANTER: Compassionately, Kumagai repeats Buddha's name in his heart as he moves behind Atsumori and lifts Buddha's sword that will sever earthly ties!

A stage assistant takes Kumagai's fan. Kumagai moves behind and just to one side of Atsumori. He draws his long sword and raises it above his head and then slowly lowers it.

In appearance like a precious jewel.

Gently, Kumagai places his hand on Atsumori's cheek and turns his head [fig. 3.73].

Overwhelmed by pity and remorse, his heart breaks, he hesitates.

His sword trembling, Kumagai turns away, trying to gain control. Atsumori closes his eyes and bows his head again. Kumagai raises his sword, his face anguished.

The hand that holds high the great sword weakens, his mind dissolves in tears. It is not possible to strike. Thus agonized time slips away from Kumagai—

Suddenly the drum and cymbals sound "battle alarm." To continuous clapper beats, Kumagai looks down the rampway and poses in a strong protective stance.

—when from the opposing hill, Hirayama!

Hirayama rushes onto the rampway followed by two soldiers. At the seven-three position, he mounts a small platform that has been placed there by two stage assistants. It is decorated with a pine tree and indicates a hilltop some distance away.

HIRAYAMA: Kumagai! You! Kumagai!! Traitor! You capture a Heike general and are about to let him go? Kill them, men, kill them both! (*He poses.*)

CHANTER (*Chants without shamisen accompaniment*): He hurls out abuse! Kumagai starts with surprise! What should he do? He stands in silence.

Kumagai starts, then slowly looks down at Atsumori, eyes wide with shock. He lowers his eyes and stands immobile, deep in thought.

ATSUMORI: Ah, will you fail, Kumagai? Do not let this chance pass and earn a coward's disgrace. Quickly, cut off my head and prove yourself.

Atsumori looks up at Kumagai, and Hirayama sits ostentatiously on a camp stool placed beside the platform by a stage assistant.

CHANTER (*To shamisen accompaniment*): It destroys his heart looking with unseeing eyes into the noble face turned up to him!

KUMAGAI (*Deeply aware of the irony of his words*): My only son, called Kojirō, whom you match exactly in age and appearance, was wounded in this morning's battle leading the attack, so I was forced to lead him to our battle camp. (*Glances covertly at Hirayama*) Deeply concerned, out of a father's love for his son, I could not help but reflect that taking your life here will cause your mother and your father—Tsunemori—grief.

His voice breaks into sobs. He turns away from his son.

CHANTER (*To shamisen accompaniment*): Brave warrior though he is, tears flow uncontrolled.

ATSUMORI (*Faces Kumagai*): Dull-witted Naozane. You would abandon companions as villains and welcome enemies as friends.[4] Take my head quickly and pray for my soul in death. If not, I will kill myself.

Atsumori takes up the dagger in front of him. Kumagai rushes forward and seizes Atsumori's hand to stop him.

KUMAGAI: Do not do it.

ATSUMORI: Will you disgrace yourself, coward?

KUMAGAI: But I—

Kuriage

ATSUMORI (*Gently*): Then cut off my head. Well?

KUMAGAI: Well?

BOTH (*Alternately, increasing in speed until they are speaking simultaneously*): Well, well, well, well, well!

ATSUMORI (*Agonized voice*): Do it quickly! Behead me!

4. A saying used in the noh play *Atsumori* to quite a different effect.

Atsumori rises on one knee, pulls loose his hair, bites hard on it to control himself, and then sits cross-legged with his hands clasped in prayer.

KUMAGAI *(Now calm and resolved)*: If father and son both pray for each other's salvation, in future lives they will surely dwell together on the same lotus blossom. Hail Amida Buddha. Hail Amida Buddha. Hail Merciful Buddha.

CHANTER *(Sings in a highly emotional voice to shamisen accompaniment)*: His head falls to the ground!

Kumagai decapitates Atsumori with a single, swift stroke, to loud shamisen and double clapper beats. Atsumori falls backward. A stage assistant covers his head with a black cloth and places a property head beside the body.

Though shameful in people's eyes

Kumagai wipes the sword in the crook of his arm, sheathes it, and sinks to his knees. Afraid to look, he gropes blindly for his son's head.

—cradling the precious head in his arms, he raises his voice in an anguished cry!

The gidayū shamisen plays. Kumagai rises to his knee, holds the head in front of him, and looks at it. He falls back with an anguished scream to double clapper beats. He then rises and faces Hirayama.

Nori

KUMAGAI: No other than Kumagai Jirō Naozane has severed the head of Imperial Prince Atsumori, unmatched among the Heike clan! *(Thrusts the head forward)* Witness it!

HIRAYAMA *(Rises and gazes at the head)*: I, samurai Hirayama, witness the act!

KUMAGAI *(In a hoarse scream)*: Victory!

HIRAYAMA: Victory!

SOLDIERS: Victory!!

Drums and cymbals at rear of the rampway play the battle alarm pattern as Hirayama strides up the rampway and out, followed by the soldiers. Kumagai watches and, in the ensuing silence, gradually relaxes. The wave patterns begin softly, creating an atmosphere of suspense.

CHANTER *(To shamisen accompaniment)*: Is it unquenchable longing for her husband that rouses Princess Tamaori, lying faint on the sand?

Tamaori pulls herself painfully from the beach grasses toward Kumagai.

TAMAORI *(Weakly)*: Ah, wait, please. What cruel person has killed Prince Atsumori? At least let me see his face one final time as a remembrance.

CHANTER *(To shamisen accompaniment)*: Speaking in a faint voice, deeply wounded, she approaches Kumagai, who is embracing the head.

KUMAGAI *(Cautiously)*: Who asks for Prince Atsumori?

CHANTER: "Ah, to meet him," is her dying breath.

TAMAORI *(Clutching her wound)*: I am Prince Atsumori's betrothed, Princess Tamaori.

FIGURE 3.74. In both the bunraku (left) and the kabuki versions of the play, Tamaori, now blind, cradles the head of Atsumori in her arms. (Photos by Aoki Shinji.)

KUMAGAI *(Turns around, surprised)*: Is it Atsumori's bride, Princess Tamaori?

TAMAORI: He is dead? Then his head— *(she gropes blindly for Kumagai)*. My eyes! I can't see!

KUMAGAI *(Softly)*: You can't see?

He kneels beside her and passes his hand before her eyes. When she makes no response, he sighs, relieved that she cannot give them away.

How pitiful. Here is the head—of Prince Atsumori.

CHANTER: As it passes from hand to hand, she catches her breath and cradles it on her lap, near death with pain.

Kumagai gently places the head in her lap. She embraces it weeping [figure 3.74]. Drums and cymbals sound "battle alarm," and Kumagai rushes toward the rampway and looks into the distance.

TAMAORI *(Faintly)*: Dearest Atsumori, it is pitiful that your life should come to this; I longingly sought you everywhere since you departed for battle. When the Genji warrior Hirayama seized me and forced his love on me, I tried to slay him by surprise, but being a woman, as you can see, I was wounded. Dearest Atsumori, we two share the same sad end together,

CHANTER *(Plaintively)*: "At least I want to die seeing your face as we part," she thinks, but—

She places the head on ground before her but loses track of it. She gropes frantically, then gasps with pain and falls back, clutching her breast.

—her heart fills with the pain of her dreadful wound.

TAMAORI: I cannot even see—how inconsolable!

CHANTER: Lovingly she strokes the head, cherishing a memory of his final words to her, "afterward," spoken in the evening as the flute played.

TAMAORI (*Shaking with pain as she cradles the head*): Although our love was unfulfilled in this life, in future lives it assuredly will last eternally.

CHANTER:

"I am bound to you in love, my husband," she says,
pressing the head to her face, folding it to her breast,
her mind driven to distraction,
uncontrolled voice rising

She weeps distractedly and falls forward.

in the cries of Suma Bay's sea plovers.
Sleeves dipped in an ocean's tide of tears
ebbing now as life's breath ebbs,
seeing that the time of death has come
her life expires.

She desperately strains for a final glimpse of Atsumori, then falls dead to the ground, holding the head tightly to her breast.

KUMAGAI: How sad it is that two noble young people, like budding flowers who knew nothing of life but springtime days at court, should come to this. Their bodies now lie on lonely Suma Bay, too remote for any visitor to honor their graves.

CHANTER: He weeps tears of bitter grief.

Kumagai begins to cry, checks himself, and looks cautiously down the rampway for signs of soldiers. Noh drums play mountain echo, and rolling thunder is heard. Kumagai kneels beside Tamaori and, to double clapper beats, tries to take the head. She holds it tightly in death, and he is forced to bend each finger gently to release it.

KUMAGAI (*Softly*): Let worldly attachments be dissolved that you may enter Buddha's Pure Land. Hail Amida Buddha. Hail Amida Buddha.

CHANTER (*Quietly, extremely slowly, and in a free tempo to shamisen accompaniment, mountain echo drum pattern, and distant rolls of thunder*): There is no escape for it, there is none.

With reverence, Kumagai places the head on a tree stump.

Taking Atsumori's cape, he covers her body, and places Atsumori's imperial corpse beside hers.

He places Tamaori's body on a raft of small logs, half hidden in the rushes at stage left, and spreads over her the bright red cape that had covered Atsumori's armor. Then he cuts a piece of cloth from his own purple cape, carefully wraps Atsumori's head in it, and replaces the head on the tree stump. He takes off his purple cape and, with the help of a stage assistant, holds it in front of Atsumori, who moves onto the raft. The cape is spread over Atsumori. The instrumental music continues as Kumagai, profoundly depressed and moving as if in a dream, finds his spear and uses it to push the raft gently out to sea. He watches the raft as it moves away, then drops his head and sobs. His black horse enters at stage right. Kumagai crosses over to it.

Gathering the reins and securing them, tightly cinching the saddle

With the help of a stage assistant, Kumagai secures Atsumori's armor onto the saddle. To instrumental music, Kumagai continues his long pantomime, picking up Atsumori's dagger, long sword, and helmet, looking at each and sighing before fastening it to the saddle. Last, he picks up the head.

cradling the head in his bow arm, he grasps the bridle with the other hand. Hearing the melancholy clop of hoof against rock brings to mind the sadness of that parting in the Dandoku Mountains.

KUMAGAI *(Leading his horse to stage center):* When Prince Siddhartha's young groom said farewell to his master

CHANTER: eons ago[5]

The horse rears and paws. Kumagai turns his back to the audience to calm the horse.

amid falling tears.

With one arm around the horse, a sobbing Kumagai gazes at his son's wrapped head and then falls to the floor. The horse nuzzles him. The drum and cymbals sound "battle alarm." Rising, Kumagai grasps the bridle firmly with one hand, cradles the head with the other, and assumes a strong pose to loud triple clapper beats. He holds this pose as the curtain is closed to a loud rushing (kakeri) pattern played by the offstage shamisen, hand drums, and flute; a wave pattern by the large drum; and accelerating beats by the clackers. The music fades away. A sharp clack.

5. Alluding to the sorrow of his young groom when the historical Buddha, Prince Siddhartha, left to seek enlightenment.

Yotsuya Ghost Stories

Act 2 of *Tōkaidō Yotsuya kaidan* by
Tsuruya Namboku IV (1755–1829)

Translated by Mark Oshima

When *Yotsuya Ghost Stories* was first produced at the Nakamura Theater in Edo in the summer of 1825, it was part of a two-day double bill with its acts intermingled with those of *Chūshingura*. The first day's performance included *Chūshingura* through act 6 (the act translated in this anthology) and the first three acts of *Yotsuya*. Act 3 was repeated on the second day, along with the latter halves of each play. Consequently, the world of *Yotsuya Ghosts Stories* was identified with that of *Chūshingura*: Iemon, like Kampei, is a former retainer of the dead Lord Enya, and Kihei is in the service of the enemy Kō no Moronao. Iemon has also killed his wife's father, an act that Kampei was convinced that he had committed. The result of this juxtaposition was, of course, that *Yotsuya* became a commentary on *Chūshingura*: it problematizes the virtue of loyalty, the value of the traditional vendetta, the role of women, and, as this is very much a Tokugawa-period play, the power of wealth. The relationship between the two plays was important to *Yotsuya*'s initial success. Since that performance, however, the two plays have seldom been presented together, and the relationship is no longer considered particularly important.

Yotsuya is a prime example of both raw-life pieces (kizewa mono) and ghost plays (*kaidan*), two specialties of its author Tsuruya Namboku IV (1755–1829). In addition to portraying society at its cruelest and most decadent, Namboku also mocks kabuki conventions in bizarre and gruesome ways. For example, the hair-combing scene (*kamisuki*), in which a woman dresses her lover's hair with tender and erotic care, is a staple of kabuki love plays. Oiwa's hair combing is a grotesque parody of such scenes. Another kabuki technique that Namboku repeatedly uses is the quick change (*hayagawari*), in which a single actor plays several roles, changing from one to another with incredible speed. In the original production of this play, Onoe Kikugorō III played the roles of Oiwa, Iemon, and Yomoshichi, who kills

Iemon in act 5. Only acts 2 and 3 are commonly performed today, but they allow actors—like the current Ichikawa Ennosuke—who revel in such techniques, to play both Oiwa and Kohei.

Mark Oshima suggests that Namboku's use of gruesome detail and spectacular stage effects, set off with a wicked sense of humor, is never gratuitous. Namboku combines the most common with the most unusual stage effects to express the play's principal themes. For example, the revolving stage is effectively used in *Yotsuya Ghost Stories* to contrast the poverty of Iemon, the masterless warrior, with the splendid wealth of Itō Kihei, the warrior-class doctor. The supporters of the two warring masters are depicted on the two sides of the stage as it goes around and around. This physical image is repeated in the next act when the bodies of Oiwa and Kohei (both played by the same actor) are displayed nailed to either side of a door floating down the river, first one corpse, then the other exposed. The relationships among these four characters—Iemon, Oiwa, Kihei, and Kohei—are complex and ever-changing.

For his descriptions of stage business, Oshima drew on current performance practices. To help the reader envision the performance, he includes directions to the actor called *omoiire*, a term used in scripts to indicate that an actor is to react nonverbally to display a psychological state. The actor can choose the specific physical actions or expressions to use. For example, the script might say "react angrily" (*haradatashiki omoiire*) or, in Edo times, might simply include a small circle to indicate an *omoiire*. When an actor assumes such a pose, there is usually a short pause in the action; hence these poses have somewhat the same function as close-ups in films. An annotated text is available in Gunji 1981.

TAMIYA IEMON: a masterless samurai (rōnin), a former retainer of
    Lord Enya

OIWA: his wife, who has just had a baby

KOBOTOKE KOHEI: Iemon's servant, loyal to Lord Enya

HOTOKE MAGOBEI: the father of Kohei

AKIYAMA CHŌBEI: a masterless samurai and Iemon's crony

SEKIGUCHI KANZŌ: a masterless samurai and Iemon's crony

BANSUKE: Kanzō's servant

TAKUETSU: a masseur, working for Iemon

ITŌ KIHEI: a rich doctor in the service of Lord Kō no Moronao, an enemy
    of Lord Enya

OYUMI: Kihei's widowed daughter

OUME: Oyumi's daughter

OMAKI: a nurse in the Itō household

TOKURAYA MOSUKE: a pawnbroker, whose name means "House of Profit"

MUSICIANS

Music-room (geza) performers

ACT 2, Scene 1

Tamiya Iemon's house

*The residence of Tamiya Iemon, a masterless samurai who lives in a shabby tenement
in Yotsuya, a neighborhood in the great capital of Edo (now Tokyo) occupied by poor
and masterless samurai. Many of them must swallow their pride and do craftwork at
home to make ends meet. The set has gray walls with cracked and peeling plaster and
a sliding, freestanding lattice door at stage right. Outside, a flat depicts the wall of a
neighboring estate. Inside is an area of bare floorboards, where people take off their
footwear, and then an area with a straw mat to represent tatami. At stage left is a
room surrounded by closed sliding-paper screens. In the center of the back wall, a
doorway leading to the back of the apartment is covered with a long split curtain,
and to stage right of the doorway are some sliding panels covering a closet. There are
a few sparse furnishings: a square paper floor lamp, a dirty white standing screen,
and a small brazier with a teapot on it.*

*As the curtain is pulled aside, lively shamisen and percussion music suggests the
bustle of commoner life and the dispute occurring on stage. Iemon sits on the floor
of the main room gluing triangles of paper onto the partially covered bamboo frame
of an umbrella. His clothing is that of a commoner, but his bearing reveals that he
once was a samurai. He listens coldly, not interrupting his work, as Magobei, the
father of Iemon's servant Kohei, and Takuetsu, a masseur, bow apologetically at his
right. Magobei wears a plain cotton kimono, and his wig is flecked with gray. He*

crouches on all fours. Takuetsu has the shaved head of a masseur and sits between Iemon and Magobei, trying to mediate their dispute [figure 3.75].

FIGURE 3.75. Tamiya Iemon's house in *Yotsuya Ghost Stories*. Takuetsu, a masseur, addresses Iemon, who is busy making an umbrella. (Photo by Aoki Shinji.)

TAKUETSU: Master Iemon, please listen! You are quite right, but please try to be a bit more understanding. It's all my fault. I made the mistake of introducing Kohei to you when you needed some help. I take full responsibility, so please give me a day or two to try to settle the matter.

IEMON *(Stops working and speaks deliberately)*: No, no, this is a matter that can't wait. Kohei is an embezzler and a thief. When he is caught, my samurai spirit will not be satisfied until I execute him. *(Pointing to the half-finished umbrella)* Every since I lost my master, I've had to make umbrellas just to get by. Me, a samurai! Look at this! Do you think I do this for fun? Iemon, his retainer, would be a fine samurai today. Now do you understand the situation? *(To Magobei)* You there! You're his father. Everything depends on what you have to say. Stop acting like a senile old fool. *(He rises and threatens Magobei.)*

MAGOBEI: Oh, no, no, you are quite right. There is nothing I could possibly say to defend what my son has done. You said that Kohei stole something. If I may, I would like to ask what he took.

IEMON: It's nothing someone like you would know anything about. He stole a packet of rare Chinese medicine called Sōkisei that has been passed down in the Tamiya house for generations. It's priceless; you won't find it anywhere else. The medicine is so potent that if someone has lost the use of his legs, this drug will enable him to walk right before your eyes. My stipend was cut off when my master's household was disbanded, and I haven't received a cent since then. Even so I have never let that medicine out of my hands. That is what Kohei stole. *(Picks up a short, badly made sword)* Look at this thing. This is all that Kohei left behind. He took my family's greatest treasure and left me with a rusty penknife. My friends are furious at what happened and left early this morning to try to track down Kohei. I'd be out there too, but I can't leave my wife, since she just had a baby and is still weak. That's why I needed help around here and took Kohei into my service. He's certainly been more trouble than he's worth! Just thinking about it makes me furious. When I get my hands on him, I'll take care of him once and for all. Takuetsu, you're his guarantor. You're responsible for what he's done. Do you understand what I'm going to do? *(As Iemon talks to Takuetsu, Magobei mulls over what he has learned—omoiire.)*

TAKUETSU: You are only right to feel that way. You accepted the introduction of this humble masseur and took Kohei into your service, only to have him steal from you and flee. And what a time to run off, just when poor Oiwa has given birth and has not yet recovered her health. How could Kohei abandon you at such a time? I can find nothing to say to apologize. Magobei, oh Magobei! What do you think?

MAGOBEI: I don't quite know what to say. Kohei has never amounted to much, but I always thought that he was honest. I'm shocked that he stole something. A family heirloom? A priceless packet of (*omoiire*) medicine?

TAKUETSU: That is strange, isn't it? Stealing cash is normal, but who steals medicine?

MAGOBEI (*To himself*): Hmm, now that his real master is so sick, maybe he thought this was his only hope.[1]

IEMON: What?

MAGOBEI: I mean, what Kohei did was unforgivable.

IEMON: Listen, old man. That medicine may not look like much, but it's very rare. A druggist would pay at least a dozen gold pieces on the spot. My medicine is even more valuable because it has a certificate guaranteeing its authenticity. The medicine and the certificate have been handed down through my family for generations. There's nothing like it anywhere else. However, I'll give you a chance. You can have a couple of days to try and find Kohei yourself. If you don't find him by then, you can give me what the medicine is really worth — fifteen gold pieces. Got it? That's fifteen gold pieces. Find him or you owe me a fortune.

MAGOBEI: Thank you. I'll find him, and I'm sorry for what my son has done. (*To Takuetsu*) Forgive me for having caused you so much trouble.

TAKUETSU: It's not your fault. It's troublesome, but I got us into this situation in the first place. This is just one of those things that happens when you try to help someone. No wonder more people aren't helpful.

Magobei puts on his straw sandals and gets ready to leave. The background music, which has been playing since the scene opened, ends.

IEMON: Remember, two days. Come here the instant you hear anything about Kohei. I can make things difficult for you if you try to hide anything.

MAGOBEI: I understand. (*To Takuetsu*) Doctor, thank you for everything. (*Bows his way out*) Good-bye.

Magobei departs down the rampway, muttering as he goes. Takuetsu prepares medicine for Oiwa and takes it into the enclosed room at stage left.

IEMON: No cash, not even enough to keep up appearances, yet she's dumb enough to go and have a kid. If you want sweet innocence, that's what you'll get.

Lively lion dance (shishi mai) music is played by the shamisen and percussion in the music room. Akiyama Chōbei, dressed in tattered clothing but wearing the two swords that indicate his samurai status, comes racing down the rampway to the front door.

1. Kohei's former master, Matanojo, is another retainer of Lord Enya of the *Chūshingura* story. Matanojo is extremely ill, and Kohei is desperate to get the medicine so that Matanojo can recover enough to participate in the vendetta.

CHŌBEI: Iemon, are you there? We found Kohei!

IEMON: Chōbei! You saw him?

CHŌBEI: Yes. I knew he lived somewhere across town, maybe on the other side of the river. I captured him just before he reached the bridge. Here's the packet of drugs he stole. (He passes over a small packet wrapped in a small cotton cloth.)

IEMON: Thank you. Where is that damn Kohei?

CHŌBEI: He's with Kanzō. Ah, it sounds like they're here.[2]

The lion dance music begins again. Sekiguchi Kanzō, his servant Bansuke, and Kohei enter down the rampway. Kohei's hands are tied with a coarse rope, his hair is disheveled, and his clothing is torn. In improvised dialogue, he apologizes profusely, but Kanzō and Bansuke tell him that he won't get away with it as they pull him roughly onto the main stage.

IEMON: Kanzō, thank you for all your trouble. I heard the details from Chōbei. Your work is greatly appreciated. Ah, Bansuke, is it? Thank you for your efforts.

BANSUKE: Thank you, sir. You must feel better now. (*He removes the rope from Kohei.*)

TAKUETSU (*To Kohei, who sits, his head hanging in shame*): Here, here. For your sake I've gone through a lot of trouble, too. Even your old father had to be called in. What got into you?

KOHEI (*Slowly lifting his head*): Doctor, I owe everything to your kindness in finding me this position. Instead of showing the proper gratitude, I've made things difficult for you, all because I was seized by a sudden impulse. And now my father has been drawn in, too. I guess he must have gone home already. I'm sorry to hear that. He must be worried sick about me. Master, since Chōbei took back the medicine, and I didn't touch anything else, please have mercy and forgive me. I beg you (*omoire*).

IEMON: That's ridiculous. When a servant disobeys his master, it cannot be overlooked. A dishonest and insubordinate servant has to be punished properly. We'll have to find just the right treatment for you.

KANZŌ: Iemon, I've been thinking about some of the things he said. I hear that his old master was a samurai in Lord Enya's house, where you also served. Remember Oshioda Matanojo, the most loyal samurai in the whole house? Kohei's entire family was in his service. You'd never guess that someone who used to work for such an honest person would go so bad, would you?

IEMON: Do you mean the same Matanojo I knew in Lord Enya's mansion? Kohei used to serve him? Is that true?

KOHEI: Yes, everything you say is true. For generations my father's family has served Matanojo's family. When Lord Enya's house was disbanded, Matanojo became a masterless samurai. Then recently he became very ill. I entered your service to help support him. My wife, my father, and even my little boy

---

2. Important characters are almost always mentioned or heard offstage a few seconds before they make their entrances. This enhances the dramatic effect of their actual appearance.

have gone to work also. We all want to do whatever we can to help him now that he's facing hard times, but we are so poor that we can't do very much. I wanted desperately to cure him, so I attempted to steal the medicine. I did it for the best possible reasons: I stole out of loyalty to my master. I thought there could be no higher cause. Even so, the fact that you found me out must be heaven's punishment. Please forgive me.

IEMON: You mean you stole my family heirloom for your master's sake? Did Matanojo order you to do that?

KOHEI: No, no. He knows nothing about it. I did it myself, thinking that it was the only loyal thing to do.

IEMON: It doesn't matter whether loyalty or insanity made you do it. If you steal, you're a thief. Is there some law saying thieves can get off if they're properly loyal? What a ridiculous idea! At least I have the medicine back now. I might have spared you if you had paid me something for it. But you didn't give me a cent. For the theft of the medicine, I will break all of your fingers, one by one.

CHŌBEI: That sounds like fun. Can we start right now?

KANZŌ: Ten fingers instead of taking his life? That's letting him off too easy.

BANSUKE: Since I'm an apprentice, let me try breaking one too—for the practice.[3]

IEMON: Come on, help me. (*They surround Kohei. Takuetsu tries to stop them.*)

KOHEI (*omoiire—entreaty*): Stop it! I have to take care of my parents. What can I do if my hands are useless?

ALL THREE (*Kanzō, Bansuke, and Chōbei*)[4]: What do we care?

KOHEI: Mercy! Mercy! Show some kindness. Please, I returned the medicine.

IEMON: Shut up! Gag him!

ALL THREE: OK, OK. (*The three surround him, and Bansuke takes a handkerchief and ties it over Kohei's mouth.*)

BANSUKE: That should keep him quiet.

KANZŌ: After we finish with the fingers, how about pulling his hair out?

CHŌBEI: That's a good idea.

They mime kicking and beating him. The blows are emphasized with sharp clapper beats. Music announces the appearance on the rampway of Omaki, a wet nurse serving in the neighboring household of rich Dr. Itō Kihei. She is accompanied by a servant bearing a large barrel of sake and a stack of lacquered boxes filled with food—expensive ceremonial gifts celebrating the birth of a child. She carries a gray cloth bundle that we later learn contains a baby's yellow-and-black-checked kimono. She comes to the front door.

OMAKI: Is anyone home? May I come in?

ALL THREE: Who could that be?

IEMON: Someone's here. Stick Kohei in the closet.

ALL THREE: OK, OK. Get in there.

---

3. Bansuke is played by one of the apprentices of the actor playing Iemon.

4. Lines attributed to these three are not spoken entirely in unison. Usually one or another of them speaks, with the others joining in for the last few words or for a laugh together at the end of the line.

They drag Kohei to the closet at stage right, slide the door open, throw him in, and close the door.[5] In a passage not translated here, Omaki presents the gifts and a packet of medicine she claims will cure Oiwa. She goes into the room at stage left to attend the mother and child. Tokuraya Mosuke, a pawnbroker, enters and demands the repayment of five gold pieces plus the rental for a mosquito netting, bedding, and a padded nightgown. Iemon is forced to give the pawnbroker his precious medicine and the accompanying document instead of the five gold pieces.

MOSUKE: Well, now that's cleared up (*slips the packet into his kimono*). Now the rentals. I'll just take the mosquito net and the bedding. Excuse me (*stands*).

IEMON: What are you doing? You're still taking the other things?

MOSUKE: Yup. If you don't pay another gold piece, I can't clear the account. Excuse me. (*He heads toward the room at stage left, but Omaki comes out and stops him.*)

OMAKI: Pray wait a moment, tradesman. Do not force your way into a sickroom. If I heard correctly, it's some matter of money, is it? Here, this will probably do. Go away and leave the things here.

She hands Mosuke a paper-wrapped bundle, somewhat more than the amount that is owed. Iemon is surprised and wonders what he will have to do in exchange.

MOSUKE (*Examining the packet*): Hey, this is too much.

OMAKI: Shh, there's no need to wake up the mother. Well, sir?

MOSUKE: Uh, well, I'm speechless. This is truly a great favor, ma'am.

IEMON: After all this help, there is no way to show my thanks.

OMAKI: Please, there is no need to worry about it. Well, I must take my leave now (*goes toward the door*).

MOSUKE: I'll walk you to the street.

IEMON (*To Omaki*): Nurse, thanks. You've been a great help.

OMAKI: My best wishes to all of you. (*The music that began with her entrance ends.*) Well, Mosuke?

MOSUKE: After you.

Omaki and Mosuke exit up the rampway to lively music. The rest are silent for a moment, impressed with the generosity of Itō Kihei and his household. The music slows and continues quietly during the following dialogue.

CHŌBEI: Well, Iemon, we've been getting a lot of help from the Itō mansion. You probably should go over there and say a few words of thanks.

IEMON: Maybe I should, but I can't do it.

CHŌBEI and KANZŌ: What do you mean?

IEMON: Itō Kihei is a retainer of our enemy, Lord Kō no Moronao. Our master is dead and his retainers have been expelled from his mansion and scattered. Meanwhile, Kō no Moronao lives in the best part of town in a rich mansion. I was once a retainer of Lord Enya, who was a victim of Lord Moronao's evil plots. Even after all they've given us, I can't go to my enemy's house.

---

5. The closet has an exit at the back so that the actor can exit and change into the costume and makeup for Oiwa, whose role he also plays.

CHŌBEI and KANZŌ: You're right, that is a problem. (*During this time the baby starts crying in the room at stage left.*[6] *Takuetsu hears him.*)

TAKUETSU: Oh, no. That child again.

IEMON: That brat cries a lot. Maybe the fleas are getting at him.

The music becomes languid to suggest the atmosphere of a sickroom. Iemon pushes open the downstage sliding screens to reveal Oiwa sitting on the cotton bedding looking sick and weak. There is a room-size mosquito net hanging from the ceiling and a small folding screen to protect the bed from drafts. An amulet for safe birth hangs around Oiwa's neck, and she is holding the baby—a doll—and patting it on the back. Iemon looks at Oiwa.

Oiwa, are you better today? How do you feel?

CHŌBEI and KANZŌ: We came to visit you.

OIWA (*omoiire—contemplating them*): You are very kind. Please excuse me. They say one always feels ill after giving birth. But perhaps because of the strange weather we've been having lately, I feel even worse than usual (*omoiire—she does not really think that it is because of the weather*).

Takuetsu helps her into the main room. She puts the baby on a cushion and covers it with a robe.

IEMON (*Noticing the handsome kimono covering the baby*): Oiwa, I've never seen that kimono before. Did you make it?

OIWA: This came a moment ago from the Itō mansion with the warm wishes of the widow Oyumi. Husband, please go and thank them.

IEMON (*omoiire—hesitation*): Is that so? They've been so generous it's embarrassing. I don't understand why.

CHŌBEI: Look here, it's like I always say. What's past is past. Tamiya Iemon, now you're a masterless samurai. Forget about ideas like duty and avenging former masters and go over to the mansion.

OIWA: He's right. You really must go over to the mansion and thank them.

IEMON (*Broods on Oiwa's words*): You're right, Oiwa, I have to go, but I shouldn't go alone without you.

OIWA: If you must go with someone, take those two along.

CHŌBEI: Yeah, we'll go—

KANZŌ: together with you. (*The music stops.*)

IEMON: Well, as they say, the sooner, the better. Let's go.

KANZŌ: Yeah, let's go.

BANSUKE: I'll be your retinue.

TAKUETSU: And I'll look after things while you're gone. It's best for you to go and express your gratitude.

IEMON (*Puts on his two swords and an old short formal jacket*): I'm going, but I haven't fixed anything to eat yet. Could you do it?

TAKUETSU: Yes, yes. I'll take care of everything.

IEMON: Remember, keep your eye on the closet. (*Points to Kohei's sword*) He thinks that thing makes him look important. (*To Oiwa*) This medicine to help

---

6. The sound of the crying baby is produced by an offstage actor.

your circulation came from the Itō mansion. You'd better take it. They said it was an old family secret. (*He hands over the packet of powdered medicine [figure 3.76].*)

OIWA: Oh? A little while ago the nurse said something about some medicine. Please give it to me. When the water is ready, I'll take it. (*Slips the medicine into her kimono*) Come back quickly.

IEMON: I'll come right back. Let's go. (*To Takuetsu*) Remember to make dinner.

TAKUETSU: I understand.

IEMON: I'm going now, Oiwa.

OIWA: Please come back as soon as you can.

IEMON: What would keep me there? Let's go.

FIGURE 3.76. Having donned a crested short coat (*haori*) to go to Kihei's house, Iemon hands the packet of "medicine" to Oiwa. Costumes for kizewa mono are closer to contemporary fashion than are those of other types of plays. (Photo by Aoki Shinji.)

Moderately lively music plays as Chōbei, Kanzō, and Iemon, with Bansuke in attendance, exit up the rampway, and Takuetsu goes through the door to the back of the house. The sound of a temple bell increases the feeling of loneliness.[7] The shamisen music begins again, slowly and pensively, as Oiwa stares after the men.

OIWA: Iemon has been mean to me from the moment we were married. He didn't even look pleased when I told him his baby was a boy. Every day from dawn to dusk he complains that the "brat" is nothing but a nuisance. He grumbles that for him, a baby is just another mouth to feed. He says things like that even when he knows I can hear him. (*She hugs herself to endure her emotional pain*) Living in this house is constant torture, with little wounds that never heal. (*She recalls the reason that she must stay with Iemon*) But I must remember that Iemon promised to help me attack my father's murderer.[8] (*She stops and weeps, then continues to cry as she says*) If I can just endure this a little while longer, I will be able to leave this evil man. Please, please, let us avenge my father's murder soon.

She pauses in fervent prayer, but at this point a decorative tortoiseshell comb stuck in her hair drops to the floor. She picks it up and looks at it.

This tortoiseshell comb was my mother's. Look at the cheerful swirl of chrysanthemums and the beautiful old-fashioned silver work. Even though we need money desperately, I will never give up this comb. But since I had my

7. In addition to suggesting the striking of the hour, the temple bell is used to indicate a lonely or foreboding mood and to emphasize actions.

8. In act 1, Oiwa's father, who learned that Iemon had stolen from his master, demanded that Iemon give up Oiwa. Wanting to keep her, Iemon killed her father and then cynically promised to avenge his death if Oiwa remained with him.

FIGURE 3.77. Oiwa comforts her baby, pours the "medicine" into her hand to eat it, and then drinks the remaining powder in a cup of hot water. These actions are accompanied by background music and the ominous sound of a temple bell. (Photos by Aoki Shinji.)

baby, I've been so sick—I feel so weak I'm not sure I can live. If I die, I want my sister Osode to have it to remember our mother. It's the only thing from our mother that I still have left.

She gazes at the comb. The baby starts crying. She picks him up and comforts him and returns him to his cushion [figure 3.77].

Oh, I'm dizzy again. It must be my bad circulation. I hope that the powder will help.

To slow background music, she picks up the packet of medicine with a prayer of thanks. Ominously, the action is emphasized by the boom of the temple bell. She lays down the package and picks the comb off the floor and puts it back in her hair. Oiwa walks unsteadily to the little brazier where there is a pot of hot water, fills a teacup, and returns to sit beside the baby. She unfolds the packet and puts it carefully back on the floor, then wipes her hand with a handkerchief. She pours the medicine directly onto her hand, happily lifts both hands to her forehead in a gesture of gratitude and then takes the medicine. She taps the remaining medicine from the packet into the teacup and gulps it down. After another gesture of thanks with the empty packet, she wipes her mouth.

I'm sure I'll feel better now. Here, my precious little boy (*she dangles the new kimono in front of the baby to amuse it*). You got something nice today, didn't you? I wonder who made it, little Oume? The nurse?

Without realizing it, she drops the kimono but continues to wave her hands. After a moment she notices the kimono on the floor, picks it up, dangles it in front of the baby, but drops it again. She notices that her fingers are numb and begins to rub them. Suddenly she gasps as she feels a sharp pain in her chest and starts to moan as her face begins to burn with fever.

Oh, oh, oh, oh! Now that I took the medicine I feel worse. Oh! My face is burning. It's never felt like this before. Oh, the pain, the pain.

She huddles on the floor in pain. Just then, there is a sharp pounding on the door of the closet where Kohei is tied up.

TAKUETSU (*Enters from the back and, since Oiwa is hunched over, at first is totally unaware of what has happened to her*): Oh Oiwa, shall I fix some soup? (*She lifts her head, and he can see that she has changed, but the room is too dark to see clearly.*) This is awful. What happened, what happened to you? How pale you are, even your face looks different.

OIWA: I took the powder and right away— Oh, it hurts, it hurts.

TAKUETSU: It started to hurt after you took the medicine? The draft is bad for you, come over here.

He bends over her and starts to scream at the sight of her face but quickly recovers and rubs her back, being careful not to look directly at her face, which the audience still cannot see. The baby begins to cry, and Takuetsu goes to comfort it, but then Oiwa cries out in pain, and he runs back to her. Just as he is running back and forth between them, the closet door slides open and Kohei (a stand-in actor, as the "real" actor is playing Oiwa) tries to get out.

Hey, hey! Don't try to escape! (*Slides the closet door shut and tries to decide what to do*) If I take care of one thing, the other two will get away from me. (*A sharp strike of the wooden clackers*)[9] What a time to be housesitting.

He ponders his situation. Oiwa is in pain. Takuetsu puts the baby in the room at stage left and closes the door. He tries to comfort Oiwa, patting and massaging her back. The action is punctuated by the sound of the temple bell as the stage revolves.

Scene 2

The Mansion of Itō Kihei

Lively folk music sounds as the stage revolves to reveal the grand and luxurious home of the rich doctor Itō Kihei. The interior is on a low platform and is surrounded with a veranda with a step down into the garden, which covers the downstage half of the stage. There is an alcove at stage left with a precious scroll and a flower arrangement. In the garden there is a wattle fence with an elegant rustic gate at stage right and a stone lantern and water basin by the veranda at stage left. Iemon is seated at center stage with Chōbei and Kanzō to his right. Behind them sit Oyumi and Omaki. Oyumi is a middle-aged woman wearing a somber kimono befitting a widow. Omaki is the nurse of Kihei's granddaughter Oume. There are sake cups in front of the men and containers of sake by the women. Chōbei and Kanzō enjoy the banquet while Bansuke performs a folk dance in the garden below. Kihei is seated at far stage left. He is dressed in the restrained colors of a prosperous retired man and wears glasses with round black frames. He is carefully washing gold coins in a large copper basin and putting them away in a small wooden box. When the stage stops turning, Bansuke tumbles and everyone laughs. Bansuke joins the banquet, and the scene

9. Usually the end of a scene is marked by one sharp blow of the wooden clackers (*ki*) just before the last important line of the scene. Then some bridging action continues as the stage revolves. Here, Takuetsu runs around semicomically trying to tend to Oiwa, Kohei, and the baby.

begins with some improvised light conversation about the private lives of the actors on stage. Servants in formal divided skirts bring in three covered soup bowls on trays, which they set in front of Chōbei, Kanzō, and Bansuke. They are young retainers, and their appearance suggests that this is a samurai household.

IEMON (*Observing Kihei's actions*): Sir, are those sword ornaments you are cleaning?

KIHEI: No, nothing so important. These are just some old coins I inherited from my father. If I don't wash them from time to time, the gold and silver gets all tarnished. This is about all an old retired man can do anymore. Ha, ha, ha.

IEMON: Not a bad job to have.

ALL THREE (*Kanzō, Bansuke, and Chōbei*): Let us give you a hand. Ha, ha, ha.

OYUMI: It's not much, but please have some soup and a cup of sake.

OMAKI: Please do have a drink.

ALL THREE: You're going to too much trouble. But Iemon doesn't have a tray.

BANSUKE: Here, let me. (*He tries to pass his tray to Iemon.*)

OYUMI: Oh no. We have something very special for Mr. Iemon. Please, it's not much, but go ahead and eat.

CHŌBEI: Let's eat then. (*They lift the lids of their soup bowls. To their astonishment, the bowls are filled with gold coins [figure 3.78]*) This is a real delicacy.

KANZŌ and BANSUKE: We're much obliged.

OYUMI: We've invited Mr. Iemon so many times. Now that he has graciously accepted our invitation and you have been kind enough to come along with him, please have as much as you like. We are happy that you like our humble meal. Omaki, give them another helping if they want one.

OMAKI: As you wish. Please don't hesitate to ask.

ALL THREE: What a great banquet. *They put the money away in the breasts of their kimono.*

KIHEI: Now that we've taken care of your companions, what shall we serve you, Iemon, our eminent guest of honor?

IEMON: It must be something special. *The music stops.*

OYUMI: If you are ready, we can serve you, but—(*looks at the others meaningfully*) if you will excuse us for a few moments.

KANZŌ and CHŌBEI: We understand. Let's give them some time alone.

OYUMI (*To Omaki*): Please take care of our guests.

OMAKI: Let me show you around the grounds.

The background music becomes slower and more deliberate. Omaki leads Chōbei, Kanzō, and Bansuke through the curtained door at the rear. Oyumi exits as well. Kihei puts the coins he has been washing on the lid of the box and slides it over in front of Iemon.

KIHEI: Please be kind enough to accept these, Iemon.

IEMON: Why are you giving me all this money? (*omoiire—looks pointedly at Kihei. The music stops.*)

OYUMI (*From behind the curtained door*): Let me explain the matter to you.

The slow and deliberate background music begins again to underscore the important section that follows. She leads her daughter, Oume, through the doorway. Oume is wearing a kimono with long flowing sleeves, the dress of a young, unmarried girl. Oyumi seats Oume at far stage right, and Iemon looks at her.

This girl is Oume, my daughter by my late husband Mataichi.

KIHEI: Oume is my dearest granddaughter. By some mysterious fate, she fell in love with you the first time she saw you and began to suffer from love sickness. One day we thought it would do her good to get outside, and so we all went to the Asakusa Temple. There she miraculously—

OYUMI: saw you again. She was happy for the first time in so long. Well, my daughter, now you can finally say what you have kept hidden in your heart for so long.

FIGURE 3.78. Chōbei and Kanzō, who accompanied Iemon on his visit, remove the lids of their soup bowls and discover that the bowls are filled with gold coins. A sake bottle sits on the floor beside the dinner tray. Because they are guests, they sit on cushions. (Photo by Aoki Shinji.)

She leads Oume to sit at Iemon's side. The music stops as Oume poses shyly (omoiire), then the music begins again.

OUME: After I have worried my dear mother so, how could I hide anything? One day shortly after you moved into this neighborhood, Mr. Tamiya, I caught a glimpse of you, and from that moment—from that moment—I was yours. Since then, full of longing, I have done nothing but dream of you.

OYUMI: From dawn to dusk, she was so consumed with love that she kept to her bed. Every day her face and body grew thinner before my very eyes. I constantly questioned her to find out what was wrong. Finally she told me about you, the man she could not forget.

OUME: But you are married. I did not dare to hope my wish could be granted; I tried to be firm and put you out of my mind. However, when two people are linked by fate, it is impossible to forget. Let me be your servant or even your scullery maid. I wouldn't mind. Anything, just let me stay by your side. (*Bows to Iemon—omoiire.*)

KIHEI: It is just as you have heard. If possible, I would like to have you as my son-in-law. Please grant my Oume's request.

OYUMI: My daughter has become obsessed with you. Listen to her, she says she would even condescend to live as a commoner. She would be Oiwa's servant or your mistress. But this is a samurai household, and such a breach of class could not be kept secret. (*To Oume*) Now that my husband is dead, you are all I have left. How can I allow you to do such a thing? (*omoiire*)

IEMON: Your daughter's feelings leave me quite speechless. But I was adopted as the heir to the Tamiya family, and duty binds me to my wife Oiwa. It is all heartbreaking (*the music stops*), but unfortunately—

KIHEI: So you deny my granddaughter's request?

OYUMI: It is only right that you refuse her. And now, Oume, we must be resigned to forgetting about Iemon.

OUME: Yes, I'm resigned to it. I've made my decision, and I will prove it to you now—(*takes a razor from her sash*). Hail Amida Buddha (*bends over and tries to cut her throat, but they all stop her*).

KIHEI (*The music continues*): You have acted virtuously. Your heart's desire was not granted and so—

OYUMI: you decided to die with honor. My daughter's spirit is worthy of a samurai. How sad that your prayers could not be granted.

CHŌBEI (*Appears at the door at the rear of the stage*): Hey, Iemon, you're making a big mistake. Look, Oiwa's going to die sooner or later. After she's gone, you're going to need a wife anyway. So why don't you make these two nice people happy and go ahead and change your nest? That's what you really should do.

IEMON: No, no. Even if it makes me rich, it's not right for me to abandon Oiwa. That's the one thing I couldn't do. (*The music stops for a tense, silent pause— omoiire.*)

KIHEI (*Turning decisive, he takes all the gold from the box and presents it to Iemon*): Please, kill me. Please kill Kihei, kill this poor old man (*omoiire*).

IEMON (*Puzzled*): What are you talking about? I know that it must be a shock for Oume to be refused, but why are you asking me to kill you?

KIHEI: There is something else I must tell you. (*Slow deliberate music*) I found my granddaughter's suffering pitiful, but I knew that because you already had a wife, getting you to marry her might be difficult. I considered all kinds of plans, and finally, without telling Oyumi anything, I sent a disfiguring poison to Oiwa, falsely claiming it was medicine. I thought that the problem would solve itself as soon as her beauty disappeared. Your love for your wife would vanish, so you would divorce her and marry my granddaughter. I kept this evil plan to myself and sent a medicine for circulation—which was really a poison—by way of the nurse. I knew that it would ruin her face but leave her life untouched. It would leave her alive! I clung to that fact, telling myself that it wouldn't be such a great crime. However, matters have not worked out as I hoped. I am responsible for a great tragedy. (*The music stops*) It is for this reason that I want you to kill me.

OYUMI: You thought up this evil plan all for the sake of my poor young child?

OUME: This is how I am being punished for my sinful desires.

KIHEI: If you are able to forgive me, all my family's gold is yours.

CHŌBEI: It would be a big mistake not to take what's on your plate.

KIHEI: Vent your fury by killing me!

OYUMI: No! Not here in your own house.

OUME: It is better for me to die.

She tries again to kill herself, but Oyumi stops her.

KIHEI: Will you forgive me?

IEMON: I, I—

OYUMI: If you die, how can I protect this child all by myself?

IEMON: Well—

KIHEI: Then kill me!

IEMON: I, well,

OYUMI and KIHEI: well, well

IEMON: well

ALL THREE: well, well, well, well.

The preceding lines are spoken more and more intensely, culminating in this chorus of "wells"—sa in Japanese—which rises and falls in pitch and volume.

KIHEI: I have done a monstrous thing.

OYUMI *(Forcefully)*: Please, give us your answer.

IEMON *(omoiire)*: I have made my decision. I will leave Oiwa and take your granddaughter's hand [figure 3.79].

KIHEI: Then you will give your consent?

OYUMI: You are granting—

CHŌBEI: this child's wishes?

IEMON: In exchange, I have a request myself.

KIHEI: And that request is?

IEMON: Recommend me to Lord Moronao as a retainer.[10]

KIHEI: Done. I would have done that even if you hadn't asked, now that we all are one family.

IEMON: If I take your granddaughter, we will be father and son-in-law. From this moment, I will change my name from Tamiya to Itō.[11]

OYUMI: As they say, "the sooner, the better."

KIHEI: We'll have the wedding ceremony tonight. Do you agree?

IEMON: Certainly. *(To himself)* Hmm, maybe I can put the blame on that masseur that comes in to see Oiwa.

KIHEI: What?

IEMON: Oh, nothing. I suppose we can discuss the details later.

CHŌBEI: First things first. Now you should exchange wedding cups. I'll be your go-between.

OUME: Oh, I'm blushing *(omoiire)*.

OYUMI: She's still a bit shy.

OUME: Oh.

FIGURE 3.79. With her mother, the nurse, and her grandfather looking on, Iemon agrees to take Oume as his wife. Itō Kihei's mansion is one side of the revolving stage, contrasting with Iemon's house on the other, as shown in figure 3.75. Oume wears the arrow-patterned (*yagasuri*) kimono typical of daughters of wealthy merchants. (Photo by Aoki Shinji.)

10. Many masterless samurai dearly wished to find service in a samurai household so that they could serve in a position befitting their social rank and receive a stipend. For Iemon, this is perhaps the most attractive aspect of marrying Oume, even though Moronao was responsible for his former master's death.

11. Iemon announces that he will be adopted into the Itō clan and serve Lord Moronao. It was a common practice to adopt sons-in-law as heirs.

KIHEI: Well, son-in-law? (*Takes out a marriage cup. Oume bashfully clings to Iemon.*)

IEMON (*Changing his tone and putting his hand on Oume's shoulder*): Now that you are my wife (*the music begins*), I'll swear my oath to you on my sword. (*He takes his dagger and solemnly taps it against his sword. He looks at Oyumi and Kihei.*)

OYUMI and KIHEI: A blessing on you both.

They clasp their hands in prayerful thanks. The temple bell sounds. The music increases in volume and tempo as the stage revolves. The actors continue to celebrate the marriage as they are carried out of sight.

Scene 3

Tamiya Iemon's House

The stage returns to the first scene. The large drum plays wind patterns (kaze no oto), which derive from the sound of wind rattling the wooden sliding doors and shutters of the houses of commoners. There is also the sound of chirping insects. In a brief passage not translated here, Takuetsu lights a lamp, sees how horribly Oiwa's face has become disfigured, and staggers out to buy some lamp oil. He collapses in fear at center stage and finally makes it out the front door. He collapses again on the rampway and tries to stand several times, but his legs keep collapsing under him. Finally he runs off. Oiwa takes the baby into the room at stage left; the audience still has not seen her face.

A popular song is played, and the temple bell sounds. Iemon staggers down the rampway, tipsy from drink. He pauses at the seven-three position and looks toward the house, concerned about how things will turn out. He stops outside the gate.

IEMON: Kihei claimed the drug wouldn't kill her, only change her appearance. If she's—I'll look for myself first.

He goes through the front door and enters the house. Languid music plays, evoking the heat of summer.

OIWA (*Calling from inside the room at stage left*): Takuetsu, are you back with the oil already?

IEMON: What oil? It's me.

OIWA: Is that you, Iemon?

Iemon opens the sliding paper screens in front of the room at stage left. Oiwa is still hidden by the mosquito netting, which is almost opaque.

IEMON: How are you feeling? Did the medicine help your circulation?

OIWA: It helped my circulation, but as soon as I took it, I broke out in a terrible fever. My face felt like it was on fire.

IEMON: The fever felt the worst in your face?

OIWA: Yes, it's all numb now. (*She comes out of the mosquito netting. There is a horrible swelling above Oiwa's right eye.*)

IEMON (*Shocked at her appearance*): Oh, it's changed, it's changed, it's changed. It changed so quickly.

OIWA *(Weakly)*: What's changed?

IEMON: What I was saying was that—that while I was at Kihei's, your face has changed, the color has come back into your cheeks. It must be the effect of the drug. Yes, yes, you look like you're getting better *(omoiire)*.

OIWA: I don't know if my face looks better or worse. I feel just the same. It's been like this day after day without a break. Oh, Iemon, I'd rather die! Iemon, if I died now, I would leave this world with no regrets—except for my child. It is only pity for my child that keeps me tied to this wretched existence. Husband, if I die, please don't marry again, at least for a while.

IEMON: I'll marry if I feel like it.

OIWA: What?

IEMON *(Decisively)*: I'll find a new wife right away. I'll get a better wife than ever. So what? There are plenty of people who get married again.

OIWA *(Shocked)*: Iemon, you are cruel! You were born heartless. I always knew what you were like. I married you because—

IEMON: you needed help to avenge your father's murder. Well, I don't feel like getting involved. Avenging murder is old-fashioned. Leave me out of it. We got married because you wanted a swordsman, but I'm not interested.

OIWA: What? So now— but you—

IEMON: So I don't feel like it anymore. What are you going to do about it? If you don't like it, leave. Go find someone else who has the time to waste on vendettas. Vendettas make me sick.

OIWA: If you refuse me, I have no one else to turn to. I am a woman alone. I suppose I should have expected you to fail me. If you want me to go, I will go. But what about the child? Are you going to have your new wife take care of our baby?

IEMON: If you don't want a stepmother to have him, take the brat with you. I'm not giving up a chance for a good new wife for the sake of a stupid baby. But I need some cash; something came up. Do you have something you can lend me? Is there anything around here we can pawn? *(Looks around and sees the ornamental comb on the floor)* Why don't I take this? *(Picks it up)*.

OIWA *(Grabbing it from him)*: That's the comb my mother left me. I will never let that out of my sight.

IEMON: You won't, will you? Well, my new woman doesn't have a nice dress comb, so she keeps asking me to buy her one. What's wrong with giving her this one?

OIWA: This is the one and only thing I can never give up.

IEMON: Then give me something I can buy a comb with. Also, I need to dress up tonight, so I need to get my good clothes out of hock. Lend me something! *(The music stops)* Come on, make it quick. *(Shoves her.)*

OIWA *(Ponders—omoiire. The languid music begins again)*: There's nothing left to speak of, but perhaps this? *(She takes off her outer kimono, leaving herself dressed only in a thin, pale gray underkimono, which makes her look more ghostlike)* I'm sick, but since you asked for something, I'll give you this. *(She hands it to Iemon, who also grabs the new kimono from the baby.)*

IEMON *(Examining the two pieces of clothing)*: This won't bring enough. I need more. Isn't there anything else? How about the mosquito netting? (*He takes it down and starts to go.*)

OIWA (*Clutches at the net*): Wait, wait! Without a mosquito net, my baby will be eaten alive by mosquitos as soon as it gets dark. (*She takes back the net.*)

IEMON: If the mosquitos start eating him, your job as a parent is to chase them away. That's what filial piety means.[12] Let go! Let go! I said, let go!

He tugs roughly. Oiwa is dragged along the floor with the net. Finally he kicks her, the blows emphasized by beats on the board, and pulls the net away. He takes a few steps and looks back at her. Oiwa lets out a cry and holds up her hands; her fingertips are covered with blood, showing that her nails have been torn away.

IEMON: This still isn't enough, you stingy bitch!

A popular song and a temple bell are heard as Iemon goes up the rampway, stops at the seven-three spot, and looks up as he calculates how much he can pawn the items for. Then he exits.

OIWA (*Stands*): Iemon! Iemon! I can't let you have the mosquito net. (*Goes to the door*) He's already gone. He took the only thing I could not give up. Even though I'm as weak and sick as I am, I hung on to it for dear life for the sake of my child. Nothing could have made me agree to part with that net. How violently, violently, the net and my fingernails were torn away. (*Stares at her blood-covered fingers*) Iemon, you are so cruel. How sorry I feel for my poor baby when I think about his being your flesh and blood.

She broods, and the languid music begins again. The baby cries. Oiwa stands unsteadily, looking around. She finally pulls out a small brazier and wearily starts burning incense to drive away the mosquitos. This continues for a while. Iemon reappears on the rampway with the kimono and mosquito netting slung over his shoulder. He has Takuetsu in tow.

TAKUETSU: Master, master, you're going too far. If you do that, everyone will talk about me and Oiwa.

IEMON: I'll fix it all if you do your part right. (*He whispers his plan in Takuetsu's ear.*)

TAKUETSU: Then you're going to have the wedding tonight?

IEMON: Keep it quiet. Here. (*He shows him a small gold coin wrapped in paper.*)[13]

TAKUETSU: You're giving me this gold coin?

IEMON: Do it right, and it's yours. (*He gestures with his sword to show what will happen if Takuetsu refuses.*)

TAKUETSU: Yes, I understand. (*After Iemon has exited up the rampway*) What a mess I'm in now! (*Enters the front door of the house*) Oiwa, oh, Oiwa. I'm sorry to have kept you waiting so long. Here's the oil. (*He picks up the lantern.*)

12. Probably an ironic reference to the story in the *Twenty-Four Examples of Filial Piety*, in which a boy protects his father from mosquitoes at night by lying exposed, attracting all the mosquitoes away from his sleeping father.

13. Iemon has the gold coins he received from Kihei, but he is pawning Oiwa's things to get her to leave him of her own volition or at least to throw her into Takuetsu's arms.

OIWA *(Resignedly fanning the incense burner)*: You're back? So soon? After you left, Iemon came and took away the mosquito net.

TAKUETSU: Back to the pawnshop, eh? Tsk, tsk, how very thoughtless of him. What will happen to you and the baby without it? Well now, look at you. My, my, how thin your kimono is.

OIWA: Even though I'm sick and shouldn't get chilled, Iemon forced me to give him my kimono.

TAKUETSU: Really? How unfortunate. What hard times you've been through. Instead of all that trouble, wouldn't it be better to find another man? Think about it. *(Thinks a moment)* I used to read palms. Let me look. *(Goes to Oiwa, takes her hand, and looks intently at the palm)* Look at this, there's an unlucky line running all through your palm. According to this, your husband will give you endless pain. It says here that you should cut off this line; that is, you should cut off all ties with that man. *(As he says this, Oiwa looks at Takuetsu. He sees her face, gasps, and turns away.)*

OIWA *(Jumping up in surprise and saying firmly)*: What are you trying to do? Remember, I am the wife of a samurai. If you try anything like that again, I won't forgive you the next time.

TAKUETSU: Wait, wait! Your faithfulness will only hurt you. Iemon lost his love for you long ago. If you insist on staying with him, it will lead to nothing but more misfortune. I'm the man for you.

OIWA: What? Rather than patiently enduring hardships with my rightful husband, I should turn to you? Explain yourself. What are you saying? Are you trying to lure me into adultery? You insolent creature! Even though I'm nothing but a woman, I am the wife and the daughter of samurai. Do you think you can get away with talking that way to Oiwa? *(Picks up Kohei's sword, deftly unsheathes it, and confronts Takuetsu)* There must be a reason you are doing this, tell me!

TAKUETSU *(Shaking)*: Put that down, it's dangerous! You'll get hurt!

He tries to grab Oiwa's hand. They struggle back and forth. Finally he grabs the sword, tosses it into the room at stage left, and holds her down in a seated position. We later learn that the sword lands against the pillar of the room, with the tip sticking out.

Listen, listen. It was all a lie. What I said just now was all a lie. Really, calm down! It's not the way I said. Even a poor wretch like me wouldn't want a woman with your awful face. I don't know why this was fated to happen, but on top of your sickness, now your face. It breaks my heart.

OIWA *(omoiire—gradually beginning to suspect what has happened)*: My face? Along with the fever there was a sudden pain, could that have—?

TAKUETSU: It is a woman's fate to be deceived. That miracle drug for your circulation you got from Kihei was all a trick. It was a poison for changing people's faces, an extraordinary poison. When you took it, your face changed and now you look like an ugly, evil woman. Didn't you know that? How pitiful. *(He goes to the back of the room and takes her mirror off its stand)* Here, here, if you want to know, look at this. Look at your face in this.

He stands behind her and holds up the mirror to her face. She doesn't want to look, but he forces her to.

OIWA: Ahh, my face is gray, as gray as my kimono. (*She turns away, then with new determination takes the mirror herself, drops to her knees, and looks carefully*) What has happened to my face? Is this my face? Have I really changed into a demon? Is this truly my face?

She holds the mirror at various angles, hoping that the image will change. She huddles on the floor and cries, leaving the mirror on the floor beside her.

TAKUETSU: This play had another author (*the music begins again*), Kihei's granddaughter Oume. She wanted Iemon to be her husband, but her family all knew that Iemon already had a wife. Kihei has gold to spare and thought he could buy Iemon, but he worried that perhaps Iemon had some feeling of loyalty to you. To make absolutely sure he wouldn't be refused, Kihei tricked you with this medicine. He thought that if your faced changed, your husband's love would run out. Poor Oiwa, you innocently took the medicine, not knowing a thing. What an unhappy situation.

Her face has been gradually revealing her growing fury as she looks intently at her image in the mirror. The following is spoken with great deliberateness.

OIWA:
I never guessed the truth these gifts concealed,
sent day after day by our good neighbor Itō Kihei.
My heart swelled with thanks.
Even when the wet nurse came, the destroying poison in her hand,
to force me to my ruin, I clapped my hands in gratitude.
Now each time I think of it, my heart fills with shame.
They must laugh and laugh at me.
Bitter, oh how bitter, is this humiliation. (*She lies on the floor sobbing.*)

TAKUETSU (*Drawing near as the music stops*):
Iemon has run out of love for you.
As bridegroom of the house of Itō, he plotted to rid himself of you.
"Play my wife's lover," he ordered.
I replied, "Never!" and up came his sword.
So we have no choice but to play out our little comedy.
He stripped you of your robe, cruelly tearing it away.
But now the truth is revealed.
Tonight! The wedding is tonight.
By pawning your things,
money for the preparations fell into the bridegroom's hands.
He ordered me to seduce you and to flee with you as lovers do,
so that when he leads his bride here, you won't be an obstacle for them.
I was to be the made-to-order lover,
but that terrible face of yours keeps tender passion down.
Forgive me, please forgive me.

OIWA (*Strengthening her resolve*): Now all that is left to me is suffering and death.

But while I still have breath, I must go and thank Master Kihei properly. (*She stands unsteadily and begins to stagger to the front door.*)

TAKUETSU (*Rushes over and crouches in front of her*): No, no! If you go out looking like that, people will think you are a madwoman. (*Pushes her back*) Your clothing is torn and—your—face—

Together they take three steps with the last three words, which are spoken rhythmically. He stops and inadvertently looks up at her face, shrieks, and looks down. They are just at the spot where the mirror is still lying on the floor. Takuetsu and Oiwa freeze and stare at the mirror together, transfixed by the horrible image.

FIGURE 3.80. Oiwa, now aware of her disfigured face, nonetheless begins blackening her teeth in preparation for going out. (Photo by Aoki Shinji.)

OIWA (*Takes the mirror and looks carefully*):
How frightful is the hair of the woman in the mirror.
I must blacken my teeth as married women do.
Then I must dress my hair.
I must look proper to give Kihei and Oume, parent and child,
one small word of thanks.
(*Quietly*) Bring me my tooth blackening.

TAKUETSU: But you are still sick and weak. You've just given birth. It's not safe for you to go out.

OIWA: It's quite all right. Bring my tooth blackening quickly.

TAKUETSU: But—

OIWA (*Firmly*): I said, bring it right now.

TAKUETSU (*Startled by her firmness*): Yes.

Dokugin[14]   *A solo singer accompanied by a shamisen begins singing a plaintive song. Takuetsu brings the lantern, a large metal container, and a stick of blackening. Oiwa sets up the mirror on a stand and sits down in the center of the main room. She rinses her mouth, wipes her teeth dry, and then applies the blackening [figure 3.80]. It was customary for married women to blacken their teeth, but Oiwa has not done this since giving birth. She messily covers the corners of her mouth, which makes it look as though her mouth is monstrously wide. The baby, who has been sleeping in the other room, starts to cry. Takuetsu tries to comfort him and put him to sleep. The first verse of the song comes to an end, but the shamisen continues*

14. Often a musical scene is underscored with a sensuous musical solo (*dokugin*). This might be a meeting between lovers or a scene with a woman alone at her makeup mirror. In this case, Oiwa acts out a kind of parody of the latter kind of scene.

FIGURE 3.81. Clappers strike to emphasize the dripping of blood that Oiwa wrings from her hair. Her hairline has receded, revealing the grotesque bump on her forehead. (Photo by Aoki Shinji.)

playing background music. Takuetsu clears away the utensils while Oiwa spreads some paper on the floor and takes her comb from her kimono.

OIWA:

> My precious comb, all that is left from my mother.
> After my death, this comb must go to my sister, Osode.
> This is my one remaining wish.
> My father, my husband, my sister, and I
> all are tied together by bonds thousandfold.
> As I dream of the one thing I can do for my sister,
> let the teeth of this comb pass through my hair
> and straighten out its tangled strands.

The second verse of the song begins. Oiwa has Takuetsu cut the cord holding her hair in place. She sweeps her hair forward over her head and beings combing it. Hair comes out in great handfuls.[15] The hair piles up on the floor, augmented by a stage assistant who pushes more hair up through a hole in the stage floor. The second verse of the song ends. When Oiwa sweeps her hair back, her hairline has receded considerably, leaving the grotesque swelling above her right eye totally exposed. This action is emphasized by doro-doro drum patterns, which suggest strange occurrences. She drops the comb on the pile of hair.

> Every moment is uncertain, as the end comes for Oiwa.
> But one thing is sure, the moment I die he will marry that girl.
> I can see the scene right before my eyes.
> Now I have nothing but hatred for you, Iemon,
> and hate for the house of Kihei, hatred for the Itō family.
> None of you shall ever escape to a life of peace.
> The more I think about it
> the more my heart is filled with bitter, bitter hatred.

She picks up the pile of hair and tries to go to the door, but Takuetsu stops her, pushing her back with the standing screen. He looks up at her face and, in shock, drops the screen, which falls at Oiwa's feet, angling toward the audience. Oiwa's face twists with fury, and she begins to wring her bundle of hair. Blood drips from the hair onto the white screen in front of her. Clappers strike to emphasis the dripping of blood [figure 3.81].

TAKUETSU (*Seeing the blood and shaking*): Ahh, ah, ah, ahh. She's squeezing blood from her hair.

15. Scenes of combing hair (*kamisuki*), often with a woman dressing her lover's hair, are intimate and erotic moments. Here again is a grotesque parody of a kabuki tradition.

OIWA: My fury will not rest until it reaches its goal!

TAKUETSU: Oiwa, please, please!

He grabs Oiwa and tries to stop her, unintentionally letting go of her and sending her tottering into the room at stage left. Oiwa tries to reenter the main room and accidentally cuts her throat on Kohei's sword stuck in a pillar [figure 3.82]. She gestures with painful spasms, emphasized by the sharp clanging of a prayer bell. Finally, she collapses on the floor and dies.

TAKUETSU *(Shaking)*: Oh no, no. Kohei's sword was there. I wanted to stop her, but not like this. Oh, oh, how awful, awful, awful.

FIGURE 3.82. After Oiwa runs into Kohei's sword, a prayer bell clangs to emphasize Oiwa's spasmatic gestures before she falls down dead. (Photo by Aoki Shinji.)

Doro-doro drum patterns and the noh flute played breathlessly produce an eerie effect. A rat—represented by a stuffed doll on a long pole manipulated by a stage assistant—appears and tries to tug at the baby. Takuetsu shoos it away.[16] A green spirit flame floats near Oiwa's body.

I can't stay here any longer!

The terrified Takuetsu runs out the front door, continually slipping and falling in his haste. Iemon enters the rampway dressed in a magnificent formal costume and runs into Takuetsu.

IEMON: It's my good masseur. How did it go? Did you run away with Oiwa? Did things go according to plan?

TAKUETSU: Ah, ah. You ordered me to do that, but it just didn't work. It didn't work.

IEMON: Then she hasn't gone away yet? What a useless old fool you are. I just came from the marriage ceremony at the Itō mansion. I was sure you would have taken her away by now. Tonight they are bringing over the new bride. If Oiwa is still in there, it will be a problem. This is awful!

TAKUETSU: It was awful, it was awful, awful, awful. That rat was awful!

He shivers and exits up the rampway.

IEMON *(Looking after him)*: That idiot went off just babbling about some rat without telling me what happened. Who can I use in his place as an excuse for chasing Oiwa out? *(omoiire—thinking)* Wait, I know. I'll turn my servant Kohei into her lover and drive the two of them out. In any case, tonight Oume will be coming. *(Reaches the front door)* Oiwa, Oiwa, where are you? Oiwa,

16. The rat represents Oiwa's spirit, since she was born in the year of the rat. In the first performance, this was a more elaborate scene with a cat, thought to be able to raise the spirits of the dead, appearing and then being pursued and killed by a huge rat.

Oiwa. (*Notices the crying baby on the floor and jumps in surprise*) One more step and I would have crushed him. Oiwa, Oiwa![17] (*Picks up the crying baby*) Hey, Oiwa, Oiwa. (*Sees her body*) Oh, oh, oh, oh, oh. This is Oiwa with Kohei's rusty old sword in her throat. Did he kill her? But he was in the closet. (*Omoiire, then puts the baby down, opens the closet, and pulls out Kohei.*) He's still tied up just as before, then he didn't—(*omoiire*). In any case, he'll get the blame for killing Oiwa. (*He unties Kohei.*)

KOHEI: Master, what a monster you are.

IEMON: What the hell are you talking about?

KOHEI: You may have bound my hands and gagged me, but I know that hounding Oiwa to death in that miserable way was all your doing. Takuetsu told Oiwa everything about the plot between you and your neighbor Kihei. He told her about the poison that disfigured her. How could you drive out your wife at a time like this, all for your own advancement? Do you really think you can prosper that way? You're the lowest scum!

IEMON: Shut up! Peon! Oiwa was killed with your sword. You killed her. You killed your master's wife. You killed her! You killed her! You killed her!

KOHEI: That's insane! I was tied and gagged. How could I?

IEMON (*Shouting*): But look! Look! Your hands are moving now. You must have killed Oiwa! Murderer!

No matter what Kohei says, Iemon refuses to listen to him. They continue to argue, ad libbing. Kohei suggests that he be given the medicine in return for being labeled a murderer. Iemon refuses.

IEMON: I have no choice. You, you are Oiwa's enemy, and I must avenge her death. You killed her, so you are a murderer. Anyway, how could I let you live after you heard all about our plot? Here, pass on to the next world pushed by Tamiya's sword. (*Strikes him.*)

Tachimawari *They struggle in a dancelike stylized manner. Lively music plays as they fight, posing dramatically from time to time. Kohei defends himself desperately, throwing everything he can get his hands on, including umbrellas. Finally, wounded in several places, Kohei clings to Iemon [figure 3.83].*

KOHEI: I guess even during just one night's employ, if one fights with one's master—

IEMON: justice strikes you with your master's sword. That's why I'm killing you, slowly. You are Oiwa's enemy! Die! Die!

After a struggle, Kohei collapses to the sounds of a Buddhist wooden gong. Chōbei, Kanzō, and, later, Bansuke enter down the rampway. After being told what has happened, they carry the bodies out the back door.

Stately entrance music is played for a grand procession up the rampway. Two servants enter holding large lanterns marked with the crest of the actor playing the role of Kihei. Kihei, dressed in a formal coat and divided skirts leads Oume by the

---

17. In early performances, several puppet rats entered. The first one grabbed the baby's clothing and tugged, and the others lined up, each grabbing the tail of the one in front. They attempted to carry off the baby, but Iemon chased them away.

hand. Behind them, Omaki is accompanied by two servants bearing silk bedding and a six-section folding screen. They arrive at the front door.

KIHEI *(Slightly tipsy from the wedding sake):* Master Iemon, Master Iemon. It's Kihei.

IEMON: Well, well, good sir. You're here already with Oume. Come in, come in.

OUME: Oh please, wait. We have been married as you promised, but I feel funny moving right into your house so soon.

KIHEI: Don't worry. Iemon made a mistake by not having anyone to look after Oiwa, but fortunately, we're all one family. Even if it does go a little against samurai practice to bring everything over before we've had a public ceremony, we brought the screen and the bedding anyway. Don't worry.

OMAKI: You are undoubtedly right, but remember how young the girl is. She has not yet come of age.

KIHEI: If I say not to worry! *(He pulls Oume into the house, and they all sit down)* By the way, Iemon, is it true that Oiwa and you know who?

FIGURE 3.83. Bleeding and battered, Kohei clings to Iemon, who holds the sword that killed Oiwa. (Photo by Aoki Shinji.)

IEMON: When I told you about it at the wedding, I had the wrong man. It was actually my servant Kohei who was having an affair with her. When the two were discovered, she ran off with her lover, leaving her baby behind. Oume, tonight, if my new father-in-law will allow it, I would like you to stay here.

KIHEI: Ah, so she did have another man? Among samurai, that sort of thing just will not do. But as far as we are concerned, the timing was perfect. Congratulations, congratulations!

OMAKI: I'm sure you are right, but I'm surprised that she left the house when she was still so sick. Well, I guess that certainly is a marvel. But what are you going to do about the little boy?

IEMON: That really is a problem.

KIHEI: Well, for that very reason, I'll stay here starting tonight and help you out. Early tomorrow morning, the nurse will come and help too. Omaki, spread out my bed.

OMAKI: As you wish. *(She spreads out the bedding at stage right and puts the large folding screen around it)* Master, I've prepared your bed over here.

KIHEI: Then where will the young couple sleep?

IEMON: Let's use my old bed. It will serve that faithless old wife of mine right.

KIHEI: Of course, of course, what a fine idea. Here Oume, this is your good luck charm. Take care to keep it around your neck. *(He hands her a red charm.)*

OUME: I'll never let go of it. I'm scared of Oiwa.

OMAKI: I know you are, but put her out of your head, at least while you are in your wedding bed.

IEMON: Don't worry about it. Who would dare to say anything against people as important as we are?

OMAKI: No, no. Of course, no one could object. Now here you go. (*Takes Oume by the hand and leads her to the bed in the room at stage left*) Tonight your wishes will come true at last.

OUME: I know you're right, but when I remember that for my sake, poor Oiwa—

OMAKI: Now hush or your wishes won't come true. (*She closes the sliding doors. The baby starts to cry.*)

IEMON: What a time for the kid to—

KIHEI: Ah ha. I may not be able to give any milk, but tonight I'll be the child's wet nurse. I'll keep him with me tonight.

He picks up the baby, cradles him, and retires to the bed at stage right.

IEMON: Father-in-law, thank you for everything.

OMAKI: What shall I do?

KIHEI: Go and tell my daughter that everything is all right here.

OMAKI: As you wish. Well, my deepest congratulations.

IEMON: Good night, nurse.

OMAKI: Enjoy your wedding night.

To a lively song and the tolling of the temple bell, Omaki, preceded by the servants carrying the lanterns, exits up the rampway. Kihei pulls the screen closed around his bed. Iemon, left alone, is pleased with the turn of events.

IEMON: Now it's off to the bridal bed with an innocent girl who's never done anything. Well, let's start her out right.

Eerie flute music plays, and the temple bell tolls. Iemon enters the room at stage left and slides open the doors so the interior is visible to the audience.

Oume, I'm sorry I've kept you waiting. (*Oume sits, looking down at the floor*) Listen, my bride, there's no reason to stare at the floor. Even if you feel bashful, come, lift up your face. Tonight is the night that all your dreams come true. Here, look happy. Look at me, smile, and say, "Now you're my husband." (*He draws closer.*)

OIWA: Yes, Iemon, you are my husband. (*She lifts up her face. The red charm is around her neck, but the face is that of Oiwa. She glares with hatred at Iemon and cackles. Iemon picks up a sword from nearby, draws it, and strikes her, immediately closing the screen door behind him. A wooden head is tossed onto the stage.*[18] *Light doro-doro drum patterns are heard.*)

IEMON (*Looks closely at the face*): Oh no, no, no. That was really Oume. I acted too quickly!

Still holding the sword, he runs over to the screen at stage right and pulls it aside.

18. Or the head of the actor playing Oume sticks out of the floor through a trap door as though it were the decapitated head. Rats might come onstage and surround the head.

Inside, Kihei is sitting up, his face turned away from the audience. He is wearing a thick padded jacket and is holding the baby. Iemon goes over to him.

Father-in law! Father-in law! Something terrible has happened. By mistake—

Kihei turns his head: it is Kohei, his mouth stained. He glares at Iemon.

KOHEI: Master, master, give me the medicine.

IEMON: Oh no! You're Kohei! And now you're killing the baby!

Iemon cuts off Kohei's head. The blood-stained head of the actor playing Kihei emerges through a trap door. A snake emerges from Kohei's hips, crawls toward the head, and coils around it.[19]

(*Looking closely*) That was really my father-in-law. I can't stay in this cursed place!

He runs to the front door. The door is closed, so he slides it open. But the door slides shut by itself. Iemon opens the door again and runs out only to stop suddenly. With one hand, he grabs his collar as though pushing away some unseen force tugging him back. With the other hand, he reaches forward desperately in the direction he wants to go. This movement is punctuated by a doro-doro drum pattern. He pushes away whatever it is and starts running again, only to be stopped and to run backward several steps. Another doro-doro pattern is played. The forward and backward movements alternate with increasing rapidity until Iemon is standing in one place, desperately trying to move. Finally, he is pulled back into the house, spins in a circle, and sits down hard in the middle of the floor. Doro-doro drum patterns sound, and green spirit flames float in the air in front of him. Iemon stiffens and shouts.

You spiteful spirits!

The clacking of the wooden clappers begins to mark the end of the act.

Hail Amida Buddha, Hail Amida Buddha, Hail Amida Buddha—

The two green spirit flames hover in the air. Iemon clasps his hands together, praying fervently as the curtain is pulled shut.

19. Kohei was born in the year of the snake.

The Hamamatsu-ya Scene

From act 3 of *Benten kozō* by
Kawatake Mokuami (1816–1883)

Translated by Samuel L. Leiter

Kawatake Mokuami, the last of the major traditional playwrights, was sometimes called the "bandit playwright" (*shiranami sakusha*) because he so often used thieves and other outlaws as the subjects of his plays. *Benten the Thief* (Benten kozō), also called *The Five Bandits* (Shiranami gonin otoko) and *The Story of Aoto and the Gorgeous Woodblock Print* (Aotozōshi hana no nishiki-e),[1] is a good example. The play was first performed in 1862 at the Ichimura Theater in Edo (now Tokyo), with an all-star cast including the future Onoe Kikugorō V (1844–1903) as Benten. This Kikugorō was the grandson of Kikugorō III, who starred in the first performance of *Yotsuya Ghost Stories*.

The heart of most plays featuring thieves is an extortion or blackmail scene (*yusuriba*), which in *Benten the Thief* is set in a dry goods store called the Hamamatsu-ya. This is presented as an upscale textile shop in Kamakura, although a contemporary audience would recognize the scene as the Nihonbashi area of Edo. (Censorship made it safer not to set plays in the shogun's castle town.) As is so often the case in kabuki, things are not what they seem, and the climax of the scene is the revelation that Benten is not the young daughter of a samurai he appears to be. His name-announcing speech ends in one of kabuki's best-known poses, revealing an incongruous, half-male half-female figure. The plot is further contorted, for the samurai who unmasks Benten as a thief is none other than the leader of the gang, who goes on to extort even more money from the hapless shopkeeper.

Although the full play consists of eight scenes in five acts, only three scenes are usually performed today, including the Hamamatsu-ya scene from act 3. Act 4 (Seizoroi no ba) is a colorful mustering of the bandits at Inase River, where each announces

---

1. This is the title under which the play is listed in most Japanese encyclopedias. It refers to an earlier play by Sakurada Jisuke III (1802–77) about the historical Aoto Fujitsuna (thirteenth century) and to the woodblock print that inspired Mokuami's play.

his name and reveals his character with theatrical flourishes. The first scene of act 5 (Gokurakuji sammon) makes use of elaborate stage effects: Benten flees to the roof of the enormous temple gate at Gokurakuji, pursued by a group of constables. After a valiant struggle, he holds them at bay and commits seppuku standing up. As he plunges the dagger into his abdomen, the great roof tilts slowly backward (with Benten still on it) to reveal the upper story of the temple gate where the leader of the robbers, Nippon Daemon, is sitting peacefully. The gate is then raised to reveal the lower level, and a historical figure rises on a trap in front of the gate. This is a visual allusion to an earlier play, *Kimmon gosan no kiri*, about the famous bandit Ishikawa Goemon and the shogun Toyotomi Hideyoshi.

In his memoirs, writing about the inspiration for this play, Kikugorō V claims that he saw a set of woodblock prints by Utagawa Toyokuni III (1786–1864) depicting himself and several other popular actors as bandits and asked Mokuami to create a role in which he could look like the image in one of the prints. There is some doubt about the accuracy of that account, but it does suggest the close relationship between prints and the kabuki stage. This play, which seems "realistic" in comparison to most earlier kabuki, is actually structured rather like an illustrated Edo book, with one tableau following another and theatrical "self-portraits" receiving more attention than the intricacies of the plot. This is clearly presentational theater.

For this anthology, Samuel Leiter revised his translation of this scene from the version published in 1979 in his *The Art of Kabuki: Famous Plays in Performance*. That work also includes a translation of act 4 and valuable information about variant performance practices. The translation is based on an acting script provided by the Tōhō Producing Company, which was used for the production at the Imperial Theater (Teikoku gekijō) in Tokyo in December 1974. Most of the stage directions are also from that production. The editor abridged the piece slightly, especially the stage directions.

Members of the gang of thieves:
BENTEN KOZŌ: disguised as a samurai's daughter
NANGO RIKIMARU: masquerading as a samurai called Yosohachi
NIPPON DAEMON: leader of the gang, masquerading as a samurai
The Hamamatsu-ya textile shop:
KŌBEI: the shop owner
SŌNOSUKE: the owner's son
YOKURŌ: the chief clerk
TASUKE, SAHEI, and other clerks
Others:
SEIJI: a fireman
Shop boy from the teahouse

MUSICIANS

Music-room (geza) performers

ACT 3, Scene 1
The Hamamatsu-ya Scene

After wooden clackers have been struck at intervals for several minutes, the nagauta-style tune "Echigo Lion" is sung to the accompaniment of the stick drum by performers in the music room at stage right. Soon the clackers return, beating faster and faster as the curtain is pulled across the stage to reveal the Hamamatsu-ya, a prosperous textile shop in the Yukinoshita section of Kamakura. The shop interior takes up most of the stage. A platform about eighteen inches high occupies the upstage area, with a small room enclosed with shōji screens at stage left. The rear wall has a sliding door at the center, and to the right are shelves laden with dry goods. Adjoining the shop at stage right is a small teashop run by the Hamamatsu-ya for the convenience of its customers. The navy blue curtains hanging in its two doorways bear the shop's emblem and its name.

Behind a low latticework screen in front of the shelves, the officious chief clerk, Yokurō, is going over the business accounts in a ledger. He is acted in the semi-comical tradition of the clerk-villain. Nippon Daemon, leader of the gang of thieves, has arrived at the shop disguised as a samurai and has gone into the back room. The tone of a lively, bustling shop is set by a brief passage during which several customers are rapidly served. After the last customer leaves, the Echigo Lion music fades, and Yokurō crosses to the large brazier at left center.

The nagauta music from the dance play The Heron Girl *is heard from the music room, and the curtain at the end of the raised rampway through the audience is loudly swished aside, signaling the entrance of Benten Kozō and Nango Rikimaru. Benten is disguised as a samurai's daughter, in a long-sleeved black kimono with a*

*red obi, both decorated with chrysan-
themum patterns.*[2] *Nango Rikimaru,
a fellow thief and extortionist, is
disguised as Benten's samurai man-
servant, Yosohachi. He wears two
swords tucked samurai style in his obi.
Whenever he sits, he places the long
sword on the ground at his left, hilt
facing forward, repositioning it when
he moves. Benten precedes Nango
down the rampway, gesturing demurely with a white fan. They stop at the
seven-three position on the rampway,
and Benten speaks, using the falsetto
tones of a female impersonator.*

FIGURE 3.84. When Benten, dressed as a woman, and Nango arrive
at the Hamamatsu-ya, the clerks rush about to welcome them. Benten
is dressed as a city girl, in a kimono with long *furisode* sleeves, whereas Nango's kimono is tucked up (*hashiori*) high under his striped haori.
(Photo by Aoki Shinji.)

BENTEN: Yosohachi, where is the
  Hamamatsu-ya textile shop?

NANGO *(Speaking with a deep, powerful voice in a very formal, self-
  important manner):* It's right ahead, miss.

BENTEN: Now, remember, you must not mention that I am shopping for my
  wedding robes.

NANGO: Why not, miss?

BENTEN *(Shyly, hiding his face with his fan):* Because I'm so embarrassed.

NANGO: In that case, I won't say a word about it. Let's move on. *(They walk to
  the shop entrance while shamisen music plays softly in the background)*
  Pardon me!

*The clerks look up and stumble over each other in their eagerness to wait on this
impressive pair. Some ad-libbing is acceptable. The overlapping of the following
lines creates the effect of humorous confusion [figure 3.84].*

SAHEI: Welcome!

TASUKE: Please come this way!

YOKURŌ: Here, here! Please come right in, miss.

SAHEI: No, no. This way, this way.

NANGO: Ah, now, now! Will you please be quiet? You'll drive me out of my mind!

YOKURŌ *(Chasing away the clerks with a yardstick):* That's right, will you all shut
  up? *(To Nango, officiously)* Well, now, we've got beautiful, really beautiful
  goods in stock. But first, please step into our shop.

*Benten and Nango remove their sandals at the entrance and enter the shop. Benten
sits at stage center with Yokurō and Nango at either side.*

---

2. The chrysanthemums (*kiku*) on the kimono indicate the role's connection with the Kikugorō line
of actors. Onoe Kikugorō V was Benten at the first performance of this play in 1862, and the play has
remained a favorite in his family.

Fine weather we're having today, eh?

Shouts in the direction of the tea shop.

Let's have some tea here!

SHOP BOY: Y-e-e-e-s!

He enters immediately, carrying two cups of tea on a small black lacquer tray, which he puts by Benten and Nango, and then sits at Nango's right side.

YOKURŌ: Now, what would you like to look at?

NANGO: Please show us some Kyoto-style woolen brocade obi fabric, some scarlet crepe for undergarments, and some scarlet dappled fabric as well.

YOKURŌ: Certainly, certainly. Clerks, bring out the Kyoto-style woolen brocade, scarlet crepe, and also some scarlet dappled fabric.

CLERKS: Y-e-e-e-s! (*Speaking in unison, they rush out.*)

YOKURŌ: The fabrics will be here in a minute. (*Pause*) They say the kabuki is really booming these days. Do you go to the theater, miss?

BENTEN (*Shyly*): Yes, I do. I recently saw a play at (*names the theater where this production is being given*).

YOKURŌ (*Rubbing his hands in glee*): You did, did you? Do you have any special favorite among the actors? Let's see if I can guess who it is. I'll bet it's that young star who steals all the girl's hearts (*names the actor playing Benten*), isn't it?

BENTEN (*Still shy*): No, I hate that actor with a passion.

YOKURŌ (*Undaunted*): Wrong, huh? Then it must be (*names the actor playing Nango*), right?

BENTEN (*Embarrassed*): Yes.

NANGO: But I hate that actor with all my heart! You really are a theater buff, aren't you? I'll bet you have a favorite actor, too.

YOKURŌ: I sure do (*names himself*)! I enjoy the theater more than my daily meals. (*Calling the clerks in singsong fashion*) Let's have those goods here, on the double!

CLERKS (*In unison*): Here we come!

The clerks enter carrying bolts of cloth and open boxes filled with piece goods, which they place near Benten. One of them carries two tall floor lanterns with the word Hamamatsu-ya on each and places them at either end of the upstage platform. The clerks busily take out the fabrics and hand them to Benten for his examination. He shows those he likes to Nango, who also examines them.

YOKURŌ: Sorry to have kept you waiting.

The clerks appear to be conversing with one another, although we don't hear what they are saying.

BENTEN: Which one of the dappled fabrics do you like, Yosohachi?

NANGO: Whatever pleases you is fine with me.

BENTEN: I do like this one with the hemp-leaf design.

NANGO: We should select one with an auspicious design, since it's for your wedding, after all.

YOKURŌ: Ah, it's for a wedding, is it?

BENTEN *(Embarrassed)*: Oh. Now didn't I tell you not to mention that?

NANGO: Well, it slipped out.

YOKURŌ *(Figuring on his abacus)*: These fabrics would come to . . .

Benten stealthily slips a piece of scarlet crepe out of his sleeve and drops it in the fabrics in front of him, mixes it in with the others, and then removes it, tucking it into his kimono at the breast.

SAHEI *(Leaning over to Yokurō, just before Benten's action)*: Hey, Yokurō-san, she really makes me drool.

YOKURŌ: Now that's uncalled for.

The clerk to Yokurō's left has noticed Benten's deliberate actions and, aghast, is tapping Yokurō and whispering to him fiercely. Yokurō motions to the clerks, and they instantly gather up all the fabrics and run inside. The shop boy takes the empty teacups and returns to the teashop. One clerk runs to the teashop to summon a fireman, Seiji, who is there. The clerks all come back in and stand in a row at upstage left. Benten and Nango act as though nothing were happening.

NANGO *(Casually)*: We'll take two bolts of the patterned fabric, three of the woolen brocade obi fabrics, and also the scarlet crepe. Please figure out what it all comes to. We're going to visit the Hachiman Shrine and will pick up everything on our way back.

Benten and Nango rise to leave, Nango replacing his sword in his obi, but Yokurō stops them.

YOKURŌ: Please wait a moment.

NANGO: What should we wait for?

YOKURŌ: You haven't been joking with us, have you?

NANGO: What do you mean, "joking"?

YOKURŌ: Please hand over the scarlet crepe you stole.

The fireman, Seiji, has entered from the teashop and stands at stage right, barring the entrance. He wears a fireman's leather happi *coat over his kimono, as well as tight leggings and dark split-toe socks [tabi]. The music, which has been playing throughout the scene, fades.*

SEIJI *(Nastily)*: Don't tell me a fine-looking young lady like yourself has been caught trying to steal!

CLERKS: It's a dishonest world we live in, eh, Seiji?

NANGO: What is this? My young mistress a thief? *(Slowly)* You'll be sorry you have such careless tongues in your heads!

YOKURŌ: We do business all year long and are never mistaken.

SAHEI: If you say you're innocent, we'll simply take off your clothes and search you.

TASUKE: You'd better hand it over.

CLERKS: Before something unpleasant happens to you!

SEIJI: Don't think you're going anywhere. Sit down. I say, SIT DOWN!

He pushes Nango down by pressing on his right shoulder. The clapper is beaten sharply to emphasize the movement.

FIGURE 3.85. The fireman Seiji holds down Nango as Yokurō retrieves the cloth and strikes Benten on the forehead. Benten's obi is tied in the *furisage* style. Seiji wears a happi coat and snug *momohiki* trousers. (Photo by Aoki Shinji.)

BENTEN (*Plaintively*): Oh, Yosohachi, what shall we do now?

NANGO: There's nothing to worry about. These beasts called you a thief, but I won't leave until your name is cleared.

YOKURŌ: What? You won't leave until her name is cleared? You seem pretty good at saying such things.

NANGO: As you are at calling people thieves.

YOKURŌ: Still holding to that line, are you? Well, you'll change your tune now.

He crosses over to Benten and pulls the cloth from his breast. The clapper now beats at each strong movement.

Where did you get this from? You're going to get it!

The Echigo Lion music begins again as the clerks rush over to thrash Benten. Seiji holds Nango back [figure 3.85]. Yokurō strikes Benten on the forehead with his abacus while the fireman and clerks force Benten and Nango into a position near the upstage platform, where they form a wall around them. Yokurō flails at Benten with his abacus, using stylized gestures to suggest this action. Sōnosuke, son of the shop's owner, enters hurriedly from the right, dressed in a fine light blue kimono with a three-quarter-length haori jacket. His is the delicate manner of the young male role. His wig bears the forelock of an adolescent, and he speaks in a rather high-pitched voice. While Benten is being beaten, a stage assistant dressed in black enters to help Benten with makeup and wig adjustments.

SŌNOSUKE: What's going on here? What's all the fuss about?

YOKURŌ (*Joining him at center stage*): Don't get upset now, but we caught these two in the act of stealing.

SŌNOSUKE: What? Thieves in this shop? What did they steal?

YOKURŌ: A piece of scarlet crepe fabric. (*Turning to the others*) Beat them good!

The others have been scarcely moving, so as not to distract from the other stage action. At this cue, however, they begin to ad-lib and make threatening movements. The next line is heard above the din and must be held and greatly emphasized to bring the moment to a rhythmic climax.

NANGO (*To beats of the clapper, he strikes a pose on one knee, thrusting out his hands to either side as if parting a wall, palms outward, fingers stretched*): Hold on, hold on, HOLD ON!

Two clerks move to the right and two to the left as Benten crouches low at center stage just below the platform, keeping his back to the audience and covering his forehead with a piece of white tissue paper.

You insist on calling us thieves, do you? Is that the cloth you say we stole? (*Points to the cloth on the floor.*)

YOKURŌ: Don't play dumb.

NANGO: We bought that cloth at the Yamagata shop. If you look at it carefully, you'll see that their mark is on it.

YOKURŌ (*Looking at the cloth and realizing his error*): Ahhh! The mark is that of the Yamagata, a mountain drawn inside a circle. This really is from their shop.

SAHEI: We called them thieves.

TASUKE: But it was something from another shop.

CLERKS: Yes, yes, yes (pause).

NANGO: Furthermore, Mr. Chief Clerk, I have proof of the sale right here.

He withdraws a receipt from his kimono and holds it in his left hand, pointing to it with the right. Drawing out his words with great emphasis, he continues.

Now, do you still insist on calling us thieves?

YOKURŌ (*Staring at the receipt*): I don't know what to say.

NANGO: Let's have an end to this thief business (*with emphasis*), shall we?

TASUKE: Sure.

He pauses. All the clerks and Sōnosuke now kneel and bow low in apology. Seiji, the fireman, however, merely lowers his eyes and does not prostrate himself. The stage assistant has helped Benten change his wig, without the audience noticing the switch. The new wig has only the rosette decoration inserted in the forelock, and the topknot is made to look somewhat awry. Shamisen music begins to play softly in the background and continues throughout most of the scene, highlighting the action.

SŌNOSUKE: My name is Sōnosuke, and I am the son of the owner of this shop. The clerks appear to have made a dreadful error and to have treated you very badly, so I must beg you on hands and knees to accept my deepest apologies. Please find it in your hearts to forgive us.

CLERKS (*Bowing low*): We beg of you to do so.

NANGO: What? (*Angry*) Now everyone is begging for forgiveness. It was easy enough for you to accuse innocent people of being crooks, wasn't it?

SŌNOSUKE: What you say is perfectly justified, sir, but please have pity and forgive us.

He rattles on, ad-libbing phrases begging forgiveness, overlapping with Nango's next line.

NANGO: Shut up, shut up, SHUT UP! To speak frankly, my mistress here is the daughter of Hayase Mondo, vassal of Nikaidō, lord of Shinano. She is engaged to a member of a powerful family from Akita and will soon be married. Do you think you can simply label her a thief and let it go at that?

SŌNOSUKE: We are deeply mortified at our mistake, sir.

NANGO: You fools don't understand a thing. Call your master. I said, call your master. CALL YOUR MASTER!

KŌBEI (*Offstage*): Yes, yes, I will be with you in a moment.

Plaintive shamisen music is played in the music room as Kōbei enters and crosses

FIGURE 3.86. A stage attendant has unobtrusively helped Benten change wigs. This simpler one has a "scar" attached. A hair ornament lies on the floor by Benten's hand as "she" looks up, revealing the disfigurement to the shopkeepers. (Photo by Aoki Shinji.)

down to the left of center. He gestures to Sōnosuke to move over for him and bows low to Nango.

NANGO: Well! I guess you must be the master himself, eh?

KŌBEI: I am Kōbei, the owner of this establishment. I overheard what happened and am at a loss as to how I can make amends for the rash behavior of my clerks. Please think of some way I can gain your forgiveness.

NANGO: If it were up to me, I might accept your apology, since it comes from the master of the house. (*Slowly and seriously*) But I'm afraid—

KŌBEI: I beg you to tell me how I can make this up to you.

NANGO: I can do nothing. (*Slowly draws Benten to his side*) Here master! Take a good look at this scar.

He has Benten raise his face, revealing a deep scar on his forehead [figure 3.86]. All are astonished at the sight. Kōbei points to Benten while looking at the clerks.

KŌBEI: Ahhh! You've scarred this young lady's face!

CLERKS (*Perplexed*): Yaa, yaa, yaa!

NANGO: As I've just said, my mistress is engaged to be married, but I can hardly bring her home with a gash on her face. It's unfortunate, I know, but I seem to have no alternative than to sever the head of each and every one of you and then commit ritual suicide right here.

He raises his sword and holds it perpendicular to the ground at his left.

Prepare yourselves!

BENTEN (*Slowly, while bent over with his hand to his head*): Yosohachi, isn't there some less violent way to settle this affair?

NANGO (*Putting down his sword*): There's nothing that can be done. If we settle this peaceably, news of it will leak out one day, and what excuse can I offer for my behavior then?

SEIJI (*Ingratiatingly*): Beg pardon, Mr. Samurai, but would you mind stepping over here?

NANGO (*Crosses over to the right, to Seiji*): Here I am.

SEIJI: It will only take a minute.

NANGO: Well, what is it?

SEIJI: From what I gather, that clerk made a rather serious error. There's really no excuse for what he's done. But what purpose would there be in lopping off our heads like a bunch of pumpkins? You can make up some excuse, like your mistress fell on her way home or something fell off a roof and hit her or something else like that, can't you? In return, we'll be glad to give you something nice for your troubles. Can we call it a deal?

NANGO: Wait a moment. (*Turns to Benten*) Shall I accept his offer, miss?

BENTEN (*She appears to be weeping quietly*): I suppose it's only right that we should.

NANGO (*Pauses*): Since that's what you want, I'll accept.

SEIJI: You will forgive us? Thank you very much. (*Bows slightly*) Please wait a moment.

NANGO: My mistress has been hurt, and I have been struck so!

These words are spoken as Seiji rises and crosses quickly to Kōbei, where he kneels. He looks meaningfully at Kōbei, and the latter reaches into his kimono to withdraw his wallet. He also takes the wad of paper from the breast fold of his kimono and, removing one sheet of paper, begins to wrap some coins from his wallet in it.

SEIJI: Hey, chief clerk, you'd better be more careful from now on. (*To Kōbei*) And you'd better keep a close watch on these clerks of yours.

Kōbei hands a packet of ten ryō to Seiji, who takes the money to Nango.

Sorry to have kept you waiting. I realize this isn't much, but please take it and leave us alone.

NANGO (*Picks up the money, opens the paper, and looks at it. Then, menacingly*): You said there'd be something worth our while; is ten ryō what you meant?

SEIJI (*Furious*): I sure did. I sure did! What's wrong with ten ryō?

NANGO: I thought we could settle this matter privately, but (*growing angry*) if my master should hear of it, it could be my neck! (*Puts the money down.*)

SEIJI: We've given you ten ryō. If you're not happy, you can leave without it.

NANGO: I'm not leaving, so what do you propose to do? I'm not selling my life for pocket money. I'll take (*stretching the words*) one hundred ryō (*pauses and then adds quickly*) or I'll take nothing!

SEIJI: What the—? You won't sell? You won't sell? Well, we won't buy! Get out! (*Turns to the clerk seated nearest him*) Tasuke, give this money back to your master. Well, you just said you were going to lop off our heads, right? You think you're tough because you carry two swords, huh? I'll tell you what! You can begin with me! Go ahead! Start chopping! Start chopping!

This is said quite quickly. Toward the end of the speech, the fireman stands, throws off his jacket, pulls back the lower flaps of his kimono, revealing black leggings, and squats cross-legged on the ground in a position of defiance.

NANGO (*Reaching for his sword*): If that's what you want—

The clerks rush over and hustle Seiji out into the teashop. As they do so, Seiji throws down his pocket towel, which is white with blue polka dots, at Nango's feet. The following lines, spoken as the fireman is being pushed out, sometimes are mingled with ad-libs.

YOKURŌ: Control yourself, Seiji!

CLERKS: Hold it, will you? Hold it!

When the clerks come back into the shop from the teashop, they quickly wipe off the soles of their split-toe socks with pocket towels.

NANGO (*Standing, ready to draw his sword*): Now that I have had one disgrace heaped upon another, I cannot leave without drawing blood. Get ready to lose your heads!

KŌBEI: Please, please wait a moment. (*Pauses*) A little while ago you said we hadn't given you enough money to make up for what has happened to you here. Money cannot buy a man's life, but somehow it may heal the wounds you have suffered. Well, well, please wait a second.

He gestures to Sōnosuke, who nods and takes a packet of one hundred ryō out of his breast fold and hands it to Kōbei, who places it by Nango.

Please forgive us.

NANGO (*Opens the packet and looks at the money, smiling*): It's not easy to forgive you, but since you're resigned to your fate, I'll accept these one hundred ryō.

All the shop people are bowing low.

KŌBEI: Then may we bring this matter to a close?

NANGO: As you wish.

KŌBEI: Then we all can

CLERKS: breathe a sigh of relief.

NANGO: We've stayed longer than we expected

BENTEN: but the matter has been settled without incident,

NANGO: so let us be off at once.

KŌBEI: Farewell to both of you.

NANGO: Thanks (*pause*) for everything.

The pair rise and begin to leave, Nango holding Benten's hand. Just then, Nippon Daemon enters through the upstage doors. He wears hakama, a haori jacket, and an unusual black headpiece [figure 3.87].[3] Since he is disguised as a samurai, he carries two swords and holds a closed fan in one hand. His is a bold and powerful presence, and his words stop Nango and Benten in their tracks.

NIPPON: Wait a minute, samurai. Wait *one* minute, please.

A clerk moves a cushion for Nippon to sit on and places a small tobacco box near him.

NANGO (*To Benten*): He's a pretty impressive samurai. (*To Nippon*) Do you have some business with me that you ask me to wait?

NIPPON: I do.

NANGO: And that business is?

NIPPON (*Meaningfully*): Well, well. Please take a seat.

Benten and Nango sit down, puzzled.

I heard everything that's been going on here, and you are to be commended

3. This black cloth headpiece (*zukin*) is called *Sōjūrō zukin* because it was created by Sawamura Sōjūrō I (1685–1756). It is considered the most striking of all kabuki cloth head coverings and became so popular that it was adopted by people in daily life.

for your generous act of pardoning these people.

NANGO: It was not easy to forgive them, but as I am in the company of my young mistress here . . .

NIPPON: All the more why this shop has been fortunate. It appears that I have unexpectedly run across a strange relation; you did say you are a member of the Nikaidō clan (*pauses*), didn't you?

NANGO: Correct! This lady is the daughter of Hayase Mondo, vassal to Nikaidō, lord of Shinano.

NIPPON (*Louder*): Are you quite sure of that?

NANGO (*Suspicious*): Why all these questions?

NIPPON (*Angry*): Because you're an imposter!

NANGO: What did you say?

FIGURE 3.87. As Benten and Nango are about to leave with their payment, Nippon Daemon enters from the back room wearing a dark haori, hakama, and hood (*Sōjurō zukin*). He and Nango each carry two swords. Kōbei and Sōnosuke are seated to the right. (Photo by Aoki Shinji.)

Shamisen music begins to play in the background.

NIPPON: I happen to be steward to Nikaidō, lord of Shinano. My name is Tamashima Ittō. I know of no one called Hayase Mondo in our family (*pauses*), and this fair young lady who says she is engaged is clearly a man.

BENTEN: Eh?

This is accidentally spoken in a male voice, but Benten immediately resumes his female voice.

Why, how can you say that I am a man?

He has been bent low at center stage all this while, pressing his forehead with a piece of paper. He remains so for the following dialogue.

NIPPON: Even though you say you're a woman and are quite good looking, I caught a glimpse of tattooing all over both your arms.

BENTEN: Oh!

NIPPON (*Sure of himself*): You are a man, aren't you?

BENTEN: Well, well, I . . .

NIPPON: If you insist you're a woman, how would you like us to examine your breasts?

This section builds in intensity and speed, with some overlapping of lines at the end. It is a major climax of the scene.

BENTEN: Well, well, I . . .

NIPPON: Tell us who you are!

The music fades out.

Kuriage *One voice overpowers the other until they join together in chorus.*

BENTEN: Saa, saa

NIPPON: saa, saa, saa

BOTH: saa, saa, saa!

NIPPON: You fake! Answer me!

He holds the final vowel. Nippon slaps his fan to the floor to emphasize the moment. Benten has practically collapsed. He is now the center of attention as the audience waits to see what he will do. Slowly, very slowly, he raises his face to the audience. The pause before he speaks may take as long as ten seconds. He seems to be struggling with his emotions. The white paper in his right hand flutters rapidly. As he leans over, his decorative rosette falls out of his hair to the ground. When he finally speaks, his manner changes completely to that of the brash, arrogant young "son of Edo." The contrast with his previous impersonation is striking.

BENTEN: Well, Nango (*pause*), no need for these disguises anymore. They've caught on to our game.

NANGO (*To Benten*): You're an impatient son of a bitch, aren't you? Couldn't you have waited a little longer?

BENTEN: Don't be an ass. They know I'm a man, so why do I have to stand on ceremony? Mr. Samurai here has guessed my true sex, so (*a pause and a derisive gesture of flipping his right hand*) I beg your pardon.

He begins to untie his obi cords. Nango, too, starts to change his appearance. Stage assistants enter and crouch behind the actors to help them [figure 3.88]. The actor creates the impression of delight in the feeling of being unbound from the extremely restricting female kimono. He opens the cord holding his long red underkimono in place and, stretching in a great yawn, for a moment reveals his male body underneath. Beneath his undergarments Benten wears a white loincloth and bellyband. He fans himself with his kimono folds and shakes his cramped legs. The business is accompanied by a good deal of humorous ad-libbing between Benten and Nango. Benten then sits down, cross-legged, at center stage. Nango has taken off his swords, his haori, and his hakama. He wears only a rather seedy-looking light brown kimono. His topknot has been pushed to the side so as to look disheveled.

Hey, chief clerk, how about a pipe and some tobacco over here?

The frightened Yokurō brings a pipe and a small box of tobacco taken from behind the large brazier at stage left, cautiously places it by Benten, and then scoots away quickly to the left.

YOKURŌ (*At stage left, shocked*): I thought he was a woman, but he was only an impostor!

CLERKS: Yaa, yaa, yaa.

Benten removes the sleeve of his outer kimono from his left shoulder, leaving the patchwork-patterned underkimono visible on his left arm and shoulder. The stage assistant adjusts the folds of his disheveled kimono on the ground around him, making a pleasing arrangement of the fabrics. Benten picks up a pipe and the polka dot pocket towel thrown down earlier by Seiji. He lights his pipe during the following lines. Nango, seated stage right and slightly upstage of Benten, does likewise. Benten speaks in a nasty, biting, arrogant voice, lengthening his vowels for effect. The shamisen plays in the background.

BENTEN: As you know, I came here disguised as a woman to wring some money out of you. I blew all our dough gambling in Akita and didn't even have a penny for a cup of soup, so thinking to earn myself a lousy ten ryō, I rented this woman's getup. I get by pretty good acting as a woman, so things would have gone nice and smooth if my cover hadn't been blown. This all ought to give you a good belly laugh. (*Smokes his pipe.*)

FIGURE 3.88. Stage assistants help Nango (left) and Benten (center) change their costumes. Benten's gestures reveal that he is really a man happy to be released from the restrictions of female clothes. (Photo by Aoki Shinji.)

YOKURŌ: No matter how I look at him, I keep seeing the young lady. Well, you sure are a brazen

CLERKS: character, aren't you?

BENTEN: Anyway, I came here in disguise. My neck is slender, but my nerve is thick.

NANGO: Hey, what's all this chatter about thick and thin, anyway? You sound like you're selling potatoes.

BENTEN: Right. And you can take your pick.

NIPPON: Even though your disguise has been discovered, you carry on as though nothing had happened. You must be the greatest con man of them all!

The music fades.

BENTEN: Hmm. You still don't know who we really are, do you?

YOKURŌ: You're obviously some no-good bum.

CLERKS: But we don't know who you are.

BENTEN (*Boldly and with dramatic emphasis*): If you still don't know (*slight pause*), then lend me your ears.

Pause. This is the most famous speech in the play, known to many Japanese by heart. Benten performs a wide variety of gestures with his pipe during its delivery [figure 3.89]. First, to get the audience's attention, he taps the pipe sharply on the brazier. This is said to be a trick borrowed from the storytellers who always rapped on their stands with their fans before beginning their tales. Satsuma bushi, a kind of shamisen accompaniment normally found in history plays, begins to play in the background. Meanwhile, Nango, having dropped his disguise, sits arrogantly smoking with his right hand while he keeps his left in the pocket of his right sleeve. Benten begins to speak while twirling his pipe around and around on the fingertips of his right hand, a trick requiring a good deal of manual dexterity, though he does

FIGURE 3.89. Benten gestures with a pipe as he makes his famous speech announcing his true identity. (Photos by Aoki Shinji.)

it quite casually. His voice rises and falls in regular poetic meter during this stylized speech. The last line culminates in a famous pose.

> In the words of the notorious bandit,
> Ishikawa Goemon,[4] we thieves are
> countless as Shichirigahama's sands.
> It was there I, too, plied my nighttime trade
> on the Isle of Enoshima,[5] near the
> abbey of Fuchi, while apprenticed to
> a local lord, I would steal and gather
> in my tiny bowl the pennies offered
> to the Buddha by the Edo pilgrims,
> then gamble freely with them and even
> further pile up loot by pilfering a
> hundred or two from the offertory box.
> My crimes piled up as well, and I went from
> theft to theft, robbing the sleeping pilgrims

4. This popular thief was executed along with his son by being boiled in oil on a riverbank in Kyoto in 1594. Plays about Goemon include puppet plays by Chikamatsu Monzaemon and Namiki Sōsuke, a kabuki play (*Kimmon gosan*) in which a superhuman Goemon challenges Toyotomi Hideyoshi (called Hisayoshi in the play), and a nineteenth-century play (*Keisei Hamanomasago*) featuring a female Goemon.

5. Both Shichirigahama and Enoshima are near Kamakura. The goddess Benten is worshiped on the island.

at the Iwamoto Temple, but my
quick-fingered reputation caught up with me,
and I was booted off Enoshima.
Next, I dressed in drag to trap married men
and blackmail them, playing the badger game
and then, here and there, extorted and conned
using the vocal tricks I picked up
in Terajima from my old granddad[6] —
so if you want to know my name, it's

*He taps the brazier with his pipe to remove the
tobacco.*

Benten Kozō Kikunosuke — that's who!

*He makes a wide swinging gesture with the pipe
and then slams it down at his side. At the same
time, he draws his left arm into his sleeve. The
name Kikunosuke is delivered in a greatly height-
ened manner, almost sung, with the syllable* no
*being spoken in a higher pitch than the rest, the
voice then dropping sharply for* suke. *As soon as
that last syllable is uttered, Benten thrusts his left
arm out of the breast of his kimono in a fist held
near the right knee, forcing the garment to drop
from his shoulder, revealing an arm and shoulder
covered with tattoos of blooming cherry blossoms.*

FIGURE 3.90. Benten removes his inner kimono, revealing his tattooed "skin," a painted or dyed body stock-
ing. This is the beginning of a dramatic pose, called the
Revelation Pose (*mie*), which is emphasized with beats
of the clapper. (Photo by Aoki Shinji.)

*Simultaneously, he grabs the big toe of his left foot and brings the foot up over the
knee of his right leg [figure 3.90]. He finishes with a revolving motion of the head
timed to the beating of the clapper. He glares, crossing one eye. Tattoos covering his
thighs are visible. This pose is called the Revelation Pose. As Nango begins to speak,
Benten slowly relaxes, after having held his pose for about five seconds, and begins
smoking again.*

NANGO *(Remaining seated):*
I, his partner and instigator, have
gambled and plundered from the shadows of
Fuji to Ōiso, Koiso, and Odawara.[7]
Born a fisherman acrost the waves, I
snatched the loaded dice presented to the
fishermen's patron deity aboard the
mother ship and gambled with them, flinging

6. Terajima is in modern Tokyo. More important, however, it was the home of Onoe Kikugorō III,
the grandfather of Kikugorō V, who played Benten in the first production of this play.

7. These three places are along Sagami Bay and serve as the gateway to the Hakone region around
Mount Fuji. Ōiso has a bluff with a fine view of the mountain, and Odawara was a castle town in the
Edo period.

down the dice like an anchor plunging in
the sea, grabbing the pot, raking off a
kickback. My steel-like nerves didn't flinch at
the thought of the dark, hell-like sea beneath
my feet, or of spending time in jail,
and I wouldn't stop at stealing the ship
itself. My crimes are as heavy as a
ship's speed is slow. Today you'll find me in
the east, tomorrow in the west, never
staying in one place long.

Reaching a minor crescendo.

I am Nango Rikimaru (*pause*),
and don't forget it!

He glares fiercely as he speaks, rhythmically moving his head and pipe to accentuate the pose.

NIPPON: You're from that five-man gang of Nippon Daemon's we hear so much about, aren't you?

BENTEN: Right. I'm the scrap end of the five thieves.

This is spoken in a highly rhythmic manner, which accentuates each syllable of the names, as Benten points to his left hand with his pipe and, starting with the thumb of his left hand, closes his fingers one by one until all the fingers are closed.

First, there's Nippon Daemon, Nango Rikimaru, Tadanobu Rihei, Akaboshi Jūzō, Benten Kozō (*pause*); I'm the last of the lot.

NANGO: To get right down to it, we won't be going anywhere with this. Here's the one hundred ryō we squeezed you for.

He turns and tosses the money to Kōbei, who is seated on the platform upstage of him.

BENTEN: Well, now that you've found us out, you can call the police. I've even put on a nice new loincloth for the occasion.

NANGO: I'm also ready for anything, come what may! Hey, boy! Let's have some tea!

SHOP BOY (*From inside the teashop*): Y-e-e-e-s!

BENTEN: Sounds like a ghost in there, doesn't it?

NANGO: His answers do take forever, don't they?

BENTEN: Yeah.

SHOP BOY (*Stands at Nango's right*): Here's your tea.

NANGO: What? You dare serve tea while standing? (*Takes a sip and spits it out*) Ptu! Do you think I can drink burned tea?

He tosses the tea in the boy's face. The boy is startled, then raises the round teatray in his right hand as if to strike Nango, and pauses. Nango glares at him menacingly; the boy thinks the better of it and runs off to the teashop, wailing. Nango tosses the teacup by the entrance, and the boy picks it up on his way out.

SHOP BOY: Waaaa!

BENTEN: Well, the sooner all this is finished, the better. We'd appreciate it if you'd get moving, tie us up, and hand us over to the cops before it gets dark. We don't know if we'll ever return to this corrupt world as we are, but we can guarantee (*to Nippon*) that as a token of our gratitude, we'll have no problem in visiting your place, my kind friend, even if we've lost our heads.

NANGO: Stop talking as if you're afraid to die.

NIPPON (*Considering what they've said*): Your skillful masquerade has been discovered, so what do you do? Do you rise and leave, disconsolate? No. You have the nerve to say "Turn us over to the cops!" If it wouldn't cause this family trouble, you two would soon breathe your last.

He grabs his sword with his left hand.

BENTEN (*Mocking*): How's this? How's this? Playing around with his sword? Did he say he would kill us? Go ahead, have fun! It's always been my ambition to see two heads chopped off at one stroke by an amateur getting his sword rusty on my blood.

He points to and strikes his left arm as if chopping it.

NANGO: Right you are! Right you are! How glorious it will be to die on these nice tatami mats and be carried out of (*pointing outside*) this shop like heroes!

BOTH: Remember, you get no money if you fail to draw blood! Go ahead, we're waiting!

They turn on their knees simultaneously and face right on a slight diagonal.

NIPPON: If that is what you want.

He takes his sword and begins to rise. Kōbei and Sōnosuke instantly gesture to stop him. They bow low to address Nippon.

KŌBEI: Please wait a moment, sir. If you murder these two scoundrels, our names will be dragged through the mud and

SŌNOSUKE: we realize how furious you must be, and they certainly are a wicked pair

KŌBEI: but we ask you to forgive them.

NIPPON: Yes, I have been angry, but from the beginning I had no taste for this affair. (*Puts his sword down.*)

KŌBEI: Then you'll forgive them?

NIPPON: Yes, I will.

SŌNOSUKE: Oh, thank you very much.

BENTEN: Well, are you going to kill us quickly or not?

NANGO: If you're turning us in instead . . .

KŌBEI: Now listen! (*He rises, crosses to Benten's left, and sits down.*) Keep a civil tongue in your heads! I'll be the one who says whether you are to be bound and handed over to the police. Since I'm in business and don't want a fuss, I'll overlook everything and let you go just as you are.

BENTEN (*Speaking over his shoulder*): No sir! We won't leave!

KŌBEI: And why not?

BENTEN (*Gesturing with his pipe*): I said I was the daughter of Hayase Mondo of the Nikaidō clan (*he shifts his position so that he is sitting on his left hip with his right leg out to the right, knee raised, while his left leg is under him; he leans on his left hand*) and dressed like this to prove it. My ruse was discovered, so I gave you back the one hundred ryō I stole from you. Right? You haven't lost a penny, but me—I'm called a thief, beaten by a mob, and get a goddamn scar on my forehead (*points to it with his pipe*). What do you propose to do about that?

KŌBEI: Well, as for that, I suppose I must apologize, and if it will help settle the affair, I'll give you a tidy sum that should soothe your feelings.

BENTEN: Let's talk the matter over. If we can come to an understanding, we'll be happy to leave.

KŌBEI: Wait a second, please.

Kōbei takes some money from his wallet and wraps it in a sheet of paper. While waiting, Benten ad-libs with Nango, asking him to look at his gash, telling him how much it hurts, and receiving his friend's commiseration; he also curses the clerk and his abacus.

It's not much, but please take it and leave us alone.

He puts down the money beside Benten, who picks it up and puts his arm back in his underkimono sleeve so that he will be more properly dressed for the moment.

BENTEN (*Breezily*): Thank you, Master, thank you. I understand very well the kind of trouble we've caused for you, your being such a respectable man and all.

As he talks, he looks at the money. Realizing it is, after all, only a small amount, he expresses surprise. His manner has now changed.

Eh? Hey, Master, you said you'd give us a tidy sum, but you couldn't have meant only twenty ryō, could you? How do you think we'd feel if people said that Benten Kozō and Nango Rikimaru had flopped at blackmailing a dry goods shop and came away with only ten ryō apiece? Here's your money back!

Puts it down with a thud and slides it over toward Kōbei; he then turns away.

KŌBEI (*Threatening*): If it's not enough, I'll think of something else.

BENTEN: Yeah! I'm not after pocket money, you know.

Kōbei attempts to get Benten's attention, saying, "Please, please."

NANGO: Now, now, Benten, we can probably get thirty or forty ryō out of him if we press him long enough, but we'd have to hang around here until it was too late. Let's take this cash and go, OK?

He crawls on his knees over to Benten.

BENTEN: Hey, Nango, you're not yourself tonight, are you? How can we leave with only ten ryō apiece?

NANGO: True enough, true enough.

At this point there is a great deal of ad-libbing between the pair, Benten refusing to accept the money and Nango urging him to take it. The exchange lasts a few seconds, speeds up, and reaches a climax when Nango states the following, loudly and slowly.

But remember (*pause*), the master here was just talking about certain measures he might have to take.

Nango is at Benten's right, elevated slightly above him on his knees. He speaks slowly and emphatically.

The money will come in handy if the cops ever get their hands on us.

At the end of this speech, he is rhythmically pointing his hand at the money near Benten. There is a long pause, then the pair nod knowingly at each other.

BENTEN: Well (*taking the money*), it's a shame I had to get scarred for nothing more than pocket money.

He points to his forehead, acting as if he had suffered great pain.

NANGO: I guess you're right, having to leave like this and all.

This following section requires a considerable amount of ad-libbing as Benten and Nango rise and begin to dress for the road. Nango busies himself at the rear with the bundle they are to carry. He is assisted by the stage assistant who has brought out a dummy set of swords wrapped in fabric to substitute for the hakama and swords removed earlier. Benten removes his outer two kimono and wears only his red undergarment, which he adjusts by tucking it up at the rear. He looks at himself and says what a fool he looks like. Nango offers him his haori jacket, which Benten puts on and poses with. Then Nango tells Benten he can't go out with a woman's wig on, since he looks ridiculous. Benten puts his hands to his head in surprise as if to say, "Oops! You're right" and, getting an idea, takes the polka dot towel and places it on his head, knotting it under his chin. He turns to Kōbei.

BENTEN: Don't worry, we'll be back. I mean twenty ryō is a mere drop in the bucket these days. I'm sure your shop can provide a better price, master.
KŌBEI: Now, please be reasonable
SŌNOSUKE: and leave us alone.
BENTEN: We're going, but we'll be back from time to time.
YOKURŌ: Not on your life!
BENTEN: That's a laugh! You may have told me to stay away, but I'll be back when my money runs out. (*To Yokurō*) You've got a mouth like a tea spout, you little runt!

He and Nango move to the entrance of the shop. Nango steps into his sandals, but Benten notices that his have red thongs.

Hey, boy! How the hell can I wear red sandals? Let me have those white ones. (*Points to a pair lying nearby.*)
SHOP BOY: They're the head fireman's.
BENTEN: I don't give a damn if they're the head's or the tail's! Give 'em to me!
SHOP BOY (*Bringing over Seiji's sandals for Benten*): Yes, sir.
BENTEN (*Turning slightly to Nippon*): One day, Mr. Samurai, I'll pay you back for this.
NIPPON: Anytime you have a complaint . . .
BENTEN: I won't forget!

YOKURŌ (*Turning to face Benten*): Come back the day before yesterday! (*Pushes Benten's shoulder.*)

BENTEN: What the . . . ?

He turns and aims a sharp slap at Yokurō's cheek; the clapper accentuates the blow.

YOKURŌ: Aiii!

He falls to the floor in a sitting position, below the platform, with his back to the audience.

BENTEN: How do you like that? (*To those in the shop*) Hope I haven't caused you too much trouble.

He thrusts his hands inside his kimono, keeping them at his chest, his sleeves dangling. Nango holds the bundle over one shoulder and puts his other hand inside his kimono, too. They casually proceed to the rampway, ad-libbing freely. The lines that follow are mainly from the acting script, but they are merely a skeleton on which the actors embroider their improvisations. Nango and Benten stop at the seven-three position. Shamisen music in the narrative style known as shinnai bushi is played in the music room.

BENTEN: The clouds look pretty big. It'll probably rain again tonight.

NANGO: Hey, are you sure you haven't forgotten something?

BENTEN (*Puzzled*): We've brought everything with us.

NANGO: Since we didn't divide it yet, let's do it now.

Realization dawns, and Benten immediately slips his hands into his sleeves and searches there for the money. He takes out the packet, holding it forth, his hand protruding from the breast of his kimono.

BENTEN: Right. This is your share.

He flips some coins into Nango's hand, also thrust forth from his kimono at the breast. They quibble a bit over their spoils. Then, referring to the bundle that Nango is carrying.

That load is a real pain, isn't it?

NANGO: Why don't we play The Priest Holds the Bag?

BENTEN: How do you play that?

NANGO: Whenever a blind masseur comes along, the other person must carry the load.

BENTEN: OK, it's fine with me.

Nango hands Benten the bundle. They begin to walk very slowly. A masseur enters the rampway tapping his blind man's cane [figure 3.91]. He is bald and wears a simple gray kimono and wooden clogs. A blue hand towel is tucked into his obi on one side and a cylindrical whistle on the other.

MASSEUR (*Singing out*): Massage, acupuncture!

BENTEN (*Happily*): A masseur. Here, you carry it. (*Gives the load to Nango.*)

NANGO: That was fast, wasn't it?

The masseur stops, seeming to have forgotten something, and turns back the way he came.

Hey, the masseur is leaving. Now it's your turn (*hands the load to Benten*).

BENTEN: Son-of-a-bitch masseur.

He puts load on his shoulder and begins to sing in the shinnai bushi style as he strolls up the rampway, his eyes downcast, almost closed. Meanwhile, the masseur, having felt for his whistle and towel and realizing that he had them with him all the time, turns to go on his original route. Nango sees him coming and holds his sleeves out, making a wall so that Benten does not see the masseur go by. Benten is singing.

Amari doyoku na, mada mada.

MASSEUR (*Now almost at the stage proper*): Massage, massage, acupuncture!

FIGURE 3.91. In their lighthearted exit, Nango and Benten exchange a bundle of clothes each time a blind masseur passes them. Their kimonos are worn tucked up (*hashiori*) in the nonchalant, uneven style often affected by dandified gamblers. Benten has put on Nango's short coat and has a hand towel (*tenugui*) wrapped around his female wig. Nango and Benten wear zōri, and the masseur is wearing low geta. (Photo by Aoki Shinji.)

BENTEN: Ah! A masseur, huh? (*Tries to give the bundle to Nango.*)

NANGO (*Not taking it*): Yeah, but your singing canceled the deal.

BENTEN: Damn and double damn!

The two casually stroll off the rest of the way while the masseur, blowing his whistle, exits at stage right. The shamisen begins playing.

KŌBEI (*To Nippon*): If it hadn't been for you, sir, they would have gotten away with one hundred ryō.

SŌNOSUKE: Without your help, we could never have avoided being robbed.

KŌBEI: We would like very much to give you something for your trouble; if you would be kind enough to step into the rear of the shop for a cup of sake.

NIPPON: Since you put it like that, it would be rude to refuse.

KŌBEI (*Bowing gratefully, as do the others in the shop*): Sir.

NIPPON: Then I shall (*taking up his sword*) be glad to accept.

Music and singing are heard from the music room. Sōnosuke crosses to the center doors, kneels, and opens them for Nippon to go through. The curtain is pulled across the stage on this tableau as the clackers are struck together faster and faster.

A Maiden at Dōjōji (Musume Dōjōji)

A dance piece

Translated by Mark Oshima

The Dōjōji story, which appeared earlier in this anthology in a noh version, is also presented in various forms on the puppet, kabuki, and folk stages.[1] The main bunraku version, *Hidakagawa iriai zakura* (1759; The cherry trees along the Hidaka River), was composed by Chikamatsu Hanji and others. In that variation, a young girl, Kiyohime, falls in love with an imperial prince, who, for political reasons, is disguised as the priest Anchin. Its most popular scene, sometimes performed as a dance piece in kabuki, depicts Kiyohime's transformation into a serpent as she crosses the Hidaka River (figure 3.92). A kabuki version entitled *Yakko Dōjōji* features a dancer who is revealed to be a male kyōgen performer, and another variation, *Meoto Dōjōji*, presents both a male and a female dancer. The original reason for using a male dancer was a pragmatic one. The last play (*Kin no zai Sarushima dairi*, 1829), by Tsuruya Namboku, who also wrote *Yotsuya Ghost Stories* (translated here), was supposed to end with a standard Dōjōji scene featuring a woman; however, the onnagata became ill, and Utaemon IV, an actor who specialized in male roles, agreed to do the role as a man.

The best-known and most enduring kabuki version is *A Maiden at Dōjōji* (Kyōganoko musume Dōjōji, or simply Musume Dōjōji).[2] The play originated with the great onnagata Segawa Kikunojō I (1693–1749), who was particularly talented at transforming noh plays into kabuki-style pieces. In 1731, after having created kabuki versions of *Hagoromo* and *Shakkyō*, Kikunojō performed *Courtesan Dōjōji* (Keisei Dōjōji) at the Nakamura Theater in Edo (now Tokyo). In this rendition of the story, the bell is raised to reveal not a demon but a beautiful courtesan who recalls

---

1. The autumn 1992 edition of the journal *Bekkan Taiyō* (The sun: special issue) is devoted to *Dōjōji* and contains pictures of various dance and folk forms.

2. Kyōganoko refers to a kind of dappled cloth (*kanoko*) produced in Kyoto, the home of Nakamura Tomijūrō I (1719–1786), who first performed the starring role.

her life in the pleasure quarters and then depicts the torments of the hell where her ghost is suffering. Combining this work and another popular version, *Sanakida Dōjōji*, produced by Kikunojō in 1744, Nakamura Tomijūrō I created *A Maiden at Dōjōji* in 1753. Tomijūrō, perhaps the greatest onnagata in kabuki history, changed the main character from a dignified courtesan to a young girl (*musume*) and substantially lightened the tone. This version, although it has changed considerably over the centuries, has retained its popularity and is now the single most important dance piece (shōsagoto) in the kabuki repertory.

In *A Maiden at Dōjōji*, the noh story of feminine desire becomes a backdrop for a series of separate dances, each with a distinctive atmosphere conveyed by different musical accompaniments, costumes, and movements and employing different hand props—a fan, a mirror, a small towel, hats, a drum, tambourines, and a demon's mallet. In the course of the dances, many different characters emerge briefly—a young girl, courtesans from various parts of Japan, a woman in a boudoir, a fox, and a

FIGURE 3.92. Kiyohime poses at the edge of the river (top) in the bunraku version of the Dōjōji story (*Hidakagawa iriai zakura*). As she swims across, she is transformed into a serpent (bottom). (Photos by Aoki Shinji.)

demon. Mark Oshima suggests that these fragments of character are not so much aspects of the fictional Kiyohime as they are different faces of "woman" projected on the screen of the role of the young woman. The high point of the piece is the central lament (*kudoki*), which is danced with a white silk towel (*tenugui*), cotton replicas of which are then distributed to the audience by the dancer and the priests.

In his translation, Oshima describes the nature of the dances and their importance. However, even his careful annotations still indicate only about half the movements performed. The translation is based on the text found in Gunji 1980. The descriptions of the dance movements are based on current performance practices.

CHARACTERS

HANAKO: a shirabyōshi dancer, but in reality, the ghost of Kiyohime
ODATE GORŌ: a name for the role of Demon Queller
Priests

MUSICIANS

Gidayū chanters and shamisen players
Nagauta chanters and shamisen players
A noh ensemble of flute and drums
Music-room percussionists and sound effects

A Dance Piece in One Act

The main curtain is drawn open to the sound of wooden clackers, revealing a large bell hanging at stage left. The rest of the scene is hidden by a curtain with horizontal red and white stripes. The priests enter along the runway wearing white robes with black aprons and wigs that represent shaved heads. They carry Buddhist rosaries.

PRIEST 1 *(Walking down the rampway)*: Have you heard, have you heard?
OTHERS: We've heard, we've heard.
PRIEST 1: Have you heard, have you heard?
OTHERS: We've heard, we've heard.

The priests enter the main stage and line up across the stage facing forward, with Priest 1 at stage left.

PRIEST 2: You keep saying, "Have you heard, have you heard?" Have we heard what?
PRIEST 1: I'm asking whether you have heard that there is to be a dedication ceremony for the new bell today?
PRIEST 2: I thought you were asking if we heard that the head priest has another girlfriend.
PRIEST 3: Just thinking about how long the head priest will drone on reciting sutras makes my stomach turn.
PRIEST 4 *(Holding out jug of sake)*: I've brought a healing elixir for that problem.
OTHERS *(In surprise and delight)*: Oh, oh!
PRIEST 5 *(Holding out some cooked octopus)*: And I've brought a sacred canopy.[3]
OTHERS: Oh, oh!
PRIEST 6: Then shall we nibble at the sacred canopy,

---

3. A *tengai*, a canopy hung above a Buddhist altar, has long, dangling straps that resemble the legs of an octopus. Buddhist priests are prohibited from eating fish or meat and drinking alcoholic beverages. Compare the similar dialogue between Black Cloud and White Cloud in the opening scene of *Saint Narukami*, translated in part 1.

PRIEST 7: and sip at the healing elixir,

PRIEST 1: and take our places,

ALL: to keep watch.

Travel passage (michiyuki)[4] *The priests sit in two rows facing the audience while to the left of them, at stage right, a temple gate is set out by the stage assistants. A wheeled platform covered with a bright red ground cloth on which the Takemoto musicians are seated is pushed onstage. The ensemble usually consists of three chanters and three shamisen players, although the narration is largely a solo by the main chanter, accompanied by a single shamisen. The other musicians join in the more lyrical passages to intensify the musical texture.*

TAKEMOTO CHANTERS:

The moon shimmers on all the inlets of the sea;
white mists snake through the plains of scrub pine.
I try to hurry, but the wind holds me back,
reaching out at my long waving sleeves,
making my graceful white hood flutter.

The sharp sound of the noh flute from the music room signals the entrance of Hanako on the rampway. She is wearing a black kimono with a pattern of flowering cherry branches. Her obi sash has circle designs, and she has on a white cap of the type worn by women to keep dust off their hair when they go outside. She carries a small gold fan. She stops at the seven-three position and poses, looking slightly left, inclining her head, and then turning slightly to the right.[5]

My clothing is in disarray from my journey;
how embarrassed I am.
Perhaps people will guess at the turmoil in my heart.

Hides behind her sleeve.

I think of my sacred oaths of fidelity to the one I love.

Makes a prayer gesture with her hands.

Lost in the single-minded hope that the gods will grant my prayer,
I hurry by the magnificent clouds of cherry blossoms.

Looks to both sides, admiring the blossoms.

Along the way, people laugh at my distraction,

Bashfully hides behind her fan.

in the sky the seagulls laugh in derision as well—
laugh on, laugh on!

4. The travel passage was added after Tomijūrō I's time. It has been regularly performed; however, over the years actors have used different forms of narrative music to accompany their entrances. The version described here is probably rather late. Even though the music and lyrics have changed somewhat, the images, and hence the choreography, have probably remained roughly the same.

5. This *kubifuri* head movement is often used to animate poses (mie) that are the high points of kabuki dance. Although this section has more movements related to the narrative than do other parts of the dance, even in mimetic moments—such as when Hanako weeps or expresses hatred for the bell— the point is less to express character than to create a series of poses.

FIGURE 3.93. The shirabyōshi dancer Hanako, dressed in a black kimono with a cherry blossom design, pauses at the seven-three spot on the rampway. The chrysanthemum (*kiku*) motif on her obi and inner kimono and the nested-fan pattern in the silver hair ornament are references to the actor playing the role, Onoe Kikugorō. Hanako is looking into a mirror and arranging her hair, to the front of which is pinned a folded head cloth (*bōshi*). (Photo by Aoki Shinji.)

She points and rotates her finger coyly as though chiding them.

I remember being parted from my love
    at daybreak,

Pillows her head on her sleeve.

    parted by the hateful toiling of the bell
    at dawn.

Raises her fist in the direction of the bell.

    May the bell shatter; may its clapper
    break—

Holds out her fan to represent the log used as a bell clapper.

    it dammed the river of my love and
        stopped the flow of my passion.

She hits her left hand with the fan and makes a small circle on the rampway, staring fixedly at the bell. Then she sits, taking a small folded sheaf of tissue papers and a hand mirror from the bosom of her kimono and adjusting her hair to the accompaniment of a popular song [figure 3.93]. A bamboo flute and small gong playing in the music room join the Takemoto musicians to add to the liveliness of the atmosphere.

    A woman in love is like a plover drenched
        by the sea,
    each and every night she wrings out her tear-soaked sleeves, *shongae*.[6]

The actor takes a piece of the tissue paper, coyly rolls it into a ball, and tosses it into the audience.[7] She holds the ends of her long kimono sleeves and gestures with them during the second verse of the song.

    On nights when I meet my love, the ravens call from treetops.
    As they caw, "How sweet, how sweet," we draw each other close, *shongae*.

The mood changes again, becoming melancholy.

    As we share a pillow, the dawn bell startles us to wakefulness.
    Outside, the lonely cry of the geese fills the sky over the empty fields.

She stands up and makes a circle on the rampway, shading her eyes with her fan as she looks up, as though watching the birds in the sky.

6. *Shongae* is a meaningless, rhythm word (*hayashi kotoba*) used to emphasize the end of each of the song's stanzas.

7. The paper becomes a keepsake from the actor for the person who catches it. This illustrates the simultaneous presence of the performer as both a character and a star in kabuki.

Am I the only one so persecuted by the bells?
Do I hate an innocent bell?

She poses, holding her sleeves in front of her, weeping, and shaking with emotion.

But when I count my resentments, each time a bell has hurt me,
the crimes outnumber the grains of sand on the road—

She approaches the stage.

the road along which I hurry to the place
where the cherries blossom early.
Already I have arrived at Dōjōji Temple;
I have arrived at none other than the famed Dōjōji.

As the music ends, the platform on which the Takemoto musicians sit is pushed off-stage. The dancer goes and stands outside the gate at stage right. On the other side of the stage, the priests all stand in a group.

PRIEST 1: Have you all noticed that nice smell?

OTHERS: Yes, yes.

PRIEST 2: I'll go take a look. (*Goes and peers at the woman*) What a wonderful smell. (*Returns to the other priests*) A beautiful woman is here.

PRIEST 1: Where, where? (*Looks at her*) You're right, she is certainly beautiful. Who do you think she could be?

PRIEST 2: I think she is a shirabyōshi dancing girl.

PRIEST 3: No, she can't be a dancing girl, she looks like a sweet young thing.

HALF OF PRIESTS: Dancing girl, dancing girl!

OTHERS: Sweet young thing, sweet young thing.

PRIEST 1: It's no good arguing about it. I'll ask her myself. Hey there, you woman standing there. Are you a shirabyōshi dancer—

PRIEST 2: or are you a sweet young thing?

PRIEST 1: Pray tell us who you are.

OTHERS: Pray tell us who you are.

HANAKO: I am a shirabyōshi dancer living in this region.

PRIEST 1: What business does a dancing girl have here at our temple?

HANAKO: I have heard that a new bell is to be dedicated and have traveled long and far to see it. Please allow me to dance for the dedication of the bell.

PRIEST 2: We might be able to allow you to worship

PRIEST 3: if you will answer our questions first.

HANAKO: I will respond to your questions if you will let me worship the bell.

PRIEST 4: Then we shall proceed. Even the worst sinner,

PRIEST 5: the greatest fool—

HANAKO: can be aided by Monju's wisdom.[8]

PRIEST 6: Willows are—

HANAKO: green.

PRIEST 7: Cherry blossoms—

HANAKO: pink.

8. Monju is the bodhisattva associated with wisdom.

PRIEST 8: A dancing girl is a—

HANAKO: dancer.

PRIEST 9: What is a "sacred canopy?"

HANAKO: A concealing hat.

PRIEST 10: No, it's an octopus.

HANAKO (*Holds out her fist*): Priests, what is this?

PRIEST 11: That's a shell fist.[9]

HANAKO: In my hand is a sparrow.

PRIEST 1: They say a sparrow dances until it's a hundred years old.[10]

PRIEST 2: Are you suggesting that we dance?

HANAKO: Is this sparrow dead or alive? Take a guess.

PRIEST 3: If we say that it's alive, you'll crush it.

PRIEST 4: If we say that it's dead, you'll let it fly free.

HANAKO: Look at this. (*Opens her hand.*)

PRIESTS: There's nothing there!

HANAKO: If you think it's there, it's there.

PRIESTS: If you think it's not there, it's not there.

HANAKO: Substance is emptiness;

PRIESTS: emptiness is substance.

HANAKO: Please let me in to worship the bell.

PRIEST 1: After all that you have said,

PRIEST 2: we will allow you in.

PRIEST 1: Come in, come in.

PRIESTS: Yum-yum!

The priests murmur in appreciation of her beauty in a most unpriestlike manner.

PRIEST 1: Fortunately, there happens to be a court cap here. Please put it on and dance.

PRIESTS: Dance, dance!

HANAKO: I hear and obey.

A priest hands Hanako the gold-colored court cap, which is on a ceremonial tray. She takes it and exits stage right to change her costume. While she is gone, the priests discuss types of dances and the history of dance. Some of this is ad-libbed, so their comments change from production to production. When the dancer is ready, there is a signal from offstage, and to the solemn sound of the noh flute from behind the red and white curtain and a tinkling bell and booming drum from the concealed music room at stage right, the priests go and sit on either side of the stage. When they are seated, the clappers strike once, and the curtain is raised to reveal Hanako wearing the gold court cap and a red kimono. The backdrop is a landscape filled with cherry trees in full bloom. A large nagauta ensemble of chanters and shamisen players sit on a long platform covered with a red cloth. In front of them is a percussion ensemble, including a stick drum player, and two or three players each of the hip and

9. The Japanese word is *sazae*, a shell shaped like a fist. Like all shellfish, it also has slightly erotic connotations in Japanese.

10. This is based on the maxim "A sparrow does not forget how to dance even if it reaches a hundred," meaning that the things learned when one is young are never forgotten.

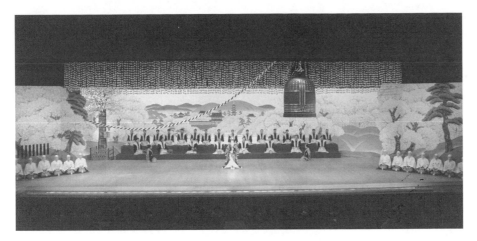

FIGURE 3.94. Hanako, the priests, two stage attendants (*kōken*, kneeling), and the nagauta and noh musicians (*debayashi*) are surrounded by cherry blossoms and the hanging bell (*kane*). (Photo by Aoki Shinji.)

shoulder hand drums, as well as a few noh flutists. All the musicians are wearing formal kamishimo costumes with cherry blossom patterns, so that it appears almost as though the blossoms from the backdrop had spilled out onto them [figure 3.94].

Shirabyōshi dance

NAGAUTA CHANTERS *(To noh-style shidai music.)*
    Other than the ephemeral cherry blossoms,
    there is only the eternal pine.
    Other than the ephemeral cherry blossoms,
    there is only the eternal pine.
    The sky begins to darken,
    how the sound of the temple bell will resound.

To the sharp sound of the hip drum, Hanako slowly begins to approach the bell, staring at it fixedly and moving faster and faster until she is directly under it.

Rambyōshi *She turns and, to the accompaniment of cries from the drum ensemble, begins this dance adapted from the noh play. Facing forward, she lifts her right foot, moves it to one side, then to the other, and sets it back down. She repeats this movement with her left foot and looks up sharply at the bell [figure 3.95]. Holding out her fan, a large formal noh fan—different from the delicate fan used in the travel passage—she makes a wide circle and sings. The percussion ensemble accompanies her movement, but the rhythm is unrelated to her singing.*

HANAKO:
    Obeying an imperial command,
    Lord Michinari first raised these sacred walls,
    and because the temple was his work,
    they called it Dōjōji.[11]

---

11. The characters for Michinari can also be pronounced "dōjō"; *ji* means "temple."

FIGURE 3.95. Hanako performs as a shirabyōshi dancing in a gold court cap (*eboshi*) and red kimono with long sleeves (*furisode*) and a hanging (*furisage*) obi. At the left, she performs the rambyōshi dance from the noh theater, raising her feet and then looking up at the bell. At the right, she looks up at the sky before throwing her cap up over the bell rope (in some traditions); she has already loosened the cap's cords. (Photos by Aoki Shinji.)

Fast dance (kyūnomai) *The noh flute and drums accompany this dance, which Hanako performs with her fan, circling the bell with formal movements taken more or less from noh-style dancing. Suddenly, the bright sound of the shamisen enters, and the chanters begin to sing quickly and rhythmically, changing the mood as Hanako stamps her feet to add to the rhythm.*

NAGAUTA CHANTERS: There are many things to hate about the sound of a temple bell.

The mood changes again, and the ensemble sings in a slow, rather solemn version of nagauta-style singing.

"The bell tolls at the beginning of the night,

She gently taps her left sleeve with the open fan.

telling of the impermanence of all things;

Holding her left sleeve to the front, she slowly takes a few steps.

the bell tolls in the middle of the night,

She circles slowly in place, bending forward and looking at her fan first low in front of her and then raised high as she bends backward; she taps her sleeve again.

telling that all that lives must die.

She walks slowly forward again. From this point, the dancer's movements are not directly related to the words. She gestures with her fan and stamps from time to time to the rhythm of the shamisen.

The dawn bell resounds with the destruction of all;
the evening bell resounds with the infinite joy that greets
those who leave the world of mortal pleasure."[12]
All hear these bells, and none is surprised.
I have cleared away the five clouds of mortal delusion

Waves her open fan.

and spend the night gazing at the clear moon of enlightenment.

12. These lines are based on a section of the noh play *Miidera*, translated in part 2.

She gazes into the sky, loosens the court cap's cords, and removes it, tossing the cords of the cap over the bell rope. The court cap hangs on the rope until it is later taken away by a stage attendant.[13] *The dancer poses solemnly, turns around, looks at the bell, and then walks upstage. There, a stage attendant adds a silver tiara to the dancer's wig. In keeping with the spectacular setting of the play, the stage attendant is dressed in a formal costume (kamishimo). While this is going on, there is a shamisen interlude accompanied by the solemn tinkling bell and booming drum from the music room.*

"My heart does not speak (iwazu katarazu)" *The next section is a lively dance with hand gestures. Unlike the previous sections, it is performed in pure kabuki style. The text resembles a popular song and has no direct relationship to the Dōjōji story except as it describes the feelings of a woman about a man. The dancer depicts an energetic young girl, and the only gestures directly related to the text suggest the tangles in her hair, an image for troublesome feelings of love.*

NAGAUTA CHANTERS:

My heart does not speak, it does not tell tales,
but the tangles in my hair and the pain in my heart
all come from your faithlessness.
So it is that all men are fickle.
Even though it is the felicitous season
when people sing in praise of cherry blossoms,
what my lover told me contained meanings false,
double as my waving sleeves.
Even when I am with a man in the pleasure quarters,
my mind wanders to the one I love.
So it is that all women are fickle.
One raised in the capital is as beautiful and pure
as the blossom of the lotus.[14]

A stage attendant suddenly pulls out some threads, and Hanako's red kimono is removed to reveal a pale blue one. She lies on her side, languidly holding one sleeve behind her, and poses.

Bouncing ball dance (mari uta) *The shamisen music, accompanied by bamboo flute and drum, plays a long, rhythmical, instrumental passage. The dancer mimes taking a ball from her sleeves or mimes gathering cherry petals to form a ball. Kneeling, she mimes bouncing the ball as she circles on her knees, resuming a full standing position as the lyrics begin. This is both a virtuoso section for the dancer and an opportunity to express the lively innocence of a young girl. During the following passage, the dancer alternately mimes actions that evoke the characteristics of different pleasure quarters and again bounces the imaginary ball. As is usually the case with Japanese catalogs, this list of pleasure districts is replete with puns on the place-names.*

13. These are the stage directions followed by the Utaemon line of actors. For other lines of actors, a stage assistant removes the cap after the dancer loosens its cords.

14. In the mid-eighteenth century, when Nakamura Tomijūrō I first performed this dance, Kyoto women were famous for their beauty and refined manners, and nearly all onnagata came from the Kyoto–Osaka area.

NAGAUTA CHANTERS:

> In the quarters of love
> a concealing straw hat,
> an indispensable accessory for samurai,[15]

Mimes carrying swords.

> in this land of spirited women with pride:
> Edo's Yoshiwara.

She waves her fist and then circles, miming an elegant yet haughty, high-ranking courtesan.

> The capital, full of blossoms,
> gently cultured with the sound of poetry:
> Kyoto's Shimabara.

She takes out a pocket mirror, looks at herself, slips it back into her kimono, and then circles, waving her sleeves.

> Who does a courtesan bed down with
> in Fushimi's Sumizome quarter?[16]
> Solemn black robes match the dark of twilight,
> mortal sins and salvation:
> the bells of Shumoku-machi.

Mimes striking a bell.

> From the four pleasure quarters of Osaka
> are tree-lined crossroads along which I commute
> to the pleasure district of Nara

Mimes carrying a palanquin.

> with its stands of child apprentices.[17]
> The early blooming blossoms by their chambers[18]
> reveal the true color of sensuality.
> One, two, three, four

Mimes bouncing a ball.

> dewy nights and days of snow.

Protects herself with her sleeves.

> The road through the narrow pass,[19]

15. Samurai were not supposed to visit the pleasure quarters, so they conventionally concealed their identities with large, conical straw hats that could be rented at the gate to the Yoshiwara.

16. Sumizome and Shumoku-machi were two pleasure districts in Fushimi, a town on the southern edge of Kyoto. There are puns on all three names: *fushi* can mean "to lie down"; *sumizome* means "ink-stained" and is used to describe the black robes of priests; and *shumoku* indicates the log used to strike a temple bell.

17. Osaka's Shinmachi pleasure district had four blocks and Nara's pleasure quarter was called *kitsuji*, which means "tree crossroad." This leads by association to the next phrase, *kamurodachi*, which refers both to a stand of pines and to the young girls who were apprentices of courtesans.

18. *Muro,* which means "chamber," was also the name of the pleasure district in Hyogo.

19. "Narrow pass" is a pun on the place-name Shimonoseki.

which my lover travels nightly,
as we come to know each other intimately,
our relationship becomes as full and round
as the Maruyama district in Nagasaki.[20]

She stands facing front and draws a circle with her hands.

Love at first sight became an unbreakable
    bond.

The dancer and the priests exit, and the shamisen ensemble performs an instrumental interlude.

String of hats (kasa odori)   *When the dancer returns, the top of her kimono has been pulled down to reveal another light blue underkimono. She has a flat, round, red hat on her head and holds a similar hat in each hand. Her entrance is accompanied by an instrumental prelude played by the shamisen and stick drum.*

NAGAUTA CHANTERS:
    Plum blossoms *san san*
    and cherry blossoms,
    which is the older brother, which the
        younger?

She holds out first one hat, then the other, then waves them over the hat on her head, creating bewildering patterns.

    They can't be told apart,
    the colors of the flowers.

FIGURE 3.96. Hanako poses at the end of the hat dance, with red hats spread out to each side of her in a serpentine design. Two layers of the light blue kimono are visible, one above and the other below the obi. (Photo by Aoki Shinji.)

Each hat opens out into a string of three. The dancer waves them over her head and then poses with them all in a line, a pattern vaguely reminiscent of a serpent [figure 3.96]. The dancer exits stage right as the shamisen and stick drum repeat the prelude to this song.

Priests' dance   *All the priests, except for the two most senior, come out with the tops of their white robes slipped off their shoulders and tucked around their waists to reveal red underrobes covered with white circles with charcoal gray sleeves. They are wearing pink headbands, and the hems of their robes are tucked up (hashiori) into their sashes to reveal yellow leggings. They carry openwork parasols studded with clusters of cherry blossoms. They line up across the stage and dance in pairs to the second verse of the song [figure 3.97].*

    The lovely iris has two shades,
    which is the older sister, which the younger?

20. Maruyama is the pleasure district in Nagasaki and also means "round mountain."

FIGURE 3.97. The priests dance with openwork parasols decorated with cherry blossoms. Their kimono are tucked up into their sashes, revealing yellow leggings. (Photo by Aoki Shinji.)

> They can't be told apart,
> the colors of the flowers.

The priests suggest the iris with the closed umbrellas, then open them, spinning them sideways to suggest wheels and waving them in the air as they walk around each other in pairs. They divide in the middle and exit to either side during the following passage.

> From the east and from the west
> all come to gaze at the flowerlike face
> and so, and so.
> Each glance makes it seem more lovely,
> the face of the beautiful maiden.

At the end of this section, Priest 1 and Priest 2 come out, still in their white robes. One attracts the other's attention by pointing in various directions and then mischievously poking him in the eye. A mimed fight ensues, and the two priests exit on opposite sides of the stage. The other priests return in their white robes and take their seats on either side of the stage. There is a long, spectacular interlude by the shamisen ensemble, and then the stage is hushed for the following section, the emotional high point of the dance.

Lament (kudoki)[21]   *The dancer returns dressed in a lavender kimono and carrying a white tenugui towel decorated with the actor's crest.*

NAGAUTA CHANTERS:

> I began learning about love from books,
> and ended up learning more than enough from experience.

21. In performance, this section shows kabuki dance at its best. The dancer creates the intimate atmosphere of the boudoir. At some moments, the movements illustrate the words of the song, and at others, the words and movements operate independently. The tension and relaxation created by the divergence and convergence of the music and dance build a richly varied rhythm that focuses the audience's attention on suspended moments that highlight the facial expressions of the actor, like a series of cinematic close-ups.

FIGURE 3.98. Dressed in a lavender kimono, Hanako performs the Lament dance with a tenugui. At the left, she begins by spreading the towel; the double-fan crest is that of the actor Onoe Kikugorō. At the right, she is covering her eyebrows to suggest marriage (married women shave their eyebrows). (Photos by Aoki Shinji.)

Standing, she holds the center of the tenugui with her lips and spreads out the ends with both hands [figure 3.98]. She then faces the back of the stage, leans back, and looks behind her.

For whose sake did I redden my lips and blacken my teeth?[22]

She sits on the floor, mimes putting on makeup, and then gazes into a mirror suggested by the tenugui.

It was all to show my devotion to you.

She holds one end of the tenugui and gently tosses it front and back and then twirls it in a circle.

Oh, the joy! How happy I was.

She looks and then bashfully hides her face; poses facing the back and looking behind her again, this time holding the tenugui around her arm.

You said that we would be like this, so I endured patiently.

Puts the tenugui around her neck, tucking the ends neatly inside the lapels of her

---

22. Blackening teeth was customary for married women but was also done for cosmetic reasons, to keep teeth from looking an unsightly yellow next to pale powdered skin.

FIGURE 3.99. Now in a yellow kimono and dancing with a little drum (*taiko*), Hanako leans over backward and makes foxlike gestures with her hands at mention of the fox shrine of Inari. (Photo by Aoki Shinji.)

kimono and links her little fingers in a gesture that suggests the lovers being united.

> Are all the written vows we exchanged false?

Holds out the ends of the tenugui as she poses, faces back, and then, reaching behind her, poses while holding out the loose ends of her obi sash.[23]

> It was unbearable not knowing your feelings;
> I had to come and see you.
> Having vowed never to be jealous,
> I became accustomed to hiding my feelings.

She mimes clapping her hands with joy at seeing her lover, leading him in, and making him sit and listen to her; her hands pushing back and forth delicately suggest a fight between them, which leads her to sit, looking soulful and teary-eyed.

> Now, after all that has happened, I think how cruel you are.
> Is a woman worthless?

Waves her sleeves in delicate feminine gestures.

> My husband, lord and master,[24]
> I do not know what is in your heart.
> I do not know what is in your fickle, fickle heart.

Puts the tenugui around her shoulders again, holding out the ends as she takes a few steps.

> How hateful, how hateful!

Suddenly the music slows, and her movement freezes. She stares and starts to turn slowly in the direction of the bell, her stare increasing in intensity as she begins to breathe deeply with emotion and looking tearful.

> She sinks into tears.

The dancer begins to weep but hides her face with the cloth and then instantly covers up this revelation of her feelings by waving the tenugui as the music again becomes animated.

> How heavy and soaked with dew are the fragile petals of the cherries.
> One brush, and the blossoms scatter in this delicate, beautiful landscape.

The dancer tosses out cotton hand cloths similar to the tenugui as souvenirs for the audience. The priests continue to toss out cloths as the dancer exits.

23. This is the third time that this pose appears, but each time it is varied slightly. The same exact pose does not usually appear twice in one piece.

24. Even though Anchin never married Kiyohime, this is beside the point, since this song depicts the loyalty of a woman to the man that she loves.

Mountain catalog (yama zukushi)[25]   *The dancer comes out with the sleeves of the previous kimono slipped off from her shoulders to reveal a yellow underkimono with a pattern on each sleeve showing one large drum of the type used in gagaku court music. The dancer has a drum tied around her waist and dances, alternately beating the drum rhythmically and making graceful gestures with the drumsticks.*[26]

NAGAUTA CHANTERS:

How engaging are the views of nature in the four seasons.
Mount Fuji, the greatest mountain in all the empires of Asia.
Is it snow that covers the mountains?
No, it is delicately colored clouds of blossoms,
here in Yoshino, famous for its thousand cherry trees.
The wind blows and blows on Storm Mountain.
Looking out over the mountain peaks in early morning light
we can see Nakayama and Ishiyama, famous from poetry of old.
At the farthest reach of sight is Matsuyama,
and beyond is Oeyama, the haunt of dangerous demons.
Even though the road that leads to Ikuno is long and hard,
once there, one can tread the path that leads to love
in the mysterious stretches of smoky Mount Asama
or perhaps spend a night of love at Mount Arima.
Our prayers will be answered at the fox shrine of Inari.

To eerie drums sounds, the dancer bends backward, making fox gestures with her hands [figure 3.99].[27]

Hand dance (te odori)   *The dancer exits and returns with her upper kimono still folded down, but the revealed underkimono is either red or purple and the sleeves no longer have drum patterns. The bamboo flute joins the musical texture to suggest an atmosphere of folk dance. The dancer beckons a lover and waves her hand happily in a light-spirited dance.*

NAGAUTA CHANTERS:

A prayer in good faith is sure to be granted.
The god of the clan looks fondly on me.
If we make a promise to the god of Izumo,
then soon as husband and wife we will share a pillow.
Love within the pleasure quarters reveals
the uncertainty of this floating world.
While claiming that he deeply loves me,
he has a rendezvous with anyone who beckons.
How handsome he is, how infuriating.

25. The text is a series of wordplays and allusions to famous mountains in Japan. Since mountains are traditionally considered sacred and full of supernatural power, it is appropriate that the nonhuman nature of the dancer's character becomes a theme here.

26. Unlike noh, in which prop instruments are not sounded, the dancer here produces sounds both on the drum and with the drumsticks on the floor.

27. Foxes were believed to have supernatural powers, as exemplified in the travel scene from *Yoshitsune and the Thousand Cherry Trees*, translated here. This reference suggests the dancer's identity as a ghost.

FIGURE 3.100. At the end of the Tambourine dance (*suzu daiko*), Hanako, in a white kimono, stares up at the bell. (Photo by Aoki Shinji.)

Tambourine dance (suzu daiko)   *In this section, she dances with two tambourines, flat, wooden rings with bells attached. She shakes them rhythmically as she gestures. The clatter of the tambourines competes with the lively music, which increases in speed as she dances.*

> A peony is deep with feeling;
> the garden blushes, colorfully,
> a woman reddens her lips.
> How gentle she looks, how elegant her figure,
> so beautiful, so beautiful.
> In the soft rains of May,
> the young maidens, the young maidens,
> sing as they plant rice,
> their skirts and sleeves become damp.

The dancer stares at the bell [figure 3.100].

> The flowerlike figure's hair falls in tangles.
> Each time I think of it,
> I recall how hateful it is.

Circles around the bell as it is lowered.

> She touches the dragon-shaped top of the bell,

The priests line up along the bell cord, an arrangement that represents the tail of a serpent.

> and seeming to fly, she carries the bell away
> and disappears.

The dancer mounts the bell and poses dramatically on top of it as the curtain is pulled shut [figure 3.101].

ALTERNATIVE ENDING[28]

Demon quelling (oshimodoshi)   *Instead of appearing on top of the bell, the dancer stands under the bell as it is lowered and is spirited offstage through a door in the back of the bell for a costume change while the priests perform this comic interlude.*

PRIESTS: Save us, save us!
PRIEST 2: What was that noise?
PRIEST 3: It seemed to come from the bell tower.
PRIEST 6: Something terrible has happened. The bell (*kane*) has fallen.
PRIEST 1: What? Money (*kane*) has fallen? Pick it up.
OTHERS: Where is it, where is it?

---

28. This ending was not part of the original version of the piece. An early reference to it dates to 1793, and it is thought to have developed from an old tradition of aragoto heroes getting rid of evil spirits. It is now performed only on rare occasions.

FIGURE 3.101. Hanako mounts the bell and poses, thereby indicating the end of the play. The line of priests under the bell rope suggests the tail of a serpent. (Photo by Aoki Shinji.)

PRIEST 2: It's not money, it's the temple bell.

OTHERS: Oh no!

PRIEST 1: At least no one was hurt.

PRIEST 4: Now the only thing that we can do is follow the teaching of our master and try to raise the bell with our prayers.

PRIEST 1: In that case

PRIESTS: we shall pray.

To a lively, rather comic musical version of the exorcism from the original noh play, the priests sing and dance a prayer to raise the bell. Finally, the bell rises, and the dancer, who has reentered the bell through the door at its back, appears, her face hidden by a robe over her head. In one hand she holds a mallet like the ones carried by spirits in the noh theater. Moving from stage left, she slowly confronts the line of priests. As she faces each one, he ducks off to the side. When she reaches the center of the stage, she uncovers her face and poses, revealing herself as the ghost of Kiyohime. To indicate her demonic nature, she wears florid kumadori makeup, a large bushy wig, and divided skirts.

Tachimawari *The demon moves slowly across the stage, waving her mallet gently. Singly and in small groups, the men face her with cries of "Yaa!" They then do backward flips, landing with their legs sticking up in the air in a V shape. The movements are accentuated by beats on the board. From time to time, the demon freezes in a mie pose. Finally, the action comes to a stop, and all pose. Suddenly there is a shout from behind the curtain at the end of the rampway.*

GORŌ: Wai-ai-ai-t!

Gorō appears on the rampway. He is an aragoto hero with florid red kumadori makeup to indicate his strength. He wears clogs and carries a huge length of bamboo, presumably to fight the evil spirit. He stands at the seven-three position on the rampway.

GORŌ: How strange. A monster has appeared on the holy rampway along which I,

Odate Gorō Terusada, am traveling. Before the petals of this sacred garden turn to dust, you'd better disappear!

DEMON: Never! (*She goes to the rampway.*)

The two characters stand next to each other on the rampway and then move their heads in unison in a movement called "five heads" (itsutsu-kubi). With drum beats accenting the movements, they both look right and left, then, at a faster tempo, right, left, and right, ending with a pose. The two fight briefly on the rampway and then enter the main stage. There, they face each other and ritually trace out the character for "big" in the air, the demon using her mallet, Gorō with his bamboo pole.[29] Finally, the demon poses on a red two-level step at stage left while Gorō poses at stage right. The priests line up beside the demon in a line that suggests a serpent, and the curtain is drawn shut.

29. The character for "big" (*dai*) begins the phrase *daikyūka*, a wish for good fortune, which was often written at the end of play scripts in hopes of ensuring a full house.

Glossary of Theatrical Terminology and Index to Illustrations

This glossary contains the theatrical terms used in the anthology and also serves as an index to the illustrations. Definitions are found under the Japanese entries, with the terms that often appear in English listed for cross-reference. Those words in small capital letters within the definitions appear as main entries in the glossary. Many of the terms have several meanings, but only those used in this anthology are given here. Finally, the references to figures are selective, not exhaustive.

ADO Secondary role for kyōgen actor(s). See also SHITE; WAKI.

ADOAI Secondary role for kyōgen actor(s) in the interludes (AIKYŌGEN) of noh plays. Figure 2.31. See also ADO; KOADO; OMOAI.

AGED MODE See RŌTAI

AGEMAKU See MAKU.

AGEUTA A noh term for a common segment of sung, metered poetry in plainmatch (HIRA-NORI), beginning in the upper register. Often follows SAGEUTA.

AI Abbreviation of AIKYŌGEN.

AIKATA Kabuki music patterns (GEZA ONGAKU) played by the shamisen alone to produce emotional and atmospheric effects. Compare NARIMONO.

AIKYŌGEN (or simply *ai*) The kyōgen interlude in a noh play or the kyōgen actor performing the interlude. May also refer to interludes in kabuki plays. Figures 1.20, 2.15, 2.19, 2.21, 2.31. See also ADOAI; OMOAI.

AKUBA An evil or rough woman role type (YAKUGARA) in kabuki.

AME NO OTO Rain sounds, a kabuki music pattern (GEZA ONGAKU) played by the large drum.

Amijima See *Shinjū Ten no Amijima*.

AMI NO DAN A dance with a net performed in the noh play *Sakuragawa*. See also DAN NO UTA.

ANIMALS See DŌBUTSU.

ARAGOTO Bravura or "rough" style of acting in kabuki; distinctive to Edo and particularly to the Ichikawa Danjūrō family. Also used in the puppet theater. Figures 1.4, 1.16, 1.32–34, 3.6, 3.12–14. Compare WAGOTO.

ARAGOTO-SHI A kabuki role type (YAKUGARA); performed in bravura style (ARAGOTO).

ARMOR See YOROI.

ASHIRAI In noh, noncongruent instrumental music to accompany actions of the SHITE or TSURE, such as quiet entries, movement from bridgeway to stage, or onstage costume change.

ASHURA See SHURA MONO.

"At the Farmhouse" scene See *Kanadehon chūshingura*

ATSUITA A brocade kimono worn by male and demonic characters, which usually has geometric designs and strong color contrasts. Figures 2.9, 2.11, 2.39–40. Compare KARAORI.

Atsumori A noh play. Figures 2.7–11. Compare *Ichinotani futaba gunki*.

AWAZU An abbreviation of HYŌSHI AWAZU.

BABA Old woman; a puppet head (KASHIRA) with a brown satin head cloth and white or gray hair in a bun. Figure 3.40.

BATA-BATA [TSUKE] Continuous beats; a TSUKE pattern of continuous beats that emphasizes the rapid entrance or exit of a character in kabuki.

BATAN [TSUKE] Double beats; the two-beat, basic TSUKE pattern used to emphasize actions such as a sword stroke or a person falling.

BATTARI [TSUKE] Triple beats; the three-beat, basic TSUKE pattern often used to accentuate head movements during a MIE. The second, right-hand beat is a soft, often almost inaudible grace note.

Battles of Coxinga, The See *Kokusen'ya kassen*.

BELL MELODY See KIN [AIKATA].

Benten Kozō The kabuki play containing the "Hamamatsu-ya" scene. Figures 3.84–91.

BINAN The white headdress worn by female characters in kyōgen. Figures 2.49, 2.55, 2.57–59.

BIWA A lutelike instrument producing harsh sounds used to provide rhythmical accompaniment for recited narratives such as HEIKYOKU.

BIWA HŌSHI Biwa priests; male entertainers, usually blind and tonsured, who recited narratives—particularly of battle tales (HEIKYOKU)—accompanying themselves on the BIWA.

BOAT See FUNE.

BŌSHI A piece of cloth placed over a kabuki actor's forehead or just above it; created to enhance the looks of actors when they were required to shave their forelocks. Bōshi are usually made of crepe or silk and are worn in a variety of styles. Figures 1.29, 3.93.

BŌZU KATSURA The bald-head, bonze wig (KATSURA). Figures 1.26–28, 3.91, 3.101.

BRAVURA STYLE See ARAGOTO.

BRIDGEWAY See HASHIGAKARI.

BROCADE ROBE See KARAORI.

BUAKU A fierce kyōgen mask (KYŌGEN MEN) used for demons and fierce deities.

BUGAKU Court dance imported from the continent before the eighth century. Elaborately costumed and masked figures perform slow, stately dances to instrumental music called GAGAKU. Figure 1.2.

BUKKAERI A version of a quick change in which only the top of a new kimono is revealed. The KŌKEN pulls out threads to make the top half of the costume fall down over the OBI and skirt of the inner kimono. Figures 1.32, 1.37, 3.36–38. Compare HIKINUKI.

BULGING-EYED, GOLD MASK See ŌTOBIDE.

BUNGO BUSHI A style of narrative musical (JŌRURI) founded by Miyakoji Bungo (1660?–1740). Blamed for encouraging too many love suicides, the topic of many of Bungo's passionate and suggestive pieces, bungo bushi was prohibited in 1739. Bungo's disciples developed SHINNAI BUSHI, TOKIWAZU, and other popular styles.

BUNRAKU Refers both to the Bunraku theater group, the major commercial puppet troupe headquartered in Osaka at the Bunraku National Theater, and more broadly to the traditional Japanese puppet theater.

BUNSHICHI The most important male puppet head (KASHIRA). Its strong lines suggest bravery and some powerful hidden grief. The eyeballs, eyebrows, and, in some variations, the mouth all move. Figures 1.5, 3.73.

Busu The Delicious Poison, a kyōgen play. Figures 2.45–47.

BUTAI Stage. See also HANAMICHI; HASHIGAKARI; MAWARI-BUTAI; ŌDŌGU; SERI. Figures 1.11, 1.13–14, 2.1, 2.48, 2.50, 2.61–62, 3.15, 3.41, 3.51, 3.58, 3.75, 3.97.

CHANTBOOK See UTAIBON.

CHIGUSA A kabuki music pattern (GEZA ONGAKU) for love scenes played by shamisen and bells.

CHIRICHIRI KATSURA Curly-haired wigs (KATSURA) worn by strong men in kabuki. The "hair" is actually made of fine wire. Figures 3.61, 3.73.

CHOBO The shamisen player and chanter playing GIDAYŪ BUSHI for kabuki adaptations of puppet plays. They sit on a small platform on stage left or in a rattan-screened music room above the exit at stage left. See also DEGATARI.

CHŌKEN A three-quarter-length garment of gauze weave. It usually has embroidered or gold-leaf designs on the sleeves and center back and is often worn in the second act of noh plays when a long instrumental dance (MAI) is performed. Figures 1.21–22, 2.2, 2.9–10, 2.16.

CHŪKEI The spread-tip fan used in noh and plays based on noh. Closed, it looks like a capital Y because the ribs to which the paper is attached are spread outward. The fan's design usually is related to the character carrying it. Leading kabuki characters, such as daimyō and nobles, also use a chūkei. Figures 2.10, 2.20. See also MAKE-SHURA; YAMAMBA. For gestures using a fan, see ŌGI.

CHŪ NO MAI Medium dance; a long instrumental noh dance (MAI) performed in a moderate tempo. It is considered the "standard" MAI and is danced in a wide variety of plays, including *Atsumori*. Figure 2.10. See also JO NO MAI; KYŪ NO MAI.

CHŪNORI A technique used in the kabuki and puppet theaters to enable an actor or a puppeteer holding a puppet to "ride the air (chūnori)" suspended from an almost invisible wire.

CHŪNORI[JI] Half match, one of the three basic congruent song (HYŌSHI AU) rhythms in noh music. Each syllable matches a half beat. It is used for moments of vigorous intensity, such as the final dances in warrior pieces.

Chūshingura See *Kanadehon chūshingura*.

Cicada, The See *Semi*.

CLACKERS See HYŌSHIGI.

CLAPPERS See TSUKE.

CLOSING STAMPS See TOME-BYŌSHI.

CONGRUENT See HYŌSHI AU.

CONTINUOUS BEATS See BATA-BATA [TSUKE].

Coxinga See *Kokusen'ya kassen*.

CRAZED-PERSON PLAYS See KYŌRAN MONO.

CURTAIN See MAKU.

DAIKYOKU Major works of the Izumi school of kyōgen performers: *Kanaoka*, *Hanago*, and *Tsurigitsune*.

DANCE TO INSTRUMENTAL MUSIC See MAI.

DAN NO UTA An important danced section of a noh play. The dance is performed to song with instrumental accompaniment, and the focus is often on the manipulation of a prop. Dan no uta are often performed as SHIMAI. See also AMI NO DAN; KANE NO DAN; KASA NO DAN.

DANSHICHI A puppet head (KASHIRA) used for strong, usually bad, middle-aged men such as Gonta in *Yoshitsune sembon zakura*. The eyes move laterally and the mouth opens. Compare ŌDANSHICHI.

DEBAYASHI The appearance on the kabuki stage of the music-room (GEZA) musicians (HAYA-SHI) and NAGAUTA performers for dance pieces. The shamisen players sit at stage right, the chanters at stage left, and the hayashi on the lower step of the platform. Figures 3.94, 3.97. Compare DEGATARI.

DEGATARI The appearance onstage of the shamisen players and chanters. This is the normal practice in the contemporary puppet theater. In kabuki, GIDAYŪ performers (CHOBO) may appear onstage or behind a screen while other JŌRURI players normally play onstage. Figures 1.13, 1.15, 1.34, 3.32. Compare DEBAYASHI.

DEHA In noh, instrumental entrance music, including the stick drum (TAIKO), for deities, ghosts, and spirits. In kabuki, deha refers to both the similar music played by GEZA and important entrances down the HANAMICHI.

DEITY PLAY See WAKI NŌ [MONO].

Delicious Poison, The See *Busu*

DEMON PLAY See KIRI NŌ; ONI KYŌGEN.

DENGAKU Early rice-planting songs (TAUEUTA) and other rural rituals contributed to the development of dengaku (field music) noh, which eventually combined with SARUGAKU to become the classical noh theater.

DIVIDED SKIRTS See ŌKUCHI.

DŌBUTSU Animals. Figures: fox, 3.34; horse, 3.69, 3.71; shrike and clam, 3.7; tiger, 3.12–14.

DŌGU The general term for properties and scenic elements. Hand-held properties are called "small dōgu" (KODŌGU). In kabuki and the puppet theater, the sets are called "large properties" (ŌDŌGU). Stage properties in noh are called TSUKURIMONO ("built things").

Dōjōji A noh play. Figures 2.30–36. Compare *Musume Dōjōji*.

DOKUGIN A vocal solo. In kabuki the soloist is often accompanied by a shamisen, and the song is usually melancholy.

DOMESTIC PIECES See SEWA MONO.

DONCHO See MAKU.

DORO-DORO A kabuki music pattern (GEZA ONGAKU) played by the large drum for the entrances and exits of supernatural beings.

DOUBLE BEATS See BATAN [TSUKE].

DRUM See TAIKO; TSUZUMI.

DRUM INTERLUDE See UCHIKIRI.

DYNAMIC MODE See TSUYOGIN.

EBISU KAKE Early puppeteers connected with the Ebisu Shrine at Nishinomiya (between modern Osaka and Kobe) and specializing in plays about the deity Ebisu. See also NINGYŌ ZUKAI.

EBOSHI A type of black (occasionally gold) lacquered hat in various styles worn by priests, warriors, noblemen, SHIRABYŌSHI, and others. Figures 1.18, 2.24, 2.32, 2.42–44, 3.52, 3.63, 3.95.

ECHIGO JISHI Echigo lion music, a folk dance depicting a lion as performed by a street entertainer from Echigo and the kabuki music and dance based on it.

Eguchi A noh play. Figure 2.6.

FAN See ŌGI.

FAST DRUM PATTERNS See HAYATSUZUMI.

FEMININE MODE See NYOTAI.

FIFTH CATEGORY [NOH PLAYS] See KIRI NŌ.

FINAL DANCE See KIRI.

FIRST CATEGORY [NOH PLAYS] See WAKI NŌ.

First Note of Spring, The See *Yoshitsune sembon zakura*

FOOTWEAR See GETA; TABI; WARAJI; ZŌRI.

FOURTH CATEGORY [NOH PLAYS] See YOBAMME MONO.

FUE Generic term for flute. Figure 3.3. See also NŌKAN.

FUKAI A middle-aged woman's mask used in noh by the Kanze school of actors. Figure 2.20.

FUKEOYAMA A kabuki role type (YAKUGARA) for old women and a puppet head (KASHIRA) for middle-aged or old women.

FUKIWA-MAGE The wide topknot of a woman's wig (KATSURA) looped over a large drum-shaped ornament. An elaborate HANAGUSHI (flower comb) is pinned in the front of the wig for a princess or young lady of high birth. Figures 1.29–30.

Funa Benkei A noh play. Figure 2.6.

FUNAZOKO The sunken stage area on puppet stages. The funazoko (ship's bottom) is seven feet wide and fourteen inches below floor level and is used for street or garden scenes.

FUNE Boat; a popular stage prop. Figures 1.8, 1.13, 2.5–6, 2.24, 2.29, 3.8–10, 3.61, 3.66.

FURE A formal announcement in noh, performed by the AIKYŌGEN.

FURI Gestures and dance movements; puppets' stylized representations of ordinary human actions, and pantomimic movement in kabuki dance, usually accompanied by song. Kabuki dance is a combination of MAI, ODORI, and furi. *Furi-tsuke* (adding furi) is the general term for choreography in kabuki.

FURISAGE [MUSUBI] Style of tying a woman's OBI with long ends hanging down in back. Figures 1.9, 3.85, 3.95.

FURISODE A young woman's kimono with long, flowing sleeves. Figures 1.9, 1.30, 3.84, 3.95.

FURYŪ ODORI Decorative dancing; large processions of masked dancers in ornate costumes with decorated props singing popular songs. Popular in the late sixteenth and early seventeenth centuries. Compare NEMBUTSU ODORI; NEMBUTSU FURYŪ.

Futari daimyō Two Daimyo, a kyōgen play. Figures 2.42–44.

GAGAKU Court music imported from the continent before the eighth century. The gagaku ensemble—including a variety of percussion, string, and wind instruments—plays independent concerts and accompanies court dance (BUGAKU).

GASSHŌ The prayer pattern (KATA) used in noh. Figures 2.12, 2.18.

GE NO EI A sung segment in noh with a highly inflected melody centering on the lower register, characteristically used to deliver a poem.

GENTA A male puppet head (KASHIRA) used for handsome young men. A special pox-marked version is used in *The Miracle of the Tsubosaka Kannon*. Figures 3.35, 3.45, 3.47, 3.53.

GENZAI MONO Living-person play in noh. Specifically, this refers to fourth-category noh plays (YOBAMME MONO) featuring a living male character, often performed without a mask; however, masked plays such as *Shunkan* also belong to this category. More broadly used to refer to GENZAI NŌ.

GENZAI NŌ In contrast to noh about spirits and ghosts (MUGEN NŌ), genzai noh refers to plays featuring people alive in the dramatic present.

GETA Wooden clogs of varying heights worn by head puppeteers and by kabuki characters for outside wear. Figures 3.11, 3.91. See also WARAJI; ZŌRI.

GEZA Music room; a small room for musicians screened from the audience by a rattan blind that allows the performers to see out. Figures 1.7, 3.3, 3.58. See also DEBAYASHI; GEZA ONGAKU; HAYASHI.

GEZA ONGAKU Music played in the GEZA. In both the puppet theater and kabuki, geza music includes sound effects and background music; however, this music is much more important in kabuki than in the puppet theater. In kabuki, the geza houses NAGAUTA chanters and shamisen players as well as flute and percussion instruments (NARIMONO). Of the approximately eight hundred named kabuki music patterns, the following appear in this anthology: AME NO OTO, CHIGUSA, DORO-DORO, HARU WA HANAMI, HAYAFUE, HAYATSUZUMI, ISHIDAN, KAKEIRI, KAMINARI OTO, KAZE NO OTO, KIN, KODAMA, MIUKI SANJŪ, NAMI NO OTO, NANAKUSA, ŌDAIKO-IRI, TAKI NO OTO, TSUKKAKE, YUKI NO OTO.

GHOST-OF-WARRIOR PLAYS See SHURA MONO.

GHOST PLAYS See MUGEN NŌ.

GIDAYŪ [BUSHI] A style of narrative music (JŌRURI) established by Takemoto Gidayū (1651–1714). Gidayū is the basic music of the puppet theater; when used in the kabuki theater, it is often referred to as Takemoto.

GIGAKU A performing art imported in the sixth century that included a procession of masked figures followed by dances and mimes accompanied by flutes, drums, and cymbals. The lion dance (SHISHI MAI) was a featured part of the performance.

GOBANDATE The five categories of noh plays (WAKI NŌ, SHURA MONO, KAZURA MONO, KIRI NŌ, YOBAMME MONO) codified sometime in the Edo period. A full, formal program consists of one play from each category, plus the ritual piece *Okina* and four KYŌGEN plays.

GŌGIN See TSUYOGIN.

GOHEI A purification wand, made of a stick of bamboo with folded white paper attached, used as a ritual instrument in Shinto ceremonies and as a hand prop. Figures 1.16, 1,23, 2.5. Gohei also refers to similar strips of folded paper hung to mark off sacred space. Figures 1.2, 1.31, 2.2, 3.49–50.

GUNTAI Martial mode; a dynamic style of dancing used for vigorous male and supernatural roles in noh. Figure 2.11. See also SANTAI.

HACHIMAKI Headbands worn mostly by men. In noh, white headbands tied in the back are worn over the masks of warriors. In kabuki, headbands are worn in a variety of male and a few female roles and may be tied in the front. Figures 1.4, 1.6, 2.10. Compare KAZURA OBI.

HAKAMA Soft, pleated trousers worn by musicians, stage attendants, and some characters in all theater genres. Kyōgen hakama are usually patterned. Hakama may be ankle length (*hambakama*) or very long (*nagabakama*). They differ from ŌKUCHI and HANGIRI by the lack of stiffeners in the back panels and the generally slimmer line. Figures 1.6, 2.35, 2.53, 3.11, 3.46, 3.49, 3.87. See also KUKURI-HAKAMA; SASHINUKI.

HALF-BEAT DRUM RHYTHMS See CHŪNORI[JI].

"Hamamatsu-ya" scene See *Benten Kozō.*

HANA BŌSHI One of three different head coverings worn with the special mask created for *Shunkan.*

HANAGUSHI Flower comb; a wide, elaborate comb with three to five rows of flowers pinned into a female wig. Figures 1.29–30, 1.43, 3.32–33, 3.70.

HANAMICHI Rampway; the raised gangway in a kabuki theater that extends from front stage right through the audience to the back of the auditorium. Some plays, such as *Saint Narukami*, may have two rampways, one on the right and the other on the left. The rampway is occasionally used in the puppet theater. Figures 1.7, 1.13, 1.34. See also HASHIGAKARI; SHICHI-SAN.

HAND DRUMS See KOTSUZUMI; ŌTSUZUMI.

HANGIRI Divided brocade skirts with pleats in front and stiffened backs decorated with bold designs in either brocade or gold or silver leaf. They are worn by strong people and deities. Figures 1.16, 1.23, 2.40. Compare ŌKUCHI and HAKAMA.

HANNYA A noh mask (NŌMEN) used for the ghosts of jealous women. Figures 2.4, 2.35.

HAORI A short coat; still worn today over kimono. Figures 1.24, 3.76, 3.84, 3.87.

HAPPI A short coat. In noh plays and for noh-based characters, it has bold designs in gold thread and is used for strong, supernatural characters or to represent armor. In kabuki, a simpler, dark-colored version is worn by firemen and craftsmen. Figure 3.85.

HARU WA HANAMI Spring flower viewing; a delicate, kabuki music pattern (GEZA ONGAKU) played by a shamisen.

HASAMI KUSA A noh hand prop consisting of a stick with grasses or reeds attached to it. Figures 2.5, 2.7–8.

HASHIGAKARI Bridgeway; the roofed walkway that extends on a slight diagonal from the back of a noh stage to a curtained exit at stage right. Three pine trees (*wakamatsu*) are placed in front of this walkway. Figures 1.11, 2.1, 2.13, 2.29. Compare HANAMICHI.

HASHIORI The hem (*hashi*) of a kimono or yukata is often held or folded (*ori*) and tucked into the OBI to make it easier to walk or simply to display the (male) legs. Figures 3.84, 3.91.

HASHIRA-MAKI A wrap-around-the-pillar pose (MIE) in kabuki. Figure 1.32.

HATARAKI [GOTO] Action pieces; short dances to instrumental music in noh and kyōgen that usually include some mimetic action, such as the shouldering of the burden in *Yamamba*, or express the state of mind of a character, as in the KAKERI performed in crazed-person plays (KYŌRAN MONO). Varieties include MAIBATARAKI (figure 1.23), INORI, KAKERI, RAMBYŌSHI, TACHIMAWARI. Compare MAI.

HAYAFUE (also *hayabue*) Fast flute; lively entrance music in noh played in the second act for the appearance of a dragon god or a vigorous deity such as the thunder god in *Kamo*. The flute is accompanied by the drums. Also a kabuki music pattern (GEZA ONGAKU) played by a flute.

HAYAGAWARI Quick-change technique, used in kabuki when actors playing more than one role in the same scene must change costume and makeup quickly. The costumes are rigged in advance to make this possible. For example, the OBI may be sewn on the kimono itself.

HAYASHI [KATA] Musicians; hayashi is used especially for the noh flutist and drummers, and for the instrumentalists in the GEZA of kabuki. Figures 2.12, 2.39, 3.97. See DEBAYASHI.

HAYATSUZUMI Fast drum; a kabuki music pattern (GEZA ONGAKU) played by the hand drums and flute.

HEADGEAR See KABURIMONO.

Heike nyogo no shima A puppet/kabuki play that includes the "Shunkan on Devil Island" scene. Figures 3.56–68. Compare *Shunkan*.

HEIKYOKU Recitation of episodes from *The Tale of the Heike* to BIWA accompaniment. Traditionally performed by blind men called BIWA HŌSHI. See KATARIMONO.

HENGE MONO Transformation pieces; a type of kabuki dance in which the main actor changes roles and costumes several times. See also HAYAGAWARI; HIKINUKI.

HIKINUKI Literally, "pull and take off"; a quick onstage costume change. Basting threads are pulled out by the KŌKEN to remove an outer garment as an actor performs. Compare BUKKAERI.

HIKKOMI In kabuki, an important exit up the rampway (HANAMICHI).

HIP DRUM See ŌTSUZUMI.

HIRANORI Plainmatch, the standard congruent (HYŌSHI AU) song rhythm in noh music. Twelve syllables are sung to sixteen half beats. See also AGEUTA; SAGEUTA; SHIDAI.

HITAMEN Maskless; refers to noh actors performing without masks. The face remains motionless and masklike. Figures 2.7–8.

HITATARE A matching wide-sleeved jacket with kimono-style collar and long or short HAKAMA. In kabuki, elaborately patterned hitatare are worn under armor (YOROI). Figure 3.73.

HITORI ZUKAI See TSUME.

HON'I Essential characteristics, a poetry term adapted by Zeami and other noh composers.

HONJI MONO A type of SEKKYŌ BUSHI in which the main character is revealed to be a manifestation (*suijaku*) of a deity (*honji*).

HONKADORI Allusive variation. A classical poetic technique adapted in noh plays.

HOTOKE MAWASHI Early puppeteers who were connected with temples and who presented tales about Buddhist deities and related themes. See also NINGYŌ ZUKAI.

HYŌSHI AU Congruent rhythm; a noh song style in which the syllables of the text correspond to specific beats of the drums. There are three types: HIRANORI, CHŪNORI, and ŌNORI. Compare HYŌSHI AWAZU.

HYŌSHI AWAZU Noncongruent rhythm; a noh song style without a fixed relationship between the syllables of the text and the beats of the drums. Compare HYŌSHI AU.

HYŌSHIGI (or simply ki) The hand-held wooden clackers used in kabuki and the puppet theater to signal such functions as the opening and closing of the curtain and the changing of sets. Figure 3.4. Compare TSUKE.

Ichinotani futaba gunki A puppet/kyōgen play including the "Suma Bay" scene. Figures 3.69–74. Compare Atsumori.

IMAYŌ Popular songs of the Heian and Kamakura periods, sung professionally by female SHIRABYŌSHI performers, but also by aristocrats themselves at elite entertainments.

INORI MONO A group of noh plays in which a vigorous action piece (HATARAKI) enacts the exorcism (inori) of a female demon by one or more monks. Figure 2.36. Failed exorcisms occur in kyōgen. Figures 2.49–50.

INSTRUMENTAL INTERLUDE See UCHIKIRI.

INTERLUDE See AIKYŌGEN.

INTONED SPEECH See KOTOBA.

IRO In narrative singing (JŌRURI), an intermediate mode of recitation between speechlike (KOTOBA) and sung (JI) passages. Often used as a transition between the two styles.

ISHIDAN [NO AIKATA] Rocksteps; a kabuki music pattern (GEZA ONGAKU) played by the hand drums and shamisen used for battle scenes.

ISSEI A noncongruent (HYŌSHI AWAZU) song that may immediately follow ISSEI ENTRANCE MUSIC or precede a danced segment (MAI).

ISSEI ENTRANCE MUSIC A type of subdued entrance music in noh played by the flute and hand drums used for the appearance of the SHITE (and TSURE, if any) in either act of a noh play. Compare SHIDAI ENTRANCE MUSIC.

ITCHŪ BUSHI A Kyoto style of narrative music (JŌRURI) with a dignified and elegant melodic line founded by Miyakodayū Itchū (1650–1724). Primarily a form for private entertainments, it was used on the kabuki stage in Kansai and Edo most often in the eighteenth century.

ITSUTSU-KUBI Five heads; a movement pattern in kabuki.

IWAZU KATARAZU My heart does not speak; the name of a lively passage in Musume Dōjōji. The text resembles a popular song, and the dance gestures are rarely related directly to the words.

Izutsu A noh play. Figures 2.12–17.

JI In JŌRURI, ji refers to sung sections, as distinguished from KOTOBA and IRO. Figure 2.12. See also JIUTAI.

JIDAI MONO Period pieces, one of the two major categories of plays in the puppet theater and kabuki. These plays portray historical events and often have larger-than-life heroes. Figures 1.26–34, 3.7–14, 3.56–74. Compare SEWA MONO.

JINSEN A war fan with a red sun on a gold or silver background used in kabuki and the puppet theater. Figure 3.71. See also ŌGI; MAKE-SHURA.

JITORI (also jidori) Repetition by the noh chorus (JIUTAI) of the words of a SHIDAI.

JITSUAKU Evil samurai; a villainous role type (YAKUGARA) in kabuki.

JIUTAI (also ji) The noh chorus composed of six to twelve SHITE actors. Also the text chanted by the chorus. A smaller group of kyōgen actors serve as the chorus when one is needed in kyōgen.

JO NO MAI A slow, graceful dance to instrumental music (MAI) in noh. Most often occurs in third-category women plays such as *Izutsu*. See also CHŪ NO MAI; KYŪ NO MAI.

JŌRURI Originally the name of the heroine of a sung narrative composed in the sixteenth century, as well as the style of music used for that piece, jōruri came to be a general term for the puppet theater and for various styles of narrative music for shamisen and voice associated with the puppet and kabuki theaters. See also BUNGO BUSHI; GIDAYŪ; ITCHŪ BUSHI; KATŌ BUSHI; KIYOMOTO; NAGAUTA; ŌZATSUMA; SHAMISEN; SHINNAI BUSHI; TOKI-WAZU.

JŌZA Shite spot; the spot on the noh stage closest to the HASHIGAKARI, where the SHITE often stands. Figures 2.5, 2.14, 2.17.

JŪROKU Sixteen; a young man's mask in noh. Figures 2.9–10.

JUZU Buddhist rosary; used by priests in all theatrical genres. Figures 1.26, 1.30, 2.34, 2.51.

KABUKI A major genre of theater that developed in the early seventeenth century. The word *kabuki*, originally meaning something like "slanted," was used to refer to outlandish behavior or dress, and came to be written with three Chinese characters meaning "song-dance-art."

KABUKI JŪHACHIBAN Eighteen kabuki pieces selected by Ichikawa Danjūrō VII that emphasize the ARAGOTO style of the Danjūrō line. Because of this jūhachiban (18 pieces) has come to signify an acting family's artistic forte. *Saint Narukami* is one of these plays.

KABUKI ODORI Kabuki dance. The term was used to describe the performance of *Okuni* in Kyoto in 1603, an event used to date the beginning of kabuki.

KABURIMONO Headgear, includes hats (EBOSHI, KAMMURI, KASA, TOKIN), crowns (TENGAN), and head clothes or hoods (BŌSHI, ZUKIN). See also HACHIMAKI; KAZURA OBI; TENUGUI.

KADOZUKE Ritual performances enacted at the gate (*kado*) of private homes. Figure 3.48.

KAGO Palanquin. Figure 3.41.

KAGURA Shinto ritual performances, including music, song, dance, and some mime. In noh, kagura also refers to a type of dance (MAI) representing the ritual performance. Figure 1.1.

Kagyū The Snail, a kyōgen play. Figures 2.51–54.

KAKEAI A noh segment sung in noncongruent style (HYŌSHI AWAZU), with the shared lines becoming shorter and shorter until the chorus takes over.

KAKEGOE The calls made by noh drummers to mark the rhythm. In kabuki, kakegoe refers to words of praise shouted by members of the audience.

KAKEIRI Hurried entrance; a kabuki music pattern (GEZA ONGAKU) played by the stick drum and hand drums.

KAKERI An action piece (HATARAKI) danced in noh and kyōgen plays about the ghosts of warriors (SHURA MONO) or crazed people (KYŌRAN MONO) to depict suffering or distraction.

Kamabara The "Sickley" Stomach, a kyōgen play. Figures 2.55–57.

KAMINARI MASK The kyōgen mask used in *Thunderbolt* (Kaminari). Figure 1.24.

KAMINARI OTO Sound of thunder; a kabuki music pattern (GEZA ONGAKU) played by a large drum.

Kaminari Thunderbolt, a kyōgen play. Figures 1.24–25.

KAMISHIMO (sometimes read *jōge*.) A costume with a broad-shouldered vest (KATAGINU) and matching, ankle-length HAKAMA. Worn by musicians, chorus, chanters, and puppeteers as well as male characters. Figures 2.12, 3.5, 3.33, 3.37. Kyōgen kamishimo have narrower kataginu that do not necessarily match the patterned kyōgen hakama. Figures 2.15, 2.42. Compare NAGA-KAMISHIMO; SUŌ.

KAMISUKI Hair combing, a scene in kabuki in which a woman combs a man's hair. The scene usually expresses love or sorrow. It is parodied in *Yotsuya Ghost Stories*. Figure 3.81.

KAMMURI Elaborate, black court caps. Figures 1.41, 2.16–17.

Kamo A noh play. Figures 1.16–23.

Kanadehon chūshingura The Treasury of Loyal Retainers, a puppet/kabuki play containing the scene "At the Farmhouse." Figures 3.39–47.

Kanaoka A kyōgen play. Figures 2.58–59.

KANE Bell; a popular prop. Figures 2.5, 2.21–22, 2.30–36, 3.94, 3.97, 3.101.

KANE NO DAN The bell dance in the noh play *Miidera*. See DAN NO UTA.

Kanjinchō A kabuki play based on the noh play *Ataka*. It is one of the KABUKI JŪHACHIBAN. Figure 3.5.

KANJIN NŌ Subscription noh; large, public performances of noh for which admission was charged. Originally held to raise funds for a religious institution or for public works, but later the performers themselves benefited.

KARAORI A brocade outer kimono worn by female characters. The richly colored material usually has floral motifs. It may be worn in KINAGASHI, KOSHIMAKI, NUGISAGE, or TSU-BOORI styles. Figures 1.19, 2.6, 2.18.

KARIGINU Hunting cloak; a three-quarter-length, outer garment for male characters with a rounded neckline and double-width sleeves. Always worn with ŌKUCHI or HANGIRI divided skirts. Figures 1.18, 2.61, 3.1.

KASA Various types of large, umbrella-like, round hats used in all theaters. A favorite hand prop (KODŌGU) for dances. Figures 2.2, 2.49, 3.32–33, 3.35, 3.44, 3.96. Also umbrellas used as props. Figures 1.4, 2.50, 3.75, 3.77, 3.82, 3.91, 3.97.

KASA NO DAN A hat dance performed in the noh play *Ashikari*. See also DAN NO UTA.

KASA ODORI A kabuki dance using a string of hats. Figure 3.96.

KASHIRA A large, wildly flowing wig worn by supernatural beings in noh and noh-related works. Varieties are white (*shirogashira*), figure 2.37; red (*akagashira*), figures 1.23–24, 2.35; and black (*kurogashira*), figures 2.24, 2.26. In the puppet theater, kashira is the general term for puppet heads. See also BABA; BUNSHICHI; DANSHICHI; FUKEOYAMA; GENTA; KŌMEI; MATAHEI; MUSUME; ŌDANSHICHI; SAMBASŌ; SHIRADAYŪ; SHŌJŌ; SHUNKAN; SHŪTO; TAKEUJI; TSUBUSHI SHIMADA; WAKAOTOKO.

KATA Fixed forms or patterns of performance. In noh and kyōgen, kata is most commonly used to refer to movement patterns. In kabuki and the puppet theater, kata refers to fixed forms in general and especially to forms created by specific kabuki actors for specific roles. Figures 1.6, 2.10, 2.40–41, 2.51–52. See also GASSHŌ; SHIORI; TOME-BYŌSHI. Compare FURI.

KATAGINU A vest with broad shoulders worn with HAKAMA. Worn by musicians and puppeteers as well as characters. Figures 2.12, 2.15, 2.43, 2.46, 2.53, 3.5. See also KAMISHIMO.

KATANA General term for sword. Figures 1.1, 2.5, 2.11, 2.43, 3.13, 3.22, 3.30, 3.64–65, 3.72–73, 3.82–83, 3.87.

KATANUGI The right (left for archers) sleeve of the outer robe of warriors is slipped off the arm, rolled up, and inserted in the waistband (OBI). Figure 2.9. Compare NUGISAGE.

KATARI A relatively long, spoken narrative passage. Figure 2.15.

KATARIMONO A general term for recited narratives such as HEIKYOKU and JŌRURI. Compare UTAIMONO.

KATŌ BUSHI A genteel style of narrative music (JŌRURI) founded by Temmanya Tōjūrō (1684–1725) of Edo. Used today as the narrative accompaniment for the kabuki play *Sukeroku*.

KATSURA (also *kazura*) The general term for wigs; in noh, it is usually pronounced kazura and refers specifically to the type of wigs worn by women. Katsura may have wounds attached. Figure 3.86. See also BŌZU KATSURA; CHIRICHIRI KATSURA; FUKIWA-MAGE; KASHIRA; KUROTARE.

KATSUREKI GEKI Living-history kabuki plays first produced by Ichikawa Danjūrō IX (1838–1903) that emphasize historical accuracy and the recent past.

KAZE NO OTO Sound of the wind; a kabuki music pattern (GEZA ONGAKU) played by the large drum pattern.

KAZURA See KATSURA.

KAZURA MONO Woman plays; plays in the third of the traditional five categories of noh plays (GOBANDATE). Usually considered the most elegant (YŪGEN) plays.

KAZURA OBI Decorated headbands worn by female characters. In noh, the headband is worn under the wig and hangs down the back. Figures 1.19, 2.6, 2.18.

KAZURA OKE See SHŌGI.

KEISEI GOTO Plays about courtesans or prostitutes, made popular by the actor Sakata Tōjūrō (1644–1709).

KENTOKU A kyōgen mask (KYŌGEN MEN) with pop eyes and prominent teeth.

KI See HYŌSHIGI.

KIN [AIKATA] Bell melody; a kabuki music pattern (GEZA ONGAKU) played by a shamisen.

KINAGASHI A style of draping a small-sleeved kimono so that it fits snugly around the body, forming a brocade V at the neck. Figures 1.19, 2.6.

KIRI Refers to the final section of an act or play or to the final play in a program. If the final section of a noh play is danced, it may be performed independently as a SHIMAI.

KIRIDO The small door at the back of the stage-left wall of the noh stage used for inconspicuous entrances and exits. Figures 1.11, 1.17, 2.1.

KIRI NŌ The last of five traditional categories of noh plays (GOBANDATE). Performed at the end of a day's program and often featuring a supernatural being or demon. *Yamamba* is an example.

KISERU The traditional long, slender tobacco pipe, a favorite hand prop in kabuki and the puppet theater. Figures 3.16, 3.18, 3.40, 3.89.

KIYOMOTO An Edo style of narrative music (JŌRURI) that takes its name from Kiyomoto Enjudayū (1777–1825) and is widely used in kabuki both for dance pieces and as musical accompaniment. See also SHAMISEN.

KIZEWA MONO Raw-life pieces; kabuki plays depicting the lower strata of society first written by Tsuruya Namboku IV (1755–1829). Figures 3.75–91.

KOADO Tertiary role in kyōgen plays. See ADO.

KODAMA Mountain echo, the name of a kabuki music pattern (GEZA ONGAKU) played by a shoulder drum.

KŌDAN A type of traditional storytelling developed in the Edo period involving the recitation of nonhumorous narratives, often about historical or military events. The narratives, which include some gestures similar to those of RAKUGO, are generally performed in a stylized, lecturelike tone. The style and contents of these two storytelling forms have often intermingled.

KODŌGU Hand-held properties. See GOHEI (wand), HASAMI KUSA (grass), JUZU (rosary), KATANA (sword), KISERU (pipe), MIZUOKE (pail), SAKE, SASA (bamboo grass), TAIKO (drum), TSUE (staff), UCHIZUE (demon's mallet). General drawing: figure 2.5; figures of other kodōgu: baby (doll), 3.26, 3.77; baskets, 3.57–58; blood, 3.81; boat poles and oars, 2.6, 3.9; clothing and cloth, 3.24, 3.85; conch shell, 2.53; dishes, 3.77–78, 3.87; futon, 3.24; gun, 3.43; human head, 3.2, 3.75; mallet and needle, 1.25; medicine, 3.76–77; mirror, 3.80, 3.83; octopus, 1.26; paint, 2.58–59, 3.80; palaquin, 3.41; paper articles, 1.33, 2.27–28, 3.22, 3.47, 3.49, 3.62, 3.93; plaque, 3.13; rake, 3.58, 3.64; sickle, 2.55–57; spider web, 2.62; vajra, 1.16; zabuton, 3.77, 3.79–80. Compare ŌDŌGU; TSUKURIMONO.

KOGAKI The label in noh and kyōgen for named variant renditions of a play incorporating adjustments in text, dance, music, or costume.

KOKATA (also *koyaku*) Roles played by children. Figures 2.23, 3.26, 3.69, 3.72.

KŌKEN Stage attendants who assist actors with costume and props, prompt them, and even take over the performance should an accident occur. In noh, kyōgen, and kabuki dance pieces, they wear formal kimonos with crests and divided skirts (HAKAMA). For other kabuki pieces, they dress in black (KUROGO). Figures 2.8, 2.30, 2.33, 3.94.

Kokusen'ya kassen The Battles of Coxinga, a puppet/kabuki play. Figures 3.7–14.

KOMAI Small dances, which in kyōgen are danced to song; for example, the AIKYŌGEN performs a komai to a song about toys in the noh play *Miidera*. Figures 2.19, 2.54.

KŌMEI A rather rotund male puppet head (KASHIRA) with gentle, noble features and movable eyes. It is used for Michizane in *Sugawara and the Secrets of Calligraphy*, Yuranosuke in *Chūshingura*, and Mongoemon in *Amijima*. Figures 3.1, 3.18.

KO-OMOTE A noh mask for young women. Used for the TSURE and some SHITE roles. Figures 1.19, 2.4.

KOSHIMAKI A style of wearing a kimono wrapped around the hips with an underkimono showing at the top. Figures 2.36, 3.13. Compare KINAGASHI; TSUBOORI.

KOSHI OBI A narrow sash worn around the waist with decorated stiff ends hanging down in front. Figures 2.8, 3.1, 3.5.

KOTOBA Sections of noh and JŌRURI texts recited in speechlike patterns rather than being sung (JI).

KOTSUZUMI Shoulder drum; the smaller of the two hourglass-shaped hand drums is held by the left hand near the right shoulder and struck with the fingers of the right hand. It produces a wider range of sounds than does the hip drum (ŌTSUZUMI). Figures 1.12, 2.3, 2.32.

KO-UTA A type of popular medieval song that was both incorporated into KYŌGEN plays and derived from the texts of the plays.

KO-UTAI Brief sections of noh texts chanted outside the context of a full noh performance.

KŌWAKA [MAI] A medieval performance art that rivaled noh in popularity in the fifteenth and sixteenth centuries but has since died out. Male entertainers danced to drum rhythms and recited battle tales.

KUCHIBARI A special needle inserted at the side of a puppet's mouth to catch the sleeve or a hand towel in gestures of weeping.

KUDOKI In noh, a noncongruent song centering on the lower pitches and usually expressing lament or sorrow. In the puppet theater and kabuki, kudoki are often climatic and highly dramatic scenes. See also SHINNAI BUSHI.

KUDOKI-GURI In noh, a KURI segment that precedes a KUDOKI.

KUKURI-HAKAMA Kyōgen hakama; patterned, ankle-length HAKAMA—tied up just below the knee and worn with leggings. Figures 2.21, 2.31. 2.43, 2.51.

KUMADORI A distinctive style of kabuki makeup using red, black, and blue lines in a large variety of designs to emphasize a character's strong personality. It was developed by the Ichikawa line of actors to enhance their ARAGOTO style of acting. Figures 3.6, 3.12–13.

KURI A short noh segment with noncongruent singing of metered poetry. It incorporates the highest set pitch (also *kuri*) and ends with a long embellished syllable.

KURIAGE In kabuki, a vocal technique in which at the climactic part of a dispute, two or more performers simultaneously repeat a set phrase such as *saa, saa, saa* (well, well, well). In the puppet theater, a related melodic technique.

KUROGASHIRA See KASHIRA.

KUROGO Black costume and gauze hood suggesting invisibility, various forms of which are worn by puppeteers (NINGYŌ ZUKAI), kabuki stage attendants (KŌKEN), and stage assistants (KYŌGEN KATA). Figures 1.13, 3.2, 3.88.

KUROTARE A wig with long black hair hanging below the shoulders, worn by male or female deities and the ghosts of warriors. Figures 1.22, 2.10.

Kusabira Mushrooms, a kyōgen play. Figures 2.48–50.

KUSE A relatively long segment of a noh play that is its aural highlight. The chorus (with a single line in the middle by the SHITE), accompanied by drums, presents important textual material in congruent song, moving through the low, middle, and high registers and concluding in the low register. The SHITE may remain seated (*iguse*) or dance (*maiguse*) during this segment. Figure 2.41. See also KUSEMAI.

KUSEMAI A medieval female performance art with a lively rhythm that integrated song and dance. The noh actor Kannami (1333–84) studied with the kusemai dancer Otozuru (dates unknown) and incorporated the rhythms and structures of her art into noh.

KYŌGANOKO MUSUME DŌJŌJI See *Musume Dōjōji*.

KYŌGEN Refers both to the major theatrical genre of kyōgen and to the actors who perform it. Kyōgen actors also perform some roles in noh plays and the interlude (AIKYŌGEN) between acts of noh plays. Kyōgen (literally, wild words) also refers to play scripts in kabuki. Figures 1.24–25, 2.42–60.

KYŌGEN KATA Actors who perform kyōgen, a comic genre of classical theater. In kabuki, a kyōgen kata was originally a low-ranking playwright, but now he is a stage manager who dresses in black (KUROGO) and supervises the progress of the entire performance. His responsibilities include prompting the actors and beating the clackers (HYŌSHIGI). Figure 3.4.

KYŌGEN MEN Kyōgen masks. See BUAKU; KENTOKU; OTO MASK; USOFUKI.

KYŌGEN SPOT The spot at the stage end of the HASHIGAKARI where the AIKYŌGEN sits when not performing. Figures 2.1, 2.28, 2.31–32.

KYŌJO Crazed woman; a female character in noh plays who has become crazed through obsession or possession. The mother in *Miidera* is an example. Figures 2.18, 2.20, 2.22–23.

KYŌJO MONO Plays featuring a crazed woman (KYŌJO). See also KYŌRAN MONO.

KYŌRAN MONO Crazed-person plays in noh that feature a character who has become deranged or distraught through the loss of a loved one and who expresses a frenzied state through song and dance. Some of the earliest crazed-person plays were about men, but crazed-woman (KYŌJO) plays such as *Miidera* became more common and now make up about three-quarters of the total. Figures 2.18–23. Similar plays are found in kyōgen, for example, *Hōshigahaha*. See also KAKERI; KYŌJO; OTOKO MONOGURUI.

KYŪ NO MAI A rapid-paced dance to instrumental music (MAI) in noh. In *Dōjōji* it is performed after the RAMBYŌSHI to the music of a flute and hand drums. A kabuki version appears in *Musume Dōjōji*.

LARGE DRUM See ŌDAIKO.

LEAPING EXIT PATTERN See TOBI ROPPŌ.

LIVING-PERSON PLAYS See GENZAI MONO.

MACHIUTAI In noh, a variety of AGEUTA sung by the WAKI at the beginning of act 2 as he waits for the SHITE to reappear.

MAEJITE The SHITE in the first act of a noh play.

MAI The general term for circling dances in which the feet remain close to the floor, such as the dances in noh and kyōgen. Compare ODORI; FURI. In noh, mai or *maigoto* refers specifically to abstract dances performed to instrumental music alone. These dances share a basic choreography, varying mostly in music and tempo. See also CHŪ NO MAI; JO NO MAI; KYŪ NO MAI; OTOKO-MAI; SANDAN NO MAI; TENNYO NO MAI. Two variations, *gaku* and KAGURA, include special dance and music patterns suggesting BUGAKU and KAGURA. Compare HATARAKI.

MAIBATARAKI A vigorous action piece (HATARAKI) in noh and kyōgen danced by deities and demons, such as the thunder god in *Kamo*. Figure 1.23.

Maiden at Dōjōji, A See *Musume Dōjōji*.

MAI KYŌGEN A category of kyōgen plays that mime and/or parody noh plays. *Semi* is an example. Figure 2.60.

MAKE-SHURA In noh, a defeated-warrior fan (CHŪKEI) depicting a red sun setting into waves. Figure 2.11. Compare JINSEN.

MAKI-KAKUSHI Queue concealer; a small black lacquered hat covering the topknot. It is worn with RYŪJIN-MAKI. Figure 3.61.

MAKU Curtain. In kabuki and the puppet theater, a large traveler curtain (*hikimaku*) is pulled open and closed at the beginnings and ends of acts; a variety of drop curtains (*donchō*) may also be used. Figures 1.10, 1.26, 3.11. The noh stage has only a striped lift curtain (*agemaku*) at the end of the HASHIGAKARI. Figure 2.13. The kabuki HANAMICHI has a similar lift curtain at its end.

MALE DANCE See OTOKO-MAI.

MARI UTA A kabuki dance in *A Maiden at Dōjōji*, in which the actor expresses the innocence of a young woman by miming the bouncing of a ball.

MARTIAL MODE See GUNTAI.

MASKS See KYŌGEN MEN, NŌMEN.

MASSHA RAIJO A type of lighthearted RAIJO entrance music used for the appearance of the deity of a subordinate shrine (*massha*), such as the AIKYŌGEN in *Kamo*.

MATAHEI A puppet head (KASHIRA) usually used for good-natured, unassuming male characters; the eyebrows and mouth move. Figure 3.40.

MATSUBAMME MONO Kabuki versions of noh plays. These dance pieces are performed with a set modeled on the noh stage, which also has a pine tree (*matsu*) painted on the back wall. *Kanjinchō*, performed by Ichikawa Danjūrō VII in 1840, was the first such piece.

MAWARI-BUTAI Revolving stage; first effectively used in a kabuki play by Namiki Shōzō in 1578, it has become a standard feature of kabuki theaters. Figures 1.14, 3.67.

MEDIUM-TEMPO DANCE See CHŪ NO MAI.

MELODIC MODE See YOWAGIN.

MELODIC SONG See YOWAGIN.

MICHIYUKI Travel song. In noh, this is a passage describing a journey by either the WAKI, who generally sings an AGEUTA and performs a few symbolic gestures, or the SHITE or TSURE, who also may dance. In kabuki and the puppet theater, a michiyuki is a danced scene or act. Figures 3.28–29, 3.32–38.

MIE A dramatic pose assumed at climactic moments by puppets and especially by kabuki actors. A series of preparatory movements, usually including the circling of the head, leads to the holding of a dramatic pose with a fixed glare that may include crossing the eyes. Mie are usually accompanied by the beating of wooden clappers (TSUKE). Group mie are often performed as the curtain closes. In SEWA MONO, the term *kimari* replaces mie. Figures 1.4, 1.32, 1.39, 3.13–14, 3.36, 3.45, 3.90.

MIGAWARI The substitution of one person, often one's own child, to enable the escape of another; a standard scene in puppet and kabuki plays. The substitution of Kumagai's son for Atsumori in *Ichinotani futaba gunki* is an example.

Miidera A noh play. Figures 2.18–23.

MIKO Shinto priestess who may perform KAGURA. Figure 1.1.

Miracle of the Tsubosaka Kannon, The See *Tsubosaka Kannon reigenki*.

MISCELLANEOUS [NOH] PLAYS See YOBAMME MONO.

MITATE A popular Edo-period technique by which, through visual and textual allusions, one thing is made to seem like something else. A young maiden may be identified with the famous eighth-century poet Ono no Komachi, or the poses in a felicitous piece may resemble a crane flying over Mount Fuji.

MIUKI SANJŪ A kabuki music pattern (GEZA ONGAKU) played by the shamisen.

MIZUGOROMO A three-quarter-length, wide-sleeved gown of light silk or gauze worn fastened with a belt by male characters and left hanging loose for female characters. The shoulders may be stitched together in the back to shorten the sleeves (*katageru* or *kata o toru*). Figures 1.20, 2.2, 2.7–8, 2.20–21, 2.23, 2.31, 2.51, 3.5.

MIZUOKE Bucket or pail, a popular prop. Figures 1.19, 2.13, 2.25.

MO A train worn over the robes of a high-ranking lady. Figure 3.70.

MOMOHIKI Snug dark trousers always worn with a HAPPI coat by firemen or artisans. Figure 3.85.

MON A family crest; mon appear on the kimono of musicans, puppeteers, and some kabuki and puppet characters, as well as on some props. Figures 1.4, 1.6, 1.18, 1.38, 3.5, 3.35, 3.76, 3.98.

MONDŌ In noh, a spoken segment in the form of a dialogue, most often between the WAKI and the SHITE. Figure 2.14.

MONO NO TSUKUSHI A catalog or list of things; a poetic technique adapted in theatrical texts. For example, the list of bells in *Miidera*.

MONOGI ASHIRAI Instrumental music to accompany an onstage costume change.

MŌSHIAWASE A partial run-through of a noh or kyōgen play in lieu of a dress rehearsal.

MOUNTAIN ECHO PATTERNS See KODAMA.

MUGEN NŌ Noh plays featuring deities, the spirits of plants and animals, and the ghosts of humans. Compare GENZAI NŌ.

Mushrooms See *Kusabira*.

MUSUME Young girl; an immobile puppet head (KASHIRA) used for girls fifteen to twenty years old. Has a KUCHIBARI. Figure 3.40.

Musume Dōjōji A kabuki dance drama. Figures 3.92–101. Compare *Dōjōji*.

NADAI [SHITA] Actors' ranks. Nadai (named actors) are those whose names appeared on the theater billboards in the Edo period; the names of nadai shita (lower-ranked nadai) were not advertised. The current testing system enables actors to advance, although the children and disciples of nadai actors are still favored.

NAGABAKAMA See HAKAMA.

NAGA-KAMISHIMO Matching broad-shouldered vest (kataginu) and long HAKAMA worn by townsmen in kyōgen plays and as informal samurai garb in kabuki. Figures 2.38, 2.55. Compare KAMISHIMO and SUŌ.

NAGAUTA A genteel style of narrative music (JŌRURI) for shamisen and voice that developed in the late seventeenth and eighteenth centuries into the basic kabuki style.

NAMI NO OTO Sound of waves; a kabuki music pattern (GEZA ONGAKU) played by the large drum. It is used when the curtain opens and closes on seashore scenes and when characters enter and exit.

NANAKUSA Autumn grasses; a kabuki music pattern (GEZA ONGAKU) played by the shamisen.

NANORI Announcement of a name; a spoken segment in noh in which a character introduces himself. Most often it is performed by the WAKI when entering or immediately after a SHIDAI. Figure 1.18.

NANORI FLUTE A flute solo (*nanorifue*) announcing the entrance of the WAKI, who then introduces himself (NANORI).

NANORI ZASHI A segment announcing a name (NANORI), performed in a recitative style (SASHI).

NARIMONO The instruments (except the shamisen) played in the GEZA. These include flutes, drums, and other percussion instruments. Figure 3.3. Also, the music (GEZA ONGAKU) played by these instruments. Compare AIKATA.

NARIMONO-SHI Players of all the musical instruments in the music room (GEZA) except the shamisen. Also called HAYASHI KATA.

Narukami "Saint Narukami," a scene from the kabuki play *Narukami Fudō Kitayama zakura*. Figures 1.16, 1.26–34, 3.6.

NEGI Shrine attendants who sometimes performed SARUGAKU noh.

NEMBUTSU An invocation of the name of Amida Buddha with the words *namu Amida butsu.*

NEMBUTSU FURYŪ A syncretic form combing NEMBUTSU ODORI and FURYŪ ODORI, which led directly to the development of kabuki.

NEMBUTSU ODORI A group dance during which the NEMBUTSU was chanted and Buddhist hymns were sung accompanied by drums, gongs, and rattles. This dance was advocated by the priest Kūya (903–972) and popularized by Ippen (1239–1289). See also FURYŪ ODORI.

NIKYOKU In noh, nikyoku refers to song and dance, which Zeami labeled the basic arts of the genre. See also SANTAI.

NINGYŌ ZUKAI Puppeteers; three are required to manipulate the puppet for a major character, one for a minor character (TSUME). Figures 3.2, 3.11, 3.43, 3.49, 3.52. See also EBISU KAKE and HOTOKE MAWASHI.

NINJŌ MONO Noh plays of the fourth category (YOBAMME MONO), centering on human feelings (ninjō). *Shunkan* is an example. Figures 2.24–29.

NOBORIHIGE A cheerful, bearded kyōgen mask (KYŌGEN MEN) used for deities. Figure 1.20.

NOCHIJITE The SHITE in the second act of a noh play.

NŌGAKE BUTAI Temporary stages for puppet performances built on a newly harvested field or on the grounds of a shrine.

NOH (also *nō*) The earliest fully developed theatrical genre in Japan, noh combines music, dance, text, mime, costumes, and props. It was created in the fourteenth century (when it was known as *sarugaku*) and continues to be performed today.

NŌKAN The noh flute, also used in other theatrical forms; a transverse instrument made of strips of bamboo with a highly idiosyncratic scale and sets of overtones. Figures 2.3, 2.12.

NŌMEN Noh masks. Figure 2.4. See also FUKAI; HANNYA; HITAMEN; KO-OMOTE; ŌTOBIDE; SHAKUMI; SHUNKAN; WAKAONNA; YAMAMBA; ZŌ-ONNA.

NONCONGRUENT See HYŌSHI AWAZU.

NORI "Riding" (*nori*) the rhythm; in kabuki and the puppet theater, this refers to acting and speaking to the rhythm of the shamisen, whereas in noh and kyōgen, nori usually refers to the rhythms of the drums.

NORIJI In noh, a sung segment in wholematch (ŌNORI) rhythm, usually accompanied by three drums. Often used with supernatural characters or to express highly charged emotional states.

NOSHIME A small-sleeved silk kimono worn by male characters. Old men wear plain colors, and lower-class samurai, yamabushi, and many kyōgen characters wear stripes or plaids. Figures 2.8, 2.38, 2.53, 3.5.

NOTTO In noh, energetic instrumental music characterized by the steady beating of a shoulder drum. It is used to represent part of an exorcism in *Dōjoji*. See also INORI MONO.

NUGISAGE (or *nugikake*) Wearing an outer robe with the right sleeve off the arm and hanging down the back, to indicate work or madness. Figures 2.6, 3.70. Compare KATANUGI.

NUIHAKU Embroidered, satinlike, small-sleeved kimono, often with a silver or gold leaf pattern. Usually worn folded down at the waist (KOSHIMAKI) by female characters. Figures 2.32, 2.36. Compare SURIHAKU.

NUREBA Sensual love scenes in kabuki. Figure 1.29.

NYOTAI Feminine mode. In noh, a quiet style of dancing used for female characters and to depict the gentle side of male characters. Figures 1.21–22, 2.16–17. See also SANTAI.

OBI A narrow, wide, or padded sash worn around the waist of both men's and women's kimono. May be tied in a variety of ways at either the front or the back. Figures 3.18, 3.20, 3.58, 3.85, 3.95. See also FURISAGE; KOSHI OBI; TOMBO-MUSUBI.

ŌCHŌ (or *ōdai mono*) In kabuki and the puppet theater, period pieces (JIDAI MONO) that feature Heian-period courtiers. *Sugawara and the Secrets of Calligraphy* is an example. Figures 1.35–43.

ŌDAIKO A large, barrel-shaped stick drum placed on its side and played with two sticks in the kabuki music room (GEZA). Its patterns include AME NO OTO; DORO-DORO; ISHIDAN; NAMI NO OTO; TAKI NO OTO. Figure 3.3. Compare TAIKO.

ŌDAIKO-IRI A kabuki music pattern (GEZA ONGAKU) in which the large drum (ŌDAIKO) plays with the stick drum (TAIKO) and flute.

ŌDANSHICHI A puppet head (KASHIRA) for warriors of violent temperament. It was first used for Watōnai in *Coxinga*. Its mouth, eyes, and eyebrows all move. Figures 3.7, 3.13. See DANSHICHI.

ŌDŌGU Sets in kabuki and the puppet theater. Figures 3.7, 3.10, 3.15, 3.28, 3.32, 3.41, 3.56, 3.66–67, 3.75, 3.79, 3.84, 3.92, 3.94, 3.97.

ODORI Dance; originally referring to dance using leaps and jumps, in contrast to MAI, the circling, ground-hugging type of dance used in noh. Odori now generally refers to kabuki dance. See also FURI.

ŌGI The general term for fan. Fans are carried by most characters in all theatrical genres as well by the musicians (figures 2.5, 2.12, 2.15) and are used in a wide variety of gestures (figures 1.22, 1.35, 2.10, 2.23, 2.25–26, 2.40–41, 2.45–46, 3.21, 3.36–38, 3.84, 3.96). See also CHŪKEI; JINSEN; MAKE-SHURA; YAMAMBA.

ŌGUCHI See ŌKUCHI.

OIE MONO (also *sōdō mono*) Period pieces (JIDAI MONO) about struggles for succession (sōdō) in the major samurai houses (oie) during the early Edo period, although they are usually set in an earlier historical period (SEKAI). *Chūshingura* is an example. Figures 3.39–47

ŌKAWA See ŌTSUZUMI.

OKINA Old man; the ritual performance tradition of this name depicts an old man, a young man (SENZAI), and SAMBASŌ and is associated with the origin of theater in Japan. Versions of this ritual are performed in all theaters. Figures 2.61, 3.52.

ŌKUCHI (also *ōguchi*) Wide divided skirts with pleats in the front and stiffened in the back. White ōkuchi are the most common; red or purple ōkuchi are worn by young female characters; and green, blue, or patterned by young warriors. Figures 1.18, 2.7, 2.10.

OMIGOROMO A brocade robe fastened with elaborate gold cords and with a stand-up collar of a different design. Worn as leisure clothes by high-ranking characters in bunraku and kabuki. Figure 1.43.

OMOAI Designation for the primary AIKYŌGEN actor within a noh play. Figures 2.19, 2.21, 2.31. Compare ADOAI.

OMOIIRE A term used in kabuki scripts to indicate that an actor should react nonverbally to display a psychological state. The script may indicate the type of reaction, for example, an angry reaction (*haradatashiki omoiire*), or it may simply signify omoiire with a small circle.

ONI KYŌGEN Demon plays in kyōgen such as *Kaminari* (Thunderbolt).

ONNAGATA (also *oyama*) A kabuki actor who specializes in female roles, and the general term for female roles in kabuki. See also YAKUGARA and compare TACHIYAKU.

ŌNORI Wholematch; a type of congruent song (HYŌSHI AU) with a relatively steady beat in which a syllable is matched to a whole beat. It usually occurs toward the end of a play. Compare HIRANORI and CHŪNORI.

ŌSATSUMA See ŌZATSUMA.

OSHIMODOSHI Queller of demons; a type of ARAGOTO performance and the role type (YAKUGARA) that performs it. The character, carrying a bamboo stick, repels a raging demon or demon. *Musume Dōjōji* has an alternative ending that includes an oshimodoshi.

ŌTOBIDE A noh mask (NŌMEN) for powerful deities, such as the thunder god in *Kamo*; it has bulging eyes and a wide-open mouth with a prominent red tongue. Figures 1.16, 1.23.

OTOKO-MAI Male dance; a lively noh dance (MAI) for unmasked male roles. Accompanied by a hand drum and flute, and performed in a strong martial style (GUNTAI), it is somewhat faster than the quick dance (KYŪ NO MAI).

OTO MASK The comical, round-faced kyōgen mask (KYŌGEN MEN) of a young girl that is used for special roles, such as the princess mushroom in *Mushrooms* (Kusabira). Figure 2.49.

OTOKO MONOGURUI Crazed-man plays in noh. See also KYŌRAN MONO.

ŌTSUZUMI (also *ōkawa*) Hip drum; the larger of the two hourglass-shaped hand drums is held on the left knee and struck with the fingers of the right hand. Figures 1.12, 2.3. Compare KOTSUZUMI.

ŌZATSUMA (also *ōsatsuma*) A style of intense narrative music (JŌRURI) founded by Ōsatsuma Shusendayū (1695–1759). The school has disappeared, but NAGAUTA musicians still perform in the ōzatsuma style when accompanying ARAGOTO pieces. Figure 1.34.

PALANQUIN See KAGO.

PERIOD PIECES See JIDAI MONO.

PINTOKONA A somewhat effeminate lead male role (YAKUGARA) in kabuki.

PIPE See KISERU.

Poison See *Busu.*

PROPS See KODŌGU; TSUKURIMONO.

QUICK FLUTE PATTERN See HAYAFUE.

RAIJO Noh instrumental music played by a flute and three drums for the exit of the MAEJITE. See also MASSHA RAIJO.

RAIN PATTERN See AME NO OTO.

RAKUGO A traditional form of storytelling in which a single seated performer (*hanashika*)—with just a fan, a towel, and his tongue—presents a story by taking on the voices and gestures of the various characters involved. The scenes of humorous dialogue about daily urban life lead up to an *ochi* (a pun or gag), which abruptly closes the story. Compare KŌDAN.

RAMBYŌSHI Erratic rhythm; an action piece (HATARAKI) with flexible rhythms controlled by the drummer watching the movements of the dancer. The rambyōshi of *Dōjōji* is famous. Figures 2.32, 3.95.

RAMBYŌSHI UTAI A sung segment at the end of the RAMBYŌSHI dance.

RAMPWAY See HANAMICHI.

ROCK STEPS PATTERNS See ISHIDAN.

RONGI A noh dialogue in metered verse chanted in congruent rhythm (HYŌSHI AU). After an exchange of lines between two actors or an actor and the chorus, the chorus ends the segment.

RŌTAI Aged mode; a style of dance in noh used to portray old people. It combines fragility with spiritual strength. See also SANTAI.

RYŪ A school of performers. There currently are, for example, two schools of kyōgen actors and five schools of noh SHITE actors (SHITE KATA). Musicians also belong to ryū.

RYŪJIN-MAKI A special puppet and kabuki style of SUŌ worn by strong samurai serving as messengers from the nobility. The left sleeve, decorated with a large crest, is stiffened with bamboo splints; the right is removed, wrapped around a stick, and folded behind the back; and the trousers are tucked up in puffs high on the legs. Figures 3.61, 3.63.

SAGEUTA A noh segment of metered poetry sung in plainmatch (HIRANORI) in a low register. Compare AGEUTA.

Saint Narukami See *Narukami.*

SAKE Rice wine. Sake and its containers are often used as props (KODŌGU). Figures 1.26, 3.59, 3.78.

SAMBASŌ Masks and puppet heads used in various traditions for the character of this name; associated with OKINA. Figures 2.61, 3.48, 3.51–52.

Sambasō A puppet piece. Figures 3.50–52. See also OKINA.

SAMISEN See SHAMISEN.

SANDAN NO MAI In kyōgen, a dance to instrumental music modeled on the three-part (*sandan*) version of the noh CHŪ NO MAI.

SANTAI The three basic modes of dance identified by Zeami: the aged (RŌTAI), feminine (NYOTAI), and martial (GUNTAI). See also NIKYOKU.

SARUGAKU (or *sangaku*) An entertainment imported from China that included acrobatics, magic, music, dance, comic pantomime, and trained-animal acts, especially with monkeys (*saru*), now often labeled "old sarugaku" (*ko-sarugaku*). From the fourteenth century onward, sarugaku or sarugaku-nō was used as the general term for the noh theater as developed by Kannami and Zeami. See also DENGAKU.

SASA Bamboo grass; a hand prop (KODŌGU) in noh carried by crazed women (KYŌJO). Figures 2.5, 2.20.

SASAKAKE A strip of cloth decorated with pompoms hanging down the center back and both sides of the front, to indicate that the wearer is a YAMABUSHI. Figures 2.48, 2.51, 3.5.

SASARA A large, rattlelike instrument made of bamboo and used to accompany such entertainments as SEKKYŌ BUSHI.

SASHI Recitative; a noh segment of unmetered poetry set to a noncongruent rhythm. Sometimes used for lyrical monologues.

SASHINUKI A style of wearing HAKAMA tied up at mid-calf. Figures 3.42, 3.73.

SECOND CATEGORY [NOH PLAYS] See SHURA MONO.

SEGMENT See SHŌDAN.

SEKAI Conventional settings or "worlds" (sekai) populated with selected historical and fictional figures used by many puppet—and, particularly, kabuki—playwrights in creating new plays. By setting contemporary plots in earlier periods, the playwright could add new levels of meaning and avoid being censored by government authorities.

SEKKYŌ BUSHI Sermon ballads; narratives recited by itinerant entertainers accompanied by a variety of musical instruments, initially a SASARA and gongs (SHŌ). See also HONJI MONO; KATARIMONO.

Semi The Cicada, a kyōgen play. Figure 2.60.

SENZAI The young man depicted in the OKINA ritual tradition. Compare SAMBASŌ. Figure 3.50.

SEPPUKU (also *harakiri*) Traditional warrior suicide performed by cutting open the abdomen. Suicide scenes are popular in both kabuki and the puppet theater. See also SHINJŪ. Figure 3.46.

SERI Stage traps, used in kabuki from the mid-eighteenth century onward to raise and lower actors, settings, and props. The one on the HANAMICHI is called SUPPON. Figure 1.14.

SEVEN-THREE POSITION See SHICHI-SAN.

SEWA MONO Domestic pieces; puppet and kabuki plays that emphasize elements of the ordinary lives of contemporary people, mostly townspeople. Made popular by Sakata Tōjūrō's (1688–1703) courtesan plays (KEISEI GOTO) and Chikamatsu Monzaemon's (1653–1724) love suicides (SHINJŪ), domestic pieces became one of the two major play types. Figures 3.15–31. See KIZEWA MONO; ZANGIRI MONO. Compare JIDAI MONO.

SHABERI A noh segment in stylized speech (KOTOBA) without accompaniment; usually performed by an AIKYŌGEN explaining a situation. Often followed by a MONDŌ with the WAKI.

SHAGIRI In kyōgen, a music pattern played by a flute to accompany an actor's movements, usually at the end of a play.

SHAKUMI A noh mask, for a woman in her twenties. Figures 2.31–32.

SHAMISEN (also *samisen*) A banjolike instrument imported into Japan in the sixteenth century, the shamisen was modified to become the main instrument accompanying narrative songs. A large thick-necked, thick-body version is used for the puppet theater's GIDAYŪ style of JŌRURI; the smallest version is used for NAGAUTA, central to kabuki; and a middle-sized version is used for TOKIWAZU and KIYOMOTO music. Figures 1.15, 3.97. Compare BIWA.

SHAMISEN HIKI Shamisen player. Figures 1.15, 3.97.

SHARE A punning passage in kabuki.

SHICHI-SAN The seven-three position on the kabuki rampway (HANAMICHI), so named because it is seven-tenths of the distance from the entrance and three-tenths from the stage. Actors often stop to pose here, and a stage trap (SUPPON) permits unusual entrances. Figures 3.57, 3.71, 3.91, 3.93.

SHIDAI A song in HIRANORI rhythm sung by the WAKI or SHITE upon entering the noh stage. It has a fixed metrical form, and the first line is repeated. After the entering player has completed the song, the chorus repeats the first and last lines in noncongruent song in a lower key (JITORI). See also SHIN NO SHIDAI. Compare ISSEI.

SHIDAI ENTRANCE MUSIC Quiet instrumental music in noh announcing the entrance of the WAKI or SHITE. See also SHIN NO SHIDAI; SHŪ NO SHIDAI.

SHIKATA-BANASHI In kabuki, a type of narration using hand gestures to illustrate some of the content.

SHIKIGAKU Ceremonial music. The official ceremonial entertainment of the elite class. BUGAKU and GAGAKU filled this function in the Heian period, noh and kyōgen in the Tokugawa period.

SHIMAI Dance demonstration; selected sections of noh plays danced by a single actor to the accompaniment of chanters (usually five) without instruments. The dancer wears a crested kimono and HAKAMA and carries a fan. Props are seldom used.

SHINJI Sacred matters, performances intended for the deities. Humans may be present as onlookers.

SHINJŪ Lovers' suicide; a popular scene in kabuki and puppet plays. Figure 3.31. See also SEPPUKU.

SHINJŪ MONO Lovers' suicide pieces; a category of kabuki and puppet plays in which a man commits suicide with his lover, who is usually from the pleasure quarters. A type of SEWA MONO. Figures 3.15–31.

Shinjū Ten no Amijima The Love Suicides at Amijima, a puppet/kabuki play. Figures 3.15–31.

SHIN KABUKI New kabuki; plays written since 1868 that attempt to "modernize" kabuki, usually by using Western dramatic or plot elements.

SHINNAI BUSHI A style of narrative music (JŌRURI) named for the Edo musician Tsuruga Shinnai (1747–1810). Especially noted for the suggestive tone of its music for lamentations (KUDOKI), it influenced other styles of kabuki music and is still used in a few pieces.

SHIN NO ISSEI A stately type of ISSEI ENTRANCE MUSIC to announce the appearance of a deity in WAKI NOH and the heavenly maiden in *Hagoromo*.

SHIN NO SHIDAI A long, solemn type of SHIDAI ENTRANCE MUSIC used for the entrance of a deity in WAKI NOH. The sung SHIDAI that follows has a congruent JITORI and a second repetition (*sambengaeshi*) of the text.

SHIORI A graceful movement pattern that represents weeping. One or both hands are raised to eye level. Figure 2.28. See also KATA; FURI; KUCHIBARI.

SHIRABYŌSHI Female entertainers of the Heian and medieval periods who wore male court caps and white (*shira*) robes, danced to percussion accompaniment, and sang songs, including IMAYŌ. They are portrayed in many traditional plays. Figures 2.31–32, 3.95.

SHIRADAYŪ An immobile puppet head (KASHIRA) named after the father of the triplets in *Sugawara and the Secrets of Calligraphy*. It represents a good-natured, rather humorous country man. Figure 1.35.

SHIROGASHIRA See KASHIRA.

SHIROGASHIRA KOGAKI A variant performance practice (KOGAKI) using a white (*shiro*) head-piece (KASHIRA) such as the one used for *Yamamba*. Figures 2.37–41.

SHISHI MAI Lion dance; imported from China and incorporated into many performance arts.

SHITE Literally, *doer*; refers to the main role in noh, kyōgen, and early kabuki.

SHITE KATA Noh SHITE actors who perform the shite, TSURE, KŌKEN, chorus (JIUTAI), and most KOKATA roles. There are currently five schools (RYŪ) of noh shite actors: Kanze, Hōshō, Kita, Komparu, and Kongō.

SHITE SPOT See JŌZA.

SHŌ A variety of small metal gong. Written with a different Chinese character, shō refers to a bamboo mouth organ used in GAGAKU.

SHŌDAN Segments; the primary units of a scene in noh plays. Each has a characteristic form of language, rhythm, melody, instrumentation, and kinetic structure. The term was coined by Mario Yokomichi (b. 1916).

SHŌGI (also called *kazura oke*) A large, round, black, lacquered container with a lid that is often used as a stool in noh and as both a stool and a prop in kyōgen. Figures 2.5, 2.9, 2.40, 2.45–46, 2.58.

SHŌJŌ A rather lean and angular puppet head (KASHIRA) used for male roles. Named after Kan Shōjō (aka Sugawara Michizane). Figures 1.35–37.

SHOSA GOTO Dance plays in kabuki that were developed in the eighteenth century first for ONNAGATA and then for male roles (TACHIYAKU) as well.

SHOULDER DRUM See KOTSUZUMI.

SHUKŌ Plot. Traditional kabuki playwrights considered plot (shūko) and world (SEKAI) to be the two basic elements of play construction. Shukō refers to the way that the playwright plots the events and characters drawn from the sekai. It includes creating new characters and/or situations and applying conventional plot elements (for example, see MIGAWARI) to the materials from the sekai.

SHŪNEN MONO Resentful attachment pieces; a category of noh plays featuring a person (most often female) who suffers (often in hell) because of resentment toward her lover. *Dōjōji* is an example. Figures 2.30–36. Compare SHŪSHIN MONO; YOBAMME MONO.

SHUNKAN The name of a character, a puppet head, and a noh mask designed to present him. The head has a lot of facial hair and movable eyes and eyebrows (figure 3.68), and the mask has deeply set gold eyes (figure 2.4).

Shunkan A noh play. Figures 2.24–29. Compare *Heike nyogo no shima*.

Shunkan on Devil Island See *Heike nyogo no shima*.

SHŪ NO SHIDAI A type of SHIDAI ENTRANCE MUSIC.

SHURA-BA Battle scene in the puppet and kabuki theaters. See also SHURA MONO.

SHURA MONO Noh plays featuring the ghosts of warriors. They are performed second in the traditional five-play program (GOBANDATE). Shura (or Ashura) refers to the realm of fighting beings where warriors were thought to go after death. *Atsumori* is an example. Figures 2.7–11.

SHŪSHIN MONO Devoted attachment pieces; a category of noh plays featuring a person who suffers because of devotion to a lover. *Kayoi Komachi* is an example. See also SHŪNEN MONO; YOBAMME MONO.

SHŪTO Father-in-law; a puppet head used for stubborn men.

"Sickley" Stomach, The See *Kamabara*.

Snail, The See *Kagyū*.

SŌDŌ MONO See OIE MONO.

SŌJŪRŌ ZUKIN A dark hood worn by major male characters such as Nippon Daemon in *Benten Kozō*. Created by Sawamura Sōjūrō I (1685–1756), these hoods became so popular that people began wearing them in daily life. Figure 3.87.

SŌKA (also *sōga*) A thirteenth-century song genre that influenced noh. Anthologies of sōka were compiled in Kamakura, and the songs were particularly popular with the warrior class.

STAGE See BUTAI.

STEADY BEAT See ŌNORI.

STICK DRUM See TAIKO.

STOOL See SHŌGI.

Sugawara denjū tenarai kagami Sugawara and the Secrets of Calligraphy, a puppet play. Figures 1.16, 1.35–43.

SUICIDE See SEPPUKU, SHINJŪ.

Sukeroku A kabuki play. Figure 1.4.

"Suma Bay" scene See *Ichinotani futata gunki*.

SUMIBŌSHI A pointed head covering often used by religious characters. Figures 2.12, 2.24, 2.29.

SUŌ Matching long-sleeved top and long HAKAMA worn as ordinary male attire. Figures 2.24, 2.26, 2.38. See also RYŪJIN-MAKI.

SUPPON The small stage trap (SERI) at the seven-three (SHICHI-SAN) spot on the HANAMICHI. It is used for the entrances of ghosts, sorcerers, and other unusual characters. Figure 3.57.

SURIHAKU A narrow-sleeved kimono decorated with gold or silver leaf. Usually worn as an undergarment. Figure 2.36. Compare NUIHAKU.

SUZU Bell rattle; used in dances, especially in ritual performances. Figures 1.1, 2.61, 3.51.

SUZU DAIKO Rattle drum; a tambourine. Figure 3.100.

SWELLING BEATS See UCHIAGE [TSUKE].

SWORD See KATANA.

TABI Split-toe socks. Noh actors wear white ones; kyōgen actors, light yellow. In kabuki, they may be colored or even patterned. Figures 2.40, 3.73.

TACHIMAWARI Stroll; a type of action piece (HATARAKI) in noh, in which the dancer circles the stage to the left to noncongruent instrumental music. The stick drum may be used in the accompaniment. Figure 2.41.

TACHIYAKU Leading male roles in kabuki. See also YAKUGARA, and compare ONNAGATA.

Tadanori A noh play. Figure 1.6.

TAIKO General word for drums struck with drum sticks. In noh and related plays, a squat, barrel-shaped drum played with a wooden resonator and whose skins at the top and bottom are lashed together with cords. It is played with two sticks alternately. In noh the taiko is used only in some plays, and then only in the second half. Figures 1.12, 2.3, 3.3, 3.50. Compare KOTSUZUMI; ŌTSUZUMI; ŌDAIKO. A taiko is also a small stick drum used as a prop. Figures 1.16, 1.25, 3.34, 3.99.

TAKEUJI A puppet head (KASHIRA) used for old men, often country folk. Figure 3.43.

TAKIGI NŌ Noh performed outdoors by the light of bonfires and/or torches. Figure 2.2.

TAKI NO OTO The sound of a waterfall; a kabuki music pattern (GEZA ONGAKU) played by the large drum (ŌDAIKO).

TARE A long-haired noh wig in black (KUROTARE), white, or occasionally brown. Figures 1.21, 2.11.

TATE In kabuki, specific movements used in fighting; also a scene based on these movements. Some two hundred movements for hand-to-hand combat and fighting with a sword, spear, or lance have been codified and named.

TAUEUTA Rice-planting songs; ritual songs included in early DENGAKU and still performed today. Figure 1.3.

TAYŪ A general term meaning something like master, tayū was used for the lead actor or head of a noh troupe and for the highest-ranking ONNAGATA in kabuki and hence for courtesan roles (YAKUGARA) originally played by the onnagata. In the puppet theater, tayū refers to the chanter. Figure 1.15.

TENGAN Heavenly crown; an elaborate headpiece topped with a new moon or a phoenix that is worn by female deities and heavenly beings. Figure 1.21.

TENNYO NO MAI Heavenly maiden dance; a three-part medium dance (CHŪ NO MAI) in noh performed by a TSURE or KOKATA presenting a heavenly maiden. The stick drum plays in the instrumental accompaniment. Figure 1.21. See also MAI.

TENUGUI A small rectangular hand towel used as a handkerchief, head covering, or dance prop in kabuki and the puppet theater. Figures 3.2, 3.17, 3.29, 3.54, 3.91, 3.98.

TE ODORI Hand dance; the name of a dance segment with graceful hand movements in *Musume Dōjōji.*

TE SARUGAKU Amateur and semiprofessional (or unofficial) noh actors, as well as the plays performed by them.

TESURI Three partitions of different heights that run the width of the puppet stage, concealing the puppeteers' lower bodies and serving as a floor or ground on which the puppets appear to walk or sit. Figures 3.7–8, 3.23, 3.43.

THIRD CATEGORY [NOH PLAYS] See KAZURA MONO.

Thunderbolt See *Kaminari.*

THUNDER PATTERN See KAMINARI OTO.

TOBI ROPPŌ Leaping exit pattern in kabuki. Figure 1.34.

Tōkaidō Yotsuya kaidan Yotsuya Ghost Stories, a kabuki play. Figures 3.75–83.

TOKIN A small, round, black cap worn by YAMABUSHI. Figures 2.48, 2.51, 3.5.

TOKIWAZU A style of narrative music (JŌRURI) founded by Tokiwazu Mojidayū (1709–1781) following the prohibition of BUNGO BUSHI in 1739. It is important in kabuki as both a narrative style and as music for dance pieces. See also SHAMISEN.

TOMBO-MUSUBI The ARAGOTO style of tying a wadded OBI. Figure 1.27.

TOME-BYŌSHI The stamps indicating the end of a noh play. They are performed at the SHITE SPOT by the SHITE or the WAKI, or at the end of the HASHIGAKARI by the shite. Figure 2.17. See also KATA.

TORIMONO Held object; in ritual performances, an object such as a rattle, branch, or purification wand, into which a sacred force will descend. Figures 1.1, 1.16. See also GOHEI; SUZU.

TŌSHI (KYŌGEN) Full-length production; the performance of an entire puppet or kabuki script (KYŌGEN), or a least a large amount of it, rather than only one or two scenes or acts, which is common practice today.

TŌYOSE Battle alarm; a kabuki music pattern (GEZA ONGAKU) played by the large drum and cymbals.

TRIPLE BEATS See BATTARI.

TSUBOORI A style of wearing a kimono tucked up at the waist. Figures 2.6, 2.32. Compare KINAGASHI; KOSHIMAKI.

Tsubosaka Kannon reigenki The Miracle of the Tsubosaka Kannon, a puppet/kabuki play. Figures 3.53–55.

TSUBUSHI SHIMADA A puppet head (KASHIRA) for a mature commoner woman. Figures 3.53–55.

Tsuchigumo A Mibu kyōgen play. Figure 2.62.

TSUE Walking sticks, often used as props. Figures 2.5, 2.39, 2.41, 3.7, 3.11, 3.32–33, 3.53, 3.91.

TSUKE The beating of clappers on a square wooden board placed on stage left in both kabuki and the puppet theater. Patterned beats emphasize the sounds of a movement (falling, running, fighting) and accentuate MIE poses. The KYŌGEN KATA strikes the tsuke. Tsuke patterns include BATA-BATA, BATAN, BATTARI, UCHIAGE. Figure 3.4. Compare HYŌSHIGI.

TSUKE-UCHI The person striking the TSUKE. Figure 3.4.

TSUKIZERIFU Arrival announcement; in noh, a short segment in speech by the WAKI announcing his arrival at his destination. Usually follows a MICHIYUKI.

TSUKKAKE Sudden movement, a kabuki music pattern (GEZA ONGAKU) played by the large drum, stick drum, and flute.

TSUKURIMONO Stage properties in noh. Large objects such as bells (KANE), boats (FUNE), huts, and the like that are carried in by the stage attendants. Figures 1.17, 2.5–6, 2.14, 2.16, 2.22. Compare KODŌGU; ŌDŌGU.

TSUME (also *hitori zukai*) Puppets for minor characters manipulated by a single puppeteer. Figures 3.8, 3.14, 3.34. See also NINGYŌ ZUKAI.

TSURE Companions; supporting roles to the noh SHITE, played by SHITE KATA. All secondary females roles are tsure, because WAKI do not wear masks. Compare WAKIZURE.

TSUYOGIN (also *gōgin*) Dynamic mode; a noh singing style based on the intensity of the voice variation rather than on exact pitch. It is used for strong characters and intense passages. Compare YOWAGIN.

TSUZUMI Hand drum. See also KOTSUZUMI; ŌTSUZUMI.

TWO-BEAT CLAPPER PATTERN See BATAN [TSUKE].

Two Daimyō See *Futari daimyō*.

UCHIAGE [TSUKE] Swelling clapper beats (TSUKE); a long pattern that accompanies the major MIE in a kabuki play.

UCHIKIRI Drum interludes. In noh, a brief hand drum passage that interrupts the chanting.

UCHIZUE Demon's mallet; a prop or KODŌGU. Figures 2.5, 2.34–36.

UMBRELLA See KASA.

USHIRO-BURI A movement pattern for puppets and kabuki designed to display the beauty of the back of a woman's kimono. Figure 1.9.

USOFUKI (also *usobuki*) A kyōgen mask with pop eyes and a puckered mouth; used for non-human spirits such as those of the cicada or a mushroom. Figure 2.60.

UTA A general term for a song or poem. In noh it refers specifically to a segment of metered poetry sung in congruent rhythm to drum accompaniment. See also AGEUTA and SAGEUTA.

UTAIBON Chantbooks; noh scripts with notes for performers (especially amateurs) published by each school of SHITE actors. Early texts had simple melodic notations to remind players what to do; modern texts include more detailed musical notation as well as information about costumes, masks, dance, and meanings of words.

UTAIMONO A general classification for songs, including IMAYŌ and SŌKA. Compare KATARI-MONO.

WAGIN See YOWAGIN.

WAGOTO A gentle, understated kabuki acting style for young lovers and nobles, which contrasts sharply with ARAGOTO. It was created largely by Sakata Tōjūrō and is particularly popular in Kansai. Figures 1.4, 3.15, 3.57.

WAKA Classical court poetry, often quoted in drama, most frequently in noh.

WAKAONNA A young woman's mask in noh (NOH MEN). Figure 2.16.

WAKAOTOKO Young man; the puppet head (KASHIRA) for a naive young man.

WAKASHU Young man's kabuki, which flourished in the early seventeenth century but was then banned.

WAKAUKE A sung segment in noh that serves as a transition between a WAKA and a NORIJI.

WAKI Secondary role in noh; now played by specialized waki actors (*waki-kata*), who never wear masks and hence are limited to middle-aged male characters, often priests or courtiers. A few plays, such as *Rashōmon*, have major roles for waki actors. If there is more than one waki role, the others are called WAKIZURE. There are currently three schools of waki actors. In some noh-related kyōgen plays, the secondary role is called waki rather than ADO. Compare SHITE.

WAKI NŌ [MONO] Deity plays; the first of the five traditional categories of noh (GOBANDATE) are auspicious, celebratory pieces usually featuring a Shinto deity. *Kamo* is an example.

WAKI SPOT The place at front stage left of the noh stage where the WAKI usually sits, especially when he is not part of the action. Figures 2.1, 2.14.

WAKIZURE Companions of the WAKI. Compare TSURE.

WARAJI Straw sandals, though actually made of cloth for stage wear. Figures 3.35, 3.42, 3.73. See also ZŌRI; GETA.

WATARI-SERIFU (also *watari-zerifu*) Pass-along dialogue; a kabuki technique in which a group of actors divide the lines, speaking the last line in unison.

WATERFALL PATTERN See TAKI NO OTO.

WAVE PATTERN See NAMI NO OTO.

WIG See KATSURA.

WOMAN PLAYS See KAZURA MONO.

YAGASURI Arrow-patterned kimono worn in kabuki by the daughters of samurai serving in court or by the daughters of wealthy merchants. Figure 3.79.

YAKUGARA Role types in kabuki; the two major divisions of male (TACHIYAKU) and female (ONNAGATA) are subdivided into numerous categories, including the male roles ARAGOTO-SHI, JITSUAKU, OSHIMODOSHI, PINTOKONA and the female roles AKUBA, FUKEOYAMA, TAYŪ.

YAMABUSHI Mountain ascetics; popular characters in all forms of theater, especially kyōgen, which has a whole category of yamabushi plays. See also TOKIN; SASAKAKE. Figures 2.48, 2.51, 2.54, 3.5.

YAMAMBA The main character in the play *Yamamba* and a special mask and fan used for that play. The mask has many variations. Figures 2.4, 2.37. The fan depicts a silver moon amid clouds. Figure 2.41.

Yamamba A noh play. Figures 2.37–41.

YAMA ZUKUSHI Catalog (*tsukushi*) of mountains. Used as the name of a passage in *Musume Dōjōji*.

YATSUSHI A favorite kabuki situation in which a man disguises himself, often to go to the pleasure quarters. Also a name for the role of actors in this situation.

YOBAMME MONO Fourth-category noh plays. Includes KYŌRAN MONO, NINJŌ MONO, SHŪNEN MONO, SHŪSHIN MONO.

YŌGŌ NO MATSU Epiphany pine; the pine tree painted on the back of the noh stage and on backdrops for kabuki plays based on noh (MATSUBAMME MONO). Figures 1.11–12, 2.25–26.

YOROI Armor. Real armor was not allowed on stage in the Edo period, so costumers designed armor based mostly on earlier types. Noh and kyōgen do not use armor. Figures 3.36, 3.71–73.

Yoshitsune sembon zakura Yoshitsune and a Thousand Cherry Trees, a puppet/kabuki play containing the MICHIYUKI, "The First Note of Spring." Figures 3.32–38.

Yotsuya Ghost Stories See *Tōkaidō Yotsuya kaidan*.

YOWAGIN (also *wagin*) Melodic mode, a noh singing style based on a tonal scale and used for most women and gentlemen. Compare TSUYOGIN.

YŪGEN The concept of profound and refined beauty that Zeami adapted from WAKA aesthetics and made into a theatrical ideal.

Yuki A noh play. Figure 2.2.

YUKI NO OTO Sounds of snow, a kabuki music pattern (GEZA ONGAKU) played by the large drum (ŌDAIKO).

YUSURIBA Extortion scene; a conventional scene popular in kabuki KIZEWA MONO. "The Hamamatsu-ya Scene" from *Benten kozō* is an example.

ZA Medieval guilds of performers. The term has continued to be used in connection with troupes and theaters.

ZANGIRI MONO Cropped-hair pieces are a type of SEWA MONO created in the late nineteenth century to include new, Western-influenced customs. Compare KIZEWA MONO.

ZŌ-ONNA A type of female noh mask with a refined, almost other-worldly expression, used for young though relatively mature women and those with a divine nature. Figure 1.21.

ZŌRI Flat footwear with a thong between the toes worn by both men and women in kabuki. Noh and kyōgen actors wear only split-toe socks (TABI), and female puppets do not normally have feet. Figures 3.63, 3.91. See also GETA; WARAJI.

ZUKIN A variety of hats and hoods. Deities of subsidiary shrines in kyōgen wear the tall *massha zukin* (figure 1.20), and commoners such as a country doctor and servants wear the *nōriki zukin* (figures 1.24, 2.19, 2.31). See also SŌJŪRŌ ZUKIN.

Selected Bibliography

Works in Japanese

This section includes all the Japanese works cited and the reference books most often referred to in preparing this volume. All books were published in Tokyo unless otherwise noted.

Asahara Yoshiko and Kitahara Yasuo. 1994. *Mai no hon*. Shin Nihon koten bungaku taikei 59. Iwanami shoten.

Atsumi Seitarō, ed. 1928. *Nihon gikyoku zenshū*. Vol. 28. Shun'yōdō.

Baba Akiko, Masuda Shōzō, and Ōtani Jun. 1985. *Kurokawa nō no sekai*. Heibonsha.

Fukami Katsurō. 1933. *Nōgaku gushō seika*. Kyoto: Hinoki Shoten.

Gunji Masakatsu, ed. 1978. *Buyōshū kabuki on-steeji*. Vol. 25. Hakusuisha.

———. 1981. *Tōkaidō Yotsuya kaidan*. Shinchō Nihon koten shūsei 45. Shinchōsha.

Hattori Yukio, Tomita Tetsunosuke, and Hirosue Tamotsu, eds. 1983. *Kabuki jiten*. Heibonsha.

Itō Masayoshi, ed. 1983–1988. *Yōkyokushū*. 3 vols. Shinchō Nihon koten shūsei 57, 73, 79. Shinchōsha.

Koyama Hiroshi, ed. 1960–1961. *Kyōgenshū*. 2 vols. Nihon koten bungaku taikei 42, 43. Iwanami shoten.

———. 1987. *Nō kyōgen: Kyōgen no sekai*. Iwanami shoten.

Koyama Hiroshi et al., eds. 1973, 1975. *Yōkyokushū*. 2 vols. Nihon koten bungaku zenshū 33–34. Shōgakukan.

———. 1987–1988. *Yōkyokushū*. 2 vols. Zenyaku Nihon no koten 46, 47. Shōgakkan.

Matsuzaki Hitoshi et al., eds. 1993–1995. *Chikamatsu jōrurishū*. 2 vols. Shin nihon koten bungaku taikei 91, 92. Iwanami shoten.

Nagata Kōkichi. 1983. *Ikite iru ningyō shibai*. Kinseisha.

Nishino Haruo and Hata Hisashi, eds. 1987. *Nō kyōgen jiten*. Heibonsha.

Nogami Toyoichirō. 1949–1951. *Kaichū yōkyoku zenshū*. 6 vols. Chūōkōronsha. Reprint 1971.

Nomura Mansai. 1929. *Shinsen kyōgen shū*. Vol. 1. Wanya shoten.

Nonomura Kaizō. 1935. *Kyōgen buyōshū*. Yōkyokukai shuppanbu.

Nonomura Kaizō and Andō Tsunejirō, eds. 1931. *Kyōgen shūsei*. Shun'yōdō. Revised and expanded edition published by Nōgaku shorin, 1974.

Omote Akira and Amano Fumio. 1987. *Iwanami kōza nō, kyōgen*. Vol. 1: *Nōgaku no rekishi*. Iwanami shoten.

Omote Akira and Katō Shūichi. 1974. *Zeami Zenchiku*. Nihon shisō taikei 24. Iwanami shoten.

Sanari Kentarō, ed. 1931–1933. *Yōkyoku taikan*. 7 vols. Meiji shoin. Reprinted 1964 and 1983–1984.

Shigetomo Ki. 1958. *Chikamatsu jōruri shū*. Nihon koten bungaku taikei 49. Iwanami shoten.

Shuzui Kenji and Ōkubo Tadakuni. 1959. *Chikamatsu jōruri shū*. Vol. 2. Nihon koten bungaku taikei 50. Iwanami shoten.

Tada Manabu. 1977. *Jūyō mukei minzoku bunkazai: Mibu kyōgen*. Seibunsha.

Toita Yasuji, ed. 1955. *Kabuki meisakusen*. Vol. 2. Sōgensha.

Tsunoda Ichirō and Uchiyama Mikiko. 1991. *Takeda Izumo, Namiki Sōsuke jōrurishū*. Shin Nihon koten bungaku 93. Iwanami shoten.

Wada Eiko. 1976. "*Atsumori* no kuse to *Genji* yoriai." *Nō: Kenkyū to hyōron*, July, pp. 13–15.

Yokomichi Mario, and Omote Akira, eds. 1960–1963. *Yōkyokushū*. 2 vols. Nihon koten bungaku taikei 40, 41. Iwanami shoten.

Yūda Yoshio, ed. 1965. *Bunraku jōruri shū*. Nihon koten bungaku taikei 99. Iwanami shoten.

Works in Western Languages

This section includes all Western-language works cited, translations of Japanese literary works mentioned, and selected books on Japanese theater. The fullest bibliography of Western-language works on Japanese theater is that in Ortolani (1990).

Adachi, Barbara Curtis. 1978. *The Voices and Hands of Bunraku*. Tokyo: Kōdansha.

———. 1985. *Backstage at Bunraku: A Behind the Scenes Look at Japan's Traditional Puppet Theater*. New York: Weatherhill (a revised version of Adachi 1978).

Araki, James T. 1964. *The Ballad-Drama of Medieval Japan*. Berkeley and Los Angeles: University of California Press. Reprint, Rutland, VT: Tuttle, 1978.

Berberich, Junko Sakaba. 1989. "The Idea of Rapture as an Approach to Kyōgen." *Asia Theater Journal* 6:31–46.

Bethe, Monica, and Karen Brazell. 1978. *Nō as Performance: An Analysis of the Kuse Scene of Yamamba*. Cornell East Asia Series 16. Ithaca, NY: Cornell University East Asia Program.

———. 1982. *Dance in the Noh Theater*. 3 vols. Cornell East Asia Series 29. Ithaca, NY: Cornell University East Asia Program.

Bethe, Monica, and Richard Emmert. *Noh Performance Guides*. Tokyo: National Noh Theater:

———. 1992a. *Matsukaze*, with Royall Tyler.

———. 1992b. *Fujito*, with Royall Tyler.

———. 1993. *Miidera*.

———. 1994. *Tenko*.

———. 1995. *Atsumori*, with Karen Brazell.

———. 1996. *Ema*.

———. 1997. *Aoi no ue*.

Brandon, James R., trans. and ed. 1972. *Traditional Asian Plays*. New York: Hill & Wang.

———. 1975. *Kabuki: Five Classic Plays*. Cambridge, MA: Harvard University Press. Paperback reprint, Honolulu: University of Hawaii Press, 1992.

———. 1982. *Chūshingura: Studies in Kabuki and the Puppet Theater*. Honolulu: University of Hawaii Press.

___. 1997. *Noh and Kyōgen in the Contemporary World*. Honolulu: University of Hawaii Press.

Brandon, James R., William P. Malm, and Donald H. Shively. 1978. *Studies in Kabuki: Its Acting, Music, and Historical Context*. A Cultural Learning Institute Monograph. University Press of Hawaii East–West Center and University of Michigan Center for Japanese Studies.

Brandon, James R., trans., with Miwa Tamako. 1966. *Kabuki Plays: Kanjinchō and the Zen Substitute*. New York: Samuel French.

Brazell, Karen, ed. 1988. *Twelve Plays of the Noh and Kyōgen Theaters*. Cornell East Asia Series 50. Ithaca, NY: Cornell University East Asia Program.

de Poorter, Erika. 1986. *Zeami's Talks on Sarugaku: An Annotated Translation of the Sarugaku Dangi with an Introduction on Zeami Motokiyo*. Amsterdam: J. C. Gieben.

Dunn, C. U. 1966. *The Early Japanese Puppet Drama*. London: Luzac.

Ernst, Earle. 1956. *The Kabuki Theatre*. New York: Grove Press.

Gerstle, Andrew C. 1986. *Circles of Fantasy: Convention in the Plays of Chikamatsu*. Cambridge, MA: Council on East Asian Studies.

Gerstle, Andrew C., Kiyoshi Inobe, and William P. Malm. 1990. *Theater as Music: The Bunraku Play* Mt. Imo and Mt. Se: An Exemplary Tale of Womanly Virtue. Ann Arbor: Center for Japanese Studies, University of Michigan.

Goff, Janet. 1991. *Noh Drama and* The Tale of Genji: *The Art of Allusion in Fifteen Classical Plays*. Princeton, NJ: Princeton University Press.

Gunji, Masakatsu. 1970. *Buyō: The Classical Dance*. New York: Walker/Weatherhill.

___. 1970. *Kabuki*. Tokyo: Kodansha.

Hare, Thomas Blenman. 1986. *Zeami's Style: The Noh Plays of Zeami Motokiyo*. Stanford, CA: Stanford University Press.

Harich-Schneider, Eta. 1973. *A History of Japanese Music*. Oxford: Oxford University Press.

Hoff, Frank. 1978. *Song, Dance, Storytelling: Aspects of the Performing Arts in Japan*. Cornell East Asia Series 15. Ithaca, NY: Cornell University East Asia Program.

Honda, Yasuji. 1974. "*Yamabushi Kagura* and *Bangaku*: Performances in the Japanese Middle Ages and Contemporary Folk Performances." Trans. Frank Hoff. *Educational Theater Journal* 26:192–208.

Huey, Robert N. 1983. "*Sakuragawa*: Cherry River," *Monumenta Nipponica* 38:295–312.

Inoura Yoshinobu and Kawatake Toshio. 1981. *The Traditional Theater of Japan*. Tokyo: Japan Foundation.

Irwin, V. R., ed. 1972. *Classical Asian Plays in Modern Translation*. Baltimore: Penguin Books.

Jones, Stanleigh H. Jr. 1976. "Hamlet on the Japanese Puppet Stage." *Journal of Teachers of Japanese* 11:15–36.

___. 1981. "Experiment and Tradition: New Plays in the Bunraku Theater." *Monumenta Nipponica* 36:113–131.

___. 1983. "Puccini Among the Puppets: *Madame Butterfly* on the Japanese Puppet Stage." *Monumenta Nipponica* 38:163–174.

___. 1985. *Sugawara and the Secrets of Calligraphy*. New York: Columbia University Press.

___. 1993. *Yoshitsune and the Thousand Cherry Trees: A Masterpiece of the Eighteenth Century Japanese Puppet Theater*. New York: Columbia University Press.

Keene, Donald. 1951. *The Battles of Coxinga*. London: Taylor Foreign Press. Paperback edition, New York: Columbia University Press, 1990.

___. 1961. *Major Plays of Chikamatsu*. New York: Columbia University Press. Paperback reprint 1990.

___. 1965. *Bunraku: The Art of the Japanese Puppet Theater*. Tokyo: Kodansha.

___. 1966. *Nō: The Classical Theatre of Japan*. Tokyo: Kodansha.

___. 1970. *Twenty Plays of the Nō Theatre*. New York: Columbia University Press.

___. 1971. *Chūshingura: The Treasury of the Loyal Retainers*. New York: Columbia University Press.

___. 1976. *Worlds Within Walls: Japanese Literature of the Pre-Modern Period, 1600–1867*. New York: Holt, Rinehart and Winston.

___. 1984. *Dawn to the West: Japanese Literature in the Modern Era (Poetry, Drama, Criticism)*. New York: Henry Holt.

___. 1990. *Nō and Bunraku: Two Forms of the Japanese Theater*. New York: Columbia University Press (a paper reprint of the text with a few of the photographs of Keene's 1965 and 1966 books on bunraku and noh).

___. 1993. *Seeds in the Heart: Japanese Literature from Earliest Times to the Late Sixteenth Century*. New York: Henry Holt.

Kenny, Don. 1968. *A Guide to Kyōgen*. Tokyo: Hinoki shoten.

___. 1989. *The Kyōgen Book*. Tokyo: Japan Times.

Kim, Yung-hee. 1994. *Songs to Make the Dust Dance: The* Ryōjin hishō *of Twelfth-Century Japan*. Berkeley: University of California Press.

Kominz, Laurence R. 1995. *Avatars of Vengeance: Japanese Drama and the Soga Literary Tradition*. Michigan Monographs in Japanese Studies. Ann Arbor: Center for Japanese Studies, University of Michigan.

Komparu Kunio. 1983. *The Noh Theatre: Principles and Perspectives*. New York: Weatherhill/Tankosha.

Law, Jane Marie. 1992. "Religious Authority and Ritual Puppetry: The Case of *Dōkumbo Denki*." *Monumenta Nipponica* 47:77–97.

___. 1993. "Of Plagues and Puppets: On the Significance of the Name Hyakudayū in Japanese Religions." *Transactions of the Asiatic Society of Japan*, fourth series, Vol. 8: 108–132.

___. 1995. "Puppet as Body Substitute: *Ningyō* in the Japanese *Shiki sanbasō*." In Jane Marie Law, ed., *Religious Reflections on the Human Body*. Bloomington: Indiana University Press.

Legge, James. 1861–1872 *The Chinese Classics, with a Translation, Critical and Exegetical Notes, Prolegomena, and Copious Indexes*. 8 vols. London: Trübner.

___. 1882. *Yi Ching*. Oxford: Oxford University Press.

Leiter, Samuel L. 1979a. *The Art of Kabuki: Famous Plays in Performance*. Berkeley and Los Angeles: University of California Press.

___. 1979b. *Kabuki Encyclopedia*. Westport, CT: Greenwood Press.

___. 1997. *New Kabuki Encyclopedia*: A Revised Adaptation of *Kabuki jiten*. Westport, CT: Greenwood Press (a revised and expanded version of Leiter 1979b).

Malm, William P. 1959. *Japanese Music and Musical Instruments*. Rutland, VT: Tuttle.

___. 1963. *Nagauta: The Heart of Kabuki Music*. Rutland, VT: Tuttle.

Martzel, Gérard. 1982. *La Fête d'ogi et le nō de Kurokawa*. Paris: Publications orientalistes de France.

Matisoff, Susan. 1978. *The Legend of Semimaru, Blind Musician of Japan*. New York: Columbia University Press.

McCulloch, Helen Craig. 1959. *The Taiheiki: A Chronicle of Medieval Japan*. New York: Columbia University Press.

___. 1968. *Tales of Ise: Lyrical Episodes from Tenth-Century Japan*. Stanford, CA: Stanford University Press.

___. 1985. *Kokin Wakashū: The First Imperial Anthology of Japanese Poetry*. Stanford, CA: Stanford University Press.

___. 1988. *The Tale of the Heike*. Stanford, CA: Stanford University Press.

McKinnon, Richard N. 1968. *Selected Plays of Kyōgen*. Tokyo: Uniprint.

Mishima Yukio. 1973. *Five Modern Nō Plays*. Trans. Donald Keene. New York: Vintage Books.

Morley, Carolyn Anne. 1993. *Transformations, Miracles, and Mischief: The Mountain Priest Plays of Kyōgen*. Cornell East Asia Series 62. Ithaca, NY: Cornell University East Asia Program.

Motofuji, Frank T., trans. 1966. *The Love of Izayoi and Seishin: A Kabuki Play by Kawatake Mokuami*. Rutland, VT: Tuttle.

Nippon gakujutsu shinkōkai, trans. 1955–1960. *Japanese Noh Drama*. 3 vols. Tokyo: Nippon gakujutsu shinkōkai. Vol. 1 reprinted as *The Noh Drama*. Rutland, VT: Tuttle, 1973.

O'Neill, P. G. 1958. *Early Nō Drama: Its Background Character and Development 1300–1450*. London: Lund Humphries.

Ortolani, Benito. 1990. *The Japanese Noh Theatre: From Shamanistic Ritual to Contemporary Pluralism*. Leiden: Brill. Paperback, Princeton, NJ: Princeton University Press, 1995.

Philippi, Donald L. 1968. *Kojiki: A Record of Ancient Matters*. Tokyo: University of Tokyo Press. Copublished with Princeton University Press, 1969.

Pound, Ezra, and Ernest Fenollosa. 1917. *The Classic Noh Theatre of Japan*. New York: Knopf. Reprint, New York: New Directions, 1959.

Pronko, Leonard C. 1967. *Theater East and West: Perspectives Towards a Total Theater*. Berkeley and Los Angeles: University of California Press.

Quinn, Shelley Fenno. 1993. "How to Write a Noh Play: Zeami's Sandō." *Monumenta Nipponica* 48:53–88.

Raz, Jacob. 1983. *Audiences and Actors: A Study of Their Interaction in the Japanese Traditional Theater*. Leiden: Brill.

Rimer, J. Thomas, and Yamazaki Masakazu, trans. 1984. *On the Art of the Nō Drama: The Major Treatises of Zeami*. Princeton, NJ: Princeton University Press.

Sakanishi, Shio. 1960. *Japanese Folk-Plays*: The Ink-Smeared Lady *and Other Kyōgen*. Rutland, VT: Tuttle.

Scott, Adolphe Clarence. 1953. Genyadana: A *Japanese Kabuki Play* and Kanjincho: A *Japanese Kabuki Play*. Tokyo: Hokuseido.

____. 1956. *The Kabuki Theater of Japan*. London: Allen & Unwin.

____. 1963. *The Puppet Theatre of Japan*. Rutland, VT: Tuttle.

Seidensticker, Edward G. 1976. *The Tale of Genji*. 2 vols. New York: Knopf.

Shaver, Ruth M. 1966. *Kabuki Costume*. Rutland, VT: Tuttle.

Shimazaki Chifumi. 1972. *The Noh*. Vol. 1. *Kami(god)-Noh*. Tokyo: Hinoki shoten.

____. 1976, 1977, 1981. *The Noh: Sambamme Mono (woman noh)*. 3 vols. Tokyo: Hinoki shoten.

____. 1987. *The Noh*. Vol. 2: *Battle Noh*. Tokyo: Hinoki shoten.

____. 1993. *Warrior Ghost Plays from the Japanese Noh Theater*. Cornell East Asia Series, 60. Ithaca, NY: Cornell University East Asia Program.

____ 1995. *Restless Spirits from Japanese Noh Plays of the Fourth-Group*. Cornell East Asia Series 76. Ithaca, NY: Cornell University East Asia Program.

Shively, Donald H. 1953. The Love Suicide at Amijima: A *Study of a Japanese Domestic Tragedy by Chikamatsu Monzaemon*. Cambridge, MA: Harvard University Press.

____. 1978. "The Social Environment of Tokugawa Kabuki." In Brandon et al., 1978:1–61.

____. 1982. "Tokugawa Plays on Forbidden Topics." In Brandon, 1982:23–57.

Sieffert, René. 1979. *Nō et Kyōgen*. 2 vols. Paris: Publications orientalistes de France.

____. 1954. "Mibu-kyōgen." *Bulletin de la maison franco-japonaise*, new series 3:117–51.

Sigée, Jeanne, trans. 1979. *Les Spectres de Yotsuya: Drame en cinq actes* by Tsuruya Namboku. Paris: L'Asiathèque.

Smethurst, Mae J. 1989. *The Artistry of Aeschylus and Zeami: A Comparative Study of Greek Tragedy and Nō*. Princeton, NJ: Princeton University Press.

Suzuki Tadashi. 1986. *The Way of Acting: The Theatre Writings of Tadashi Suzuki*. Trans. J. Thomas Rimer. New York: Theatre Communication Group.

Tada Tomio. 1991. "Noh: The Well of Ignorance" (text for performance). National Noh Theater.

Tamba, Akira. 1981. *The Musical Structure of Noh*. Trans. Patricia Matoréas. Tokyo: Tokai University Press.

Teele, Rebecca, comp. 1984. "Nō/Kyōgen Masks and Performances." *Mime Journal*, 1984.

Thornbury, Barbara E. 1982. *Sukeroku's Double Identity: The Dramatic Structure of Edo Kabuki*. Ann Arbor, Michigan: Center for Japanese Studies, University of Michigan.

Tyler, Royall, ed. and trans. 1978a. *Granny Mountains: A Second Cycle of Nō Plays*. East Asia Series 18. Ithaca, NY: Cornell University East Asia Program.

___. 1978b. *Pining Wind: A Cycle of Nō Plays*. East Asia Series 17. Ithaca, NY: Cornell University East Asia Program.

___. 1992. *Japanese Noh Dramas*. New York: Penguin Books.

Ueda, Makoto, trans. 1962. *The Old Pine and Other Noh Plays*. Lincoln: University of Nebraska Press.

Waley, Arthur, trans. 1921. *The Nō Plays of Japan*. London: Allen & Unwin. Reprint, New York: Grove Press, 1957.

Watson, Burton. 1968. *The Complete Works of Chuang Tzu*. New York: Columbia University Press.

Yasuda, Kenneth. 1989. *Masterworks of the Nō Theater*. Bloomington: Indiana University Press.

Other Works in the Columbia Asian Studies Series

Translations from the Asian Classics

The Complete Works of Chuang Tzu, tr. Burton Watson   1968

The Romance of the Western Chamber (Hsi Hsiang chi), tr. S. I. Hsiung. Also in paperback ed.   1968

The Manyōshū, Nippon Gakujutsu Shinkōkai edition. Paperback ed. only.   1969

Records of the Historian: Chapters from the Shih chi of Ssu-ma Ch'ien, tr. Burton Watson. Paperback ed. only.   1969

Cold Mountain: 100 Poems by the T'ang Poet Han-shan, tr. Burton Watson. Also in paperback ed.   1970

Twenty Plays of the Nō Theatre, ed. Donald Keene. Also in paperback ed.   1970

Chūshingura: The Treasury of Loyal Retainers, tr. Donald Keene. Also in paperback ed.   1971

The Zen Master Hakuin: Selected Writings, tr. Philip B. Yampolsky   1971

Chinese Rhyme-Prose: Poems in the Fu Form from the Han and Six Dynasties Periods, tr. Burton Watson. Also in paperback ed.   1971

Kūkai: Major Works, tr. Yoshito S. Hakeda. Also in paperback ed.   1972

The Old Man Who Does as He Pleases: Selections from the Poetry and Prose of Lu Yu, tr. Burton Watson   1973

The Lion's Roar of Queen Śrīmālā, tr. Alex and Hideko Wayman   1974

Courtier and Commoner in Ancient China: Selections from the History of the Former Han by Pan Ku, tr. Burton Watson. Also in paperback ed.   1974

Japanese Literature in Chinese, vol. 1: *Poetry and Prose in Chinese by Japanese Writers of the Early Period*, tr. Burton Watson   1975

Japanese Literature in Chinese, vol. 2: *Poetry and Prose in Chinese by Japanese Writers of the Later Period*, tr. Burton Watson   1976

Scripture of the Lotus Blossom of the Fine Dharma, tr. Leon Hurvitz. Also in paperback ed.   1976

Love Song of the Dark Lord: Jayadeva's Gītagovinda, tr. Barbara Stoler Miller. Also in paperback ed. Cloth ed. includes critical text of the Sanskrit.   1977

Ryōkan: Zen Monk-Poet of Japan, tr. Burton Watson   1977

Calming the Mind and Discerning the Real: From the Lam rim chen mo of Tsoṇ-kha-pa, tr. Alex Wayman   1978

The Hermit and the Love-Thief: Sanskrit Poems of Bhartrihari and Bilhaṇa, tr. Barbara Stoler Miller   1978

The Lute: Kao Ming's P'i-p'a chi, tr. Jean Mulligan. Also in paperback ed.   1980

A Chronicle of Gods and Sovereigns: Jinnō Shōtōki of Kitabatake Chikafusa, tr. H. Paul Varley.   1980

Among the Flowers: The Hua-chien chi, tr. Lois Fusek   1982

Grass Hill: Poems and Prose by the Japanese Monk Gensei, tr. Burton Watson   1983

Doctors, Diviners, and Magicians of Ancient China: Biographies of Fang-shih, tr. Kenneth J. DeWoskin. Also in paperback ed.   1983

Theater of Memory: The Plays of Kālidāsa, ed. Barbara Stoler Miller. Also in paperback ed.   1984

The Columbia Book of Chinese Poetry: From Early Times to the Thirteenth Century, ed. and tr. Burton Watson. Also in paperback ed.   1984

Poems of Love and War: From the Eight Anthologies and the Ten Long Poems of Classical Tamil, tr. A. K. Ramanujan. Also in paperback ed.   1985

The Bhagavad Gita: Krishna's Counsel in Time of War, tr. Barbara Stoler Miller   1986

The Columbia Book of Later Chinese Poetry, ed. and tr. Jonathan Chaves. Also in paperback ed.   1986

The Tso Chuan: Selections from China's Oldest Narrative History, tr. Burton Watson   1989

Waiting for the Wind: Thirty-six Poets of Japan's Late Medieval Age, tr. Steven Carter   1989

Selected Writings of Nichiren, ed. Philip B. Yampolsky   1990
Saigyō, Poems of a Mountain Home, tr. Burton Watson   1990
The Book of Lieh-Tzū: A Classic of the Tao, tr. A. C. Graham. Morningside ed.   1990
The Tale of an Anklet: An Epic of South India—The Cilappatikāram of Iḷaṅkō Aṭikaḷ, tr. R. Parthasarathy   1993
Waiting for the Dawn: A Plan for the Prince, tr. and introduction by Wm. Theodore de Bary   1993
Yoshitsune and the Thousand Cherry Trees: A Masterpiece of the Eighteenth-Century Japanese Puppet Theater, tr., annotated, and with introduction by Stanleigh H. Jones, Jr.   1993
The Lotus Sutra, tr. Burton Watson. Also in paperback ed.   1993
The Classic of Changes: A New Translation of the I Ching as Interpreted by Wang Bi, tr. Richard John Lynn   1994
Beyond Spring: T'zu Poems of the Sung Dynasty, tr. Julie Landau   1994
The Columbia Anthology of Traditional Chinese Literature, ed. Victor H. Mair   1994
Scenes for Mandarins: The Elite Theater of the Ming, tr. Cyril Birch   1995
Letters of Nichiren, ed. Philip B. Yampolsky; tr. Burton Watson et al.   1996
Unforgotten Dreams: Poems by the Zen Monk Shōtetsu, tr. Steven D. Carter   1997
Sutra on the Expositions of Vimalakirti, tr. by Burton Watson   1997

Modern Asian Literature Series

Modern Japanese Drama: An Anthology, ed. and tr. Ted. Takaya. Also in paperback ed.   1979
Mask and Sword: Two Plays for the Contemporary Japanese Theater, by Yamazaki Masakazu, tr. J. Thomas Rimer   1980
Yokomitsu Riichi, Modernist, Dennis Keene   1980
Nepali Visions, Nepali Dreams: The Poetry of Laxmiprasad Devkota, tr. David Rubin   1980
Literature of the Hundred Flowers, vol. 1: *Criticism and Polemics*, ed. Hualing Nieh   1981
Literature of the Hundred Flowers, vol. 2: *Poetry and Fiction*, ed. Hualing Nieh   1981
Modern Chinese Stories and Novellas, 1919 1949, ed. Joseph S. M. Lau, C. T. Hsia, and Leo Ou-fan Lee. Also in paperback ed.   1984
A View by the Sea, by Yasuoka Shōtarō, tr. Kären Wigen Lewis   1984
Other Worlds; Arishima Takeo and the Bounds of Modern Japanese Fiction, by Paul Anderer   1984
Selected Poems of Sŏ Chŏngju, tr. with introduction by David R. McCann   1989
The Sting of Life: Four Contemporary Japanese Novelists, by Van C. Gessel   1989
Stories of Osaka Life, by Oda Sakunosuke, tr. Burton Watson   1990
The Bodhisattva, or Samantabhadra, by Ishikawa Jun, tr. with introduction by William Jefferson Tyler   1990
The Travels of Lao Ts'an, by Liu T'ieh-yün, tr. Harold Shadick. Morningside ed.   1990
Three Plays by Kōbō Abe, tr. with introduction by Donald Keene   1993
The Columbia Anthology of Modern Chinese Literature, ed. Joseph S. M. Lau and Howard Goldblatt   1995
Modern Japanese Tanka, ed. and tr. by Makoto Ueda   1996

Studies in Asian Culture

The Ōnin War: History of Its Origins and Background, with a Selective Translation of the Chronicle of Ōnin, by H. Paul Varley   1967
Chinese Government in Ming Times: Seven Studies, ed. Charles O. Hucker   1969

The Actors' Analects (Yakusha Rongo), ed. and tr. by Charles J. Dunn and Bungō Torigoe 1969

Self and Society in Ming Thought, by Wm. Theodore de Bary and the Conference on Ming Thought. Also in paperback ed. 1970

A History of Islamic Philosophy, by Majid Fakhry, 2d ed. 1983

Phantasies of a Love Thief: The Caurapañcāśikā Attributed to Bilhaṇa, by Barbara Stoler Miller 1971

Iqbal: Poet-Philosopher of Pakistan, ed. Hafeez Malik 1971

The Golden Tradition: An Anthology of Urdu Poetry, ed. and tr. Ahmed Ali. Also in paperback ed. 1973

Conquerors and Confucians: Aspects of Political Change in Late Yüan China, by John W. Dardess 1973

The Unfolding of Neo-Confucianism, by Wm. Theodore de Bary and the Conference on Seventeenth-Century Chinese Thought. Also in paperback ed. 1975

To Acquire Wisdom: The Way of Wang Yang-ming, by Julia Ching 1976

Gods, Priests, and Warriors: The Bhr..^gus of the Mahābhārata, by Robert P. Goldman 1977

Mei Yao-ch'en and the Development of Early Sung Poetry, by Jonathan Chaves 1976

The Legend of Semimaru, Blind Musician of Japan, by Susan Matisoff 1977

Sir Sayyid Ahmad Khan and Muslim Modernization in India and Pakistan, by Hafeez Malik 1980

The Khilafat Movement: Religious Symbolism and Political Mobilization in India, by Gail Minault 1982

The World of K'ung Shang-jen: A Man of Letters in Early Ch'ing China, by Richard Strassberg 1983

The Lotus Boat: The Origins of Chinese Tz'u Poetry in T'ang Popular Culture, by Marsha L. Wagner 1984

Expressions of Self in Chinese Literature, ed. Robert E. Hegel and Richard C. Hessney 1985

Songs for the Bride: Women's Voices and Wedding Rites of Rural India, by W. G. Archer; eds. Barbara Stoler Miller and Mildred Archer 1986

A Heritage of Kings: One Man's Monarchy in the Confucian World, by JaHyun Kim Haboush 1988

Companions to Asian Studies

Approaches to the Oriental Classics, ed. Wm. Theodore de Bary 1959

Early Chinese Literature, by Burton Watson. Also in paperback ed. 1962

Approaches to Asian Civilizations, eds. Wm. Theodore de Bary and Ainslie T. Embree 1964

The Classic Chinese Novel: A Critical Introduction, by C. T. Hsia. Also in paperback ed. 1968

Chinese Lyricism: Shih Poetry from the Second to the Twelfth Century, tr. Burton Watson. Also in paperback ed. 1971

A Syllabus of Indian Civilization, by Leonard A. Gordon and Barbara Stoler Miller 1971

Twentieth-Century Chinese Stories, ed. C. T. Hsia and Joseph S. M. Lau. Also in paperback ed. 1971

A Syllabus of Chinese Civilization, by J. Mason Gentzler, 2d ed. 1972

A Syllabus of Japanese Civilization, by H. Paul Varley, 2d ed. 1972

An Introduction to Chinese Civilization, ed. John Meskill, with the assistance of J. Mason Gentzler 1973

An Introduction to Japanese Civilization, ed. Arthur E. Tiedemann 1974

Ukifune: Love in the Tale of Genji, ed. Andrew Pekarik 1982

The Pleasures of Japanese Literature, by Donald Keene   1988
A Guide to Oriental Classics, eds. Wm. Theodore de Bary and Ainslie T. Embree; 3d edition ed. Amy Vladeck Heinrich, 2 vols.   1989

Introduction to Asian Civilizations

Wm. Theodore de Bary, General Editor

Sources of Japanese Tradition, 1958; paperback ed., 2 vols., 1964
Sources of Indian Tradition, 1958; paperback ed., 2 vols., 1964; 2d ed., 2 vols., 1988
Sources of Chinese Tradition, 1960; paperback ed., 2 vols., 1964
Sources of Korean Tradition, paperback ed., vol. 1, 1997

Neo-Confucian Studies

Instructions for Practical Living and Other Neo-Confucian Writings by Wang Yang-ming, tr. Wing-tsit Chan   1963
Reflections on Things at Hand: The Neo-Confucian Anthology, comp. Chu Hsi and Lü Tsu-ch'ien, tr. Wing-tsit Chan   1967
Self and Society in Ming Thought, by Wm. Theodore de Bary and the Conference on Ming Thought. Also in paperback ed.   1970
The Unfolding of Neo-Confucianism, by Wm. Theodore de Bary and the Conference on Seventeenth-Century Chinese Thought. Also in paperback ed.   1975
Principle and Practicality: Essays in Neo-Confucianism and Practical Learning, eds. Wm. Theodore de Bary and Irene Bloom. Also in paperback ed.   1979
The Syncretic Religion of Lin Chao-en, by Judith A. Berling   1980
The Renewal of Buddhism in China: Chu-hung and the Late Ming Synthesis, by Chün-fang Yü   1981
Neo-Confucian Orthodoxy and the Learning of the Mind-and-Heart, by Wm. Theodore de Bary   1981
Yüan Thought: Chinese Thought and Religion Under the Mongols, eds. Hok-lam Chan and Wm. Theodore de Bary   1982
The Liberal Tradition in China, by Wm. Theodore de Bary   1983
The Development and Decline of Chinese Cosmology, by John B. Henderson   1984
The Rise of Neo-Confucianism in Korea, by Wm. Theodore de Bary and JaHyun Kim Haboush   1985
Chiao Hung and the Restructuring of Neo-Confucianism in Late Ming, by Edward T. Ch'ien   1985
Neo-Confucian Terms Explained: Pei-hsi tzu-i, by Ch'en Ch'un, ed. and trans. Wing-tsit Chan   1986
Knowledge Painfully Acquired: K'un-chih chi, by Lo Ch'in-shun, ed. and trans. Irene Bloom   1987
To Become a Sage: The Ten Diagrams on Sage Learning, by Yi T'oegye, ed. and trans. Michael C. Kalton   1988
The Message of the Mind in Neo-Confucian Thought, by Wm. Theodore de Bary   1989

PL
782
E5
T73
1998

Traditional Japanese
  theater.

$49.50

WITHDRAWN

DATE		

PL
782
E5

CARROLL COMMUNITY COLLEGE LMTS

Traditional Japanese theater.

00000009298134

Learning Resources Center
Carroll Community College
1601 Washington Rd.
Westminster, MD 21157

BAKER & TAYLOR

MAR 1 0 1999